P9-CQB-905

HISTORY

OF THE

FREE CHURCHES OF ENGLAND.

HISTORY
OF THE
FREE CHURCHES
OF
ENGLAND

1688—1891.

FROM THE REFORMATION TO 1851
By HERBERT S. SKEATS

WITH A CONTINUATION TO 1891
By CHARLES S. MIALL,
AUTHOR OF "HENRY RICHARD, M.P., A BIOGRAPHY."

LONDON
ALEXANDER & SHEPHEARD, FURNIVAL STREET
JAMES CLARKE & CO., 13, FLEET STREET.

PREFACE.

"THE History of the Free Churches of England" was brought out in a library form by Mr. Skeats in 1868, and met with so much acceptance that, in the following year, a second edition was called for, which was ere long exhausted. It was the intention of my friend to have thoroughly revised the volume, with a view to a further issue; but this object was unhappily frustrated by his untimely death in 1881. Since that time down to the present day there have been frequent demands for a work which, in a consecutive narrative of facts and opinions, should convey a correct, impartial, and lively description of the important part played by the Free Churches in the development of the English nation from their earliest formation, and the present volume is intended to supply that want in as complete a form as possible.

In undertaking to revise so unique a work, and bring down the History to the present day, I have been fully conscious of the delicacy of the task. Apart from the inherent difficulty of attempting to build upon the foundations of another man, there is the added difficulty of adequately preserving essential continuity, which in this case is increased by Mr. Skeats's original style of treatment. His History is no mere compilation. It is the outcome of most laborious research; and the vast material thus accumulated has been moulded and utilised with the skill, insight, and industry of an accomplished historian. There is abundant evidence that the author aimed at rigid impartiality, and this is as manifest in his critical estimate of the work and opinions of the earlier Nonconformists as in his judgment on the acts and tendencies of the Established Church. "Nothing extenuate, nor set down aught in malice," seems to have been his motto. His conclusions are not hasty or prejudiced, and for all of them adequate reasons are given. In revising his work I have been scrupulous to preserve its characteristic features. Here and there it has been necessary to correct some statements by the light of new information, to tone down a few needlessly strong expressions, and to omit some superfluous matter. But substantially the History remains as Mr. Skeats wrote it. Its fine, incisive, and vivacious style, and the force and beauty of its sketches, have been reverently preserved.

The narrative of Mr. Skeats comes down to 1850. For the remaining five chapters I am solely responsible. Though I cannot aspire to his literary finish and faculty of perspective, I have found some assistance in a contemporary knowledge of the events described, and in a personal acquaintance with many of the actors who cross the stage. It has been necessary, in dealing with those events, to adopt a somewhat different method from that of my predecessor. The marvellous expansion of Nonconformity, the abundance of the material that might be utilised, and a necessarily restricted space, have made much compression inevitable. That there has been so little opportunity for comment on current events may be no disadvantage to the reader. If, to some people, the story may appear fragmentary, it is owing to the absolute necessity of selection. To others it may seem that too much prominence is given to the political history of Nonconformity; but, in this respect, I have simply been guided by the facts of the case. Combined agitation and action in and out of Parliament have been a foremost characteristic of Dissent during the last forty years. The remarkable—indeed, unprecedented—victories gained in the interests of religious equality, though faintly remembered now, are worthy of being put on record in a complete form as an essential part of our national history. These legislative concessions, it must be generally admitted, have not injured the Church of England. They are not only themselves just, but they have tended to assuage the bitterness engendered by ecclesiastical monopoly and the intolerance it produces; and their substantial fruits, it may be added, are enjoyed by Nonconformists who shrink from being classed with "Political Dissenters."

In his original Preface—and the same thought pervades his book—Mr. Skeats reasonably claims that the best features in the political and social constitution, and the mental as well as the religious life, of England can be traced to the direct or indirect influence of the principles of Dissent; in other words, to the fuller recognition of those natural rights in respect to free thought and free religious action, which are the patrimony of no particular sect. Step by step, not without severe and protracted struggles, these claims have been, to a considerable extent, realised. Their results are now under the guardianship of a phalanx of Free Churches, that are conscious of their growing power, flanked by the mass of outside opinion which, in the course of generations, they have, to so large an extent, created. Although in this matter there can be no retrogression, there is still an imperative need to frustrate all stealthy schemes for placing the Established Church in a position of absolute independence, so long as it retains connection with, and receives the patronage of, the State. This History sets forth with emphasis the portentous evils and dangers of that unbridled sacerdotalism which is once again re-asserting its pretensions. In this direction the Free Churches have yet a great work to do. I shall greatly rejoice if a further issue of this historical narrative should help to strengthen their resolution. Not only the spirit of the age, but influential allies within the Church are on their side, if they actively utilise them. To Nonconformists especially seems to be committed the task of grappling with these reactionary tendencies, seeing that the Evangelical party has become increasingly quiescent. Happily, with all their differences, the leading Nonconformist bodies are drawing closer together at a period when such union for such an object must be irresistible.

Some few of the topics I have dealt with, though of real interest, had almost passed from my recollection till refreshed by a study of the volumes of the *Nonconformist* and contemporary publications, and will probably be entirely new to the majority of readers. But no research has been spared to present all sections of the narrative in as complete a form as possible. For the most part it has been found necessary to advert in a very cursory fashion to the many eminent Nonconformists who have passed away during the period under review, notwithstanding the temptation to expatiate on their distinctive qualities and conspicuous services; while it has been useless attempting to discuss such recent and significant events as the Congregational International Council, the scope of the Free Education measure, the more general action taken by many of the Free Churches in connection with various social reforms, and many other indications of revived religious activity. The year 1888 —the Bicentenary of the Revolution that brought legislative relief to Dissenters—was fixed upon as a goal, but, owing to the interlacing of events, it has been found practically impossible to draw a hard and fast line, while some of the Nonconformist movements of the last three years have been full of significance and hopefulness.

In sketching the course of these latter-day events I have been much indebted to the facilities kindly afforded by the authorities at the Congregational Memorial Hall and the Baptist Mission House, and for valuable assistance from experienced members of the Wesleyan Methodist Connexion and the Society of Friends, and from the Secretary of the Unitarian Society, and to various other friends, such as Mr. J. Carvell Williams, for help and suggestions and the loan of books. In the midst of my labours a volume, entitled "The Interregnum," by Mr. F. A. Inderwick, Q.C. (Sampson Low, Marston, & Co.), came into my hands, containing a most interesting and elaborate sketch of legislative, social, and religious life in England during the Commonwealth era, based on official documents, letters, and newspaper reports, which throw a flood of light upon the characteristics of that period, and show that many valuable reforms were suggested by Cromwell, such as free education, which have been only realised by subsequent generations. Unfortunately the book only reached me when the sheets dealing with the events of the Commonwealth had already passed through the press.

CHARLES S. MIALL.

9, Cathcart Hill, Junction Road, N.
September, 1891.

CONTENTS.

CHAPTER I.

INTRODUCTORY—REVIEW OF ECCLESIASTICAL HISTORY FROM THE REFORMATION TO THE REVOLUTION.

refused by Presbyterians—Liberty of Conscience in the Parliamentary Army; "Prides's purge"—Religious freedom under the Commonwealth; "The Triers"—Cromwell and Milton on toleration—Popular errors as to the culture and manners of the Commonwealth Puritans—Religious zeal among the Baptists; Powell and Kiffin—Rise of the Quakers; Fox persecuted during the Protectorate by Presbyterians and Independents—Charles II.; the Savoy Conference—Ejectment of two thousand clergymen (1662)—Act of Uniformity and draconic legislation—Rapid increase of Nonconformists—Their sufferings—Savage persecution of the Quakers—Attempts at Comprehension—James II.—Penn as a courtier—Imprisonment of the Seven Bishops and the "Declaration"—Dissenters sympathise with them ... ... pp. 1—69

CHAPTER II.

The Revolution to the Comprehension Bill, 1688—1689.

Eminent Nonconformists prior to 1688-89—The Bishops and Dissenters—Numerical strength of Dissent—Character of Nonconformist preaching—Academies for Dissenting ministers—Declaration of the Prince of Orange on toleration—His reception by the clergy and by Dissenters—Twelve bishops vote against his taking the Crown—Debate on Coronation Oath—Oath of Supremacy and Allegiance and Corporation Act—The nonjuring bishops and clergy—The clause abolishing sacramental tests defeated—The Whig families now the rulers of the nation—Bishop Burnet's views on toleration and comprehension—Relations of Tillotson, Tenison, and Stillingfleet to Nonconformists—Religious liberty in the House of Commons—Dissenters expecting a Comprehension scheme, mainly indifferent to Test and Corporation Acts—Toleration Act passed—Its provisions—The Quakers denounce all compulsory exactions—John Locke's "Letters on Toleration" strike at the root of all State churches—Comprehension Bill in the House of Lords—A Commission appointed—Proposed alteration in services, &c.—Prorogued and dissolved without result—Opinions on the failure of the scheme ... pp. 70—119

CHAPTER III.

THE COMPREHENSION BILL TO THE OCCASIONAL CONFORMITY BILL, 1689—1704.

CHAPTER IV.

THE CHURCH IN DANGER AGITATION TO THE DEATH OF QUEEN ANNE. 1704—1714.

CHAPTER VI.

FROM THE ORGANIZATION OF THE DISSENTING DEPUTIES TO THE ESTABLISHMENT OF METHODISM. 1732—1744.

CHAPTER VII.

THE REVIVAL OF RELIGION IN WALES.

CHAPTER VIII.

From the Establishment of Methodism to the Second Agitation for the Repeal of the Test Acts. 1744—1793.

CHAPTER IX.

FROM THE SECOND AGITATION FOR THE REPEAL OF THE TEST AND CORPORATION ACTS, TO THEIR REPEAL. 1792—1828.

CHAPTER XI.

FROM 1848 TO 1860.

CHAPTER XII.

FROM 1860 TO 1870.

CHAPTER XIII.

FROM 1870 TO 1880.

CHAPTER XIV.

FROM 1881—1891.

CHAPTER XV.

VARIOUS FREE CHURCHES. A RETROSPECT.

A History
OF THE
Free Churches of England.

CHAPTER I.

INTRODUCTORY.—REVIEW OF ECCLESIASTICAL HISTORY FROM THE REFORMATION TO THE REVOLUTION.

THE struggles of English Nonconformists up to the time of the Revolution have been so often and so ably described, that it may seem to be unnecessary to add one more page to that painful yet honourable history. No Englishman can look back upon that history without shame, but no Nonconformist can recall it without pride. The conduct both of the State and the Church of that period are now uniformly condemned both by Statesmen and by Churchmen; and if it is necessary, for the purposes of this History, that I should pass it in review, I wish it to be understood that I hold neither the State nor the Church of the present day responsible for acts then committed. It might seem superfluous to make this remark, were it not the case that, when the facts of those times are recalled, they are often treated as though the present historical descendants of the old ecclesiastical parties were, in some manner, accountable for them. No person of common sense dreams of taunting the advisers of Queen Victoria with the acts of Charles the Second's ministers, but many persons, who are possessed of strong common sense in other matters, esteem it to be a natural thing to taunt the Established Church of the present day with the acts of the Established Church of three hundred years ago. And so, on the other side, there are men combining high literary culture and ordinary common sense, who seem to imagine that they have turned the flank of their opponents' position if they have proved that the Independents of the Commonwealth were persecutors, and that they not only had no objection to tithes and Church-rates, but held firmly by the theory of a State-established religion. In so far as I may find occasion to repeat the history of religious persecution I shall do it with no such purposes as these. Men may be responsible, in no small degree, for the character and the acts of their descendants, but not for the character or the acts of their forefathers.

In reviewing the ecclesiastical history of England, from the Reformation to the Revolution, the changes in government, doctrine, and service which the Established Church successively underwent naturally claim the first attention. What is most remarkable in connection with these changes is the comparative readiness with which the more important were received, and the strenuous opposition which the less important, after a time, encountered. When Henry the Eighth founded a new Church* in England, excepting from those who remained faithful to the Romish communion, he met with no opposition to his claim to be the "supreme head" of that Church. The explanation of this fact is natural enough, although it has not been recognised by the historians of that period. The doctrine of regal supremacy in ecclesiastical matters had been familiar to Englishmen

* I use this expression advisedly, and I imagine that none but eager controversialists will dispute its accuracy. "The existence of the Church of England," says the late Bishop of St. Asaph, "as a distinct body, and her final separation from Rome, may be dated from the period of the divorce."—Short's "History of Ch. of England," p. 102.

for many generations. It had been successfully maintained, up to a certain point, by the greatest of the Plantagenet kings, and ably vindicated by Wycliffe, one of whose cardinal "heresies" was the denial of the supremacy of the Pope.* All that Henry did was to apply and extend a doctrine that had long been filtering through the minds both of the aristocracy and of the commonalty. Hence the otherwise inexplicable circumstance that his assumption of unlimited supremacy excited only what may be described as a professional opposition. Most of the bishops voted against the Act† vesting the sole ecclesiastical prerogative in the Crown; but only Gardiner resisted its extreme application when the King suspended all the bishops from their episcopal authority, and, of his own sovereign will, afterwards restored it to them. The gallows and the stake made short work of those of the inferior clergy who resisted the new law; and, long before the death of Henry, his spiritual leadership was effectually established. In that age, indeed, there seemed to be no alternative between the supremacy of the Pope and the supremacy of the King. The minds of the best of men, as is the case with some even in these days, were so warped by ancient ecclesiastical precedents that none dreamed of an ultimate appeal to Holy Scripture. St. Paul, if he were consulted, was to be interpreted by Augustine, St. John by Jerome, and St. Peter by the Popes; and to the interpreters, as a matter of course, was given the principal authority. A Church of Christ, independent, as such, of human control, and existing apart from statecraft, was an idea almost impossible to that age. If entertained at all, it could only have been by men as humble in life as in spirit, such as afterwards arose to assert the spiritual character of the kingdom of Christ upon earth.

* Vaughan's "Wycliffe," p. 211. † 25 Henry VIII., cap. 21.

It was not more difficult to compel obedience to the theological dogmas of the new Church, for they differed but little from those of Rome. The King himself undertook to settle what the people should believe, and, with this view, drew up a set of Articles of Religion These Articles, while they enjoined belief in the "whole Bible" and the Three Creeds, also declared that Baptism was necessary to salvation; that the opinions of all "Anabaptists" were detestable heresies; and that Auricular Confession and Priestly Absolution were commendable. The doctrine of Transubstantiation was set forth without reserve, as also was that of Purgatory, and Prayers to the Saints were commended. On the other hand, the doctrine of Justification by Faith was recognised. The decision of the dignitaries of the Church on these points was what the decision of State functionaries customarily is. Expressed in vernacular English, it was—"We believe whatsoever we are commanded to believe." But a step was taken which undermined many of the Articles, and was almost equally fatal to the doctrine of the Royal supremacy. The King not only authorised a translation of the Bible into English, but ordered a copy of it to be set up in each of the churches. This act, however, was soon felt to be a political blunder, and after seven years it was substantially recalled.

Before furnishing his subjects with such a potent weapon against the system which he had determined to establish, King Henry issued the "Injunctions." He, who was the slave of his own lusts, enjoined the clergy to exhort the people to "keep God's commandments," and to give themselves to the "study of the Scriptures, and a good life." In the "Institution of a Christian Man," the bishops laid down, at greater length, the creed of the Reformed Church, which was further vindicated in the "Necessary Doctrine." Having thus explained and apparently demonstrated the absolute truth of the new theological system, it only remained to enforce it. Some denied the corporeal presence, and were accordingly sent to Smithfield. In order to strengthen his power, the King allowed his Parliament to assume the functions of a Convocation by debating for eleven days the doctrines of Christianity. This debate issued in the adoption of the law of the "Six Articles," which set forth, in the strongest language, the presence of the natural body and blood of Christ in the Sacrament of the Lord's Supper, sanctioned Communion in one kind only, denied the right of Marriage to the priesthood, enforced vows of Chastity, allowed Private Masses, and declared Auricular Confession to be both expedient and necessary. The most fearful penalties were attached to any opposition to these doctrines. The least was loss of goods ; the greatest, burning at the stake, which was the punishment for denying the first of the Articles. The law was now let loose against both Protestants and Catholics, but with peculiar vengeance against the former. Catholics were only hanged, Protestants were burned ; Fisher was sent to the gallows, Anne Askew to the stake. And so the new Church was founded. The work begun by one royal profligate was, a hundred and thirty years later, fittingly finished by another. Henry the Eighth's natural successor in ecclesiastical politics was Charles the Second.

No change took place in the ceremonies of the Church in the reign of Henry the Eighth. A Commission had been appointed in 1540 to examine into them, but no action was taken upon its proceedings. The Services in use were of several kinds, and varied according to ancient custom. York had its custom distinct from Exeter, and Hereford and Lincoln from Bangor and Sarum. The first step in the direction of uniformity was made in the second year of Edward the Sixth, when an Order of Communion was published. The word "Mass" was now dropped, and the cup was restored to the laity. In the same year appeared the first Book of Common Prayer, which was adopted by Parliament, and ordered to be used, without having been submitted to Convocation. It was compiled, with a few important alterations, from the old Missals. The compilers had, however, left some questions open, and there was doubt as to what was meant in certain portions. The book, therefore, was ordered to be revised. On this revision the German Reformers exercised some influence, which appears in the omission, in the second book, of Prayers for the Dead, the doctrine of Transubstantiation, and in the adoption of simpler ecclesiastical vestments—the second rubric forbidding the use of any vestments excepting the rochet and the surplice.* For the second time Convocation was not consulted, and the new order of worship was published without having been submitted to its decision. Those who, in later days, have expatiated on the claims of this body seem to have forgotten history. In the settlement of the Protestant religion in England Convocation was altogether ignored by the State. The use of the second book was enforced by a second Act of Uniformity. The State having, in two years, changed its opinions, required all the people to do the same.

The greater simplicity of the second Service-book was probably, in some measure, due to the bold position assumed by the first Nonconformist, John Hooper, Bishop of Gloucester. History, while it has done justice to the character and the abilities of this eminent man, has not done similar justice to his opinions. He appears on its page as a conscientious opponent of all ecclesiastical ceremonies and habits not expressly warranted by Scripture,

* See Cardwell's "Two Prayer Books of Edward VI., compared."

as a sufferer for his opinions on this subject, and as a martyr for the Protestant religion. But he was more than this. All Protestants and Puritans have been accustomed to hold his name in reverence, but it belongs in a more especial manner to the English Nonconformists of the nineteenth century. It was Hooper's voice that first publicly proclaimed the principles of religious freedom. He stood alone amongst the English Protestants of his age in denying the right of the State to interfere with religion. While Edward the Sixth, acting under the advice of his council, was submitting to Parliament Acts of Uniformity, and compelling assent to new Articles of Religion,* Hooper was publicly denying the right of any king to interfere in the government of the Church. "Christ's Kingdom," he says, "is a spiritual one. In this neither Pope nor King may govern. Christ alone is the governor of his Church, and the only lawgiver." He told the people, in words proclaimed to thousands at Paul's Cross and in various parts of the kingdom, that their consciences were bound only by the Word of God, and that they might, with it, judge "bishop, doctor, preacher, and curate." "The laws of the civil magistrate," he elsewhere says, "are not to be admitted in the Church."† Preaching before the King he called for the restoration of the primitive Church, and demanded the abolition of all vestments, crosses, and altars. It is a wonder that such a man should have been asked to accept a bishopric; but, next to Latimer, he was the greatest and most popular preacher of his day; and his zeal not only for

* "The forty-two Articles of Religion of this reign, which are substantially the same as those now in force, were issued without consulting either Parliament or Convocation." Burnet, vol. iii., p. 210.

† "A Declaration concerning Christ and his Offices." Early Writings, p. 82.

the Reformation, but for a further reformation, knew no bounds. And the young King liked him. Hooper was a man peculiarly calculated to fascinate such an open, frank, and tender nature as that of Edward. He was one of the few ecclesiastics of his age who was more than an ecclesiastic. He did not imagine that, in assuming the office of a preacher of the Gospel, he was bound to quench all the natural instincts of humanity. He loved children. Of a candid and truthful moral disposition, generous in his sympathies, just in his desires, an ardent and eloquent preacher, he was a man who seemed to be, above all his contemporaries, born to be the apostle of the new religion. Had King Edward and Hooper lived, the Reformation would probably have been completed.

For Hooper to be offered a bishopric under the first Act of Uniformity was for him to refuse it. He declined to take the oath of supremacy, and he "scrupled the vestments." The oath was altered by the King, and large personal liberty in wearing the "garments of Popery" was, it must be said, generously offered him; but he loved his conscience more than any honours, and esteemed the cause of the Reformation of more value than many bishoprics. The King, Cranmer, and Ridley remonstrated with him. He took advice of the German and Swiss Reformers, and they, while holding his opinions of the vestments, advised him, for the sake of religion, to accept the bishopric; but he still declined. Then he wrote against the Papal observances, and was committed to the Fleet, from whence he came forth giving up a little but holding much, and was consecrated Bishop of Gloucester. In this capacity, for four years he visited and preached as bishop had never done in England before, and seldom, if ever since, and so won the crown of a martyr. Such was the man who sounded the first note of that controversy which was afterwards to test the English Church, and who laid the foundation of English Puritanism.

All times of persecution, and all ages which have been distinguished by an intemperate zeal for external uniformity, have been marked by the prevalence of notorious immorality. The age of Edward the Sixth was no exception to this rule. While the King's council was framing theological propositions, and compelling, for the first time in the history of England, "subscription" to them, enforcing laws for wearing red habits by some on some days, and white and black habits by others on other days, changing the laws themselves within two years, and burning, hanging, or imprisoning all those who could not change their consciences as fast as their rulers could theirs, immorality flourished like a green bay-tree. "Lying, cheating, theft, perjury, and whoredom," says Bucer, in his letter to Hooper,* "are the complaints of the times." Bishop Latimer said that England was "infamous for whoredom" beyond any other part of the world. "Profaneness and immorality," says a Church historian who is not given to exaggeration in the use of language, "had now an unlimited range." "The courtiers and great men," writes another, "indulged themselves in a dissolute and licentious life, and the clergy were not without blemish."†

The reformation of the English Church never passed beyond the line drawn by the death of Edward the Sixth. It has, on the contrary, rather receded from it. There can be no doubt concerning the intentions of the reformers of that reign.‡ They wished for a further reformation. Had they lived the royal supremacy would probably have been relinquished; the idea of enforcing uniformity by legal pains and penalties would have been surrendered the

* Collier, vol. ii., p. 294. † Neal, vol. i., p. 78.

‡ The testimony on this point is indisputable. See Neal, vol. i., p. 79.

theory of episcopacy, as it is now held and stated, would have been consigned to the pages of history only, and the Reformation would have been as complete in England as it was in the German States.

It might have been expected that there would have been a rebound from the persecutions endured in the reign of Mary, and a sudden leap from Romanism to a more extreme Protestantism; and, under a sovereign of any character but Elizabeth's, this might have been the course of history. But that Queen had inherited too much of the disposition of her father, Henry the Eighth, to surrender the smallest of her royal prerogatives. Her unwillingness to assume the title of "Supreme Head" of the Church, while she retained the whole prerogative of headship, and her willingness to take the title of "Supreme Governor" only, have been much commented upon; but it requires a preternatural acuteness to detect any real difference between the two titles. The English legislature certainly has never recognised that difference,* and Elizabeth acted with all

* In the Act relating to First Fruits and Tenths (2 and 3 Anne, cap. 11), the two Houses addressed Queen Anne in the following terms:—"Inasmuch as your Majesty, taking into your friendly and serious consideration the mean and inefficient maintenance belonging to the Clergy in divers parts of this your kingdom, has been most graciously pleased out of your most religious and tender concern of the Church of England (whereof your Majesty is the 'Supreme Head' on earth)," &c. On May 3rd, 1717, the Lower House of Convocation made a representation to the Upper House relating to Bishop Hoadley's Sermon on "The Nature of the Kingdom and Church of Christ,"—a sermon the doctrine of which was that Christ alone was Head of His Church. The Lower House, on this occasion, condemned Bishop Hoadley's sermon, because its tendency was to "impugn and impeach the regal supremacy in causes ecclesiastical," in maintenance of which, said the House, "we offer the following particulars:—That whereas His Majesty is, and, by the statutes of this realm, is declared to be, 'Supreme Head' of the Church." Palin's "History of the Church of England," cap. 17.

the autocratic authority of headship and regal supremacy. From the reign of the second Tudor to the reign of the last Stuart the great object of the Crown was to retain its supremacy over all the actions of the subject.

During the forty-four years of the reign of Elizabeth the whole power of the Crown was exercised, in regard to ecclesiastical matters, with two distinct purposes. The first was to subject the Church to its "governor;" the second to suppress all opinions differing from those which had received a special patent of protection. The first wholly succeeded; the second entirely failed. The Prayer Book and Articles of Elizabeth do not materially differ from those of Edward. The only difference of any importance relates to the vestments, which were ordered to be the same as those used in the second year of Edward. This change was adverse to a further reformation, and it was confirmed by a third Act of Uniformity, which the Queen took care should not be a dead letter. She heard of some who did not wear the habits, and who even preached against them, and Parker was at once ordered to enforce the law. Then the exiles who had returned from the Continent, flushed with hope and ardent in the cause of the Gospel, found that the agent was not less cruel than the sovereign who directed him. The Primates of the English Church have always been selected for their willingness to be the passive instruments of the Government. Cranmer's chief work had been to celebrate and then to undo royal marriages, to carry out the law of the Six Articles, to publish the Bible, when it pleased the king that his subjects should read it, and to recall that book when the sovereign found that its circulation was becoming dangerous to his pretensions. Parker's office was to carry into execution the law which made it criminal not to conform to the Prayer Book, and high treason itself to refuse to take the oath of spiritual supremacy. A hot-headed, intolerant, arbitrary, and vindictive man, he was the model of an Elizabethan archbishop. So zealously did he set about his work that he shocked the statesmen of his age,* and at last shocked even Elizabeth herself.

The attempt to enforce the Act of Uniformity excited instant resistance, and the Church was "turned into a great shambles."† Those who, soon afterwards, came to be denominated "Puritans" were the first to suffer; but at Cambridge there arose one whose character, genius, controversial ability and persistency of purpose made the Puritan controversy famous throughout Europe. Thomas Cartwright, their leader in the reign of Elizabeth, had preached the doctrines of Puritanism with boldness and vigour for some time before he was silenced. Multitudes in the University town and its neighbourhood crowded to hear him, for he united in an equal degree the finest qualities of the scholar and the preacher. "The sun," said Beza, "doth not see a more learned man."‡ The Church historian Fuller does not hesitate to bear similar testimony to Cartwright's high character and great abilities.§ Whitgift, an almost equally able disputant, attempted to answer him, and failing to convince either the preacher or his hearers, used his power as Vice-Chancellor to dismiss him from the University. Cartwright, indeed, held doctrines more dangerous to the established order than many of the Puritans. He took no part in the controversy respecting the habits, and, indeed, objected to the whole order of Church government and patronage. He denounced the hierarchical system, and demanded that the people should have liberty to choose their own ministers. On other subjects he

* Burleigh's Letter to Grindal in Strype's "Grindal," p. 281.
† Sherlock on "Judgment," p. 119.
‡ "Church History," b. x., p. 3.
§ "Clark's Lives," p. 19.

anticipated most of the views and practices which were afterwards enforced by the Presbyterian party in the time of the Commonwealth. The controversy between Cartwright and Whitgift was carried on with equal vigour on both sides; but Whitgift had one advantage,—he was in power.

It does not come within the scope of this work to review at any length the progress of the Puritan struggle. It was a struggle against all that was Romish in the Protestant Church. Every doctrine and ceremony which could not be authenticated by reference to the Scriptures was assailed by the Puritans. Diocesan Episcopacy was the foremost question; then came the baptismal ceremonies, the churching of women, church discipline, episcopal ordination, the use of the cross in baptism, of caps and surplices in preaching, of the ring in marriage, and of organs in church music. It may be a matter of wonder at the present time how some of these matters could have been debated with such excitement; but there lay at the bottom of all of them the greater question of the ultimate supremacy of the Divine or of human law. And, besides, the Puritans knew, or thought they knew, that each and every one of the doctrines and practices which they condemned was a side entrance back to the Church of Rome. Hence they felt that they were fighting both for their God and for their country.

The greatest struggles took place on two questions—that of Episcopacy and that of the vestments; and on both the persecuted had the private sympathies of the men who persecuted them. The claims of Episcopacy had not then become hardened into an absolute theory. The present theory of the Church of England on this subject was held at that time only by members of the Roman Catholic Church. Cranmer favoured Wycliffe's doctrine that bishops were not a distinct order. In the "Necessary Erudition" —a book drawn up by a committee of bishops and clergy, and published, by royal command, as an authoritative exposition of the doctrines of the Church—it is stated that there are only two orders of the Christian ministry, presbyters and deacons, and that the Episcopal character is included in the former. Archbishops and bishops were declared to be of human appointment only.* Whitgift treated the whole question of the form of Church government as a matter of indifference, maintaining, in reply to Cartwright, who advocated the exclusive authority of the Presbyterian system, that Christ had left the external polity of His Church an open question. It was not until near the close of Elizabeth's reign that the theory of Episcopacy which now prevails in the Established Church was even mooted. It was in 1588, when all the fathers of the Reformation were dead, that Bancroft, then chaplain to Whitgift, first maintained that bishops were an order distinct from presbyters—or, as he called them, priests—and were superior to them by Divine law, and that it was heresy to deny the doctrine.‡ Whitgift said that he wished this were true, but could not believe it. A theory so flattering to human vanity was not, however, likely to remain unrecognised by those whose position it would most favourably affect; and accordingly, in another generation, Diocesan Episcopacy was claimed to be of Divine institution, and the only Scriptural form of Church government.

The Puritans denied not merely the expediency, but the lawfulness of this form. They preached and wrote against it with the same vigour as they had done against the "Popish garments." The difference between the two parties was not so wide then as it afterwards became; but Episcopacy was part of the system established by law, and

* Records of the Reformation in Burnet.

† Whitgift's "Answer" (A.D. 1572) and "Defence of the Answer" (A.D. 1574).

‡ Neal, vol. i., p. 494.

no mercy was shown to any man who dared to oppose the smallest part of that system.

It was the same with respect to the vestments. Neither the bishops nor the clergy were very zealous for them; they would have given them up as willingly as they would have retained them, but they wore and therefore defended them. Latimer, Ridley, and Cranmer derided them; Jewel could compare them only to actors' dresses; Grindal tried to get them abolished; Parker gloried in not having worn them at his consecration; Sandys, Bishop of Worcester, said that they "came from hell;" the laity hated them, and, says Whitgift, would "spit in the faces" of the men who wore them; but they, too, were part of the system established under the Act of Uniformity, and, although Parker himself disapproved of them, he hunted to banishment, to prison, or to death all who openly did the same. The question of the habits has, since that time, undergone a change somewhat similar to that which has come over the question of Episcopacy. An "ultra-ritualist" could not have been met with either in court or church in Queen Elizabeth's days, but in the days of Queen Victoria Ritualism is a gospel in itself.

Public opinion was thus clearly on the side of the Puritans, and yet they failed to do more than to create a party. They did not shake, for one moment, the foundations of the Church, or the smallest of its ornaments. Not a single concession was made to them. Looking at their controversy, from this distance of time, it would be harsh and ungenerous to say that they did not deserve success. The Puritans were men of the noblest intellectual attainments, the greatest scholars of their age, and of the loftiest piety. Like their successors a hundred years later, they must also have been aware that for them to be suspended from preaching, was for the best preachers to be silenced, and that at a time when preaching was never so much needed. For thousands of the pulpits were empty, and in many parts of the country a sermon could not be heard within a distance of twenty miles, or from one six months in the year to another. They must have reckoned on this amongst other deprivations; or did they, knowing the extent of public sympathy with their views—having repeated evidence that the House of Commons agreed with them, and being aware that all the foreign reformers were pleading their cause—expect a relaxation of the laws? There is no evidence to this effect. There is not a sentence in all their writings expressing the assurance of ultimate victory. They do not seem, at any time, to have had a gleam of certain hope. They acted as they did, with a forlorn courage, knowing that there was no issue for them but punishment or death, yet meeting both when they came with an abounding happiness which was certainly denied to all their persecutors. Probably not one of these—Henry, Elizabeth, Parker, or Whitgift—but would gladly have exchanged his death-bed for that of the commonest Puritan that was dying in the Gate prison or the Compter.

There must be a reason, apart from the character of the governing power, why Puritans within the Church have never succeeded. The reason is probably to be found in the fact that they never essentially differed from the dominant party. Both were almost equally intolerant. Parker and Whitgift persecuted the Puritans; but if Cartwright had been in Whitgift's place he would have dealt out equal persecution to Baptists and Independents. They who had suffered imprisonment on account of their opinions actually remonstrated with statesmen for releasing Roman Catholics from confinement. They held a purer doctrine than their opponents, but none the less did they require it to be enforced by the "authority of the magistrate." But the habit of theological thought was then, as for generations afterwards, essentially dogmatical. The best of the Puritans looked to the Scriptures for rules rather than for principles—for propositions rather than for examples. Christianity was with them merely an historical development of Judaism; and therefore, while they believed in the sacrifice of Christ, they equally believed in the laws of Moses. The sacred writings were rough materials out of which they might hew their own system. The stones were taken in equal parts out of the books of the Old Testament and the New; the latter being dug for doctrine and the former for precept. Amongst all the works of the early Puritans there is not one on the character or life of Christ, nor one which gives any indication that they had even an imagination of the wholly spiritual nature of His kingdom. They pleaded with tears for liberty of conscience, while they would have denied it to the first "Anabaptist" whom they met. It was no wonder that they did not gain their end, and that they scarcely hoped to gain it.

There were at that time men who were esteemed guilty of a greater crime than Puritanism. A Presbyterian church had been formed at Wandsworth, in 1572, and it had the honour of being the first silenced "conventicle." Wandsworth was then a quieter and a pleasanter place than it is now, and those who went there may have gone for rural retirement as well as for personal safety; but Parker's hounds of law tracked them, and they were dispersed. No greater punishment, at that time, awaited them, for they were not "Anabaptists" or "Brownists." Dutch Anabaptists * had been caught and burned in Henry

* The Dutch Anabaptists of this period had little in common with English Baptists, excepting an objection to infant baptism. These and the Münster Baptists are no more to be confounded with English Baptists than are Greek with English or Armenian Episcopalians. It erved an obvious purpose, however, in Elizabeth's reign to do so.

the Eighth's time, and perished in the same way under Elizabeth; but the English Baptists and Independents had not hitherto attracted much public notice. It has been asserted that a Baptist church existed in England in 1417.* There were certainly Baptist "churches" in England as early as 1589,† and there could scarcely have been several organised communities without the corresponding opinions having been held by individuals and some churches established for years previous to this date. With respect to the Independents, certain "congregations" are spoken of by Foxe ‡ as established in London in 1555, and it is possible that they were Independent, but more probable that they were Puritan. It is now clearly established that an Independent church, of which Richard Fitz was pastor, existed in 1568.§ In 1580 Sir Walter Raleigh spoke of the Brownists as existing by "thousands." In 1583 Brownists and Anabaptists are freely classed together. Which really appeared first in point of time can be only a matter of conjecture.

But although Richard Fitz was the first pastor of the first Independent church in England, to Robert Browne belongs the honour of founding the denomination. This man's character has been assailed with almost equal virulence by Church and Nonconformist writers; but, although he is proved to have been naturally of a passionate, dogmatic, and weak nature, no charge against his piety has been successfully established.|| His moral courage and his

---

* Robinson's "Claude," vol. ii., p. 54.

† Dr. Somer's Reply to Barrowe, quoted in Ivimey's History, vol. i., p. 109.

‡ Vol. iii., p. 114.

§ "Congregational Martyrs." Art., Richard Fitz, *pass.*

|| The best estimate of the character of Browne is to be found in Fletcher's "History of Independency," vol. ii., cap. 3.

willingness to bear suffering in testimony of his sincerity were amply shown by his life. If, like Cartwright, he eventually returned to the Church, he did what ought not to excite surprise. The wonder is, not that human nature was so weak in him, but that it was so strong in others.

With one exception Browne held all the views which distinguish modern Independents. It was many years before this body adopted the principles of religious freedom in their widest application. Browne himself, who was extravagant in many of his opinions, believed that the power of the civil magistrates ought to be exercised in favour of a Scriptural religion. Both Barrowe and Greenwood—next to Penry, the noblest martyrs of Independency—fully acknowledged the supremacy of the Crown in Ecclesiastical matters. It is the singular and distinguished honour of the Baptists to have repudiated, from their earliest history, all coercive power over the consciences and the actions of men with reference to religion. No sentence is to be found in all their writings inconsistent with those principles of Christian liberty and willinghood which are now equally dear to all the free Congregational Churches of England. They were the proto-evangelists of the voluntary principle.*

On Independents and Baptists the hand of Archbishop Whitgift, the Jeffreys of the Episcopal bench, fell with double vengeance. He choked the prisons with them, and from prison hailed their most eminent leaders to the scaffold, the greatest crime of which they were guilty being the denial of the supremacy of the Crown as it was then exercised. In the eyes of Churchmen, however, the Independents and Baptists were heretics beyond any of

* The Author is not connected with the Baptist denomination; and has therefore, perhaps, greater pleasure in bearing testimony to undoubted historical fact.

their age. The one party denied the Scriptural warrant, and even the priestly efficacy, of Infant Baptism. The doctrine of these men cut at the roots of Priestism, and was fatal to the very idea of a National Church. For, how could there be a National Church, if only "believers" were to be baptised; and if priests did not, by the magic of baptism, make all infants Christians, was not their principal function gone? The frantic opposition of the clergy to these revolutionists can be easily understood. Even the best of the Puritans could not endure them, and employed their pens to revile both their characters and their opinions. With scarcely less violence were the "Brownists" attacked. The characteristic creed of the Baptists was adult believers' baptism. They were as thorough Independents as were the Brownists, but Independency was not the most prominent feature of their belief. Browne, however, had given such prominence to this distinctive doctrine that those who accepted it were publicly marked off, both from Puritans and from Episcopalians. It was, as even then taught, a doctrine which was fatal to an order as distinct from an office in the Christian ministry. The Puritan system was one of a mixed ecclesiastical oligarchy, in which the clergy held life-peerages, and were superiors in rank, as well as in work, to the people. The Independents denied the scripturalness of any such distinction. A man, with them, was a minister no longer than he had the care of a separate congregation. The sole authority for his office was his spiritual fitness and the consent of the people to whom he ministered. Other ministers and churches had nothing to do either with him or with them, but they gladly, and from the first, welcomed the co-operation and approval of similar organisations in their choice and work. They differed, therefore, as much or more from the Puritan clergy as the Puritan clergy differed from the Episcopalians; and the

Puritans took pains to let it be known that they had as little sympathy with the "schism" of the Brownists as they had with the "heresy" of the Anabaptists.

The doctrines of these men were set forth with great clearness in their defences before the ecclesiastical authorities as well as in their works. Their mode of stating them, if sometimes offensive,* was generally, from its extreme simplicity, exceedingly winning. Jeered at and browbeaten in Courts of High Commission and Star Chamber by archbishops and bishops, they defended themselves with a humility which became as well as adorned their belief.

These were the men whom the civil and ecclesiastical authorities of the latter part of Queen Elizabeth's reign judged to be not fit to live. The laity, generally, cared little for them, and the Queen suffered herself to listen to the promptings of her clerical advisers. They were, therefore, imprisoned for months and years in the foulest gaols, beaten with cudgels, some left to die of fever and sores, while others were hanged. Barrowe, Greenwood, and Penry, the three great witnesses for Independency, met the latter fate. They were all just and holy men, but the character of Penry was of an order which times of the fiercest persecution apparently can alone produce; for, only at such periods are certain characters tested to their utmost. Penry seems to have stood that test until his soul was purified from all the dross of human nature. He was a man of Johannine disposition, yet of a most indomitable energy; a scholar, but also an evangelist; of as intense reflective faculty as a mystic, yet as active as a pioneer; overflowing with domestic affections, but absorbed with the love of souls; and serving his Divine Master as though

* Barrowe, when before the Commission, called Whitgift, to his face, a "beast" and a "monster." It was true; but the words, probably cost him his life.

that Master had no other servant to do His work. He was the Christian apostle of Wales, a country then, although four bishops had charge of it, and "livings" abounded, in a state of worse than heathen barbarism, for the clergy set an example of the grossest vices and of the foulest living.* Penry was hanged, and Whitgift was the first to put his signature to the warrant for his execution.

The Independents and the Baptists took up the weapons against the Established Church as the Puritans were dropping them. The vestment controversy had worn itself out. The old leaders of it were dead or had conformed. What law failed to do with many others the power of a master intellect had accomplished. Jewel had, in the early part of this reign, in an "Apology" for the Church of England, built a barrier of reason and Scripture against the pretensions of the Church of Rome; Hooker now undertook a similar work in behalf of the principles of an Established Protestant Episcopalian religion. In an age when nearly all learning and culture were on the side of the Puritans, Independents, and Baptists; when most of the ministers of the Established Church "were the basest of the people," and had been taken from the lowest occupations,† Hooker must have seemed an ecclesiastical Ajax, and time has not diminished his greatness.

But it is unfortunate for Hooker's reputation, that in the controversy which occasioned the writing of the "Polity" he should have so closely imitated his archdiocesan Whitgift, in his controversy with Cartwright. Not being able to silence Cartwright by argument, Whitgift had silenced him by authority. Travers was as learned a man as Hooker, and as great a scholar. He was predecessor to Hooker in

---

* Rees' "History of Nonconformity in Wales." Int. chap.

† "Supplication of the Puritans to Parliament." Neal, vol. i., p. 483; and "Survey of the State of Religion." Ib., pp. 477-78.

point of time, as a Temple lecturer, although inferior to him in position. It might be an unseemly thing, and it was illegal, for the same pulpit to be used in the morning by Hooker to preach Conformity, and in the evening by Travers to preach Puritanism, and it was unseemly that they should attack each other. But wars of oral disputation were at that time as common as pamphlet wars have since become. They were arranged beforehand with all the formality of a tournament. Luther had engaged in one such war; Bucer in another. They were still more common a century later, when Pædobaptism and anti-Pædobaptism divided the Nonconformist body, and public disputes were invited on both sides. But Hooker became annoyed. Travers was a man of quicker, if not profounder, intellect than he, readier at attack and more adroit in fence. Hooker moved slowly. His thought might be, as it was, majestic in its march and grand in its sweep, but it was deficient in celerity of action. He complained to the authorities, and Travers was silenced and ejected, but afterwards Hooker seems to have become ashamed of the course which he then took. His "Polity" occupied the whole of his subsequent life, and those who, since then, have maintained the power and authority of the Church to command human obedience, and to enforce penalties for the non-observance of her laws, have always drawn the best of their arguments from the great armoury of the "Ecclesiastical Polity."

The foundations, rites, and ceremonies of the Established Church being settled as against Roman Catholics on the one hand, and Puritans, Independents, and Baptists on the other, and the press and pulpit being closed against any replies, an attempt was next made definitely to settle her particular system of theological doctrine. Whether, as has been supposed, the language of the Articles was so chosen as purposely to leave them open to different interpretations, is, and always will be, a matter of dispute. Like the Catechism, they are of Lutheran origin,* and are therefore not essentially Calvinistic. As far as they go, they will bear a Calvinistic interpretation better than any other ; but where Calvin's system, as on the doctrines of Predestination, the Atonement, and Inspiration, is particularly explicit, the Articles are particularly vague. The presumption is that, like everything else connected with the new Establishment, they were intended to be a compromise. But theological compromises, however they might have suited Cranmer, did not suit Whitgift. A preacher of the University of Cambridge, sympathising with the doctrines of the lately-risen Arminius, had ridiculed Calvin's theory of Predestination and Perseverance. Whitgift, to settle the controversy, issued the nine propositions known as the "Lambeth Articles," in which the doctrine of Predestination is stated with a naked repulsiveness of language only since surpassed by Toplady. "God," said Whitgift, "has, of his own good will and pleasure, from all eternity, reprobated some men to death ; men cannot be saved if they will, and a person predestinated to life, whatever his sins and relapses, shall inherit that life." Whitgift, however, was not supreme head of the English Church, and he had no sooner published his dogmatic decisions as to the counsels of the Almighty from eternity, and which he declared to be "already established by the laws of the land," than Elizabeth commanded them to be recalled. The Queen might, or might not, have been a "hyper-Calvinist." She was, on the whole, likely to be one. Her government was based upon the Calvinistic principle of politics. She predestinated sound Churchmen, whatever might be their

* This is conclusively shown in Archbishop Lawrence's "Bampton Lectures."

personal profligacy, to a heaven of place and profit, and Puritans and Anabaptists, whatever might be their personal piety, to pains and penalties. She might naturally, therefore, be supposed to approve of Whitgift's Articles, but they raised painful and troublesome questions. Perhaps they made her ask herself whether she was a "justified person," having, as such, "full assurance and certainty" of the remission of her sins, and, doubting it, may have decided that a system which doomed herself to a worse punishment than she had been able to inflict on all the heretics in her kingdom—from Wielmacker and Ter Voort, the unhappy Anabaptists whom she had burned at the stake, to Penry, the last Brownist whom she had hanged—however true it might be, should not be declared to be the doctrine of the Church of which she herself was the supreme head.

The controversy between Calvinists and Arminians, although never entirely ceasing, and never likely now to cease, did not again attract prominent notice until the Arminian Laud succeeded the Calvinistic Whitgift, when an Irish Episcopalian Synod framed articles in exact accordance with Whitgift's, a House of Commons decided in favour of Calvinism, and the question was so debated at solemn public conferences that no one, we are informed, left them as Arminians, who had not gone thither in the same opinion;* which is not at all unlikely. But from Whitgift's time the Puritans were distinguished by their rigid creed as well as their rigid life, and the Archbishop, who had spent his most vigorous years in rooting out that party, must have found, just before he died, that in his last attempt at enforcing uniformity, he had given greater unity to his own adversaries. Calvinistic Puritans afterwards brought to the block an archbishop whose Arminianism was, in their

* Neal, vol. ii., p. 170.

eyes, one of his greatest sins, and Whitgift was one of their authorities.

It was just previous to this controversy that Elizabeth took the step to which reference has already been made. She cleared the gaols, and, by substituting banishment in place of imprisonment for non-attendance at church, drove both Brownists and Anabaptists from her kingdom. No event has had a greater influence on the government of the world and the success of the Christian religion than the transplantation of Englishmen which then commenced. What Elizabeth intended to do, and no doubt thought she had done, was to secure her dominions, for all time to come, from being troubled by Separatists. But absolutism in a State is as short-sighted as intolerance in a Church, and in the Tudor Queen absolutism and intolerance were combined. What, therefore, she did do was to plant nurseries of freedom, destined, at a future period, to be fatal to the very principles of political and ecclesiastical government whose permanency she had thought to secure.

Amongst those who went forth to find new homes in the free cities of the Continent, were Francis Johnson and Henry Ainsworth, who, in 1596, published "A Confession of Faith of certain English people living in the Low Countries, exiled." The church at Amsterdam, of which these men were joint pastors, was apparently the first English Independent church founded on the Continent; and was the first which issued a public confession of its faith. This document, which consists of forty-five articles, contains an elaborate explanation of the views of the English Independents at that period. It commences with a protest against the constitution and worship of the Established Church, and the means by which that Church was upheld. It then goes on to expound the nature and constitution of a Christian Church, the exposition being supported by numerous Scripture proofs. The articles on this subject differ materially, on only two points, from the principles and practices of most modern Congregationalists. All infants, it is stated, should be baptized or received into the Church "that are of the seed of the faithful by one of the parents, or under their education and government."* On this subject great difference of opinion afterwards arose, but the first Independents held the creed of the Presbyterians, both of that and of the present age. They also adhered to the doctrine that it was the official duty of princes and magistrates to "suppress and root out, by their authority, all false ministries, voluntary religions, and counterfeit worship of God. Yea, to enforce all their subjects, whether ecclesiastical or civil, to do their duties to God and men."† Worshipping in a back lane in Amsterdam, and having had experience beyond most men of what was meant by the "suppressing" and "rooting out" of religious opinions, this Church was yet as intolerant as that which they so fiercely assailed.

What influence it was which, for a time, stayed the more active persecutions of the Nonconformists towards the end of the reign of Elizabeth can only be conjectured; but there is evidence that as the Queen grew older her disposition became more tender. She had endured much pain and remorse, and had not the old hardihood to inflict pain on others. With Parker and Whitgift to carry out her behests and find new victims to the law, she had left Fox and Coverdale to linger out their lives in misery and die in poverty. She had silenced the best preachers of Christian truth, and she had filled all the prisons in England with the men of most eminent piety and learning. Then, until her

* Articles xxxv. and xxxvii. Hanbury's "Hist. Memo," vol. i., pp. 96, 97.

† Article xxxiv., Ib.

death, there was a limited toleration. There was reason to expect that, when James came to the throne, this toleration would be continued, or perhaps extended; but none as yet knew the character of Elizabeth's successor. James the First has to be considered in these pages only as the head of the Established Church. That Church had already enjoyed the honour of having the grossest of voluptuaries for its supreme head; it was now to enjoy the honour of having one of the greatest liars and drunkards of his age in the same position. The prelates accepted him with devout gratitude. The more his character became revealed to them the greater appeared to be their satisfaction. When he almost swore at the Puritans, Whitgift declared that his Majesty spake by the especial assistance of God's spirit, and Bancroft that he was melted with joy, for that since Christ's time such a king had not been. When he drivelled they held up their hands in amaze at his wisdom. The two parties fully understood each other. James had quite sufficient cunning to detect the ambitious designs of the prelates, and the prelates had sufficient learning and knowledge of the theory of morals to know that they were dealing with a dissembler and a fool. But it served their purposes to play into each other's hands. The king could put down Puritanism in the Church, and "harry" all Brownists and Anabaptists out of the land; and the bishops, in their turn, could exalt the supremacy of the monarch.

The Puritans of James's reign were a different order of men from those of Elizabeth's. They were more numerous, but more moderate, and very few of them went as far as Cartwright had gone. The grievances complained of in the "Millenary" petition from the Hampton Court Conference included, certainly, the cap and surplice, and the ring in marriage; but they did not touch on the regal supremacy or on Episcopacy. They objected to portions of the baptismal service and to confirmation; they wished the Lord's-day to be kept more holy; they asked for a more godly ministry and for a restoration of Church discipline; for pluralities to be abolished; and, lastly, that the Calvinistic Articles of Whitgift might be declared to be the creed of the Church of England, and that uniformity of doctrine might be prescribed. King James answered them at the Conference with denial and abuse. Church writers, in dealing with this subject, have felt compelled to employ language of shame and indignation at the conduct of the King and the bishops at this period, which a Nonconformist would almost hesitate to use.* It is obvious, from the whole proceedings, that the Conference was summoned for a purpose opposed to its ostensible aim. It was not intended to bring the two parties in the Church into harmony, but to give occasion for casting out one of them. It led, however, to results which none probably had anticipated. Reynolds, the Puritan, had suggested a new translation of the Bible, by his Majesty's special sanction and authority. The vanity of the King was touched, and the great work was executed. If the knowledge of the Gospel was extended, and practical religion was strengthened, by this act, the next step had a contrary tendency and effect. In the year after the Hampton Court Conference Convocation met to frame a new set of Canons. These laws—laws so far as the clergy are concerned—still deface the constitution and character of the English Episcopalian Church. Most of them are obsolete, for they have been virtually repealed by the Legislature, and only those which can be brought to bear against Dissenters are observed by

* Marsden's "Early Puritans," chap. x. Hallam's "Const. Hist.," i., 404.

the clergy, who have sworn to obey them all. They are now little else than monuments of the intolerance of a past age, and of the combined immobility and timidity of the ecclesiastical establishment of the present day.

The exiles also addressed a humble supplication to the King, in which, in admirably chosen words, they stated their faith, and asked for toleration. One article of this statement relates to the maintenance of the Christian ministry, and is decisive as to the opinions of the earliest Independents in favour of the voluntary support of religious worship. This doctrine, as will be seen, was subsequently re-affirmed, while unlimited religious freedom was still unrecognised. In the course of their history during the next hundred years this position of the Independents was reversed. They allowed the lawfulness of tithes and of a compulsory support to the Christian religion, but claimed a more perfect liberty of worship.

King James did not consider this petition worth his notice. Once more, therefore, uniformity was rigidly exacted, and once more, but for the last time, the fires of Smithfield were lighted. Bartholomew Legget, who had been convicted of Arianism, was the last to suffer in this place, and a month later, in May 1612, Edward Wightman met the same death at Lichfield. He had been convicted of a multitude of mysterious heresies, the principal of which were Anabaptism and Arianism. After this, imprisonment was substituted for death, and books instead of bodies were burned. The change marks one step towards increased religious liberty. Puritans were now tolerated, but to Brownists and Anabaptists a severer measure was dealt out. Archbishop Bancroft was to James what Parker had been to Elizabeth, and those Separatists who could not be imprisoned were banished.

It was under this new reign of terror that a second

exodus took place to Holland from inhabitants principally of London and Lincolnshire. Amongst them and their followers were some whose names are written in many histories,—such as John Robinson, the scholar and pastor, whose figure so often adorns the annals of Independency, and stands so prominent in the history of the Pilgrim Fathers; William Brewster, the future governor of the new colony; and John Smyth and Thomas Helwys, the most prominent of the Baptists of this period. When Smyth joined the Church at Amsterdam, it was already torn with dissension, and the course which he took added to its divided state. He declared himself to be a Baptist, and because the Church allowed infant baptism, denounced it as participating in spiritual adultery. The Independents, in their turn, denounced Smyth and his party as "heretics," and excommunicated them.* If the whole controversy on both sides is read, most persons will come to the conclusion that the blame of this first and fatal division of the Independent body into Pædobaptists, and Antipædobaptists, ought to be equally divided amongst both parties. If one more than another should be condemned it is Smyth, whose violent language alone would have justified the violent measure by which he was expelled.

Smyth and Helwys at once formed a Baptist Church, whose members, forty-two in number, drew up a confession of their faith, which is remarkable for two points—its Anti-Calvinism, and its Anti-State Churchism. The former is exhibited in treating of Original Sin, Predestination, and

* Francis Johnson writes:—"About thirteen years since, this Church, through persecution in England, was driven to come into these countries. Awhile after they were come hither, divers of them fell into the heresies of the Anabaptists, which are too common in these countries; and so persisting, were excommunicated by the rest." Hanbury, vol. i., p. 110.

Free Will, on which subjects the Arminian view was taken; the latter in the declaration that the office of the magistracy is not ordained in the Church. Smyth and his followers held also some doctrines nearly approaching to those afterwards affirmed by the Society of Friends. On the subject of the relation of the magistrate to the Church, as on other subjects, Smyth himself afterwards published a fuller confession, in which he disputed the right of the civil magistrate to meddle with religion or matters of conscience. This is decisive as to the more advanced opinions on this subject of the early Baptists.* Helwys returned to England about 1612, and formed in London the first General or Anti-Calvinistic Baptist Church. All Baptists at that period apparently held the sentiments of Smyth and Helwys on subjects which divide the Calvinistic and Arminian sections of the Christian world.

John Robinson had joined the Church at Amsterdam, but soon afterwards left it to found in Leyden a new

* In writing this, I have not overlooked the Humble Supplication for Toleration, attributed to Jacob, published on behalf of the Independents in 1609; nor the Pamphlet entitled "Religion's Peace; or a Plea for Liberty of Conscience," by Leonard Busher, a Baptist, and published in 1614. Mr. Hanbury ridicules Dr. Price for having, in his History of Nonconformity (vol. i., pp. 522-23), taken credit to the Baptists for being the first, as shown in Busher's Pamphlet, to bring forth to public view, the principles of religious liberty, and refers to the "Humble Supplication," published five years before, as proof that the Independents were the first to do this; but Mr. Hanbury does not distinguish between even toleration and liberty, much less between toleration and equality. The "Humble Supplication" acknowledges the power of the Sovereign in "overseeing, ruling, and censuring particular Churches," and requests that subordinate civil officers may be appointed to demand and receive of each Church accounts of their proceedings. This is not asking for, or dreaming of, religious liberty, and only for toleration in a most limited and degraded sense. The doctrine of "Religion's Peace," on the other hand, is as unequivocal as is that of Smyth.

Independent Church, the mother Church of the Pilgrim Fathers of New England. No name in the history of Independency shines with greater lustre than his. To him the Churches of that communion were indebted, until the time of Owen, for the ablest vindication of their principles, as against the Church of England on the one hand, and the Baptists on the other. He was a man of profound scholarship, high culture, and of a largeness of heart which was, at that time, less common among the Separatists than many other qualities. As a theological disputant he was quick and vigorous. None of the Separatists lacked moral courage, but Robinson had a higher courage than most, if not any, of his brethren. The most conspicuous fault of the Separatists was excessive dogmatism. It was impossible for any of them to err; impossible for any who differed from them to hold the truth. They were all infallible in their judgments, and none but they knew the whole counsel of God. When this failing did not become a vice, as it sometimes did, it was not without its service. It was the almost inevitable result of the circumstances in which the Separatists were placed. They were in constant conflict with a supreme authority, which was not exercised in favour of what they judged to be the truth. If they had not been doubly sure that they, and they only, held the truth, they could never have withstood the power which was arrayed against them. If that faith and confidence often—or, indeed, generally—degenerated to dogmatism, was it not natural that it should do so? To doubt was, with them, to be lost. They did not fight with the measured pace and nice rules of courtier duellists, but Agag "was hewed in pieces," and the Christian Hector was dragged round the applauding field by the Christian Achilles who had slain him.

Robinson was a man of finer mould and higher temper. He could strike with equal swiftness, and generally with surer accuracy than most of his rivals. He was unworthy of himself in his controversy with the Baptists,* but who had been worthy of himself in that dispute? In most of his controversial, and in all his ethical writings, there is an equal breadth and purpose He could assail the Church of England without reviling her. He could treat of morality and philosophy with a learning, a wisdom, and a calmness second only to Bacon's. His faith was perhaps more assured than that of some who used more assertion, but it was further removed from dogmatism. He could write—a great thing in those days to do—"If in anything we err, advise us brotherly. Err we may, alas! too easily, but heretics, by the grace of God, we will not be." And when Robinson bade the Pilgrim Fathers God speed, his memorable last words were—"I charge you, before God and His blessed angels, that you follow me no further than you have seen me follow the Lord Jesus Christ. If God reveal anything to you by any other instrument of His, be as ready to receive it as you were to receive any truth by my ministry, for I am verily persuaded the Lord hath more truth yet to break forth out of His holy word. For my part, I cannot sufficiently bewail the condition of those reformed Churches which are come to a period in religion and will go, at present, no further than the instruments of their reformation. The Lutherans cannot be drawn to go beyond what Luther saw. Whatever part of His will our God has revealed to Calvin, they will rather die than embrace it; and the Calvinists, you see, stick fast where they were left by that great man of God, who yet saw not all things. This is a misery much to be lamented." No man, probably, at that time, but Robinson could have given expression to thoughts such as these, for

* He denounced all Anabaptists as "Vile heretics and schismatics."

no other man possessed his spirit. He was honoured to be the pastor of the Pilgrim Fathers, and from his Church went forth those also who founded anew in England the Independent denomination. From John Robinson's congregation at Leyden came Henry Jacob, to form in London in 1616 what, at one time, was termed the first Independent Church. Probably it was the only Church at that period, those that went before having been rooted out by James and his prelates.

We now see two, but only two, Free Churches certainly established and existing in England in the latter part of the reign of James the First. And at this period two questions rose into prominence, the discussion of which served, in no small degree, to aid in the development of a freer thought, and a more devout religious life. The first was the history and origin of tithes. Selden had written his book, proving the purely human authority for this impost, which so exasperated the prelates that the author was compelled to apologise for its publication. Yet his work is now the highest authority on the subject, and its principal contention has been accepted by the greatest jurists and statesmen of England. In the same year another question was forced upon public attention. One of the petitions of the Puritans had been for a better observance of the Sabbath. This question had begun to excite attention in Elizabeth's reign by the publication of Dr. Bound's book on the obligations of the Lord's-day. This author was inclined to Jewish Sabbatarianism, but so were the Puritans, and his work had, for that age, an extraordinary circulation. There was certainly a necessity for the moral obligations of the Christian day of rest being explained and enforced. Sunday, in England under Elizabeth, was what Sunday was in France under Napoleon the Third. It was the gala day of the week—a day for sport and pleasure, dancing and theatrical entertainments, riot and debauchery. Bound's treatise was exercising great influence, but it was an influence which tended in favour of Puritan doctrine and life. This was enough for Whitgift, and it was at once prohibited. The Archbishop having declared that such a theory of the Sabbath did not agree with that of the Church, every copy of the book was called in, and the author was ordered not to reprint it. Bound's work, however, gave an impetus to what are called Sabbatarian views, which has never ceased in England, and it was the text-book of the Puritans in the next and succeeding reigns. The author's views would, by most persons now, be considered somewhat too Judaical, and the contrast between them and those set forth in one of the most recent works on this subject* is a fair measure of the gap which lies between the drift of Puritan thought in the seventeenth and the nineteenth centuries. Bound's book was reprinted in 1606, and it largely influenced the Puritanical observance of the Sunday. It appears to have been some time before James saw this, but when he saw it he determined to counteract it. The "Book of Sports" was issued, and the people were informed by royal authority that Sunday was not to be a day mainly for religious rest and worship, but for games and revels. What there was, however, of religious sentiment and feeling in the nation revolted at the order to publish from the pulpits of England this indulgence, and even Whitgift's successor, Archbishop Abbott, himself forbade it. The Puritans now, for the first time, defeated the king, and, for the first time, royal authority was set at naught. In conquering him the Puritans first became conscious of their real strength and power, and learned that resistance to a monarch might, after all, be successful.

The events of no period of English history have been

* Dr. Hessey's "Bampton Lectures."

more fully described than those of the reign of Charles the First and the Commonwealth. Charles prepared the way for his own overthrow and execution by his lofty pretensions and his habitual bad faith and perjury. Other Stuart sovereigns were faithless, but he lied on system, and the vice cost him his crown and his life.

At the same time the way was prepared for the sacrifice of the Established Church. The "Book of Sports" was again issued, "out of a pious care," said the King, "for the service of God." Scotland was excited to rebellion by the imposition of Episcopacy, and Convocation was invested with unlimited power to make ecclesiastical laws. All "sectaries" were again brought under the extreme penalty of law, and the doctrine of the divine right of Kings and of passive obedience was accepted without reservation. I toleration was not to be allowed against the sectaries, there was some occasion, apparently, for new laws. The Independent Church formed by Jacob, but now presided over by another pastor, was still in existence. From it, in 1633,* there was a withdrawal of Baptists, who formed the first Particular or Calvinistic Baptist Church in England, and were the first to practise baptism by immersion; for, hitherto, the controversy between Baptists and Independents had had relation to the subjects only of baptism, and not to the mode. There were, at this period, four other Baptist Churches in England, and probably also one at Olchen, in Wales.† A little later Laud notices vindictively the existence of "several Anabaptists and other sectaries" at Ashford, in Kent, while Bishop Hall, in 1641, called attention, in the House of Lords, to the existence in London and the suburbs of "no fewer than fourscore congregations of several sectaries, instructed by cobblers,

* Wilson's "Dissenting Churches," vol. i., p. 41.

† "Thomas's History," p. 3.

tailors, felt makers, and such like trash." Hall was alarmed at such a state of things, and prophesied the rise of Jack Cades, Jack Straws, and Wat Tylers, if such people were not put down.*

But it was not the "sectaries" who rose against Charles. The House of Commons, which declared war against him, was a house of Churchmen only,† gentlemen of rank, wealth and territorial position. The bishops, and afterwards the clergy, suffered with him because they had identified themselves with his cause, and because their pretensions were as opposed to the preservation of liberty as were the King's. There can be no doubt that the Episcopal form of Church government is more consistent with civil tyranny than any other form. Wherever it has existed its adherents have cast the weight of their influence into the scale of despotism. The reason for this is not difficult of explanation. It consists in the fact that the Episcopal form of government demands a greater surrender of personal liberty in religion than any other system. It exalts authority at the expense of right. In Charles's time, as often since, the English Episcopacy sought the apparent interests of its order, and of its order only. What wonder that, with their recent history in view, the people should have determined, while they held the King in check, at the same time to suppress the Episcopalian religion and all connected with it?

The progress of Free Christianity can be clearly traced through the period which followed, but it was far more apparent than real. The religion partially established by Parliament and the Westminster Assembly of Divines was simpler, more strict in form, and finer in essence than that

* Collier.

† The testimonies of Clarendon and Baxter on this point are too well known to be cited.

which had been overthrown; but this is the best that can be said of it. Politically, its establishment was expedient—for the sympathy and aid of the Scots could scarcely, at that time, have been dispensed with—but religiously it was a blunder. The Presbyterian State Church, where, as in London and Lancashire, it exercised coercive power, proved to be quite as intolerant, and, to the majority of the people, less pleasant than had been the Episcopalian. Assemblies of Divines have never been celebrated for practical wisdom, moderation, or charity; and of all assemblies, that of Westminster, which sat for six years, and held one thousand one hundred and sixty-three sittings, showed the least of these qualities. The imposition on the nation of the Solemn League and Covenant was a more odious infraction of religious liberty than the imposition of the whole of the Prayer Book and Thirty-nine Articles; for it was enforced on laymen as well as on the clergy. The longer and shorter Catechisms are admirable summaries of the doctrines of ultra-Calvinism, and the Confession of Faith is a work of masterly theological exposition, but what is to be said of the proposed enforcement of these on a whole nation?

The Baptists took no part in this Assembly, for it was tacitly decided that their doctrine concerning Infant Baptism prevented them from sitting in it. The position taken by the few Independents, five or six in number, who were nominated to it, has only lately been thoroughly understood.* It was not favourable to a very extensive degree of religious liberty. How could it be, when at their entrance they had to sign the solemn League and Covenant, by which they engaged to extirpate all "heresy and schism" from the land? Yet they let it be distinctly understood that they were not in favour of complete toleration. A petition

* See Fletcher's "History of Independency," vol. iv., cap. 1.

was presented to the Assembly by "an old Anabaptist at Amsterdam," against the Covenant, and in favour of "full liberty of conscience to all sects." It contained, no doubt, some wild sentiments, but not so wild as the Covenant must have appeared to the majority of Episcopalians. Nye and Thomas Goodwin, the leaders of the Independent party, were the most vehement in their denunciations of this petition. The Independents also prayed to be included in the proposed new national Church, the conditions being that the power of ordination should be reserved to their own congregations, and that they might be subject, in Church censures, to Parliament, but not to any Presbytery. They offered, if this were conceded, to allow the State to limit the number of their congregations. The Presbyterians replied, saying that if such a toleration were allowed to Independents it must be allowed to all other sects, and taunted Nye and his party with the fact that they were asking for more than their brethren in New England were willing to permit.* The noblest words uttered by the Independents in this assembly were uttered by Jeremiah Burroughes, in reply to the refusal of the Presbyterians to grant even this concession. "If," he said, "their congregations might not be exempted from that coercive power of the classes, if they might not have liberty to govern themselves in their own way, as long as they behaved peaceably towards the civil magistrates, they were resolved to suffer, and go to some other place in the world where they might enjoy their liberty. But while men think

* There are many misunderstandings concerning the persecution of the sects by the New England Independents, arising from the confusion between the Pilgrim Fathers and the Puritans. The former never persecuted. The latter, as in England, were avowed State Churchmen. The distinction is pointed out in Palfrey's "History of New England," and in a tract entitled, "The Pilgrim Fathers not Persecutors," by B. Scott, F.S.A., London, 1866.

that there is no way of peace but by forcing all to be of the same mind, while they think the civil sword is an ordinance of God to determine all controversies of divinity, and that it must needs be attended with fines and imprisonment to the disobedient, there must be a base subjection of men's consciences to slavery, a suppression of moral truth, and great disturbances in the Christian world." * With these words the endeavour to comprehend Independents in the proposed new national church came to an end. Few though they were in number, the Independents probably prevented this scheme being realised. They were incessant in exposing the evils of a coercive Presbyterianism, and in this they succeeded. Before the nation they were the sole advocates of greater liberty of conscience. They stood in the breach against the advance of a new State Church, which, if better in many respects than the old, would have been worse in other respects. The final result was, that while uniformity of external worship, by the imposition of the "Directory," was enforced, no system of Church government was established. Episcopalianism was made impossible; but neither the bishops nor the ministers of the old persuasion were rooted out, as the sectaries had been under all previous governments.

The attempt at comprehension had thus signally failed. Almost as soon as this was evident both the Parliament and the Assembly were dispensed with. The latter had long lost all moral influence. The wit of Selden had made it ridiculous, and the denunciations of Milton had exposed its tyrannical tendency. And, there was growing up a public distrust of Puritanism. The instruction to the Assembly to frame, if possible, a scheme of comprehension which should allow full liberty of conscience, had been moved in the

* Neal, vol. iii., p. 309.

House of Commons by Oliver Cromwell, and its failure was certainly one of the leading causes of his assuming the reins of government. With the liberty then allowed to them by law, the Nonconformists had recently increased both in numbers and in influence. They had what they had never before enjoyed—a clear stage. The greatest statesmen were Independents; the army was filled by members of the same body; Fairfax's regiment especially, being almost entirely composed of them. Led by Cromwell, St. John and Vane in Parliament, with Milton as their literary champion, they had nothing more to fear. If the Baptists were not so well represented in the legislature, they had large influence in the army. The Lord Deputy Fleetwood, Oliver Cromwell's son-in-law, Major-General Harrison, Major-General Ludlow, and Colonel Hutchinson were Baptists. It is scarcely to be wondered at that an army so composed should resent the proceedings of the Parliament and the Assembly. At the time, therefore, that the power of both these bodies seemed to be at their height, the army made complaint and demanded a general indulgence for tender consciences. They asked that the taking of the Covenant be not imposed, and that all orders and ordinances tending in that direction should be repealed. They protested against any "compulsory" religion, stating that "the ways of God's worship are not all entrusted to us by any human power." The Presbyterians on the other hand insisted on the establishment of their own religion only, upon "a covenanted uniformity," and upon the extirpation of the sects. A third party was represented by the King, who after two years' negotiation consented to most of the views of the Presbyterians. It was at this period that the army, seeing that everything for which they had fought, including liberty of conscience, was about to be wrested from them, sent in a remonstrance to the legislature. It was not attended to; Fairfax at once marched on London, and on December 6th, 1648, Pride "purged" the House of Commons. From this time Cromwell and the Independents held the reins of government.*

If the Presbyterians protested against one thing more vehemently than another in the prospect which was now before the nation, it was against toleration. The army had asked for a conference on the subject of the coercive power of the magistrate in matters of religion. The Presbyterians, instead of granting the request, drew up two formal documents, warning them of the consequences of men being guided by the "impulses of the Spirit." "We will not," said the army, "have any restraint laid on the consciences of men for religious differences." The Presbyterians replied that this would but make way for the "toleration of all heresies and blasphemies." It is significant to notice amongst the names of those who gave their assent to these views some of the most eminent of the men who, with the two thousand ejected ministers, were, fourteen years later, thrust from the Established Church because the toleration which they had denied to others was now denied to them. William Gouge and Thomas Manton, Edmund Calamy, William Spurston, Edmund Stanton, and Andrew Janeway believed, at that time, that toleration was a doctrine born of hell.

The establishment of the Commonwealth was an era in religious liberty, and England, under Cromwell's government, experienced a degree of freedom which had hitherto been unknown. All who petitioned for liberty of conscience

* It is remarkable that so few modern writers should have drawn attention to the intimate connection of the question of religious liberty with the events which led to Pride's "purge," the execution of Charles, and the establishment of the Commonwealth. Rushworth, and Neal following him, have clearly pointed it out.

were granted it. Considering the political position which they occupied, the Episcopalians were, on the whole, tenderly treated—much more tenderly, indeed, than they had ever treated those who differed from them. In many parts of the kingdom the reading of the Book of Common Prayer, although contrary to law, was tolerated. The few who left the Church were mercifully dealt with. They were not deprived of all means of living, and Usher and Pearson were still allowed to preach. Political Presbyterianism had received its death-blow at the battle of Dunbar, but although its adherents were the worst enemies of the Commonwealth and the Protectorate, they were allowed freely to disseminate their views, and to defend the "Solemn League and Covenant." They were associated with Independents and Baptists as "Triers" of the qualities of ministers, and by their "trials" they purged the pulpit of the vicious, the profane, and the ignorant; though Owen says that worthy as well as unworthy men were ejected, such as Pococke. Presbyterians and Independents, and a few Baptists, took the places of these men, and Christianity was preached throughout the land with a zeal and an energy which had never before been known. The doctrine of the State on the subject of religious toleration was indicated in the declaration of the Council of State in 1653, the thirty-sixth and thirty-seventh articles of which provided "that none be compelled to conform to the public religion by penalties or otherwise; but that endeavours be used to win them by sound doctrine, and the example of a good conversation;" and that "such as profess faith in God by Jesus Christ, though differing in judgment from the doctrine, worship, or discipline publicly held forth, shall not be restrained from, but shall be protected in, the profession of their faith and exercise of their religion, so as they abuse not this liberty to the civil injury of others, and to the actual disturbance of the public peace on their part, provided this liberty be not extended to Popery or Prelacy, or to such as, under a profession of Christianity, hold forth and practise licentiousness." Tithes also were proposed to be abolished, in order that "a provision less subject to scruple and contention" might be made.* The views of the State on this subject were unquestionably in advance of those of the nation, and it is probable that they were in advance even of the opinions of most of the Independents of that period. For Burroughes thought that if the magistrate should choose to interfere, it was lawful to assist and second the sentence of subverters of the faith. Owen, in his sermon on "Toleration," went no further than the title of his discourse, affirming in it his adherence to the principle of a State Church, while the Savoy Conference of 1658, which was attended by more than two hundred ministerial and other delegates from a hundred Independent Churches established throughout England and Wales, and of which Owen, Goodwin, Nye, and Caryl were members, said, only, that "professing Christians, with their errors, which are purely spiritual and internal, and overthrow not civil society, are to be borne with, and permitted to enjoy all ordinances

* I cannot refrain from quoting the words of a Church historian, the Rev. J. B. Marsden, on these declarations :—"Wise men," he says, "musing in their closets, had for some time questioned the wisdom, if not the justice, of compelling the dissatisfied to embrace the religion of the greater number, and making their dissent a crime. But Cromwell was the first who dared not merely to give expression to the doubt, but to enrol the principle itself with the fundamental laws of England. Received with hesitation at the time, denounced by Presbyterians as little short of blasphemy, spurned by the Parliament of Charles II. with the same indiscriminate contempt with which all Cromwell's legislation was trampled under their feet, it still survived. The plant grew, for it was watered by the rains of heaven, and tens of thousands have reposed beneath its quiet shade."

and privileges, according to their light, as fully as any of their brethren who pretend to the purest orthodoxy." They further declared that "if they had the power which any of their brethren of different opinions had desired to have over them, or others, they would freely grant this liberty to them all.* This seems to be unexceptionable, and, as far as toleration only is concerned, it is so; but when Dr. Thomas Goodwin delivered this declaration to Richard Cromwell, he said, on behalf of the Savoy Assembly, "We look at the magistrates as *custos utriusque tabulæ*, and so commit it [the Gospel] to your trust, as our chief magistrate, to countenance and propagate." † It was such sentiments which drew down upon the Independents the scornful rebukes of Milton. The laymen, in fact, as has generally been the case, were in advance of the clergy on this subject. Vane, one of the greatest of the Independent statesmen, had said, "The province of the magistrate is this world and man's body; not his conscience or the concerns of eternity."‡ Cromwell probably only waited for time in order to apply this principle to the practical government of the nation.

No just estimate of this period of ecclesiastical history can be formed without taking into consideration—first, the characters of the principal actors in it and their intentions, and, secondly, the results of their work. The figure of Cromwell stands in the foreground. No man's character was better indicated than his by his features and his attitude. He was notably a rugged, firm, enthusiastic, sincere, and affectionate man. That he was not a hypocrite, as some have judged, is proved by the fact that his feelings retained their natural force and freshness to the last moment of his

* Orme's "Owen," p. 180. † Ib., pp. 182-183.
‡ "Meditations," A.D. 1655.

life ; and this can be the case with no hypocrite. Of all his qualities his will was the strongest, and, next, his family affections. Occasionally, his enthusiasm seemed to overbalance his judgment, but this was not really the case; for although it appeared to excess in his words, it never influenced him to a rash act. What is remarkable in Cromwell, considering his ecclesiastical relationships, is, that while he imposed, from temporary necessity, his own form of civil polity on the nation, he never cared to impose upon it his own form of ecclesiastical polity. The explanation is that he was not, in any sense, a theorist. The breadth of his intellect was equal to its strength; and though not a cultured man, he had all the essential qualities of cultured men. He could bear with differences of opinion; and although he had power to suppress, he chose to tolerate and encourage them. Politically, he was a monarchist by tradition and feeling, and would have restored Charles if he could have done so with safety to the nation. He became a dictator from necessity. There is no evidence, however, that he cared for power as such, and he never used it but for what he judged—with a larger judgment than any man who had gone before him was capable of exercising—to be for the good of his country. Ecclesiastically he was an Independent, but he never forced Independency on the nation. He was willing to tolerate even Jews—a thing at that time almost unheard of in Christendom ; and he allowed Usher to preach almost within a stone's throw of Whitehall. With a sagacity which would have been justified by events had he lived longer, or had his son been competent for government, he used his influence mainly for the better political education of the people. He cast off even his oldest friends for this, and made enemies equally amongst pure republicans, democratic levellers, and army leaders. It was the same with respect to religion. He would not impose Presbyterianism, and the Presbyterians therefore hated him. Many of the Baptists were "red republicans," and they, in their turn, were estranged. He, himself, kept in the way which he judged would be for the permanent advantage of his country, actuated in his work by a strong patriotism and a fervent religious feeling. Such a man, dying before half his task was accomplished, was not likely to be well reported of by many, either of his contemporaries or his successors. What he hoped to have done was to change the character of the nation, and he lived only long enough to disturb it. As soon as he was dead "the sow went back to her wallowing in the mire."

As Cromwell was at the head of the government of his age, so Milton was at the head of its literature. One remark applies to both—they stood, from the greatness of their genius, comparatively alone. Milton appears to have been an Independent in Church government, a Baptist so far as the distinctive creed of the Baptists was concerned, with theological beliefs inclined to Arianism. He cannot be identified with any of the denominations, and in the later years of his life he attended no place of public worship. He was above the sects, and appears to have loathed their mutual jarrings. Of his controversial works the utmost that can be said is that he defended the Commonwealth with his pen as successfully as Cromwell defended it with his sword. He gave to the Government the services of the loftiest genius and the most varied scholarship, adorned by all the manners of a courtier. What is most pertinent to remark in connection with his support of Cromwell and Cromwell's government is, that they could not have been of the character which it was once the fashion to ascribe to them, or Milton would not have identified himself with their cause.

The names and labours of the religious leaders of this age belong to the Christianity of the English nation. Foremost amongst them were the disputatious but zealous Baxter, the scholarly Owen, the gentle Howe, the liberal Goodwin, the solid Manton, and the active Powell. The Church of Christ never possessed abler or purer ministers than those of the Commonwealth, or men who gave themselves up with greater ardour to the work to which they had consecrated themselves. They gave a new character to the religious life of their country.

Much has been written of the vulgar and hypocritical character of the religion of this period. No doubt religious affectation prevailed to a great extent; but the representations which have come down to us from Tory writers are charged with the grossest exaggerations. The religious leaders of the Commonwealth have been stigmatised as a company of ignorant and canting fanatics. Ignorant they were not, canting some of them probably were, but they were not more fanatical than the High Churchmen of their age. Their learning alone has made their time as illustrious as any in the history of their country. No man was a greater patron of letters than the Protector. Oxford and Cambridge became, under his auspices, seats of study more profound and exalted than had been known since their foundation. "The love of deep learning was now, for the first time, widely diffused."* Under Owen's Vice-Chancellorship at Oxford, Wilkins and Boyle were pursuing their philosophical studies, and Locke and South were being educated. Goddard the physician, Gale the philologist, Seth Ward the mathematician, Pococke, the greatest Oriental scholar in Europe, with John Howe and Stephen

* Marsden's "Later Puritans," p. 386.

Charnock, were in the same University. Some of these men were Independents, some were Presbyterians, and some were Episcopalians, for Cromwell never sacrificed the interests of learning to the prejudices of the sects. At Cambridge, Cudworth was teaching, and Poole, Stillingfleet, and Tillotson obtaining that learning with which they were subsequently to adorn their church. If a comparison of times be made, it will be found that no period of English history was more fruitful in the most exalted genius and the most profound scholarship than that of the Commonwealth era.

Nor were the manners of the age as destitute of dignity and grace as is generally supposed. The Nonconformists were not the melancholy and sour-visaged race that historians have delighted to portray. Addison has handed down to us* a picture of Puritan manners in the person of a "very famous Independent minister" who lived in funereal state, and exhibited nothing but "religious horror" in his countenance. The genial humourist describes a saint of that age as abstaining from all appearance of "mirth and pleasantry," and as "eaten up with spleen and melancholy;" but no such impression as this is to be obtained either from their portraits, their writings, or the memoirs of their lives. Gravity was certainly a characteristic of their manners; but it was not unmixed with pleasantry and humour. Some, like the leaders and followers of the highest fashion in the present day, chose to wear their hair cropped, but the majority of those whose portraits have come down to us were remarkable for their flowing ringlets. Milton, Colonel Hutchinson, Selden, and Owen are fair representative men, and they were all distinguished by their graceful dress, their

* "Spectator," 494. The divine is supposed to be Dr. Thomas Goodwin.

curling hair, and their polished manners.* In their own times, indeed, they were abused for their gaiety. "Yea," said Bastwick, of the Independents, "you shall find them with cuffs, and those great ones, at their very heels, and with more silver and gold upon their clothes and at their heels (for these upstarts must now have silver spurs) than many great and honourable personages have in their purses."† Anthony Wood brings a charge against Owen that, instead of being a good example to the University, he scorned all formality, and describes him as "like a young scholar, with powdered hair, snake-bone band-strings, or band-strings with very large tassels; a large set of ribands pointed at his knees, and Spanish leather boots, with large lawn tops, and his hat mostly cocked." ‡ Cromwell himself, when Whitelocke told him, on his return from Sweden, how he had amused the members of his Embassy with music and dancing in the long winter nights, expressed his emphatic approval of "such very good diversions."§ One of the most popular preachers of the Commonwealth was Henry Smith, whose sermons, like Latimer's, abound in broad English humour. Milton, who appears to have thought that his works would

* The following is Mrs. Hutchinson's portrait of her husband:—"He could dance admirably well, but neither in youth nor riper years made any practice of it; he had a skill in fencing, such as became a gentleman; he had great love to music, and often diverted himself with a viol, on which he played masterly; had an exact ear and judgment in other music; he shot excellently in bows and guns, and much used them for exercise; he had great judgment in paintings, graving, sculpture, and all liberal arts, and had many curiosities of value in all kinds. . . . He took much pleasure in improvement of ponds, in planting groves, and walks, and fruit trees, in opening springs, and making fish ponds." "Memoirs," p. 23. Col. Hutchinson was an "Anabaptist."

† "The Utter Routing of the Independents." Preface.

‡ "Athenæ Oxon." ii. 556.

§ "Whitelocke's Embassy," ii. 438.

be read only by the Puritan section of his countrymen, wrote not only the "Paradise Lost," but "L'Allegro" and "Comus." The controversial writings of the age are distinguished by their quickness of wit and their felicity of classical illustration. It is true that some sanctioned laws for the suppression of certain pastimes, revels, and theatrical entertainments; but those amusements had been conducted in a manner which no decent man would now tolerate. The difference in morals and manners between the Nonconformists and the Cavaliers was that, while the former anticipated the pure and refined life of the English gentleman of the nineteenth century, the latter were as dissolute and licentious as the ancient heathens.

The Baptists of this period were inferior as a sect to others in learning, but their activity in preaching the Gospel, and their zeal in defence of religious freedom, were probably superior. The mantle of Penry had fallen on Vavasour Powell, who was evangelising Wales and forming Churches, most of which appear to have been of an unsectarian character, in various parts.* William Kiffin, a wealthy London merchant, was their chief pastor in the metropolis, and had great influence with Cromwell, as well as, afterwards, with the two Stuarts. John Canne and Hansard Knollys were using their pens with vigour and success in favour of a free Nonconformity, and Tombes, a man of learning and great controversial ability, was defending Baptist views against Baxter, and preaching with vigour in the Midland Counties. All through England the activity of religious effort was remarkable, and it was adorned, for

* This was the case with many of the early Nonconformist Churches. The Pilgrim Fathers' Church, at Southwark, was originally an unsectarian Church and had Baptist ministers. Wilson's "Dissenting Churches," vol. iv., p. 122, and "Crosby," vol. iii., p. 40.

the most part, by such human graces as commonly attend profound scholarship and unaffected piety. Nor ought it to be forgotten, in justice to the Independents of the Commonwealth, that it was they who first conceived the duty of foreign missionary effort. It was on July 27th, 1648, that an ordinance was passed in Parliament,* constituting a corporation under the title of "The President and Society for the Propagation of the Gospel in New England." This was the first Missionary Society formed in England, and was the parent of the present Society for the Propagation of the Gospel in Foreign Parts.

A new faith, however, now appeared. It had the reception usually accorded to new faiths, and its leaders appeared even to court persecution. The Society of Friends dates its origin from this period. No religious community ever had more vigorous or consistent founders. George Fox, to whom it owes its origin, was no doubt an indiscreet man; but such indiscretion as his may well be overlooked, in comparison with the purity, the enthusiasm, and the piety of his life. No man was more maligned than he; and the creed of no sect was so grossly caricatured and misrepresented as the creed of the "Quakers." The doctrines of the Baptists had only lately been tolerated; but here were doctrines that went far beyond those, which, to many, had once appeared to be utterly inconsistent with Christianity. The demand made upon the charity of Christians of all sects was greater than they could bear, and there was, for once, unanimity in denunciation. Baxter, not for the first time in his life, became the bell-wether of theological detraction. He was always ready for controversy; but in controversy with the Quakers he was not merely ready, but eager. He had some hope of the ultimate salvation of Baptists, but he doomed all Quakers, without reserve, to

* Scobell's "Acts," cap. 45.

utter damnation. Owen, also, used his authority as Vice-Chancellor at Oxford to sanction the whipping of two Quaker women for speaking in church, denouncing them, at the same time, as blasphemers and abusers of the Holy Spirit.* Much of this language was simply retaliative, for George Fox and those who became his disciples denounced all the forms of worship then in practice, and "bore testimony" against them in a manner which was calculated to excite both anger and revenge. "Steeple houses," as they termed the Churches, were an abomination; a paid ministry was unscriptural; tithes were without warrant either from religion or from justice; † the Sacraments were done away with; and, above all, they declared that men had not merely the light of Scripture, but an "inward light" communicated by God's Spirit, whereby they might discern the truth. Allied to these opinions were some that were not less unpalatable to those who heard them. Such was the assertion that all oaths are sinful; that the civil government had nothing to do with marriage; that no manner of respect should be paid to rank; and that it was unlawful for a Christian to take up arms, or even to make use of physical force, for his own or his country's protection. The characteristic doctrines, however, of Quakerism resolved themselves into two—the "inward light" and the essential spirituality of religion. Religion, the Friends maintained, had its origin in the communion of the spirit of man with the Spirit of God, and therefore neither needed, nor could properly be expressed by, forms and ceremonies. They abjured all that was tradi-

* Sewell's "History," pp. 90, 91.

† The Quakers were the first people who assailed with anything like power or persistency the injustice of tithes and Church-rates. They did this from the outset. In their early tracts all the modern arguments against these imposts are anticipated.

tional and all that was merely external in worship. Had they abstained from attacking other sects they would probably, in the time of the Commonwealth, have been left alone; but when they attended places of worship and publicly assailed both the preachers and their doctrines, they excited an animosity which fell little short of fury. Though whipped and imprisoned, put in stocks, pilloried, and made subject to every personal indignity, they still increased in numbers with an unexampled rapidity. During the Protectorate three thousand one hundred and seventy-three Quakers were imprisoned, thirty-two of whom died in confinement. Their persecutors were, for the most part, Presbyterians and Independents. Whenever their sufferings were brought officially before Cromwell he appears to have given orders for their relief. It was at the time of one of Fox's numerous imprisonments that he first met the Protector. The two men, each equally remarkable, and each capable of appreciating the peculiar greatness of the other, talked largely of God's ways, and Fox was dismissed and set at liberty with an expression of Cromwell's personal good-will. All Quakers were then ordered to be set free, and men were forbidden to harm them. Liberty of public meeting was, however, denied them; but Quakers were the least likely of all men to obey such a law. They defied the law, met and preached, and, from the Baptists especially, gathered large numbers of converts. So they laid the foundation of one of the most respected and useful of all the Christian communities. Those who will be at the trouble of reading their own expositions of their own faith will hardly fail to acknowledge that the Quakers obtained a firmer grasp than others of one or two central Christian truths, and that their "testimony" was necessary to the complete exhibition of the Christian religion. Much of their distinctive theology has unconsciously been absorbed into the current theology of the present day. The advent of Quakerism was a test of the degree of religious liberty enjoyed under the Commonwealth and the Protectorate.

No one can doubt that the Restoration under Charles the Second was popular with the nation, and especially popular with the Presbyterians, to whom, indeed, he owed his return. Cromwell had offended this body, beyond forgiveness, by frustrating their schemes of ecclesiastical domination. They had detested the tolerant character of his government, and they now, spite of his debauched habits, welcomed the Stuart. They again looked forward to a modified National Church, in which they might retain their livings and probably regain their coveted ascendancy. They were assured not merely of toleration, but of indulgence for tender consciences. Had not the King given his word? Had he not said it in the Declaration from Breda, which was signed with his own hand? Their joy was great when ten of their number were appointed Court chaplains; still greater when they knew that five bishoprics were kept open for them. Although the old Liturgy and all the old clergy had been restored, they were sanguine enough to wait upon the King, and ask his interposition for removing the differences in the Church—that is to say, the differences between the Episcopalians and themselves. They obtained, in reply, a second Declaration, in which a modified and temporary liberty of Nonconformity was granted, which, however, the House of Commons refused to sanction. There can be little doubt that Charles would have consented to a large degree of religious freedom. Like most men of his stamp, he had a generous and easy nature, and preferred not to be troubled with ecclesiastical matters. This, however, was not Clarendon's disposition, nor was it Sheldon's. While the King sported with his mistresses, the statesmen and the ecclesiastics ruled the people, and there was no intention on their part to allow the smallest indulgence to the most tender conscience.

It was probably only to save the public honour of the King that the Savoy Conference was held. This Conference was a repetition of that at Hampton Court, and its secret object was the same—namely, to keep all Puritans and Presbyterians out of the Church. The presence of Baxter, with his argumentative disposition, would have prevented the success of any such assembly; but had Baxter not been a member—and the most conspicuous member—of the Conference, its issue, while it might have been delayed, could scarcely have been different. His demands were not dissimilar from those of the earlier Puritans,* and their reception was the same. The Book of Common Prayer was made less, rather than more, palatable. The ecclesiastical authorities decided, with expressions of hatred and contempt for those who were suing to them, that there should be no alteration in the formularies of the Church, which would be likely to keep within its borders any who differed from the old ecclesiastical constitution.

Neither the Independents nor the Baptists took any part in the Savoy Conference. They did not ask for, nor apparently, did they desire, any comprehension within the Church. They pleaded only for toleration. The Presbyterian Commissioners took no note of their existence. They do not appear even to have considered what effect their proposed revision of the Prayer Book would have on other Christian communities. No one who has read Baxter's controversial works—the most abusive even of that age—will believe that he would willingly have consented to the toleration of Baptists or Quakers. Had the Church

* See "Documents relating to the Settlement of the Church of England under the Act of Uniformity," edited by the Rev. George Gould, 1862.

of England been reconstituted in accordance with the desires of the Presbyterian party in this Conference, the result, in all likelihood, would have been such a State Establishment as was contemplated by the Westminster Assembly, which refused to allow of more than a limited toleration, even to Independents. As it is not in the nature of ecclesiastics to become more liberal in proportion as they are invested with power, it is very possible that the Act of Uniformity, which must have been passed to give authority to the revised Prayer Book, would have been followed by other Acts, not very dissimilar in character from those which followed the enforcement of the unreformed Book. The Puritans were saved from this disgrace by their own ejectment.

The history of this Ejectment has been often and eloquently told. The passing of the Act of Uniformity, considered as an enactment instigated by the State Church, was a fatal blunder; considered as an essential element in the development of the Free Churches of England, it was the most happy event that could have taken place. For, where Nonconformists could formerly be counted only by the score, they could now be told by the thousand. Until 1662, the opponents of the State Church were few, and those few were localised. They were now spread throughout every part of the kingdom, and wherever there was an ejected pastor there was public sympathy with him. But the lives and the preaching of Howe, and Owen, and Baxter, and Caryl, and Bates, and Manton, with their two thousand brethren, would have counteracted all the external influences which the authority of the State had given to those who had conformed. Sheldon, in spiritual power, could never have successfully competed with any of the men whom he had aided to cast out of the Church. He, and the majority of his episcopal brethren, were ecclesiastics only—unscrupulous politicians with clerical titles, who, to aid their own ambitious purposes, banded themselves together to uphold the worst of all English Governments. But they soon discovered that the Act of Uniformity had not decreased the influence of the ejected ministers. It had, on the contrary, increased it. In many cases, perhaps the majority, the ejected remained where they were, and preached to the same people. The chief difference between their former and their present position was a difference of external circumstances. They did not preach in a certain building, nor had they a fixed maintenance; all besides remained as it had been, excepting that the sacrifice which they had made for conscience' sake had increased towards them the respect and affection of the people.

It was resolved to break this spiritual power. During the remainder of Charles the Second's reign the aim of the ecclesiastical authorities was to extinguish Nonconformity. First, in 1661, was passed the Corporation Act, after which no Nonconformist could hold office in any municipal body; in 1662 the Act of Uniformity silenced their ministers; in 1663 the Conventicle Act was passed, by which no Nonconformist could hold a meeting where more than five persons in addition to the family were present; in 1665 all Nonconformist ministers were prohibited, by the Five Mile Act, from coming within that distance of any corporate borough; in 1670 the Conventicle Act was extended, the penalties under it were increased, and informers encouraged; in 1673 the Test Act was passed, after which all employment, civil, naval, or military, under the Government, was denied to Nonconformists. The revival of the Act for the burning of heretics would have been an appropriate addition to these laws, but Sheldon did not suggest it. Long and weary imprisonments, banishment, and starvation satisfied even the Episcopal bench.

Some hundreds of Free Churches date their existence from this period. It was the period, also, when the distinguishing principles of the various sects may be said to have been finally established in literature. Stillingfleet, the greatest ecclesiastical lawyer and antiquarian of his age, was beginning to denounce the sin of schism; Baxter, as though he were a whole college of divines, poured forth defences and expositions, answers and rejoinders, at the rate of sometimes eight and sometimes ten in one year, on Conformity and Nonconformity, Peace and Schism, Baptism and Popery, Calvinism and Arminianism; David Clarkson, with a mind stored with patristic lore, assailed the theory of Diocesan Episcopacy; and John Owen, with massive and sinewy brain and exhaustless learning, so built up the principles of Congregationalism that, if all the works on that subject which have since been written were destroyed, the Congregational Churches of England could stand behind his treatises as behind an impregnable rampart. Amongst the Baptists, Benjamin Keach did eminent service by the publication, amongst other works, of a Christian catechism, for which he was sent to the pillory, and from thence to gaol; Delaune perished in prison for his "Nonconformist's Plea"; and John Bunyan arose to expound and defend the principles, if not of a liberal theology, at least of a liberal ecclesiastical rule.* The Quakers were represented with equal ability. At this period was brought out the Catechism and the "Apology" of Robert Barclay, a man of eminent piety and equally eminent learning, and the first treatises of William Penn. Exegetical and devotional theology was cultivated with similar zeal. The "Pilgrim's Progress," the "Saint's Everlasting Rest," the

* Bunyan advocated "mixed communion" principles, and his Church was an unsectarian one.

"Redeemer's Tears," the "Living Temple," and "No Cross, No Crown," belong to the time of the Stuart persecution.

The sufferings of ministers and people during this period were unspeakable. Their congregations were scattered; they were fined, pilloried, imprisoned, and banished. Many Presbyterians took refuge in the Church; others identified themselves more closely with the Independents, and the denomination, as such, began to decline. The Independents and Baptists gave up their meetings or met by stealth, while watchers, stationed on roofs, or as outposts in the streets, gave warning of the approach of informers. The members of one denomination alone continued, by meeting openly and without concealment, to defy and not to evade the law. These were the Quakers. The brutality with which the members of this sect were treated exceeded anything known in the recent history of persecution in England. Their meetings were broken up by the military, and their attendants stunned by bludgeons or hacked by swords. The female members were stripped and flogged with shameless indecency. In 1662, more than four thousand Friends were in prison in England, five hundred of whom were crowded into the prisons of London.* Hundreds died, and many more were banished to the West Indian settlements. In spite of all this, they continued openly to meet and preach, not once reviling their persecutors. And when, in 1672, an "Indulgence" was granted to Dissenters, and a return ordered of all such prisoners as should be released, George Whitehead, a Quaker, waited on King Charles, and obtained his promise of pardon to such as were imprisoned. None had been more vehement against the Quakers than Bunyan, yet he obtained his release from gaol through

* Sewell's "History," vol. ii., p. 2.

Whitehead's exertions. "Our being of different judgments," said Whitehead, "did not abate my compassion or charity, even towards those who had been my opposers in some cases. Blessed be the Lord God, who is the Father and fountain of mercies; whose love and mercies in Christ Jesus to us should oblige us to be merciful and kind one to another."* Bunyan was the first Nonconformist minister licensed to preach in England. It was fit that a man whose genius and pulpit eloquence were of matchless order should occupy such a historical position, and it is a proof that no degree of persecution, short of extermination, will root out religious opinions, that in ten months after the "Indulgence" was issued, three thousand five hundred licences to preach and to hold meetings were granted.

It was previous to this that another and probably sincere endeavour towards comprehension was made. The initiative was taken by the Government, and immediately responded to by the leaders of the Presbyterian party. Baxter and Manton did not, on this occasion, forget the Independents. Baxter informed the Lord Keeper that it was now possible to include this body and all sound Christians in the Establishment, but the suggestion was received with no favour. Terms of comprehension were however agreed upon, one of which was that ceremonies should be left indifferent. All who were not comprehended were to be indulged, the names of the ministers and of every member of their congregations being registered.

It is impossible to say whether Howe and Owen gav authority to Baxter to make such concessions, but Baxter, in 1667, was in correspondence with Owen concerning a union between Presbyterians and Independents. Baxter took the first step towards this object. Christian union may be said

* Offor's "Bunyan," Hansard Knollys' ed. pp. 62—65.

to have been his hobby, but no man was less fit to promote it than himself. He was for ever framing concordats, but never yielding in the least either to Episcopalians or to Independents. He was induced to open a correspondence with Owen in consequence of the publication, by the latter, of a Catechism of Church worship and Discipline, in which Owen laid down the doctrine that Christian Churches have not the "power of the keys," or, in other words, that ministers of the Gospel do not derive their office to preach and rule from the Churches, but from Christ Himself.* Twice before had Baxter made similar proposals, and now he was engaged in another scheme of general comprehension. Nothing came of either, and the purity of the Independent Churches, if it was ever endangered, was saved from compromise.

In 1673 and 1674 Baxter made new proposals for union with the Church, which he again thought might "take in the Independents"; but he must have known, after all, little of their polity if he supposed—as he appears to have done—that they would have accepted in its substance the Book of Common Prayer, and subjected themselves to the authority of a political hierarchy. It is noticeable that the whole of these proposals were made on behalf of the Church with the view of "strengthening the Protestant interest," and counteracting the growth of Popery. The statesmen and bishops of those days felt, what has been manifest ever since, that the Established Church alone is no preservative against the errors of Romanism. Baxter's amendments to the Prayer Book would have taken out of that volume all, or nearly all, that is distinctively Roman Catholic in origin and influence. That they were accepted at the time by such men as Tillotson, Morley, Stillingfleet,

* Orme's "Owen," pp. 235—237.

Sir Matthew Hale, the Earl of Orrery, and the Lord Treasurer is a sufficient indication that the Prayer Book was considered, not by Presbyterians and Independents alone, to encourage the growth of Popery.

During the next fifteen years Protestant Dissenters were alternately persecuted and coaxed. James the Second, whatever may have been his vices, was on the whole in favour of religious liberty. It is customary to assume that his sole design in permitting toleration was to gain an ascendancy for his own sect, but there is trustworthy evidence of the general liberality of his opinions. Almost as soon as he ascended the throne he released all who were in prison for conscience' sake, by which act no fewer than fifteen hundred Quakers alone were set at liberty. When, in 1687, this body sent a deputation to thank him for his tolerant spirit, the king replied, "Some of you know—I am sure you do, Mr. Penn—that it was always my principle that conscience ought not to be forced, and that all men ought to have liberty of their consciences, and what I have promised in my declaration I will continue to perform as long as I live; and I hope, before I die, to settle it so that after ages shall have no reason to alter it."* Unfortunately, the King, while right as to the end he had in view, was wrong as to the means which ought to be adopted to attain it. He believed in governing without a Parliament, and the English people had decided, in the time of the Commonwealth, that the prerogative of the legislature was superior to that of the monarch. The King could pardon offences against the law, but he could not suspend the law.

The attitude assumed by some Dissenters towards the Crown at this period has been the subject of severe denun-

* Sewell, vol. ii., p. 333.

ciation, and the conduct of William Penn and the Quakers generally has been held up to the most unmerited opprobrium. The great historian of this and the succeeding reign was not the first who accused Penn of partiality to the Stuarts. The accusation was made in Penn's lifetime, and replied to by him. He admitted his daily visits to the palace, and states how it was he became so intimate with the monarch. His father had been admiral when the King was lord-high-admiral, and had left Penn to James's guardianship, receiving from him a promise to protect the young Quaker as far as possible from the inconveniences to which he would be subjected in consequence of his religious profession. Penn made use of his friendship to promote the progress of religious freedom. No man had done more than Penn to prove his faithfulness to this principle. Like the Barclays—David and Robert—he was born a gentleman, and had received the most cultured education which Oxford University could bestow. He was a fellow student with Locke and Villiers at Christ Church, when John Owen was Dean. He had all the polished manners of a courtier. His father was a favourite with Charles and James, and no man had better prospects of receiving substantial proofs of royal friendship. From a sense of religious conviction, he gave up the whole of this, and attached himself to the most unpopular sect in Christendom. What influence he had he afterwards used to shield the members of his own denomination from the vengeance of the law. As the founder of the Commonwealth of Pennsylvania, he made himself an undying reputation in the history of the world. His wisdom and justice as a statesman were a new revelation of humanity and religion to the savages by whom he was surrounded. His consistency as a friend of religious equality was made evident by the constitution of his Commonwealth, the first words of which were as follows:—"In reverence to God, the Father of light and spirits, the Author as well as the object of all divine knowledge, faith, and worship, I do, for me and mine, declare and establish, for the first fundamental of the government of this country, that every person that doth or shall reside therein shall have and enjoy the free profession of his or her faith and exercise of worship towards God in such way and manner as every such person shall in conscience believe is most acceptable to God." The man who could first originate and then impose such a statute was not likely to be a favourite with many of the ecclesiastical parties of James the Second's time.

But Penn and the Quakers were not the first to thank the King for his lenity. The Presbyterians, Independents, and Baptists were before them. When the Declaration of 1687 in favour of liberty of conscience was issued, and the prison doors thrown open, it was natural that there should be a spontaneous burst of gratitude to its author. At first the Dissenters did not see what would be the consequences of recognizing the legality of the Declaration; when they did, notwithstanding the renewed sufferings to which they might be exposed, they took part against it. It was owing solely to the persecuting spirit of the Church that a general toleration had not long before been granted. Yet when the seven bishops refused to read the Declaration, and were sent to the Tower, Independents, Baptists, and Quakers vied with each other in showing them sympathy. No doubt they acted at that time from mixed motives. None of them—not even Penn—was in favour of the toleration of Roman Catholicism. No man who valued the civil liberties of England dreamed of giving a foothold to the professors of that intolerant creed. Three generations had not sufficed to wipe out the memory of its curse on England. Thousands still living could recollect the Vaudois massacres; and the streets of London were at that moment crowded with sufferers from the revocation of the Edict of Nantes. Is it a wonder that the most tolerant refused to tolerate the creed of men who, whenever they were in power, persecuted to the utmost limits of persecution?

It is stranger that the Nonconformists should have declined to recognize the legality of the Indulgence because its exercise was opposed to the constitution of England. What was the constitution to them, that they should have been willing to make even the smallest sacrifice for it? Its history was written with their own blood. They were excluded from its pale. They existed but to be fined, imprisoned, and banished. Yet they freely and almost unanimously resisted any encroachment upon it, even when that encroachment was made in their own favour. There were, however, reasons for this attitude. The first was a fear that, if the King's claims were not resisted, his prerogative might ultimately be exercised in favour of the restoration of Popery as the established religion. They would not have suffered much more, in such an event, than they had recently suffered from the establishment of Protestant Episcopalianism; but they believed that religion would suffer. The second reason was of a political character. The Dissenters were the brain and muscle of the constitutional party. The right of resistance—passive or active—to despotism had come down to them as their most precious inheritance. All their ecclesiastical organizations were founded on a recognition of the rights of the people, and it was not probable that they would surrender those rights to a Stuart. By their co-operation with the bishops, when their weight might have turned the scale of public opinion in favour of the King, they assisted to save the liberties of their country. From the time of the arrest of the seven bishops, James's authority as a monarch was gone, and the temporary union, in a period of common danger, of Conformists and Nonconformists, for the safety of the State, gave promise that when a new Government should be established, the legal security of toleration would be one of its first works.

With the end of the reign of James the Second, the experiment of forcing one form of religion upon the English people ceased. Every means which the despotism of the State and the intolerance of the favoured sect could devise to secure an entire conformity had been adopted. The Crown and the dignitaries of the Established Church had united to put down all freedom of opinion. The fire of the stake had been lighted, the gallows had been erected, and the prisons choked in order to strike terror into the minds of all who dissented from the one sect. During the whole of this period scarcely one bishop or clergyman had lifted up his voice against such inhumanity. The members of the hierarchy of what was declared to be the only Christian Church in England, with hardly an exception, employed their influence to make the fires hotter, to give increased employment to the hangman, and to swell the numbers in the gaols. Yet the Nonconformists grew and increased. Their doctrines became every year more readily accepted, until it was seen that a despotic Church was as opposed to the interests of religion and humanity, and as inconsistent with the rights of mankind, as a despotic State. And, in looking back upon the history of their country, it must have struck the most superficial observers that the worst instruments of bad government had always been the instruments which had been employed for ecclesiastical purposes. Elizabeth and Whitgift, James the First and Bancroft, Charles the First and Laud, Charles the Second and Sheldon, were names that could not but be associated together. The sympathy of the Established

Church with the despotic rule of the Tudors and the Stuarts was now a matter of history. It remained to be seen whether it would oppose or support a practically new dynasty, which entered on its reign with the promise of a constitutional government and the toleration of ecclesiastical differences.

CHAPTER II.

THE REVOLUTION TO THE COMPREHENSION BILL, 1688—89.

IT is seldom that those who fight the battles either of political or of religious liberty live to see the reward of their labours, and this was especially the case with many of the most eminent of the earlier advocates of religious toleration. When James the Second was expelled from England, those who had laboured with the most ardent zeal and untiring devotion for this consummation of their work had entered into their rest. John Milton had died, "in mean circumstances," eleven years before King Charles the Second's death, and immediately after that monarch had formally recalled the Indulgence of 1672, and given orders for the effectual suppression of all conventicles. In 1677 Dr. Manton, who had been one of Cromwell's chaplains, and who had suffered imprisonment for his Nonconformity, was also called to his rest. Two years later died Matthew Poole, a professor at Oxford University with Owen, and whose labours in Biblical criticism remain, at the end of two centuries, undimmed in splendour; and, at the same time was called away, Dr. Thomas Goodwin, president of Magdalen College during the Protectorate, and who had attended Cromwell's death-bed. The next year died Stephen Charnock, chaplain to Henry Cromwell, and one of the gentlest preachers of his age. In 1681 Thomas Gouge, who had devoted his life and fortune to the evangelization of the Welsh, who gave to that people a Bible in the vernacular, and whose character Archbishop Tillotson compared, for his eagerness in doing good, to "the glorious character of the Son of God," also died. Nearly six years before the Revolution entered into rest Dr. John Owen, the greatest champion of Independent principles that ever adorned the denomination. David Clarkson, Owen's successor in the ministry, and almost his equal in learning and in public service, died in the year before the Revolution. Delaune the Baptist had perished in prison, and Canne and Knollys, of the same religious body, had not lived to see one of their principles obtain public toleration after the Protectorate. Only a few months before William the Third landed in England, John Bunyan, who had suffered more than any, also died. The greatest popular preacher in England since Latimer and until Whitefield, who had endured Jeffrey's abuse, and who had spent a fifth portion of his life in gaol, lived neither to see his preaching legalized, his persecutor meet his reward, nor one of the laws under which he had suffered repealed. These, and the thousands who had died in prison without leaving a name behind them, had made the continuance of an intolerant ecclesiastical policy impossible, and prepared the people for a more liberal and patriotic government.

But if the principal "witnesses" for religious freedom did not live to enjoy that rest from controversy which is so refreshing to the Christian man who is a controversialist only from necessity, neither did their opponents live to see the triumph of their adversaries. The race of intolerant prelates and arbitrary statesmen had also died out. Sheldon, the last conspicuous representative of religious intolerance, had long lain beneath his monument in the parish church of Croydon. Their successors had, for the most part, been chosen on account of the moderation of their ecclesiastical sentiments. Clarendon had died in exile and disgrace, and no statesman of equal power, ability, and independence, holding his principles, had succeeded to him. The high character, the zealous labours, the controversial ability, the steadfast adherence to their views, and the unselfish patriotism of the Nonconformists, had changed the temper of all parties. In a time of common danger, even the bishops had welcomed them as their friends, and had loudly declared their desire for more liberal ecclesiastical laws.

The bishops went, indeed, almost beyond this. In their petition to James against publishing the Declaration for liberty of conscience, they had declared that their "averseness" proceeded not from any want of due tenderness to Dissenters, in relation to whom, they said, they "were willing to come to such a temper as shall be thought fit, when that matter shall be considered and settled in Parliament and Convocation."* After their acquittal, Sancroft, Archbishop of Canterbury, publicly counselled the bishops and clergy of his province to have a very tender regard to "their brethren" the Protestant Dissenters, to visit them at their houses, and to receive them kindly at their own; to discourse to them civilly; to persuade them, if it was possible, to join the Church, but, under any circumstances, to unite heartily and affectionately with them in prayer for the blessed union of all the Reformed Churches.† Privately, the bishops told every one that they were about to adopt a new policy towards Dissenters. "I do assure you," said one writer of the time, "and I am certain I have the best grounds in the whole world for my assurance, that the bishops will never stir one jot from

* Burnet's "Own Times," p. 470, *note*.

† "Papers relating to the Affairs of England," vol. i. 1688. Birch's "Tillotson," pp. 155, 156.

their petition; but that they will, whenever that happy opportunity shall offer itself, let the Protestant Dissenters find that they will be better than their word."* Another writer, who was afterwards elevated to the Episcopal bench, candidly acknowledged the errors of the Church in her former persecutions, and confessed that "the wise and generous behaviour of the main body of Dissenters had given them so just a title to our friendship, that we must resolve to set all the world against us if we can ever forget it, and if we do not make them all the return of ease and favour, when it is in our power to do it."† Such promises, made in foul weather, were destined to receive only the ordinary fulfilment.

The condition of Protestant Dissent at the commencement of the reign of William the Third was remarkable for its strength and purity. Some estimate of the number of its adherents may be formed from the circumstance that two hundred and seventy-three Congregational and one hundred and twenty-two Baptist Churches now existing date their origin from before this period.‡ The Presbyterians were to be found probably in still greater numbers,§ and in London, Lancashire, Yorkshire, Cheshire, and the Northern counties generally, they predominated over all the other denominations. The Quakers appear to have been almost as numerous as either the Baptists or the Independents. Their places of worship, especially in the metropolis, were large and well attended, and their missionary spirit was inferior to that of no other sect. With the exception of the Quakers', the

* "Calamy's Abridgement," pp. 629, 630.

† Burnet's "Apology."

‡ Reckoned from the Congregational Year Book and the Baptist Hand Book for 1866.

§ Burnet says that the Presbyterians and Independents were three-fourths of all Dissenters. "Own Times," p. 438.

"meeting-houses," as they were termed, of the denominations were guarded by trusts of a general character, which neither specified the sect to which they belonged, nor the doctrines which were to be preached. They were secured by deeds to the congregations of "Protestant Dissenters" worshipping in that place, who were allowed to choose such person as minister as a majority might elect. No creeds, confessions, or articles of belief were subscribed to by either ministers or churches,* but declarations of their faith, made at general assemblies or conferences, were common to all Dissenters. The creed of the Presbyterians and Independents was in accordance with the Westminster Assembly's Catechism; while the Baptists were perhaps equally divided between Calvinism and Arminianism. Arianism, or Socinianism, had, as yet, only individual professors. It had existed in England from the time of the Dutch Anabaptists, but no attempt had been made to found an organization on its basis.

The form of public service of all the denominations, excepting the Baptists, was substantially the same as that which prevails at the present day. The Baptists, like the Quakers, had conscientious scruples against public singing, which were scarcely overcome at the end of half a century from this time.† Books were written to prove that the only Scriptural singing was from the heart, and that women especially ought no more to sing than to speak in Church.‡ In one or two places where singing was at all allowed, it was agreed to sing only once, and that after the last prayer was ended, so that those who disapproved of the practice might have an opportunity of leaving the meeting; but even

---

* Wilson's "Historical Inquiry," p. 3.

† "Ivimey's History," ii. 373.

‡ Marlow's "Discourse against Singing."

this compromise created dissatisfaction.* Anointing with oil seems to have been common among the Baptists of this period.† That denomination was also already divided on the subject of open and strict communion.

Of the general character of Nonconformist preaching, if judgment may be given from such printed sermons as have come down to the present time, it may be said that the Presbyterians excelled in doctrinal, the Independents in exegetical, and the Baptists and Quakers in experimental discourses. Neither of the former were remarkable for brevity, while the minuteness with which they divided and subdivided their sermons has made it difficult for modern readers to take any pleasure in them.‡ "My next," wrote Bolingbroke to Swift, "shall be as long as one of Dr. Manton's discourses, who taught my youth to yawn, and prepared me to be a High Churchman, that I might never hear him read, nor read him more." § Yet Manton was not one of the most tedious of preachers. The length of their religious services was not, probably, so great as in the time of the Commonwealth, but, according to modern tastes, it was inordinate. Philip Henry, one of the purest men and most instructive preachers of that age, began family worship on Sunday at eight o'clock, "when he read and expounded pretty largely, sung a psalm, and prayed," and this service was eagerly attended by others than the members of his own family. At nine o'clock public service began, which did not conclude before noon, after which there was a rest

---

* Keach's "Breach Repaired," 1689. The practice described existed in Keach's own Church, at Horsleydown, but it divided the Church.

† "Kiffin's Life," p. 33

‡ This methodical style is well described by Burnet, "Own Times," p. 102.

§ Burnet, *note*, p. 106.

of an hour and a-half. He then read and commented on a chapter of Scripture, catechised the children, expounded the catechism, and preached another sermon.* This is a fair sample of public religious service amongst Nonconformists at this period.

But whatever might have been the minor characteristics of their preaching, the eminence of the intellectual and spiritual power of the older Nonconformist preachers can even now be gauged, and it was fully recognised not only by that "middle class" which is ordinarily said to be the support of Nonconformity, but by the most refined and cultivated sections of society. The barrier which, through the lust of social as well as ecclesiastical predominance, the Established Church has since successfully raised between the Nonconformists and the upper classes of society was, at that time, neither so high nor so impregnable as it now is. Owen's church, while it included some of the still living leaders of the Commonwealth, such as Lord Charles Fleetwood, Colonel Desborough, and Colonel Berry, included also many of the aristocracy, amongst whom were the Countess of Anglesea, Sir Thomas Overbury, and Lady Haversham; whilst amongst Owen's most intimate friends were Lord Orrery, Lord Willoughby, Lord Wharton, the Earl of Berkeley, and Sir John Trevor.† When Manton preached in Covent Garden Church the Duke of Bedford was his constant hearer, and remained his friend until his death.‡ Dr. Bates was in intimate intercourse with King William, Archbishop Tillotson, the Earl of Nottingham, and his father, the Lord Chancellor Finch. Baxter was acquainted with all the leading men of his age, and would

* Matthew Henry's "Life of Philip Henry," p. 105.

† Orme's "Owen," pp. 277—289.

‡ Calamy.

be found discussing philosophy, at Acton, with Sir Matthew Hale; terms of concordance, at Dublin, with Archbishop Usher; politics, in London, with Lord Lauderdale; and divinity with the Earl of Balcarres; while Oxendon Street Meeting-house was built, in large part, through the contributions of the aristocracy.* Howe held a social position equal to that of either Baxter or Owen. He was on visiting terms with many of the aristocracy, was a close correspondent of Lady Rachel Russell, and a personal friend of Archbishop Tillotson.† All the leading Nonconformists had free personal access to William the Third.

This intimacy, although it did not result, on either side, in any compromise of opinion or of position, had the effect of moderating the spirit of controversy. Illustrations of this are to be found in the controversial works of Stillingfleet and Tillotson, and Baxter, Howe, and Owen. Stillingfleet, by his repeated charges of schism against Nonconformists, provoked replies from the leading Presbyterian and Independent divines, but even Baxter met him with moderation, and Owen was chivalrous. Tillotson, in a sermon preached before the King, had indiscreetly committed himself to the statement of opinions which, in their logical issue, involved the persecution of all Nonconformists. While it was necessary, on account of the royal command, to print this discourse as it was delivered, the author candidly assured Howe of his regret at having so expressed himself, and in a subsequent edition of the sermon, carefully modified its language. It was the suggestive and acute remark of a writer of that age, that the high personal honour and piety and the generous dispositions of such men as Stillingfleet and Tillotson worked greater harm to the Nonconformist

* Calamy, p. 688.
† Birch's "Tillotson" and Rogers's "Life of Howe."

interest, as such, than anything which mere policy could have devised.*

The education of Dissenting Ministers was conducted in private academies. One of the first resources of those who had been ejected by the Act of Uniformity was to take to teaching; and, although contrary to law, they formed schools in all parts of the country. The Universities, for the first time in English history, were closed against a section of the people, but no enactments could recal the learning which the ejected ministers had received from them. Their academies appear to have been numerously attended, and their students, drawn from all sections of society, to have received an exact and a "liberal" education. It was scarcely to be expected that such proceedings should not be looked upon with jealousy, and accordingly we find even Tillotson approving of the suppression of such academies as were conducted by members of either of the Universities.† It was thought that no person who held a University degree could legally, without breaking the oath which he had taken not to lecture at any place in England excepting in Oxford or Cambridge, assume the office of a teacher. The Nonconformists objected to this interpretation of the oath, and, although sometimes obliged to remove their residences, maintained their academies in large numbers and great efficiency. Amongst the most memorable of such teachers were William Janeway and Philip Henry. Upwards of twenty academies are known to have been in existence at the time of the Revolution.‡

Of the character of the religion both of Nonconformists and Churchmen, the impartial testimony of one of the most

* Birch's "Tillotson," p. 32, *note*, and Du Moulin's "Appeal."

† Birch's "Tillotson," p. 246. Toulmin's History, chap. iii.

‡ Dr. Toulmin has given the most complete account of the early academies of Dissenters. See chap. iii. of his History.

moderate and charitable of Churchmen may be accepted without question. The gentle and sainted Archbishop Leighton had remarked of the Church of England, in Charles the Second's reign, that its administration, both in relation to the ecclesiastical courts and pastoral duties, was the most corrupt he had ever seen; * and Bishop Burnet observes of the clergy of his own time: "I must own that the main body of our clergy have always appeared dead and lifeless to me, and, instead of animating, they seem rather to lay one another to sleep." The Nonconformists, on the other hand, he commends for their "great zeal," and observes of the Baptists especially that they were generally "men of virtue, and of an universal charity." The predominants and the predominated naturally differed. In the one party, persecution had ensured piety; in the other, privilege had begotten indifference, luxuriousness, and pride.

While the intentions of the Prince of Orange and his party were as yet unknown to the Court of St. James', Fagel, the pensioner of Holland, had written a letter explaining the sentiments of the Prince and Princess on the subject of religious toleration. In this letter, which was soon circulated throughout the kingdom, it was stated that they consented to grant "a full liberty to Dissenters, but that they would not consent to the repeal of the laws which tended only to the securing the Protestant religion, such as those concerning the tests, which inflicted no punishment but only an incapacity of being in public engagements, that could not be complained of as great severities." In writing this, Fagel wrote what he knew would be acceptable to Dissenters. In the first place, it was at that time fully intended to bring about a comprehension of the Presbyterians and the Independents in the Established Church,

* Burnet's "Own Times."

and it was known that these two principal sections of the Nonconformist body, providing that the Church services were modified, were willing, for the sake of Christian unity, and what was considered to be the strength of the Protestant interest, wholly to unite with the Church. In such an event, the tests which it was proposed to retain would bear only upon Baptists, Quakers, and Roman Catholics. The former two sections had little political influence; the latter, it was unanimously agreed, could not, without putting the State itself in peril, be trusted with any civil or political power. This letter satisfied the Church leaders, as well as Dissenters. The former felt that, with the tests still in force, their position of supremacy could not be endangered by any ecclesiastical party which might choose to remain outside their own pale. The people saw in it the assured safety of the Protestant religion, and a promise of peace to the kingdom. These pledges were renewed and extended on the landing of the Prince of Orange in England. The first public act of William, on setting foot on English soil, was to issue a declaration, in which he stated that it was his intention to preserve the Established religion; to unite to the Church, by the best means which could be devised, all such as were divided from it; and to suffer all others, who would live peaceably, to enjoy a due freedom of conscience. No one doubted that the Prince would keep his word, and those who enjoyed his most intimate confidence well knew that he was prepared to go beyond it.

William had not been many days in England before he received decisive proof that some of the clergy were not disposed to welcome him. The Bishop and the Dean of Exeter left that city as soon as he entered it, while the whole of the clergy stood aloof from him.* When the

* Burnet's "Own Times," p. 500.

Declaration was read in the cathedral, all the officials hurried from it. On the first Sunday, Burnet, the Prince's chaplain, was called upon to preach before him. No man more merited this honour, for none was more devoted to William's interests or had been more useful in promoting them than this able, skilful, and large-minded man. James, at this very time, was expressing his own confidence in and obligations to the bench of bishops, telling them how sensible he was that they had shown themselves "zealously concerned" for him.* When, however, James had left England, and the loss of his cause was patent to almost every man, the bishops did not hesitate to throw themselves, for the time, into the arms of William. Sancroft, Archbishop of Canterbury, Lamplugh, Archbishop of York, and five bishops, were amongst the peers who met at the Guildhall, in the city of London, on the 11th of December, 1688, to take upon themselves the government of the country until William should arrive. They forthwith issued a declaration that they had determined to join with the Prince of Orange, both for the protection of the Church and for securing due liberty of conscience to Dissenters.† Lamplugh was the bishop who hastened to James when William entered Exeter, for which service he was promoted, on the 15th November, to the archbishopric of the northern province. Twenty-six days afterwards he thus publicly joined the standard of the Prince! Nothing, however, was more remote from the intentions of the bishops and the clergy than to accept the Prince of Orange as King. The highest post they were inclined to assign to him was that of Regent; while many would have been satisfied if, after doing duty as an armed mediator between the Church and James, they

* "Kettlewell's Life," p. 81.

† "London Gazette," December 13, 1688.

could have sent him back to Holland. The opinion of this party was that it was the Prince's prime duty to look to the special interests of the Established Church, rather than to the general interests of the nation.

It was quite consistent with such views that the bishops and the clergy should personally welcome the Prince. The day after William's arrival in London, all the bishops who were in town, with the exception of Sancroft, who declined to go, waited upon him. The clergy of London, with Bishop Compton at their head, and several Dissenting ministers, followed. The Dissenters had not had time to organize a separate deputation. The bishop, therefore, spoke of their presence, stating that they united with the clergy in welcoming the Prince to England. Compton had always treated the Dissenters with respect, and, excepting Trelawney, Bishop of Bristol, was probably the only prelate present who was disposed to enter heartily into the Prince's views. Scarcely a month after this, Evelyn visited Sancroft at Lambeth Palace, where he found the Bishops of St. Asaph, Ely, Bath and Wells, Peterborough and Chichester, debating the state of the nation. "They were all," he says, "for a regency."* The Dissenting ministers waited some days before they presented a separate address; but on the 2nd of January they waited on the Prince. The Duke of Devonshire and Lords Wharton and Wiltshire introduced them; Howe acted as their spokesman. The illness of Baxter and Bates prevented their presence, and they were thus unable to take part in a ceremony which could not but have yielded to both intense gratification. In their address, the Nonconformist ministers expressed their "grateful sense of the Prince's hazardous and heroical expedition," and of the "favour of Heaven" upon it; they

* Evelyn, iii. 263.

esteemed it "a felicity that the patriots of the nobility and gentry had concurred in the design," and that the adminis tration of public affairs "was devolved into hands which the nation and the world knew to be apt for the greatest undertakings"; they promised to promote the views of the Prince to "their utmost endeavours"; they prayed to the Almighty to preserve his person, and to grant success to his efforts for "the defence and propagation of the Protestant interest throughout the world"; they apologized for not having paid their duty earlier, and stated that they did not now appear "on a distinct account, but on that only which was common to them and to all Protestants"; and lastly—referring to the absence of Baxter and Bates—they said that while some of "eminent note" were prevented by age or infirmity from being with them, these ministers concurred in the same grateful sense of a common deliverance. The Prince at once caught the tone of this address, and answered that he came on purpose to defend the Protestant religion, and that he should endeavour to promote "a firm union amongst Protestants." Nothing could have been in better taste than the language of the ministers. While the bishops and clergy could never keep out of sight the defence of the religion as established by law, the Dissenters made no reference whatever to their own painful position. They distinctly disclaimed appearing on their own account. They spoke as Protestant Englishmen only, anxious, before their own grievances were considered, that the government of the nation should be placed on a safe and satisfactory basis. Their reference to "the propagation of the Protestant interest throughout the world"—whatever meaning such words might cover—was only natural in addressing a Prince who had been, during the whole of his life, and was now especially, looked up to as the great champion of that interest, the embodiment of the Protestant thought, and the leader of the Protestant armies of Europe. This was more than a skilfully-designed reference to the Prince's secret object of ambition; it was an acknowledgment of his great public services as a European statesman, and an expression of trust in his capacity and his policy. William frankly accepted it as such, and at the same time gave expression to what he knew was in their thoughts, although from delicacy of feeling, they had not expressed it.

When, on the 22nd of January, the Convention Parliament met, the state of feeling existing amongst the bishops and clergy was more fully disclosed. Sancroft refused to appear in it. Nothing could move him from that determination. It was in vain that Lord Halifax, who had been elected to preside over the proceedings of the peers, conjured him, as the Primate of the Established Church, to attend; and said that the House of Lords sent him an order to appear in his place. It was in vain that his friends remonstrated with him, and plainly hinted that he was guilty of a cowardly desertion of them all.* Sancroft was determined to be no party to any course of action which would lead to the deposition of James. His stubborn and persistent refusal proceeded from an obstinate man, whose weakness was strengthened and whose obstinacy was confirmed by that favourite doctrine which Churchmen had so often proclaimed since the Restoration—the Divine right of all kings. It is only doing justice to his memory to add that Sancroft's course of action did not proceed from any jealousy concerning the extension of religious liberty. When he was reminded that he was pledged to the relief of Protestant Dissenters, he answered at once that the bishops had no intention of evading their obligations in that respect, but that this was a matter to be settled in Convocation. The High Churchmen

* "Clarendon Correspondence," ii. 248. Tanner, MSS. 27, 16.

were thus, before William was on the throne, giving clear indication of their intention to set up the claims and privileges of their own order as against the paramount rights of the State. No class of men in history have so often forgotten that they are Englishmen as the clergy of the Established Church.

But although Sancroft did not attend in his place, many of the other prelates had no such hesitation. The Primate could move in neither direction; but he could and did influence the conduct and the votes of others. This influence, however, was not felt in the House of Commons, which in one sitting resolved, without going to a division, that James had abdicated the government, and that the throne had thereby become vacant. This resolution was at once communicated to the other House; but it was only after prolonged debates and conferences between both Houses that their concurrence was secured. When the first vote was taken on the question that the Prince and Princess of Orange be declared King and Queen, fourteen bishops were present, of whom twelve voted against it, and only two, Compton and Trelawney, in its favour.* These two gave to the vote the small majority which it received, the numbers being forty-nine against and fifty-one for it.

By this time it had become evident that the clergy, as a body, were opposed to the new settlement. They had supported the bishops in their arguments in favour of a Regency,† and were now in an "ill-humour" with everything. So manifest was their disaffection that members of the House of Commons felt compelled to notice it. Sharp, Rector of St. Giles's and Dean of Norwich, had preached a sermon on Popery before the House, on January 30th, and had the bad grace, notwithstanding that the legislature

---

* "Clarendon Correspondence," ii. 256. † Burnet, p. 513.

had declared the throne vacant, to pray for "his most excellent Majesty." Maynard, the Nestor of the House, who had sat in all the Parliaments from the first of King Charles the First, charged the Dean with a breach of the vote, and expressed his opinion that he should not receive the thanks of the House for his sermon. "Almost all the clergy," cried Sir John Thompson, "do the same thing." The Speaker ruled that the preacher had contradicted the vote of the House.* The temper of the clergy was again alluded to in the debates on the King's speech. "I think," said Maynard, "that the clergy are out of their wits, and I believe if the clergy should have their wills, none of us would be here again."† It is not difficult to assign a cause for this feeling. Neither William nor Mary were hot Episcopalians. On the first Sunday after arriving in London, William had attended the worship of the Established Church, and partaken of the Communion. He pledged the word of a man, whose honour both as a gentleman and a statesman had never been impeached, that he would maintain the religion established by law, but it was well known that he was not an Episcopalian by conviction. In his own country he had been a Presbyterian; but he attached little, if any, importance to forms of worship or church constitutions. He would listen to preachers of any sect, and although holding most of the Evangelical tenets was inclined to Latitudinarianism. But, while he did not drink or swear like James the First, was not untruthful like Charles the First, was not dissolute like Charles the Second, nor a tool of France and the Jesuits like the second James, he was beloved by the clergy less than either of these men. It was natural that he should be accused of favouring the Presbyterians, although it would be difficult to tell in what

* Grey's Debates, Jan. 30. † Ib., Feb. 20.

manner he favoured them. His fault was, that he intended to keep faith with Dissent as well as with the Church, and the clergy knew that he would keep it. Ecclesiastical intolerance in the clerical order is generally, although not always, co-existent with negligence in the performance of religious duties. The clergy of this period are described, by one who knew them well, as pluralists, non-resident, busybodies, news-mongers, frequenters of ale-houses, intemperate, and as of weak and small understanding.* The moral power of such men must have been very feeble, but the nature of their office appears, notwithstanding, to have cast, as has so often been the case, a glamour over the minds both of statesmen and people. One man, however, was insensible to this fascination; that man was the Prince of Orange.

The feeling with respect to the Established Church as a part of the Constitution of England, was first manifested in the debates on the Coronation Oath. It was moved, as an addition to the old oath, that the King should swear that to the utmost of his power he would maintain the Protestant religion established by law; to which it was replied that he should also maintain the Protestant religion not established by law. But what was meant by "law"? Did it mean the laws in being when the oath was taken, in such a strict sense that the Sovereign was never to consent to an alteration in them,† or such laws as the legislature might, from time to time, see fit to make? In order to settle this point, it was further moved that the King should swear to maintain the Protestant religion as it is, or shall be, established by law. But what was meant by "established"? and

* "Kettlewell's Life," p. 91.

† This, as is well known, was the view taken by George III. and George IV. in the case of the Irish Church and the laws affecting Dissenters.

might not these words be as effective with regard to all as to one particular Church? "What," said one speaker, "is established by law, may be overthrown by law;" and he suggested the use of the words, "according to the laws for the time being." Ultimately, and notwithstanding a warning that these words would imply a forgetfulness of the promises made to Nonconformists, the Commons agreed to the phrase "as it is now established by law." An amendment adopted in Committee, substituting the words "Protestant religion professed by the Church of England," was subsequently rejected. On the third reading, Mr. Pelham moved a further proviso, to the effect that no clause in the Act should be so understood as to prevent the Sovereign from giving his assent to any measures for alterations in the discipline or the forms of the Church, but it was unanimously considered that the words already adopted did not restrict his liberty in this respect. Mr. Pelham's amendment, therefore, was not persisted in.* The tone of the debates on this question indicated, throughout, a recognition of the just claims of Dissenters; and it is evident that the words of the oath were not intended to prevent any subsequent alteration in the constitution of the Established Church.

The Oaths of Allegiance and Supremacy were next discussed. It was proposed, on the introduction of this question, that the Corporation Act should, at the same time, be abolished—"an Act," said one speaker, of "as much intrinsic iniquity as any Act whatever;"† but it was thought desirable to deal with this question separately. No debates excited greater interest than those on this important measure. It was well known that many of the bishops and

* Grey's Debates, March 25—28, 1689.

† Speech of Sir Robert Howard, Grey's Debates, Feb. 25, 1688-9.

clergy entertained conscientious scruples against taking the oath to William and Mary. Amongst them were some of the highest influence and the most spotless integrity, who considered that no earthly power could absolve them from the oath which they had already taken to King James. Were they and their whole order to be exempted, and thus allowed, if they should think proper, to conspire together for the return of the Stuart? There was no difference of opinion in the legislature on this point. In the House of Commons there existed a strong feeling against the clergy as a body, and it was resolved to make no exceptions in their favour. But there is more than one way of imposing an oath. The Lords were in favour of the oath being privately tendered to the clergy by an Order in Council, which, obviously, might have led to some persons being omitted. The subject was gravely debated in formal conferences between both houses, but the firmness of the Commons triumphed. The Act provided that those who did not take the oaths before the 1st August, 1689, should be dispossessed of their benefices; the only modification being that the King was at liberty to allow such of the clergy, not exceeding twelve in number, as might refuse to take the oaths, an allowance of a third part of their present income.*

The wisdom and magnanimity of William were never more conspicuously shown than on this occasion. On March 16th, he went down to Parliament, and earnestly recommended that the Test and Corporation Acts should be abolished, and all Protestants admitted to public service. If this were done he was willing to dispense with the Oath of Allegiance from the bishops and clergy who were already

* The proceedings of the conferences are fully reported in Grey's Debates.

in possession of office. No one has charged the King with mixed, much less with unworthy motives, in making this proposal. It was the natural suggestion of a generous and trustful mind. It may, indeed, have occurred to him that, with the aid of Dissenters in office,* he need not fear the enmity of a portion only of the clergy; and, on the other hand, he might have been confident that even his most bitter clerical enemies could not but be favourably affected towards him by this expression of his trust in their loyalty, and his consideration for the tenderness of their consciences. But William did not yet know the English people. By asking greater liberty for Dissenters he enraged all Tory Churchmen; while, by suggesting a generous treatment of the bishops and clergy, he offended his own friends, who knew better than he, the danger of trusting implicitly to the forbearance of the clergy. His speech therefore did harm to both the parties whom he would have befriended. The Act took no notice of Dissenters, and bore with all the justice of the severest law on the position of the clergy.

Eight bishops and more than four hundred of the clergy refused to take the oath. It should be possible, at this distance of time, to pass an unprejudiced judgment on the characters and the acts of the non-jurors. At their head was Sancroft, Archbishop of Canterbury, a man of unblemished moral and religious character, but weak in purpose, and narrow in his judgment and sympathies. Next to him in influence, and superior in spiritual character, was Thomas Ken, Bishop of Bath and Wells, the

* "It was their (the clergy's) dissatisfaction that made the King more inclinable to favour the Dissenters, whom he generally looked upon as better affected to his person and title."—Kennett's "History," iii. 518.

author of the celebrated "Morning Evening, and Midnight Hymns." A man of gentler disposition or more saintly life than Ken never adorned the Christian Church, and none can suspect the motives which induced him to throw in his lot with the non-jurors.* The remaining bishops were Thomas, of Worcester; Lake, of Chichester; Turner, of Ely; Lloyd, of Norwich; Frampton, of Gloucester; and White, of Peterborough. Thomas and Lake died immediately afterwards; and Sancroft, who somewhat ostentatiously retired to a cottage at Fressingfield, soon followed them. Turner became implicated in a conspiracy to restore James, and the sympathies and prayers of all of the new sect were unhesitatingly given to the dethroned monarch. Ken refused to dissever himself from the Church; but Sancroft had no hesitation in denouncing the whole of the hierarchy and clergy who took the oaths as schismatics. He joined with the other non-jurors in obtaining James's license to proceed with the consecration of new bishops,† thus defying the Government, and inviting persecution from it. There was no occasion, however, for the State to stretch out its arm in order to punish the non-juring clergy. Some reverence was felt for the personal character of many of them, but public opinion was not in their favour. If the rank of a few was high, their numbers were small. During the time of their probation the press teemed with pamphlets concerning the injury which might result to the State and the Church if they refused to take the oaths. Burnet used his persuasive powers to the utmost. Stillingfleet, forgetting the sin of schism in Dissenters, turned the whole of his controversial battery against the stubborn members of his own Church. When the day of probation passed, it was

* "Ken's Life." By a Layman. Page 364.

† Lathbury's "History of the Non-jurors," p. 97.

found that the Government was not endangered nor the Church rent in twain by the defection of even eight bishops. The State was, in fact, the stronger for the slight danger to which it had apparently been exposed. It had asserted the superiority of the civil to the ecclesiastical power in the Church of its own creation; it had ventured to depose from office men who claimed the authority of their office from God Himself, and to deny to them the right of exercising any of their functions.

The non-jurors were pre-eminently the sacerdotalists of their age. Their favourite doctrine was, that the clergy were independent of the "lay power"*—a doctrine true of the Church, but not of the clergy of any State-established Church. In the course of years this doctrine blossomed into semi-Romanism, and the non-jurors claimed to be members of the "Catholic," as distinguished from the Protestant Church; advocated Transubstantiation; the mixing of water with wine in the Communion; and the supreme authority of the Church over all persons, "though never so great."† Finding themselves cut off from intercourse with Episcopalians at home, they fruitlessly endeavoured to promote a union with the Greek Church. Reduced in numbers, and brought into general contempt, they eventually quarrelled amongst themselves; and what little respect has been accorded to them was lost by their participation in the rebellion in favour of the Pretender in 1745, after which they gradually sank into oblivion. But like all zealots, the non-jurors were as severe in life as in doctrine. Whatever may be said of their disaffection to the State, none could accuse them of spiritual heresy. Although intolerant amongst the intolerant, they were pure in life, correct

* Dodwell's "Independency of the Clergy of the Lay Power," 1697.
† Lathbury's "History of the Non-jurors," pp. 313—15.

in mcrals, and numbered amongst them men of great learning.*

It became evident, in the debates on the Oath of Allegiance Bill, that there was no disposition in either House of Parliament to do justice to those who had by general admission contributed to save the nation. When the Bill had been read a second time in the House of Lords, it was resolved that a Select Committee be appointed to draft a clause which should abolish the Sacramental Test as a qualification for enjoying any office, employment, or place of trust under the Crown. The Committee drew up this clause, but it was at once rejected by a large majority. Seven peers—but seven only—Delamere, Stamford, North and Grey, Chesterfield, Wharton, Lovelace, and Vaughan, entered their protest against this vote expressing their opinion that a hearty union amongst Protestants was a greater security to Church and State than any test that could be invented, and that greater safeguard ought not to be required from such as held office under the Crown, than from the Members of Parliament, none of whom were obliged to receive the Sacrament in order to enable them to sit in either House. A more moderate proposal met with a similar fate. It was moved that any person should be sufficiently qualified who, within a year of his admission to office should receive the Sacrament of the Lord's Supper, either according to the usage of the Established, or of any other Protestant Church. The terms of this motion were fixed so as to prevent the qualification of Roman Catholics. It was obviously open to serious objection on religious grounds. Had it been adopted it would have operated as a premium

* Two of the ablest and most accurate of our national historians were non-jurors—Jeremy Collier, the author of the "Ecclesiastical History of England," and Carte, who wrote a history of England. Law, the author of the "Serious Call," was also a non-juror.

on the profession of personal religion amongst Dissenters, as well as in the Church; and although Lord Wharton, himself a Presbyterian of sincere religious character, voted for it, there is some doubt whether it could have received the sanction of the Dissenting leaders. This proposal was however, like its predecessor, rejected by an overwhelming majority, six peers protesting against the rejection. These were Lords Oxford, Lovelace, Wharton, Mordaunt, Montague, and Paget, who argued that it was a "hard usage" of Dissenters; that it deprived the kingdom of the services of many fit and able men of unquestionable loyalty: that it raised a suspicion of the insincerity of the many promises which had been made to them; that it was an unjust humiliation of them, a profanation of the Sacrament, a violation of the spirit of Christianity, and an infliction of punishment where no crime had been committed.* The protest had, however, no effect beyond the vindication of the personal sincerity of the protesters.

A similar fate awaited the action taken in the Commons. A Bill was introduced into this House for the repeal of the Corporation Act, which was allowed to pass a second reading. But on going into Committee an instruction was moved that no alteration be effected in the laws respecting the Sacrament. As this motion, if carried, would have defeated the sole object of a Bill which the House had already sanctioned, it could scarcely have seemed probable that it would meet with success. But, while there was a vindictive opposition to the measure among the Tory party, there were trimmers and half-hearted men—waiters on the opinions of the ministers—amongst the Whigs. They agreed that no vote should be taken on the merits of this motion. In place of it, the adjournment of the debate was

* "Collection of Protests," pp. 64, 65.

proposed and carried by a hundred and sixteen to a hundred and fourteen votes. The same influence which brought about this division prevented the Bill from making any further progress. It therefore became a "dropped order." Once and once only in the lifetime of the generation who then sat in the House of Commons was this subject revived. That was after the Toleration Act had been passed, when the Corporation of London appeared by its Sheriffs before the bar of the House with a petition that Dissenters might bear offices as well as others.* This city, which had sheltered the "Five Members," which had set the example of public addresses to the Head of the State by expressing its confidence in the Protector's government, had found money enough to carry on the war of the Parliament; had taken the first step to secure the government on the flight of James; and had been the bulwark of civil and religious freedom for generations, made the only public protest during that period against the injustice of the enactments to which Dissenters were subjected.

The explanation of the course taken on these questions is to be found in the position of parties in the State and the Church. Whatever amount of indebtedness might have been felt towards the King, it is certain that he was not personally popular. His grave, cold, and reserved manners repulsed the courtiers who had participated in the revels of the court of Charles the Second. William cared nothing for palace gaities. His ill-health obliged him, almost as soon as he came to England, to seek a residence outside the metropolis. He cultivated few personal intimacies among Englishmen, rarely confided to them his purposes, and seldom took their advice. This course could not, as is generally represented, have proceeded wholly from tem-

* Grey's Debates, June 24th, 1689.

perament, for he trusted without reserve those in whom he had confidence; but, unfortunately, excepting Burnet and Tillotson, these persons were not Englishmen. Like many men who have consecrated themselves to a great public object, he had very few personal sympathies. What he most cared for was sympathy with his ideas, and these were not the ideas of the people by whom he was surrounded in England. They followed him in his foreign policy, because they knew that he was the only man in Europe who could cope with the French King, and that the safety of England as a State, and the permanency of the new Government, depended on the manner in which that policy was carried out. William the Third brought to the consideration of domestic matters the same breadth and strength of intellect which enabled him to be the master of the political future of Europe, but not quite the same sagacity. Foreigner though he was, he had larger and more patriotic purposes respecting England than almost any of the statesmen around him. His was the only vision that was not disturbed by party and personal prejudices; but he showed a lack of sagacity by not sufficiently taking such prejudices into consideration. Although a greater statesman than any Englishman of his day, he was by no means so great a politician as many men of smaller intellect; and it soon appeared that the statesmen who sat in his council made him miserable by their opposition to his plans and preferences. They seemed to delight in humiliating him. No Sovereign of England, before or since his time, ever endured so much personal mortification as this great "deliverer" of the nation from the despotism of the Stuarts and the anarchy of another civil war. What real gratitude was felt towards him was shown by the manner of his burial. He had the meanest funeral of any King who ever sat on the English throne.

Considerations of public policy occasioned, no doubt, much of the treatment to which William was exposed. It was desirable to show, and show frequently, that the relations of ruler and people were changed from what they had been—that in fact the King was now only nominally a ruler, that the three branches of the Legislature held the sovereign power, and that the chief magistrate's functions were limited by their will and pleasure. The despotic powers of the Tudors and the arbitrary pretensions of the Stuarts were gone, and gone for ever. The statesmen of the Revolution had the difficult and delicate task committed to them of adjusting the new relations. To their firmness were owing the solidity of the throne and the liberty of the nation, but little can be said in praise of their delicacy. If the people had cared to think much about the subject, they would have found that nearly the whole power formerly claimed by the monarch of the country was now being absorbed by the great territorial families, and that their chief safety consisted in the ambition and the mutual jealousies of those families. The Revolution practically substituted a mild oligarchy for an intolerable despotism, and from that time to the present this feature of the government of England has undergone but little modification. During the reign of William the great Whig families, with a few exceptions, were naturally the rulers of the nation, and their sympathies were, as they had always been, with the Nonconformists. But even amongst these men, the influence of the clergy, Jacobite although it was, was powerful. It was better for the sake of the public peace that the clergy should approve than disapprove of the policy of the statesmen, and that, as far as might be consistent with the general welfare, or even a little beyond such pure patriotism, their good-will to the new government should be gained. Such families as the Devonshires and the Bedfords would nearly always be found voting right; but the Halifaxes, who had joined the new government simply because it was successful, would, as it suited their own purposes, support an increased religious liberty one day and deny it the next; while the Earl of Nottingham, Secretary of State, who had the largest influence amongst the peers, was a Tory. The clause for abolishing the Sacramental Test was thrown out in the Lords by the votes of Whigs, and the votes of Whigs decided the fate of the Corporation Bill in the Commons. Both these decisions were probably given, not on the merits of the question at issue, but from a desire to diminish the growing disaffection of the Church and the clergy.

There were some clergymen of eminence, however, who did not share in the general feeling respecting either the government or the Dissenters. The best representative of the political feeling of the general body of the clergy at this period was South, Prebendary of Westminster, whose rich and lofty, if sometimes coarse and turgid, eloquence has earned for him deserved distinction as one of the greatest orators of the English Church. No preacher of his day, and few preachers since, could decorate Christian truth so gracefully and gorgeously—could make the love of God seem so winning, or the powers of the world to come so terrible as Dr. South. But he loathed Dissent and Dissenters. The coarsest words in the English language were scarcely coarse enough to express his scorn and hatred of those "schismatics." He had more charity for the greatest sinner before him, than even for a Howe or a Bates. When he spoke on this subject he became inflamed with passion, and his mouth poured forth a torrent of invective. What South said, five-sixths of the clergy felt. There was, however, a minority which included in its ranks men of equal, though of a different order of ability from

South, who were possessed of very different feelings. Most prominent in this section was Burnet, who, in acknowledgment of his sincere Christian character, his devotion to the duties of his ministerial office, as well as in reward for his great services in promoting the Revolution, had now been created Bishop of Salisbury. An ardent Whig and a severe rebuker of the vices of the clergy of his time, no man was both more respected and more hated than this active, learned, and liberal-minded man. His weaknesses undoubtedly drew upon him some contempt. He was garrulous, and like all garrulous men, sometimes too plain-spoken. He was also credulous, and too easily prejudiced; but these faults are as nothing in comparison with the excellencies of his character, and his great public services. Burnet was the personal confidant of both William and Mary, and his suggestions and advice contributed in no small degree to the success of their enterprise. A Whig of the Whigs, when Whiggism meant devotion to one's country at the risk of life and fortune, he was an unswerving advocate of popular rights as opposed to arbitrary authority. His Protestantism was more than a creed; it was a principle of his religion. His liberality of sentiment would be esteemed even in this age; in his own it was exceptionally conspicuous. While he deplored any separation from the National Church, he advocated, with a zeal and energy which was the secret of half the odium of which he was the object, an unlimited toleration. In the pulpit, in his place in the House of Lords, and in the press, through good report and through evil report, from the first Liberal administration of King William to the last Tory administration of Queen Anne, he never failed to advocate the application of this principle to the legislation of his country. His works on the "Thirty-nine Articles," the "History of the Reformation," and the "History of His Own Times," are part of the national literature, and his example as a bishop was a legacy to his Church. A more laborious, charitable and useful prelate, or a more active preacher never adorned the English Episcopacy.

Next, in personal, and superior in some respects in public influence to Burnet, were Tillotson, Tenison, and Stillingfleet. Tillotson and Tenison, successively Archbishops of Canterbury, had much in common. Both were liberally inclined; but Tillotson was by far the greater man of the two. He was one of the most chaste and pious, and at the same time, one of the most popular, of preachers; he was active in promoting all measures tending towards an increased toleration; he cultivated largely the personal friendship of Dissenters, and was the leader of the Liberal Church-party who sought, by a revision of the formularies and the constitution of the Church, to bring back to her fold those who had left it. Tenison possessed less mental power, but equal liberality of sentiment. Stillingfleet, Bishop of Worcester, was superior to both of the archbishops in learning, and in love of disputation somewhat resembled Baxter. But although he had raised a controversy with Dissenters on the subject of "Schism," no man was more respected by them. All these were, as were all William's bishops, somewhat latitudinarian in theology; but the latitudinarianism of that day meant nothing more than moderate Calvinism.

The most cultured intellect and unblemished patriotism in the House of Commons were also in favour of the largest degree of religious liberty. Serjeant Maynard, the veteran leader of the Liberal party, now past ninety years of age, had seen too much of the fatal folly of persecution to resist any measure for the relief of conscience and the restoration of natural religious rights. The grandson of John Hampden was found on the same side. Somers, who spoke for the first time in this Parliament, and who was destined soon to attain to the highest eminence of statesmanship, never faltered in his loyalty to the principles of English liberty. In the same roll was to be found the great name of Sir Isaac Newton, who, although apparently a silent member, gave his uniform support to such measures as most tended to the higher elevation of his country. How was it that, with such a weight in favour of a more enlarged liberality, one House of Parliament decided to retain the Test Act, and the other the Corporation Oath?

The opposition of the clergy to all liberal measures has already been referred to; but their opposition was not the only cause of this failure. The truth is that neither the people at large nor the majority of the Dissenters cared about them. Dissent, however in certain districts it commanded respect, in consequence of the high character of its representatives, was not popular. This was sufficiently shown on William's death, when the lower classes all over the country threatened to pull down the meeting-houses.

In fact, the people far preferred the chatty, easy-going, careless "parson" to either the severe and scrupulous Presbyterian, the godly and painstaking Independent, the zealous but generally unlettered Baptist, or the ardent but strange Quaker. The preacher who allowed them to live as they might choose, who did not preach too censoriously about sin, who was ready with his absolution at the last moment of life, and who professed to give them, with the sanction of the State and all the bishops, an easy entrance to heaven after death, was the preacher for them. Besides this, the English have, of all people, the strongest feeling of loyalty. The Tudors were popular with them in spite of their vices, and the Stuarts notwithstanding their crimes.

For another reason the most influential of the Dissenters were indifferent to the proceedings of the legislature. A

Bill was already under discussion having for its object the union of the Presbyterians, and possibly the Independents, with the Church. If it should be successful, the Test and Corporation Acts would not affect them, but only the smaller and more unpopular bodies of Baptists and Quakers. Some amongst the Presbyterians had not, even yet, very large views concerning toleration, and they were the most conspicuous representatives of the "Dissenting interest." While, therefore, these Bills were under discussion, they stood still. In the absence of all external pressure on the legislature, excepting from the King, and in view of the spirit of the clergy, now just beginning to raise the cry of the "Church in Danger," it cannot be a matter of surprise that these measures should have been defeated. No one in all the Parliamentary debates questioned the undoubted loyalty of Dissenters; the doubt was as to the loyalty of the Church. Both proposals, therefore, were sacrificed to the twin Molochs of political disaffection and ecclesiastical supremacy.

The last act of the nonjuring bishops as peers of Parliament, was to propose two Bills—one for the toleration and the other for the comprehension of Dissenters. In doing this they vindicated the sincerity of their promises, and furnished proof that their conduct did not proceed from personal animosity to the King; for on no questions did William feel more strongly than on these two. The Earl of Nottingham, on behalf of the Government, took charge of both these measures. The first was entitled "An Act for exempting their Majesties' Protestant subjects, Dissenting from the Church of England, from the Penalties of Certain Laws." It passed the House of Lords without objection, and reached the House of Commons in May, 1689. That assembly, however, had its own Bill on this subject, entitled "An Act for Liberty and Indulgence to Protestant

Dissenters," and on May 11th both Bills were read a second time. There was no substantial difference between the two measures, and on the question that the House do go into Committee, it was agreed, out of respect to the Lords, that their Bill only should be proceeded with. So important a measure was probably never so briefly discussed. The first speech made upon it was by Hampden, who remarked that every man was in favour of indulgence to Dissenters, and that little needed to be said on the subject. "The empire of religion," he continued, "belongs to God," and he showed that those nations which had refused to acknowledge this principle had been injured by such a policy. He deprecated certain theological references in the Bill, but expressed his hearty agreement with the clause which excluded Unitarians from toleration. After two or three unimportant speeches, the measure was ordered to be committed. Two days subsequently the report of the Committee was brought up by Mr. Hampden. There was some debate on the proposal to allow Quakers to make an affirmation instead of taking an oath; "but," said Colonel Birch, "these sort of people have been in the shambles these twenty years;" and he added that he had never supposed they would have accepted such a Bill.* It was also urged that the measure should be limited to seven years; but the House made no alterations in it, and on the same day May 17th, it finally passed.

During the passage of the Bill through the legislature, the last appeal for an enlarged toleration was issued. John Howe, in an anonymous publication, entitled "The case of the Protestant Dissenters represented and argued," laid down, in clear and stately language, the right of Dissent.

* There is a curious passage in George Fox's "Journal" of this month, in which he describes how he attended the House of Commons and saw the members to arrange terms for Quakers.

He based this right on the natural claims of conscience, on the human origin of those forms and ceremonies which divided Dissenters from the Church, on the unnatural cruelty of the laws by which the supremacy of the Church had been enforced, and on the known patriotism of Dissenters. In this publication, Howe affirmed that the generality of Dissenters differed from the Church of England in no substantials of doctrine or worship, or even of government, provided that the government were so managed as to attain its acknowledged end. He also argued against the unreasonableness of excluding Dissenters from any participation in civil affairs. "We tremble," he said, "to think of the sacramental test brought down as low as to the keeper of an alehouse." "Never," he added, "can there be union or peace in the Christian world till we take down our arbitrary inclosures, and content ourselves with those which our common Lord hath set."

This Act, which subsequently received the popular title of the "Toleration Act," gave, as may be supposed from the temper of the times in which it passed, the smallest possible advantage to Dissenters from the established religion. The only Dissent which it recognised or allowed was dissent from forms and ceremonies; it allowed none from the established doctrines of the Church. The preamble recited that its object was to give some ease to scrupulous consciences, in order that Protestants might be more united in interest and affection. It exempted Dissenters, on condition of their taking certain oaths against the Papal rule and supremacy, from the operation of those laws of Elizabeth compelling attendance at parish churches; on the same condition it exempted them from any past defaults against those laws, and provided that they should not in future be prosecuted for their Nonconformity. No assembly of persons meeting for religious worship was allowed to hold such meeting in any place the doors of which were, at the time, secured by locks, bars, or bolts; nothing was to exempt Dissenters from payment of tithes or other parochial duties; if any person elected to a parochial office objected to take the oaths, they might serve by deputy; all Dissenting preachers and teachers were required to take the oaths and subscribe, before a general or quarter session, all the Articles of Religion excepting the thirty-fourth, thirty-fifth, and thirty-sixth, or neglecting to do so, were subjected to the penalties of the Act of Uniformity and the Conventicle and Five Mile Acts of Charles the Second; the names of such persons as had so subscribed were to be registered and they were to be charged a fee of sixpence for such registration; those who scrupled at the baptizing of infants were exempted from the obligation to subscribe to the Article respecting Infant Baptism; all Dissenting ministers so qualified were not to be liable to serve on juries or to be appointed churchwardens or overseers; anyone going to a Dissenting place of worship might be called upon at any time, by a justice of the peace, to take the oaths, and if he refused, was forthwith to be imprisoned without bail, and to be punished as a "Papal recusant;" "certain other persons"—referring to Quakers—who scrupled at the taking of any oath, were allowed to substitute for it a promise and declaration in the terms of the oath, subscribing at the same time a profession of their belief in the Trinity and in the Divine inspiration of the Scriptures; all the laws until that time in force for frequenting Divine service on the Lord's-day were to be executed against all persons who did not attend some place of religious worship; Dissenting as well as Church congregations were to be protected from disturbance during public service; no Dissenting congregation was to be permitted to assemble until the place of worship had been certified before the bishop of the diocese, his archdeacon, or a justice of the peace; and, lastly, all Papists and all who denied the doctrine of the Trinity were wholly excluded from the benefit of the Act. The Dissenters as a body, we are informed, received this measure with thankfulness and content.* The only people who were dissatisfied with it were the Quakers, who continued from this time forward, year after year, to denounce, in the most emphatic language, tithes and Church rates, and all compulsory exactions for the support of religion. Howe, as soon as the Act was passed, addressed to Churchmen and Dissenters an exhortation to peace and charity, counselling them no longer to "bicker" about forms, ceremonies, or Church constitutions, but to adopt such a course of conduct as might lead to a closer ecclesiastical union.†

In addition to the Quakers, there was one man who did not view the Toleration Act with complacency. It has been supposed that the terms of the Act were negotiated by John Locke; if so, we know that he considered them most inadequately to meet the claims of justice.‡ Locke, although not a Dissenter, had been trained under Dissenting influences. "Educated," says Sir James Mackintosh, "amongst English Dissenters during the short period of their political ascendancy, he early imbibed from them that deep piety and ardent spirit of liberty which actuated that body of men." § Cast out from Oxford soon after the Restoration, he took refuge in Holland, where, in 1688, he

* Calamy's "Baxter," p. 653. "Life of Howe," p. 163.

† "Humble Requests to Conformists and Dissenters touching their Temper and Behaviour towards each Other, upon the lately passed Indulgence." 1689.

‡ Lord King's "Life of Locke," i. 327.

§ Sir James Mackintosh's Miscellaneous Works: Art. "Locke."

composed, in Latin, his First Letter on Toleration. He came to England with the Prince of Orange. Soon after the Act was passed this Letter was translated and published in English. It was the first publication in which the principles of religious equality were described and defended by a Christian philosopher as well as a Christian statesman. Locke's mental constitution peculiarly fitted him for the dispassionate treatment of such a subject. His intellect, while it was clear and penetrating, was neither cold nor unsympathetic. He was endowed with the highest order of the reasoning faculty, but his breadth of vision was equal to its accuracy and its strength. The founder of the school of English experimental philosophy, he led the way to a revolution in the principles of mental science. All the strength and freshness of his intellect he brought to bear on the discussion of the relation which should subsist between civil governments and the human conscience. His motive, however, in writing on this subject was not merely to settle a question in political philosophy. He was a devout, religious man, as well as an exact thinker; and he felt that the religion of Jesus Christ did not, and could not, sanction any form or degree of persecution. Locke had an inflexible sense of right, and his mind revolted at the suggestion that injustice could ever promote the interests of the Christian religion.

In the first of the letters referred to, the writer described the mark of a true Church with an insight, fulness, reverence, and felicity of illustration that is not surpassed by any enlightened theologian of the present day. Thus, on the relations of Church and State, he says: "All the life and power of religion consist in the inward persuasion of the mind; and faith is not faith without believing. The civil magistrates' power consists only in outward force, and it is impossible for the understanding to be compelled to the belief of anything by such a force; even if the rigour of the law could change men's opinions it would not help to the salvation of their souls." The real schismatics, Locke argues, are not the men who separate from an established religion, but the men who, professing that religion, violate, by their want of charity, and by their carnal desire for supremacy, the precepts and the spirit of Christianity. This Letter was followed by two others, on the same subject, in which the position taken by the writer was defended with equal acuteness and power. In other writings Locke gave what may be termed the moral history of state-churches. In the religion established by Jesus Christ, he remarked, such outward ceremonies as had been common amongst the ancients, and which were always conducted by an order of men called "priests," were almost dispensed with, and pompous rites were abolished. Since then, its ministers, who, like the ancients, also called themselves priests, had assumed to themselves the parts both of the heathen priests and the philosophers, and had combined to enlist the secular power on their side. They had been the cause of more disorders, and tumults, and bloodsheds, than all other circumstances put together. He traced the divisions of Christendom, and the persecution to which men had been subjected, to the assumption by the clergy, supported by the magistrates, of sacerdotal power, although the Scriptures plainly showed that there was nothing which a priest could do which any other man could not also do.*

The treatises of Locke bore the same relation to the age in which they appeared as those of Milton had borne to a previous generation. Both writers addressed the rulers of the State with a common object, and both aimed to establish sounder principles of government. While priests and

* Locke's Common-place Book. Art. "Sacerdos."

presbyters alike were laying claim to supernatural power and arbitrary authority, Milton, in wrath and indignation, exposed the pretences of both parties. When the popular will had, in relation to the control of the civil government, successfully asserted its power, he would have had it to assert itself, with equal intensity against all ecclesiastical usurpation. To make sacerdotalism appear as odious to others as it did to himself, he arrayed it in the most repulsive garb which his imagination could suggest. When the civil government again became unsettled, Locke endeavoured to do what Milton had done. The style and manner of Milton would have been unsuited to the circumstances of the Revolution. The possessors of power both in Church and State now professed to be animated by a conciliatory spirit. Locke therefore addressed them in the calm voice of philosophy. His purpose was not to arouse indignation, but to persuade the judgment and the conscience. As far as his own generation was concerned he failed, but the lovers of freedom in all subsequent times have drawn from his works a strength which, but for him, they could not have attained.

Nothing could have been more opposed to the principles of government laid down in Locke's writings than the ecclesiastical law of England as settled by the Toleration Act. This Act, while it repealed former laws which had had for their direct object the extinction of all Dissent, legalised it and gave it a social standing. But care was taken that this standing should be as low as possible. The right of all persons to think for themselves in matters of religion was now finally recognised by the law of England, but those who chose to exercise this right were, at the same time, deprived of a portion of their civil privileges. The State expressed its solemn and deliberate judgment that such men could not be trusted. It did not believe this;

but the statesmen of the Revolution sacrificed Dissenters to appease the jealousies and the fears of the lower order of the clergy. In 1687 the Dissenters had voluntarily surrendered their liberties, in order to save the State; in 1689 the State, ostensibly for its own safety, limited those liberties within the narrowest bounds which, with any pretension to honour, it could define. But if, relatively to Dissenters, the Toleration Act was an unjust and ungenerous measure, relatively to the State it was an almost infinite concession. In passing it the civil government declared that it had been vanquished; that conscience had conquered law; that a system of absolute repression had failed, and could no longer be continued. Henceforward the Church was not to be armed with the sword to kill, but with the stave alone to punish and distress. The contest between it and Dissent was not to be one for existence on the one side and extermination on the other, but for equality in the one and supremacy in the other. In order that the Church might prosecute this new warfare with success she was armed and equipped at the expense of the State. She had the exclusive privileges of office and power, and her endowments were anew secured to her. The Dissenters, like the Christians who were sent into the Roman amphitheatre, were defenceless.

At the same time that the Toleration Bill was brought into the House of Lords, the Bill for the "Comprehension" of Dissenters in the Established Church was also introduced. Six times during the preceding hundred years had steps been taken to bring about this result. Some of these proposals had failed from the insincerity of the Government and the Church, and others from the want of general interest in the subject. It seemed that on this occasion there could be no such failure. The Crown was known to be warmly interested in the scheme, and some of the most eminent of the Church dignitaries were not merely favourable to it, but anxious for its success. The only quarters apparently from which opposition could be expected were the House of Commons and the clergy. The Bill introduced by the Earl of Nottingham to the House of Lords was entitled "an Act for uniting their Majesties' Protestant subjects."* The preamble recited that the peace of the State was "highly concerned" in the peace of the Church, and that it was most necessary, in the present conjuncture, for that peace to be preserved. In order, therefore, to remove occasions of difference and dissatisfaction amongst Protestants it was provided that no subscription or declaration should be required from any person but the declaration against the Papacy, and that the declarant approved "of the Doctrine and Worship and Government of the Church of England by law established as containing all things necessary to salvation"; but this was subsequently altered to an engagement to "submit to the present constitution of the Church of England," with an acknowledgment that "the doctrine of it contains in it all things necessary to salvation," and a promise "to conform to the worship and the government thereof as established by law." The declarant was also required to promise that in the exercise of his ministry he would preach and practise according to such doctrine. No oaths were to be required on admission to a benefice but the oath of fidelity to the present settlement of the Crown, and the oaths concerning residence and simony. Schoolmasters also were required to take the former two oaths. Persons taking any degree, fellowship, headship, or professorship in the Universities were to take

* When Lord Macaulay wrote his History this Bill had not been seen by more than "two or three living persons" (chap. xi.). It has since been reprinted in the "Report of the Subscription Commission for 1865." Parl. Paper, 3,441. Sess. 1865.

the same oaths, and also to engage, in the words required of clergymen—excepting, in the case of laymen, the latter portion of them—to conform to the Established religion. There was also a clause to the effect that, with the imposition of the bishop's hands, Presbyterian ordinations should be considered valid; but this clause was struck out. It was next provided that, excepting in the royal chapels and the cathedral and collegiate churches, no person should be compelled to wear a surplice during the performance of any of his ministerial duties, but only a black gown. Compulsion to use the sign of the Cross in baptism was abolished, and parents were allowed to take the office of godfathers and godmothers. Kneeling at the Sacrament of the Lord's Supper was left to the option of the communicant. Lastly, as the liturgies and canons of the Church were capable of being altered so as to "conduce to the glory of God and the better edification of the people"; as the ecclesiastical courts were defective in their jurisdiction, particularly in respect to the removal of scandalous ministers; as Confirmation should be solemnly administered, and a strict care exercised in the examination of candidates for the ministry, their Majesties were petitioned to issue a Royal Commission to the bishops and clergy, not exceeding thirty in number, for the purpose of making alterations in the liturgy, the canons, and the ecclesiastical courts, and to present such alterations to Convocation and Parliament "that the same may be approved and established in due course of law." This Bill did not pass the Lords without some difficulty. The clauses relating to kneeling at the Sacrament occasioned, says Burnet, "a vehement debate,"* and a strenuous opposition was made to the proposal to include only members of the clerical order in

* "Own Times," p. 531.

the Commission. When the vote was taken on this proposal the numbers were found to be equal, and therefore, according to the rule of the House, the amendment was negatived. The Marquis of Winchester, Lord Mordaunt, and Lord Lovelace entered, however, their protest against this vote, in which they expressed their opinion that it was a humiliation of the laity; that it unduly exalted the clerical order; that it was a recognition of the Romish principle of the clergy alone having a right to meddle in religion; that it would be a greater satisfaction both to Dissenters and to the legislature if lay lords and commoners were included in the Commission; that the clergy had no authority but such as was given to them by the laity in Parliament; and that it was contrary to historical precedents.

When the Comprehension Bill reached the Commons it was allowed to lie on the table without discussion. Instead of proceeding with it, the House passed a resolution requesting the King to summon a meeting of Convocation, and the Lords seconded the request. This was acceded to at the suggestion of Tillotson, who had intimate relations with his Sovereign. That prelate's sincerity in promoting Comprehension cannot be questioned, but the step which he advised proved fatal to the success of the scheme.* Tillotson's motives had reference to the character of the Church. He thought it desirable that the stigma of its being a mere "Parliamentary religion" should be taken away from it, and that, therefore, liberty should be given it to revise its own constitution. The King, no doubt, saw in the suggestion, a means of conciliating the clergy, and therefore yielded to it.

* Burnet was very angry at the address of the Commons, and prophesied that if Convocation were summoned it would be "the utter ruin" of the Comprehension Scheme. Reresby's "Memoirs," p. 344.

In accordance with the terms of the Bill the Commission was first nominated. It consisted of ten bishops and twenty divines, and included men of all parties in the Church. Amongst them was Lamplugh, Archbishop of York; Compton, Bishop of London; Burnet, Bishop of Salisbury; Stillingfleet, Tillotson, and Tenison. Tillotson and Stillingfleet appear to have taken the initiative in all the proposals which were laid before this body. Before the Commission met Tillotson drew up a list of the concessions which, in his judgment, the Church would be willing to make. All ceremonies, Tillotson thought, should be left indifferent; the liturgy should be revised, the Apocryphal lessons left out, and the Psalms re-translated; the terms of subscription should be altered in accordance with the clauses of the Bill on that subject; the canons should be revised, the ecclesiastical courts reformed, persons ordained in foreign reformed Churches should not be re-ordained, and Presbyterian ordination should be considered valid.* The Commissioners met on October 3rd, and in six weeks held eighteen meetings, some of them of several hours' duration, besides holding various sub-committees. A diary of their proceedings was kept, and a copy of the Prayer Book used by them in their revision is still in existence.†

Nothing could have exceeded the conscientious and scrupulous care, or the spirit of conciliation, which characterised the labours of this Commission. They had before them all the works of Nonconformists, from Elizabeth's time to their own, in which exceptions had been taken to

* Birch's "Tillotson."

† These papers were inaccessible until recent years. Calamy knew of their existence, but could not see them. Tenison desired them to be deposited in the Lambeth Library, but to be kept secret. They were published, on the motion of Mr. James Heywood, M.P., in Parl. Paper 283, Sess. 1854.

the services and the constitution of the Church. The whole of the Prayer Book was considered sentence by sentence, and alterations were made throughout every part. The proceedings do not appear to have been always of an amicable character. Six of the Commissioners never sat, one attended only twice, and three others left after the third meeting. The whole of these belonged to the High Church party. The attendance, however, was still very considerable, and always included five or six bishops. Neither Burnet, Tillotson, nor Tenison was once absent. The labours of the Commission resulted in the adoption of an entirely reformed service, and in the revision of several of the most important laws and ceremonies of the Church, the whole amounting to nearly six hundred alterations. The Apocrypha was discarded; the word "priest" was altered to "minister"; the "Lord's-day" was substituted for "Sunday"; the use of the surplice was left optional; the Athanasian Creed was so explained as to diminish the effect of the damnatory clauses; there was to be no obligation to kneel at the communion, or to use the cross in baptism; the marriage service was purged of its indecencies and the words of the contract modified; the absolution service was so changed that it was impossible for it to sanction Romish doctrine; in the burial service the objectionable phrases relating to the "sure and certain hope" of the everlasting happiness of the departed were changed to an expression of belief in the resurrection of all the dead, and in the eternal life of all who might "die in the Lord." Ordination by presbyteries was acknowledged to be valid, and the ordination service so altered that the gift of the Holy Ghost, which the words now ascribe to the bishop, was made a matter of prayer only, the Commissioners expressing their judgment that the form then, and now, in use was imported into the Church of England service in the "darkest times of

Popery." In addition to these, several alterations were made in the collects, the litany, the catechism, and other portions of the service. These changes were made not merely to satisfy Dissenters, but, as Stillingfleet remarked, they were "fit to be made were there no Dissenters" whatever.*

The Commission finished its labours on the 10th November, and on the 21st of the same month Convocation met. The Upper House was, as a whole, well disposed for peace and unity. Sancroft being under suspension, it was presided over by Compton, Bishop of London, who had been one of the most active members of the Commission, and whose antecedents were all in favour of a conciliatory policy. The Lower House gave, at its first sitting, proof of an opposite temper. The liberal party had hoped to secure Tillotson as prolocutor, but it appeared that the members had been already canvassed by the High Church and Jacobite party in favour of Dr. Jane, of Oxford, who had ceased to attend the meetings of the Commissioners, on the ground that he was not satisfied with its authority, and that, after having given his assent and consent to the contents of the Prayer Book, he did not see how he could make an alteration in them. Jane was elected, and with his election the hopes of all liberal Churchmen died away. It was with great difficulty, after this, that the Lower House could be prevailed upon to consent to an address to the King. It was proposed by one of its members that the non-jurors should sit with them. The Bishop of London spoke warmly in favour of indulgence and charity, but on this question he spoke to deaf ears. All the indulgence and charity of the Lower House were accorded, not to Dissenters, but to those who stood in the strongest political and

* Parl. Paper "Alterations," &c., 283, p. 103, Sess. 1854.

ecclesiastical opposition to them.* They spent their time in considering what books they should condemn, and in creating occasions of difference with the Upper House. It was useless to lay the scheme of revision before this body. To prevent unseemly spectacles, Convocation was prorogued until the January of the next year, when, with Parliament, it was dissolved. No attempt was afterwards made to revive this subject.

The failure of this scheme perpetuated, to a great extent, Nonconformity in England. The Presbyterians never ceased to regret this issue of the labours of the Comprehension Commission. Baxter protested, in his latest works, that the body to which he belonged was in favour of a National State Church. He disavowed the term Presbyterian, and stated that most whom he knew did the same. They would be glad, he said, to live under godly bishops and to unite on "healing terms."† He deplored that the Church doors had not been opened to him and his brethren, and pleaded urgently for a "healing Act of Uniformity." Calamy explicitly states that he was disposed to enter the Establishment if Tillotson's scheme had succeeded.‡ Howe also lamented the failure of the plan.§ It is uncertain to what extent the Independents shared in this feeling, but it is unquestionable that they were generally considered to be willing, on certain terms, to unite with the Church. They formed a portion of the deputation of ministers which waited on the King after his coronation, when Dr. Bates said, on behalf of the whole body, that they were now

---

* Lathbury's "History of Convocation," p. 332. Procter's "History of the Common Prayer Book," p. 159. Kennett, iii. p. 555.

† Baxter's "National Churches," p. 68, A.D. 1691.

‡ Calamy's "Own Life," i. 208.

§ Calamy's "Howe," p. 163.

encouraged to hope for a firm union of Protestants by the rule of Christianity being made the rule of Conformity. "We shall cordially," said the ministers, "embrace the terms of union which the ruling wisdom of our Saviour has prescribed in His Word." Such an union, they added, would make the Church a type of Heaven. On the same day they addressed the Queen, and besought her to use her influence to compose the differences which then existed, and that the terms of union might be those in which all Protestant Churches were agreed.* It was stated, however, that the Independents seemed incapable of anything but toleration, and that they could not be brought into the Church excepting by such concessions as would shake its foundations. But, in the judgment of many men, the concessions made by the Commissioners were sufficient to do this. Calamy's assertion that the scheme, if it had been adopted, would, in all probability, have brought into the Church two-thirds of the Dissenters,† indicates the almost entire agreement of the Independents with the Presbyterians concerning the expediency of accepting it. Had Owen been alive, their sympathies might have been restrained; but no man since his death had taken, or was qualified to take, his place.

The Comprehension scheme failed, not because of the disaffection of Dissenters, but because of the opposition of the Church. While it was under discussion, pamphlet after pamphlet appeared against it, in which the plan was denounced as tending to division rather than to union, and as undermining and "pulling down" the Church. The Universities declared against it. South declaimed against the "rabble" being admitted, and compared the proposals for union to

* Calamy's "Baxter," pp. 623–24.
† Calamy's "Baxter," p. 655.

letting a thief into a house in order to avoid the noise and trouble of his tapping at the door. It seems also to be certain that the statesmen who publicly advocated it were privately opposed to it. Even those who were most eager in its promotion came afterwards to the conclusion that its failure was owing to a "very happy direction of the providence of God,"* for that, in all probability, it would only have strengthened the schism of the non-jurors, and have given occasion to a stronger opposition to the government. That its virtual rejection was a breach of faith to Dissenters no one questioned. "All the promises," says Burnet, "made in King James's time were now entirely forgotten."

In a different sense from that intended by Bishop Burnet, "the happy providence of God" in this matter may be acknowledged by all Dissenters and most Englishmen. The absorption into the National Church of two-thirds—and those the most learned and influential—of the Dissenters of that period, would have been a public calamity. It is true that the Church to which they would have given their adhesion would have been a reformed Church. No suspicion of Romanism could henceforth have attached to it, and it would have afforded no foothold to men whose sympathies were with the doctrines of Rome while their offices were in the Church of England. But the strength of English Protestant Dissent would have been broken, and its influence both in its political and its ecclesiastical relations—on the religion of the people and on the character of public legislation—have been fatally diminished.

* Burnet's "Own Times," p. 544.

CHAPTER III.

THE COMPREHENSION BILL TO THE OCCASIONAL CONFORMITY BILL. 1689—1704.

TOLERATED, but still under the frown of the State, all classes of Dissenters began at once to make the most active use of their newly-acquired liberty. Some official statistics were at that time published of the relative numbers of Conformists, Nonconformists and "Papists" in England which would indicate that Dissenters were about 4.4 per cent. of the Churchmen—evidently a ridiculous under-estimate. It was, however, the opinion of some that Dissent would die out with the generation then existing;* and, looking at the age of its living leaders, and at the little prospect there seemed to be of men of equal power and influence rising to take their places, this opinion may have appeared, even to many of their own number, a not unreasonable one. Nonconformists did not, however, act as though there was any such probability. The most aggressive, and, in some respects, the most successful body at this period, was that of the Quakers. Fox, Barclay, and Penn were still living. Although nearly seventy years of age, Fox's zeal was as ardent as ever it had been. Years of imprisonment and labour were, however, telling on his constitution. The meetings which he attended now made him feel "wearied and spent,"† His work was nearly finished, and in little

* This was Burnet's statement to Calamy as the opinion of the "great men of the Church."—Calamy's "Life of Howe," p. 129.

† Fox's "Journal," vol. ii., p. 340.

more than another year he, also, was to join the dead witnesses. No man then living had done more than he in preaching the Gospel, and in planting and watering new Christian communities. What was said of him by the friend of Milton was not in excess of the merits of his extraordinary character and work. Fox was, says Ellwood,* a "heavenly-minded man;" valiant and bold for the truth; immovable in principle as a rock, but patient in suffering, forgiving in disposition, gentle to the erring, and "tender, compassionate, and pitiful to all in affliction." He had a wonderful acquaintance with the Scriptures, and was a bold and vigorous yet plain preacher. His zeal knew no bounds, and his love and charity were as great as his zeal. Like many great orators, Fox probably owed much of his popular power to his commanding stature, his "graceful countenance," and his admirable voice. His natural fitted with his spiritual qualifications to make him the founder of a sect, and he did not die until he had seen its tenets spread throughout large portions of England and America.

Although Robert Barclay, whose defence of the doctrines of the Quakers has not, during two hundred years, been superseded by any similar work of equal ability and scholarship, was now also approaching his end, other prominent leaders of the Friends were in the prime of life and the fulness of activity. Amongst them were Penn, whose political influence was equal to that of any man outside Parliament, and George Whitehead, one of the most earnest of preachers. The Quakers at this period were remarkable for their extensive use of the press. Penn was equally conspicuous as a writer and as a negotiator. His history of the Society is now out of date, but his expositions of their doctrines were very numerous and are still of value. White-

* Fox's "Journal," vol. ii., p. 369.

head, however, was probably their best literary controversialist. The documents of the Society, as well as the registries of the Bishops' Courts, give proof of the rapid progress which Quaker principles made immediately after the passing of the Toleration Act. Between 1688 and 1690 licenses were taken out for no fewer than a hundred and thirty-one new temporary, and a hundred and eight new permanent places of worship for this Society. Sixty-four of these were in Lancashire alone.* In their Yearly Epistles the Friends are repeatedly congratulated on the "prosperity of the truth in many counties," on the opening of new places of worship, and on the willingness of people to receive their doctrines.†

The old leaders of the Baptist denomination were, for the most part, men greatly advanced in years. Foremost amongst them was William Kiffin, merchant, and once alderman of London, the first pastor of the Devonshire Square Church, and the "father of the Particular Baptists." Kiffin had suffered distress and imprisonments under the reigns of the last three Stuarts, but his great wealth and social position brought him at last into consideration at Court. Charles the Second did not think it beneath him to "borrow" ten thousand pounds from Kiffin, and James the Second endeavoured to use him as an instrument to bring over the Dissenters to his views. The sturdy Nonconformist, on the last occasion, gave the King a rebuke which silenced his tongue and flushed his cheek. Two of the old man's grandsons had been hung by Jeffreys in the "bloody assizes." James would have brought him over to his interests by nomination to office, but Kiffin excused himself from age, adding, with tears, "the death of my grandsons gave a wound to

* Parl. Paper, No. 156, Sess. 1853.
† Yearly Epistles, 1687 and 1690.

my heart which is still bleeding, and never will close but with the grave." The King, we are told, was struck with the rebuke. A total silence ensued, while his countenance seemed to shrink from the remembrance. He replied, however, "I shall find a balsam for that sore," and then turned away.* Kiffin was an able and faithful preacher, and a man of unbounded benevolence. At this time he was about seventy-five years of age, and he lived until the last year of King William's reign. His portrait does not bear out the once current impression concerning the Baptists of that age. With skull-cap and flowing ringlets, with moustache and "imperial," with broad lace collar and ample gown,† he resembles a gentleman cavalier rather than any popular ideal of a sour-visaged and discontented Anabaptist.

A still older man than Kiffin was Hanserd Knollys, minister of the Church at Broken Wharf, Thames Street. Knollys was originally a clergyman of the Established Church, but had now been connected with the Baptists for fifty years. He, too, had known from experience what bitter persecution was. The High Commission Court in Charles the First's time had followed him to New England. Under Cromwell he had met with favour; but was illegally arrested for preaching in favour of baptism at Bow Church, Cheapside. After this he was stoned out of the pulpit in Suffolk by fanatical Presbyterians; but in London he gathered one of the largest of Nonconformist congregations. He was committed to Newgate for eighteen weeks in Charles the Second's time, and again, in the same reign, imprisoned in the Compter. Knollys was, perhaps, the most active minister in the Baptist body—preaching for

* Noble's "Cromwell," ii. 463.

† See his portrait in Wilson's "Dissenting Churches," i. 403.

forty years, in prison and out of it, seldom less than three or four times a week. His scholarship adorned all his sermons and his writings. When the Toleration Act passed he was ninety-one, and he survived it for two years.*

Benjamin Keach, pastor of the Church in Goat Yard Passage, Horsleydown, was at this time in the height of his power. He, too, had suffered under the Stuarts. For publishing a Child's Instructor he was imprisoned and pilloried at Aylesbury, and for years afterwards was hunted from place to place. He was pre-eminently the controversialist of his denomination. His published works, some of which are of great religious value, were more than forty in number.†

Out of London, Andrew Gifford, of Bristol, occupied the most eminent position amongst Baptist ministers. Like many others of that age, he had been a constant preacher in parish churches until he was silenced by the Act of Uniformity. He was the most active and intrepid evangelist in the West of England, and was remarkably popular amongst the colliers of that district, who, on the approach of officers to apprehend him, would disguise him as a labourer so that he should not be recognised. The narrative of his imprisonments and escapes from apprehension, and of his travels to preach the Gospel, during which he would swim any river that obstructed his way, reads more like romance than history. He was actively engaged in the Duke of Monmouth's rebellion, but fortunately escaped the punishment which fell on most of those who were implicated in that transaction. Gifford appears to have had a remarkable moral power, which often awed both his gaolers and the civil authorities. He took a most prominent part in the organization of the Baptist body.

* Knollys' "Own Life." Wilson's "Dissenting Churches," ii. 562-71.

† Wilson, iv. 243-250.

Soon after the Toleration Act was passed the Baptists held a general assembly of their churches in London. It was summoned by a circular signed by Kiffin, Knollys, Keach, and four others, and its object was to discuss the general state of the denomination. It appears from the terms of invitation that the Baptist body was at that time in a remarkably depressed state. Its condition was openly deplored, its power, life, strength, and vigour having, it was stated, to a great extent, departed.* The registries of the Bishops' Courts confirm this statement. Scarcely any—if any—denomination appears to have made so little progress after the passing of the Toleration Act. While the total number of Nonconformist places of worship licensed in the two years from 1688 to 1690 was nearly one thousand,† the number avowedly belonging to the Baptists was only sixteen.‡

This assembly was attended by delegates from more than a hundred churches in thirty counties of England and Wales. Thirteen of these were in London, one in Cornwall, and no fewer than thirty-five in Devonshire, Somersetshire, and Wiltshire, where, at that period, owing mainly to Gifford's labours, the chief country strength of the denomination lay. It is noticeable that Lancashire sent only one delegate to this meeting, and that Yorkshire was altogether unrepresented, there being, at that time, no Baptist church in the whole of that large county.§

The proceedings of this assembly appear to have been

* Ivimey, i. 479.

† Namely, temporary, 796; permanent, 143. Parl. Paper.

‡ The great majority (503) were registered without any specifications, and 158 as "Protestant Dissenters" only. It is possible that some of these were Baptist, but I think that they were nearly all Presbyterian and Independent.

§ Hunter's "Life of Oliver Heywood," p. 413.

marked by great humility and harmony; and they give a most favourable impression of the ardent and sincere religious character of the Baptists of this period. With regard to ecclesiastical government, it was resolved that they had no authority to impose any belief or practice upon any of the Churches, and that all they could do was to offer counsel and advice according to the Scriptures. It was decided to raise a common fund by way of "free-will offerings" for the support of the ministry in poor districts, for home evangelization, and for the education, in classics and Hebrew, of ministerial students. It was recommended that weak Churches existing in the same neighbourhood should unite together for the better support of the ministry, and for the better edification of each other; and it was agreed that ministers were entitled to an adequate maintenance; that there should be a "proper ordination" of ministers; that Baptists should be at liberty to attend churches of other denominations; but that persons who, being members of Baptist Churches, communicated in the Established Church, should, after admonition, be rejected. Those who did not attend the ordinary fixed meetings of the Church were to be reported, and those who did not contribute to its expenses were to be "withdrawn from." Excesses of apparel in ornaments and dress, including "long hair and periwigs," were condemned; and the Lord's-day was considered to be sacred to worship. Two distinctively doctrinal articles were also adopted—one in favour of the "reconciliation, adoption, or justification" of all who have a living faith, and the other as to the sufficiency of the Holy Spirit alone for the continuance of a Christian ministry. A formal approbation was expressed of a book to advocate the maintenance of ministers; and, lastly, the assembly passed a declaration against the government of James and an acknowledgment of their thankfulness for that which had been established under William.* A Confession of Faith and an Epistle to the Churches were also adopted. In the latter, the general decay of religion was dwelt upon, recommendations were made in accordance with the resolutions of the meeting, and a general fast-day was appointed.

The Confession of Faith consisted of thirty-two articles relating to theological doctrines and Christian ethics. The former would now be considered of ultra-Calvinistic tone. The doctrine of the Divine decrees was pushed to its uttermost application, even "infants" being classed in the two orders of the "elect" and the non-elect. Marriage within the degrees condemned by the law of Moses was held to be "incestuous." Liberty of conscience was declared to be a natural right, and all infringements upon it contrary to the Word of God.†

The repeated reference in these proceedings to the necessity of a sufficient maintenance for the ministry was caused by the fact that most of the Baptist ministers of the period were supported, not by their churches, but by some trade or profession. Some of the most eminent were schoolmasters. The churches frequently supplemented the incomes of these men by small subscriptions. But although the Baptists were not mindful of their obligations in this respect, and had therefore a comparatively unlearned ministry, the incomes of all Dissenting ministers were extremely small. Oliver Heywood, one of the most celebrated of the Presbyterians of the time, received only twenty pounds a year;‡ Sylvester, one of the most respected of the same denomination in London, seldom received as much as ten pounds a quarter, and Calamy began his ministry with a similar stipend.§ One feeling

* Ivimey, i. 478-501.

† Crosby, iii. Appendix 56, 111.

‡ Life, p. 391.

§ Calamy's "Own Life," i. 360.

only could have sustained them under such circumstances —the feeling that, whatever became of them, they must obey their consciences in preaching the Gospel. Some ministers, however, such as Baxter and Bates, often from having married women of fortune, enjoyed good incomes; but this was a rare exception to the general rule.

Similar association meetings were held in several following years, from the proceedings of which it appears that a project for raising a common fund for the education of the ministry and the assistance of poor churches was attended with some success. County associations were also formed. In 1692 it was resolved, for convenience, to divide the general association into two—one section meeting in London, and the other at Bristol. In the same year, and before the division took place, the question of public singing was brought forward. It had been agreed, between the two parties who were opposed on this subject, to submit it to the authoritative decision of seven ministers, who made their report to this assembly. The referees unsparingly condemned the unchristian manner in which the controversy on this question had been conducted by both the parties to it, and exhorted them to humble themselves before God for their want of mutual forbearance and charity. They advised that all the books that had been written should be called in, their further circulation stopped, and that nothing more should be published on the question.* No resolution concerning the merits of the points at issue was proposed. The result of this proceeding was that the public discussion of the question died out. Each church pursued the practice which it most approved, until, in the course of years, no opponents of public singing were left.

* Ivimey, i. 520—523.

While the Particular Baptists were thus organising their resources, the General Baptists were not less active. The strength of this body appears to have lain mainly in what are now called the Home Counties and in the Midland District. Of their ministers, the most eminent were Dr. William Russell and Matthew Caffin. Dr. Russell, who had been educated at the University of Cambridge, was a man of eminent scholarship and no less eminent controversial ability. Public and private disputation, indeed, seem to have been, if not his chief, at least one of his chief pleasures. He assailed Quakers with an animosity which was only equalled in the retorts which he provoked. All who held the doctrine of Infant Baptism were equally the objects of his attack. Caffin, also, was a University man, having studied at Oxford. To him, many of the churches in Kent, Surrey, and Sussex owe their existence. Caffin was at one time charged with heresy on the subject of the Trinity, and the discussion of his views appears to have given the first impulse to the subsequent movement in favour of Unitarianism amongst the General Baptists. All, however, that he did, was to define, or attempt to define, the exact relations of the divine and the human elements in the third person of the Trinity. He was exonerated from the charge of heterodoxy; but those who had brought the charge against him, and those who had supported it, withdrew from the majority and made a breach which was not healed for several years.*

The General Baptists had, like their brethren of the same denomination, their Assemblies, which met from time to time, chiefly in London, Buckinghamshire, and Northamptonshire. Some amongst their body appear to have keenly felt their separation from those who agreed with them on all points but such as were involved in the distinction

* Crosby, iv. 328—342. Ivimey, i. 548—554.

between Calvinists and Arminians. They felt, to use their own words, that they were "looked upon as a people degenerated from almost all other baptized congregations," who, therefore, were "afraid to have affinity with them" in Christian work. In order to remove some prejudices and to open the way to reconciliation and fellowship, the churches in the county of Somerset agreed, in 1691, upon a Confession of Faith.* In this Confession the doctrine of original sin, considered as an inherent taint, or as a sufficient cause of eternal condemnation, is denounced as both unscriptural and irrational; and the doctrine of reprobation is also abjured. The grace of God is declared to extend to the whole world, and if any man fall short of salvation it is not because God, but because the man himself has so willed it; while the preservance of the saints is declared to be dependent on their own conduct. This Confession, which is a clear and, in some places, an eloquent statement of the doctrines of the General Baptists, closes with a specific reference to the nature of the kingdom of Christ, and the means by which that kingdom should be sustained. "We believe," say these churches, "that this kingdom ought not to be set up by the material sword, that being so exceeding contrary to the very nature of Christianity." For this reason they decline to have any communion with those "that own the setting up of this kingdom by such means; believing that His spiritual kingdom, which is His Church here on earth, ought not to be set up or forced either by the sword or any civil law whatsoever, but by the preaching of the Gospel, which is the Sword of the Spirit and the Word of God." † Clearer or more decisive language on this subject has never been

* Crosby, iii. 259, iv. Appendix i.
† Art. xxvii. Crosby, iv. Appendix i., pp. 41, 42.

held, and it cannot be a matter of surprise that no attempt was made to "comprehend" such men in an Established Church.

From the year immediately succeeding the passing of the Toleration Act to the end of the reign of William the Third the history of the Baptist denomination, as a whole, was not a history of progression. Judging from the language held in the circular letters adopted at the Association meetings, the general state of religion was not satisfactory. While, however, these representations may be considered to be correct, it is a question whether the apparent declension proceeded from actual decay of religious feeling, or from the subsidence of political and ecclesiastical excitement. Many a man will cheerfully and heroically suffer who will not steadily work, and it is possible that the Baptist denomination at this period was comprised largely of such men. But, if this was the fact, it is strange that the same characteristic should not have been found in the other three Nonconformist bodies. So far was this from being the case that the Presbyterians, Independents, and Quakers, in the earlier years of the reign of William and Mary, made greater comparative progress than they have ever made since that time. A Quaker writer of about this period describes the Baptists as having great love and affection for their religion, but as wanting in unanimity and agreement amongst themselves, and rash and morose towards such as differed from them.* Any testimony from this quarter, written at a time when Quakers and Baptists were engaged in hot disputes, is to be received with some reserve; but the published writings of the Baptists of the latter part of the seventeenth century substantiate the general accuracy of this description.

* Gerard Croese's "Collection," p. 76. Quoted in Crouch's "Sufferings," p. 145.

The Independents and the Presbyterians, having relinquished nearly all expectation of such a reform in the Established Church as would enable them to enter its communion, began to open in all parts of the kingdom new places of worship. The trusts of many of the Presbyterian meetings were so framed that the buildings could afterwards be used by the Established Church; but the majority of their places of worship were not of a permanent character, most of the licences taken out applying to rooms in private houses. The edifices which were erected by these, the two wealthiest sections of Dissenters, were of the plainest character, and were generally situated in the meanest thoroughfares. Very few were registered as "Independent," a fact which may be accounted for by the circumstance that the two denominations were now drawing more closely together, and making arrangements for an amalgamation on terms by which the distinctive principles of each were to be virtually sacrificed.

It is impossible to tell which party took the initiative in this project, but it is evident that both were almost equally anxious for its successful realisation. The Independents were comparatively ill-represented at this time. Their three most eminent ministers were Matthew Mead, of Stepney; Isaac Chauncey, of Mark Lane, who had succeeded David Clarkson as pastor of Owen's Church; and Stephen Lobb, of Fetter Lane.

Matthew Mead, whom Howe describes as "that very reverend and most laborious servant of Christ," * occupied the highest rank amongst the Independent ministers. He had been appointed to the living of Shadwell by Cromwell, but had been ejected by the Act of Uniformity. Soon after he went, in common with many ministers of that age,

* Funeral Sermon for Mead. Title, 1699.

to Holland, where he became acquainted with the Prince of Orange, and earned such great respect from the Dutch community that the States presented him with the four pillars which stood in front of the meeting-house at Stepney. He had one of the largest congregations in London, and was as indefatigable in Christian work as he was amiable in spirit. In consequence of his mild temperament, and the moderation of his opinions, he was probably more intimate with Churchmen and Presbyterians than any other minister of his denomination. He possessed, for more than forty years, the intimate confidence and friendship of Howe; and when, at the close of the century, he died, the strongest personal link between the Presbyterians and the Independents was broken.

Chauncey added little strength to his denomination. Although a learned, he was not a popular man; and he alienated most of his congregation by too frequently addressing them on ecclesiastical order and discipline.* Lobb's character is rather difficult to estimate. Unequivocal testimony is borne by his contemporaries to his personal piety, and he had been well trained for the ministerial office. But he was a Jacobite Dissenter. He had publicly defended James in the exercise of his arbitrary powers; he had advised the king to prosecute the seven bishops; and he was a notorious favourite at the Court of the Stuarts, and therefore not a great favourite with his own people.†

With the exception, therefore, of Mead, the Independents had no highly qualified leader. On the other hand, nearly all the old Presbyterian leaders were still living, and it appeared certain that, if an amalgamation should take

* Wilson's "Dissenting Churches," i. 289—291.
† Ib. iii. 436–446.

place, that powerful and influential body would ultimately absorb the Independents. Baxter drawing, as he himself said when the Toleration Act passed, "to the end of this transitory life," was now taking "half-duty" with Matthew Sylvester, and about to be confined to his house, where, however, he still preached twice a day, and from whence he was to issue in the two years of life that remained to him thirteen works, in addition to the hundred and twenty-five which he had already published. Neither the brain nor the heart of this old Goliath of Presbyterianism had suffered with age; his immense labours had not even yet wearied him, nor, although he had grown more catholic and his charity was much more extensive than it had been,* was he tired of controversy. He had filled the largest space of any ecclesiastic of his generation, and he filled it until the year of his death. The great old man lived to see one dream of his life apparently fulfilled, in the settled concord of two at least of the Christian sects.

Next to Baxter stood Bates, the "silver-tongued," who had now taken Baxter's place in the public representation of Dissenting interests. Bates shone in the qualities in which Baxter was especially deficient. Mild, polite, affable, and courteous; full of charity; eloquent, yet chaste in his oratory, and a rare conversationist, his social influence was surpassed by none. Side by side with Bates stood Howe, then in his sixtieth year. This great man was one of the few who was venerated as much by his contemporaries as by his successors. Time, which commonly adds increased lustre to the memory of the good, has not been able to magnify any of the qualities for which Howe was so conspicuous. His strong and capacious intellect, his sublime elevation of thought, his flowing eloquence, the holiness of his life, the dignity and courtesy of his manners,

* Calamy's "Baxter," p. 677.

and the humour of his conversation, won for him from the men of his own time the title of the "great Mr. Howe." After serving Cromwell as a court chaplain, and being often engaged by him in affairs of State, Howe, at the Restoration, took his part with the ejected Puritans. Latterly he had been pastor of the Presbyterian Church in Silver Street. His Presbyterianism, however, was of the most moderate character, for his charity embraced all sects. Nor could he consent to excommunicate the Church of England, with whose most eminent scholars and divines he lived on terms of frank and friendly intimacy. He statedly communed with Churchmen, and repeatedly defended the practice.

Dr. Samuel Annesley, formerly lecturer at St. Paul's, and rector of St. Giles', Cripplegate, one of the most humble of men and pathetic of preachers, was now pastor of the Presbyterian Church at Little St. Helen's. Matthew Sylvester, Baxter's biographer, with whom Baxter was co-pastor, and one of the most profound of theological thinkers, was minister at Carter Lane. The youngest in point of residence amongst the Presbyterian ministers was Dr. Daniel Williams, who had been for about a year pastor of the New Broad Street Church. Williams's reputation had, however, preceded him from Dublin, where he had preached for twenty years. He at once took a distinguished place amongst the London brethren, and, in matters of controversy, soon became their acknowledged leader. This eminent divine, and no less eminent scholar, was, besides Howe, the only man then living who almost invariably adorned the cause which he advocated by combined candour and charity. As the founder of the Divinity scholarships and of the valuable library, both of which still bear his name, Dr. Williams' memory has now been held in grateful reverence by students and scholars for two hundred years.

No greater preachers than the Presbyterian ministers of this period ever adorned the pulpits of the metropolis. In the suburbs they were represented by men of scarcely less eminence than those who were known as the city ministers. In the south, Nathaniel Vincent, a scholarly man, but chiefly remarkable for his quickness of wit and redundancy of good humour, occupied the pulpit of St. Thomas's, Southwark. Vincent Alsop, "the South of Dissent," preached at Princes Street, Westminster; while Thomas Doolittle, the principal trainer of young men for the ministry, and who built the first Dissenting place of worship in London,* was a preacher in Finsbury. In the provinces this denomination could boast of John Flavel in Devonshire; of Oliver Heywood in Lancashire; of Philip Henry in Cheshire; and of those who were not ministers, the Ashurst family in London, and Lady Hewley in York, all of whom were steadfast adherents and liberal supporters of the Presbyterian system.

The whole of the ministers in London threw themselves with great ardour into the proposals for union with the Congregationalists. Howe is said to have had a principal share in drawing up the terms of agreement, which were ultimately settled, at the beginning of 1691, by a committee of six Presbyterian and six Congregational ministers. Amongst the former were Howe, Williams, and Annesley, and amongst the latter Mead, Chauncey, and Lobb. The terms were afterwards published under the title of "Heads of Agreement assented to by the united ministers in and about London, formerly called Presbyterian and Congregational; not as a measure for any national constitution, but for the preservation of order in our congregations, that cannot come up to the common rule by law established." The "heads" are

* Circ. 1666, in Monkwell Street, Finsbury. This place of worship is still standing.

nine in number. The first relates to the constitution of the Christian Church, in which the right of each particular congregation to choose its own officers is recognized; but ministers and elders are to "rule and govern," and "the brotherhood are to consent." This was an old Presbyterian formula, dating as far back as the days of Field and Wilcox, in the reign of Queen Elizabeth. The second relates to the ministry, who are to be, in all cases, elected by the churches, after the advice, "ordinarily requisite," of neighbouring churches. It is also stated to be "ordinarily requisite" that the pastors of neighbouring churches should concur in the ordination of the ministers. In this article the distinctive feature of Presbyterianism—the power of the Presbytery—is entirely abandoned. "Censures" form the subject of the third article, which contains a simple statement of the nature of church discipline. In the article on the communion of churches, frequent meetings between the several Christian communities are recommended, both for worship and for counsel. The next subject dealt with is that of "Deacons and ruling Elders." Of the latter it is said that, while some are of opinion that there is such an office, and others think the contrary, "we agree that this difference make no breach amongst us." The subject of the sixth article is "Synods," and it is recommended that in order to concord, and in weighty and difficult cases, synods should be called for advice and consultation, and that particular churches should have a reverential regard for the judgment of such meetings. Obedience to civil magistrates is inculcated under the succeeding head. Of confessions of faith it is remarked that it is sufficient if a church acknowledges the divine origin of the Scriptures, and owns the doctrinal parts of the Articles, or the Westminster or Savoy Confessions. Lastly, it is declared that Christians of other communities should be treated with respect; and that all who have the essential requisites for church communion should be received without troubling them with disputes concerning lesser matters.

Both denominations, it will thus be seen, relinquished some of their distinctive opinions. The Congregationalists expressed their agreement with the Presbyterians as to the government of each church being vested in the ministers and elders; and the Presbyterians surrendered the doctrine of the authoritative power of synods.* On the whole, however, the Congregationalists gave up less than their brethren of the more powerful denomination. What is chiefly remarkable, however, in connexion with this attempted settlement of the differences between the two sects, is the circumstance, that the consent of the churches to the arrangements made was not applied for by either party. No "lay" representatives were concerned in drawing up the "heads"; and the creed and constitution of all the churches were fixed without any consultation with them. The amalgamated bodies described themselves as the united "ministers" only; and although they were pastors settled over two different Christian organizations, they decided, of their own accord, to dispense with the characteristic titles which those organizations had assumed. It must, of course, be taken for granted that the churches tacitly assented to these arrangements; but the manner in which they were made contrasts as strongly with the habits of the Baptist associations of the same period, which were invariably attended by lay delegates, as with the modern practice both of the Presbyterian and of the Congregational communities.

* It is worth notice that, while the Episcopalians of the United States have accepted the revised Prayer Book of 1689, the Congregational and a large section of the Presbyterian Churches of that country are, for the most part, governed in accordance with the "Heads of Agreement" of 1691.

The scheme of union was joyfully accepted in several parts of the country. In London the union was formally celebrated by a sermon preached by Matthew Mead, on "Two Sticks made One," in which the preacher declared that now the day of reproach had been rolled away from the Christian Church, and earnestly conjured the ministers to manifest and preserve their accord. Flavel, as soon as he saw the heads of agreement, exclaimed, "Lord, now lettest Thou Thy servant depart in peace;"* and in a subsequent sermon alluded to them as "those blessed sheets." There can be no doubt of the sincere and great delight of most of the ministers throughout the country at this event; and, although the scheme came to a quick and unhappy conclusion, the annual meetings of the two denominations, commenced at this time, were continued in some countries for more than a century.†

Two events speedily occurred to disturb this fraternal feeling, and virtually to dissolve the union. Some Congregational ministers in London—Nathaniel Mather, pastor of Lime Street Church, and one of the committee who framed the "heads," being the most conspicuous—had never heartily accepted it. He is accused, in fact, of having been unwearied in hindering and breaking it.‡ At all events, within a year of the formation of the union, two discussions on points of doctrine and order arose. The first was excited by the preaching of the Rev. Richard Davis, of Rothwell, in Northamptonshire. Mr. Davis was a Congregational minister holding high Calvinistic or rather Antinomian opinions, believing and preaching that repentance was not necessary to salvation, that the elect were

* Flavel's "Life and Remains."

† Hunter's "Life of Heywood," p. 357.

‡ Dr. Williams's Works, iv., p. xii.

always without sin, and always without "spot before God." Notwithstanding these views, Davis was an active and untiring evangelist. Where the sustenance or the progress of religious life was at stake he made light of ecclesiastical traditions and established church order, and was the first amongst the Congregationalists who broke the bounds of ordination. Wherever he made converts he justified them in maintaining Christian fellowship together, and in allowing one amongst their number to preach to them, whether they had the sanction of neighbouring churches or not. The attention of the united ministers was soon called to Mr. Davis's proceedings. The country brethren solicited their judgment upon the subject, and quickly obtained it. Both the doctrine and the practice of Davis were severely condemned. The city ministers, acting as a metropolitan synod, sat in judgment upon him, and, as though they were a Sanhedrim, virtually cast him out from their midst as unworthy of any Christian communion, stating at the same time, as is common in such assemblies, that "they would earnestly pray for his repentance." Unfortunately, however, for the interests of the newly-formed union, their judgment was not received by all persons as authoritative and binding. Davis himself repelled it. His vindication,* although characterised by what many persons would consider to be extreme theological views, was, on the whole, in better taste than the attack which had been made upon him. He successfully defended his evangelistic work, and the right of Christian men to continue what he had begun. The controversy threw eleven counties into disorder, and before a year had passed away the Congregationalists had begun to be weaned from the union. The ministers could not have made a more fatal mistake than by interfering in

* "Truth and Innocency Vindicated." 1691.

this question. They knew all along that many Congregationalists were jealous of the union. Knowing it, they deliberately gave occasion for suspicion.

In the midst of the excitement connected with this controversy, another and a graver one arose. Dr. Crisp, an Antinomian divine of the Commonwealth period, had written several works in defence of the views held by the school of theology to which he belonged. His son, wishing to republish his father's works with previously unpublished manuscripts, conceived the notion of requesting some of the most eminent of the London ministers to certify to their genuine character. The ministers, Howe—strangely enough, considering his characteristic prudence—amongst them, did what was requested. Crisp's works, therefore, went forth to the world with what many conceived to be a recommendation from the leaders of the moderate Calvinistic party.* Amongst those who did not sign this certificate, and who probably was not asked to sign it, was the acute and wary controversialist, Baxter. It is more easy to imagine a veteran rat deliberately entering an unbaited cage, than to imagine Baxter putting his hand to such a document. If he hated anything more than Quakerism it was Antinomianism, which all through his life he had assailed with unfailing vigour and constancy. No sooner, therefore, had Crisp's works appeared than, after remonstrating with those who had so rashly given them such surreptitious importance, Baxter prepared once more to enter his old and favourite field of controversy. In deference, however, to the earnest solicitations of Howe, he refrained from publishing what he had written. Howe

* I cannot help agreeing with Mr. Henry Rogers that this was nothing but a disgraceful trick of Crisp's son; but it is incomprehensible that the London ministers should have fallen into such a trap. —Rogers's "Life of Howe," pp. 271—273.

at once cleared his own reputation by writing a recommendation of Flavel's "Blow at the Root," a work against Antinomianism, just about to be published. This, however, did not repair the mischief which had been done, and accordingly Dr. Daniel Williams was requested to undertake a formal refutation of Crisp's doctrines. This work appeared in 1692, under the title of "Gospel Truth, Stated and Vindicated." Prefixed to the first edition was a recommendation from Bates, Howe, Alsop, and thirteen other Presbyterian ministers, to which thirty-two other signatures, including those of Doolittle, Sylvester, and Edmund Calamy, were added in the second edition.* No Congregationalist, however, would sign this recommendation. Both Bates and Williams requested Mead's signature, but he refused —first, on the ground that he did not judge it prudent to sign, and ultimately because he disapproved of its doctrines.† It became, therefore, very evident that the Presbyterians and the Congregationalists did not hold the same theological opinions. The variance was at once made public by virulent attacks from Chauncey, Mather, and Lobb on Williams's doctrines relating to free grace and justification. The controversy which ensued lasted for more than seven years, during the whole of which period the London ministers were torn by angry dissensions. In 1692 Chauncey withdrew from the united ministers. Honesty, truthfulness, and charity were now equally sacrificed. The Congregationalists denounced the Presbyterians as no better than Arminians and Socinians; and the Presbyterians retorted by fixing upon their opponents the stigma of Antinomianism. Howe tried to hush the storm by preaching on the carnality of religious contention, but this time he preached in vain. The united ministers also

* Williams's Works, iii., pp. 3, 4.

† Ibid, iii., p. 281.

endeavoured to stem the torrent. In three successive years they issued three statements of doctrine to meet the various phases which the debates assumed; but each statement only gave rise to fresh disputes. They were, however, still more than sixty in number, and the whole of their moral support was given to Williams, who, it must be said, was worthy of the confidence they gave to him. Failing to silence him in argument, some persons now attacked Williams's moral character. He met the disgraceful charge by courting an examination into his whole life, from which he came out with augmented reputation. An open rupture between the two bodies now took place. In 1694 the Congregationalists excluded Williams from the Merchants' Lecture at Pinners' Hall. This lecture had been founded by some wealthy London tradesmen for the purpose of holding week-day morning services, to be conducted by the most eminent of the Dissenting ministers of the metropolis. The lecture was always largely attended, and had been of eminent use, both in a religious and in an ecclesiastical sense. To prevent further contentions the Presbyterians now withdrew, and, with the aid of the majority of the subscribers, established a new lecture at Salters' Hall, the lecturers being Bates, Howe, Alsop, and Williams. The old lecture was continued by Mead, Cole, and four other Congregationalists. Mead appears to have remained with some reluctance, and afterwards regretted that he had not gone with the Presbyterians.*

This disastrous controversy raged, at best, around doctrines the reception or rejection of which can scarcely be said to

* The old Merchants' Lecture was subsequently transferred to New Broad Street, and afterwards to the Poultry Chapel. It is now delivered at the Memorial Hall, Farringdon Street. The Salters' Hall lectures were discontinued. One of the last lecturers was Dr. W. B. Collyer, of Peckham.

have influenced the Christian character. There can be no doubt that the Presbyterians at this time were more moderate Calvinists than the Congregationalists, and that the epithet of "Baxterians" was not inappropriately applied to them; but as Baxterianism included the Articles of the Church of England, and the confessions of Dort and Savoy, their moderation was certainly limited. What they did not believe was the doctrine of absolute reprobation, held in the sense that persons were condemned irrespective of their character and faith. They did not believe that sinners were pardoned without repentance, or that the Saviour so stood in the sinner's place, that God ever looked upon him as a sinner. The last point was the point most vehemently debated in this controversy. The question was—Was there a change of persons, or only of person in the redemption? and according as this was answered, and the sense in which the answer was understood, the controversialist was classed as an Arminian, or even Unitarian, on the one side, and as an Antinomian on the other. Mather went so far as to state that believers were as righteous as Christ Himself, and the Congregational body supported Mather. By-and-bye the question came to be less one of doctrine than of meaning. It might be stated to be, what did Dr. Williams mean? Williams replied, and was almost told that he did not mean what he said. At last a happy thought occurred to Lobb. He believed that Stillingfleet, Bishop of Worcester, the greatest controversialist in the Church, and whose views had been referred to by the Presbyterians, would not approve of Williams's views of justification, and that Dr. Jonathan Edwards, who had recently "unmasked" Socinianism, would be able to detect that doctrine in Williams. He therefore made an appeal to these divines to give their judgment on the controversy. Both men generously consented, and both pronounced, without reservation, in favour of the entire orthodoxy of Williams. Stillingfleet finally advised that the Congregational ministers should formally repudiate the charge of Antinomianism. The advice was taken, and in 1698 a "Declaration" was published. Williams, at Lobb's request, responded in 1699, with an "End to Discord," clearing himself from the imputation both of Socinianism and Arminianism. Peace followed, and the ministers met together again, but the scheme of an organized union of the denominations had become a thing of the past.*

The spirit of intolerance exhibited during the progress of this controversy was not confined to mutual recrimination. Though the Presbyterians successfully vindicated themselves from a charge of Socinianism, which could never have been honestly brought against them, there was no doubt that Socinianism was spreading. The doctrine of the Trinity had been discussed in the Established Church. Dr. Wallis, a Professor at Oxford University, had endeavoured to prove its truth by mathematical demonstration, and had given, in doing so, ample room for a reply. The question being thus brought to the surface, the Socinians took advantage of the opportunity, and openly assailed Trinitarianism. Howe joined in an attempted explanation, but, although a master of metaphysics, lost himself in metaphysical subtleties. Sherlock, Dean of St. Paul's, defended the doctrine, but, in

* I do not pretend to have read all the pamphlets and sermons connected with this controversy which were published during these eight years; and if, as I did, anyone should make an attempt to do so, he will, I think. do as I have done—speedily relinquish it. I have read, however, all that Williams wrote; the Declarations of the Ministers; a part of Chauncey and Lobb's publications; Stillingfleet's and Edwards's Letters to Williams; the account in Bishop Bull's "Life"; in Calamy's "Howe" and his "Own Times"; in Dr. Toulmin's "History"; and in Mr. Joshua Wilson's "Historical Inquiry." The above narrative is based on these works.

doing so, only laid himself open to the ironical criticism of South, that he had furnished the world with three deities. The principal Socinian at this period was Thomas Firmin, a wealthy London merchant, of high reputation for benevolence, who expended part of his fortune in the distribution of books in favour of his doctrines, and the remainder in works of charity. The literature of this small but increasing party was well written and moderate in spirit. Tillotson was never forgiven by the Trinitarians, because, while preaching against the opinions of Socinians, he had once praised in high terms their manner of conducting controversy. "They are a pattern," he said, "of the fair way of disputing; they argue without passion, with decency, dignity, clearness, and gravity."* The legislature, the clergy, and the Dissenting ministers had no such charitable opinions of this sect. The first had already excluded them from the benefit of the Act of Toleration; and the House of Commons now voted an anonymous work, entitled "A clear confutation of the Doctrine of the Trinity," to be a blasphemous libel, and ordered it to be burned by the hangman. The clergy, for the most part, agreed with South that the Socinians were "impious blasphemers."† The Dissenting ministers appear to have held opinions of a more moderate character, but of a similar tendency. In 1697 they waited on the King, and urged him to interdict the printing of any work in favour of Socinian doctrines. In the next year the Commons addressed the King, beseeching him to take measures to root out vice and immorality, and to give orders for the suppression of all books containing assaults on the doctrine of the Trinity, or on any other fundamental article of faith. The same year an Act was passed prohibiting all such publications. Any

* Birch's "Tillotson," p. 427. † Ib. p. 428.

person found writing, printing, publishing, or circulating any works, or preaching against the doctrine of the Trinity, was condemned to lose nearly all the privileges of citizenship; he could neither sue nor be sued, and neither bequeath nor receive property. He was disabled for ever from holding any public office, and he was to be imprisoned for three years without bail. The merciless severity of this Act appears to have excited no criticism and no remonstrance. Even the plain teaching of history was not once thought of. The history of the city where Servetus was burned was ignored. The men who had urged the passing of this law did not even dream of such a theological Nemesis as that their own direct ecclesiastical descendants should, in less than two generations, almost universally embrace the creed which they thus attempted violently to stamp out.

The future relations of the various Dissenting bodies to each other were for a time settled by the terms of concord established at the close of this controversy. The Quakers stood aloof from all intercourse with other denominations. There is no proof that the Baptists had, as yet, united with others in any public matters; the Presbyterians and Congregationalists were on terms of friendly intimacy with each other, and, when interests common to Dissenters as such required to be represented or defended, uniformly acted as one body. The theological creeds of the several parties were also clearly defined. It remained to determine in what relation they should stand to the Established Church. On this question there were the greatest differences, both of opinion and of action. The principles of the Quakers and Baptists prevented them from holding any religious communion with members of the State-Church. Members of some Baptist churches were forbidden to enter, on any pretence whatever, the established places of worship; inter marriage and social intercourse with Episcopalians were equally prohibited.* Of the practice of the Congregationalists there appears to be no record, but, in all probability, it was milder than that of either the Quakers or the Baptists. The Presbyterians not only, in some instances, practised what was then termed "Occasional Conformity," but publicly advocated it; but this was more characteristic of London than of the country. Many of their leaders, indeed, appear to have hesitated in taking any steps which might give fixity to the separation of the Presbyterians from the Church. When Edmund Calamy requested Howe to be present at his public ordination, Howe not only refused, but thought it necessary to take the advice of Lord Somers as to the expediency of any such service taking place. Bates also, notwithstanding an admission to the effect that separation from the Church was not only justifiable, but necessary, as circumstances then stood, declined a similar request.† The older Presbyterians still looked on the Church with affection, and would have done nothing either to bring her into disrepute, or to separate themselves entirely from her communion.

Circumstances now arose which compelled them to defend their position. According to the Act of Uniformity, no person who was not a communicant of the Established Church could hold any municipal office; but with the Presbyterian practice, a person could be a communicant, and yet be a Dissenter. In 1697, Sir Humphrey Edwin, on being elected Lord Mayor of London, carried the regalia of his office to Pinners' Hall, which was then used by a Congregational church. The circumstance excited considerable irritation amongst Churchmen. It was described

* Robert Robinson's "Lecture on a Becoming Behaviour in Religious Assemblies." The above were Articles of Communion in the Baptist Church at Cambridge at this time.

† Calamy's "Own Life," i. 338—348.

as a reproach to the city, and a crime against religion. It was on this occasion that Daniel De Foe, for the second time, took up his pen to treat of an ecclesiastical question. De Foe was born of a Dissenting family, and had received a classical education at one of the best of the Dissenting academies. His ecclesiastical principles were Presbyterian, but he does not appear to have identified himself very closely with any particular congregation. As yet, he was a comparatively unknown man. He had, however, some years before, taken part in public questions. He had joined the Duke of Monmouth's rebellion, and had successfully exerted his influence to dissuade Nonconformists from accepting James's offer of indulgence. He was noticed amongst the royal regiment of volunteer horse, composed for the most part of Dissenters, who went out to welcome William and Mary on their first state visit to the city.* Since that time he had been engaged in, and had failed in, business, and was now accountant to the Commissioners of glass duty. De Foe saw, in Sir Humphrey Edwin's conduct, an inconsistency which was reproachful to religion. Probably he also saw, for his vision was constantly, and with singular accuracy, projecting itself into the future, that the practice of Occasional Conformity must, if persisted in, tend to the destruction of Nonconformity. He therefore published a remonstrance with Edwin,† in the terse, vigorous, and pungent style which made him the most effective and the most celebrated political writer of his age. De Foe set aside, altogether, the question whether Nonconformity was right or wrong, but argued that when a man conformed he practically denied the lawfulness of his

* Oldmixon, iii., p. 36. Wilson's "De Foe," i., p. 189.

† "An Enquiry into the Occasional Conformity of Dissenters in Cases of Preferment." 1697.

Dissent; while at the same time, in dissenting, he was condemning the sinfulness of Conformity. If he could conscientiously commune with the Established Church, his conscience ought to allow him to become a member of that Church, and he was guilty of the sin of schism if he did not. De Foe examined the various reasons which might induce a person occasionally to conform. He might hold his act of communion to be a civil act only; but, inquired De Foe, How can you take it as a civil act in one place, and a religious act in another; is not this playing "bo-peep with God Almighty?" Or, a person might occasionally conform from patriotic motives, but the author plainly expressed his entire disbelief in the existence of persons who were willing to "damn their souls to serve their country"; and was of opinion that the power of God was omnipotent enough to protect a nation without the perpetration of any sin.

No notice appears to have been taken of this pamphlet on the occasion of its first publication, but three years afterwards, in 1701, another Dissenter, Sir Thomas Abney, a member of Howe's church, was elected Lord Mayor. Having qualified himself for office by taking the Lord's Supper in an established church, Sir Thomas afterwards communed with the members of Howe's congregation. De Foe thereupon republished his "Enquiry," with a preface dedicated to Howe, in which he asked that minister whether this practice of alternate communion was allowed by him or by Dissenters in general, and, if not, he conjured him by his tenderness for the weakness of others, by his regard to God's honour and the honour of the Church, to censure it, in order that the sincerity and purity of Protestant Dissenters might be vindicated. If it were allowed, he desired Howe to give his reasons in defence of the practice. Howe replied in a pamphlet, the publication of which all who venerate that great man's name must regret.* De Foe had addressed Howe in terms of the utmost respect; Howe replied with insinuations and with abuse. His pamphlet abounded in personalities. He suggested that the writer of the "Enquiry" must be a Fifth Monarchy man, and openly stigmatised him as of a "stingy, narrow spirit." Nor did he avoid gross misrepresentation, which, however, must have arisen from carelessness rather than from intention. It is strange, also, to notice that he did not give a direct reply to De Foe's question. He declined to say whether or not he approved of Occasional Conformity, but, instead, suggested a number of hypothetical cases in which a person might be justified in that practice. Howe's argument conveys—and was evidently intended to convey—the impression that he considered the questions at issue between Church and Dissent as of minor importance. He closed by remarking that if De Foe's judgment were true, truth, accompanied by De Foe's temper, was much worse than any Occasional Conformist's error. De Foe at once published a rejoinder,† in which, after remarking on the tone of Howe's reply, he assailed the position taken by him with the keenest logical acumen. Like many other controversialists, the two writers argued from different premises and with different objects, and would never have agreed. Logically, De Foe was right, but Howe did not try the position by the rules of logic. He tried it by the test of Christian sympathy—a sympathy which, in some cases, may be only another name for personal inclination or even for laxity and indifference, but may also be of a higher character. If De Foe, in his rejoinder, had tested Howe's

* "Some Considerations of a Preface to an Enquiry, &c.," by John Howe. 1701.

† "A Letter to Mr. Howe by way of Reply, etc." 1701.

arguments by Howe's own justification of Nonconformity, published twelve years before, he would have placed this antagonist divine in a painful position. The fact, however, that Howe did not openly state that he himself approved of Occasional Conformity, while it is known that, privately, he approved of and defended it,* appears to be a sufficient indication that he did not feel his position to be logically tenable. With De Foe's second pamphlet the controversy on this subject was, for the present, closed.

The tendency of public opinion towards the close of William the Third's reign, so far from being in favour of an increased measure of toleration, was for a limitation of the liberty already enjoyed by Dissenters. By the death of Mary they had lost the protection of a Queen of large and liberal views, and of the most kindly feelings towards themselves. Tillotson and Stillingfleet were also dead; the Tories had obtained possession of power, and the clergy were advancing in their pretensions. The King, having had sufficient experience of the temper of Convocation when the Comprehension scheme was under discussion, had not summoned that body to meet for business for ten years. In the interval a claim was put forth to the effect that Convocation had a right not only to meet whenever the Houses of Parliament met, but to sit and transact business without the royal license. This doctrine was boldly advocated in a "Letter to a Convocation Man," published anonymously in 1694, but known to be from the pen of Dr. Binkes. Its novelty was only equalled by its audacity. In the Act of Submission of 1532 Henry the Eighth had required the clergy to consent that no constitutions, canons, or ordinances of Convocation should be enacted or enforced without the King's consent, nor unless the King should first

* Howe's "Letter to Boyse." Rogers' "Life of Howe," p. 295.

license the clergy to assemble, and give to their decisions his assent and authority.* In the next year an Act was passed subjecting the clergy to fine and imprisonment if they assembled without the royal writ. From that period it had been the established law that a writ was necessary to meet; that another writ was necessary to allow of business; that after business had been transacted, it could not take effect without the confirmation of the sovereign; and that, even with the sovereign's own authority, no canons could be made against the laws and customs of the land or the King's prerogative. The claim now advanced was, in effect, that the clergy were entitled to the same powers which they had enjoyed before the Reformation, and that, in fact, there neither was, nor should be, a royal supremacy. The nature of this demand, which, if it had been acceded to, would have put the ecclesiastical laws and the religious liberties of Englishmen into the hands of the Jacobite clergy, was at once seen. The letter was replied to by Dr. Wake, afterwards Archbishop of Canterbury, in an elaborate work, in which the authority of the Crown was sustained with great learning and ability.† Wake, in return, was charged with surrendering the rights of the Church, and an endeavour was made to prove that the Act of Submission did not involve the royal supremacy to the extent that had been supposed. Binkes was now silent, a far abler man having undertaken to defend the cause of the clergy. This was Dr. Francis Atterbury, a clever, learned, witty, but ambitious and unscrupulous clergyman, who was afterwards appointed by Queen Anne Bishop of Rochester, and who was ultimately banished the kingdom for intriguing to

* Fuller's History, v., p. 189. Before this period the Archbishop had been accustomed to summon the Provincial Councils, for which no license was required.

† Lathbury's "History of Convocation," pp. 110, 111.

restore the Stuarts. Atterbury maintained that the Convocation had a perfect right to sit, and to make canons, without the permission of the sovereign, but he convinced few excepting the non-juring and Jacobite clergy of the accuracy or success of his arguments. So able a controversialist, however, could not remain unanswered. Bishop Burnet, Bishop Kennett, and a host of inferior writers took the field against him, and ultimately Wake, in a second work, summed up the whole case. But while the upholders of the rights of the sovereigns of England were indisputably successful in maintaining their position in argument, the High Church party were equally successful in the main object for which this controversy was provoked. They did not destroy the King's prerogative, but they compelled him to summon a meeting of Convocation. This step was taken on the advice of his Tory ministry, and assented to by Tenison. Convocation met in the spring of 1701. The Lower House at once gave proof of their High Church spirit. It had always been assumed, up to this time, that the archbishop could prorogue both Houses, but the Lower House now refused to be prorogued by him, treating his authority as well as his acts with open contempt. They claimed to sit when and as long as they chose; they openly defied the episcopal bench; and proceeded, without asking for the Royal license, to transact business of the most important character. Toland, a free-thinker, had pnblished a book in disparagement of the divine nature of Christianity. This work was seized upon, extracts from it were selected, a so-called synodical censure of it was passed, and the proceedings reported to the Upper House Such an assumption of independent authority could scarcely be overlooked. The bishops at once took legal advice concerning the power of the Lower House to perform such an act. The opinion of the lawyers, which was entirely against the possession of such a right, and hinted at the possibility of the penalty of the Act of Submission having been incurred, was communicated to Convocation by the archbishop, and the body was again prorogued.

Similar scenes took place all through the summer. From the condemnation of Toland's book, the Lower House proceeded to deal with Bishop Burnet's "Exposition of the Articles." They represented that it tended to introduce such a latitude and diversity of opinions as the Articles were framed to avoid; that it was opposed in many places to the received doctrine of the Church; and that it contained propositions which were dangerous to the Establishment. What were the passages complained of was not stated. Burnet asked that these representations might be received in order that he might reply to them; but it is obvious that if the bishops had consented to this step they would have acknowledged the right of the Lower House to make such a representation. In place of doing this they passed a series of resolutions, in which the power of the Lower House to censure any work was denied; their censure of the "Exposition of the Articles" denounced as defamatory and scandalous, and the author of that book formally thanked for his great service to the Church of England. After this, prorogation followed on prorogation, until, by the dissolution of Parliament, Convocation also was dissolved.* The new body, was, however, possessed of no better temper than the old. From the first day of its meeting to the last it did little else but dispute concerning its rights and privileges. The death of the King put a brief termination to "these sandalou s and offensive proceedings." †

* Lathbury's "History," cap. xi.

† These are Archbishop Tenison's own words. "Tenison's Life," 97—99.

There was more in this memorable controversy than appeared upon the surface. Those who have read with any attention the works of the lower order of the clergy of King William's reign, will scarcely fail to have perceived that the doctrines which were advanced during the discussions which took place on the powers of Convocation and the relative authority of the Episcopacy, had a political as well as an ecclesiastical bearing. The bishops and the clergy belonged to different political parties. The former were for the most part ardent and steadfast adherents of the Revolution. They had, indeed, been selected for their known political sympathies. They were personally attached to the King, and they threw the whole weight of their influence in support of the measures which he was known to favour. The clergy, on the other hand, were Tories. They hated equally the Revolution and its promoters. They despised every bishop who had been nominated to his see by the revolutionary King. Any ecclesiastical measure that was approved by Tillotson, Tenison, or Burnet was sure, on that account, to receive their opposition. They delighted to disparage every man who had received a single mark of favour from William. It was this feeling which gave its animus to the Convocation controversy. The clergy flouted the authority of the bishops, not because they were bishops, or because of their power as such, but because they were King William's bishops. While they treated Tenison with contempt, they reverenced every non-juror who had once held the episcopal office.

Queen Anne was no sooner seated on the throne than it became evident that the liberties of Dissenters were in danger of serious restriction. The High Church tendencies of the Queen were well known, and it was confidently anticipated that she would view with favour the desire of the clergy to limit the operation of the Toleration Act. Dissenters were everywhere insulted; their ministers could scarcely walk the streets with safety; High Church ballads, all ending with the refrain of "Down with the Presbyterians," were composed and sung by drunken mobs under newly-erected Maypoles. "Queen Mary's Bonfires" were hinted at for the effectual extirpation of obstinate schismatics; people talked of pulling down the meeting-houses as places that should not be suffered to exist; and at Newcastle-under-Lyne they carried this desire into execution.* Two things, however, operated as a restraint on the indulgence of this intolerance. The first was the increased numerical power and social influence of Dissent. In the twelve years from 1688 to 1700, Dissenters had taken out licenses for no fewer than two thousand four hundred and eighteen places of worship.† De Foe, who knew as much, if not more, of their condition than any other man, reckoned their number at this period at no fewer than two millions,‡ and states that they were the most numerous and the wealthiest section in the kingdom; § but notwithstanding their great activity and the wide surface of the kingdom over which they had spread their network of Christian organizations, it is quite impossible to accept this estimate. The second circum-

* Calamy's "Abridgment," i., 620; and "Own Life," i. 460. De Foe's "Christianity of the High Church." Ded.

† Parl. Return, 156. Sess. 1853.

‡ De Foe's "Two Great Questions," in the first series of the collection of his writings, p. 394. This estimate entirely conflicts with a Government return in 1689, from which it would appear that in that year the Dissenters of England were reckoned to be little more than 111,000. Yet three years later they were set down at two millions! These two statements are irreconcileable. In the first case there was no doubt every disposition to minimise the numbers, and in the second a tendency to exaggerate. Still, there must have been a great increase of Dissenters in the interval.

§ "Christianity of the High Church." Ded.

stance in their favour was that they were known to approve of the renewal of hostilities with France, which, soon after the accession of Anne, declared in favour of the Pretender. The Queen herself, however, treated them with contempt. The first occasion on which the three Denominations of Presbyterians, Congregationalists, and Baptists * united together for a common public purpose was on the accession of Anne to the throne, when a deputation, headed by Dr. Daniel Williams, waited upon her. Either their address displeased her, or she did not care to assume a courtesy which would not sincerely express her own feelings. She heard the deputation in silence. Not a word of thanks nor a promise of protection escaped her lips. Since the time of James the First, the Dissenters had not been treated with such scant courtesy, and they must have left the royal presence with an increase of the cloudy apprehensions which a contemporary writer states to have generally prevailed amongst them.† In her first speech to Parliament, indeed, the Queen promised to protect the Dissenters so long as they conducted themselves peaceably towards the government, but she added that members of the Established Church would enjoy her favour. At the close of the session she deigned to be more distinct. She promised to preserve and maintain the Act of Toleration, but she again added, "My own principles must always keep me entirely firm to the interests and religion of the Church of England, and will incline me to countenance those who have the truest zeal to support it." This was nothing less than the offer of a royal

* In this year, also, the body termed "Ministers of the Three Denominations," was formed. The committee consisted of four Presbyterian, three Congregational, and three Baptist ministers. —Ivimey, iii., 42.

† Calamy's "Own Life," i. 460.

premium upon High Churchism, and it is therefore scarcely to be wondered at that, from this time, High Churchism became the popular form of religion.

Neither the condition of political parties, nor the apparent tendency of public affairs, was calculated to dispel the apprehensions entertained by the Dissenters. Within two months of her accession to the throne, Queen Anne had dismissed from office nearly every statesman who had enjoyed the confidence and favour of William. The names of Halifax, Somers, and Orford, the great leaders of the Revolution, were struck from the Privy Council list. The conduct of public affairs was placed in the hands of Marlborough and Godolphin, both men of Tory sympathies, but less extreme in their views than other members of their party. The House of Commons was "full of fury against the memory of the late King, and those who had been employed by him."* Its political sympathies were unmistakably shown by the election of Harley, once a Presbyterian and a Whig, and now a Tory Churchman, to the Speakership. Above any of these in influence—for, at this time she commanded the Queen herself—was the wife of Marlborough, chief favourite at Court, who, during the early part of this reign, set up and pulled down men at her pleasure. This woman's politics were guided mainly by considerations of interest; but it happened that those interests were sometimes identical with those of the nation. Undoubtedly, she was no friend of the Jacobite party, and she saw that the fortunes of her husband and family could not be advanced by the return of the Stuarts or the promotion of extreme Toryism. Although she occupied this confidential position with a Tory Queen, the Countess of Marlborough was herself an ardent Whig. More than Somers or Halifax, she was the leader of the

* Burnet's "Own Times," p. 719.

party, and so successfully, by means of Court intrigue, did she lead it, that she soon had the satisfaction of seeing a change in the administration of affairs.

Before this was brought about it was determined to make the Dissenters feel the effect of the death of their protector The Church party raised a cry for the suppression of the Dissenting academies and for the repeal of the law which allowed Occasional Conformists to hold public offices. A clergyman named Henry Sacheverell was chosen to discharge the preliminary work of inflaming the passions of the people. Sacheverell had qualifications which eminently fitted him for such a part. He was a man of hot and angry temperament, unscrupulous in his language, and fierce in his style of denunciation, but totally destitute of either learning, education, or refinement. He had all the bad qualities of a demagogue united to all the worst qualities of a bigot. He was, as are most men of his class, both bold and cunning. His cunning taught him that he might rise to popularity, if not to eminence, by pandering to extreme Church prejudices; by preaching up the wrongs of the clergy; by denouncing, with holy horror, the schism of Dissent, and by warning the nation of the danger to be expected from the encouragement of men whose ancestors had rebelled against and brought to the block the "lawful King" and "martyred saint" and sovereign, the direct ancestor of the Royal lady who then sat on the throne. Sacheverell's first attempt in this direction was made in a sermon preached before the University of Oxford, on June 3, 1702.* In the slipshod style which characterized all his writings, Sacheverell referred to the Dissenters and their

* "The Political Union: a Discourse, showing the dependence of Government on Religion in general; and of the English Monarchy on the Church of England in Particular."

friends as enemies of the Commonwealth and State. "Apostates and renegadoes to their oaths and professions," &c. In another sermon preached before the judges at assize, in the same city, the same firebrand made formal complaint of Dissenting academies as being dangerous to the Church and State, and as "fountains of lewdness," from which were "spawned all descriptions of heterodox, lewd, and atheistical books"; their supporters were described as "worse monsters than Jews, Mohammedans, Socinians, or Papists"; and the State was asked to pass a law for the suppression of "such a growing mischief." Sacheverell was followed by Samuel Wesley, a clergyman who attacked the educational institutions of Dissenters as being both immoral in their character and disloyal in their tendency. The last author was replied to with great force, and his character exposed, by Mr. Samuel Palmer, a Dissenting minister of Southwark—a man in every way competent to such a task. The controversy between Wesley and Palmer extended through four years. The former—the father of the celebrated John Wesley—was as unscrupulous and abusive as Sacheverell himself. The mildest words in which he could describe Dissenters were "villains," "hypocrites," and "murderers."* There can be no doubt that the success of the Dissenting academies had drawn away many from the Established Church as a religious institution, and that their natural tendency and effect were the perpetuation of an educated and learned ministry. But this was not the only

* Those who may be curious to see the spirit in which Dissent was attacked, and the style of controversial writing which was deemed both allowable and respectable at this period, can scarcely do better than read the three pamphlets of Wesley. The first was called "A Letter from a Country Divine, concerning the Education of Dissenters in their Private Academies in several parts of the Nation"; the second was "A Defence of a Letter" (1704); the third, "A Reply to Mr. Palmer's Vindication" (1707).

grievance. It was asserted "that they endangered the success of the two national Universities." To prove this point Wesley explicitly refers to the numbers of nobility and gentry who would have sought their education at one or other of the great seats of learning, "had they not been intercepted by these sucking academies." After stating the numbers who had been trained at certain well-known institutions, he adds that, on the whole, "there must have been some thousands this way educated." The reply to such an attack was very obvious. "It is the Church of England's own fault," said Palmer, "that we stand excluded from the public schools"; and he appealed both to the Universities and to the Colleges to remove the barrier which prevented Dissenters from taking advantage of the acknowledged benefits which they offered. It appears from this writer that Dissenters had made formal proposals for admission at Oxford and Cambridge. He states that they had expressed their willingness to be content with some of the inferior Colleges and Halls, and to submit to any civil or moral tests, and indignantly exclaims against the injustice of their exclusion.* Sacheverell met at this point with another antagonist, Mr. James Owen, who reminded him that, from the reign of Elizabeth to that of Charles the First, the degrees and preferments of the Universities were conferred without distinction of parties or opinions, and in reply to a taunt levelled at the ignorance of Dissenters, aptly and pertinently remarked that, while it was made one of the causes of prejudice and partiality, the Dissenter "was not allowed the benefit of a learned education to cure him of this vice." "He excludes them," said the author, "from the fountain of learning, nor will he allow them to drink water out of their own cisterns. He would have them

* Palmer's "Vindication," pp. 11, 12. 1705.

punished for using the means of knowledge, and yet damns them for the prejudices of ignorance." The right to participate in the advantages of the Universities was, it will thus be seen, affirmed, as strongly by the generation of Dissenters who, by the operation of the Act of Uniformity, were the first to be excluded, as it has been, till recently, by their descendants.

Sacheverell's party, however, found in Daniel De Foe an abler and more astute opponent than was either Palmer or Owen. De Foe was now rising with rapid strides to the height of his reputation as a political writer. Shortly before the death of William he had published the exquisite satire of the "True-born Englishman," in which those who were for ever carping at the King on account of his foreign birth were shown a not very flattering image of themselves. De Foe had, previous to this, enjoyed the friendship of the King, and by this service had laid him under a debt of gratitude. But De Foe's politics were not popular, and he took no pains to earn applause. If, amongst any people, he might have expected encouragement, it should have been amongst the Dissenters, for he was the only vigorous and constant advocate of what, at that time, was understood to be religious freedom. But by the majority of Dissenters he was treated with undisguised contempt. Calamy sneeringly alludes to De Foe as "a certain warm person, who thought himself well qualified for the management of any argument." * It was the policy of the clerical leaders of Dissent at this period not to advance any claims for further political concessions. Considering the threatening aspect of the dominant High Church party, it is possible that this was a prudent attitude. The principal representatives of Dissent were in frequent communication with the members

* "Own Life," i. 464.

of the Government and other parliamentary leaders, and no doubt shaped their public action according to the advice which they received. Excepting, therefore, in matters relating exclusively to ecclesiastical polity, they preserved a prudent, if not a dignified, silence. If they prided themselves in anything, it was in being "moderate." When, at this very time, as well as afterwards, proposals were made to the Legislature for the abridgment of their liberties, this course was referred to as an argument in favour of their retention of the position which the law had already given to them. But it unfortunately happened, as, under similar circumstances, it has generally happened, that this argument was of no avail. However highly the statesmen of this period may have appreciated a quiet policy, and however sincere they may have been in advising and eulogising it, they had no hesitation in sacrificing the Dissenters when party necessities made such a sacrifice desirable. So far, therefore, from anything having been gained by the adoption of a "moderate" course, much had been lost. The rights and principles which had been held in abeyance, or had ceased to be actively urged, lost ground. The fruit of "moderation" and quiet was retrogression and weakness. To the policy generally adopted in this reign, however prudent it may have seemed, and however conscientiously it may have been taken up, is, in part, to be attributed the rapid decline of Dissent in the next and immediately succeeding generations.

De Foe was no party to such a policy. If he was conspicuous for the possession of one quality more than another, that quality was fearlessness. He was accused by persons of a more timid disposition of not being apt to consider consequences.* The fact is, he never considered

* Calamy's "Own Life," i. 464.

immediate consequences. He seemed able to see past any present disadvantages that might arise from the recommendation of a particular course of action to what would be its ultimate issue. Temporary sacrifices, temporary unpopularity, or the excitement of temporary anger weighed nothing with him. In regard to ecclesiastical politics, he had, what no other Dissenter of his day appears to have possessed, a firm and far-sighted policy—a policy which he carried out almost alone, at the cost of fortune, health, and reputation, but the wisdom as well as the courage of which posterity has gratefully vindicated.

De Foe met Sacheverell's furious denunciation of Dissent, and apostrophe to the "bloody flag" of persecution, by a satire so delicate that for a time it deceived those against whom it was directed into the belief that it was written on their own side. "The Shortest Way with the Dissenters" belongs to the period in the history of English literature at which were produced the "Tale of a Tub," "Gulliver's Travels," and the "History of John Bull," and takes equal rank with either of those memorable satires. That, out of the circle of persons of literary pursuits, it is not so widely known and read as are the popular writings of Swift and Arbuthnot, is owing to the fact that it takes the form of an ordinary and apparently grave political tract, instead of a humorous narrative. In politics—and especially ecclesiastical politics—De Foe felt too deeply to allow the humorous to predominate over the serious. While he was not averse to pleasing the fancy, he was intent on convincing the reason. He was incapable, in his political writing, of subordinating his purpose to the instrument by which he chose to accomplish that purpose. Whenever, especially, he was engaged in attacking High Churchism, he was almost savagely earnest. A kind of Mohawk ferocity was a characteristic of most of the party writing of this age; and it was not an uncommon circumstance for people who were attacked by the pen to threaten a reply by the sword; * but De Foe rose above the ordinary level of party warfare. He saw, in the High Churchmanship of this reign, a power which threatened, if it was not resisted with all the vigour of which the mind was capable, to be fatal to the liberties of Englishmen; to undo, as was sometimes openly promised, the work of the Revolution, and arrest, perhaps, for generations, the progress of the people towards a more liberal government and a more religious life.

The author commences "The Shortest Way with the Dissenters" with a history of Dissent, in which its rebellious tendency and tyrannical character are described in exaggerated Sacheverellian style. The "purest Church in the world," he says, has borne with it, "with invincible patience," and a "fatal lenity." "Charity and love," he adds, "are her known doctrines." He then examines the reasons given by Dissenters for their continued toleration. They are numerous, but so were the Huguenots, and yet the French king disposed of them; but the more numerous they are the more are they dangerous, and the greater need there is to suppress them. If it be said that there is need of union in time of war, there is the greater need at such a time to take security against private enemies; and heaven, by depriving them of their "Dutch Sanctuary," had clearly made way for their destruction. The popular objection that the Queen had promised them toleration was worth nothing, for the promise was limited by the safety of the Church; and although there might be no immediate danger to that institution, if the present opportunity was not taken it might be too late hereafter to do the work. He proceeds to ridicule the laws imposing fines and imprisonments for not attending church,

* Both De Foe and Swift, as is well known, received frequent threats of assassination.

and in sarcastic allusion to the "Occasional Conformists," says that they who will go to church to be chosen sheriffs and mayors would go to forty churches rather than be hanged. "If one severe law were made, and punctually executed, that whoever was found at a Conventicle should be banished the nation, and the preacher be hanged, we should soon see an end of the tale. They would all come to Church, and our age would make us one again." After comparing the Church to Christ crucified between two thieves, he concludes :—"Let us crucify the thieves. Let her foundations be established upon the destruction of her enemies, the doors of mercy being always kept open to the returning part of the deluded people. Let the obstinate be ruled with a rod of iron. Let all true sons of so holy and oppressed a mother, exasperated by her afflictions, harden their hearts against those who have oppressed her."

This work was no sooner issued from the press than it was caught up, and circulated with eager zeal by the High Church party. De Foe himself says, that "the wisest Churchmen in the nation were deceived by this book. Those whose tempers fell in with the times hugged and embraced it; applauded the proposal, and filled their mouths with the arguments made use of therein." Some Dissenters even were taken aback, and from the popularity with which it was greeted, began to fear that they were in considerable danger. When, however, the fact came out that it was written by a Dissenter, with a view to expose the designs of the High Church party, and that it was nothing but a satire, a hot fury took possession of the men who had allowed their passions to cheat their judgment as to its real character and intention. In press and pulpit the autho was now denounced as a malignant slanderer. Hounded on by the rage of the clergy, the Government undertook to ascertain who was the writer of the pamphlet—a task in which, by the Earl of Nottingham's perseverance, they quickly succeeded. A State prosecution against De Foe was immediately commenced. A proclamation was issued and a reward of fifty pounds offered for his apprehension. In this proclamation the "Shortest Way" is stigmatized as a scandalous and seditious pamphlet, and after the fashion of the "Hue and Cry," De Foe's personal appearance is minutely described. The House of Commons ordered the pamphlet to be burned in New Palace Yard by the common hangman. De Foe had, before this, prudently retired from the scene, but on learning that both his printer and publisher had been apprehended, he voluntarily surrendered himself. He then wrote a brief vindication of his work, and threw himself on the justice of the Government. He was tried at the Old Bailey on February 24th, 1703. The Attorney-General, Sir Simon Harcourt, who prosecuted, appears to have treated him in the style in which State prisoners were treated before Jeffreys. De Foe frankly admitted his guilt, and was sentenced to a fine of two hundred marks, to stand three times in the pillory, to be imprisoned during the Queen's pleasure, and to find sureties for his good behaviour for three years. The leader of political Dissent was thus dealt with in the "shortest way," and his satire proved, by the sentence on himself, not to have been a libel.

It is to the disgrace of the majority of the Dissenters of that period that, so far from defending or supporting De Foe, they did nothing but heap reproaches upon him. They affected to believe that he intended his work as a serious production, forgetting, as he well says, that he must then have designed to place his father, his wife, his six children, and himself in the same condition. He appears to have felt this conduct far more severely than the effect of his sentence. For, although forsaken by his own people, the public, in place of treating him as a criminal, honoured him as a hero. When he appeared in the pillory they greeted him with shouts of applause; they hung what was intended to be the instrument of his disgrace with garlands of flowers, and plentifully supplied him with refreshments. De Foe himself, summoning all his moral courage to meet his position, turned it at once to advantage by composing a "Hymn to the Pillory," in which, in clever rhyme, he satirized his opponents and prosecutors, and vindicated his pamphlet. He occupied his whole time while in Newgate in publishing more pamphlets, and in collecting his works, until, after he had been in prison for more than a year, Harley put himself into communication with him, with a view to secure his literary services for the Ministry, and the Queen sent relief to his family, and set him free. It was during this imprisonment that De Foe established his "Review," a journal of politics and general information, published on an average about three times a week, written wholly by himself, and printed at his own risk. In the pages of the "Review" are, for the first time in English literature, to be seen the style and scope of the modern newspaper article. Questions of domestic and foreign politics, of education and morals, of arts and sciences, and of trade and commerce, were treated with a fulness of information, sincerity of purpose, and vigour of style which, if the politics advocated had been popular, would have obtained, even from the contemporaries of De Foe, as much respect and reward as they secured malignity and fear. De Foe came out of Newgate the scoff of the polite wits, but with the consciousness that after the controversy on the "Shortest Way," no "bloody flag" could, in his time, be reared in England. The High Church party had concentrated their vengeance on his single person. The conduct of the Government in this case has been freely censured, and no words are strong enough to describe the arbitrary injustice with which they treated De Foe.

Between the publication of Sacheverell's sermon and De Foe's caustic reply, an attack was made on the liberties of Dissenters from another quarter. On November 4th, 1702, the members for the Universities of Oxford and Cambridge brought into the House of Commons a Bill for the prevention of Occasional Conformity. This measure was supported by the whole strength of the Tory and High Church party, and was carried through the Commons by an immense majority. The clergy successfully exerted themselves to inflame the passions of the people to their highest point in order to ensure the passing of the measure.* The Tories, however, in prosecuting this Bill, were not animated entirely by motives of religious intolerance. The "Occasional" Bill, from its first to its last introduction, was mainly a party measure. The Whigs, in many parts of the country, where the corporations returned members to Parliament, were, to a great extent, dependent for their election on the Dissenting members of those corporations. On the fidelity of these members they could always rely. But if the Occasional Bill were passed, no Dissenter could, in future, be a member of any corporation. The Whigs, accordingly, fought against the Bill with stubborn tenacity. The character, however, of the opposition to it, was as mixed as were the feelings which had led to its promotion. There were as sincere friends to religious liberty amongst the statesmen of the Whig party as there were sincere opponents to it amongst the Tories. Both parties, also, could raise the same cries of the welfare of the nation, and the welfare of the Church. The one party believed that the

* "Among those who were hottest in this affair were the clergy, and a crowd of women of the lowest rank, inflamed, as it were, with a zeal for religion."—Cunningham's "Great Britain," i. 318.

first could be secured only by excluding from its service the extreme adherents of the doctrine of resistance, and that the second would never be safe while Dissent was permitted to exist. The other party believed that the security of the State was best promoted by the goodwill of all the people to the laws, and that the Church had gained, and would still gain by preserving a mild and tolerant attitude towards those who differed from her. In the Bill that passed the Commons there was much which might reasonably have suggested hesitation even to the warmest partizan of the Church. It prohibited any person who did not statedly commune in the Established Church from holding any civil, military, or naval office whatsoever. Not only every admiral, general, judge, alderman, town councillor, or high officer of state, but every common soldier and sailor, every bailiff, every cook and scullery maid in the Royal household was required to be a member of the Established Church. The Bill further provided that if any person holding such an office should, at any time after receiving his appointment, attend any Conventicle or religious meeting other than one conducted according to the liturgy and practice of the Church of England, he should forfeit the sum of onc hundred pounds, and five pounds for every day that he continued in the occupation of his office: and he was at the same time adjudged to be incapable, during the remainder of his life, of holding any public employment.*

The House of Lords at this period was not greatly affected by the prevailing High Church passion. It was, to a considerable extent, a house of William the Third's creation, and most of the bishops had owed their nomination to that liberal monarch. When, therefore, the Occasional Bill came up, that assembly proceeded to make modifica-

* Boyer' "Annals," i. 173—177.

tions in some of its most offensive provisions, and to add to it clauses which were calculated to make its operation less extensive and less permanent. The Bill, in this amended shape, was sent down to the Commons, who at once requested a free conference with the other House. On the evening of this prolonged and celebrated meeting, Dr. Calamy waited on Bishop Burnet, upon whom he urged the claims of the occasional Conformists with such apparent success that he concluded "it might answer very good ends for some of us sometimes to wait on great men." *

The conference between the two Houses was managed with great ability on both sides. It was opened by the representatives of the Commons, who denounced, in strong terms, the "scandalous practice" of occasional Conformity, and exposed, in vivid language, the dangers besetting the monarchy and the Church from the existence and encouragement of Dissent. This mode of argument was an unhappy one, for it threw upon the managers for the Lords the necessity of defending Dissent. The Lords had sent their ablest and most eminent men to manage this interview. The Duke of Devonshire represented the old landed aristocracy of the nation; Somers and Halifax the statesmen of the Revolution; and Bishop Burnet the Episcopal Bench. While the Lords admitted that it was a scandal to religion that persons should conform to the Church only for the sake of obtaining a place, they did not admit Dissent from the established religion to be such an evil as the Commons had represented it to be. They considered that Dissenters differed from Churchmen "only in some little forms," and that they should be charitably dealt with. They also argued that the principle of toleration had already produced such visibly good results—had, in fact,

* "Own Life," i. 473, 474.

contributed so much to the security and reputation of the Established Church, and had so diminished the number of Dissenters—that it was unwise to trench upon it. They then proceeded to vindicate Nonconformists from the charges of disloyalty and schism. The Commons had said that Dissenters had never wanted the will, when they had the power, to destroy the Church and State; this, replied the Lords, is "hard and untrue, since in the last and greatest danger the Church was exposed to, they joined with her in all imaginable zeal and sincerity." The Commons had denounced separation from the Church to be schism, and, therefore, a spiritual sin; the managers of the Upper House replied that "the Lords cannot think the Dissenters can properly be called schismatics." With regard to one of the amendments, by which it was proposed to exempt workhouses from the operation of the Bill, the Lords somewhat satirically remarked that "it could never be conceived that the distribution of some Presbyterian bread to the poor, and Dissenting water-gruel to the sick, could ever bring prejudice to the Church of England." Finally, they advocated the practice of a charity such as the Almighty had both allowed and commanded,* and repeated that, owing to the exercise of such a charity, Dissent was "visibly abating all over the nation," and that nothing but severity could prevent its final absorption into the Church. The Commons rejoined, but the Lords adhered to most of their amendments, and the Bill accordingly fell through. For this issue the Dissenters were mainly indebted to Archbishop Tenison, who framed, and resolutely persisted in retaining, the Lords' amendments;† and to Bishop Burnet, who was one of the principal spokesmen in the conferences

* Boyer's "Annals," i. 178—200; Chandler's "Debates," iii., *pass.*
† "Tenison's Life," p. 102.

with the Commons. Burnet felt the gravity of the political issue involved. "Had the Bill passed," he says, "we had been all in confusion, and our enemies had had the advantage."* The Court strained its utmost to secure the success of the measure. The greatest number of peers that had ever at that time been brought together—one hundred and thirty—met to decide upon it. The Queen's husband, Prince George of Denmark—although himself a Lutheran and an occasional Conformist—was compelled to vote for it, while he exclaimed to one of its opponents, "My heart is vid you!" But even this vote and example failed to secure a majority, and the Court, at the end of the session, had to acknowledge itself defeated in the one measure which it most desired to carry.

It was not to be expected, under such circumstances, that this question would be allowed to rest; but, during the close of one Parliament and the opening of another, a change had come over the temper of the Court. During the whole of the summer the Duchess of Marlborough had been intriguing for the restoration of the Whigs, and exerting her influence with the Duke to induce him to coalesce with that party.† When the Queen, in November, 1703, met the two Houses of the Legislature, the effect of this influence was immediately apparent. "I want words," she said, in the last paragraph of her speech, "to express to you my earnest desires of seeing all my subjects in perfect peace and union amongst themselves. Let me, therefore, desire for all that you would carefully avoid any heats or divisions that may disappoint me of that satisfaction, and give encouragement to the common enemies of our Church and State." The Commons replied

* "Memorial to the Princess Sophia," p. 91.
† Coxe's "Life of Marlborough," cap. xviii.

in words which merely echoed this wish ; but the reply of the Lords was couched in the most emphatic and threatening language. "We, in the most solemn manner, assure your Majesty," they rejoined, "that we will not only avoid, but oppose whatsoever may tend to create any disquiet or dissension amongst your subjects." All parties knew that this language referred to the Occasional Bill ; but the fact that the Court seemed disposed to evade this question only served to inflame, to a greater height, the passions of those who had determined that it should pass. Accordingly, in the same month that the Parliament was opened, a new Bill was brought into the House of Commons. It was of a more moderate character as regards penalties than the former measure, but not less offensive in its political tendency. Its fate in the Upper House was worse than the fate of the Bill of the preceding year. Archbishop Tenison and Bishop Burnet led the majority of the bench of bishops to vote against it. Burnet, especially, distinguished himself by the warmth of his opposition ; but, although he opposed it because, he says, he had long looked on liberty of conscience as one of the rights of human nature antecedent to society, it is certain, if his speech has been correctly reported, that, while he used his utmost power to throw out the Bill, he expressed himself favourable to the exclusion of all Dissenters from public offices. He defended, that is to say, the practice of occasional Conformity because he judged it to be consistent with Christianity, and favourable to the progress of the Church. With regard to the latter point, he repeated the argument which he had urged at the conference between the two Houses in 1702. "Toleration," he said, "has not only set the Dissenters at ease, but has made the Church both stronger and safer, since God has so blessed our labours that we see the Dissenters lose as much strength as we gain by it. Their numbers are abated, by a moderate computation, at least a fourth part, if not a third." * The lay Lords spoke not less vigorously against the measure. On a division, the second reading was rejected by seventy to fifty-nine. In the majority were fourteen, and in the minority nine, bishops. The Duke of Marlborough gave a silent vote in its favour, and used his influence to prevent the Bill becoming law. Both he and Godolphin had now become aware that the interest really at stake in this Bill was not the interest of the Church, but of the nation, and that it was impossible to dispense with the aid of Dissenters in securing a constitutional government.

By this decisive rejection of a measure which the majority of the Commons and nearly the whole of the clergy had resolved to pass, popular excitement was raised to its utmost pitch. The vote of the bishops drew down upon them unmitigated abuse. They were denounced as traitors to the Church and enemies to religion. The Queen and the Prince came in for their share of vituperation.† "I wish," writes Swift to Stella,‡ "you had been here for ten days, during the highest and warmest reign of party and faction that I ever knew or read of upon the Bill against Occasional Conformity, which, two days ago, was, upon the first reading, rejected by the Lords. It was so universal that I observed the dogs in the streets were much more contumelious and quarrelsome than usual; and, the very night before the Bill went up, a committee of Whig and Tory cats had a very warm and loud debate upon the roof of our house. But why should we wonder at that, when the very ladies are split asunder into High Church

* Boyer's "Annals," ii. 179. † Burnet's "Own Times," p. 741.
‡ December 16, 1703.

and Low, and, out of zeal for religion, have hardly time to say their prayers. For the rest, the whole body of the clergy, with a great majority of the House of Commons, were violent for this Bill."

The controversy was now, for a time, transferred from the Legislature to the people. Clubs and societies were formed all over the kingdom to take measures for securing the success of the Bill when it should next be brought before Parliament, and the press teemed with pamphlets on both sides of the question. The Friends, the Baptists, and a large proportion of the Congregationalists, as they judged communion with the Church to be unlawful and unscriptural, took no part in the controversy; but it was otherwise with the Presbyterians, who occupied a high social position, were conspicuous for their wealth, and held many civil offices. It is not a little singular to find, amongst the reasons urged by this party for the continuance of occasional Conformity, the argument which Burnet employed with such force in the House of Lords. Not satisfied with justifying the practice by the authority of ecclesiastical and political precedents, they gravely and earnestly argued that it should be allowed to continue because it strengthened the Established Church and depressed the Dissenting interest. They acknowledged the truth of the statements that occasional Conformity had weakened them, and that on account of the practice their adherents were fast leaving their communion;* but, with strange inconsistency and fatal blindness, they still advocated it. De Foe alone, writing from Newgate, set forth the question on the only principles which a Nonconformist could consistently urge. He condemned the practice, as he had done in his controversy with Howe, as both hypocritical in its character

* "Moderation a Virtue," p. 29.

and injurious in its tendency, and maintained that no respectable Dissenters would be affected by the Bill. Taking the broad ground of religious equality, he denounced the intolerance which made either temporary or permanent churchmanship a qualification for any public office. In answer to a violent pamphlet from the pen of Sir Humphrey Mackworth, he showed that the Established Church of England was, in this respect, the most intolerant church in Christendom.* He asked, was it just that a Dissenter should be excluded, for any consideration, from places of profit, while he was compelled to serve in places of trouble—was it just that he should be pressed as a sailor, and be made incapable of preferment; that he should maintain his own clergy and the clergy of the Church; pay equal taxes, and yet not be thought worthy to be trusted to set a drunkard in the stocks? "We wonder," he cried, "that you will accept our money or our loans." He had no fear that Dissent would be endangered by the passing of the Bill, for its foundation was lodged in God's especial providence; it would be strengthened by it, and its professors would learn to live like people under the power of those who hated them.† In none of De Foe's works is there so much passionate indignation as there is in this scornful rebuke of ecclesiastical intolerance and "politic Dissent." That the author did not stand alone in his views is evident from the fact that this pamphlet passed through four editions in less than a year.‡ He had also an able coadjutor in a Dissenting minister named Stubbs, who roused the indignation of the moderate party by comparing them to a neuter gender in religion, and by calling upon

---

* "Peace without Union." 1703.

† "An Inquiry into Occasional Conformity." 1703.

‡ Wilson's De Foe, ii. 137

them to choose at once between God and Baal.* No publication of this period, however, was of greater weight than one written by John Shute, afterwards Lord Barrington, in which the service of the Protestant Dissenters to the State, their necessary antipathy to an absolute Government, and the liberality of their principles, were stated with the greatest completeness.

The Church party in the Commons met, in 1704, with a determination to carry matters with a high hand. The Occasional Bill, still more modified, was accordingly tacked to the Land-tax Bill, on the credit of which Marlborough had just concluded a treaty with Prussia. It was taken for granted that the Peers would not reject a measure on the passing of which the national faith had been pledged, and the success of the war depended. But the High Church party had, in the extravagance of their zeal, over-reached themselves. They were deserted by their own friends, and the tack was rejected by 251 to 134 votes. This, however, did not dishearten them. The Bill, without the tack, was still persisted in, and again carried through the Commons. When it made its appearance in the Lords, Anne herself went down to hear the debate. Her presence had the effect of exciting the orators to unusual vehemence, even on this question; but it was understood that, at present, she did not desire that the Bill should pass. It was rejected by a majority of thirty-four, Marlborough and Godolphin both voting against it. From this time the extreme Tories were nicknamed "Tackers"; their violence had made them unpopular; the Whigs were slowly rising to power, and the Occasional Conformity Bill slept the long sleep—for such a measure—of seven years.

* "For God or Baal; or, No Neutrality in Religion. Preached against Occasional Nonconformity."

CHAPTER IV.

FROM THE CHURCH IN DANGER AGITATION TO THE DEATH OF QUEEN ANNE, A.D. 1704—A.D. 1714.

THE resolute and repeated attack against the civil rights of Dissenters, as described in the last chapter, had thus, owing to the exigencies of party, failed of its purpose. It was not, however, the only assault that was made upon them at this period. At no time was a more strenuous effort made to bring back, by the legitimate weapons of argument, the moderate Dissenters to the Church than in the last years of King William's, and the earlier years of Queen Anne's, reigns. The whole argument at issue, between the Church and the moderate party especially, was set forth on the part of Churchmen with a keenness of intellect, a fulness of learning, and a candour of spirit which, at such a period, when the tempers of men had become softened by mutual charity, were likely to tell with successful force on the ranks of Dissent. There were many, and those the men of strongest brain and highest character, who had long been convinced that the best means to strengthen a church were those which were most in accordance with Christianity itself. Tillotson, Tenison, Burnet, Stillingfleet, and Patrick were conscious that the attitude which the Established Church had hitherto assumed towards those who differed from her communion, had been a blunder as well as a crime. Persecution had only strengthened the persecuted. How was it possible that men—and especially good men—should be attracted towards a church which had always borne to them a forbidding aspect; which had been little more than an incarnation of Pagan vices, instead of Christian virtues; and whose history had been signalized by repeated acts of the most deliberate oppression and cruelty? Instead, therefore, of invoking the vengeance of the civil magistrate, and calling for more penal laws, the new order of Churchmen seriously prepared themselves to meet the Dissenters with their own weapons. In place of a collection of Acts of Parliament they published a "Collection of Cases," which were written to recover Dissenters to the Communion of the Church.* Here Sherlock, Dean of St. Paul's, Williams, Bishop of Chichester, and Freeman, Dean of Peterborough, discoursed of the terms of communion in things indifferent in religion; scrupulous consciences were attempted to be quieted, and their doubts satisfied by Sharpe, Archbishop of York; objections to the Book of Common Prayer were answered by Dr. Claget; Fowler, Bishop of Gloucester, undertook to show that the accordance, in certain particulars, of the Established Church with the Church of Rome, was no sufficient reason for Dissent; Hooper, Dean of Canterbury, vindicated his Church from the imputation of Romanism; and Tenison persuasively urged the interests of Protestantism as a reason why there should be no separation from the Protestant State Church. These "Cases," twenty-three in number, are singularly free from many of the vices of theological controversy. They are characterised by great intelligence of treatment and fairness of argument, though they are uniformly dull and prolix. But that this was not considered a great fault is shown by the fact that the Collection speedily passed through several editions. In conjunction with other circumstances, it is not at all improbable that these writings helped to thin the

* "A Collection of Cases" &c., 1698.

ranks of Dissent. Men who were already disposed to conform would at least find an excuse for taking the final step in the heavily-marshalled but friendly arguments of these exemplary controversialists.

The publication of Calamy's "Abridgment of the Life of Baxter" gave occasion for a revival of the respective claims of Church and Dissent. Calamy, in one of the chapters of his work, had stated, in plain and unexaggerated language, the reasons why Dissenters such as Baxter had separated from the ecclesiastical Establishment. His justification of this Dissent was received as an attack on the Church, and was answered with no little vehemence by a clergyman named Olyffe, and by Benjamin Hoadly, afterwards Bishop of Bangor.* Hoadly wrote with the hope of conquest animating his heart. He avowedly treated of those questions only which separated such men as Calamy from the Church, and thought it quite possible to convince them of their error. Hoadly was the best specimen of Broad-churchmanship in his time; and if any writer could have succeeded in such an enterprise as the one he had undertaken, he would certainly have done so. The logical faculty in his intellectual constitution being subordinate to sentiment, he was a man of catholic principles respecting creeds. He held many views in common with Dissenters concerning thc relative rights of peoples and sovereigns, and Church and State, and was an open and fearless disputant. With all this he had utterly miscalculated the nature and character of moderate Dissent, and in attacking Calamy had equally miscalculated the strength of his adversary.

Edmund Calamy was now the principal representative of Dissent in the metropolis. It was his pride to consider

* "The Reasonableness of Conformity." 1703.

that he was descended from "moderate" Dissenters, and to be a "moderate" Dissenter himself. His grandfather and his father belonged to the Two Thousand who were ejected by the Act of Uniformity of 1662; and their descendant adopted, with little alteration, the faith of his celebrated ancestors. "I had," he says, in the "Life" of himself, which has often been quoted in these pages, "moderation instilled into me from my very cradle."* When he had become celebrated for his preaching, Bishop Burnet consulted him as to the opinions, in ecclesiastical matters, of "the more moderate sort of Dissenters," "with whom," he remarks, "I was known to be most conversant."† Calamy's Dissent, however, was not less firm or conscientious because it was "moderate." The line which divided him, and perhaps the majority of Dissenters of this period, was not so broad as that which divided the Congregationalists, Baptists, and Friends, who were occasionally classified together under the title of "high Dissenters" from the ecclesiastical Establishment, but it was as distinctly marked. Being narrower, it could be more easily stepped across, and accordingly most, if not all, of the secessions to the State Church were from the moderate or old Presbyterian ranks. But in the instances in which this Dissent was not merely hereditary or accidental, but conscientious, it was clung to with a tenacity quite as intense as that which characterised the more extreme sections. It may be difficult to explain why it should have been the case, but it is evident that the class to which Calamy belonged considered their Dissent to be of a superior order to that of their brethren. Ecclesiastically, if not religiously, it was reckoned as of higher birth; it was more aristocratic in its pretensions; its adherents

* "Own Life," vol. i. 72. † Ib. 470.

were more wealthy, and occupied a better social position; it stood nearer to the great, popular, and patronised Establishment than did the more unfashionable sects. There was, accordingly, the slightest tinge of Pharisaic pride in its attitude towards meaner brethren. The Congregationalists, Baptists, and Friends might be good men, but they were not "moderate."

Calamy was the ablest and best representative of the last generation of Puritans. He appears, from the indications afforded in his "Own Life," to have been a man of courtly manners and affable address, shrewd in his dealings with men, and politic in his management of public affairs. He was one of a class who never allow their zeal to outrun their discretion. He was an eminently "safe" man. While, however, he was possessed, in a large degree, of the merely prudential virtues, he was not wanting in higher qualities. He was an active pastor, an unusually successful preacher, and a good and accurate scholar. The historical literature of Dissent is more indebted to him than to any other man. His "Life of Baxter," his memorial of the two thousand ejected ministers, his defences of the character of the Puritans from the attacks of Archdeacon Echard and of Walker, and his "Own Life," are works which have laid, not merely English Dissenters, but all Englishmen under obligation to him. Nor was his own generation less indebted to him for the promptitude, vigour, and success with which he met Olyffe and Hoadly, in vindication of the principles of "moderate Nonconformity." The first portion of this work was published in 1703.* Hoadly was irritated with it, and immediately addressed "A Serious Admonition" to Calamy, which was followed by a treatise on the "Reasonableness of Conformity," and this by a defence of the "Reasonableness."

* "Defence of Moderate Nonconformity."

Calamy also added two works to his first, the third of which was published in 1705. These works are remarkable for two characteristics. The positions sustained by the author are nothing but the old positions of the Puritans, in advance of which Calamy had not moved one step. The general ground taken was that the Established Church was unscriptural in its constitution and its ceremonies. But if this were the case, how could Calamy defend occasional Conformity? The Presbyterians, in fact, pulled down their own arguments by their practice. When they observed conformity they did so on the plea that there was little difference between the two communions; when they justified their Dissent they did so because of the greatness of that difference. The second characteristic of Calamy's Defence is its masculine style. It is the first exposition of the reasons of Dissent written in modern English—the English of Addison and Pope, as distinguished from that of Shakespeare and Hooker.

But this mode of controversy did not satisfy the High Church zealots. Arguments which could not be enforced by a more effective weapon than reason were held by them in contempt. Having failed in all their appeals to the legislature, they now raised the cry that the Church was in danger; not, it was insinuated, from Dissenters alone, but from the Crown itself. Anne's temporary desertion of them, in the case of the Occasional Conformity Bill, had stung them to the quick. One writer was found bold enough to put in print what the clergy talked about only at home, or at most in the coffee-houses. This was Dr. Drake, who, in a pamphlet entitled the "Memorial of the Church of England," attacked, with furious animosity, the Queen's ministers, the bishops, and all who had contributed to the failure of High Church tactics. The nation, remarked Drake, had for a long time abounded with sectaries; the sons of those who had overturned both Church and State, and who were heirs of their designs, yet remained in the country. The Church, the author went on to say, would be strong enough to encounter these men but for the treachery and supineness of its members. The Head of the Church was inclined only to forgive and forget; she gave them comfortable speeches and kind assurances, while her prime minister gave them his countenance. The bishops were preaching indifference, and had extinguished the noble spirit which had animated their predecessors. Politicians were told that it was dangerous to rely too much on the apparent supineness of the clergy, or on their passive principles, for it was not to be expected that they would long bear to be used as they had been, or see the party in power courted at their expense; for the Church was in danger. Here, at last, was found a cry which, like the war-whoop of an American Indian, was sufficient to excite the whole clerical race to do final battle. Every pulpit at once echoed with it. In the coffee-houses nothing was spoken of but the Church's danger. With such a cry the Whigs could be extinguished and the Dissenters exterminated. Drake's pamphlet was a repetition of De Foe's "Shortest Way" without its satire. Those who dreaded the consequences of its publication denounced it as a forgery. It was a second part of the "Shortest Way," and it was not written by a High Churchman. De Foe himself greeted its appearance with undisguised expressions of gratification. He publicly thanked the author for convincing the world that what he had said ironically was now declared to be true literally.* Reviewing the history of the High Church party from the accession of the Queen to the time of this publication, he showed that Drake's doctrines were the goals to which they had always tended.† Pamphlet

* Review, ii. 266-270. † "The High Church Legion." 1705.

now followed pamphlet. The grand jury of Middlesex, Ashhurst the Presbyterian in the chair, made a presentation against Drake's pamphlet. By their order it was burned before the Royal Exchange, the Sheriff of London attending to witness the burning. This ceremony, a stupid relic of the *auto-da-fé*, was almost as frequently witnessed in the "Augustan age" of Queen Anne as it had been in that of Queen Elizabeth. What a revolution in thought had occurred between the two periods may be seen by the burning of the "memorial." Drake, in Elizabeth's days, would have been made a bishop, and Calamy and his books would probably have shared the fate of Penry and his works. But the Presbyterian could now preach within ear-shot of the Queen's palace, while the High Church bigot saw his pamphlet condemned to the greatest public ignominy. The fact might have suggested both to High Churchmen and to Presbyterians, that burning books did not, as they seemed to think, annihilate thoughts.

The legislature which had been so zealous in prosecuting De Foe could scarcely ignore Dr. Drake. On December the 5th, 1705, on the motion of Lord Halifax, the House of Lords took into consideration the alleged danger of the Established Church. The debate was led by the Earl of Rochester, who stated his belief that such danger existed. He ascribed it to the Act of Security in Scotland, which, while it established Presbyterianism as the national religion, had not tolerated Episcopacy; but this, as it was subsequently pointed out, was not a correct description of the ecclesiastical condition of Scotland; for Episcopacy, although not endowed, was tolerated in the same sense that Dissent was tolerated in England. Another reason assigned by the speaker was that the Occasional Bill had not passed; and this, indeed, was the exciting cause of the cry. The Earl of Halifax, in deriding the affected anxiety of Churchmen, called attention to the fact that, soon after the accession of William the Third to the throne, the cry of the Church in danger began, and that it had been continued all through that sovereign's reign. The suggestion conveyed by this remark was, no doubt, sufficiently obvious to those who heard it. It was, that a Church of England, framed according to the ideal of the High Church party, could not co-exist with a constitutional government, and that its old pretensions were opposed to those rights of the subject which it was the design of the Revolution to establish. The Bishop of London recognised this suggestion by immediately adding, that in the doctrines contained in a sermon which had been recently preached before the Corporation of London, by Hoadly, in which the right of resistance to a bad government was sustained with all the boldness of which Hoadly was so capable, he saw a source of danger to the Church. Burnet, with his quick and ready wit, aptly recalled to recollection that Compton, since his appointment to the Episcopal office, was the bishop who himself had taken arms against James by joining the revolutionary standard at Nottingham. "His lordship," therefore, remarked Burnet, "ought to be the last man to complain of that sermon, for, if its doctrine was not good, he did not know what defence his lordship could make to his appearing in arms." Sharpe, Archbishop of York, drawing an arrow from Sacheverell's quiver, gravely suggested that the greatest danger was to be apprehended from the increase of Dissenters, and particularly from the many academies which they had established. The archbishop followed up this attack by moving, almost in Sacheverell's words, that the judges be consulted as to what laws were in force against such seminaries, and by what means they could be suppressed. Sharpe found in Lord Wharton an ironical seconder. Wharton's memory was as apt and faithful as Burnet's. He remembered that Sharpe himself had had his two sons educated at a Dissenting academy. Hough, Bishop of Lichfield and Coventry, said that "if a source of danger existed anywhere, it was to be found in the clergy, and the clergy only." This closed the debate, and it was then formally resolved, "That the Church of England, which was rescued from the extremest danger by King William the Third, of glorious memory, is now, by God's blessing, in a most safe and flourishing condition, and whosoever goes about to suggest and insinuate that the Church is in danger under her Majesty's administration, is an enemy to the Queen, the Church, and the kingdom." This resolution was at once communicated to the House of Commons, where the van of the High Church party again led the attack on Dissent. But in vain, the Commons sustained the resolution of the Lords by a majority of fifty-two. The next step was the issue of a proclamation by the Queen, which recited that several persons, endeavouring to foment animosities, and to cover designs which they dared not publicly own, had "falsely, seditiously, and maliciously" suggested the Church to be in danger. Order, therefore, was given to all judges, justices, magistrates, sheriffs, mayors, and bailiffs, to "apprehend, prosecute, and punish" such persons. Again the High Church party suffered defeat, and again was supplied fresh stimulus to take, on the earliest occasion that might offer, their revenge on the Dissenters.

It had been, for many years, the desire of the most ardent patriots and greatest statesmen, to bring about a legislative union between England and Scotland. In 1706, owing partly to the management of Lord Barrington and De Foe, who had been sent to Scotland for the purpose, the northern Parliament had agreed to the proposed terms of this union. On the 10th January, therefore, in this year, a Bill was introduced into the House of Lords for sanctioning the union. No manner of objection but one was offered to this great measure, that one being the possibility that the presence of Presbyterian Peers and Commoners in the Parliament of Great Britain would tend to endanger the safety and supremacy of the Church of England? The clergy at once took alarm. The Lower House of Convocation, which was then sitting, appointed Committees to consider the subject. But Queen Anne took the decisive step of proroguing this body for three weeks.* During this period, the measure underwent discussion in the legislature, in which its sole opponents were the members of the ultra-Church party. It was urged that there would be danger to the Church in union with a country in which Presbyterianism was established by law; that it might result in the bishops being turned out of the House of Lords; that it would be generally of the most dangerous consequence to the Church, and that Scotch members should be prevented from voting on any ecclesiastical matters. The Bill, however, passed. When Convocation again met, there was a feeling of exasperation which led the Lower House beyond the bounds of loyalty. They at once drew up a representation, protesting that no such arbitrary course had been adopted by the Crown since the Act of Submission of Henry the Eighth. The records were searched, and it was found that there were several precedents for such a step. This act of the clergy was too much even for Anne, who, herself, wrote to state that they had invaded her supremacy. Her message was received with studious contempt, and was followed by another royal prorogation.† The Dissenters, on the other hand, showed their gratification with the measure by preaching

* Lathbury's "History," p. 402. Burnet's "Own Times," p. 806.
† Lathbury's "History," pp. 402, 403.

sermons in its honour on the day appointed for a public thanksgiving, and by presenting, through the medium of the Dissenting ministers of the Three Denominations, a special address of congratulation to the Queen.*

With Marlborough and Godolphin, united with the leading members of the Whig party in power, the legislature was for two years free from the compulsion to debate ecclesiastical affairs. Such a condition of quiet was, however, ill-suited to the designs of the High Church party. In the autumn of the year 1709, Sacheverell sounded, from the pulpit of Cathedral, the first blast of a new war. In a sermon on the "Perils of False Brethren both in Church and State," preached before the lord mayor and aldermen of London, on the anniversary of the Gunpowder Plot, Sacheverell boldly attacked the doctrines of the Revolution, the course of legislation which had been pursued since that time, the men who had conducted the national affairs, and the liberties still enjoyed by Dissenters. The doctrine especially attacked was that of the right of resistance; the "false brethren" were the Whigs and the Dissenters, and those who, by their active connivance or from apathy, allowed the Whigs to govern and the Dissenters to be tolerated. He charged Dissenters with committing "the most abominable impieties," and with justifying "murder, sacrilege, and rebellion, by texts of Scripture;" they were "filthy dreamers, and despisers of dominion;" in their seminaries "atheism, deism, Lutheranism, Socinianism, with all the hellish principles of fanaticism, regicide, and anarchy, were taught;" they were "monsters and vipers," "sanctified hypocrites," "unhallowed, loathsome, and detestable." The bishops of the Church were called upon to "thunder out their ecclesiastical anathemas"

* This address is in Calamy's "Own Life," vol. ii. pp. 63, 64. Note.

against them, and all true Churchmen were exhorted to have no fellowship with their works of darkness.*

The proper way to have treated such a man as this would have been, either to have left him alone or to have sent him to a madhouse; but, unhappily, Godolphin was stung to personal resentment against Sacheverell by a contemptuous comparison of him, in this sermon, to Ben Jonson's character of "Volpone."† It was therefore decided to impeach Sacheverell before the House of Lords, for "high crimes and misdemeanors." The trial began on the 27th February, 1709. No state-trial since the impeachment of the seven bishops created such an excitement. A special court was erected in Westminster Hall, and there, on the first morning, the Lords, accompanied by the judges, the masters in Chancery, the peers' eldest sons and peers minor, the heralds, and other officers of the House, proceeded in state.‡ The Commons in Committee of the whole House, were accommodated with seats within the bar. The articles of impeachment charged Sacheverell with maintaining that the Revolution had been brought about by odious and unjustifiable means; that the toleration which had been approved by the legislature was unwarrantable, and that those who defended the liberty of conscience granted by it were "false brethren;" and that the Queen and her ministers were chargeable with general bad conduct of the affairs of the nation. Sacheverell denied the accuracy of all these charges.

In the ten days during which the subsequent proceedings lasted the populace became mad with enthusiasm for

* "Perils amongst False Brethren." 1709, *pass.*

† Swift's "Memoirs relating to the Change of Ministry."

‡ "The Tryal of Dr. Henry Sacheverell," &c. Published by order of the House of Peers. 1710.

Sacheverell, and with rage against his opponents. The man himself, who was scorned by those who were making him their tool;* who had not one of the qualities even of an able preacher; who lived on the garbage of the popular passions, suddenly found himself exalted into a hero, with a fame as celebrated, in his own country, as that of Marlborough himself. The mob, as he went every morning to the trial, surrounded his coach by thousands. His progress to and fro was as that of a conqueror. The women begged to kiss his hands; every one who passed was commanded to shout, "High Church and Sacheverell for ever!" or he was at once knocked down, his head cleft open,† or otherwise brutally maltreated. The Queen, who did not care to disguise her personal sympathy for Sacheverell, as she went every day to the Lords' to hear the arguments, met with a cordial reception. "God bless your Majesty!" cried the insane mob; "we hope your Majesty is for High Church and Dr. Sacheverell." The clergy, almost to a man, expressed their sympathy with him. The feelings of the mob were expressed in still more decisive manner than in shouts. Sacheverell's enemies were their enemies, and the men whom he had denounced were to be punished. Accordingly, the Congregational meeting-house of Daniel Burgess, near Lincoln's Inn, was pulled down, and the pulpit and pews burnt, to cries of "High Church and Sacheverell!" A bonfire was made of Earle's meeting-house, in Drury Lane, and of other churches; Salters' Hall, Shower's church, Hoadly's church and Burnet's house were threatened with a similar fate; but before this could be accomplished the military made their appearance, a

* "Duchess of Marlborough's Account," p. 247.

† Burnet's "Own Times," p. 849. "Complete History of Europe," p. 709.

few ringleaders were apprehended, and the people dispersed.*

The arguments of those who conducted the prosecution of Sacheverell, and of those members of the House of Lords who were in favour of his condemnation, were pointed mainly towards a proof of the constitutional legality and moral obligation of the doctrine of non-resistance. References were frequently made, in the course of the speeches, to the conduct of the clergy. The boldest speaker on this subject was the Duke of Argyll, who remarked that "the clergy had in all ages delivered up the rights and liberties of the people." "These proceedings of clergymen," said the Bishop of Oxford, "are of that dangerous tendency and consequence that if some effectual stop be not put to them, they will put an effectual end to our constitution." The Lords, on March 20th, by a vote of sixty-nine to fifty-two, found Sacheverell guilty, and on March 23rd condemned him to suspension from his office for three years, and his sermons preached at Derby and at St. Paul's to be burned by the common hangman.

Such a sentence, after such a trial, was equivalent to an acquittal, and so all men treated it. Sacheverell soon after made a procession through England. The University of Oxford received him with honours; at Banbury, the mayor and corporation went out to meet him; at Warwick, he was welcomed by a body of horsemen headed by the mayor and aldermen; at Shrewsbury, five thousand horsemen met him on his way to the town, and gave him their escort; at Bridgewater, the road he was to travel was lined for miles with people from all the surrounding country, the hedges were decorated with flowers, and four thousand

* Burnet's "Own Times," p. 849, 850. Calamy's "Own Life," ii. 228. "Parliamentary History," vi. 630. Perry's "History of the Church of England," iii. 222.

horse and three thousand foot constituted themselves his bodyguard; at Ludlow, riding into the town on a white palfrey, he was received with sounding trumpets and flying colours.* The Dissenters, as a matter of course, felt the vengeance of the excited mobs. At Wrexham, among other places, the effigies of the Dissenting ministers were burnt; in the same town, an effigy of Dr. Daniel Williams was buried, and an effigy of Hoadly scourged, pilloried, and then drowned.† When Sacheverell's period of suspension had expired, bells were rung, bonfires lit, and illuminations made all over the kingdom to celebrate the happy event. On the Sunday following he preached a sermon at St. Saviour's, Southwark, in which he compared his sufferings with those of Christ.‡ He was next called upon to preach before the House of Commons. The Queen rewarded him with the benefice of St. Andrew's, Holborn, one of the most valuable in the metropolis. But in the possession of a good income, and in the enjoyment of the social advantages of a high clerical position, Sacheverell's zeal expired. The world, after his promotion, heard little more from his lips of the dangers of the Church and the nation. He had, however, done enough for one man and one life to satisfy the highest ambition. Under the influence excited by his prosecution, the Whigs were hurled from power; and a vulgar sermon, preached by a comparatively illiterate man, changed the Government of the country, the fortunes of generals and statesmen, and the destinies of the nations of Europe.

If any people were at this time in danger, it was the Dissenters. Although they were still almost as active as

* Boyer's "Annals," vol. ix.

† Wilson's "Life of De Foe," iii. 109, 110.

‡ "Parliamentary History," ix. 1208.

before in opening new places of worship, they were, as has been seen from the statements made in the discussions on occasional Conformity, losing ground in two directions. Many of their ministers were seceding to the Established Church, and, in some parts of the country at least, there was a considerable decrease in their numbers. The causes of this decrease have already been hinted at; but, in addition to the mild attitude of the liberal Church party, the practice of occasional Conformity, and the absence of a sufficiently energetic assertion of their civil rights, there were other circumstances which undoubtedly had great influence in contributing to their depression. The first of these was the loss by death of all the great leaders who had been ejected by the Bartholomew Act. Few of the younger generation of Dissenters in the latter part of the reign of Queen Anne could have known anything of Baxter, Bates, Howe, Owen, Kiffin, Knollys, or Fox, except from their works or from the lips of their fathers. Personal attachment to these men kept many in the ranks of Dissent, who stayed no longer than life stayed with their old pastors. The frown of the Court could have had no less influence in deterring men from connecting themselves with any of the Free Churches. The only congregation at this time in London with which a comparatively considerable proportion of the aristocracy was still connected was Edmund Calamy's, in Westminster, and this proportion was rapidly decreasing.* It is difficult to say whether the general withdrawal of

* The Bedford family, who had formerly attended Manton's ministry, transferred themselves on his death to that of Mr. Cotton, of Dyot Street, Bloomsbury. Cotton was chaplain in the family of the Dowager Ladies Robert and James Russell; Lady Clinton also attended his ministry. —Wilson, iv. 385.

Dissenters from other circles of society, which began at this period, had much effect upon their numbers; but it certainly decreased, as it has ever since done, their moral influence. To a great degree this withdrawal was a necessary result of their exclusion from the best places of education, and of the general tone of public opinion. But it was not necessary that Dissenters should have held aloof from intercourse with literary persons. With a few remarkable exceptions, however, it was apparently the opinion of the generality of ministers now rising that it was most undesirable for religious persons to read any but technically religious books. The strictness of Puritanism, without its strength or its piety, was coming into vogue. With the death of the ejected two thousand and their contemporaries the intercourse of Dissenters, excepting for purposes of trade, with the "outer world" almost ceased. Shakespeare's plays were forbidden writings, and Bacon was a "profane" and unknown author. Addison's *Spectator* was probably unknown to nine-tenths of the members of the Free Churches. Any person reading the memoirs, diaries, and letters of this reign might naturally imagine himself to be reading of two totally different periods of English history. He would scarcely gather from any work written by a Dissenter that such men as Addison, Steele, or Pope had lived at the same time as himself.* He would infer, from the controversial writings of the great essayists, and from certain references in contemporary correspondence, that a class of people called Dissenters existed at the period when the writers were in existence, but who they

* I am aware that Watts contributed to the *Spectator*; that Grove, the head-master of the Taunton Academy, was a frequent contributor to the same periodical; and that Hughes, the friend of Addison, Pope, and Watts, also wrote for the *Spectator*, *Tatler*, and *Guardian*; but these instances were exceptional.

were he could not even guess. On the part of Dissenters this unwise and unnatural estrangement came at last to be taken as a matter of course. It had almost the influence of a holy tradition. Narrow as they were good, these men did not consider that few things could be more unfortunate for a nation than for its purest religion to be divorced from its best literature. As was plainly enough proved, also, during and immediately after the trial of Sacheverell, Dissent was as unpopular with the lower as it was with the upper classes of society. Debased and ignorant to the last degree, the labourers and mechanics of Queen Anne's reign were, in matters of belief, under the natural control of the squires and the clergy. They followed the religion which the Queen, the aristocracy, and the local gentry followed, and which they had been taught from their births was the only respectable religion.

The principal representatives of the Presbyterian ministry at this period were Dr. Daniel Williams, of New Broad Street, Dr. Edmund Calamy, of Westminster, William Tong, of Salters' Hall, John Shower, of Old Jewry, Dr. John Evans, Dr. Grosvenor, of Crosby Square, and Dr. Wright, of Blackfriars. The characters and labours of Williams and Calamy have already been noticed. Tong, before he was chosen as minister of Salters' Hall, had preached with great success at Chester, Knutsford, and Coventry, in the neighbourhoods of which, by his evangelistic work, he had laid the foundation of many other churches. His election to the Salters' Hall church, where he succeeded Nathaniel Taylor, whom Doddridge has described as the "Dissenting South," elevated him to the pastorate of the principal Presbyterian congregation, one of the wealthiest, if not the wealthiest, in London. He was a man of large learning and culture, and of exquisitely graceful manners. He is now chiefly remembered by his memoir of Matthew Henry, who succeeded him at Chester. Shower, as a preacher, excelled in pathos, and was remarkable for his gift of prayer. His publications consisted exclusively of sermons, the majority of them preached on occasion of the deaths of eminent persons. Dr. Evans was, at this time, co-pastor with Daniel Williams, and was now, probably, occupied in collecting the materials for a History of Nonconformity, which he did not live to finish, and was afterwards taken up by Daniel Neal. From his vigilance, activity, energy, and peculiar adaptation for public work, Dr. Evans was engaged in all the affairs of the Dissenters of his time,* and was one of the most effective preachers and useful writers of his denomination. At Crosby Square, where Charnock had formerly been pastor, Dr. Benjamin Grosvenor preached. He had originally been connected with the Baptists, and was a member of Keach's Church, but upon his return from his academical studies, he joined the Presbyterians. His acute intellect, cheerful temperament, graceful elocution, and devotional spirit soon raised him to the highest position amongst the Dissenting ministers of the metropolis. He was a favourite lecturer at Salters' Hall and the Weigh-house, and one of the best historical students of his day. Dr. Grosvenor's ministry extended over fifty years, from the end of King William's to the end of George the Second's reign.†

In Matthew Sylvester's old Church in Blackfriars, Dr. Samuel Wright preached. This was one of the places of worship which was nearly destroyed by Sacheverell's mob. The people afterwards removed to Carter Lane. Wright's

* Wilson's "Dissenting Churches," ii. 212—220; Harris's "Funeral Sermon," 1730.

† Crosby's "History," iv. 203. Wilson's "Dissenting Churches," i. 344.

eminence as a preacher was such that Herring, afterwards Archbishop of Canterbury, in order to learn elocution, frequently attended his ministry. The Presbyterians could also, in London, number several eminent laymen. They were largely represented in the Courts of the Aldermen and Common Council of the City, the most conspicuous being Sir Thomas Abney, in whose house Watts became a guest for nearly forty years. The family of the Ashursts had also, as it has always had, its representative in the Free Churches of the metropolis. Of all the members, however, of the Presbyterian body, De Foe was the most eminent; but he took more interest in the public relations of Dissent than in its internal organisation.

Foremost among the country ministers of this period was Matthew Henry, of Chester, son of Philip Henry, a man whose holy character dated almost from his birth. Matthew Henry was the founder of the Chester Church. No man more exemplified the graces of Christianity than he. In devotion to his ministerial work he equalled his father; the fervency of his preaching excelled that of any other person; while his "Life of Philip Henry" and his Commentary on the Scriptures have earned for him the highest reputation amongst Nonconformist divines. Henry removed in 1712 to Hackney, to take the pastorate of the Church formerly presided over by Bates, and died two years afterwards. His death, says Dr. Daniel Williams, was the subject of "universal mourning." *

There died, in the year 1710, another person whose name is intimately identified with the history of the Free Churches. This was Lady Hewley, wife of Sir John Hewley, of York. During her lifetime this eminently pious and benevolent woman was a chief supporter of the Presby-

* Tong's "Life of Matthew Henry." Williams's Works, ii. 459.

terian congregations in the north of England. Her personal charity to ministers seemed to know no limit. In 1704 Lady Hewley executed a deed conveying valuable landed property to trustees for the use of "poor godly preachers of Christ's Gospel;" for the support of the Gospel in poor places, and for exhibitions, or scholarships, in aid of the education of young men for the ministry.* Although she was a Presbyterian she placed no sectarian limit on the application either of this or her other charities. She was what in these days would be termed an orthodox Christian, or a moderate Calvinist. Whether she would have bequeathed such property under such a catholic and open trust, if she could have known that a large proportion of the funds derived therefrom would ultimately be applied to purposes which the Presbyterians of her day would have characterised by every evil name, may be honestly questioned.

Amongst the Congregational ministers of London, in the reign of Queen Anne, the name of Isaac Watts stands preeminent. On the day of the death of William III., Watts, then twenty-seven years of age, had been chosen as successor to Dr. Chauncey, of Mark Lane. It was no slight honour for any man to stand in the pulpit which had been occupied by Caryl, Owen, and Clarkson; and few of those who chose Watts, although he had been their assistant pastor for four years, could have anticipated that they had selected a minister who was destined to shed a lustre on their church equal to that which it had received from the pastorate of Owen himself. Isaac Watts had been born and cradled in Nonconformity. His father, a deacon in the Congregational Church at Southampton, was imprisoned for six

* "History, Opinions, and Present Legal Position of the English Presbyterians," pp. 114, 115. 1834. Wilson's "Historical Inquiry," pp. 250, 251.

months for his attachment to Nonconformist principles, and he drew nourishment from his mother's breast while she sat on the steps of the gaol in which her husband was confined. His genius for poetical composition seems to have been inbred, for as soon as he could write he wrote in verse. In 1705 he published his "Lyric Poems," and two years afterwards the "Hymns and Spiritual Songs." With the exception of an Essay on Uncharitableness, and a Sermon, these were, as yet, all the works by which he was publicly known; but they were sufficient to rank him amongst the most eloquent of preachers and the most original of Christian poets. The poetry of the Christian Church in England, until Watts published his Hymns, was unaccountably inferior to all the other means of religious worship. More sublime discourses have never been preached than had been preached since the Reformation. From Hooper, Latimer, and Cartwright, to Bunyan, Charnock, South, and Howe, there had been a succession of orators of the highest order of Christian eloquence. Prayer seemed to be a Divine gift to the Puritans of both ages. They were men who wrestled with God, with strong cries and tears, and who wrestled until they prevailed. But of Christian song, as an art, they knew little or nothing. Excepting in the mountains and woods, it had indeed been dangerous, until within a recent period, to exercise it. They did sing, but only a rough and uncouth doggerel. Sternhold and Hopkins, Tate and Brady, with their limping lines, and poverty stricken thought, were the Churchman's necessary choice, and the scarcely superior Patrick and Bunyan—for Bunyan the hymn-writer was not equal to Bunyan the preacher and dreamer—the almost sole refuge of the Nonconformists. Some of the finest ore of Christian poetry had been wrought into the happiest verse in the ancient and the mediæval churches, but much of it had been lost, and little of what had been left was known.

What is most remarkable is that the hymns of Protestant Germany should, apparently, have been equally unknown, though the early Reformers of Queen Elizabeth's reign, during their exile in the towns of Germany and Switzerland, must have become well acquainted with them. The Presbyterians and Congregationalists of James II.'s reign, some of whom were educated at the German Universities, and many of whom had resided and travelled for some years on the Continent, must also have been familiar with them; but no translation of them was either projected or attempted. But for the culture and enjoyment of pure devotional poetry a period of comparative rest from the struggle for mere existence is required. The Puritans of the Commonwealth drew their inspiration from the Book of Judges and the Psalms. The songs of Miriam and Deborah, and the wrathful imprecations of David, well served their need. But now that rest had been felt and enjoyed, and comparative peace had come upon the churches, there arose a half unconscious desire for better words of praise. No sooner, accordingly, did Watts's Hymns appear than they were eagerly sought for and joyfully used. They were like showers of rain on the parched earth; and from nearly all the Free Churches of England and America a new harvest of praise to God at once arose.

Dr. Johnson, who never commended when he could detract, and who grudged to acknowledge the existence of any virtue or ability in a Dissenter, has made some remarks on the devotional poetry of Watts, which, on the whole, are scarcely just or truthful; but he admits that if Watts "had been only a poet, he would probably have stood high among the authors with whom he is now associated, and that he did better than others what no man had done well."* The

* "Lives of the Poets," art. "Watts."

great critic probably read the poetry of Watts with a High Churchman's habit of thought. Its range, to him, was narrow, because it did not include many subjects which, in his public devotions, his mind had been accustomed to dwell upon. Johnson's complaint that Watts's devotional poetry lacks sprightliness is more correct, and he might have added that it was also deficient in that almost feminine softness which, since his time, has been prized as a favourite characteristic of Christian poetry. But it was equally deficient in the coarse voluptuousness which, in the eyes of a large class of worshippers, is the chief merit of devotional song. If Watts's imagination had ever associated together the ideas of Divine and of gross physical love, Watts would have shrunk with horror from expressing them. His fancy was as chaste as it was lofty, and was ever held in check by a profound and awful reverence for the character of the Almighty. His errors are, for the most part, errors of style and execution. He had not the musical ear or the delicate critical judgment of Addison. His verse is often faulty in its rhythm, and careless and inaccurate in its rhyme. From its mixed vigour and tameness of thought and expression, it is singularly unequal. But, compared with everything of their kind that had gone before, Watts's Hymns must have seemed like the addition of a new sense to the Christian worshipper.

The reputation of Watts as a poet has overshadowed his reputation as a preacher, as a man of letters, and as a philosopher; but, amongst his contemporaries, he was renowned for the latter qualities. He had, probably, the best elocution of any preacher of his generation; his sermons, while they are weighty with thought, and, as religious addresses, scrupulously faithful to the consciences of his hearers, indicate the possession of a very high order of imaginative power. It appears to have surprised even men of ability equal to his own that he could trust mainly to his extemporary power for the delivering of his discourses.* His Nonconformity, like that of nearly all his contemporaries, was, if moderate, thorough; and, as will be seen, he took an active interest in the questions which related to the religious liberties of the people. The scholarship of Watts and his acquaintance with men of letters of all description did much to redeem Dissent from the charge of narrowness and littleness. He was, as yet, unknown as a philosopher, and it was not until he had attained his greatest fame that, with a child's innocent heart, he wrote those "Divine and Moral Songs," which have since, to millions of the Anglo-Saxon race, been amongst the most precious of all the memories of child-life.

The position of Watts in the history of the Free Churches of England is one of peculiar interest. He is the link which unites the later Puritans to the founders of Methodism. As a young man, he was the intimate associate of Howe. Richard Cromwell also, after visiting the deathbed of the great chaplain of the great Protector, admitted him to the friendship of his old age, and to no house was Watts a more frequent visitor than to his. Cromwell's celebrated but eccentric granddaughter, Mrs. Bendish, was a member of Watts's congregation; and Whitefield, when at the commencement of his evangelistic work, sought his advice. Watts was a witness to the decline and extinction of Puritanism. In the generation which followed, while the Free Churches were gradually settling on a new foundation, he opposed to his utmost the united torrents of scepticism and irreligion. He lived also to see the beginning of a general revival of personal piety, to the marvellous effects of which the Free Churches of

* Johnson's Lives.

the nineteenth century owe, in greatest measure, their high character and their great numerical success.*

In the old Congregational Church in Silver Street—of which Philip Nye, of the Westminster Assembly, was the first pastor—there preached a man somewhat younger in years than Watts, but destined, in his own sphere, to achieve an equally honourable, if not an equally famous, reputation. This was Daniel Neal, who, some years later, published the "History of the Puritans."† Excepting, however, as a useful and laborious preacher, Neal, at this time, was unknown. Both Watts and Neal, as well as Dr. Evans, were educated by Thomas Rowe, the pastor of the Congregational Church at Haberdashers' Hall, and one of the most eminent tutors who have ever been connected with this body. Rowe, however, at the time of which we write, had been dead for four or five years. At New Court, Carey Street, ministered Daniel Burgess, the wit and humorist of the Congregational denomination. Burgess combined, in some measure, the characteristic qualities of Latimer and Rowland Hill. His church was the resort of the players of Drury Lane Theatre, who, if they went in sport, must often have left in pain. Burgess, we are told, seeing so many members of this profession present at his church, would often address them personally, and his ministry amongst them was so successful that not a few became exemplary Christians.‡ The Fetter Lane Church, another

* For the foundation of these remarks on Dr. Watts, I am chiefly indebted to Mr. Milner's most interesting "Life," published in 1834, and, after this, to Gibbon's "Life," to Johnson's "Life," and to the Leeds edition of his works.

† It is somewhat singular that the historian of the Puritans should have been succeeded in the same pulpit by the two joint historians of Dissent, Dr. Bogue and Dr. Bennett.

‡ Wilson's "Dissenting Churches," iii. 497.

of the oldest Congregational Churches in London, was presided over by Thomas Bradbury, a man of great pulpit power, remarkable vivacity of manner, and one of the most courageous defenders of the liberties of Dissenters. Bradbury almost equalled De Foe in his public denunciations of High Churchism, and his attachment to the principles of the Revolution was second only to his attachment to Christianity. Politics were a part of his religion, and the government of Queen Anne had no more dangerous or implacable foe than Bradbury. It is credibly stated that the Queen, who called him the "bold Bradbury," in order to purchase his silence, sent Harley to him with the offer of a bishopric. He was often mobbed, and once threatened with assassination, but, after a ministry of upwards of sixty years, lived to the end of George the Second's reign.* During his lifetime more than a hundred and fifty of his sermons were published.†

Matthew Clarke, of Miles' Lane Church, was another well-known preacher, remarkable for his high character, his reverent spirit, and his hospitable disposition. The epitaph on his tomb in Bunhill Fields is one of Watts's most elaborate efforts of this description. Sir John Hartopp, in whose family Watts had been a tutor, and whose name is familiar to all who know Watts's poetical works, was the principal layman in the Congregational denomination. He was a man of unflinching integrity and courage—a standard bearer of Nonconformity when to bear that standard was to brave certain punishment.

At the head of the Baptist denomination stood Joseph

---

* No juster epitaph was ever written than that which appears on Bradbury's tomb in Bunhill Fields—that great and holy burying-place of nearly all the eminent Dissenters of two centuries.

† Wilson's "Dissenting Churches," iii. 504-535.

Stennett, son of Edward Stennett, and his successor in the pastorate of the Seventh-day Baptist Church in Curriers' Hall, as well as the father and grandfather of two equally celebrated ministers of the same denomination. Joseph Stennett, although belonging to a religious body which was assumed to neglect human learning, was one of the greatest scholars who at that time adorned the pulpits of the Free Churches of the metropolis. His acquaintance with Hebrew and historical literature was almost unrivalled. A polished preacher, possessed of an eloquence which flowed so smoothly from his lips that it was compared by his contemporaries to a silver stream which ran along without bush or shore to intercept it,* of winning manners and gentle address, combined with the most inflexible adherence to principle, it is not surprising that he occupied a foremost position. He represented the denomination in all public affairs; he was chosen as the spokesman of the electors of the City of London when, on an important occasion, they wished to make known their wishes to their members, and was selected by the Tory Government as the only man who could influence his denomination in their favour in the political crisis which ensued on the conclusion of the peace with France. On that occasion two peers were deputed to seek an interview with Stennett in order that the London Baptists might be induced to give an expression of their approval of the political conduct of the Government. He was told that, if they would comply, it would secure them not only the esteem of her Majesty, but any favour which they could reasonably expect. Stennett unequivocally refused to use his influence for the desired object; and Dr. Williams, on behalf of the Presbyterians, taking the same course, both were warmly thanked by the leaders of

* Gibbon's "Life of Watts," p. 154.

the Whig party.* Stennett had engaged to write a history of the denomination, but did not live to complete it. John Piggott probably stood next to Stennett in public estimation. He was the founder of the Baptist Church in Little Wild Street, which, under the pastorates of Dr. Joseph and Dr. Samuel Stennett, subsequently became the principal Baptist church in the metropolis. To Dr. John Gale, the pastor of the Barbican Church, who, from his high literary culture, was the intimate associate of the most eminent scholars, the Baptists were indebted for a reply to Wall's "History of Infant Baptism." It is probably to Gale that the subsequent tendency of the General Baptists to Unitarianism is, in part, to be traced. On the subject of the Trinity Gale held opinions which, at least, were "latitudinarian." †

The Baptist Churches of London were now organised into an association, which had been formed in the year 1704. Two subjects especially occupied the early attention of this body, viz., the ordination and the education of members. It was resolved that ordination, either to the office of an elder or a deacon, by imposition of hands, was "an ordinance of Jesus Christ still in force,"‡ and it was earnestly recommended that every church should contribute to a fund for the better education of persons fitted for the ministry. It was the custom of the Baptist ministers in Queen Anne's reign to meet once a month at Deering's Coffee House, in Finch Lane, to consult concerning public measures. The public position of this denomination in the metropolis was, at this period, equal, if not superior, to that of the Congregationalists.

* "Life of Stennett." Wilson's "Dissenting Churches," ii. 595-605. Ivimey's "History," iii. 24-69. Crosby's "History," iv. 319-326.

† Ivimey, iv. 212-215.

‡ Ivimey, iii. 57.

The Quakers, throughout the whole of Queen Anne's reign, actively prosecuted their evangelistic work. Year after year they continued to bear their testimony against the maintenance of religious institutions by physical force. Their resistance to Church-rates excited the Lower House of Convocation to pray for a more speedy method of recovering this impost.* It was seldom, in fact, that it could be recovered in any manner from the Friends, who unhesitatingly went to prison rather than pay what they deemed to be an unrighteous and unscriptural demand. In every "Epistle" written at this period reference is made to their numerous imprisonments on this account. "The chief sufferings," says the Epistle of 1703, "Friends at present remain under are those of tithes, and those called Church-rates; on which accounts five have died prisoners, seventeen have been discharged, and forty-three remain prisoners, since last year's account. And we find the value of what our friends have suffered on these accounts, this last year, amounts unto about £4,200. However, we desire and hope such severities will not weaken the faith of any, nor discourage them from maintaining their Christian testimony in these and all other parts thereof."† The power which was sustained by such methods was plainly stigmatised as the power of "Antichrist,"‡ and the members of the body were exhorted to continue faithful in their "ancient testimony" against it.§ The Society was kept in vigorous life by the missionary spirit of its members. Like George Fox, the preachers of the denomination travelled throughout the length and breadth of the land, and in such a sense, that

* Lathbury's "History of Convocation," p. 384.
† "Yearly Epistles," i. 105.
‡ "Yearly Epistles," p. 127, 1710.
§ Ib. 135, 1713.

the Quakers may be justly described as the founders of the first home missionary organisations.

With respect to their civil and political position, there was an entire absence in all these religious bodies—whether Presbyterian, Congregational, Baptist, or Quaker—of any aggressive spirit. They were thankful if they could retain what they already held. They were, in fact, too profuse in their expressions of gratitude to the Queen for being allowed the very limited toleration which was accorded to them. Every year they waited on her Majesty to thank her for her protection. When Marlborough gained a victory, when peace was made, when the union with Scotland was effected, advantage was taken of the occasion to present additional addresses, in which the same thankfulness was expressed. The Quakers were not behind the other Dissenters, and, to her face, extolled the Queen for her great goodness.* All this time it was well known that Anne, had she dared, would have withdrawn every liberty from Dissenters, and have given her heartiest support to any government which would propose to legislate according to the old Stuart pattern. Every favour which royalty could confer on the Church she had conferred; every act which could propitiate the good-will of the clergy she had carefully set herself to perform. In 1704, at Burnet's suggestion, she relinquished her right to the "First Fruits," thus presenting the clergy, out of her own revenues, with a sum equal to about £17,000 per annum. This sum, denominated "Queen Anne's Bounty," has ever since been applied to the augmentation of the livings of the poorer

* Most of the addresses of this period are in Ivimey and Calamy; the addresses of the Quakers are in Sewell's "History." Dr. Watts, following the prevailing fashion, addressed an eulogistic ode to the Queen, which, however, he afterwards retracted.

clergy. In 1711, in compliance with an address from Convocation, she sent a message to the House of Commons, suggesting the erection of fifty new churches in the metropolis; and, accordingly, in May of that year, the House voted the sum of £370,000 for that purpose.* All her promotions had been of those who were notorious for their High Church zeal, their hatred of Dissent, and their opposition to constitutional government. She could suppress, as in the case of Swift, her most violent personal antipathies in order to reward men who had well served the Tory party. During the whole of her reign Queen Anne never quite gave up the hope of seeing "the Pretender" on the throne of England. She hated even to hear the name of her Hanoverian successor, and, as far as prudence would allow, guided her domestic policy, or allowed it to be guided, in harmony, not with the interests of her country, but with the traditions of her family. Nothing would have pleased her better than to see the Church governed by a second Laud and the State ruled by a second Strafford. But there was one hindrance to the success of such a policy. This was the political power possessed by the Dissenters, and the success which was attending the educational efforts of that body. If the kingdom was to be governed on Tory principles, it was necessary that the corporations should be cleared of all these men, and that they should be deprived of the power of educating the rising generation. Both these steps were resolved upon.

In 1711—the year in which the Church received its grant from Parliament—the Occasional Conformity Bill was again introduced into the legislature. Its avowed object, which was openly stated in the preamble of the measure, was the

* Boyer's "Annals," 1711, p. 374.

better security of the Church of England. It was therefore provided that no person who did not conform to the Church should be capable of holding any civil or military office; that if, after his admission to such an office, any person should be found in a conventicle or in any religious meeting consisting of more than ten persons, other than one conducted according to the rites and ceremonies of the Established Church, he should forfeit the sum of forty pounds, and be disabled for the future from holding any offices. This Bill was supported both by Whigs and Tories. It was the price paid for a coalition. The Whigs could not regain power without the active aid of the Earl of Nottingham, and he would not join them unless they consented to pass the Occasional Conformity Bill.* For this the Dissenters were unscrupulously sacrificed. The Bill was introduced by Nottingham on December 15th, passed without opposition through all its stages in three days, and received the Royal assent on the eighth day after its introduction. All that could be done to prevent its success was done. De Foe inveighed against it; Shower addressed Lord Oxford personally on the subject; application was made to every politician of influence to oppose it; but the bargain had been struck, and, as though they were beneath contempt, the Whigs ignored the services of Dissenters, and the Tories exulted in their disgrace.

Three courses were now open to those Nonconformists who were immediately affected by this measure. They could conform; they could cease to attend the public worship of their own body, and commune sufficiently often to save their places; or they could relinquish their offices, and agitate for a repeal of the law. There is no authentic

* Wilson's "De Foe," iii. 238. Coxe's "Life of Marlborough." Calamy's "Own Life," ii. 243.

record that many adopted the first course. Dr. Williams, as soon as the Act had passed, delivered an address on the duties of Dissenters at this new crisis in their history. With mournful indignation he dwelt on the temper of the Church and the ingratitude of public men; but, in his judgment, there was no alternative but for all who held office to resign their posts.* The third course was advised by De Foe, who counselled Dissenters of all classes to form a federative union, and to act independently of parties and persons. "Alas, poor people!" he cried, "when are ye to open your eyes?" Their supineness excited in him a feeling of angry contempt. "Now is the time for them," he said, "to stand upon their own legs, and be truly independent; they will soon make circumstances récover, and the figure they make differ from anything they ever made before." † This would have been unquestionably the wiser policy, for statesmen are no exception to the rest of mankind in estimating people at the value they put upon themselves. The Dissenters, as a body, chose, however, to take counsel of their prudence by adopting the second line of policy. This was the case with Sir Thomas Abney and Sir John Fryer, aldermen of London, with the mayors of several country corporations, and with justices of the peace, who decided to hold their offices and to cease their attendance at any public place of worship. The conduct of this class is stated to have been decided by the representations of the leaders of the Whig party and the Resident of Brunswick, who pledged their word that, on the death of the Queen, and the accession of the House of Hanover to the throne, the law should be repealed. Sir Thomas Abney, amongst others, ceased attendance at any public

* "An Enquiry into the Duty of Protestant Dissenters." Works, ii., p. 407.

† "Present State of Parties."

place of worship for seven years, Dr. Watts acting during the whole of that time as his private chaplain.* This course met, however, with severest condemnation from some of the Presbyterian ministers, who stigmatised it as a gross dereliction of duty, a desertion of the brethren who continued in public communion, and a virtual condemnation of those who had suffered for the Dissenting interest.†

The Occasional Conformity Act, however, failed, to a great extent, of its principal purpose. It did not materially injure Dissent, and it was necessary, if the schemes of certain politicians were to succeed, that Dissent should not only be weakened, but, if possible, extinguished. Amongst the statesmen of this period there was more than one who had conceived the bold design of destroying the Protestant succession. At the head of these were Francis Atterbury, Bishop of Rochester, and Henry St. John Viscount Bolingbroke, who had been appointed Secretary of State to the last Tory ministry of this reign—a ministry formed of Jacobite materials, and which no sooner entered on office than it began to make arrangements for securing the Pretender's succession to the Crown. While Dissent, in any form, existed it was felt to be impossible to count on the success of this reactional policy. Whoever might turn traitors to the Constitution, it was very well known that the Pretender would find his strongest and most persistent opponents in this party. Bolingbroke therefore resolved to strike at the roots of Dissent. Accordingly, on May 12th, 1714, a Bill, popularly termed the "Schism Bill," was introduced into the House of Commons. By this measure it was provided that no person should keep any public or

* Calamy's "Own Life," ii. 245, 246. Milner's "Life of Watts."
† Williams's "Enquiry." Works, ii. 454.

private school, or teach or instruct, as tutor or schoolmaster, who had not subscribed a declaration to conform to the Established Church, and obtained, from the bishop of the diocese in which he resided, a license to teach. No license was to be granted unless the applicant could produce a certificate that he had received the Sacrament, according to the rites of the Church, for the preceding year. If he taught without such a license he was, on conviction, to be imprisoned without bail.

Sectarian intolerance scarcely ever gave birth to a more scandalous proposal than that of the Schism Bill. While its precise object was to destroy Dissent, and, by destroying it, to bring in the Pretender, its actual effect would have been the extinction of the best means of religious education to be obtained at that time in England. It was a proposal to sacrifice the intelligence and religion of the people at the shrine of the Established Church. Its first blow would, of course, have fallen on the institutions established for the training of ministers. The Presbyterians had academies for this purpose at Hoxton, Taunton, and Shrewsbury; the Congregationalists at Plasterers' Hall, while throughout the country, at Bridgewater, Tiverton, Tewkesbury, Colyton, Carmarthen, Bridgenorth, and other towns, many ministers of the denomination had established private academies for ministerial education. The Baptist institution connected with the Broadmead Church at Bristol, and the Quakers' schools, would also have been extinguished. Besides these, private schools for the middle classes existed in every large town. The rapid increase and success of these institutions had been a source of alarm for many years. They had furnished a stimulus to the zeal of High Churchmen in the matter of Occasional Conformity, for the sight of a Dissenting academy inflamed the passions of men of the Sacheverell order almost to madness. The Established

Church, by the formation of the Society for the Promotion of Christian Knowledge, had done a little to overtake the ignorance of the people; but the Dissenters had, nearly a quarter of a century before, set them the example. The first school for the poor established in England was founded in 1687, in connexion with Nathaniel Vincent's church in Southwark. To the honour of the founders, it was of an unsectarian character. Children, it was stipulated, should be received into it "without distinction of parties, the general good being intended."* In 1714, in the debates on the Bill now under review, Lord Cowper stated that the schools in many country towns were chiefly supported by Dissenters, who educated Churchmen with themselves.† In the charity schools founded by the Christian Knowledge Society, all children were required to be taught the formularies of the Established Church, and to hate the existing government.‡ There was, in fact, a systematic attempt to train the children in the principles of Jacobitism.§ With the Dissenters' schools closed, and all other educational institutions in the hands of the High Church clergy, the

* Toulmin's "History," p. 430. Milner's "Watts," p. 430.

† "Parliamentary History," *in loco.*

‡ Dr. Watts, in his "Essay towards the Encouragement of Charity Schools, particularly among Protestant Dissenters," published in 1728, remarks, "Many others were formed by persons of the Established Church, to which several Dissenters subscribed largely; but at last they found, by sufficient experience, that the children were brought up, in too many of these schools, in principles of disaffection to the present government, in bigoted zeal for the word Church, and with a violent enmity and malicious spirit of persecution against all whom they were taught to call Presbyterians, though from many of their hands they received their bread and clothing. It was time then for the Dissenters to withdraw that charity which was so much abused." Works, i., p. 527.

§ This was animadverted upon with great severity by Wake, Archbishop of Canterbury, in 1716, and also by Gibson, Bishop of London.

re-establishment of the Stuart dynasty would have been a matter of comparative ease.

The introduction of this Bill excited the gravest alarm, and the Dissenters at once took active measures to prevent its being passed. Statements were written and circulated amongst members of both Houses of the legislature; Calamy addressed the bishops in a series of pungent queries; and meetings were held from day to day in the City, the Temple, and at Westminster, to concert measures of opposition; * but no time was given for agitation. The Bill was carried in the Commons, after hot debates, by two hundred and thirty-seven to one hundred and twenty-six votes, and was read three times in one day. In the Upper House, Lord Cowper, Lord Halifax, and Lord Wharton led a vigorous and almost successful opposition to it. The argument used in its favour was that it was necessary for the security of the Church. "Dissenters," said the Bishop of London, "have made the Bill necessary by their endeavours to propagate their schism, and to draw their children to their schools and academies." Lord Wharton appears to have made the ablest speech against it. He remarked that such a measure was but an indifferent return for the benefit the public had received from these schools, in which the greatest men had been educated—men who had made a glorious peace for England, who had paid the debts of the nation, and who had extended its commerce.† Three divisions were taken on the Bill. In the first it was carried by fifty-nine to fifty-four votes; in the second by fifty-seven to fifty-one; and in the third and final struggle, when both parties brought their whole forces together, by seventy-seven to seventy-two.‡

The Queen had, from the first, given the Schism Bill her heartiest encouragement. She signed it on the 25th of June.

---

* Calamy's "Own Life," ii. 282—285.

† Calamy, ii. 287. ‡ "Parliamentary History."

On Sunday, the 1st of August, it was to have been put in operation. On the morning of that day Thomas Bradbury, the Congregational minister of Fetter Lane, was walking through Smithfield, when he met Bishop Burnet. Burnet called to him from his carriage, and inquired why he seemed so troubled? "I am thinking," replied Bradbury, "whether I shall have the constancy and resolution of that noble company of martyrs whose ashes are deposited in this place; for I most assuredly expect to see similar times of violence and persecution, and that I shall be called to suffer in a like cause." The bishop, endeavouring to calm him, informed Bradbury that the Queen had been given over by her physicians, and was expected every hour to die, and that he himself was then on his way to Court. He offered to send a messenger to Bradbury to give him the earliest intelligence of the Queen's death, and arranged that, if the messenger should find that minister in his pulpit, he should go into the gallery of Fetter Lane Chapel, and drop a handkerchief. The Queen died on the same morning; and while Bradbury was preaching the messenger arrived, and dropped his handkerchief from the front gallery. The preacher made no reference to the event in his sermon, but in the succeeding prayer he offered public thanks for the delivery of the nation, and implored the Divine blessing on King George I. and the House of Hanover. He then asked the congregation to sing the eighty-ninth Psalm. It is reported that, shortly after, Bradbury preached from the text, "Go, see now this cursed woman, and bury her; for she is a king's daughter." He often, in after life, made reference to the fact that the first public proclamation of the accession of the House of Hanover to the throne was made from the pulpit of the Congregational Church in Fetter Lane.*

* Wilson's "Dissenting Churches," iii., p. 513.

With the decease of Anne the Schism Act became a dead letter. No attempt was made to enforce it. The High Church party had lost their chief strength, and the last law for the limitation of religious liberty in England had been passed. Through the fiat of the Almighty, the legacy which the revolutionary King and his statesmen had left to the country was preserved nearly intact. Henceforward, the struggle was to be, not for the preservation, but for the extension of freedom.

Almost simultaneously with the death of the Queen, three men who had devoted their great abilities to the cause of a free and constitutional government, also vanished from the page of ecclesiastical history. Tenison and Burnet lived barely long enough to see George I. ascend the throne. They both died full of years, and every generation which has succeeded them has cast its chaplet of honour on their tombs. De Foe, at the same period, relinquished his political labours. Curiously enough, De Foe was almost as much hated by the Whigs as by the Tories and Jacobites. The cause of this was his opposition to their foreign policy, and his exposure of their desertion of the Dissenters; or rather, as he stigmatized it, "the barbarity" of their treatment. The members of his own ecclesiastical party were scarcely less displeased with him for his bold rebukes of their timidity and of their continued adhesion to the men who had betrayed them. In a strain of mournful eloquence he wrote, in one of the last numbers of his "Review:" "And now I live under universal contempt, which contempt I have learned to contemn, and have an uninterrupted joy in my soul; not at being contemned, but that no crime can be laid to my charge to make that contempt my due." Of the Dissenters themselves and his relation to them, he wrote at the same time, "It is impossible for the Dissenters in this nation to provoke me to be an enemy to their interests. . . . . . Not that I am insensible of being ill-treated by them, or that I make any court to their persons. When any party of men have not a clear view of their own interests, he that will serve them, and knows the way to do it, must be certain not to please them, and must be able to see them revile and reproach him, and use him in the worst manner imaginable, without being moved. I remember the time when the same people treated me in the same manner upon the book called 'The Shortest Way,' and nothing but suffering from them would ever open their eyes. He that cleared up my integrity then, can do it again by the same method, and I leave it to Him."* De Foe warned Dissenters again of the folly of looking to politicians for their liberties, instead of to themselves and their own exertions. In a subsequent "Appeal to Honour and Justice," he reviewed his own political life from the time when, thirty years before, he had joined the standard of the Duke of Monmouth, and had cautioned Dissenters not to listen to the promises of James. This vindication is written with an affecting earnestness, which shows how much the author felt the reproaches of his friends. His life, he said, had been one of "sorrow and fatigue;" but he was desirous that his children should not be disturbed in the inheritance of their father's character. This was one of the last of De Foe's political publications. The "Review" was discontinued in the place where it had begun—in Newgate—where a second imprisonment for a second political "libel" was awarded to him. The remainder of his life, as all know, was devoted to writing works on political economy and on education, and to that marvellous series of fictions of which "Robinson Crusoe" was the forerunner. It is scarcely surprising that

* Wilson's "Life of De Foe," iii. pp 294, 295.

the Dissenters of his own day did not understand such a man. De Foe lived many generations before his time. The character of his mind and work belongs more to the nineteenth than to the seventeenth century. He was too inventive and enterprising; too original and bold; too broad; too political, and too versatile for men of "the Old Dissent." They never, therefore, understood him. And now, happily, he could lay down his political work, for religious liberty was to become a watchword given from a King's mouth.

CHAPTER V.

FROM THE SCHISM ACT TO THE ORGANISATION OF THE DISSENTING DEPUTIES.—A.D. 1714 TO A.D. 1732.

THE history of the Free Churches of England during the reign of George I. is associated with that decline in religion which immediately preceded the rise of Methodism. It commenced with a popular outbreak against the Government and the Dissenters. George was a Lutheran in religion, but on coming to the throne he expressed his firm purpose to maintain the Churches of England and Scotland as by law established. At the same time he remarked that, in his opinion, this could be effectually done without impairing the toleration, which was so agreeable to Christian charity, allowed by law to Protestant Dissenters.* The Three Denominations, in common with others, presented an address on the occasion. Nearly one hundred ministers, all clad in their black Genevan cloaks, were present. "What have we here?" asked a nobleman—"a funeral?" On which Bradbury replied: "No, my lord! a resurrection." † Dr. Daniel Williams, for the last time in his life, headed the deputation. Their address was excusably egotistic. They referred to their adherence, against al temptations and dangers, to the Revolutionary Settlement

* "Parliamentary History."
† "Monthly Repository," 1820, p. 316.

"Our zeal," they went on to state, "has been proved to be very conspicuous by those noble patriots who now surround your throne." They expressed their determination to uphold the government against all pretenders whatsoever, and thanked the King for his declaration in their favour. The King expressed his pleasure at receiving the address, and assured the ministers that they might depend on his protection.* The coronation of George was accompanied by tumults, riots, and murders, in several towns. In 1715 the Pretender was proclaimed as King James III. The cries of the "Church in Danger," "High Church and Sacheverell," and "No Presbyterianism," were now again heard. The Pretender's adherents, as though the question at issue were one of Church and Dissent—as, indeed, to some extent, it was—began at once to demolish the meeting-houses. At Oxford—then, as now, the head-quarters of High-Churchism—the places of worship belonging to the Presbyterians, Baptists, and Quakers were destroyed; the Baptist chapel at Wrexham, the Presbyterian church at Nuneaton, several churches in the county of Stafford and in other parts of England, shared the same fate.† The whole of the Dissenters, during this rebellion, rallied round the Hanoverian dynasty. At Newcastle-on-Tyne a corps of seven hundred keelmen, mostly Dissenters, were embodied for defence.‡ At Chowbent, in Lancashire, the Dissenting minister, Mr. Wood, rallied together four hundred Dissenters, armed and equipped at his own expense, and took them to join the standard at Preston—an act of loyalty which, owing to the penalties imposed by the Occasional Conformity Act, was obliged to be condoned by a special Act of

* Calamy's "Own Life," ii., pp. 299-300.

† Ivimey, iii. 121, Gough's "History of the Quakers," iv. 165.

‡ Belsham's "History of Great Britain," iii., p. 36.

Parliament.* The Dissenters, as soon as this rebellion had been quelled, waited on the King, the spokesman being, for the first time, a member of the Baptist denomination, Mr. Nathaniel Hodges.† They referred at length, in their address, to the treatment they had received, adding, with truth, that whenever there had been a design to introduce Popery and arbitrary power in England, the Protestant Dissenters had generally been the first to be attacked. The King, in reply, expressed his concern at the "unchristian and barbarous treatment" which they had received, and promised compensation.

For the first time in the history of the Free Churches an endeavour was now made to obtain an exact return of their number and distribution. This was effected, after great labour, by Daniel Neal, than whom no man, whether in respect to ability or to honesty, was more competent for such a task. Neal gives the total number of the Free Churches in England and Wales, in the years 1715 and 1716, at 1,150; but these only include Independents and Baptists, 247 only belonging to the latter. Middlesex, of course, stands first in the list; then, in succession, Devon, Dorset, Somerset, Kent, Gloucester, Yorkshire, Lancashire, Northampton, Suffolk, &c. But there is evidence that his list is imperfect. Neal states that there were no Baptist churches in Yorkshire at this period; but it is certain that Mitchell and Crossley had founded, before this, more than

* George I. c. 39. The losses of Dissenters on this occasion were represented to the House of Commons, and two years afterwards, but with great difficulty, the sum of five thousand pounds was obtained in reparation.

† Crosby, iv. 126. This circumstance gave occasion to a writer in the "Weekly Journal" to ridicule the "mean occupations" of "that dipping set of people." Hodges was afterwards knighted, and was, I think, the first Baptist who received that honour.

four in the two counties of Yorkshire and Lancashire.* The Quakers also are evidently omitted from the whole list, and in Yorkshire alone they had founded, before this period, eighty permanent churches.† If we assume Neal's list to be absolutely correct, then more than half of the churches for which licenses had been taken out between 1688 and 1710 were extinct in 1715. Taking the list as it stands, it is curious to observe the numerical relations of the different orders of Free Churches. All but one of the twenty-three Free Churches of Bedfordshire were Baptist—the fruits of Bunyan's labours; but there was not, apparently, a single Baptist church in Cornwall, Durham, Northumberland, or Westmoreland. The position of this denomination in the agricultural counties of Dorset, Hereford, Huntingdon, Lincoln, Monmouth, Sussex, Suffolk, and Wiltshire was almost equally low. In Suffolk, indeed, there was no Baptist church whatever. The list indicates a predominance of Baptist over Congregational churches in the metropolis, but takes no account of the fifty odd Presbyterian places of worship in London. On the whole, however, Neal's list, while it does not support the conclusion that Dissenters were, at that time, a majority in the kingdom, shows the great power of the voluntary principle in religion; for, as the result of little more than thirty years' toleration, and under the greatest discouragements, more than fifteen hundred places of worship had been opened and kept open.

The Quakers were the first to take advantage of the new spirit in the conduct of public affairs. By the Act of William the Third they had been allowed to make an affirmation instead of an oath. This Act was, however,

* I am aware that no existing Baptist church in Yorkshire can trace its origin to this date, and it is therefore possible that Mitchell and Crossley's labours were ultimately fruitless.

† Parl. Paper 156, September, 1853.

limited to a term of years; and as this term was about to expire, a Bill was easily passed through Parliament extending the right in perpetuity.*

It now remained to be seen whether the Whig party would redeem their promises, and several writers began to remind them of their engagements. In 1715 appeared the first claim, from the new government, for a full toleration. This was made in a pamphlet entitled "The Case of the Protestant Dissenters in England fairly stated," the author of which reviewed the history of the Test and Corporation, the Occasional Conformity, and the Schism Acts, and demanded their repeal as well in the interests of the House of Hanover as of the Dissenters themselves.† The next year Calamy wrote in favour of the repeal of the Occasional Conformity Act. With his habitual caution he asked merely for the repeal of the law which bore most harshly on Presbyterians. Others at once followed his example. At the commencement of 1717 the agitation took a shape as systematic in form as it was formidable in character. Some members of the House of Commons, indignant at the injustice which had been done to Dissenters, and at the delay which had taken place in fulfilling the promises made to them, after some conference summoned a meeting on the 20th March, which was attended by more than two hundred members, at the Rose Tavern, Temple Bar, to consider the subject. This large and influential assembly was addressed by Lord Molesworth, Sir Richard Steele, and Mr. Jessop, who remarked that the Dissenters suffered from their disabilities solely in consequence of their zeal for the Protestant succession, and urged that such friends of the Government should be placed in a position to serve them. At a subsequent meeting, it was authoritatively stated that

* Sewell's "History," ii. 469.

† Calamy, ii. 344.

the obstacles to the introduction of a Bill were now removed, and it was therefore resolved to prepare a measure for a full relief of Dissenters.*

Hoadly, who had now been promoted to the bishopric of Bangor, threw the weight of his powerful intellect into the same scale. In a sermon on the "Nature of the Kingdom or Church of Christ," preached before the King on the 31st March, 1717, he attacked the laws which limited the civil rights of any classes of Christians. The Church of Christ, he maintained, could not be protected or encouraged by human laws and penalties. Six months afterwards the King, in a passage of his speech on opening Parliament, indicated the state of his own feelings by adopting William the Third's customary language almost word for word. "I could heartily wish," he said, "that at a time when the common enemies of our religion are, by all manner of artifices, endeavouring to undermine and weaken it both at home and abroad, all those who are friends to our present happy Establishment might unanimously concur in some proper method for the further strengthening the Protestant interest, of which as the Church of England is the great bulwark, so will she reap the principal benefit of every advantage accruing by the union and mutual charity of all Protestants." This significant language, coupled with the address of the House of Lords in reply which echoed the King's sentiments in his own words, indicated that, in the judgment of the Crown and its ministers, the time had arrived when all the disabilities of the Dissenters might be removed.

Protected by a powerful party in Parliament, and with the certainty of success attending their efforts, the Dissenters now boldly took the field. Meetings were held all over the

* Tindal's "Continuation," vii. 96, 97. Fifth Edition.

country,* and on December 13th, 1718, Earl Stanhope, who had become principal Secretary of State, brought in a Bill for "strengthening the Protestant interest" by a repeal of portions of the Occasional Conformity Act, of the Schism Act, and of some clauses in the Test and Corporation Acts. His lordship, in moving the second reading of the Bill, enlarged on the equity, reasonableness, and advantage of restoring Dissenters to their natural rights, and on the probable effects of such a measure, which, he said, would strengthen the Protestant interest, and be of advantage to the Established Church. The end, in his judgment, would be that the Archbishop of Canterbury would become the patriarch of all the Protestant clergy. The authors and supporters of the penal Acts fought for their preservation with all the tenacity of a parent fighting for the lives of his offspring—one of their arguments being that to repeal them would be to break the articles of union with Scotland. No man was more vehement in his opposition than the old Earl of Nottingham, who, in William the Third's reign, had, by his own influence, prevented the repeal of the Test and Corporation laws, and who was himself the author of the Occasional Conformity Act. The debate was adjourned for five days. On the 18th December the Bill was read a second time without opposition, but on the motion for going into committee, Lord Nottingham again protested. No bishop had yet spoken upon it, and accordingly an appeal was made to the episcopal body for an expression of their opinions. Wake, Archbishop of Canterbury, the successor of Tenison and the opponent of Atterbury, at once responded by intimating that he should vote against the measure. In his judgment, also, the Acts proposed to be repealed "were the main bulwarks and supporters of the Established Church." Dawes, Arch-

* Tindal's "Continuation," vii. 224.

bishop of York, took the same side. Next rose Hoadly, who, in a speech which contained an eloquent statement of the principles of Christian liberty, said that if Dissenters were ever to be drawn over to the Church it must be by "gentle means." All religious tests, he affirmed, were an abridgment of the natural rights of men, an injury to the State, and a scandal to religion. An endeavour was made by Smalridge, Bishop of Bristol, to break the force of Hoadly's speech, but he was ably replied to by Willis, Bishop of Gloucester, and Gibson, Bishop of Lincoln. The Earl of Nottingham again warned the House that Dissenters were "an obstinate set of people, never to be satisfied." Atterbury dwelt on the hardships which Dissenters were bringing on the Church. Next to Hoadly's, however, the speech of the debate was White Kennet's, Bishop of Peterborough, who said that it was the promotion, by the clergy, of arbitrary measures and persecutions which, in Charles the First's reign, had brought contempt upon themselves and ruin on the Church and State. In ridicule of the cry of "Church in danger!" he said that, while raised for sinister designs, it merely made "a mighty noise in the mouths of silly women and children." The debate was adjourned to the 19th December. Twenty speakers, on this occasion, recapitulated the old arguments, and the Bill was then put to the vote, when it was declared to be carried by eighty-six to sixty-eight. The next day, on going through committee, the clauses relating to the Test and Corporation Acts were withdrawn, and the Bill passed the third reading by fifty-five to thirty-three. It was brought into the Commons on December 24th, and on 7th January in the next year was debated for eight hours and a half.* On a division

* Owing, it is said, to the exclusion of all strangers excepting the Prince of Wales and some peers, no report of this debate is in existence.

the Bill was carried by two hundred and forty-three to two hundred and two. It was attempted to introduce a clause the object of which was to exclude Unitarians from the benefit of the Act, but the amendment to this effect was negatived, and the Bill finally passed through committee by two hundred and twenty-one to one hundred and seventy votes.*

If the world had not had some previous experience of the inconstancy of public opinion, and the influence exercised on the fortunes of public measures by a knowledge of the views which are popular with Courts, there might be some astonishment at the contrast afforded by the divisions on this measure with those on the two Acts which it repealed. But, with the accession of George, and the increasing security of his government, the Church and Tory party exchanged a contest for perpetual supremacy for a struggle for existence. They had seen some of their most eminent members beheaded for rebellion; Oxford, the favourite minister of Anne, was in the Tower awaiting his impeachment for high treason; and Atterbury, their episcopal leader, was about to be indicted for the same offence. The opinion of the English people was slowly deciding in favour of a constitutional government, which meant, in George the First's mind, equal liberties for all, and no distinction whatever between Churchmen and Dissenters.

It appears to have been owing, in some measure, to the want of firmness in Dissenters themselves that they did not, at this time, obtain the repeal of the Test and Corporation Acts. The King was known to be in its favour, but is reported to have observed to Lord Barrington, who was considered to represent the public interests of Dissenters, that he was assured by his ministers that this point could

* "Parliamentary History," vii. 567, 590.

not be carried, and he was persuaded that the Dissenters would not insist on an act which might be prejudicial to himself.* The authority for this statement was Lord Sunderland, who had informed the King that to attempt a repeal of the Test Acts would ruin the whole Bill. At the same time assurances were given that it should soon be repealed. The Dissenters, in fact, were sacrificed, as had been the case in former periods of their history, to what was said to be the general good of the nation. As on previous occasions, they cheerfully accepted their position; and, as on previous occasions, the promises made to them were forgotten almost as soon as they were made. But they do not seem to have inquired why they, and they only, were perpetually sacrificed ostensibly for national, but often for mere party, purposes. In George the First's case there was, undoubtedly, some excuse for their willing resignation of claims which had long been recognised as both appropriate and just. The King was known to entertain a high respect for them, and a warm appreciation of their past services. His sincerity could not for a moment be doubted; and when he made the withdrawal of their claims a matter of personal favour to himself, it would have been difficult, and apparently ungracious, to refuse it. And they could hardly have suspected that, by the course they then took, they were fastening the Test and Corporation Acts on the necks of their descendants to the third and fourth generations.

The human mind seldom or never becomes enlarged in one direction only. Growth in respect to the laws of civil polity is sure to be accompanied by a similar growth in respect to the laws of ecclesiastical polity. Sacerdotalism in religion and Absolutism in politics, have generally risen and fallen together. While, therefore, the principles of

---

* Belsham's "Great Britain," iii. 132.

toleration were receiving a practical recognition from the Government, the exorbitant claims of the Church and its clergy were being dealt with in an equally effective manner. The sermon of Bishop Hoadly, already briefly referred to, on the "Nature of the Kingdom or Church of Christ," soon attracted the attention of the Lower House of Convocation. It could scarcely, indeed, in any age, have passed without criticism, for its sentiments were opposed to all the doctrines relating to the mutual relations of the Church and the State on which the ecclesiastical government of England is founded. Taking as his text the significant declaration of the Saviour, that His kingdom was not of this world, Hoadly proceeded to show that the Church of Christ was a kingdom of which only He himself was King. He was the sole Lawgiver to His subjects; He had left behind Him no visible human authority; no vicegerents who could supply His place; no interpretations upon which His subjects were absolutely to depend, and no judges over the consciences or the religion of His people. If any pretended to possess such an authority they usurped Christ's office, or ruled in their own kingdom, and not in His. If an angel from heaven were to give an account of His kingdom contrary to what Christ Himself had given, it ought, added the Bishop, to have neither weight nor authority with Christians.

Whether Hoadly, in laying down such broad principles relating to the spirituality of the kingdom of Christ, saw to what extent those principles would apply, may be doubted. His audience, probably, understood him to be preaching a sermon against the Test and Corporation Laws, and the claims of the High Church party; but the language of the bishop—who knew the full and exact value of words—had, obviously, a far broader reach than this. Is it possible that, at this time, Hoadly, flushed with the prosperity of the liberal party, and the decline of High Churchism, had sketched for himself the career of a second Cranmer, and that he preached this sermon as a tentative step in the direction of the further reformation of the English Church? He, unquestionably, had a full and clear conception of the gross inconsistency of a church which claimed to be Christian, being patronised, supported, and controlled by the State. He saw the totally unscriptural character of what was known as "Church authority," and recognised the fact that human law has no right to limit the claims of the individual conscience. If, at any time, he had indulged in the great project of purifying the Church by separating it from all which separated it, in character, from the kingdom of Christ, he abandoned it. In the worry of personal controversies, and the succession of elevation after elevation upon the episcopal bench, the Bishop of Bangor, if he ever felt it, lost the zeal of a Church reformer. He continued, throughout his life, the dreaded opponent of all who, whether in civil or ecclesiastical politics, or in theology, were disposed to advance the pretensions of collective authority in preference to individual right, and in this sense he reformed the Church of England; but he took no steps to carry into execution the precise reform sketched in his celebrated sermon. What he did was to break the neck of Church power.* In less than a month from the publication of the Bishop's sermon, the Lower House of Convocation accordingly made a representation concerning it to the Upper House. They connected with the sermon another publication of Hoadly's, entitled "A

* I have read no more, and perhaps less, than some other writers have read of the "Bangorian Controversy." It extends certainly beyond a hundred pamphlets, and any one who would thoroughly digest these would do a great service to ecclesiastical literature. I do not think that the practical influence of the controversy, in the direction indicated in the text, has ever been sufficiently recognised.

Preservative against the Principles and Practices of the Non-jurors both in Church and State," in which he had attacked, at the same time, the sacerdotal claims of the priesthood and the doctrines of the Jacobites. They complained that Hoadly appeared to deny the authority of the Church to judge, censure, or punish offenders in the affairs of conscience and eternal salvation, and to affirm that all such exercises of authority had been an invasion and an usurpation upon Christ's kingdom. If, said the Lower House, these doctrines be admitted, "there is evidently an end of all church authority to oblige any to external communion, and of all power that one man can have over another in matters of religion." They charged Hoadly with undermining the constitution of the Church and impeaching the supremacy of the King, and besought the Upper House to "vindicate the honour of God and religion," and to "assert the prerogative given to all godly princes in Holy Scripture." The Upper House had, however, no opportunity of replying to the representation. Convocation was immediately prorogued, and no further license was given to it to proceed with synodical business. The extravagant pretensions which it had put forward, and the mischievous character of its proceedings, had become offensive to the State. So rapid had been the growth of the minds of men that Jacobitism was already an anachronism in the constitution, and Convocation was dumb for a hundred and fifty years.

There was no class in England which did not feel relief from the final removal of the weights which had been placed on the free movement of human thought. In no direction was this more visible than in theology. Men everywhere felt that they were at liberty to think for themselves. The natural and immediate result of this feeling was latitudinarianism. To this movement, as natural as it was inevitable, is to be attributed the apparently sudden growth, at this period, of Unitarianism in England. Hitherto, the distinguishing doctrines of the Unitarians, although they had been actively propagated, had not, as far as can be seen, greatly influenced the religious opinions of the people. But there were many men, eminent either for great power of thought or for an enlarged benevolence, who had become more or less imbued with the spirit of Unitarian theology. The philosophy of one age is generally the theology of the next. Locke had made the philosophy of the then living generation, and its tendency was in favour of the Arian form of Unitarianism. He was accordingly denounced by the orthodox, and claimed by the Unitarians themselves. The defenders of the received belief lost themselves in a maze of metaphysical subtleties, and seldom did more than give an advantage to their opponents. In his "Reasonableness of Christianity," Locke again offended, and was again denounced, Watts, charitable as he was, accusing him of darkening the glory of the Gospel and debasing Christianity.* Locke himself, however, in a vindication, denied that there was one word of Socinianism in his work. Whatever he may have thought, he did not, either by act or word, formally identify himself with Unitarianism, but the general influence of his writings was unquestionably in its favour. If Sir Isaac Newton, as has been claimed, was also an Unitarian, he had not the moral courage to state the fact in his lifetime.† In the Established Church the elements of this doctrine could be very distinctly traced. Men who had subscribed the

* All that can be said in favour of Locke's Unitarianism has been said by Mr. Wallace, in his "Anti-trinitarian Biography," Vol. iii. Art. Locke. It is one of the questions on which there must always be some difference of opinion.

† Wallace, iii. Art. Newton.

Thirty-nine Articles, who used the Book of Common Prayer, and who repeated the Athanasian Creed, did not hesitate to express their disbelief in the Trinity, while Unitarians were charged with cowardice and with dishonesty; * but at present they did not choose to reveal themselves. When, however, a divine such as Dr. Samuel Clarke did not hesitate to argue in favour of the inferiority of the second person of the Trinity, and to defend his continuance in the Established Church by laying down, as a rule of subscription, that any person might reasonably subscribe to any formularies or confessions whenever he could, in any sense at all, reconcile them with Scripture,† inferior men need scarcely have hesitated to take, openly, the same ground. It must, however, be said that there had been plain warnings of the dangers of such a confession of faith. William Whiston, Professor of Mathematics in Cambridge University, had embraced Arianism, and was expelled the University and censured by Convocation. Samuel Clarke incurred the same censure; and although such acts were not now followed by any civil punishments, they placed a man under the ban of a large and influential section of society. In the days of which we write it was certainly more profitable, so far as this world was concerned, for a man to live in open violation of the whole of the moral law than for him to deny the truth of the Athanasian Creed. A large proportion of the clergy did the former, and held their benefices without hindrance or opprobrium. Convocation did not dream of censuring them; but if a Whiston, a Clarke, or a Hoadly—men of unstained life and transparently honest nature—gave to an old truth a new

* Edwards's "Socinian Creed," p. 185. 1697.

† Clarke's "Scripture Doctrine of the Trinity," Perry's History, iii. 305.

form, or departed from the lines laid down by law on which the thoughts of the Established clergy were to travel, a hoot of execration arose against him. Some excuse, therefore, although no justification, can be found for those persons who held the Unitarian creed remaining in the Church. One thing, at least, they lacked, without which an unpopular opinion has little prospect of becoming popular—a fearless courage. They loved their creed sufficiently to advocate it in private, but they loved their benefices more.

Of open and avowed Unitarians the most conspicuous was Thomas Emlyn, a man of devout temperament and considerable ability, who had been virtually excommunicated from the Presbyterian communion. Emlyn had been educated in Doolittle's academy, and had been pastor of a small Dissenting congregation at Lowestoft. He ascribed his change of views on the subject of the Trinity to reading Sherlock and Howe's defence of that doctrine, which, he considered, tended only to polytheism. Afterwards he went to Dublin to take the pastorate of the church formerly presided over by Dr. Daniel Williams. He did not, however, announce his change of views, which was privately discovered by a member of his congregation. He then said that if such views were obnoxious to his congregation he would immediately resign. The Dublin ministers, however, met before this resignation could be arranged, and agreed that he should not be allowed to preach again. His congregation thought it desirable that there should be only a temporary cessation of his ministry. The ministers, however, decided that he should preach neither in Ireland nor in England during the interval—an assumption of authority which Emlyn boldly refused to recognise. Two messengers—one a Presbyterian, the other a Congregationalist—were forthwith despatched to London to warn the ministers of those denominations of Emlyn's heterodoxy, and of their decision respecting him. He now published a statement of his belief. On his return to Dublin, soon after this, in February, 1702, at the instance of a Baptist of the name of Caleb Thomas, he was arrested for writing against the Trinity, tried, found guilty, sentenced to pay a fine of a thousand pounds, and to lie in gaol until the fine was paid, the Chief Justice telling him that the pillory was his due, and that if he had been in Spain or Portugal he would have been burned. The fine was subsequently reduced,* and Emlyn came to reside in England, where he lived on terms of friendship with Whiston and Clarke.†

Amongst Dissenters Unitarianism had also made some progress. It is probable that the Baptists had never been entirely free from this taint. It is not possible, however, to trace the existence of Unitarianism amongst the General Baptists to their theological creed. Arminianism does not

---

* The Archbishop of Armagh, as Queen's Almoner, claimed a shilling in the pound on this fine, and refused to take it on the reduced amount. "I thought," writes Emlyn, "that the Church was to be as merciful as the State; but I was mistaken herein."

† Wallace, "Anti-Trinitarian Biography," iii. Art. "Emlyn." This persecution called forth a sarcastic rebuke from Hoadly, who, in a preface to Steele's "Account of the State of the Roman Catholic Religion throughout the World," published in 1717, wrote, "Sometimes we of the Established Church can manage a prosecution (for I must not call it persecution) ourselves without calling in any other help. But I must do the Dissenting Protestants the justice to say, that they have shown themselves, upon occasion, very ready to assist us in so pious and Christian a work as bringing heretics to their right mind; being themselves but very lately come from experiencing the convincing and enlightening faculty of a dungeon or a fine. . . . . The Nonconformists accused him (Emlyn), the Conformists condemned him, the secular power was called in, and the cause ended in an imprisonment and a very great fine: two methods of conviction about which the Gospel is silent."

necessarily or naturally lead to either the Arian or the Socinian form of Unitarian doctrine. The connection of this body with Unitarianism was accidental, and may be traced, in the first instance, to the existence of the Dutch Anabaptists, and, in the second instance—as is the case with all creeds—to the personal influence and the writings of one or two men of unusual mental and moral power. Such a man was Dr. John Gale. Neither the Particular Baptists nor the Congregationalists evinced any tendency towards anti-Trinitarian opinions. Both these bodies professed a higher order of Calvinism than any other Nonconformist communions; but that Calvinism is, in itself, no effectual protection against the inroads of Unitarianism has been sufficiently proved by the experiences of New England and Geneva. Why these two denominations should have been free from the tendency which was affecting all other bodies may partly be explained by the fact that, with the exception of Watts, neither of them contained a man of eminently speculative mind; and Watts himself, when, after this period, he became involved in the vortex of this discussion, no sooner touched it than he also fell from the orthodox standard. The Presbyterians, however, shared equally with, if not to a greater extent than, the General Baptists, the characteristic tendency of theological thought. They were men, for the most part, of larger reading than other Nonconformists, and the writings of Whiston and Clarke had found their way amongst them.

While this movement of thought was taking place a circumstance occurred which gave to it a sudden impulse, as well as a wide, if a factitious, popularity. There were in the city of Exeter four Presbyterian churches. Amongst the ministers of these churches there was one—James Peirce, formerly a member of Matthew Mead's congregation—who was suspected of holding anti-Trinitarian views. Peirce had already made himself well known and highly respected by the Dissenters of England for his vigorous and able defences of Nonconformity against the attacks of two clergymen of the Established Church—Snape and Nichols. The most elaborate of these defences was written in Latin, for circulation amongst the Protestant Churches of Europe.* In this work Peirce compared the constitution of the Established Church, its forms and ceremonies, its ritual, and the origin and administration of its revenues with the practices which prevailed in the early ages of Christianity. This work became, in a brief period, the most popular defence of Nonconformity, and was one of two subsequently recommended by Doddridge for the education of Dissenters.

Peirce is described by Calamy, who had no sympathy with his doctrines, as a minister of good repute, and courted and beloved by his people.† He appears also to have been a man of great reading, honest judgment, and of an eminently candid mind and Christian spirit. Although he held the anti-Trinitarian doctrine, he did not think it necessary to preach it; but, for consistency's sake, he omitted from his services all phrases which implied the divinity of the three persons of the Trinity. A brother minister, however, in the course of a private conversation, finding that Peirce did not hold the orthodox view, repeated the conversation to another minister, Mr. Lavington, of Exeter, who, in his turn, felt it to be his duty to proclaim that fact amongst the people. All Exeter soon rang with

* "A Vindication of the Dissenters: In answer to Dr. William Nichols' Defence of the Doctrine and Discipline of the Church of England, &c." By James Peirce. 1718.

† Calamy's "Own Life," ii., pp. 403—405.

the information. In Peirce's own pulpit, during his temporary absence from the city, another minister charged some of the Dissenters of Exeter with "damnable heresies, denying the Lord that bought them." Peirce was then requested by three members of his congregation to preach a sermon on the nature of the satisfaction of Christ, which he did, and it appears to have pleased the majority of the people. Charges of heterodoxy, however, are not quickly abandoned, and when it was found that Peirce did not stand alone in his views, the Committee of Dissenters who, by a local arrangement, were charged with the management of the temporal affairs of the four Exeter churches, and in whom the property was vested, resolved to take up the matter. They accordingly appointed a deputation to wait upon each of the ministers, with the request that they should assert the eternity of the Son of God. Peirce could have no objection to do this, and therefore replied that he would say anything which was to be found in the Scriptures, but nothing beyond. Most of the people were now satisfied. Meantime the question was carried to London, and brought back in enlarged dimensions. At a conference of Western ministers it was proposed that another clearance should be made by another test, and this was carried by a large majority. Each minister at once declared what he believed on this subject in his own words. Peirce's declaration was, "I am not of the opinion of Sabellius, Arius, Socinus, or Sherlock. I believe there is but one God, and can be no more; I believe the Son and Holy Ghost to be Divine persons, but subordinate to the Father; and the unity of God is, I think, to be resolved into the Father's being the fountain of the divinity of the Son and Spirit." Some ministers denied the right of any body of men to demand their opinions, and refused to make any declaration. The official record of the result was, "It is the general sense of the assembly that there is but one living and true God, and that Father, Son, and Holy Ghost are the one God," "which," says Peirce, "was the sense of about two to one of the assembly." Official proceedings and records of this character have not been celebrated for settling private opinions or for quieting public controversies; and the result of the deliberations of the Western ministers was no exception to the usual rule. From this time scarcely any question was debated throughout the West of England but that of the Trinity. It was discussed in families, preached about from pulpits, written about in pamphlets, and the local journals teemed with intelligence of what was being said and done. In this condition the Exeter Committee again addressed themselves to the ministers for another declaration of their real opinions. This, however, did not satisfy the people, and it was resolved to make an appeal to London for advice.

The London ministers had already been informed of the nature and progress of this controversy. Those who obeyed the summons addressed to them by their brethren, more than a hundred and fifty in number, met, therefore, fully prepared to discuss it. But some of the most eminent of the ministers declined to have anything to do with the matter. They rightly judged that it could only end in divisions amongst themselves, and they also doubted their competency, as Dissenters, to form a court for the adjudication of such a question. Amongst those who refused to meet were Calamy, Watts, and Neal—certainly the three most eminent men belonging to the Presbyterian and Congregational denominations. The wisdom of their course was made apparent almost as soon as the assembly met. The meeting was summoned at Salters' Hall, on February 19th, 1719, and it was the general opinion that a letter of advice should be drawn up and forwarded to the

16*

brethren at Exeter. Bradbury then proposed, with the unanimous consent of the Congregational ministers, and, after hot and angry debates, it was pressed to a division, that every minister then present should, as a witness to his own faith, subscribe the first Article of the Established Church on the doctrine of the Trinity, and the answers to the fifth and sixth questions in the Catechism of the Westminster Assembly. This motion was opposed mainly on the ground that it was an imposition of a human creed, and that to impose such a creed was inconsistent with the principles of Protestant Dissent. On being put from the chair, the motion was rejected by seventy-three to sixty-nine votes, or, as was subsequently said, "the Bible carried it by four."* After this vote the minority left the conference, and resolved themselves into a distinct body. Two assemblies now met. The first, or non-subscribing assembly, was presided over by Dr. Joshua Oldfield, minister of the Presbyterian church in Maid Lane, Globe Alley, close to the spot where the Globe Theatre formerly stood. Oldfield was a man of great learning and sound judgment, and one of the most eminent of the tutors connected with the Presbyterian body Amongst the members of this assembly were John Evans, Benjamin Grosvenor, Dr. Gale, Samuel Chandler, Dr. Avery, Nathaniel Lardner, William Jacomb, and Daniel Burgess. The majority were Presbyterians, but it included a few Congregationalists and Baptists. The second, or subscribing assembly, was presided over by Thomas Bradbury. It included nearly all the Congregational ministers of the metropolis, and a majority of the Nonconformist pastors actually exercising the pastoral office. Amongst the most

* Nearly all the Congregationalists voted with the minority; the Baptists were divided by ten to nine.

eminent were William Tong, Jabez Earle, and Daniel Mayo. The two assemblies forwarded separate addresses to Exeter, each address containing "Advices for Peace." The non-subscribing ministers in their paper expressed their opinion that there were errors of doctrine sufficiently important to warrant and oblige a congregation to withdraw from the minister; that the people are the sole judges as to what these errors are; that the Bible only is the rule of faith; that no man should be condemned because he would not consent to human creeds; that no man should be charged with holding the consequences of his opinions if he disclaimed those consequences; and that, if agreement could not be arrived at, there should be quiet withdrawal without the censure of any person withdrawing. Accompanying the "advices" they forwarded a letter disclaiming their right to judge the matter at issue, as well as all sympathy with Arian doctrine. Following the letter was a statement of reasons for not subscribing, at the Salters' Hall conference, the paper relating to the Trinity. Amongst the reasons alleged were—that there was no necessity for clearing themselves from suspicion as to their orthodoxy; that it would have been taking a side against one of the Exeter parties; that no declarations, in other words than those of Scripture, could serve the cause of peace or truth; that the subscription insisted on was beyond what even the legislature required; that it would have been paying an unwarrantable regard to the Assembly's Catechism; that it would have been contrary to the principles of Protestantism, of the nature of an imposition, and a surrender of their Christian liberty. The signatories observed, in conclusion, that they were of opinion that, if such a demand were complied with, no one could tell where it would stop. To these appended documents were the signatures of seventy-three ministers.

In the following month (April 7th, 1719) the subscribing assembly forwarded their "advices for peace." It was prefaced with a declaration of faith in the Trinity, expressed in the words of the first Article of the Established Church, and the answers on that subject in the Assembly's Catechism. These were signed by forty-eight London and eleven country ministers, and eighteen other ordained or licensed preachers. Great pains and some pressure, it is said, were used to obtain these signatures. In the accompanying advices the rights of the people are stated in almost the same language as that used by the non-subscribers; the opinion is then expressed that, in such cases, neighbouring ministers might be called in for counsel; that it was proper that a minister should be asked for a declaration of his faith when that faith was suspected; that, if the attempts at union and agreement should fail, the people and the minister should quietly withdraw from each other; and that the denial of the doctrine of the Trinity was an error contrary to the Scriptures and to the faith of the Reformed Churches.

If these proceedings had terminated at this point, although they were already the subject of scandal throughout the country, no very great harm perhaps would have been done. But as the non-subscribing ministers had published their documents under the title of "A True Relation," the subscribing ministers saw fit to publish theirs, under the title of an "Authentic Account," and to these followed an "Impartial Statement." "Proceedings," "Accounts," "Animadversions," "Defences," and "Letters," now followed each other in rapid succession. The London prints opened their columns to both parties. Each side defended itself and attacked the other with a virulence and an animosity which disgraced equally their characters and their manners. Charges of deliberate lying and the gravest accusations respecting personal character were made and retorted without stint or measure. It must be said, however, that the non-subscribing party showed themselves, in their conduct of the controversy, far superior to their brethren. The subscribers were led by "the bold Bradbury," whose zealous and fiery temper communicated itself to nearly all his party. Bradbury himself penned the most violent of the whole series of pamphlets. The best controversialist was Peirce, who wrote throughout with a grave moderation of style and a charity of tone which his orthodox brethren might well have copied.

It unfortunately happened for both the parties to Salters' Hall dispute that their letters of advices were delivered just too late to be of any service. While the London ministers were disputing, the Exeter people had taken the matter into their own hands. The trustees, after consulting with seven neighbouring ministers, and without bringing the question before the church or congregation, took upon themselves to lock Peirce out of his chapel. Peirce declared that the people ought to determine this, but received the reply that, as there might be a majority in his favour, it was resolved not to consult them, and that he and his brother minister Hallett might preach at another meeting. Liberty to do this was, however, denied, and Peirce's friends, to the number of three hundred, subsequently built for him a new place of worship. The London advices were delivered after Peirce had been locked out.*

From this time Unitarianism spread with unexampled rapidity. It was unfortunate for the orthodox party that

* I have endeavoured to state the history of this controversy with absolute accuracy, but some of the narratives are so contradictory that, on some points, I may have failed to do so. The whole of the pamphlets in this controversy are perhaps seventy in number, and the greater portion, if not all, are to be found in Dr. Williams's library.

their cause, both in London and in the West, had become identified with an act of personal injustice, and something like synodical tyranny. It is impossible, however, to throw the whole blame of this transaction on one party. Peirce himself cannot escape the charge of want of ingenuousness. When his faith was questioned the most honourable course for him to have pursued would have been to offer to resign his charge. The act of the trustees was probably as illegal as it was harsh, for no trust-deeds of that time contained any specification of doctrines. The injustice to which he had been subjected rankled in Peirce's breast until his death, and, courteous although he was in print, he scarcely ever forgave those who had inflicted it upon him. For their part, while they had succeeded in one object, that of removing Peirce from his place of worship, they had utterly failed in another and a greater. They contrived to make the doctrine of Unitarianism popular, and they lived to see nearly every Nonconformist church in Exeter, and some of the principal churches in Devonshire and Somersetshire, lapse from the orthodox standard. The Presbyterian churches of London, Lancashire, and Cheshire became similarly infected. In less than half a century the doctrines of the great founders of Presbyterianism could scarcely be heard from any Presbyterian pulpit in England. The denomination vanished as suddenly as it had arisen; and, excepting in literature, has left little visible trace of the greatness of its power.

The Unitarians became, from this period, a distinct and separate denomination in England. Hitherto it had been their desire as well as their practice to worship with other persons. They held the opinion that differences in matters of doctrine, even a difference on the question of the Trinity, should not separate Christian believers. They seem to have expected that, in the course of time, the churches with which they were connected would be brought round to their own views. They do not seem to have perceived that their position, in this respect, was a false, if not a dishonest one. But the variations in the degrees in which they differed from the orthodox standard were so great that it is almost impossible to define what, at this period, Unitarianism was. Locke rejected the accusations both of Arianism and of Socinianism. Watts wrote against both these doctrines, and Peirce openly, and no doubt sincerely, stated that he belonged neither to the school of Arius nor Socinus. Yet all these rejected, in different degrees, the doctrine of the Trinity as stated in the Athanasian Creed. Whether it would have been wise and prudent not to have forced the more moderate section of the Unitarian party, to which Peirce belonged, from all ecclesiastical association with existing churches must be doubtful. Those, certainly, who remained in communion with the Established Church did not succeed in altering the doctrine of that Church. On the other hand, no notice of their existence was taken by many congregations, and a large number of those congregations subsequently became Unitarian. Their creed was, in fact, neither suppressed by the exclusion of those who held it, nor by tacit connivance in their presence. It was a development of thought,—the first form which rationalism took after mental freedom had been finally secured.

Some good came even from the Salters' Hall disputes. While the Bangorian controversy was drawing attention to the fictitious nature of the claims of the sacerdotal party in the Established Church, the Salters' Hall controversy was exciting amongst Dissenters an equal amount of attention to the mischievous character and influence of the imposition of human creeds. On this question there was little difference of opinion between the subscribers and the non-subscribers. Both parties rejected the principle of such an imposition, but disagreed as to whether the declaration concerning the doctrine of the Trinity could be correctly indicated by that title. While, therefore, the non-subscribers vigorously attacked the system of creeds, the subscribers maintained that such attacks were wholly uncalled for. None, after this controversy, ventured to suggest the framing of any system of doctrine which bore the smallest likeness to a human creed. The authority of all past compositions of this nature was gone.

The lull which succeeded to these exciting controversies extended over the lifetime of a generation. Religion, whether in the Established Church or out of it, never made less apparent progress than it did after the cessation of the Bangorian and Salters' Hall disputes. If, as was undoubtedly the case, breadth of thought and charity of sentiment increased, and, to some extent, settled into a mental habit of the nation, religious activity did not increase. The churches were characterised by a cold indifferentism. The zeal of Puritanism was almost as unknown as it was unimitated. It seems to have been impossible for the Christian men of this generation to fight with the old force of Christianity while they were being fitted into a new armour of thought. Everything was changing, and until the change was completed, and they had accommodated themselves to it, they seemed half paralysed. When the old dogmas of church authority were exploded, the Episcopalians scarcely knew what to do. The great buttress of their whole system was gone. The edifice had not been maintained with extraordinary success as a religious institution under the best of circumstances. Would it now bear the smallest extension? Episcopalians had also to meet Protestant Dissenters who were free to say anything they pleased. There was no possibility of putting

Watts in Newgate, as had been the case with Delaune and De Foe. Not merely gibbets, racks, and thumbscrews, but even the pillory was gone, and gone for ever. Men who would have liked a return of such days saw themselves frowned upon at Court, and, as a result, sneered at by the people. Church questions dropped, one after another, from public view, and, for the most part, men were glad to be rid of them.

On the part of the Dissenters this quiet and, indeed, worse than quiet condition was, for other reasons, equally natural. They had fought the last great battle for toleration, and God had given them the victory. They were sure now that they might exist, and they appear to have been grateful simply to enjoy, for almost the first time, a security that was disturbed neither by threats nor apprehensions. Their old enemy was virtually extinct; they were on good terms with governments and ministers, and none of the Georgian bishops were at all likely to make them martyrs. They existed by the side of a wholly different church from that to which they had lately been accustomed. In their judgment, therefore, the warfare against that church was over. They went to their little meeting-houses, heard their preachers, paid them, perhaps, as well as they could, and were satisfied. They admired the bishops from a respectful distance, and were very fond of quoting Hoadly. If they thought much of the deadness, ignorance, and corruption around them, they never thought of removing it. It must have seemed, indeed, too great to be removed.

Nothing that required great exertion or great sacrifice was either attempted or done during this period. The Quakers, with their habitual moral boldness and sagacity, were the only people who sought and obtained an enlarged degree of liberty. Penn, who had been, for the greater portion of their existence, their parliamentary agent, negotiating, on their behalf, terms with monarchs, ministers, and members of parliament, had died in the year 1718; but the society was not therefore left without a similar representative. Joseph Wyeth and Thomas Story were selected to take the initiative in the delicate work which was now required to be done. The form of Affirmation which had been imposed by the statute of William III. in place of an oath, for the use of Quakers in courts of law, did not, it would appear, meet the approval of some members of the body. It contained the words, "In the presence of Almighty God," which, it was objected, made it equivalent to an oath. It was, therefore, resolved to move for a new form of affirmation. Wyeth, who was well known to the King, addressed a letter on the subject to his Majesty, and secured his concurrence in their wishes. Story, who had frequently appeared, on public occasions, at Court, waited on the Earl of Sunderland, principal Secretary of State, and, from his interview, had reason for believing that the Government would support them. Next, with painstaking assiduity, the two primates were visited, and interest made with members of both houses of the legislature.* Everything being prepared for the successful passage of the measure, a petition, signed by a hundred and thirty-two persons, was presented to the House of Commons on December 14th, 1721, in which it was represented that, in consequence of the scruples of certain members of the Society, many "had fallen under great hardships by imprisonment or loss of their property," and they prayed that a Bill might be brought in for granting such a form of affirmation as might remove their difficulties. This was accordingly done, and the Bill passed through all its stages

* Gough's "History of the Quakers," part iv. 180—183.

on the ninth of the following month. On the same day it was introduced into the House of Lords, where it was opposed by Atterbury, who remarked that he did not know why such a distinguished indulgence should be allowed to men who were "hardly Christians." The Earl of Iley replied that they were Christians by Act of Parliament, at least, inasmuch as they were included under the Toleration Act; to which Atterbury angrily rejoined that to call Quakers Christians by Act of Parliament was a reflection on Christianity itself. The first reading took place with no further opposition; but when, on January 15th, the motion for the second reading was made, Atterbury again endeavoured to prove that Quakers could not claim to be Christians. After a lively debate, the Bill was carried by sixty-four to fourteen votes. Four days afterwards the House was to have gone into committee, when a petition against the measure, from some of the London clergy, was presented by Dawes, Archbishop of York. The clergy alleged that if the Bill should pass, their tithes would be in danger; that society would be injured if justice were to be administered without an appeal to God; that the enemies of Christianity would triumph when they saw such consideration made by a Christian legislature to "a set of men" who renounced the divine institutions of Christ; and that it might tend to the increase of Quakerism. The Archbishop moved that the petition be received and read. A hot and angry debate took place on this motion. Fourteen peers—seven on each side—argued the question; the Government firmly opposed the reception of such a document, and it was ultimately rejected. Sunderland then expressed the opinion that a committee should be appointed to inquire into its authors and promoters, for it was nothing but a libel. The question that the petition be rejected was again put, and carried by sixty to twenty-four, several peers, headed by the Archbishop of York, entering their protest against the decision. The Bill was then suspended, but on the fifth of March following the protest of the peers was ordered to be expunged from the records of the House. On the 18th of June the Bill finally passed by fifty-two to twenty-one votes; Wade, Archbishop of Canterbury, and Potter, Bishop of Oxford, signing a vehement protest against it.*

Nothing could more clearly indicate the change in the spirit of government and in the opinions of the people than the history of this measure. It was enough that it received, in the first instance, the opposition of the High Church clergy, and that Atterbury—now about to be impeached for high treason and banished the kingdom—appeared as its principal opponent, for it to pass by the most decisive majorities. If the Presbyterians had been possessed of anything like the courage and persistency of the Quakers, they could, no doubt, at this time have procured with ease the repeal of the Test and Corporation laws. While, however, they enjoyed the liberty of occasional conformity, and could thus qualify for office by partaking of the Sacrament according to the rites of the Established Church —joining the Church, that is to say, for half-an-hour every year and protesting against it during the remainder of their twelve months of office—they appeared to think that they had secured all that was needful and honourable.

The indifference of Dissenters with respect to their civil rights has, however, another explanation. In the next year they received a substantial mark of the royal favour. Daniel Burgess, secretary to the Princess of Wales, and, as it is supposed, son to the minister of that name, is reported

* "Parliamentary History," vii.

to have suggested to Lord Townsend that a grant from the royal purse would be highly esteemed by the Nonconformist bodies. Townsend, we are told, took the advice of Sir Robert Walpole, Chancellor of the Exchequer, and, with his concurrence, the subject was mentioned to the King. George the First, whose disposition was as generous as was his creed, immediately ordered £500 to be paid out of the Treasury for the benefit of the widows of Dissenting ministers. This grant, upon application, was afterwards increased to nearly £1,000 per annum, payable half-yearly.* Such, at least, is the public history of the origin of the "Regium Donum," but its private history is scarcely so simple. It was, in fact, a bribe to the Dissenting ministers from the statesman who declared that "every man had his price." All of them were not satisfied that the promises which they had received had been so scandalously ignored. In order to quiet them, and, at the same time, to keep them in subjection, Walpole requested to meet their principal representatives. He informed these that he wished to relieve them from their disabilities, but that the time for doing so had not yet arrived. He was the greatest friend that they had, and as a proof of his goodwill he offered them the royal bounty. "Pray," said the wily minister, "receive this for the use and comfort of the widows of Dissenting ministers, till the administration can more effectually serve your cause."† The ministers accepted the money, which was privately distributed by nine of their number. It was not, however, taken without some grave doubts as to what would be the opinion of posterity on the

* Calamy's "Own Life," ii. 465.

† These facts are taken from an article in the "London Magazine" for 1774, said to have been written by the well-known Congregational minister and tutor, Dr. Mayo. Calamy, ii. 466, note.

subject. In the fear that this secret bounty might subsequently "come to be inconveniently known," Calamy, who was one of its first distributors, attempts, in his diary, an elaborate justification of the act. It had become in his own lifetime, he says, "more known than was ever to have been desired"; but he reminds those who might afterwards hear of the circumstance that, according to Burnet, Charles II. gave similar bounties to many of the Presbyterian ministers of his reign. It is true that Baxter would not touch the money, and that he sent it back; but most of those to whom it was offered took it. "The Court," adds Burnet, "hired them to be silent, and the greatest part of them were so, and very compliant." "But," says Calamy, "there was in the reign of George I. nothing to be silent about, unless it was the continuance upon the Dissenters of the hardships they were under, of which they often complained." He remembers also that Dr. Owen received a thousand guineas from Charles II. for distribution amongst Dissenters; but he also remembers that Owen was severely blamed for receiving it. Daniel Williams, however, for refusing the offer of a similar amount, was censured for not accepting it. Calamy then asks why the Dissenters of England might not as thankfully accept such help as the Presbyterians of Ireland, to whom, in 1690, William III. ordered a royal grant, although even they were condemned for taking it.* The fear of the grant becoming publicly known is, however, a sufficient proof that Calamy himself was not satisfied with his own excuses. No one can imagine that there was an open and direct bargain between the Court and the Dissenters, but there can be as little doubt that if the latter accepted it as a free gratuity the former considered it to be a bribe. The English "Regium

* Calamy, ii. 468, 473.

Donum" had all the demoralising effects of a bribe. For more than a century and a quarter it continued to be a source of weakness, strife, discontent, and reproach.

The necessitous circumstances of many of the widows of Dissenting ministers, as well as of many of the ministers themselves, was, at this period, attracting the attention of all denominations of Dissenters. The Presbyterians and the Congregationalists established funds for their relief, with very liberal rules for their administration. In 1717 the Particular Baptists resolved to establish a similar fund. In the preliminary paper of proposal, the reason for this organization is stated to be the "great decay" of the Baptist interest in some parts of England, and the difficulty they experienced in keeping up the public worship of God "with any tolerable reputation in other parts; the great want of able and qualified persons to defend the truth, to supply those churches which are in want of ministers; the poverty and distress to which some employed in that sacred office are exposed for want of a competent maintenance for themselves and families."* It was, therefore, proposed to raise a public fund for the support and maintenance of ministers, but that it should be for the use of Particular Baptist Churches only. Nearly a thousand pounds was contributed by the six churches represented at the first meeting, but a strong objection was taken to the proposal for confining the advantage of the fund to Particular Baptists only. The principal opponent of this proposition was Benjamin Stinton, pastor of the church at Horsleydown. His protest, however, received little attention, and it was virtually resolved that if General Baptist ministers were starving, their Particular brethren must let them starve.

* Ivimey, iii. 150, 151.

Soon afterwards, in 1725, the General Baptists established, but on broader principles, a similar society.*

It was towards the close of this period that the spirit of Rationalism reached its highest development in England. Not satisfied with impugning the divinity of the Saviour, the facts of His life and the authenticity and credibility of the books of the Bible were denied. Like the Unitarian, the Deistic controversy was due to the release of the human mind from the fetters of authority, and, in its essence, was only an extension of the spirit of free inquiry. It was a challenge of the human intellect to the ability of the Christian Church to prove, by reason, the foundations of its faith. The Unitarians had denied the necessity of an expiatory sacrifice for sin in the form in which the doctrine of the Atonement had hitherto been stated; the Deists denied that the Almighty had, at any time, revealed a religion to mankind. They did not call in question the existence of a natural religion in the heart and conscience of man, but they did deny the historical foundation, the necessity, and, to a great extent, the beneficial influence, of Christianity. The books of the Bible were, to these men, either forgeries, or impositions, or both; and they challenged the Church to prove the contrary. As early as the beginning of the previous century, Lord Herbert of Cherbury had announced and defended similar views; and Thomas Hobbes, of Malmesbury, had succeeded him. Mr. Charles Blount followed. The tendency of the works of all these writers was simply to eliminate Christianity, except as an amusing system, from the

* It is significant of the circumstances of Dissenting ministers at this period that the Fund Committee of the Particular Baptists resolved not to aid any minister who was in receipt of as much as £25 a year; yet a hundred ministers were aided in the year after the fund was established.

authentic history of the world. In 1701, Toland had been censured by Convocation for his book entitled "Christianity not Mysterious." Toland, however, was scarcely a Deist, and considered himself to be a Christian. The design of his work was to prove that there was nothing in the Christian religion either contrary to, or above, reason. He systematically depreciated, however, the genuineness of the books of the New Testament, comparing them, in their character, to the spurious gospels which had made their appearance in the early history of Christianity. In 1711, Lord Shaftesbury took the same side by the publication of a work entitled "Characteristics." In this work the state of the world under the heathen and the Christian administrations was compared, and judgment given in favour of the former. In the most polished style, and with caustic irony, Shaftesbury ridiculed the characteristics of the Christian religion. "The saving of souls," he exclaimed, "is now the heroic passion of exalted spirits." Taking the ordinary ground of State-Churchmen, he, however, remarked that he considered it, indeed, "immoral and profane" to doubt the truth of any religion whatever to which the State had given its sanction. He also accepted the Scriptures, although their text was not authentic, as "witty and humorous" books; but the scheme of the Christian religion, as a whole, he considered to be an invention of the clergy for their own aggrandizement. The highest morality, he conceived, was the pursuit of virtue for its own sake, and its perfection must always be owing to belief in a God *

Contemporary with Shaftesbury was Anthony Collins, author of a "Discourse of Free-thinking," of an "Essay concerning the Use of Reason," and of a "Discourse on

* Leland's "View of Doctrinal Writers," Letters v., vi.

the Grounds and Reasons of the Christian Religion." Collins, in these works, boldly attacked the sacred writings, charging them with gross textual errors, and putting the foundation of Christianity, not on the actual life and work of the Saviour, but on prophetical fulfilments only.* Another free-thinker soon followed. This was Thomas Woolston, who selected as his ground of attack on the Christian religion the narratives concerning the miracles of Jesus Christ. In six discourses, published between 1727 and 1729, Woolston maintained that these miracles never really took place; that they are merely allegorical representations; and that the supposed life of Christ Himself was also nothing more than an allegory. The Gospel narratives he denounced as absurd and incredible, and the Resurrection as a myth.†

No sooner was the last of Woolston's discourses published than another author appeared, who argued that Christianity was, after all, nothing but a hash-up of the "Law of Nature." Dr. Tindal, who elaborated this theory, considered that the Christian religion, or such portions of it, at least, as were really historical—if any were—was an entirely supererogatory performance. The God of Nature, in His creation of man, had given him all that was needful for his spiritual existence, and any external revelation was therefore unnecessary.‡

The personal character of those who made these bold and repeated assaults on the bases of the Christian religion made their writings more influential and dangerous than would otherwise have been the case. They were, for the most part, men of great intellectual ability and of high

---

* Leland's "View of Doctrinal Writers," Letter vii.

† Ib. Letter viii.

‡ "Christianity as Old as the Creation," 1730.

attainments. They were not only virtuous men, but considered their system to be more favourable than the Christian religion to the cultivation of all human virtue and dignity. Their doctrines found thousands of willing believers. Amongst the wits and rakes Deism became a fashionable creed. Society then witnessed, on a small scale, what would be the effect of the withdrawal of the sanctions of the Christian religion from human life. All the best Christian thought of the nation was accordingly employed to make good the defences of the Gospel. Accepting issue on the ground selected by the impugners of the received doctrines, both Church and Dissenting writers undertook to prove the entire reasonableness of the Christian faith. They were quite willing that it should be brought to the bar of that intellect and judgment which the Creator had given to man. "Our religion," said Dr. Rogers, the Boyle lecturer, "desires no other favour than a sober and dispassionate examination. It submits its grounds and reasons to an unprejudiced trial, and hopes to approve itself to the conviction of any equitable inquirer."* "If in revelation," said Bishop Butler, "there be found any passages the seeming meaning of which is contrary to natural religion, we may most certainly conclude such seeming meaning not to be the real one."† Dr. James Foster, the successor of Gale, at the Barbican Baptist Chapel, held similar language. "The faculty of reason," he remarks, "which God hath implanted in mankind, however it may have been abused and neglected in times past, will, whenever they begin to exercise it aright, enable them to judge of all these things."‡

* "Boyle Lectures," 1727, p. 59.

† "Analogy of Religion," part ii., chap. 1.

‡ "Truth and Excellency of the Christian Religion," 1731. I am indebted to Mr. Pattison's Essay on the "Tendencies of Religious Thought in England, 1680-1750," for the suggestion of the above quotations.

The Deists themselves acknowledged the candour with which they were met. Collins said publicly that many of the replies to him were "written with a temper, moderation, and politeness unusual in theological controversies, and becoming good, pious, and learned men"; that the authors allowed the subject to "depend only on the force of the argument, appeal only to the reason of men for a determination, and disclaim all force and other application to the passions and weakness of men, to support and maintain the notions they advance."* With one exception, none dreamed of putting law in force to punish the authors of these works. Woolston was indicted, under the Blasphemy Act, for the publication of his Discourses, and was condemned to a year's imprisonment and a fine of a hundred pounds, but no person expressed a stronger condemnation of such a resort to force for the purpose of putting down opinion than Woolston's ablest antagonist, Nathaniel Lardner. In the preface to a "Vindication of the Miracles of the Saviour," Lardner remarked that if men were permitted to propose their objections to Christianity, no one need be in pain for the event. All force, he said, on the minds of men in matters of belief was contrary to the spirit of Christianity; and severity, instead of doing good, had always done harm.†

The most popular reply to the deistical arguments was from the pen of Sherlock, Bishop of Bangor, the old opponent of Dissenters, who selected for attack Woolston's discourses. Throwing the argument for the Resurrection of the Saviour into the form of a legal trial, Sherlock wrote a book,‡ which, if coarse and familiar in its language,

* "Scheme of Literal Prophecy Considered." Preface, p. 4.

† Kippis's "Life of Lardner," p. 15—18.

‡ "Trial of the Witnesses of Jesus Christ," 1730.

largely influenced public opinion; and, probably because it was coarse and familiar, it passed rapidly through fourteen editions. Nathaniel Lardner, then a young Presbyterian minister in Poor Jewry Lane, conceived the design of an exhaustive work on the Credibility of the Gospel History, and published, in 1727, the first part of that great performance which occupied thirty years of one of the most laborious of human lives. Lardner also defended the Miracles from Woolston's attack, in which he was followed by Dr. Zachary Pearce, of St. Martin's, London, and Smallbrooke, Bishop of St. David's. Dr. Waterland, an eminent Church scholar, replied to Tindal. Dr. James Foster surveyed the whole argument. Balguy, in "A Letter to a Deist" (1729), vindicated the beneficial influence of Christianity on moral virtue in reply to Shaftesbury. Woolston met with no fewer than twenty adversaries, the most conspicuous of whom, amongst Dissenters, were Dr. William Harris, of the Poor Jewry Church,* and Mr. Hallett, of Exeter. Watts also took the field. Next to Sherlock, however, the most popular of the opponents of Deism was Dr. James Foster, who, at this time, and for many years subsequently, occupied a foremost position amongst the preachers of the metropolis. Foster had been educated for the Dissenting ministry by Hallett, of Exeter, and had imbibed from his tutor, and probably also from Peirce, who held him in high estimation, anti-Trinitarian views. As early as 1720 he had published an essay to prove that the doctrine of the Trinity was not one of the fundamentals of Christianity. At the same time he vindicated the Resurrection of the Saviour in a sermon

* Dr. Harris, who was one of the most accomplished scholars and one of the greatest masters of the English language of his time, made a magnificent collection of works on Christian polemics, the whole of which he left, by will, to Dr. Williams's Library.

preached in reply to the objections of the Deists. The reading of Gale's work on Infant Baptism induced him to forsake the Presbyterians and to undergo adult immersion. He was subsequently elected successor to Gale, and while in charge of the Barbican Church commenced a Sunday evening lecture at the Old Jewry. Few, if any, of the Dissenting churches of this period held evening services, and Foster's lectures commanded a great and varied audience. This, however, was entirely due to the eminent and unrivalled abilities of the lecturer. Possessed of the finest elocutionary powers, a clear reasoner, chaste in his style, happy in his choice of language, combining energy with simplicity and dignity with pathos, with a voice that charmed the ear and a manner that added expressiveness to every sentence which he uttered, he both surprised and enchanted all who heard him.* Pope, who did not spare even more eminent men, has handed Foster's name down to all posterity :—

> Let modest Foster, if he will, excel
> Ten Metropolitans in preaching well.

Until Edward Irving's ministry, probably no preacher, for nearly a hundred years, enjoyed such marked popularity as this famed General Baptist minister. Subsequently, the Deistical controversy gave rise to the great works of Bishop Warburton on the "Divine Legation of Moses," and of Bishop Butler on the "Analogy of Natural and Revealed Religion;" but these works belong to the generation succeeding that of the most conspicuous early Deists.

With such an exhibition of power and of scholarship arrayed against it, it is not surprising that Deism, as an intel-

* Wilson's "Dissenting Churches," ii. 270, 282. Dr. Fleming' Funeral Sermon, p. 15.

lectual theory, was quickly beaten from the field of controversy, and that practical and vital religion did not gain from its defeat. The apologists of Christianity, in fact, were to a great extent drawn aside by the controversy in which they were engaged, from the principal work of preachers of the Gospel. They built up, with masterly ability and acknowledged success, the external defences of their faith; they proved beyond cavil the superiority of the Christian religion as a moral agent; but they did little more than this. They strangely forgot the internal evidences of the truth of Christianity. Whether Shaftesbury's sneer had or had not told upon them, they neglected, to a lamentable extent, one of the chief means of "saving souls." They fell into a habit of treating Christianity as an intellectual creed, a system of morals, and a means of virtue. In no age, probably, have so few appeals to the spiritual affections of men been made as were made during the age of Deism. As few persons are moral from considerations of reason and prudence alone, and as none can be religious without the strongest feelings of the heart going forth towards their Maker and Redeemer, it followed that the Christian preachers exercised little influence on either the morals or the religion of the people. Christianity, as an intellectual belief, was enlightened and steadied; but faith as a vital power scarcely existed in less degree. Preaching, if accurate and polished, was cold and heartless. Foster's sermons are the best illustrations of the most popular Christian oratory of the Deistic period. He was an Addison in the pulpit, but he expressed even less of Christian affectionateness than the moral essayist. Amongst, however, the most eminent of preachers and writers, Watts was one who carefully guarded himself against this danger. In three sermons on the "Inward Witness of Christianity, or an evidence of the Truth of the Gospel from its Divine Effects," Watts proclaimed the superior character of the testimony derived from the conscience and experience of man to that of any external evidence. He warned the Christian world against a religion which consisted in merely correct morals and a correct theology, "while devotion freezes at the heart;" and he vindicated zeal in the ministry of the Word from the ridicule of an age which pretended to "nothing but calm reasoning." But even Watts was careful to abjure the charge of "enthusiasm," and appealed to "common sense and reason" in defence of preaching characterised by the "movements of a sacred passion," and by a living fire.* It must be said, however, in honour of the Christian apologists of this generation, that the special work which was given them to do they did with conscientious care and unrivalled success; indeed, with such care and success, that all subsequent labourers in the same field have done little more than add, here and there, small outworks to their great system of fortifications.

As it is impossible for Nonconformity, in the circumstances in which it has been placed in England, to live and extend without its adherents possessing in an unusual measure personal piety and the spirit of self-sacrifice, its comparative decline, under the influences of the age of reason, was very obvious. Calamy mentions no fewer than twenty-five ministers, amongst whom were Joseph Butler, afterwards Bishop of Durham, and author of the "Analogy," and Thomas Secker, afterwards Archbishop of Canterbury, who seceded to the Church. Amongst the number of those who conformed were eighteen of the non-subscribing ministers in the Salters' Hall controversy, who resented the imposition of one tenet, but who had no hesitation to subscribe to the "six hundred," which are

* "Three Sermons," &c., Dedication, 1730.

reported to be contained in the Thirty-nine Articles of Religion.*

In London and the neighbourhood within the bills of mortality, it appeared that between the years 1695 and 1730 one church only had been erected, but that, by enlargements, increased accommodation had been made for four thousand persons. Twelve of the old congregations had been dissolved and ten new congregations organised; fourteen had increased, fifteen had declined, and twenty remained in about the same state. The Presbyterians (forty-four churches in number) are described as being almost equally divided between Calvinists, Arminians, and Baxterians, but principally moderate Calvinists; the Congregationalists (thirty-three churches) as all Calvinists, and the Baptists (twenty-six churches) as divided between Arminians and Calvinists, with the addition of three Socinians, of whom Foster was one. The Congregationalists are described as being greatly deficient in unity and sympathy with each other.†

---

* Calamy says:—"Some of those who had before gone over from us to the Church had been scandalous, but it was otherwise with those who now conformed. They were generally persons of sobriety and unblemished character, and might therefore be received and caressed by those whom they fell in with, with a better grace." Calamy observes that many of those who had left Dissent were soured in spirit by the change, and discovered "enmity and contempt with respect to those whose company they quitted." He adds, "It was easy to be observed and much taken notice of, that most that conformed about this time complained much of a spirit of imposition working among the Dissenters, which discovered itself in the proceedings at Salters' Hall, and on other occasions, when the debates about the Trinity grew warm."—"Own Life," ii. 503, 506.

† Palmer's MS. in Dr. Williams's Library is one of the most valuable records of the state of Nonconformity in the last century. It contains an account of the state and condition of every church, and is written with great care, but perhaps too great freedom.

While the fact of this declension was generally acknowledged, there were considerable differences of opinion concerning its causes. The first writer who directed attention to it, and who himself afterwards conformed to the Established Church, assigned it to the ignorance of Dissenters of their own principles, and to the bad management of their affairs. Amongst the proofs of the latter, he adduces, especially, the want of culture in ministers, which, he asserts, had lost them many "gentlemen."* The reply to this pamphlet proceeded from the pen of a young minister at Northampton, who had recently engaged in a work which was designed to remove any occasion for the last charge. This was Philip Doddridge, then twenty-eight years of age. He had been educated at St. Albans, by Dr. Samuel Clarke, and pressed by his tutor to devote himself to the ministry. Calling for advice and assistance on Dr. Calamy, he met from the fashionable and stately Presbyterian only a frigid reception. In 1723 Doddridge was settled as pastor of the Congregational Church in the village of Kibworth. From thence he removed to Harborough, where, at the urgent solicitation of Watts and of the ministers of the neighbourhood, he established an institution for the training of students for the ministry. In 1729 he removed to Northampton, taking his pupils with him. His gentleness of manner, his devotion of spirit, his extreme charity and conscientiousness, and the breadth and thoroughness of his learning, had already marked him out, in the eyes of those who most intimately knew him, as a man capable of great and varied service. His reply to Gough was his first publication. In it he heartily identified himself with the "Dissenting

* "An Inquiry into the Causes of the Decay of the Dissenting Interest," 1730.

cause," which, he was persuaded, was "founded on reason and truth." Doddridge agreed with Gough as to the necessity of teaching the principles of Dissent, and the injury which had been received from unscriptural impositions and uncharitable contentions. He was of opinion that more practical religion was to be found in the Free than in Established places of worship, and that it was a religious reverence for the divine authority which was their main support. Concurrently with this, he urged that preachers should not neglect the common people, who already constituted the bulk of the Dissenting interest, in order to bring back gentlemen who had forsaken them. He would rather, he remarked, have honest and godly mechanics or day-labourers in the congregations than any who would be likely to leave them from "delicacy of taste." It was evident, in his judgment, that some of those who had quitted Dissent had been influenced by merely secular views, and particularly by marrying into the Church—a custom which had given it a "fatal blow." Notwithstanding this, he commended the utmost simplicity in preaching, and was of opinion that any other style would bring about the ruin of Dissent. Such a manner of preaching greatly increased the number of Dissenters in his neighbourhood.* Another writer, immediately following Doddridge, thought that if, in local cases, Dissent was declining, it was to be attributed, amongst other things, to the fact that it was not apparently the social or commercial interest of a man to be a Dissenter, and that Nonconformists too often sent their children to Church schools.

Before this discussion was concluded the Dissenters had resolved that one mark of their civil inferiority should, if possible, be removed. In November, 1732, two meetings

* "Free Thoughts on the Most Probable Means of Reviving the Dissenting Interest," 1730.

were held at the Silver Street Chapel to consider the advisability of applying to the legislature for a repeal of the Test and Corporation Acts. At the first of these a general committee was appointed. At the second it was resolved that every church of the Presbyterian, Congregational, and Baptist denominations, within ten miles of the metropolis, should be requested to appoint two deputies. On the 29th December in the same year the first general assembly of the deputies was held. In consequence of the report presented to this body by the committee appointed at the previous meetings, in which it was stated that, upon consulting the ministers of State and others, there seemed to be no possibility that any application which might then be made to Parliament would be successful, it was determined not to take immediate action on the subject, but the Committee and the Deputies were confirmed in their appointments.* At last, therefore, there seemed to be some probability that the civil rights of Dissenters would receive something like adequate attention from themselves. An organization was now established which, if not so extensive as the one which De Foe had suggested, gave indication of increased self-respect and firmness of purpose. For the first time in their history, the Dissenters resolved to take an aggressive attitude with respect to the laws by which they were injured, and ultimately with respect also to the social disability and oppression which naturally grew out of those laws. If they had not yet lost faith in the promises of politicians, they had resolved, as De Foe had advised them, to act, in some measure, for themselves.

---

* "A Sketch of the History and Proceedings of the Deputies," &c., pp. 1—2, 1813. This was just previous to the General Election of 1734, and Walpole, to obtain the support of the Dissenters, gave them promise of future support. Belsham's "Great Britain," vol. iii. 481.

CHAPTER VI.

FROM THE ORGANIZATION OF THE DISSENTING DEPUTIES TO THE ESTABLISHMENT OF METHODISM.—1732–1744.

AFTER the General Election of 1734, when the whole strength of the Dissenters was exerted to keep Sir Robert Walpole's ministry in power, application was again made to that statesman for the repeal of the Test and Corporation Acts. His reply was characteristic. Personally, he had no objection to the repeal of these enactments, but, as a politician, he declined to identify his government with any motion to such an effect. He knew, and frankly acknowledged, his obligations to Dissenters, and also the obligation which the Crown was under to them,* but he feared to raise again the cry of "The Church in danger!" He remembered how that cry had been sufficient, in a former reign, to cast out one of the strongest ministries, and almost to endanger the Hanoverian succession; and he shrank from the probability of its renewal. This is the most reasonable explanation of his conduct. He would have served the Dissenters if he could have done so consistently with his own political interests, but, as it was, he must oppose them. For the first time, therefore, the Dissenters acted independently of the Government. They did what they could to ensure success, but

---

* Coxe's "Walpole," i. 476.

knew beforehand that they would be beaten. A Bill was drawn up and committed to the hands of Mr. Plumer, member for Hertfordshire, who moved it on the 12th March, 1736. Both in matter and manner Mr. Plumer did justice to his subject, and he was well supported in debate. When, however, Walpole himself rose, and, after eulogising the services and public spirit of Dissenters, expressed his opinion that the proposal was ill-timed, its fate was settled. On a division, it was lost by 251 to 123 votes.

It is remarkable that where the general body of Dissenters failed, the Quakers, immediately afterwards, although on another question, should again have almost commanded success. The prosecutions of this body for tithes and church-rates were so frequent, and entailed so much suffering, that they had become anxious to facilitate the processes of law by which they were convicted. Since the Act of William III., providing for the recovery of these charges in a summary way, eleven hundred and eighty members of this society had been prosecuted in the superior courts, more than three hundred had been imprisoned, and several had died in prison.* Nothing could exceed the severity with which the law on this subject was administered, or the personal hardship which was inflicted upon those who opposed it. For debts of a few shillings, which were not disputed, costs to the amount of scores of pounds were incurred, followed, in several instances, by forfeiture of all goods, and by loss of personal liberty. It was therefore determined to make a representation of their sufferings. In an address presented to Parliament, the Friends pointed out that these prosecutions were an evasion of the Act for

* Gough's "History," iv. 279. These and other particulars were separately published and brought before Parliament in the year 1736.

the summary recovery of rates, and asked that their prosecutors might, in future, be restrained from making the process of recovery so expensive and ruinous. A Bill was accordingly brought in, providing that, when a tithe or rate was not litigated, the warrant of two justices of the peace should be sufficient for the levy of a distress. Walpole gave his hearty support to this Bill, and, in doing so, roused once more the very cry which, as a statesman, he most dreaded to hear. No sooner was it before the House than "The Church in danger!" resounded throughout the land. Gibson, Bishop of London, led the way; and, in the "Country Parson's Plea against the Quakers' Bill for Tithes," endeavoured to prove that if the way of recovering these dues was made less ruinous than it was, the opposition to the payment would increase. Other pamphlets followed; circulars were sent to the clergy throughout the country to petition against the measure, and it was resolved to ask permission to appear by counsel before the House against it. This unusual liberty was accorded to both sides; but the power of the Government, although not until the measure had been debated for several days, and considerably modified, was sufficient to procure its passage. It finally passed the House by 164 to 48 votes. In the Lords it was met by every species of resistance. Arguments against its merits having failed, the plea was at last put forward that the measure had been rendered so imperfect by its manipulation in the Committee of the Commons, that it was not fit to be passed, and that there was no time left to amend it. On this ground it was rejected by 54 to 35 votes, the majority including fifteen bishops. This result greatly irritated Walpole. It was not the habit of this minister to give the support of the Government to measures likely to fail, and he had fully reckoned on his ability to carry the Bill. His mortification at his defeat is repre-

18

sented to have been extreme,* and he visited upon its author the punishment which a minister of state knows so well how to inflict. Gibson was deposed from the position of confidential adviser of the Crown on ecclesiastical questions, and received no further promotion. The elation of the clergy was as great as was the humiliation of the minister. Those of London and Salisbury voted special thanks to their bishops for the zeal and success with which they had opposed the measure. Those of London expressed their gratitude for the vigilance with which the "legal rights of the clergy had been maintained;" and those of Salisbury came forward to manifest their "grateful sense of their preservation from that strange and unheard-of infringement of their rights," and for the defence of "their just and indisputable privileges."† The "rights" of the clergy meant, in this instance, their right not to tithes or other dues, but to punish, with the greatest punishment next to that of death, those who, without compulsion, refused to pay them. Their "privileges" meant, simply, the privilege of persecution. All that the Bill, had it been passed, would have accomplished would have been to cheapen the process of recovery; but it was scarcely in the nature of ecclesiastical pride and intolerance to lessen any of the disadvantages of Dissent.

It was probably in consequence of the mortifying defeat which he experienced on this occasion that when Walpole was next applied to by the Deputies to use his influence to relieve them from the Tests, he abruptly and decidedly refused to assist them. A deputation, headed by Dr. Chandler, waited on the Minister, and, reminding him of his promises, solicited his influence in their behalf. He made, says his biographer, the usual answer, that, whatever

*Coxe's "Walpole," i. 478. †Gough, iv. 287.

were his private inclinations, the attempt was improper, for the time had not yet arrived. "You have so repeatedly returned this answer," said Chandler, "that I trust you will give me leave to ask when the time will come." "If you require a specific answer," said Walpole, "I will give it you in a word—Never!"* In spite, however, of the discouragement given by these words, it was resolved, in 1739, again to bring the subject before the legislature. The Deputies prepared for their work with systematic care and vigour. Early in the year a paper of the reasons in favour of the rights of Dissenters was issued, and a copy put into the hands of every member of the House of Commons. On March 30th a Bill was brought in. No particulars of the debate which followed are reported, but its issue was even more unfavourable than on the previous occasion. The Bill was rejected by a hundred and eighty-eight to eighty-nine votes. This result did not, however, immediately discourage its friends. The committee of the Deputies reported themselves to be satisfied, if not with the issue, at least with the character of the debate. Measures were at once taken to extend, by correspondence, the power of the Deputies in the country. Letters were sent into every county, and a general meeting of Dissenters from all parts of England summoned for the following year. It is to be presumed that this meeting, if it ever was held, advised the Deputies to discontinue their exertions. Nothing more was done, and the subject was allowed to sleep for half a century.† During this long period the Deputies were occupied in defending, often at great expense, the civil and ecclesiastical rights of Dissenters throughout the kingdom. If a clergyman refused to bury the child of a Dissenter, they put the

* Coxe's "Walpole," i. 608.

† "History and Proceedings," &c., pp. 7—12.

law in motion to compel him to do so; if Dissenting chapels were unjustly taxed, they resisted the claims that were made; if ignorant and intolerant justices refused to register places of worship, they were served with a *mandamus* from the Court of King's Bench to compel them to discharge their duty. The Deputies, also, successfully resisted demands for clerical fees and for clerical charges made for services that had never been rendered; they protected the rights of Dissenters in respect to charity schools, and saw to the legal observance of trust deeds. In a very brief period their vigilance gave them such power that a check was effectually put upon the inroads of intolerance. Much of their success was unquestionably due to the character and energy of their chairman, Dr. Benjamin Avery, a physician of London, who occupied the post of chairman and treasurer for not fewer than twenty-eight years—from 1736 to 1764.*

In 1742 a case occurred which tested the consistency of the Baptist denomination in respect to occasional conformity to the Established Church. A Mr. Baskerville, member of the Baptist Church in Unicorn Yard, had been elected to the common council of the city of London, and had qualified himself for his office by receiving the sacrament according to the rites of the Church. Being immediately remonstrated with, he defended the course he had taken, and resented what he deemed to be an interference with his own rights of conscience and of private judgment. The church at once took the advice of the London Baptist Board on the course they should pursue. At a meeting of the Board the question was brought forward, whether a person ought to be continued in Baptist fellowship who had received the sacrament in the Church of England to qualify himself for an

* "Sketch of the History," &c., *pass.*

office, when he did not incur any penalty if he refused to accept the office. The Board unanimously decided that it was absolutely unlawful for any member of a "Gospel Church" to communicate with the Established Church on any consideration whatever. The matter was then submitted to the churches individually, and they agreed, without exception, that such a person ought not to be allowed to remain in the fellowship of the church. At a subsequent meeting of ministers and deputies of all the churches, an address to the Unicorn Yard Church was agreed upon. In this address, after making an allusion to the bad example which would have been set had any sanction been given to the practice of occasional conformity, and referring, with grief, to the indulgence and growth of it amongst other Dissenting denominations, the assembly proceeded to state the grounds of their decision. They reminded the church that their forefathers had separated from the National Establishment on principle. They would submit to no ordinance or duty that was enjoined by a human authority which invaded the rights of conscience and the prerogatives of God; they did not hesitate for an instant to refuse to commune with a Church, the very frame of which was contrary to the appointment of the Lord and His Apostles, that had sprung from human policy and power alone, that assumed to itself an arbitrary right of imposing restrictions on the consciences of men, and that harboured in its bosom multitudes of people of the most corrupt principles and profligate lives. These men had been faithful to blood in their testimony: "if we, therefore," said the Assembly, "should submit to a wicked prostitution of the holy Supper for the sake of mere worldly honour or lucrative employment, we should be unworthy of the character of our ancestry, we should be exposing our profession to ridicule, we should be esteemed hypocrites, and we should draw down the righteous indignation of Heaven upon our inconsistency." The church was therefore exhorted to watch against all corruption, and to put away from it the root of bitterness. In the next year, Mr. Baskerville repeating his offence, he was formerly adjudged, after another expostulation, to be no longer a member of the church.* This decisive course saved the London Baptists from any repetition of this practice.

It was at this period that the names of three young clergymen, who, for a year or two past, had been holding extraordinary religious services in the metropolis and other towns, were becoming the subject of the familiar but prejudiced talk in all religious circles. The first of these was John Wesley. If, in early life, any one man more than another had been carefully nurtured in Church principles, John Wesley had been so nurtured. Both his paternal and his maternal grandfathers had been ejected by the Act of Uniformity of 1662. His father, however, had not only conformed to the Church, but (as we have seen) was one of the most bitter and unscrupulous opponents of Dissent. His mother, the daughter of Dr. Samuel Annesley, had also conformed. The father appears to have been a man of no more than average piety, but the mother was a woman of high principle, deep religious feeling, consistent life, and unusual intelligence. To her the Wesley family probably owed the remarkable religious and intellectual gifts with which all its members, in greater or less degree, were endowed. It is possible to trace the secret of many of John Wesley's higher characteristics, and of some of his inconsistencies, to the influences which were brought to bear upon him in early life. Saved, when an infant, as though by a miracle, from perishing in the flames which

* Ivimey, iii. 228—233.

consumed his father's house, he was led to consider himself consecrated for some great work. His mother, in consequence of it, was especially careful of the soul of her saved child. In early life John Wesley saw in his father's family that conflict between Church principles and Christian duty which he himself was afterwards to illustrate on a grander scale than any Churchman or Christian. When his father was from home, his mother insisted on taking his place as a Christian teacher and exhorter. She held public religious services, at which she read sermons and prayed with and advised the people. Her husband took alarm, first at what he considered to be the unfitness of such a proceeding in a woman, and, secondly, at the invasion of Church authority which was involved in such acts. In reply to the first, Susanna Wesley fell back on her responsibility as a Christian. She, as well as he, had a stewardship to administer; and she cared nothing for unfitness. In reply to the second objection, that she was invading the authority of the Church, she did not do what many would have done, namely, question and deny the claims of that authority, but simply pointed to the good that had been and was being effected. Exactly the same character was in her, in this respect also, that was in John Wesley. She would not yield to her husband's desire that she should discontinue her services. "Send me," she replied, "your positive command, in such full and express terms as may absolve me from guilt and punishment for neglecting this opportunity of doing good, when you and I shall appear before the great and awful tribunal of our Lord Jesus Christ." From his mother also young Wesley derived a taste for works of Christian asceticism and mysticism. Law's "Serious Call" and à Kempis's "Imitation" were two of her favourite books, and those two works became his almost constant companions. Add to this, that supernatural noises were constantly heard in his father's house, and that they were credited by all the members of the family as supernatural, and Wesley's subsequent tendency to superstition may also, in part, be accounted for. The child was, in nearly all instances, the father of the man.

Wesley, when he left his father's house for Oxford, went with somewhat vague religious impulses. He said, a few years after, of this period, as he said, after that, of the subsequent period, that he did not then know God, and that he had no true faith. When the first course at the University was nearly completed, he became strongly influenced by religious feelings. With his brother Charles and a few other members of the University, he gave up his life to visiting the poor, the sick, and the imprisoned. He read deeply and prayerfully in the Bible, and, with it, Law, á Kempis, and Taylor's "Holy Living and Dying." He fasted long and often, prayed by day and night, lived by strict "method," and became a Christian ascetic, with a strong inclination for a retired and meditative life. But although he and his friends were sneered at throughout the University as the "Holy Club," as "Methodists," and as everything else that was deemed contemptible by that school of the prophets of the Established Church, they gained too much from their work for themselves and their fellow men to swerve from it. Nor were they men, in other respects, who could be put down by coarse jokes or contemptuous tongues. Wesley was as learned and as cultured as any amongst them. He was a good classical critic, he had almost a natural capacity for logic, he had been elected to the Greek chair, and was moderator of the classes. His religious devotion adorned his academical position, and his academical position adorned his religion. Charles Wesley was younger by five years, but was giving equal promise of ability and eminence. To the "Holy Club" was soon joined another, and an equally powerful spirit. This was George Whitefield, who left the position of a beer drawer in Bristol for that of a "poor scholar" at the University. The "Imitation" had fallen, also, into his hands, and after a depth of despair almost equal to that of Bunyan, he, too, had taken hold of Christ. It is singular how both Wesley and Whitefield went through, in their earliest religious experiences, the same process, not of mental conflict, but of physical discipline. Whitefield fasted twice a week for thirty-six hours; went, like David, to his closet for prayer, seven times a day, and devoted the whole of Lent to the most laborious religious exercises. He, too, afterwards looked back upon this time as upon a time of spiritual ignorance. When he went to Oxford, before he became acquainted with the Wesleys, Law's "Serious Call" fell into his hands. It intensified equally his religious feelings and his ascetic inclinations. Soon afterwards he joined the "Holy Club," and became, next to John Wesley, its most devoted member.*

Wesley's call to Georgia to be a missionary amongst the Indians probably saved him from becoming the leader of a "Ritualistic" party in the eighteenth century. He went there with a noble and self-sacrificing purpose, but with all the ecclesiastical tendencies of a High Churchman, combined with a somewhat superstitious faith in what may be described as Christian magic. Instances of the latter are to be found in the whole of his journals. The first occurs on the voyage to Georgia. A woman who thought that she was dying, wished to receive the communion. "At the hour of her receiving," says Wesley, "she began to recover, and in a few days was entirely out of danger."† One of his

* Philip's "Life and Times of Whitefield," chap. i.
† "Journal," Nov. 10, 1736.

first acts of ministerial duty in Georgia was to baptize an infant. "The child was ill then," remarks Wesley; "but recovered from that hour."* His visit to America was a failure, and his rigid adherence to the rubrics of the Established Church, which brought upon him a law-suit, ultimately compelled him to return to England. From the Moravians on board the ship which took him out he had, however, learned one doctrine, the disclosure of which came upon him with surprise. Having occasion to consult Mr. Spangenberg, one of their pastors, he was asked, "Have you the witness within yourself? Does the Spirit of God bear witness with your spirit that you are a child of God?" Wesley says he was surprised, and did not know what to answer. "Do you know Jesus Christ?" continued the pastor. Wesley could only say that he knew He was the Saviour of the world. "But do you know that He has saved you?" The reply was simply an expression of a hope that He had died to save him. "Do you know yourself?" asked Spangenberg. "I do," replied Wesley; but he adds, "I fear they were vain words." †

Further acquaintance with the Moravians in London and in Germany strengthened Wesley's views in this direction. He saw that the Gospel to be preached was a Gospel which offered free pardon to all sinners; which proclaimed the necessity of a new birth, and gave prominence to the doctrines of justification by faith, and the witness of the Spirit. His heart grew within him as he thought of the happiness which man might enjoy, and of the salvation of which he might partake, if the Gospel were but preached to him as it might be preached. And to such preaching he determined to devote himself.

Much, however, as John Wesley's name has been identi-

---

* "Journal," Feb. 21, 1736-7. † Ib. Feb. 7.

fied, and justly so, with the great religious awakening which followed from his preaching, and from that of his followers, it is to Whitefield that the origin of the movement is more especially due. It was not Wesley, but Whitefield, who first awoke the people from the sleep of spiritual death; and it was not Wesley, but Whitefield, who first broke the bonds of ecclesiastical conventionalisms and laws. This occurred while the Wesleys were in Georgia. Whitefield was ordained in 1736. His first sermon, preached immediately afterwards in Bristol, was reported to have "driven fifteen persons mad," which simply meant that it roused several from a state of religious indifference to an intense and awful anxiety. When he next visited Bristol, in 1737, crowds of all denominations went to hear him. It was the same in London, at Gloucester, and everywhere that he went. Young as he was—not twenty-three years of age—he was now sought for in all parts of the kingdom. He preached several times in a week, and people went miles to hear him. When he left Bristol he was escorted out of the city by a multitude of horsemen and others. The beginning of the revival he himself traces to a sermon preached by himself, in this year, "on the nature and necessity of our regeneration or new birth in Christ Jesus." "This sermon," he remarks, "under God, began the awakening at Gloucester, Bristol, and London."* From this time he consecrated himself to the work of an evangelist. He preached nine times a week, and in London people rose before daybreak in order to be able to hear him, and, with lanterns in their hands, might be seen threading their way from all parts of the metropolis to the place where he was to speak. This had not lasted three months before the clergy began to oppose him. He was

* Andrew's "George Whitefield," p. 72.

emptying their dull churches, and was consequently assailed as a "spiritual pickpocket." Pulpits were now refused to him. To add to his bad odour, he was accused of visiting Dissenters—a charge which was true; for many Dissenters opened their houses to him, and welcomed him as their guest. The people, however, shared in none of the jealousy of their church leaders. When, at Wesley's solicitation, he was about to leave for Georgia, "they pressed," he says, "more eagerly and affectionately than ever upon me. All ranks gave vent to their feelings. Thousands and thousands of prayers were put up for me; they would run and stop me in the alleys of the churches, hug me in their arms, and follow me with wistful looks."

Returning from Georgia for priest's orders, after an absence of a few months from England, Whitefield found the churches of the metropolis more than ever closed to him. He was violating the diocesan and parochial systems, by expounding the Scriptures from house to house. He was doing good in violation of ecclesiastical law. He was saving souls in a fashion that a beneficed clergyman could not approve. The result was, that the greatest preacher in England could scarcely find a church in all London in which to preach. From similar motives, every church in Bristol was now closed to him. He took refuge in the prison chapel, but from this also he was soon cast out. A man who did not respect the parochial system was not considered fit to preach, even to condemned felons. Whitefield, who, although a reverent son of the Church of England, thought less of the decree of councils and of canons than Wesley, at once made up his mind as to what he should do. He waited on the Chancellor of the Diocese of Bristol, who asked him why he preached without the Bishop's licence? Whitefield replied that he thought that custom had grown obsolete. The Chancellor, he adds, then read over to him that part of the Ordination Service which precludes any minister preaching in a private house, and demanded of him what he had to say to that? Whitefield's reply had a terrible force. "There is a canon," he said, "which forbids all clergymen to frequent taverns and play at cards; why is not that put into execution?" The Chancellor answered that if complaint were made on that point, he would attend to it; and then said, "I am resolved, sir, if you preach or expound anywhere in this diocese till you have a licence, I will first suspend, and then excommunicate you."* But the Chancellor, in this instance, spoke without considering his diocesan, who gave Whitefield the necessary authority.

It was immediately after this that, for the first time, Whitefield engaged in field preaching. He determined to carry the Gospel to the savage and heathen colliers of Kingswood. "Finding," he says, "that the pulpits are denied me, and the poor colliers are ready to perish for lack of knowledge, I went to them, and preached on a mount to upwards of two hundred. Blessed be God that the ice is broken, and I have now taken the field. I thought it might be doing a service to my Creator, who had a mountain for His pulpit, and the heavens for His sounding-board, and who, when the Gospel was refused by the Jews, sent His servants into the highways and hedges." When Whitefield next addressed the colliers of Kingswood he had an audience of ten thousand. His preaching was followed by marvellous results. He could see the tears coursing down the blackened cheeks of the colliers as he spoke, and hundreds, according to his own statement, were soon

* Whitefield's "Journal," 1739.

brought under deep conviction. Whitefield's way was now open to him, and he preached wherever he could find space or standing room. At Bristol his audiences rose from five and ten to twenty thousand persons—more than all the churches together could contain. He preached once at Gloucester, but only once, for the churches of the city were immediately closed to him. From Gloucester he went to Wales, and, accompanied by Howel Harris, the founder of Welsh Methodism, held services in every part of the Principality. Here, as in England, the churches were shut against him, but the people flocked by tens of thousands to hear his voice. It was the same in the country districts of England, which he afterwards visited. At Basingstoke the landlord of the inn turned him out of his house, and the mayor forbad him to preach. There, however, he preached twice—once in a field, and once on the racecourse, for the man who had bearded the Chancellor of his diocese was scarcely likely to be frightened by the opposition of a country mayor. In very few places which he afterwards visited was he allowed the use of the church. At Oxford he was received with the characteristic wisdom and charity of the University authorities. The Vice-Chancellor sent for him. "Have you, sir," he inquired, "a name in my book here?" "Yes," said Whitefield, "but I intend to take it out soon." "Yes," replied the Vice-Chancellor, "and you had better take yourself out, too, or otherwise I will lay you by the heels. What do you mean going about alienating the people's affections from their proper pastors? If you ever come again in this manner, I will lay you first by the heels, and then these [referring to Whitefield's friends] shall follow." It is satisfactory to find that Whitefield did not meet with a similar reception from Doddridge, at Northampton, which town he visited after leaving Oxford. Doddridge received him with both kindness and courtesy. He, at least, was not afraid of his people's affections being alienated by the most powerful preaching of the Gospel. At Hertford, Whitefield was compelled to go to the common to preach; at Hitchin, the churchwardens ordered the church-bells to be rung, so that his voice, as he stood under the shadow of the church, in the market-place, might be drowned. After this he returned to London, and began his memorable mission at Moorfields, which then contained the refuse of the metropolis. Here, and on Kennington Common, his audiences consisted of as many as forty thousand persons.* Everywhere his voice was a two-edged sword, and for the first time for generations men could understand the Divine interrogation, "Is not my word like a fire, saith the Lord, and like a hammer that breaketh the rock in pieces?" From London, Whitefield once more sailed to Georgia. He remained there only a few months; but he did not leave America until he had preached in all the principal cities, breaking, in the new world as in the old, the sleep of soul in thousands of men.

It was after Whitefield had first met the colliers of Kingswood that he addressed a letter to Wesley, beseeching him to go down and preach to the people. Wesley was still holding affectionate intercourse with the Moravians. A "Society," formed to a great extent on the plan of modern Methodist class-meetings, existed in Fetter-lane. Here Wesley attended "love-feasts," which lasted all through the night; here he enjoyed "penitential" seasons; and here he was wrought up to a state of the highest devotional rhapsody. His preaching now began to be attended by those physical manifestations which have often accompanied revivals of religion. Strong men and women

* Whitefield's "Journal," 1739. Andrew's "Whitefield," cap. iv.

cried aloud, before assembled congregations, in the agony of their spirit. Fits were frequent amongst those who heard. By-and-by—sometimes in a few hours or even minutes—agony would give way to joy, terror to peace, the fear of hell to the transports of heaven, the service of the devil to an assured acceptance with God. Such phenomena—believed, at that time, to have been unprecedented—drew down on the preaching of the Wesleys a not unnatural opprobrium. They were contrary to all that had hitherto been experienced of the operations of the Spirit of God on the soul of man. Good Christians were scandalised. Wesley, however, accepted their defence; and, whatever may be thought of all such abnormal manifestations, his reply must, to a certain extent, be held to be conclusive. "You deny," he writes to his brother Samuel, "that God does now work these effects; at least, that He works them in such a manner. I affirm both, because I have heard these facts with my ears and seen them with my eyes. I have seen (as far as it can be seen) many persons changed in a moment from the spirit of horror, fear, and despair, to the spirit of hope, joy, and peace; and from sinful desires, till then reigning over them, to a pure desire of doing the will of God. These are matters of fact, whereof I have been, and almost daily am, eye or ear witness. But that such a change was thus wrought appears, not from their shedding tears only, or sighing, or groaning, but from the whole tenor of their life, till then in many ways wicked, from that time holy, just, and good. I will show you him that was a lion till then, and is now a lamb; he that was a drunkard, but now exemplarily sober; the whoremonger that was, who now abhors the very lusts of the flesh. These are my living arguments of what I assert, that God now, as aforetime, gives remission of sins; and the gift of the Holy Ghost, which may be called visions."* It is needless to say that Wesley might have obtained an explanation of all these extravagances without assigning them to the method of divine agency. But the ecstatic temperament in himself, which was communicated, by a natural law, to those whom he addressed, enabled him not only to see in all these manifestations the finger of God, but to rejoice in them. He liked excitement, he liked mystery, he liked the marvellous, and he believed with the utmost credulity, in the superhuman, or all that appeared to be so.

Such was the man who was about to follow Whitefield to Bristol; but Wesley hesitated to take this step without consulting his oracles. He wished to know the will of God respecting the matter, and, in order to ascertain it, resorted to his favourite practice of Bibliomancy. He opened the Bible once, and the text on which he stumbled was not of good omen; he opened it again, and it was worse; a third and fourth time, and it was worse still. Then he consulted the Fetter Lane Society, who had recourse to the lot, and the lot decided that he should go. Immediately afterwards the Bible was opened in several places, and every text indicated, as had been the case with Wesley himself, personal damage to him if he accepted the invitation. The little society accordingly came to the conclusion that the journey would be fatal, and Charles besought to go and die with him. But Wesley accepted the issue of the lot as the appointment of the Lord, and went.

Whitefield must have been intimately acquainted with Wesley's ecclesiastical prejudices and weaknesses, and he adopted the best method of overcoming them. He preached himself in the open air, before Wesley, and then left his coadjutor to his own course. Wesley says, "I could scarce

* "Journal."

reconcile myself at first to this strange way of preaching in the fields, of which he set me an example on Sunday; having been all my lifetime (till very lately) so tenacious of every point relating to decency and order, that I should have thought the saving of souls almost a sin, if it had not been done in a church." * How reluctant he was to follow Whitefield's example, may be gathered from an entry made four days after this: "I submitted," he says, "to be more vile, and proclaimed in the highways the glad tidings of salvation." "More vile!" Nothing could more clearly indicate, than does this expression, the rooted ecclesiasticism of Wesley's character, the utter abasement which he experienced in doing anything that appeared to be unclerical, or inconsistent with the established conventionalisms of a priest in orders. But when the churches were one after another closed to him, as they had been to Whitefield and to himself in London, and when the sheriff soon prohibited his preaching even to the prisoners in gaol, he appears to have thought little more of the vileness of proclaiming the Gospel in the open air.

From this time Methodism became an established institution. In 1739, the first Methodist "meeting-house" in England was built at Kingswood, and the first Methodist meeting-house opened in England was opened at the Foundry in Moorfields. Wesley called the congregations who used these places of worship, "societies." These societies were divided into "bands" and "class-meetings," in which spiritual exercises were indulged in and the devotional feelings cultured. Wesley's idea at this time, and for many years afterwards, was merely to revive the state of religion in the Church; but he knew enough of the condition of society in England, and of human nature, to be

* "Journal," March 29, 1739.

aware that unless those who had been brought under the awakening influence of the Gospel met together and assisted each other in keeping alive the fire which had been lit in their hearts, it must in many instances, seriously diminish, if not altogether die out. His societies, however, differed in no respect whatever from Dissenting churches, excepting that their members did not, at first, everywhere build places of worship, and did not celebrate the Lord's Supper, or have the separate administration of Baptism. But both Whitefield and Wesley were at this time Dissenters in a degree. They had openly and deliberately broken an essential law in the Church's constitution. How many more laws they might break was simply a question of time, circumstance, and conscience.

It was during Whitefield's residence in America that the first breach was made between himself and Wesley. Whitefield was a Calvinist, and he had heard from England, to his intense surprise, that Wesley was preaching against the Calvinistic doctrines. When they had separated from each other at Oxford, there was no difference of opinion between the two friends on doctrinal questions. But Wesley, in the meanwhile, had come under Moravian influences, and from the Moravian had gone to the Arminian creed. With all the ardour of a new disciple, he was not satisfied with expounding its doctrines, but made it a practice to denounce all the characteristic tenets of Calvinism. Whitefield, accordingly, wrote to Wesley expostulating against his conduct. There was no intolerance in Whitefield's disposition; of the two men he had by far the finer nature. He did not, therefore, denounce Wesley's new creed; he simply said, "I differ from your notion about not committing sin, and your denying the doctrine of election and final perseverance. I dread coming to England unless you are resolved to oppose these truths with less warmth. I dread your coming over to America, because the work of God is carried on here by doctrines quite opposed to those you hold." He besought him, with painful earnestness, not to preach as he had been preaching. "For Christ's sake, dear sir," he wrote, "if possible, never preach against election in your sermons; no one can say that I have mentioned it in public discourses, whatever my private sentiments may be. For Christ's sake let us not be divided amongst ourselves; nothing will so much prevent a division as your being silent on this head."* Next, he expressed regret at Wesley's doctrine of sinless perfection, and, with somewhat unnecessary irony, his contempt of Wesley's superstitious practice of casting lots. But Wesley would not be silent, and he would not give up casting lots. Whitefield therefore again took up his pen, and in terms of anguish thus addressed his brother in the Gospel: "For Christ's sake be not rash; give yourself to reading; study the covenant of grace; down with your carnal reasoning; be a little child; and then instead of pawning your salvation, as you have done in a late hymn-book—if the doctrine of universal redemption be not true, instead of talking of sinless perfection, as you have done in the preface to that hymn-book, and making man's salvation to depend on his own free will, as you have done in this sermon; you will compose a hymn of praise of sovereign distinguishing love, you will caution believers against striving to work a perfection out of their own hearts, and print another sermon the reverse of this, and entitle it Free Grace Indeed; free, because not free to all; but free, because God may withhold or give it to whom and when He pleases."† This letter getting, unfortunately, into print, Wesley took it with

* Andrew's "Whitefield," 117, 118.

† Southey's "Wesley," chap. xi.

him to the Foundry, at Moorfields, where it was being circulated, and before the whole congregation tore it into pieces.

When Whitefield, in 1741, returned again to London, he was received with no diminution of affection by the Wesleys. He found, however, or imagined he found, that the preaching of the two brothers had seriously damaged his reputation. "Many," he writes, "very many of my spiritual children, who, at my last departure from England, would have plucked out their own eyes to have given me, are so prejudiced by the dear Messrs. Wesley's dressing up the doctrine of election in such horrible colours, that they will neither hear, see, nor give me the least assistance; yea, some of them send threatening letters that God will speedily destroy me." * What is termed an explanation followed, when Whitefield said that the Wesleys and himself preached two different Gospels; that he could not hold out the right hand of fellowship to them; and that they must part. From this time the Methodist movement was divided into two lines: Whitefield preached Calvinism, and the Wesleys Arminianism, and both were equally successful in turning men from darkness to light, and from the power of Satan to the salvation of God. The personal friendship of the men was, however, soon renewed, and each helped the other in the work he had in hand.

The three years which Whitefield now spent in England were the years of the greatest Protestant revival that had been known since Christianity was first preached. His first work, after separating from the Wesleys, was to go to Scotland. Presbyterian sectarianism stood, for a time, in his way. The Erskines had invited him, but would not hear of his preaching in any other pulpits but those of their

* Southey's "Wesley," chap. xi.

own section of Presbyterianism. ' Why?" asked Whitefield. "Because," said Ralph Erskine, "we are the Lord's people." "I then," says Whitefield, "asked, were there no other Lord's people but themselves; and supposing all others were the devil's people, they certainly had more need to be preached to, and therefore I was more determined to go into the highways and hedges; and that if the Pope himself would lend me his pulpit, I would gladly proclaim the righteousness of Christ therein."* Whitefield, in fact, always preferred the "highways and hedges." "Field preaching," he remarked, "is my plan. I cannot join so in any particular place. Every one hath his proper gift." While, therefore, the presbytery was quarrelling about him, he took himself out of the hearing of their wrangles, and would have nothing to do with their Solemn League and Covenant. But his success amongst the people was as great as it had been in England. His audiences numbered tens of thousands; and hundreds, as the result of his preaching, appear to have undergone a change of heart. He is next found, in the year 1742, preaching at Moorfields Fair, an act which none but a man with the courage of a lion and the faith of a saint would have attempted. At six o'clock in the morning of Whit-Monday—getting, as he says, "the start of the devil"—he preached to ten thousand people. In the afternoon this number was doubled. The fair was now at its height, but large numbers left the shows to hear him. The result was that he was pelted with rotten eggs, stones, and dead cats; but he preached to the end, and announced that he would return in the evening. A merry-andrew, whose show had been forsaken, came on this occasion, to lash him with a whip, but did not succeed in doing any harm. Other attempts to stop his preaching also

* Whitefield's "Journal," 1739.

failed. When the service was over, Whitefield returned with a pocket full of notes from persons brought under concern. He therefore visited the fair again, and he left the ground with unprecedented proofs of the triumph of the Gospel over sin. Once more, during these years, he visited Scotland, where he was the principal agent in the great revival at Cambuslang; and again he went through England and Wales, meeting, in many places, with an intense spirit of opposition, but in others, with a glad and fervent reception. At Hampton, near Bristol, his presence occasioned a riot; at Axminster, the church bells were set in motion to stop him; and at Plymouth he was nearly assassinated. From this port he left again for America.

The labours of the Wesleys during this period were not less incessant or arduous than those of Whitefield; nor was the opposition to them less disgraceful. One or two clergymen had identified themselves with their work, and they were treated, notwithstanding their comparative obscurity, as the leaders of the movement themselves were treated. They were spoken of by the clergy at large "as if the devil, not God, had sent them." Some repulsed them from the Lord's table; others stirred up the people against them, representing them, even in their public discourses, as "Felons not fit to live,"* "Papists," "Heretics," "Traitors," "Conspirators against their King and country." The converts of these men encountered the same measure of obloquy. The opposition to Wesley himself was more violent. At Epworth, where his father was incumbent for forty years, and where Wesley himself was born, he was refused the use of the church, and, by the drunken successor of Samuel Wesley, denied the Sacrament because he was "not fit." The greatest opposition, however, was

* Wesley's "Further Appeal." Coke's "Life of Wesley," p. 218.

encountered in the Midland districts. At Wednesbury, Eggiston, the clergyman, incited the people to a riot, during which every Methodist—man and woman—who could be found was beaten, stoned, and pelted, and their houses dismantled. At Walsall, the mob, says Wesley, "roared at him like the roaring of the sea, and demanded his life."* But Wesley's courage and presence of mind never once deserted him. He would walk straight into the midst of the furious mob, ask what he had done to harm them, and at once begin to pray or preach. The worst and the most violent retreated before him. No men, indeed, ever possessed greater moral power than Wesley and Whitefield. Their looks were sufficient to quail the angriest mobs. As though a Divine presence manifested itself, men fell back before them, and allowed them to have their course.

The history of Charles Wesley's labours is a similar history of personal zeal, and, to a considerable extent, of popular and official opposition. Although not so good a preacher as his brother John or as Whitefield, and although extremely uncertain in the command of his power, he produced the same effect upon the people. His first great tour was in the North of England, on his way to which he preached in almost every town. At Sheffield, to use his own language, "Hell from beneath was moved to oppose us." Here he was stoned, and several of the missiles struck him in the face. The riot in this town raged throughout the night, and the meeting house was pulled down by the mob. Charles, who was even a higher Churchman than his brother, states that this riot was occasioned by sermons preached against the Methodists by the clergy of Sheffield.† The following day the rioters broke the windows of his

* "Journal," July 4, 1744.

† Steven's "History of Methodism," i. 191.

lodging. His next tour was throughout the West of England and Cornwall. At Devizes the curate led a mob against him, who played the fire-engine into his house, and broke the windows. Two influential Dissenters assisted on this occasion.* At St. Ives, the meeting-house in which he preached was gutted by the miners, who, with clubs in their hands, threatened him with instant death if he preached again. This mob was headed by the town-clerk. At Poole the churchwardens led the mob to where Charles Wesley was preaching, and drove him and his congregation from the parish.† None of these things, however, hindered him. The more they were opposed, the more these men saw the necessity for their work. Opposition did nothing but increase their zeal. "Crucify him!" cried the mob of Wednesbury at John Wesley; and there was not one of the three great Evangelists who would not have braved even crucifixion in the discharge of his work.

In almost every large town in England the leaders of Methodism had now made many converts. Whitefield had neither the inclination nor the natural faculty for organising, either into societies or churches, those who had been influenced by his preaching. John Wesley, however, had both the inclination and the faculty. No man, in any age, has exceeded him in the skill of organisation or the wisdom of administration. He resolved, first, on the formation of societies. He met, at this point, with the objection that he was creating a schism. His answer to this, to himself at least, was conclusive. He acknowledged that if by schism was meant only "gathering people out of buildings called churches," he was creating a schism; but if it meant

* Southey's "Life," cap. 14.

† The vestry-books of Poole contain, to this day, a statement of the expenses incurred at an inn for drink to the mob and its leader, for driving out the Methodists. Smith's "History of Methodism," ii. 2.

dividing Christians from Christians, it was not; for his converts were not Christians before they joined the societies, and they did not separate from Christians, unless, indeed, drunkards, swearers, liars, and cheats were Christians. All that he did was to form those who were Christians into classes, and appoint leaders to those classes, who were to watch over the conduct of every member. Over all the classes he exercised a personal superintendence, giving every consistent member a ticket or certificate of his satisfaction with his personal godliness. At the weekly meetings of the classes mutual confessions of sins and statements of religious experiences were appointed, and once a quarter a "love-feast" was held.*

Societies being established, the question of preachers came next to be considered. Wesley had always thought that preachers would be supplied from the pulpits of the Established Church, but in this he was disappointed. There was no resource, therefore, but to use laymen for this service. Charles Wesley opposed this step with all his influence, and Wesley himself accepted the necessity with the greatest reluctance. At first the laymen were allowed only to read the Scriptures, but reading soon led to expounding, and expounding to preaching. The first, in regular connection with the Society, who preached was a man named Thomas Maxfield, a member of the Moorfields Society. Wesley was absent from London at this time, but as soon as he heard that Maxfield was preaching he came up in great anger. He was met by his mother. "Thomas Maxfield has turned preacher, I find," said Wesley. Susanna Wesley—who had preached herself—replied, "John, you know what my sentiments have been; you cannot suspect me of favouring readily anything of this kind; but take

* Coke's "Life of Wesley," 228—239.

care what you do with respect to that young man, for he is as surely called of God to preach as you are. Examine what have been the fruits of his preaching, and judge for yourself." Wesley did so, and then exclaimed, "It is the Lord, let Him do what seemeth Him good." After Maxfield others arose, some of them men of great natural genius and remarkable spiritual power. Amongst them John Nelson, a Yorkshire mason, holds the first place. Nelson was almost as abundant in labour and in suffering as the Wesleys, and his influence over the working-classes, especially in Cornwall, was equal to that of Wesley himself. Nelson, also, met at the hands of the clergy and the worse part of the people the same reception as Whitefield and the Wesleys.* His preaching was of an extraordinary character. Through Yorkshire, common sense, homely wit, and intense pathos were its characteristics. The drummer of Grimsby, who had been hired by the rector to beat down Nelson's preaching on the day after the riot, was one of the witnesses of its power. After beating for three quarters of an hour, he stood and listened, and soon the tears of penitence were seen rolling down his cheeks. Men who went to mob the mason-preacher, left him in agonies of remorse. Not even Whitefield possessed more power over the common people. Without Nelson, and similar lay preachers, Methodism could not have been sustained as it was. The seeds which the leaders of the movement sowed, were, by these men, carefully matured. The few grew into many; here and there societies were added to those already existing—all, in course of time, to grow into regularly constituted Christian Churches.

The organisation of Methodism thus gradually assuming shape and completeness, required but one addition to

* Nelson's "Journal," p. 92.

assimilate it to the conventional forms of established ecclesiastical institutions. This addition was made in the year 1744. On the 25th of June in that year, Wesley summoned a conference of the clergymen and lay preachers who had identified themselves with the new movement. Six clergymen, and at least four lay preachers, attended. Wesley had many objects in summoning this conference. One was to classify the various societies into circuits; another, to settle questions of government and discipline; and a third, to come to an agreement respecting doctrine. The first and second were easily effected; the third was discussed at considerable length, but as all the men were of a catholic spirit, and recognised the Christianity of every Christian, whatever might be his creed, the conference made no shipwreck upon dogmatism. It was decided that the truth of the Gospel was very near both to Calvinism and to Antinomianism, even "within a hair's breadth;" so that it was altogether foolish and sinful, because they did not quite agree with either one or the other, to run away from them as far as possible.* One of the questions asked at the conference was, "Are we not Dissenters?" The answer was, "No. Although we call sinners to repentance in all places of God's dominion; and although we frequently use extemporary prayer, and unite together in a religious society, yet we are not Dissenters in the only sense which our law acknowledges—namely, those who renounce the service of the Church. We do not, we dare not separate from it. We are not seceders, nor do we bear any resemblance to them. We set out upon quite opposite principles. The seceders laid the very foundation of their work in judging and condemning others. We laid the foundation of our work in judging and condemning ourselves. They

* Coke's "Life of Wesley," p. 275.

begin everywhere with showing their hearers how fallen the Church and ministers are: we begin everywhere with showing our hearers how fallen they are themselves."* The refined self-righteousness with which the self-righteousness of others was thus condemned was consistent with the weaker side of John Wesley's character. When occasion served, as in defending his work from the charge of schism, he could show how "fallen" the Church and ministers were, in language which condemned them, by implication, to destruction.

The character and the labours of this conference formed an era of Methodism. A body had been constituted which assumed to itself the direction of all the affairs of the societies, determined their doctrines, and assigned to the officers their duties and the mode in which they should be discharged. Wesley had summoned to this conference those only whom he chose to summon. He had thus kept it, and, under the circumstances, no doubt wisely, in his own hands. But he had also established a precedent, and that precedent he took care, in after times, systematically to follow.

The opposition and the success which attended the Methodist movement were due to various, and in some respects opposite, causes. The Wesleys, throughout their lives, wished to walk in harmony with the Church of which they were ordained members, yet from that very Church they encountered the most malignant persecution. All ranks of the clerical order, from the bishops downwards, opposed them. One who held intimate intercourse with the bishops of the Establishment remarks that he had been an ear-witness of the treatment which the Methodists received from that body, and that, in their common discourse, their

* Coke's "Life of Wesley," p. 287.

language was not only below Episcopal dignity, but even inconsistent with common decency—an example which was followed through every rank down to the country curate.* John Wesley's own opinion of the difference between himself and the other clergy of his Church related to two questions: first, of doctrine, and secondly, of the parochial system. He maintained that his doctrine was entirely consistent with the articles and homilies of the Church; but that, with regard to the clergy generally, he differed from them in five points. They, he said, confounded justification with sanctification, whereas he believed justification to be necessarily antecedent to sanctification; they spoke of being justified by works, whereas he believed that the death and righteousness of Christ were the sole causes of justification; they spoke of good works as a condition of justification, while he believed that there could be no good works previous to a man's being justified; they spoke of sanctification as if it were an outward thing: he believed it to be an inward thing—namely, the life of God in the soul of man, a participation in the divine nature, the renewal of the heart after the manner of Him that created mankind; they also spoke of the new birth as an outward thing, as if it were no more than baptism: "I," he said, "believe it to be an inward thing, a change from inward wickedness to inward goodness, an entire change of our inward nature from the image of the devil (wherein we are born) to the image of God—a change from the love of the creature to the love of the Creator, from earthly and sensual to heavenly and holy affections—in a word, a change from the tempers of the spirits of darkness to those of the angels of God in heaven." "There is, therefore," he added, "a wide, essential, fundamental, irreconcilable difference between us;

* Archdeacon Blackburne's Works, i. 312.

so that if they speak the truth as it is in Jesus, I am found a false witness before God; but if I teach the way of God in truth, they are blind leaders of the blind."* If Wesley's description, in this case, was correctly drawn, as no doubt it was, there need be no wonder at the state of religion and morals at this period. For, according to his authority, the clergy could have had no notion whatever of what religion really was. Not only could they not have felt its power in their own hearts, but they could not have had a proper intellectual knowledge of it. And, if they had, they dared not have preached it, for their preaching would have condemned their own lives. Both the bishops and the clergy of this period were habitually non-resident; pluralities had increased to a shameful degree, and the lives of country incumbents were often openly immoral.† Whitefield and the Wesleys were a living rebuke to all this class. Their preaching tended to expose the real character of the clergy, and to bring them into contempt. The vast numbers who listened to the Methodist leaders, and the many who were converted through their instrumentality, would know, perfectly well, that their own parish ministers could have had no practical acquaintance with religion. Hence, one reason of the opposition they encountered. The clergy dreaded the exposure of their real character. The new preachers virtually pronounced them to be either grossly ignorant or grossly hypocritical. The clergy therefore stood on their defence, and, in return, proclaimed the Methodists to be nothing better, and probably worse, than enthusiasts and fanatics.

---

* "Journal," Sept. 13, 1739.

† The state of the clergy at this period has been most faithfully described by a recent Church historian, the Rev. G. G. Perry, in his "History of the Church of England," vol. iii. cap. xlii. Southey's description, in his eighth chapter of the "Life of Wesley," is almost too well known to need reference.

But this was not the only reason for the treatment which the leaders of the Methodist movement experienced. They were Churchmen, but they were not, in all things, obedient sons of the Church. A friend once, naturally enough, asked Wesley how it was that he assembled Christians who were none of his charge to sing psalms and pray, and hear the Scriptures expounded, and how he could justify doing this in other men's parishes? Wesley replied, "I know no other rule, whether of faith or practice, than the Holy Scriptures. But on scriptural principles, I do not think it hard to justify what I do. God, in Scripture, commands me, according to my power, to instruct the ignorant, reform the wicked, confirm the virtuous. Man forbids me to do this in another man's parish; that is, in effect, to do it at all, seeing that I have now no parish of my own, nor probably ever shall. Whom, then, shall I hear—God or man? Suffer me now to tell you my principles in this matter. I look upon all the world as my parish; thus far I mean, that in whatever part of it I am, I judge it meet, right, and my bounden duty, to declare unto all that are willing to hear, the glad tidings of salvation."* This was good Christianity, but it was clearly not Church of Englandism. It is Dissent, and Dissent of the oldest form. The clergy were at least enlightened enough to be aware of this. The new preachers were invading their rights, and the invasion was resented. It is not necessary to ascribe a bad motive for this resentment. Whatever the clergy did not believe, they did believe in the constitution of the Established Church, and they had a moral, as well as a legal, right to protest against brother clergymen invading their parishes. They were less to blame in this than their system; but if that system was so very bad, why did the

* "Journal," June 11th, 1739.

Wesleys so constantly tell their hearers to attend their parish churches, and insist on the members of their societies partaking of the Lord's Supper according to the rites of the Church?

Another cause of opposition is to be found in the general condition of the people. If the clergy were ignorant and debased, the people were more so. It has been justly remarked, by an acute and philosophical writer, that the preaching of Wesley and Whitefield was a test of what the people had been previously taught as Christian truth, under the tuition of their great religious guardian, the National Church; and, carrying with them this quality of a test, how were those men received? They were generally received on account of the import of what they said, still more than from their zealous manner of saying it, with as strong an impression of novelty and strangeness as any of our voyagers and travellers of discovery have been by the barbarous tribes who had never before seen civilised men.* To the mass of the people, indeed, religion was almost unknown. Their morals were, for the most part, more degraded than those of beasts. Drunkenness was not merely not frowned upon: it was fashionable. "I remember," said Dr. Johnson, "when all the decent people in Lichfield got drunk every night, and were not thought the worse for it."† The people of Wales and Cornwall were little better than heathens—uninstructed by the clergy, whom they seldom saw, and who gave them no good example when they were seen, and so ignorant as to have scarcely the knowledge of a God. Such a people were ready enough to join in a riot against the Methodist leaders. Under the same guidance they would have joined

* Foster's "Essay on the Evils of Popular Ignorance."
† Boswell's "Johnson," i. 340.

in a riot against anyone and anything. The hatred of the clergy to the Methodist leaders was an intelligent hatred; but that of the lower classes was an ignorant and brutish passion. When they listened, and came to understand or to feel what was being said to them, and why it was being said, they received the preachers with raptures, and went out by thousands to welcome them. Their human hearts then drank in eagerly the message of salvation. Before Whitefield and the Wesleys went amongst them they were like a Sahara. But no sooner did the rain of the Gospel descend upon them than the desert became like a garden, and brought forth fruit unto perfection.

The attitude of the Dissenters towards the new movement was, for the most part, one of calm observation. Their congregations were unquestionably in need of a revival of religion. The decay of piety was deplored on all sides. Joseph Stennett, the principal minister amongst the Baptists of this period, has left a vivid picture of the times in which he lived. Infidelity, he remarks, was making amazing progress; the Gospel was being reduced to only a few lectures on morality; practical iniquity was keeping pace with the corruptions of doctrine, and there was nothing but a melancholy prospect to all the friends of true religion.* The whole population, he publicly declared, was corrupted with blasphemy and profaneness, with drunkenness and lewdness, with fraud and perjury. Those who had separated themselves, in profession, from the positively wicked were filling up the cup of national guilt. Ordinances were despised, religious conversation was changed for fashionable and vicious entertainments, and family religion was neglected. It might have been supposed that, under such circumstances, the advent of the Methodist

* "The Christian Strife." A Sermon, &c., 1738.

leaders would have been eagerly welcomed; but to this there was more than one cause of hindrance. The scenes which took place during the preaching of Whitefield and the Wesleys induced many persons to hesitate in acknowledging their mission. The Wesleys also were bitter opponents of Dissent. Charles, who was always "harping on the Established Church," remarked that he would sooner see his children Roman Catholics than Protestant Dissenters. In one of his sermons he compared the shipwreck of Paul to the difficulty of being saved out of the Church of England.* Charity for sinners he had to a large extent, but none whatever for any Christian who was not a member of the Established Church. It was impossible for Dissenters to receive such a man with the good feeling which a less bitter sectarianism would have excited. There was no such difficulty, however, with Whitefield, who, though he often avowed his attachment to the Church, was as little a bigot as any man of his time. "I exhort all," he wrote to Howel Harris, "to go where they can profit most. I preach what I believe to be the truth, and then leave it to the Spirit of God to make the application."† While, therefore, the Wesleys were received with coolness by Dissenters, Whitefield often met from them the warmest welcome. When he was driven from preaching near the church at Kidderminster, the Baptist chapel was opened to him. He took counsel of Watts, and held friendly intercourse with Doddridge, who lent Whitefield his chapel. No coarse disparagement of the labours of Methodists is to be found in the writings of any of the Dissenters of this period. When Methodism was better known, and its results well attested, they gladly acknowledged the good it had effected.

* Everett's "Life of Adam Clarke," i. 83.
† Andrew's "Life of Whitefield," p. 147

The causes of the success of the new movement are not far to seek. It is mainly to be attributed, as a matter of instrumentality, to the remarkable characters of those who conducted it. The movement was originated by Whitefield. He was not the first of the "Holy Club," but he was the first who assumed an aggressive attitude. The earnestness of John Wesley would, no doubt, have compelled him, in course of time, to have had recourse to open-air preaching as a means—and as the only means—of reaching the people; but Wesley, with all his enthusiasm, was a man of cautious and deliberate judgment, and, unless Whitefield had set the example, he would have hesitated, for some time, in taking the first step in violating the established order of his Church. Whitefield had no caution. He was the impersonation of religious ardour. The preaching of the Gospel was, to him, not a duty merely, but a divine passion. This passion gave to it a character such as has been possessed by few Christian orators. It was not that his sentences were well constructed, his periods well balanced, his emphasis accurate, and his language forcible: some of these desirable but minor qualifications he did not possess in an equal degree with other great orators. But the man himself gave to every word he uttered a unique emphasis. Baptized by the Spirit of God, his whole heart yearned for the recovery of lost souls as a mother yearns for the return of a prodigal son; alive, from intense experience, both to the horrors of sin and the delights of holiness, he pleaded his Saviour's cause with a love for Him and those with whom he pleaded, which made him seem, for a time, like one possessed. Whitefield was endowed with most of the attributes of a great public speaker. Though not high in stature, and, in the first years of his work, of slight and delicate frame, his clear, exquisitely musical voice could be distinguished at the distance of a mile, and by every one of forty thousand persons in the open air. In gesture and action he equalled the most distinguished professors of the dramatic art, and his oratory was as spontaneous as it was powerful. Although he often preached sixteen times a week, he was never known, after his earliest efforts, to study a sermon. His printed discourses are loose, and, to some extent, inaccurate in style, and give no adequate conception of his genius. His most impassioned bursts of eloquence seemed to come as an inspiration. Numerous anecdotes of his power over his audience have been preserved by those who heard him. They wept as he wept, and visibly trembled with terror when he described the judgments of the Almighty. So vivid were his descriptions, and so dramatic his action, that he would make a whole congregation look around as though seeking the things he described. Whitefield's greatest weaknesses were irritability and hastiness. He was not, like Wesley, a wholly self-controlled man. But he was more warm-hearted and generous than Wesley, and he had the most catholic and unselfish temper of any of the Methodist leaders. Not, however, by any natural gift did he acquire his marvellous power over the human heart. He spent whole nights in prayer; and although he invariably rose at four in the morning, he would often, in the course of the night, get up to read and pray.

But if Whitefield gave to the new movement its first and greatest impulse, John Wesley was, unquestionably, its head and leader. Young though all these men were, their characters were fixed and formed when they commenced their work. The intensity of their religious experience had given to them a maturity which other men scarcely acquire when they reach middle life. What John Wesley was at thirty he was, with scarcely any change, at eighty. With an intellect keen, clear, and logical; a judgment whose balance was almost perfect; a will as strong as steel; cool and self-possessed, yet ardent and even enthusiastic; and an able administrator, he was, above all men, qualified to be the founder and the organiser of a new religious sect. But he added other and still greater qualities to these. He was a man capable of the most rapt devotional feeling; he possessed a conscience that never swerved from its sense of right; personal self-denial and self-sacrifice he counted as nothing; what would have been privation to others, was a rule of his life; hunger and thirst he endured with indifference; work which would have killed stronger men in a few months, brought to him no sense of weariness. Through all he felt himself to be upborne by the Divine arm, and he cared for nothing so long as he was doing his Master's will. In most respects Wesley was an entirely different preacher from Whitefield. The characteristic difference consisted in the fact that Whitefield was mainly a preacher to the passions, and Wesley to the consciences, of men. Whitefield aroused the half-dead soul by appealing to its fear, and hope, and love; Wesley, by stating the Divine claims, and the corresponding human obligations. Whitefield would make men feel, Wesley would prove them to be in the wrong. The style of their addresses was as different as was the substance. Whitefield was loose, inconsequential, dramatic, and declamatory; Wesley was chaste, accurate, and logical. There was a difference, also, of tone. Whitefield had the finer human feelings and the more tender affections; Wesley, the greater intellectual power and moral force. Whitefield could not have been a bigot; Wesley never wholly freed himself from an ecclesiasticism which, while it cannot be confounded with bigotry, is nearly allied to it. The Spirit of God, however, moved in perhaps an equal degree, both of these great but very different men. The same audiences heard them with equal delight and profit. They had sought perfect spiritual character, and spiritual power was given to them in greater measure perhaps than it had ever been given to any men since the first day of Pentecost.

Charles Wesley was, in all respects but one, the inferior of both these men. He was narrow, exclusive, and priestly. He could preach occasionally, if not often, with marvellous power and unction; but as a speaker, he was extremely unequal. On one day his sermon would be instinct with eloquent thought and moving pathos; on another, it would be dry, cold, spiritless, and childish. He was, however, of great assistance to his brother, although sometimes, owing to his priestly dogmas, of greater hindrance. Apart from his brother, Charles Wesley would probably have been known only as a learned, zealous, spiritual and active clergyman, of great intellectual capability and great poetic power, but he would never have performed the work which he did, nor have enjoyed the reputation which has actually followed him. It was at the beginning of the Methodist movement, that, in conjunction with his brother, he published his first hymns. Here he far excelled both of his coadjutors; and in depth and warmth of devotional feeling has rivalled, if not excelled, all other Christian hymnologists.

Such were the revivalists who, excepting, for the most part, by the common people, were now everywhere spoken against. Yet they were successful. But, apart from their characters, their was reason for their one especial success. The Arminianism of the Wesleys and the Calvinism of Whitefield divided the men from each other for a brief season, but none ever lived who were more tolerant of theological differences. In the first year or two of his mission, Wesley could not leave alone the doctrines of election and reprobation, but afterwards he preached few formally theological discourses. It was his boast in later life that the Methodist societies were founded on a more liberal basis than any Christian church. "They do not impose," he said, "any opinions whatever. People might hold particular or general redemption, absolute or conditional decrees. They think and let think."* "Look all around you," he added, at another period; you cannot be admitted into the Church, or society of the Presbyterians, Anabaptists, Quakers, or any others, unless you hold the same opinions with them, and adhere to the same mode of worship. The Methodists alone do not insist on your holding this or that opinion. . . . Now, I do not know any other religious society, either ancient or modern, wherein such liberty of conscience is now allowed, or has been allowed, since the age of the apostles. Here is our glorying, and a glorying peculiar to us." It was so; and none amongst the secondary causes of their success, contributed to it more than this spirit.

The spiritual influence of the Methodist leaders was not, however, limited to the lower classes. Through the influence of the Countess of Huntingdon they were brought into immediate contact with a large section of the aristocracy. This celebrated lady, after having been a frequent attendant, with her husband, on the preaching of the Wesleys and Whitefield, took Whitefield under her especial patronage. Defying all ecclesiastical order, she engaged the preacher to hold services at her own residence, which the nobility were invited to attend. They accepted the invitation in great numbers. Amongst those who heard him were the Earl of Chesterfield, Viscount Bolingbroke, the Duke of Argyle, the Earl of Aberdeen, the Duchess of Montague, Lord Lyttleton, the Duke of Kingston, the elder Mr. Pitt, and most of those who formed the Court of the

* "Works," vii. 321.

Prince of Wales.* With some of these Whitefield maintained an affectionate intercourse through life, and was of eminent use to them. To his preaching and the work of the Countess, may be ascribed the revival of religion in the aristocracy as well as in the common people.

Few women have ever deserved a noble fame so fully as the widowed Countess. Herself of high lineage, and intimately connected by marriage with the most conspicuous noble families, she had an opportunity of rendering religious service of which she took advantage to the utmost extent. Although the tone of thought amongst the aristocracy was especially unfavourable to the culture of the religious character, Lady Huntingdon lost, by her fidelity and zeal, little, if any, of her social influence. She might be smiled at, and made the butt of a few town wits, but the strength, thoroughness, and sincerity of her character generally secured for her the utmost respect. Her most intimate friends were women of her own circle and family. Next to these ranked Whitefield, the few clergy of the Established Church, such as Romaine, Venn, and Howel Harris, who were classed with the Methodist party, some of the lay preachers, and, amongst Dissenters, Dr. Doddridge, who was her constant correspondent and frequent guest. She adopted Whitefield rather than either or both of the Wesleys, because Whitefield was a Calvinist. Her faculty of organisation was almost equal, and her strength of will quite equal, to that of Wesley's. She saw, with him, that organisation was necessary to the permanence of the results which were being produced by the new preaching. She had wealth, influence, capacity, and time to frame this organisation; and she framed it. The Countess founded colleges—Trevecca

* "Life and Times of Selina, Countess of Huntingdon," vol. i., chap. vii.

and Cheshunt,—she built places of worship, she appointed ministers and she sent out evangelists; and, although in different respects, aided in founding two denominations—the Calvinistic Methodist of Wales, and the Countess of Huntingdon's Connexion in England. The latter, owing to many influences, has since become almost identified with the Congregational body. Like Wesley, the Countess had no intention of leaving the Established Church, but she had more moral courage than Wesley in respect to Church laws and ordinances. She saw no inherent difference between a layman and a clergyman, and she saw no reason why, when Christians met together, they should not celebrate the Lord's Supper. Her societies, therefore, became organised for all religious and ecclesiastical purposes much more quickly than those which Wesley directed. Wesley warded the pain of separation from himself; the Countess felt it in her lifetime. When it came, in the shape of a legal decision which compelled her to certify her buildings under the Toleration Act, she exclaimed, "I am to be cast out of the Church now, only for what I have been doing these forty years—speaking and living for Jesus Christ."* How was it that she did not remember that almost all religious earnestness, from that of early Puritanism, had met with a similar fate? How could she have expected to escape?

When the early Methodists appeared religious life was dying out in England. Even Dissent seemed to have lost its spiritual force, and with it, the power of aggression. It had, apparently, almost done the work which had been committed to it. In its first period Dissent had fought for spiritual liberty, and had won that hardest of all human battles. In its second period it had saved the country from arbitrary

* Stevens's "History of Methodism," ii. 100.

power. Statesmen and people, ecclesiastics and laymen, had now been brought round to a practical recognition of the service of Dissent to the politics, the intellect, and the conscience of the nation. Through it the English people had grown to a broader type of thought than it would have been possible for them otherwise to have possessed; for the doctrines of political liberty, of resistance to arbitrary power, and of the rights of conscience, were either the characteristic doctrines of Dissenters, or their qualities natural consequences. But it seemed impossible to make any further advance. The obstacle to this was to be removed by the infusion of a new religious life into the churches. For, in proportion as men and nations grow in religious liberty, do they grow in political liberty. Neither is the offspring of indifferences, but of belief. When—and not until that time—the churches had been baptized anew by the Spirit of God, they once more sought for the extension of civil freedom and religious equality. The power to attain this is ultimately to be traced to the Methodist movement.

CHAPTER VII.

THE REVIVAL OF RELIGION IN WALES.

REFERENCE has more than once been made, in the course of this History, to the state of religion in the Principality of Wales, and the efforts of several godly and zealous men to effect some improvement in the moral and spiritual condition of the remarkable people who inhabited that portion of Great Britain. Like Ireland, Wales had suffered not only from having been a conquered country, but from its being inhabited by a race alien to the origin, the language, and the habits of the conquerors. Probably no people placed in similar circumstances had so steadily or so successfully preserved their national characteristics as the people of Wales. It may be said that, for centuries, the land only—the bare earth on which they had lived—was kept in subjugation, for the spirit of the nation had undergone no change. They were never effectually conquered by Imperial Rome; they never, as members of the ancient British Church, bowed the neck to Papal Rome. Even the strong hand of the Normans failed for two centuries to set aside the native government; and when, at last, the last Welsh prince was defeated, all the civil rights of the conquerors were made the rights also of the conquered.

After the Reformation, so far as religion was concerned, the Welsh, like the Irish, were treated with a studied and contemptuous neglect. Their ecclesiastical revenues were, to a great extent, appropriated to augment the endowments of the Church in England or were bestowed upon English laymen. Englishmen, to whom the Welsh language was as unknown as Syriac or Sanskrit, were appointed to bishoprics, rectories, vicarages, and even curacies. These men necessarily ministered to fractions only of the people. But they were, for the most part, incapable of giving any spiritual instruction; for in morals they were as licentious as in religion they were ignorant. Towards the end of the sixteenth century, John Penry, the martyred apostle of Wales described the clergy as "unlearned dolts," "drunkards," and "adulterers." At that time, a Bishop of St. Asaph held, in addition to the revenues of his see, sixteen livings in Commendara, and only three incumbents in all the diocese resided upon their livings.* "Ye bishops of Wales," cried Penry, "seeing, you yourselves know, and all Wales knoweth, that you have admitted into this sacred foundation rogues, vagabonds gadding about the country under the name of scholars; spendthrifts and starving men, that made the ministry their last refuge: seeing you permit such to be in the ministry as are known adulterers, and thieves, roisterers, most abominable swearers, even the men of whom Job speaketh, who are more vile than the earth—do you not say that the Lord's service is not to be regarded?" † In the middle of the seventeenth century, the Rev. Rees Pritchard, Vicar of Llandovery, said that it would be difficult to decide whether the clergyman, the farmer, the labourer, the artisan, the bailiff, the judge, or the nobleman was the most daring in iniquity.‡ The picture of the state of the nation nearly a

---

* Strype's Annals. Quoted in Rees's "Nonconformity in Wales," p. 5.

† "Penry's Exhortation,' 1588, ib. p. 7.

‡ Pritchard's "Welshman's Candle," ib.

hundred years later was drawn in almost equally dark colours The Rev. Thomas Charles, of Bala, thus describes it:—"In those days the land was dark indeed. Hardly any of the lower ranks could read at all. The morals of the country were very corrupt; and in this respect there was no difference between gentle and simple, layman and clergyman; gluttony, drunkenness, and licentiousness prevailed throughout the whole country. Nor were the operations of the Church at all calculated to repress these evils. From the pulpit the name of the Redeemer was hardly ever heard; nor was much mention made of the natural sinfulness of man, nor of the influence of the Spirit. Every Sabbath there was what was called 'Achwaren-gamp'; a sort of sport in which all the young men of the neighbourhood had a trial of strength, and the people assembled from the surrounding country to see the feats. In every corner of the town some sport or other went on till the light of the Sabbath-day had faded."*

During this long period a few men had, like the prophets of Judah, lifted up their voices for their God. Besides Penry in the reign of Elizabeth, and Vavaseur Powell, in the time of the Commonwealth, three Welsh clergymen, William Wroth, rector of Llanvaches, Rees Pritchard, vicar of Llandovery, and Walter Cradock, stood conspicuous as shining lights in the spiritual darkness that enveloped the nation. Wroth was born in 1570, and was almost the first preaching incumbent in Wales.† From a man of gay and frivolous temperament he had suddenly become absorbed in the importance of the Divine message to mankind. His natural eloquence, his fervour of address, and

* "The Trysorfa," 1790. Quoted in Philip's "Life of Whitefield."

† Johnes's "Essay on the causes which have produced Dissent from the Established Church in the Principality of Wales," p. 6.

his unwearied zeal, soon made his name known throughout his native country. But he was guilty of ecclesiastical irregularities. When his Church would not hold the people who went to hear him he preached in the churchyard, for which offence he was called to account by his diocesan, who angrily inquired of him how he dared to violate the rules of the Church? Wroth, it is said, replied, with tears in his eyes, by calling the bishop's attention to the spiritual ignorance of the people and the necessity of employing every means to remove it—a reply which, for the time, availed. But he added to this offence the crime of refusing to read the "Book of Sports." Dragged afterwards by Laud before the Court of High Commission, he was summarily deprived of his benefice. Such a man was not likely to suffer mere ecclesiastical regulations or Episcopal prohibitions to influence his conduct. He still, therefore, continued to preach from house to house, and from town to town, and in 1638 founded, at Llanvaches, a church on the Congregational model. He died four years afterwards, leaving a reputation eminent for its sanctity, a title—"the blessed apostle of South Wales"—and a work which time can never destroy nor his countrymen ever forget.

Rees Pritchard—or, as he was more familiarly styled, "Vicar Pritchard"—was, if equally eminent in piety, not so unfortunate in respect to his ecclesiastical relationships. It happened that the Earl of Essex, when in his minority, resided near Llandovery, where Pritchard was born, and to his protection the vicar probably owed his immunity from persecution. His popularity was not less than that of Wroth. Vast multitudes went to hear him preach, and even the Cathedral of St. Davids was not large enough to contain the hearers. Pritchard therefore preached in the open air, and, as in Wroth's case, a charge was immediately preferred against him in the Ecclesiastical Court. He escaped punishment, but did not relinquish his labours. The tradition of Pritchard's labours has descended from generation to generation of his countrymen, amongst whom his name, at the end of more than two centuries, is still held in veneration. But he established other claims upon their gratitude than those belonging to a zealous preacher of the Gospel. He was the "Welsh Watts." His religious poetry is one of the most prized inheritances of his nation. No book in the Welsh language, it is said, excepting the Bible, has had so extensive a circulation, and, at one time, wherever the Holy Scriptures were to be found, there also was to be found the volume of "Pritchard's Poems."*

Walter Cradock, who was born in the early part of the seventeenth century, was a disciple of Wroth's, and imbibed from his spiritual teacher something of his zeal and independence. But these qualities were, at that time, an offence in the eyes of the ecclesiastical authorities. For refusing to read the "Book of Sports," he was ejected by the Bishop of Llandaff, in 1633, from his first curacy at Cardiff. From thence he went to Wrexham, where his eloquence drew crowds to hear him from the country around, and where his labours effected a signal reformation in the manners of the people. But before he had been there a year he was driven away. He is found, after this, at Llanvaire, from whence he made evangelistic excursions through all the neighbouring counties of North Wales. In the time of the Commonwealth he became a Congregationalist, and zealously defended the right of private judgment.† A hundred years after his death, the aged people amongst

---

* Johnes's "Essay," &c, pp. 12, 15. Rees's "Nonconformity," pp. 30, 36.

† Rees's "Nonconformity," pp. 51, 59.

the Dissenters of the Principality still talked of Walter Cradock.*

Excepting these men, scarcely any appeared, until just before the rise of Methodism, to enlighten the people concerning the Divine revelation to mankind, and these—the forerunners of Welsh Dissent—were frowned upon by all the ecclesiastical authorities. In common with both the earlier and the later Puritans, they were compelled to break through established rules, or to see the people die in their sins; and the judgment of those set over them appeared to be that it was better people should die in their sins than that one iota of the canon law, or the smallest of the rubrics, should be broken. The success and popularity of Wroth, Pritchard, and Cradock, apart from their religious characters, were partly due to the fact that they were eminently representative Welshmen. If the English incumbents, and their English curates, had been, what they were not, fit men to preach a pure religion, they could never have touched the hearts of the people. One of their own nation was needed to speak and to plead with them; and, as it has ever been since Christianity was first revealed, no sooner was it adequately placed before them than thousands joyfully accepted it. It is not, however, necessary to suppose that their spiritual rulers were altogether averse to their becoming a religious people. For the most part, they cared little about them. If the people had been "baptized," what more could they require? Men like Wroth, Pritchard, and Cradock, were considered enthusiasts, who were dangerous to the peaceable, if stagnant, order of things. If the religious sentiment should grow, there would be an end of non-resident bishops living upon the proceeds of dozens of livings, and of non-resident incumbents who

* Thomas's "History of the Baptist Associations in Wales," p. 3.

never saw their parishioners. The State was equally indifferent, and was not animated by any loftier principles than the hierarchy. If it had been, it would never have suffered the appointment of English prelates to Welsh dioceses, nor have overlooked the scandalous neglect of their duties of which the ecclesiastical officers of the Crown were habitually guilty. It would, at least, have seen that men fit for their special work were sent to discharge it. The native Welsh, or ancient British, race has always been marked by three characteristics—an ardent imagination, and warmth and activity of feeling. No people are more susceptible to the beauties of poetry or the charms of popular oratory, and none are more easily moved by appeals to the religious affections. Nor is the sentiment of nationality more deeply fixed, or more universally distributed amongst any of the Celtic race—where this sentiment seems to last longer than in any other race—than amongst the descendants of the earliest inhabitants of Britain. To this people, preachers, such as they were, were sent, who could have had no feelings in common with their parishioners. What wonder if they ultimately turned, almost as a whole nation, from a Church which had treated them, from the time of its birth, as aliens and outcasts, rather than as brethren and sons?*

In the early part of the eighteenth century another clergyman arose whose labours were probably of even greater practical benefit to his countrymen than those of any of his predecessors. This was the Rev. Griffith Jones, incumbent of Llandeilo and Llandouror. To this eminent man belongs the honour of establishing, long before Bell

* The causes of dissent in Wales have been most exhaustively treated by two Churchmen, the Rev. A. J. Johnes, in the "Essay" which has already been quoted in the text, and Sir Thomas Phillips, in his very comprehensive work on "Wales."

and Lancaster were born, a system of popular day-school education in Wales. Finding his own parishioners deficient in information upon the ordinary subjects of Christian doctrine and conduct, he founded a school for their benefit. The advantage of such an institution soon being made evident, he thought of the great good which would result if "a well-organised system of schools" was established throughout Wales. Aided by contributions from friends, he began to put his scheme into execution. His plan was to engage travelling schoolmasters, who should visit town after town, stopping in each as long as their services were required, and revisiting them from time to time. In order to procure proper instructors, he founded a teachers' seminary, to which he would admit none but apparently religious persons, the majority of whom, it appears, were Nonconformists. In 1741, or about ten years after their establishment, a hundred and seventy-eight of these schools were being conducted throughout the year. The result was soon apparent. Intelligence improved, manners became more civilised, and churches were better attended. Twenty years after this, when death put an end to the labours of this devoted and active philanthropist, the number of schools which had been established, at different times, and in various places in Wales, amounted to three thousand four hundred and ninety-five, and the number of scholars to more than a hundred and fifty thousand, or at least a third of the whole population of Wales. By far the larger number of the scholars in these "circulating schools" were adults, who lamented, with tears, that they "had not had an opportunity of learning forty or fifty years sooner." When Griffith Jones died he left, as has been well said, "in the religious regeneration, and the religious gratitude, of a nation of mountaineers, a memorial which will be envied most by those who are at once the proudest and the humblest of mankind." His work, however, met with much clerical opposition, and the bishops of Wales did not give him the least countenance.*

In the early period of the patriotic labours of this man a young preacher, of the name of Howel Harris, a native of Trevecca, appeared amongst the people. He had been to the University of Oxford, but had left it in consequence of the immorality of the place. Having been refused orders, because he had preached as a layman, Harris began, on his return home in 1725, to give addresses in the open air and in private houses. The effect upon the people, whom he sometimes addressed in vast numbers, was very great. As usual, he was much opposed by magistrates and the clergy, but several Dissenters kindly received him in their houses. In order to maintain the work which he had thus commenced, Harris proceeded to organise religious societies. "This," he says, "was before any other society of the kind was established in England or Wales, the English Methodists not being yet heard of." There can be no doubt, in fact, that as the system of popular education was established in Wales before it was established in England, so also the religious "societies" were set up in Wales by Howel Harris before they were originated in England by John Wesley.

When Howel Harris commenced his work Dissent in Wales was a very feeble thing. The number of Dissenting congregations in the whole Principality and the county of Monmouth, in the year 1715, was about a hundred and ten, and the actual attendants were not much more than twenty-five thousand persons. Of these the majority were Congregationalists and Presbyterians; the rest belonged to the Baptists and the Society of Friends. Most of these

---

* Johnes's "Essay," pp. 15, 25.

† Rees's "Nonconformity," &c., pp. 292, 293.

churches had sprung from the labours of Wroth, Pritchard, and Cradock. The first Baptist church, the origin of which can be clearly ascertained, was founded at Ilston, near Swansea, in 1649. The pastor of this church, John Myles, was the first who, in Wales, carried out the practice of unmixed communion.* In 1736 there were only twelve Baptist churches in the Principality, and five years later only fifteen.† In the few churches connected with the various bodies of Dissenters there was an earnest religious life, but they exercised comparatively little influence upon the character of the nation at large. Before the rise of Methodism—that is to say, before the preaching of Howel Harris—the churches were "little attended by the great mass of the people," and "indifference to all religion prevailed as widely as Dissent" has since prevailed.‡ Harris himself says that, with the generality of the people, public worship being over, the remaining part of the Sunday was spent in corrupt indulgences; all family worship was laid aside, except among some of the Dissenters; "while an universal deluge of swearing, lying, reviling, drunkenness, fighting, and gaming had overspread the country, and the clergy themselves were evidently not in earnest in their work." §

The labours of Harris excited not only the attention of his own people, but ere long secured the notice of the Methodist party in England. Whitefield put himself in communication with him; Wesley went to Wales and saw him; and the Countess of Huntingdon also visited him. He now extended his labours; and all through Wales his voice was

* Thomas's "History," &c., p. 5.
† Ib., pp. 43, 45.
‡ Morgan's "Life of Howel Harris" p. 12.
§ Johnes's "Essay," pp. 26, 27.

heard as that of a prophet crying in the wilderness. In many places he met with similar treatment to that received by the founders of Methodism in England. He was mobbed, stoned, and often in danger of his life. At Machynlleth, where he was assailed by a mob, headed by the local attorney and the parish clergyman, a pistol was fired at him, and he was driven, with sticks and stones, from the town. In Carnarvonshire he heard himself denounced by the Chancellor of the diocese as a minister of the devil; and when the Chancellor called upon the people to rise up against such a man, he was hunted from the church and the town.* But in almost all places he visited his preaching was successful. By-and-bye some clergymen took part with him, and a band was organised, resembling, in some fashion, Wesley's band in England.

Writing, in 1749, Harris relates that for seven years, in all weathers, and generally out of doors, he had preached three or four, and frequently five times a day, travelling from place to place, from ten to thirty miles in that period. Although he had not received orders in the Established Church, he strenuously adhered to its communion. He says that, for this, he was blamed by people of all denominations, and when he found some of his converts becoming Dissenters he thought it his duty "to declare against them." What he, in common with the leaders of the English Methodists, desired was that all those who were influenced by his preaching should remain members of the Established Church; but the progress of events effectually frustrated this intention. If the necessity for greater freedom of religious action than could be obtained in the Church had not compelled the disciples of Harris and of his coadjutors to separate from it, the animosity which was felt towards them

* "Stevens s History," ii. 72, 75.

by its rulers, which found expression in almost every charge that came from their pens, would have been sufficient to create alienation. The conduct of Harris was undoubtedly inconsistent. His movement was actual Dissent, and, accordingly, Welsh, like English Methodism, resulted in secession from the religion established by law. It was not long before Harris found coadjutors. Amongst these William Williams, of Panty-Celyn, was the most eminent. Thenceforward he devoted himself to itinerant preaching; and in 1716 took the bold step of administering the communion in a Welsh Methodist Chapel.

Contemporary with him was Daniel Rowlands, of Nant-cwnlle and Llangeitho, who, after preaching thirty years, was ultimately (about 1763) ejected from the Church for officiating in unconsecrated places, and for visiting other parishes than his own. The ministry of Rowlands appears to have been one of almost unsurpassed power. Persons would follow him from one church to another on the Sunday, and return home without having taken food from Sunday morning until Monday morning. After his ejection, Rowlands preached in a large place of worship built for him at Llangeitho, which became the centre of an extraordinary religious influence. Here, thousands, from every part of Wales, were accustomed to resort, some persons travelling sixty and even a hundred miles in order to hear him. The description of these remarkable assemblages, in the life of the Rev. Thomas Charles, of Bala, is not unlike that given by the Psalmist of Judah of the pilgrimage to Jerusalem. "From twenty to thirty travelled together, or in two companies, some on foot and some on horseback, both men and women. Those on foot started early on Saturday, and took a shorter course over the mountains, without any support except the food they brought with them, and their drink was pure water from the mountain springs. After hearing one or two sermons from Rowlands they returned home again, fully satisfied and abundantly repaid for all the toil of their journey." * Every county in the Principality was represented at these meetings. Llangeitho, in these days, took a position somewhat similar to that occupied by the cathedrals in the early period of English ecclesiastical history. There the new order of preachers met every month, and from it, as a centre, they went forth to evangelize the country. Speaking of Rowlands, Mr. Charles says: "His gifts and the power which accompanied his ministry were such that no hearers in the present age can form any adequate idea of them; there is no one who has not heard him who can imagine anything equal to what they were." †

The external results of the labours of these men was the organisation of numerous religious societies—the parents of the Welsh Calvinistic churches—throughout the whole of North and South Wales. In 1747 their first meeting-house was erected at Builth, in Breconshire. In the next year two more were erected in Carmarthenshire. After that they rapidly increased. In 1767 the Countess of Huntingdon founded a college at Trevecca, for the education of students, some of whom took orders in the Established Church, and became identified with the rising Evangelical party, while others remained in the Countess of Huntingdon's "Connexion," or ministered to Congregational churches. A Methodist Association, at which Whitefield was present, was held for the first time in Wales in 1743, when rules were laid down for the government of the body. From that time similar associations held periodical meetings. In the same year, Rowlands is stated to have had three thousand communicants in Cardiganshire, and Howel

* Sir Thomas Phillips' "Wales," p. 142. † Ib. p. 146.

Harris two thousand in Pembrokeshire.* Differences between Rowlands and Harris impeded the progress of Methodism for some time after this, and theological controversies had the same effect on other religious bodies, but the general progress of religion, resulting from the labours of these eminent, although discarded members of the Established Church, was without precedent. The whole aspect of the nation was changed. Religious societies sprung up in every part of the land. Dissenting churches rapidly increased in number. An effectual check was given to all amusements of an immoral tendency. The habitually warm temperament of the people began to flow, in greater and greater volume, in the channel of religious feeling. But when the early leaders of Welsh Methodism went to their rest, no provision for a permanent organisation of the forces they had created had been made. Howel Harris died in 1773, Rowlands in the same year, and Williams in 1791. As the founders of Calvinistic Methodism in Wales, Harris and Rowlands carried out the greatest work which the Almighty has given to men to perform. They began the regeneration of a whole people who, until they and their fellow-labourers appeared, were sunk in almost heathen darkness. The good they effected they effected against the will and in spite of the prohibitions of their own Church, which, as in England, and not in relation to the Methodists alone, had again exhibited herself in what was still her characteristic attitude, as the opponent of all sincere religious life, and active religious work. But whatever credit may attach to a communion from the zeal of individual members is to be attached, in this instance, to the Established Church in Wales. Although she disowned and expelled the men who were regenerating their country, their

* "Johnes's Essay," p. 36.

personal attachment to her was never lessened. It is impossible to say whether their spiritual power and success would have been greater if they had possessed less of this feeling. Their communion with the Church, and their constant professions of attachment to it, probably contributed, in the first instance, to their personal influence. It gave them, for a time, free access to churches, and gained them the ear of Churchmen. It is possible that, afterwards, its influence was not beneficial. For, when parish ministers could not address their people in the only language with which they were acquainted; when these ministers seldom even appeared in their parishes; and when their lives, if not always scandalous, were not such as to adorn an ordinary religious profession, the urgent advice to remain in the Church, if it were followed, was not calculated to conduce to the personal piety of the people. To supplement the deficiencies of the Church, or rather to supply that for which it ostensibly existed, the numerous Methodist Societies were formed. These possessed the soul, while the Church itself was only the skeleton of the community. The work of the pioneers of Welsh Methodism stopped short of the assurance of permanent success. This was obtained in the next generation, by persons whose individual sympathies were naturally freer than those of men who had been born and nurtured in the Established Church.

CHAPTER VIII.

FROM THE ESTABLISHMENT OF METHODISM TO THE SECOND AGITATION FOR THE REPEAL OF THE TEST AND CORPORATION ACTS.—1744—1793.

THE Methodist controversy was not the only controversy which attracted public attention at this period. Once more the relative merits of the Established Church and of Dissent were brought under consideration. The literature of this question received, from the active and inquiring intellect which characterised the nation during the greater portion of George the Second's reign, more important additions than had been made to it since the time of the later Puritans. The new controversy arose from a publication by Dr. Watts. When the causes of the decay of the Dissenting interest were under discussion, Watts wrote a solemn and impassioned appeal to Dissenters to live in a manner worthy of the principles they professed and the position they occupied.* He considered that these were eminently favourable to a religious life, and that therefore Dissenters were under special obligations to adorn the Christian profession. Their religious advantages he considered to be numerous and important. They, for instance, were in no danger, such as Churchmen were in, of mistaking baptism for inward and real regeneration; they were freed from the impositions and incumbrances of human

* "An Humble Attempt towards the Revival of Practical Religion among Christians." 1731.

ceremonies in Divine worship; they were not limited to set forms of prayer; they could not only worship God in their ordinary way, but could choose their own ministers; the communion of their Church was kept more pure and free from unworthy and scandalous members, and their conduct was strictly observed, and their behaviour watched with a narrow and severe eye. The real reason why they dissented from the National Church, was that they might make better improvements in religion than if they continued in her communion. What is it, he inquired, that we mean by asserting the right and freedom of conscience in our separation, but more effectually to promote the kingdom of God amongst men, to do more honour to the name of Christ in His institutions, and better to carry on the work of the salvation of souls? To be an irreligious Dissenter he counted as a degree of folly that wanted a name; for such a man got nothing by his profession but reproach and contempt in this world and damnation in the next.

Although Dr. Watts was careful to eschew ecclesiastical controversy in this work, he could not avoid frequent reference to the points of difference between the ecclesiastical constitutions of the Established and of the Dissenting communities. He also plainly stated his conviction of the unscripturalness of any National Church. The whole question of the Civil Establishment of religion he subsequently discussed in another publication.* In this—one of the most careful of all his writings—he laid down the proposition that the civil government, in its proper aims and designs, had no object beyond the benefit of men in this world, nor did the things of religion nor the affairs of a

* "An Essay on Civil Power in Things Sacred; or, an Inquiry after an Established Religion, consistent with the just liberties of mankind and practicable under every form of Civil Government." 1739.

future state come within its cognizance. No civil ruler, he held, had any right to require or command the people to profess or practise his own religion, nor to levy tithes or other compulsory dues for its support. The usurpation of the civil power in things sacred, or of the ecclesiastical power in things civil, had, he contended, produced nothing but infinite confusion, persecution, hypocrisy, slavery of soul and body, fraud and violence of every kind. With characteristic discursiveness, however, Watts proceeded to inquire whether a certain establishment of a national religion was not within the sphere of the civil government. He held that it was; that every government should make an acknowledgment of the existence of a God; that it should impose oaths; that it should employ public teachers of morality who should be sustained by taxation; and that all people should be compelled, under penalty, to hear such teachers. The ground on which he based this scheme—which he afterwards discovered to have a singular resemblance to the constitution of China—was that the law of the land on moral questions, such as theft, adultery, and truth, ought, in justice, to be made known to those who would be punished for not obeying them. Like the "Republic" of Plato and the "Utopia" of More, this scheme is to be classed with the many ingenious theories of inventive minds. It is astonishing to notice that, while Watts had every confidence that religion could take care of itself, he forgot that, in such a case, religion would certainly take care of morality; that if men could not be made religious, neither could they be made moral, by legislative machinery. Dr. Watts' declaration of anti-state-church principles was not the first that had been made by a Dissenter, but it was the first formal statement and defence of them by a Congregational minister.

It is doubtful whether Watts would have been sustained in his condemnation of Church Establishments by the majority of the Dissenters of his time. Dr. Doddridge, certainly, did not agree with him. While expressing his utmost abhorrence of all forms of persecution, and his sense of both its folly and its wickedness,* Doddridge did not hesitate to express his opinion that a civil establishment of religion, combined with its compulsory support, was not contrary to the laws of justice and equity. He held that both a regard to the honour of God and the good of society must engage the magistrate to desire and labour that his people might be instructed in what he believed to be the truth; that they could not be instructed without a public provision being made for those who instructed them; that if the magistrate had a discretionary power with respect to any branch of the public revenue he might apply it to that purpose, even though most of his people should be of a different religious persuasion from himself. He thought, however, that such an establishment should be made as large as possible, so that no worthy or good men, who might be useful to the public, should be excluded. On the critical question whether Dissenters might be properly compelled by the magistrate and the majority to assist in maintaining established teachers of whom they did not approve, he was of opinion that it stood upon the same footing with their contributing towards the expense of a war which they might think to be neither necessary nor prudent. None, he said, could reasonably blame a government for requiring such general contributions. However, if the majority should disapprove of the conduct of the government, they had the same right of resistance which they had in any other case.† Doddridge, in this instance, was influenced by the fallacy which Paley subsequently advocated, namely,

* Sermon on the "Iniquity of Persecution." Works, iii. 117.

† "Lectures on Ethics." Works, iv. 503, 504.

the resolving a question of right and wrong into one of majorities and minorities. If he had formally argued this question from an exclusively scriptural point of view, he might have expressed himself with more hesitation upon it; but it does not appear to have been one to which he attached a paramount importance. Persecution he could not but hate; but, providing an Established Church were sufficiently "large," he might even have joined it.

The two principal representatives of the Free Churches were not, however, the only persons whose thoughts were directed to this subject. By the failure of the old arguments in support of Church authority, which had been exploded during the Bangorian controversy, Churchmen were being driven to find new defences for the Establishment. Formerly, it had been sufficient to urge that they belonged to the Church of the successors of the Apostles, and had, therefore, inherited peculiar gifts, and were entitled to peculiar privileges; but this style of argument was no longer of any avail amongst intelligent men. It was necessary, therefore, to justify the connection between the Episcopalian Church and the State by another theory. This work was accomplished by a clergyman who afterwards became an eminent bishop of the Establishment. In the year 1736, the Rev. William Warburton, incumbent of Brant-Broughton, published a treatise on the "Alliance between Church and State." Warburton is entitled to the credit of framing a new and ingenious theory of this alliance. Treating the Church and the State as two separate and independent powers, he argued, from the analogy of civil government, that when the Church entered into an alliance with the State she necessarily sacrificed her independence. In return for this, she received peculiar privileges and a public endowment for her ministers. This was her benefit; but the State was equally benefited, for the

Church exerted her influence and authority on the side of public virtue and social order. The advantages of a public endowment were defended by Warburton at great length. He considered it rendered the clergy independent of the people, and did not subject them to the temptation of pandering to their passions. When Selden denied the divine authority of English tithes, he was compelled to recant his opinions, but Warburton equally abandoned that basis of ecclesiastical taxation. He considered it to be merely an eligible and convenient method of providing for the maintenance of the clergy, and he therefore approved of it. He defended the presence of "superior members" of the Church in the legislature of the nation as being a just concession to the reasonable expectations of a Church which had surrendered to the State her own independence and authority. Starting with these primary principles, he proceeded to inquire what religion should be selected for such an alliance, and replied that, from motives of policy, it should be the strongest. Such an alliance could, however, subsist only so long as the selected Church maintained its relative superiority over other sects. When that superiority should cease to exist, it would be the duty of the State to select the body which had taken the place of the other. In any case, other religious societies should have free toleration; but not so as to injure the established religion, and there should therefore be "tests." Dissenters, he argued, ought not to complain of being compelled to support the established religion, because it was maintained, not for the promulgation of any particular religious opinions, but for the benefit of the State, of which they themselves were members.

Warburton's theory was evidently constructed to suit the actual position of the English Church. It is the lowest theory of an established religion that could be framed. It ignores the difference between truth and error, and justifies the State in propagating one as well as the other. But he wrote his book, avowedly, in the interests, not of the Church, but of the State. The subject was, with him, not a religious, but a political one. That Warburton did not stand alone in this idea is proved by the sudden popularity of his treatise, and by Bishop Horsley's criticism upon it—that it was an admirable specimen of scientific reasoning applied to a "political" subject.*

While Warburton's work, singularly enough, excited no public controversy, and provoked only one public reply, Watts's "Humble Attempt" was vigorously assailed. In a series of Letters † especially addressed to "a gentleman dissenting from the Church of England," the Rev. John White, vicar of Ospring, attacked the argument of Watts that the principles of Dissent and the position of Dissenters were more favourable to the growth of piety than those of Churchmen. After denying the allegation, the author proceeded to the proof of the contrary position. He then examined the reasons of Dissent, going over the principal grounds of the old controversy on this subject. White's "Letters," written as they were in a pointed and popular style, went quickly through several editions. They found, however, an opponent far more able and astute in controversy than White himself. This was Micaiah Towgood, a Presbyterian minister of Crediton, who replied to the whole of White's letters. His work, which for three generations remained the standard treatise on this subject, and which has been more frequently reprinted, both in England and America, than any other publication of the kind, derives its chief merit from the

* Watson's "Life of Warburton," p. 57.

† "Three Letters to a Gentleman Dissenting from the Church of England." By John White, B.D. 1743.

prominence which it gives to the unscriptural character of the constitution of the Established Church. For the manner in which it exposed the subjection and dependence of the Church on the State, and the inconsistency of such a position with the rights of the Church, and in which it contrasted the character of a Christian with the character of the Established Church as such, this work had, for nearly a hundred years, no equal. Previous writers had confined their arguments mainly to a discussion of liturgies, rites, ceremonies, and other incidental characteristics of the State Establishment. Towgood, not undervaluing these points, boldly attacked the foundations on which the Church rested. He denounced it for having surrendered its Christian liberty, for being not an "ally," but a mere creature of the State. He exposed its ambitious and persecuting spirit. Subjection in religious matters, he held, was due to Christ alone, and civil governors had no right to intermeddle with them. He agreed that, with the alteration of what was unscriptural in its character, Dissenters would be glad to return to the Church. They bore it, he said, no enmity. They wished it prosperity and peace, and the glory of being formed according to the perfect plan of the primitive Apostolic Church. They wished to see it established upon a broad and catholic foundation, Jesus Christ Himself being its only Lawgiver and King. As for the Church as it was, he denied that it was any essential part of the British constitution, or that it and the State must fall together. He asked any one to annihilate, in his imagination, its present form; to suppose that its clergy, liturgy, articles, canons, ceremonies, and rites, had entirely vanished from the land; its immense revenues applied to the ease of taxation, and the payment of public debts, and the preachers to be paid only by voluntary contributions—where, he inquired, would be the essential loss to the State? Would the monarchy be overthrown, the courts of judicature shut up, parliaments no more meet, commerce and trade be brought to stagnation—because what people called their "Church" was no more?* This was the boldest suggestion that had yet been made on this subject. White added five other publications on this subject, continuing the controversy to the year 1751, but he never grappled with Towgood's leading argument in proof of the natural freedom of the Christian Church from State control. Towgood himself lived until nearly the close of the century in which he wrote, dying in 1791, at the great age of ninety-one. Though a keen controversialist he was a man of singular modesty, and he was satisfied, to the end of his life, with the pastorate of a country congregation.† The earlier editions of his answers to White were all published anonymously. His ministerial activity, his devoutness, and his public spirit were acknowledged by all his contemporaries. His service in vindication of the principles of the Free Churches has made his name one of the most eminent and honourable in their literature.

Those persons who have the most clear conception of the proper functions of the State, are also those who will be found to obey, with the greatest willingness, such laws of the State as are in harmony with the everlasting principles of justice. That the growing perception of the injustice involved in the connection between the Church and the State did not tend to alienate the Dissenters from the established Government was apparent in the rebellion of 1745. While the Jacobites and High-Churchmen received the news of the Pretender's landing with satisfaction and delight, Dissenters

* "The Dissenting Gentleman's Answer to the Reverend Mr. White's Letters," &c. 1746, 1747, 1748.

† Manning's "Life and Writings of Towgood." 1792.

of all classes at once rallied to the Crown. As soon as the news of the event was received, the Committee of the Deputies passed a resolution recommending the whole body of Dissenters throughout the kingdom to join with others of his Majesty's subjects in support of the Government. They next despatched a circular letter throughout the country, expressing their earnest desire that in view of the dangerous situation of public affairs, Dissenters would act in the most zealous manner.* This appeal was responded to with enthusiastic alacrity. Armed associations of Dissenters were formed in all parts of the kingdom; † chapels were converted into parade grounds, and ministers became voluntary recruiting officers. Doddridge was especially active in furthering this movement. He addressed letters to his friends, went personally amongst his own people in Northampton, encouraging them to enlist, and printed a private address to the soldiers of one of the regiments of foot, afterwards engaged in the battle of Culloden, encouraging them in their duty.‡ The Dissenting pulpits resounded with the call to arms, and the king was assured that, whoever besides should fail him, he might rely with confidence on the loyalty of Protestant Dissenters.§ Even the Quakers could not refrain from giving an expression of their active sympathy with the Government. Their principles forbade them to incite men to shed blood; but they contributed to the health of the regiments under the command of the Duke of Cumberland, by supplying all the soldiers with flannel for their winter campaign.‖ The reward which the Dissenters received for this service, apart from the earnest thanks of the king, consisted in their inclusion in the Act of indemnity,

* "Sketch of the History," &c., pp. 21, 22. † Ib.

‡ Orton's "Life of Doddridge," p. 208. § Ivimey, iii. 238.

‖ "Journey along with the Army of the Duke of Cumberland," p. 14.

and in the royal pardon for the rebels who had taken up arms against the Government. In accepting commissions in the volunteer army, they had incurred the penalties of the Test Act. As in the rebellion of 1715, so in this more serious crisis, they had broken the letter of the law in order to save the Crown and Government. Those who would have sacrificed both for the sake of increased ecclesiastical predominance, were still too powerful to prevent the tests from being abolished.*

From this time, and for many years, the life of the Free Churches flowed with smooth and, unless disturbed by death, with an almost unruffled course. The first amongst its eminent men to drop from their living ranks was Dr. Watts, who died in 1748. For a long period this ablest of their representatives had been in feeble and declining health, but his intellect, until very lately, had been in ceaseless activity. Judging from his writings, it would seem to have been the

* The manner in which the Dissenters were treated on these occasions was severely commented upon by Fox, in his speech in favour of the repeal of the Test Acts, on March 2nd, 1790. The great orator said that "a candid examination of the history of Great Britain would, in his opinion, be favourable to the Dissenters. In the rebellions in 1715 and 1745, this country was extremely indebted to their exertions. During those rebellious periods they had acted with the spirit and fidelity of British subjects, zealous and vigilant in defence of the Constitution; at both these periods they stood forward the champions of British liberty, and obtained an eminent share in repelling the foes of the House of Hanover. Their exertions then were so magnanimous, that he had no scruple to assert that to their endeavours we owed the preservation of Church and State. What was the reward they obtained? We generously granted them a pardon for their noble exploits, by passing an Act of indemnity in their favour. Gentlemen should recollect that, at the times alluded to, the High-Churchmen did not display such gallantry, for many appeared perplexed and pusillanimous. Hence the superior glory of the Dissenters, who, regardless of every danger, had boldly stood forth in defence of the rights and liberties of the kingdom."—*Parliamentary History.*

noble ambition of Watts to render the utmost service of which he was capable in the instruction and guidance of the human mind in all its spheres of action; and for this he was one of the few men competent both to instruct and to guide. As a mental philosopher he ranked next to Locke. Had he written only his "Logic," his essay on the "Improvement of the Mind," his "Philosophical Essays," his essay on the "Freedom of the Will," and on the "Civil Power in Religion," his name would have occupied a high and honourable place amongst the philosophical writers of his country. But he rendered greater service than this. At a time when infidelity was making the boldest assaults on the foundations of the Christian faith, he was one of the first to stand forward in defence of revealed religion. Unlike many eminent persons, however, he was as capable of commending the Gospel to the hearts and consciences of men as to the intellect. His sermons and practical writings, therefore, while they indicated a strong and polished mind, and an accurate taste, were full of chastened feeling and of close application to the conscience. Having added to his Hymns a metrical version of the Psalms of David, he had given the Church a collection of poetry for its assistance in public worship, which, with all the great additions that have since been made to that department of religious and poetical composition, has been rivalled by no other single writer. Nor was he satisfied to serve only the grown man and Christian. Watts therefore added to his Divine Songs for children, books for the guidance of their education in religion and in the most familiar of the arts and sciences. Having thus, in nearly fifty years of active life, given to his own and succeeding generations the full vigour of a mind of the highest order of Christian excellence, he died, at the age of sixty-four. He chose to rest where so many of the confessors of the Free Churches had rested, and, in the presence of an immense concourse of spectators, he was buried in Bunhill Fields. Those who attended his funeral must have felt a gratitude for his work such as can be excited by but few men. The poorest as well as the richest in intellectual gifts, the oldest Christian as well as the youngest child, might have been almost equally indebted to him. As Dissenters, they owed to him especial gratitude. In vindication of their principles he had done no more than many others, but he had, in one conspicuous manner, given strength to the Free Churches. Although of high literary renown, and brought into frequent contact with the most eminent scholars in the Established Church, he remained inflexible in his principles as a Congregational Dissenter. It was a fashion for vulgar writers in that, as it has been in more than one subsequent age, to identify Dissent with vulgarity of manners and narrowness of mind. In Watts, at least, it was seen that a man might belong to one of the most democratic sections of Dissent and write in favour of the separation of the Church from the State, and yet be a cultured scholar and a Christian gentleman.

After Watts's death, Doddridge occupied the most eminent position amongst Dissenting ministers. He had now been about twenty years at Northampton, but had not been allowed to assume the office of tutor there without opposition. He was summoned by a clergyman for non-compliance with the provisions of the Test Act respecting Dissenting teachers, but the prosecution was stopped by order of George II., who declared that he would have no prosecution for conscience' sake during his reign.* His life, since that period, had been one of singular industry and usefulness. He was the model Christian pastor and minister, and the most eminently successful tutor who

* Orton's "Life of Doddridge." Works, i. 149.

had ever been connected with the Free Churches. The seminary of Doddridge, however, was not intended only for the education of young men for the ministry: he received into it any who would go there,—noblemen's and gentlemen's sons, and persons of all religious persuasions, whether Episcopalian, Presbyterian, Unitarian, Baptist, or Congregationalist. He incurred some censure from his stricter brethren for this, and was to some extent beset by what he terms "Orthodox spies," in consequence; but he did not relinquish his system. He was consequently accused, during his lifetime—as most eminent men of his class are—by the envious and the less eminent, of looseness of theology. The fact that an Unitarian went to his seminary, was allowed to remain there as an Unitarian, was not dishonourably interfered with by his tutor, and, when he left, was an Unitarian still, was considered to indicate a lax sense of duty on the tutor's part. But Doddridge could not have done what would have pleased such men. He was a gentleman and a man of honour, and therefore his orthodoxy was suspected. Those who, wherever the Anglo-Saxon language is spoken, have read and sung his hymns; who have been brought to the feet of their Saviour by his "Rise and Progress of Religion in the Soul"; whose Christian affections have been warmed, and whose judgments have been enlightened by his "Family Expositor," may well wonder how such a man could have been even suspected by the worst-minded of his contemporaries. But Doddridge, while he held fast to the Gospel of Jesus Christ as the "anchor of his soul," held intercourse with some whom others denounced. Whitefield, as has been seen, was one of these; but Warburton, who had written a massive book to prove that Moses and the Israelites knew nothing of the doctrine of a future state, was another, and Doddridge, with Warburton's consent, had written, in a popular publication, a commendatory review of his work. Gentleness, goodness, and love were in his heart wherever he went, and if he erred it was from excess of amiability. This, however, as is natural, so far from interfering with his duty, stimulated him towards its performance. He preached regularly, and lectured before his pupils on almost every subject of human study. The accounts which have come down to us from his own pen, and from the description of his pupils, of the range and method of this teaching, give a high impression of the breadth and thoroughness of his intellectual culture. His academy took the highest rank amongst all similar institutions. Doddridge's preaching was experimental and practical rather than formally dogmatic. His theological creed is to be found interwoven in all his sermons and writings, but he evidently cared less for creeds than for a Christian life. One of his greatest services to religion in his own neighbourhood was the institution at Kettering, in the year 1741, of an association for the reformation of religion and for evangelistic purposes in Northampton. A special object of this association, it is worth noticing, was the propagation of Christianity in heathen lands.* To this movement, and to the great impulse which Doddridge's own zeal gave to all forms of religious activity in Northamptonshire, is probably to be attributed the generally high, consistent, and bold character of Dissent in the midland counties. This admirable man died at Lisbon in the year 1751. The expenses of the journey thither, taken with a forlorn hope of recruiting a constitution which, for years, had been slowly undermined by excess of zeal, were defrayed by the Countess of Huntingdon and her church friends, and his widow found means

* "The Evil and Danger of Neglecting the Souls of Men." Dedication. Works, iii. 229.

of subsistence from the same source. With the death of Watts and Doddridge the leadership of Dissent passed from the Congregational body.

The comparative inaction which followed on the death of Doddridge was broken only by a legal controversy with the City of London concerning the compulsory liability of Dissenters to serve the office of sheriff. This case is interesting as securing protection for Dissenters against the arbitrary claims of the Corporation, and for the interpretation which it gave of their rights under the Toleration Act. In 1742, a Mr. Robert Grosvenor had been elected to the office of sheriff, but, on refusing to qualify for the office by taking the sacrament according to the rites of the Established Church, he was cited by the Corporation before the Court of Queen's Bench. The defence of his case was undertaken by the Committee of Deputies, and the Court decided against the claim. To meet, as it judged, any future case of this kind, the Corporation, in 1748, passed a bye-law, imposing a fine of four hundred pounds and twenty marks upon every person who should decline standing for the office after he had been nominated to it, and of six hundred pounds upon every person who, after having been elected, should refuse to serve. The fines thus obtained were to be appropriated towards the building of a new Mansion House. The scheme was worthy of the lowest type of commercial chicanery, and the Corporation of London must have sunk infinite degrees below its ancient spirit for such a device to have been entertained for an hour. It was carried into operation with all the cunning and greed by which it is possible for such a body to be distinguished. Whenever a sheriff was required to be elected, a Dissenter was immediately nominated. One after another declined to serve, and was at once mulcted in the fine. This system had gone on for six years, during which the fines had produced more than fifteen thousand pounds, when, in 1754, a spirit of resistance was raised Three Dissenters, Messrs. Sheafe, Streatfield, and Evans were successively elected to office. On consulting the Deputies they were advised to refuse service, and to resis the payment of the fine. The Corporation at once commenced proceedings against them in the Sheriff's Court. The case against Mr. Streatfield fell to the ground, inasmuch as he was proved to be out of the jurisdiction of the Court. In 1757, after prolonged delays, judgment was given against Mr. Sheafe and Mr. Evans, who then appealed to the Court of Hustings—now abolished—of which the Recorder of the City was the sole judge. The Recorder having confirmed the judgment of the Sheriff's Court, Mr. Sheafe and Mr. Evans sued for a special commission, consisting of five judges, who, with one exception, reversed, in 1762, the decisions of the Courts below. The Corporation then brought a writ of error before the House of Lords, but before the case could be tried there, Mr. Evans, by the death of Mr. Sheafe, was left sole defendant. The case was argued at great length before the Lords on the 21st and 22nd of January, 1767. On the 3rd and 4th of February following, six out of seven judges gave judgment in favour of Mr. Evans. The decision of the Lords was then delivered by Lord Mansfield, who, in the highest strain of eloquence, expressed his abhorrence of the persecution which Dissenters had suffered, and vindicated the principles of English law with respect to religious liberty. Of the attempt of the Corporation to make two laws—one to render men incapable of serving office, and another to punish them for not serving, this eminent judge said:—"It is a trap a man cannot get out of; it is as bad a persecution as that of Procrustes: if they are too short, stretch them; if they are too long, lop them. . . . Dissenters have been appointed to the office—one who was blind, another who was bed-ridden; not, I suppose, on account of their being fit and able to serve the office." He proceeded to state his belief that these men were chosen because they were incapable of serving. In his vindication of the principles of religious liberty, the judge remarked that it was now no crime for a man to say he was a Dissenter; nor was it any crime for him not to take the sacrament according to the rites of the Church of England. For atheism, blasphemy, and reviling of the Christian religion, there have been instances of persons prosecuted and punished upon the common law, but bare Nonconformity is no sin by the common law; and all positive laws inflicting any pains or penalties for nonconformity to the established rites and modes, were repealed by the Act of Toleration; and Dissenters were thereby exempted from all ecclesiastical censures. Lord Mansfield went on to say:—"There is nothing certainly more unreasonable, more inconsistent with the rights of human nature, more contrary to the spirit and precepts of the Christian religion, more iniquitous and unjust, more impolitic, than persecution. It is against natural religion, revealed religion, and sound policy."* With this denunciation, the Corporation was ignominiously dismissed. The end of this thirteen years' prosecution found the defendant, Mr. Evans, dying, but he was sufficiently conscious to express his satisfaction at this equitable decision. To his firmness, supported by the Dissenting Deputies, is owing the fact that Church and Tory corporations, all through the kingdom, had not the legal right to use their power for the oppression of their Nonconformist neighbours.

When this cause was decided, George III. had been king for nearly seven years. By the death of his predecessor the Dissenters had lost a firm and sincere friend to their

* "History and Proceedings of the Deputies," 25, 38.

liberties. George the Second's attachment to the principles of constitutional freedom was almost the only redeeming feature in this monarch's character. He had inherited the traditions of the Revolution, and would allow neither civil nor ecclesiastical politicians to sway his mind in opposition to them. It was one of the happiest circumstances for English freedom, that the two sovereigns who succeeded to Anne were not natives of England. Had they been so, the probability is that they would have succumbed to the influences of the territorial aristocracy and of the Church, whose predominant dispositions were in favour of a more or less arbitrary system of government. As regards civil liberty, the first two Georges were constitutional from interest as well as from principle. Their maintenance of the doctrines of the Revolution was necessary to the consolidation of their dynasty, and it was not until the suppression of the rebellion of 1745 that the Hanoverian dynasty was finally secured against successful assault. George III., if he escaped some of the vices, inherited, unfortunately, few of the virtues of his grandfather. His political position was secure, and, so far as English parties were concerned, he had nothing to do but to hand it down in undisturbed safety to his children and his children's children. The Jacobites had cast their last die; they had lost all hope of changing the succession to the Crown; but the spirit of Jacobitism yet remained. Instead, however, of making a party, they adopted a wiser course; they allied themselves to the extreme section of the Tories. In George III. the Jacobites found a man after their own heart. In consequence of the shameful manner in which he had been educated, he was ignorant to almost the last degree. He was one of the most obstinate men. "I will be master," was his self-assumed motto, and any one who would let him be master was sure of his favour and patronage. Notwithstanding an early moral failing, he had, and sustained, a good domestic character—the character of a respectable farmer. He would have made a good overseer of the poor in his time, when that office was executed somewhat after the manner of a slave-driver; but by disposition, intellect, and education, he was as little fitted for a king as almost any man who ever sat on a throne. Such a personage the High Church party could work with. Their leading idea was the same—to promote and sustain prescriptive power, whether just or unjust, whether adapted to a nation's welfare—as it sometimes is—or injurious to her best interests and influence, as was the case with England during the whole of the reign of this narrow-minded, selfish, and therefore unfortunate monarch.

The state of the Church in the earlier portion of George III.'s reign was what it had been for the preceding thirty or forty years—as respects the bishops and the clergy, one of scandalous indifference to the claims of religion, as well as to the claims of ecclesiastical duty, Pluralities and non-residence were universal,* and none troubled to condemn them. Wesley and his fellow-labourers were still the objects of sarcasm and scoff, and vital religion was almost as little known amongst the clergy as amongst the people whom they taught. Yet there were men eminent for their great intellectual ability in the Established Church. Foremost amongst them was Joseph Butler, Bishop of Durham, whose "Analogy of Natural and Revealed Religion" had placed him amongst the greatest of theological writers. Butler, however, in the proportion that he excelled in his own department of thought, failed in other departments. The work by which his name has been immortalised will always remain one of

* Perry's "History of the Church of England," pp. 398, 399.

the masterpieces of human reasoning, and the greatest among intellectual defences of the Christian religion. As a preacher, however, Butler partook of the tendency of the times in which he lived. His theology was broad and liberal in tone; but, in common with many men of his school, and with most men of his peculiar intellectual culture, he preached with little religious feeling. His sermons are cold and colourless essays, as deficient in spiritual as they are superior in intellectual power.

Next to Butler, but of a later period, was William Warburton, who, after the publication of his "Alliance," attracted more attention than any other ecclesiastic. The extraordinary extent of his reading, and his brawny power of brain, are certified in his "Divine Legation of Moses," and in his many controversial works; but he wrote scarcely a single work in which he did not degrade himself by coarse and vituperative abuse of every person who happened to differ from him. Not to agree, to the minutest and most unimportant point, in all that he said, was to be paraded through the literary world as "an ass" and "a fool."* To oppose him was to be "a wretch," "a rogue," and "a scoundrel." Warburton was one of the bishops who led the opinion of the Church respecting the Methodists, whom he abused as a "new set of fanatics," and he wrote strongly against Wesley's doctrine of grace†—a controversial work which has sunk into oblivion. If, amongst other prelates, Lowth, by his learning and his wit, served to redeem the character of the Episcopal Bench, Laurence Sterne, by his profligate life and coarse if humorous writings, dragged

* See Watson's "Life of Warburton," cap. xxxiii.

† "The Doctrine of Grace; or, the Office and Operations of the Holy Spirit Vindicated from the Insults of Infidelity and the Abuse of Fanaticism." 1762.

down the reputation of the clergy. Archbishop Secker who filled the primate's chair, was inferior in ability to any of these; and as a preacher he was scarcely respectable.

Archdeacon Blackburne, at this time, scandalised the Church by writing against its doctrines, orders, and ceremonies, and yet remaining within its borders. He had the dexterous force and the happy directness of style which are necessary to the successful controversialist, and he would have wielded his powers with a moral as well as an intellectual success, if he had supported his doctrines by his practice. But when he, a Church dignitary, proceeded to denounce all creeds and confessions of faith,* to assert the right of private liberty in theological matters, and to hold up his Church to scorn and opprobrium, men, however they might acknowledge the accuracy of his judgment and the truth of his criticism, saw that he lacked the necessary evidence of moral sincerity. His works are an armoury of sharp and polished weapons of attack against the Established Church; but Blackburne himself should have been the last man to invent or to use them. Chief Justice Blackstone, who made a point, at this time, of hearing the most celebrated preachers in London, states that, in all his visits to the churches, he did not hear a sermon that had more Christianity in it than a speech of Cicero's, and that it would have been impossible for him to tell whether the preacher was a Mohammedan or a Christian.† Scattered through England were a few "Methodist" clergy, the founders of the Evangelical party in the Established Church, who laboured incessantly for the advancement of religion; but they were outnumbered by thousands, and frowned upon by all who were in authority. Of these clergy

* In "The Confessional." 1766.

† *Christian Observer*, 1858.

Fletcher of Madeley, Venn of Huddersfield, Grimshaw of Haworth, Romaine of Blackfriars, and Berridge of Everton were the chief. Hervey, the author of "Theron and Aspasia," had died in 1758. To Fletcher, Methodism in the Church owed more than it did to any except its original founders. Fervour of feeling, holiness of spirit, and simplicity of character were rarely combined in him. Venn made Huddersfield the centre of the most untiring evangelistic labours; and Grimshaw, of Haworth—that Haworth which the three daughters of a succeeding incumbent, Rev. P. Brontë, have made even more celebrated—brought thousands of Yorkshiremen to hear him preach the new Gospel. Romaine was the Evangelical preacher of the metropolis, proclaiming the "doctrines of grace" with a power that had seldom been equalled. But of all the founders of the Evangelical party, Berridge, of Everton, was the most conspicuous. He was the only one whose sermons produced the abnormal and painful physical effects which often accompanied the preaching of the Wesleys and Whitefield. His evangelistic powers were surpassed only by the three apostles of the early movement, and his eccentricity probably contributed in no small degree to his personal popularity. Berridge was possessed of a rough wit, which he used unsparingly in his public addresses, as well as in private intercourse. But he was far removed from vulgarity.

Outside the Church, Methodism was increasing with marvellous rapidity. Its preachers, going through the length and breadth of the land with an energy and rapidity never before recorded in the history of Christianity in England, left, wherever they went, new friends and converts. All these did not, however, formally identify themselves with the Wesleyan societies. The continued opposition of the clergy had aroused in many minds a corresponding spirit of antagonism to the Established Church. Lay preachers began to assert their right to administer the Sacraments, and members began to secede to one or other of the Free Churches. In this crisis it was resolved to bring the relations of the Methodists towards the Church before the Conference. This was done in 1755, and after three days' debate, which was attended by sixty-three preachers, it was resolved that, whether lawful or not, it was not expedient to separate from the Church.* This decision was arrived at mainly, no doubt, through the personal influence of John and Charles Wesley. It is easy to understand the position of the former with respect to the Establishment. He was rapidly seceding from his former Church views; he had given up apostolical succession and the divine origin of Episcopacy; he had scorned the authority of ecclesiastical law; but it would have been inconsistent with his original purpose to leave his Church. He went on, hoping against hope that the clergy would one day join him, and that, through their union, the Church itself would become one vast Methodist organisation; but none of these hopes were ever realised. As Methodism grew, it receded further and further from the Establishment, until it became necessary formally to separate from it. Nor did Wesley, in another sense, succeed. The revival of religion which ultimately took place in the Church was in the direction of Whitefield's, and not of Wesley's, theology. The forerunners of the Evangelical party were Calvinists, and more closely associated with the Countess of Huntingdon than with Wesley. But, while still determined to remain a member of the Church, Wesley candidly avowed that "he could not answer" the arguments of those Methodists who advocated secession.† But this determination need not

* "Letter to the Rev. Mr. Walker," in the "Arminian Magazine," 1779.

† Wesley's "Journal," 1755.

have excited bitter feelings towards the Free Churches. Yet, when the Baptists drew away some of his members, he could not restrain the expression of his indignation; while Charles, to whom Christian charity was an unknown feeling, railed against them as the "cavilling, contentious sect, always watching to steal away our children,"*—the very charge which the Church herself brought against the Wesleys. The decision of this Conference modified, in no degree whatever, the feelings of the clergy, and probably checked the spread of Methodism itself.†

The Congregationalists possessed, at this period, no man of a very high order of genius, but many who were more or less eminent for their scholarship and their abilities. Amongst these Dr. Thomas Gibbons, pastor of the Haberdashers' Hall Church, and one of the tutors of the Mile End Academy, occupied a conspicuous position. He was one of the most active preachers of the metropolis, and the author of a great variety of published works. His name is best known in connection with his intimacy with Watts, of whom he was the earliest biographer. At Pinners' Hall preached Dr. Caleb Fleming, almost the only Congregational minister in the metropolis who held Socinian views. Fleming was most conspicuous as an advocate of these opinions; but few men did greater service in his generation than he, in writing against the civil establishment of religion. He was the only Dissenter who replied to Warburton's

* Jackson's "Charles Wesley," cap. 20.

† "Had Methodism," Dr. Abel Stevens says, "taken a more independent stand at this early period, when it had so many intolerable provocations from the Establishment, and the popular mind so little ground of sympathy with the clergy, it is the opinion of not a few wise men that it might, before this time, have largely superseded the Anglican hierarchy, and done much more than it has for the unscriptural connection of the Church and State."—"History," i. 399.

"Alliance," and probably the first who publicly traced the increase of infidelity and of Romanism to the existence of an Established Church.* For more than forty-five years he maintained, with undiminished ardour, the cause of religious liberty. Dr. John Guise, of New Broad Street, one of Doddridge's most intimate friends, was, "though dead, yet living." He is still known as the popular author of a carefully composed paraphrase of the New Testament, and was a man greatly honoured and loved by his people. His successor at New Broad Street, Dr. Stafford, occupied also a respectable position as a metropolitan minister.

In the pulpit of Owen and Watts was Dr. Samuel Morton Savage, a man of equal learning and power, and one of the professors at the Hoxton academy. Dr. David Jennings was professor in the same academy. At Jewin Street was Joseph Hart, a man of remarkable religious experience, and a most popular minister. He is well known as the author of a volume of rather sensational hymns, abounding in extravagant expressions, but which are still prized by a certain class of religious people. Although he entered the Christian ministry at forty-eight years of age, and died eight years afterwards, he had become so known and esteemed that his funeral at Bunhill Fields was attended by no fewer than twenty thousand persons.† The Weigh-house Church was presided over by Dr. William Longford, a useful and ingenious rather than powerful preacher. He was assisted by the more eminent Samuel Palmer, afterwards of Hackney, who subsequently became one of the most eminent Congregational ministers of London.‡

A few country ministers of this denomination obtained a deserved eminence amongst their contemporaries. Dr.

* Dr. Abel Stevens' "History," ii. 232, 243.
† Ib. iii. 343, 347.
‡ Ib. i. 183, 187.

Addington, of Harborough, and Kibworth, the successor of David Some, and, some years afterwards, pastor of Miles Lane Church, London, was an admirable specimen of a devoted country minister. An impressive preacher, and a diligent and conscientious pastor, he belonged to the large class of ministers of the Free Churches, who, in the provinces at that time, adorned the profession of Christianity. Such a man also was Benjamin Fawcett, of Kidderminster, one of the successors of Baxter, and who, in his thirty-five years' ministry, almost equalled Baxter in labour and diligence. And another was Darracott, of Wellington, a man of refined manners, who attained the rare success of great spiritual influence amongst the poor of an agricultural district. The Rev. Job Orton, of Shrewsbury, the friend and biographer of Doddridge, was another of the best known and most highly respected Congregational ministers in the midland counties. His publications on religious subjects—nearly all of a practical character—were very numerous, and to his suggestion the "Nonconformist Memorial" is owing. The Congregationalists were now more eminent for teaching than for pulpit power. With considerable foresight, they had engaged their ablest men for their educational institutions. Such were Drs. Jennings and Savage, and Walker, Gibbons, and John Conder, the last three of the Mile End—afterwards the Homerton academy—under whose tutorship many of the ablest ministers of the succeeding generations were educated. Dr. Ashworth, of Daventry, whence Doddridge's academy had been removed after his death, was of equal if not greater eminence.

For theological scholarship, however, no minister amongst the Congregationalists could compare with Dr. John Gill, one of the ablest divines which the Baptist denomination has ever produced. He was elected pastor of the Baptist church at Horselydown in 1720, and continued in that position for more than fifty-one years. As a biblical commentator and a theological controversialist few persons have surpassed this able men. With a mind enriched with all the stores of biblical learning, and a brain of singular strength and capacity, he was able to do great service in behalf of the principles to which he was attached. His "Exposition of the Scriptures" is a work which can never lose all its value, and his Defences of Calvinism and Adult Baptism are, as they deserve to be, works of the highest authority in his own denomination. Gill did, for the dogmas of Calvinism, a work which was more needed in his day than it has since been. His style however, was not equal to his learning, and one of his own denomination has characterised his works as a "continent of mud."*

In Gill's church at Horselydown was a schoolmaster and deacon, named Thomas Crosby, who deserves mention as the first historian of the Baptists. Crosby wrote his work mainly to supply the deficiencies of Neal's History. The charge against Neal, that he had not done justice to the Baptists, must be acknowledged to have been correct, and Crosby's design was therefore a laudable one. He has furnished subsequent writers with many materials which would probably have perished but for his care, zeal, and industry; but, beyond this, his history is destitute of every literary excellence.

The name of Stennett had been connected with Baptist Church history for nearly a hundred years: the third of the name—Samuel Stennett—was now preaching at Little Wild Street. Not less eminent than his father and grandfather, he lived to adorn the Christian ministry, and add, by his genius and character, strength and stability to all the Free

* Robert Hall. Works, i. 125 (ed. 1832).

Churches. Samuel Stennett was, after Bunyan, the first Christian hymnologist amongst the Baptists. There is now scarcely any selection of hymns which does not contain some of his productions. In Eagle Street preached Dr. Andrew Gifford, one of the greatest antiquarians of the eighteenth century. From his remarkable acquaintance with literature, and especially with numismatics, he was chosen, in 1717, to the post of assistant-librarian of the British Museum. He was one of Whitefield's most intimate friends. Gifford, like Gill, belonged to the strictest school of Calvinists, and was an eminent favourite with the earliest Evangelical ministers, such as Romaine and Toplady.*

Just rising into prominence was a man of very different order from any of these—Robert Robinson, of Chesterton. For boldness, versatility, vivacity, and wit, this remarkable man had no equal amongst his brethren. Robinson was not a prudent man, but though intensely sincere, and one of the most ardent lovers and teachers of Christian and civil liberty who ever lived, hierarchies, priests and the superstitions and traditions by which these characteristics of corrupt Churches are mainly sustained, found, in Robinson, a vigorous and persistent enemy. He had something of the spirit which animated De Foe, united to a finer but more irregularly developed intellect. Robinson began his church life as a Calvinistic Baptist, but subsequently lapsed—without, however, relinquishing his pastorate—to anti-Trinitarian views. His writings are wanting in coherence; but they contain some of the most vigorous thought, expressed in vigorous language, to be found in ecclesiastical literature. His "Arcana," and his "History and Mystery of Good Friday," are the best of his works; his unfinished

* Ivimey, iii. 591, 613.

"History of the Baptists" is a strange and unsuccessful medley.*

Among the General Baptists there were few who had retained the theological principles of the founders of that body. A large majority had embraced Socinian views; but in 1770 a "New General Baptist Association" was formed, which adopted for its creed the characteristic principles which at one time had distinguished the denomination. The principal founder of this Association was Daniel Taylor, a man of naturally vigorous and able intellect, whose earliest religious impressions were due to the Methodists. Taylor's views on the subject of Baptism changing, he joined the General Baptist Association in Lincolnshire, and was pastor of the Church at Wadsworth, in that county. Disapproving of the theological opinions of most of his brethren in the ministry, Taylor, in conjunction with William Thompson of Boston, and nine ministers from the churches in Leicestershire and the neighbouring counties, established a new association. The distinctive creed of the new body was contained in the small compass of six articles, which declared the natural depravity of man; the obligations of the moral law; the divinity of Christ and the universal design of His atonement; the promise of salvation for all who exercise faith; the necessity of regeneration by the Holy Spirit; and the obligation, upon repentance, of baptism by immersion.† This creed especially guarded the new Association, by its third article, both from the Socinians and from the Particular Baptists. Taylor subsequently removed to London, where he became pastor of the General Baptist Church in Virginia Street, Ratcliffe Highway, and was the recognized leader of the denomination.

---

* Dyer's Life of Robinson. Robinson's Works.

† Adam Taylor's History of the General Baptists, ii. 133, 143.

He was held in high estimation, both for his abilities and for his character, by all bodies of Christians.

But neither the Baptists nor the Congregationalists, nor both combined, could at this period compare, for mental power and public service to civil and religious freedom, with the Unitarian Presbyterians. The history of the latter half of the eighteenth century is the history of the rapid growth and, on the whole, the most powerful representation of Unitarianism in England. For more than forty years had Nathaniel Lardner been labouring in defence of the evidences of the Christian religion, and was still pouring forth the treasures of his vast learning on that subject. He was now about eighty years of age, and belonged to a past generation. Next in repute stood Dr. Joseph Priestley, as distinguished for his philosophical attainments, his bold, and, to himself, perilous advocacy of liberty, as for his love of truth, his simplicity of character, and his purity of life. The theological works of Priestley are an armoury of the most advanced Unitarian doctrines; but to whatever extent he offended the great majority of his countrymen by the extremeness of his views, he could not offend them by his style of argument No more candid or gentlemanly controversialist ever defended an unpopular cause, and no man less deserved the disgraceful treatment which he received from his countrymen.

Almost equally eminent in science and politics was Dr. Richard Price, lecturer of the Old Jewry, Jewry Street, pastor of the church at Newington Green, and afterwards of Hackney. As a mathematician, Dr. Price was almost unrivalled; as a political writer on the side of liberty, no man surpassed him in vigour. He was one of the class who are the natural product of an age of arbitrary power. Possessed of a keen sense of justice and right, and of an undaunted courage, he expressed his thoughts on the political situation of his time with an energy and indignation which would have brought a fatal revenge on a less eminent man. He was the leader, in the metropolis, of those Dissenters who upheld the rights of the American Colonies in the War of Independence, and of those who most actively sympathised with the French Revolution in its earliest stages.

In the same period Dr. Andrew Kippis, the successor of Calamy and Say, was the pastor of the Presbyterian Church at Westminster. He was not eminent as a preacher; but in literature and ecclesiastical politics he held a distinguished position. He was best known by his contemporaries in these two capacities; now his celebrity is limited, for the most part, to his literary labours. As a writer in the "Gentleman's Magazine" and the "Monthly Review;" as the editor, for many years, of the last-named periodical, and as the editor of the "Biographia Britannica," Dr. Kippis rendered an unusual service. Standing at the head of two fountains of literature, he did what no man before him had done,—gave a just proportion to Dissenting politics, history, and biography. His activity on behalf of the civil rights of Dissenters was incessant. For forty years—until nearly the close of the century—no movement in connection with their common interests took place without securing his open and undaunted support.

Another name which was never missed in any movement connected with the extension of religious freedom was that of Dr. Philip Furneaux, of the Presbyterian Church at Clapham. He was celebrated for his extensive and accurate memory, to which is due the preservation of Lord Mansfield's judgment in the City of London Sheriffs' case. He was the author of an admirable essay on Toleration, in which the principles of Nonconformity were argued on the broadest ground. He also, with Dr. Priestley, defended the Dissenters, with great vigour and ability, from the malicious and unworthy attack on their principles made by Chief Justice Blackstone, in his "Commentaries on the Laws of England." Dr. Furneaux, towards the end of his life, entirely lost his reason. Dr. Samuel Chandler, of the Old Jewry, was of still greater eminence. In the contemporary histories of this period his name is to be found occupying a position similar to that formerly occupied by Calamy. He headed deputations, and more often, apparently, than any other man, presided at public and private conferences. He was far, however, from being a merely ornamental member of the Presbyterian body. He was one of the first and ablest writers against the Deists, and the author of a "History of Persecution," in which the interference of human law with religious matters was assailed as being necessarily opposed to justice, as well as to liberty. On Dissenting questions he was one of the most frequent and vigorous writers of his age. It appears, however, that Dr. Chandler would not have been unwilling, provided that the constitution of the Established Church were altered, to belong to that Church. He was, at one time, engaged with Archbishop Herring, Goold, Bishop of Norwich, and Sherlock, Bishop of Salisbury, in discussing terms of comprehension for Dissenters, in which he does not appear to have advanced very greatly, if at all, beyond the ground adopted by the later Puritans. As a writer on the Evidences of Religion, on Biblical Exegesis, and on Religious Liberty, he had few equals,* and no man, for nearly fifty years, was more honoured.† Dr. Thomas Amory, his successor in the

---

* As an indication of Dr. Chandler's industry, it may be stated that the list of his writings in the new Catalogue of the British Museum Library occupies seventeen pages. Some publications, of course, are duplicates.

† "Protestant Dissenters' Magazine," vol. 1. Wilson's "Dissenting Churches," ii. 360—385

ministry at the Old Jewry, the editor of Chandler's works and the writer of his life, carried on the same work, but while Chandler was one of the few eminent Presbyterian ministers who were not either Arians or Socinians, Dr. Amory was inclined to Arianism.

The defence of the public interests of Dissenters was at this time undertaken, for the most part, by the Unitarians. Although the creed of this section of the Free Churches was still under the ban of law, that law had already become a dead letter. No one presumed to put it in operation. There were churches which openly declared themselves to be Unitarian. Presbyterian they still were in name, and in one characteristic of old Presbyterianism they were also Presbyterian in practice. They recognised no creeds, and no confessions of faith were adopted by them. But they had abandoned the doctrinal foundations of the later Puritans. Instead of Baxter and Howe, Clarke and Whiston were their favourite authors. But, in relation to the civil liberties of Dissenters, such men as Priestley and Price were far in advance of their ancestors. It is remarkable that the class of which these eminent men were the principal representatives, instead of suffering in numbers because of their conspicuous advocacy of their liberties, were, at this time, rapidly increasing. Amongst the Congregationalists the only man who apparently took a very active interest in public questions was Caleb Fleming, and his doctrinal sympathies were with the Unitarians. The Baptists were somewhat better represented, but that body, as a whole, was not in a prosperous condition, and was largely occupied with the discussion of distinctive Baptist and Calvinistic doctrines. Two new sects had just made their appearance in England—the Sandemanians and the Swedenborgians; but, as yet, their influence on religious thought was only nominal. The Established Church, drugged by an indolent and luxurious spirit, was asleep, and, while it slept, Methodism on the one hand, and Unitarianism on the other were gaining ground on every side.

It was owing, mainly, to the existence of the Unitarian element in the Church that a movement was commenced n 1771 for the abolition of subscription to the Articles by clergymen and other professional men. In that year Archdeacon Blackburne published "Proposals" suggesting that a petition to Parliament for relief should be drawn up, and a meeting was held for organising a movement in its favour. His proposals met with considerable approval, and on July 17th a meeting of the clergy was held at the Feathers' Tavern, and a form of petition, drawn up by Blackburne, adopted. The petitioners enlarged on the rights of reason and conscience, and maintained that each man had been constituted a judge for himself in searching the Scriptures, and what might or might not be proved thereby. The cases of the clergy and of professional men were separately stated, and both parties prayed earnestly for relief.* This petition was no sooner adopted than vigorous measures were taken to procure support for it. The most active person in this work was the Rev. Theophilus Lindsey, vicar of Catterick, afterwards one of the most eminent Unitarian ministers in London, who, in the following winter, travelled some two thousand miles to obtain signatures. His success, however, was but small. Most of the clergy he found to be indifferent, while from the Methodists he met nothing but opposition.† This body, indeed, used its utmost influence to prevent the prayer of the petition being granted. Lady Huntingdon, especially, exerted herself with all her characteristic activity against it. She procured counter petitions

* "Parliamentary History," xvii. 245.

† Belsham's "Memoirs of Lindsey," p. 49.

she waited on members of the House of Commons; and she obtained from Lord North, then First Lord of the Treasury, and from Edmund Burke, a promise to oppose the Bill.*

The measure was introduced into the House of Commons on February 6th, 1772, by Sir William Meredith, who, in his opening speech, enlarged on the imperfection, absurdity, and unintelligibleness of the Articles, and stated that there was no clergyman who thoroughly believed them in a literal and grammatical sense, as he was required to do by the nature of his subscription. The most obvious line of argument against the petitioners was adopted by Sir Roger Newdigate, who asked with what face persons who had subscribed, who did not believe in what they had subscribed, and who were therefore devoid of common honesty, could come to the bar of that House. After several speeches had been delivered, Lord North stated the views of the Government. The most effective part of his speech was that which described the confusion likely to follow the adoption of the Bill. The rector, he remarked, would be preaching one doctrine and his curate another; the morning lecturer would preach in favour of the Trinity, and the evening lecturer against it. Burke followed Lord North. References having been made to the Dissenters by one speaker, who had suggested the danger to the Church which might ensue if they, also, were to be relieved from subscription, "Let him recollect," said Burke, "along with the injuries, the services which Dissenters have done to our Church and to our State. If they have once destroyed, more than once they have saved them. This is but common justice, which they and all mankind have a right to." The ablest speech in favour of the Bill was delivered, at the close of an eight hours' debate, by Sir George Savile, whose

* "Memoirs of the Countess of Huntingdon," ii. 286.

impassioned eloquence is reported to have produced an astonishing impression on the House. He derided the notion of confining the Church within the narrowest limits, and he had no fear of sectaries. "Sectaries," he cried; "had it not been for the sectaries, this cause had been tried at Rome." "Some gentlemen," he added, "talk of raising barriers about the Church of God, and protecting His honour. Barriers about the Church of God, Sir? The Church of God can protect itself." The debate ended by Lord North, in reply to Sir William Meredith, denying he had said that the Articles were conformable to Scripture. The Bill was then thrown out by 217 to 71 votes.* The motion was renewed in the two following years, and defeated with equal decision. After the third defeat several clergymen left the Church, and openly joined the Unitarians.† Blackburne, however, the promoter of the movement, retained his preferments, openly saying that he could not afford to give up his means of living. The movement, from the beginning, had no chance whatever of success. The majority of the people cared nothing for it, and statesmen and bishops were far too conservative to pull down one of the oldest foundations of the Established Church. But the rejection of the Bill did not secure any greater unity of thought than had hitherto prevailed in the Church. The Articles were signed, and not believed, just as before. It does not seem to have occurred to the Government, or to the clerical opponents of the Bill, that the scandals attending subscription might have been removed without removing subscription itself—that boys of sixteen years of age, and physicians, might, at least, be exempted from confessing their belief in the Thirty-nine Articles. The

* "Parliamentary History," xvii. 245, 296.

† Belsham's "Memoirs of Lindsay."

clergy could not reasonably have expected exemption. Church Establishments and liberty of thought cannot co-exist; or, if they do, those in the Church who exercise that liberty will always expose themselves to a reasonable suspicion of their intellectual, if not of their moral, dishonesty.

In the gallery of the House of Commons, during the first debate on this question, there sat two Dissenting ministers—the Rev. Edward Pickard, of Carter's Lane Presbyterian Church, and Dr. Furneaux. These gentlemen heard several members suggest that the Dissenters might apply, with good prospect of success, for their relief from subscription. Amongst others, Lord North remarked that, had a similar application been made by them, he should have seen no reasonable objection to it; for, said the premier, "they desire no emoluments from the Church."* Pickard and Furneaux accordingly laid the matter before their brethren, and it was resolved by the General Body of Dissenting Ministers, and the Committee of Deputies, that a Bill should be prepared and brought in. At this time the law, as defined by the Toleration Act, required all Dissenting ministers, tutors, and schoolmasters, to subscribe the doctrinal Articles. Those who did not were subject to fines, imprisonment and banishment. It was impossible for Unitarians to do this, and they therefore braved the consequences of refusal. It was now proposed to substitute for this subscription a declaration in the following words:—"That we believe the Holy Scriptures of the Old and New Testament contain a revelation of the mind and will of God, and that we receive them as the rule of our faith and practice." No time was lost in forwarding this measure, for on the third of April, in the same year, the Bill, which was in

* Belsham's "Memoirs of Lindsey," pp. 65, 66.

charge of Sir Henry Houghton and Edmund Burke, was under debate in the House of Commons. Although it gave great alarm to High Churchmen, it passed its first stage without a division, and on April 14th the second reading was carried by 70 votes to 9.* It reached the House of Lords in the next month, but was not debated until it was before the Committee of the House. Here it received the support of the most eminent men amongst the peers; Lord Chatham, Lord Camden, and Lord Mansfield, amongst the number. The weight of the Court and the Bench of Bishops was sufficient, however, to defeat it. Five bishops, headed by the Archbishop of York, spoke against it, and only one, Green, bishop of Lincoln, in its favour. "Green! Green!" exclaimed the king, when he heard of this, "he shall never be translated." † The Bill was lost by 86 to 28 votes. It was on this occasion that, in reply to Drummond, Archbishop of York, the Earl of Chatham made a memorable defence of Dissenters. The Archbishop had charged the Dissenting ministers with being men of a "close ambition." "This," exclaimed the statesman, "is judging uncharitably; and whoever brings such a charge, without evidence, defames. The Dissenting ministers are represented as men of close ambition: they are so, my lords; and their ambition is to keep close to the college of fishermen, not of cardinals; and to the doctrines of inspired apostles, not to the decrees of interested and aspiring bishops. They contend for a scriptural and spiritual worship; we have a Calvinistic creed, a Popish liturgy, an Arminian clergy. The Reformation has laid open the Scriptures to all; let not the bishops shut them again. Laws in support of ecclesiastical power are pleaded, which

* "Parliamentary History," xvii. 431.

† Dyer's "Life of Robert Robinson," p. 78.

it would shock humanity to execute. It is said religious sects have done great mischief when they were not kept under restraints; but history affords no proof that sects have ever been mischievous when they were not oppressed and persecuted by the ruling Church."

Having nearly the whole weight of the popular branch of the legislature in their favour, the Dissenters were not dismayed by their treatment in the Lords. On March 2nd, 1773, the Bill was again brought in, carried on the second reading by 87 to 34 votes, and through Committee by 69 to 16 votes, and at the last stage by 65 to 14 votes. A new feature was introduced into the question this year which threatened, at one time, to be fatal to it. Several Dissenters, including some in London, Liverpool, Bolton, Exeter, Dursley, and Wotton-under-Edge, petitioned against it, on the ground, amongst other reasons, that "if it should pass into law it would undermine the establishment of religion."* A meeting of Dissenting ministers was also held in London, at which resolutions were passed protesting against the measure. It appears from these resolutions that fears were entertained of the growth of Popery and Unitarianism; † but how the former would be effected it is difficult to see, while the latter had obviously increased and was increasing in spite of all legal prohibitions to the contrary. These petitions, however, had no weight, nor did the second successful passage of the measure through the Commons at all affect the determination of the king and the bishops. It was again decisively rejected.

From the Lords the Dissenters had, as had been their wont, appealed to the people. An admirable opportunity was given to them to re-affirm and defend the principle of religious liberty, and they took the utmost advantage of it.

* "Parliamentary History," xv. 786. † Ivimey, iv. 31, 32.

The Rev. Ebenezer Radcliffe, of Poor Jewry Lane, boldly attacked the bishops; * the Revs. Isaac Maudit, Kippis, Furneaux, Gibbons, Stennett, and Robert Robinson, asserted anew the rights of conscience. These were well-known men, and they were the customary standard-bearers of Dissent. But another name, destined to acquire an equal eminence, now appeared, namely, that of the Rev. Joshua Toulmin, Presbyterian minister of Birmingham, who, in two "Letters on the late applications to Parliament of Protestant Dissenting Ministers," ably dealt with the whole question. Most of these publications breathed a stronger spirit of defiance of the bishops and clergy than had ever before been shown by Dissenting ministers. They indicate that since the Toleration Act had passed there had been a growth, not merely of opinion respecting the claims of the Church, but of determination to resist those claims. Radcliffe, while he protested that "the oratory of all the Dissenting ministers in this kingdom could not prevail upon one man to attempt so ridiculous a project as that of pulling down the hierarchy," protested, with equal force, that he looked upon the conduct of the hierarchy with pity, indignation, and contempt. "Many Dissenting ministers," said Dr. Stennett, "cannot conscientiously subscribe the Articles, as they apprehend the civil magistrates requiring subscription to explanatory articles of faith to be an invasion upon the rights of conscience, and the sole authority of Christ as King in His Church." Kippis declared that the Dissenters now denied the right of any body of men, whether civil or ecclesiastical, to impose human tests, creeds, or articles, and that they protested against such an imposition as a violation of men's essential liberty to

* "Two Letters addressed to the Right Reverend Prelates who a second time rejected the Dissenters Bill," 1773.

judge and act for themselves in matters of religion."* But no writer more clearly illustrated this change than Robert Robinson, who, with unparalleled vigour and vivacity, attacked the whole system of human authority in matters of belief and of human legislation for the Christian Church. "Let any impartial inquirer," he said, "take up the Holy Scriptures, and ask whither do all the contents of these ancient writings tend? History, prophecy, miracles, the ceremonies of the Old, and the reasonings of the New Testament; the legislation of Moses, and the mission of Jesus Christ—to what do they tend? What is their aim? The proper answer would be, Their professed end is to give glory to God in the highest, and on earth peace and benevolence amongst men. . . . Now, to be a Christian is neither more nor less than to concur with this design." † Three years after writing this, Robinson, in the "History and Mystery of Good Friday," returned to the attack. Dealing with the hierarchy, he wrote—"Hierarchical powers have found many a state free, and reduced each to slavery; but there is no instance of their having brought an enslaved state into Christian liberty." He then proceeded to dwell upon the vices that disgraced the priesthood. They were six—ignorance, perjury, ambition, avarice, time-serving, and hypocrisy: "Perjury, he said, "if they subscribe upon oath their belief in propositions which they have either not examined, or do not believe." Avarice, "ten thousand times more tenacious of a four-penny Easter offering than of all the Ten Commandments." "What said you," he inquired, addressing a clergyman, "to the Dissenting clergy, whom you flatter and soothe, and call

* Kippis's "Vindication," p. 29.

† "Arcana; or, the Triumphs of the late Petitioners to Parliament for Relief in the Matter of Subscription." Preface, 1774.

brethren in Christ? Are they freed from oaths, and subscriptions, and penal laws? Christian liberty! thou favourite offspring of Heaven! thou first-born of Christianity! I saw the wise and pious servants of God nourish thee in their houses, and cherish thee in their bosoms! I saw them lead thee into public view: all good men hailed thee! the generous British Commons caressed and praised thee, and led thee into an Upper House, and there—there thou didst expire in the holy lap of Spiritual Lords!"

Such attacks, renewed and reiterated, the bishops of this period could, of all men, least afford to have brought against them. Nor could the Church afford to have her foundations re-examined and her breastworks so ruthlessly assailed. Whether from fear of prolonging the controversy, therefore, or from a desire of engaging the Dissenters in measures for the relief of Roman Catholics, they suddenly and unexpectedly surrendered. Preaching, on January 30th, in the year 1779, before the House of Lords, Ross, Bishop of Exeter, took occasion to express his earnest wish that toleration might be extended, and that Dissenters might have a legal security for the free exercise of their worship. Acting upon this hint, the old Bill, slightly modified, was again brought in, and passed both Houses with scarcely any opposition. The declaration, substituted by this Act* for the previous subscription to the Articles, required Dissenters, as a condition of exercising the office of minister or preacher, to assert their personal Christianity and Protestantism by their belief in the Scriptures. This was the first step for ninety years in the direction of enlarged toleration, and at the end of even this long period it could be accomplished only by a compromise.

While the attention of Dissenters was thus engaged in

* 19 Geo. III., cap. 44.

securing an extension of their ecclesiastical rights, the Evangelical party in the Established Church, combined with the Calvinistic Methodists, were absorbed in a controversy with John Wesley and some of his followers, on the relative merits of Calvinism and Arminianism. At the Methodist Conference of 1770, Wesley procured the passage of a special Minute, declaratory of the opposition of the Conference to the distinctive doctrines of Calvinism. No sooner was this Minute published than the Calvinistic Methodists took alarm. The Countess of Huntingdon believed that it was aimed at the fundamental truths of the Gospel, and publicly insisted on its formal recantation. Wesley, at the next Conference, proceeded to explain it, It had been held, by the Calvinists, that the Minute upheld the doctrine of justification by works, and Wesley now drew up another Minute, in which that doctrine was stigmatised as "most perilous and abominable." It might have been supposed that the misunderstanding would have been removed by such a frank explanation; but it unfortunately happened, as is often the case, that theological zeal outran Christian discretion. The first to exhibit this was Fletcher, of Madeley, who held ultra-Calvinism in as much abhorence as the Countess of Huntingdon held Arminianism. Fletcher, as soon as the minutes of 1770 were attacked, wrote in their justification a letter to the Hon. and Rev. Walter Shirley,* who now occupied a position somewhat similar to that of Whitefield in connexion with the Countess's labours. Fletcher attacked ultra-Calvinism with the might of a master of scriptural lore; but, at the same time, with the most gentle lovingkindness towards its advocates. Shirley replied, and Fletcher answered by a "second check." The quarrel—for it be came, in course of time, nothing better than a quarrel—was

* "Check to Arminianism," 1771.

now taken up by the partisans of both theological schools. Amongst the controversialists on the Calvinistic side were Rowland Hill, and his brother, Sir Richard. The former, one of the most successful and humorous, but most godly, preachers of the age, had been early adopted by the Countess. He was another of the great phalanx of devoted men whose earnestness was esteemed to be too great for the peace and quietude of the Established Church. After leaving Cambridge, where he had seen several of his fellow students expelled for Methodism—he being also religiously a "Methodist"—Hill was refused ordination by six bishops in succession. He then proceeded to do what Whitefield had done before him, preach in the highways and byways, and anywhere, as Berridge counselled him, where "the devil's territories" could be found. The courage of his conduct and the power of his preaching obtained for him the same reception that Whitefield and the Wesleys had met with. He was derided; his preaching was drowned with clamour and noise; he was pelted and stoned; his nearest relatives almost disowned him; but his devotion overcame all obstacles. Sir Richard Hill also fought for Calvinism in the press. He undertook to reply to Fletcher, provoking from the ardent friend of Wesley another "check."

A disputant of more thorough theological culture, in the person of the Rev. Augustus Montagu Toplady, now entered the field. None could question Toplady's piety or ability. The ultra-Calvinistic school in the Church of England never possessed a man of greater zeal, of a finer spirit of devotion, or of more acute controversial power. As vicar of the little Devonshire village of Broad Hembury, he was a living example of a devoted country pastor—a character as rare as it was precious in the generation to which he belonged. Toplady, however, while he possessed some of the best qualifications, had at the same time some of the worst vices of a controversialist. He was a laborious historical inquirer; he had a keen faculty of observation, which enabled him to detect the smallest flaw in his opponent's argument, and he could arrange his materials with skill and effect; but he was hot, vindictive, and grossly abusive. Of all the controversies which have ever stained the Christian character, that between the Calvinists and Arminians was the one most calculated to bring it into reproach and contempt; and of all Christian controversialists Toplady is the most unfavourable specimen. More Calvinistic than Calvin himself, he took a pleasure in expatiating on the severest doctrines of the great Reformer, and he was as furious as a goaded bull with his adversaries. One of these was Walter Sellon, a comparatively illiterate man, but one of Wesley's best and most useful preachers. Sellon was not nice in his choice of language, but his taste had not been cultivated, like Toplady's, by an academic education. He called Toplady very hard names, a "malapert boy," "the greatest bigot that ever existed, without one grain of candour, benevolence, forbearance, moderation, goodwill, or charity," "a wild beast," &c. Toplady took pleasure in quoting such epithets, and then returned them with double vigour. Sellon was "whitewasher in ordinary" to John Wesley; "a low mechanic," "a pigmy on stilts," and "never until now did such whining cant issue from the pen of meanness."* In such a spirit, with the exception of Fletcher, did the controversialists for six years maintain their respective theories. At its close, just before the early death of Toplady, the respective opinions of the Calvinistic and the Arminian Methodists had become settled in the minutest points of metaphysical theology; but few, in the one party, were as Calvinistic as

* Toplady's "Historic Proof of the Doctrinal Calvinism of the Church of England." Introduction.

Toplady, or, in the other, so Arminianistic as Sellon. It was the last great battle between the two systems, and its influence on the minds of those who witnessed it was probably not altogether that which the combatants would have preferred. But they were all good men, and some of the most touching and, at the same time, instructive passages in Christian biography and unchristian controversy are those which record, in Fletcher's life, his tearful interviews with Berridge and Venn, and in Rowland Hill's life his voluntary suppression of one pamphlet in which, in his own judgment, he had indulged in uncharitable censures of his opponents.*

Necessarily opposed to the system of ecclesiastical government in England, the Dissenters found themselves, at this period, equally opposed to the principles on which the king and his ministers had determined to conduct the political policy of the country. When, in 1774, it appeared probable that there might be a rupture of the peaceful relations which had hitherto subsisted between the mother country and the North American Colonies, the Dissenters almost unanimously declared their sympathy with the latter. With the principles they held it was impossible they could have done otherwise. When George the Third and his Tory ministry resolved to tax the Colonies without their consent, the descendants of the Puritans, both in Old and in New England, saw a second assertion of the arbitrary claims by which it had been attempted to levy ship-money. The very existence of Dissent in England was necessarily opposed to the exercise of such claims. For the assertion of liberty of conscience had been accompanied throughout its history with the assertion of constitutional rights. From

* Stevens's "History of Methodism," vol. ii., cap. i. ii. Benson's "Life of Fletcher." Southey's "Life of Wesley." Sidney's "Life of Rowland Hill." "Life and Times of the Countess of Huntingdon."

the time of their first existence the Dissenters had constituted themselves the guardians of these ancient liberties. They had steadfastly resisted every encroachment upon them throughout the reigns of the Stuarts, and during the yet brief period of the existence of the House of Hanover. It is of vital importance to notice that the antagonistic attitude which they deemed it necessary, for the sake of their own liberties and the liberties of their countrymen, to take during the period of the Stuart dynasty, was taken because the Crown was then encroaching upon the Constitution. What they then did was to save the rights of Englishmen from the tyranny of arbitrary power. When George the Third attempted, in respect to the North American Colonies, to exercise a degree of prerogative which had not been claimed in England since Hampden's time, the Dissenters at once, and naturally, took the side of the Colonies. Ecclesiastical sympathies had, no doubt, much weight with them, and quickened the expression of their feelings. The colonists were sons of the same fathers, and inheritors of the same principles. Was it to be imagined that English Dissenters would see them trampled upon by a prerogative-hugging king and a Tory Government, just as Charles the First and Strafford had attempted to trample upon their ancestors? With scarcely a dissentient voice the Dissenters cast the weight of their influence against the Government, and, ultimately, fully justified the course which they took.

This agitation was led by Dr. Priestley and Dr. Price. In view of the approaching general election, Dr. Priestley, in 1774, issued an "Address to Protestant Dissenters of all Denominations, with regard to the State of Public Liberty in General, and of American Affairs in Particular." In this eloquent appeal Dr. Priestley reminded the Dissenters that, while religious liberty was the immediate ground on which they stood, it could not be maintained except upon the basis of civil liberty, and, therefore, the old Puritans and Nonconformists were always equally distinguished for their noble and strenuous exertions in favour of them both. "Whenever," he warned them, "the altar of civil tyranny shall be erected, you will be the first victims." He ascribed the hostility of the Court to the Americans principally to the fact that they were Dissenters and Whigs.* He considered that the position taken by the Americans, in denying the right of the British Parliament to levy taxes upon them, was justified by the Constitution, and by the principles of liberty in general. In one striking and prophetic passage he wrote: "Because the Americans have more of the appearance of religion than ourselves, we ridicule them as hypocrites. But, if they be such hypocrites as the Puritanical party in England, whom the Royalists diverted themselves with stigmatising in the same manner in the time of the Civil War, then valour and perseverance will go hand in hand with their hypocrisy, and the history of our approaching contest will teach mankind the same lesson with our last, and show the different effects of sobriety and profligacy in soldiers. The king began with a manifest advantage in point of discipline and generals; and so may we in this war. But it soon appeared that generals and discipline are more easily acquired than principles; and, in the course of two or three years, the superiority of the Parliamentary forces was as great in one respect as in the other." †

In a tract, characterised by the most philosophic treatment of his subject, Dr. Price took similar ground. He,

* "It is remarkable that Dr. Franklin, who used this very language, and Southey also, was of opinion that 'the American Revolution must, in great part, be traced to the Puritanical origin of the New England States.'"—"Life of Wesley," cap, 27.

† "An Address, &c.," p. 15.

too, directed attention to the strength which religious principles were giving to the Americans.* "In this time," he said, "of tremendous danger, it would become us to turn our thoughts to heaven. This is what our brethren in the Colonies are doing. From one end of North America to the other they are fasting and praying. But what are we doing? We are ridiculing them as fanatics, and scoffing at religion. We are running wild after pleasure, and forgetting everything decent at masquerades. We are gambling in gaming-houses, trafficking for boroughs, perjuring ourselves at elections, and selling ourselves for places. Which side, then, is Providence likely to favour?"† Throughout the kingdom Nonconformists, as one man, held fast to their hereditary sympathies. "The Dissenters," wrote Benjamin Franklin from London, just before the war broke out, "are all with us."‡

Whatever may have been the comparatively cordial relations subsisting between many Dissenters and Churchmen in the period immediately preceding the American War, the difference of opinion on this subject divided them into camps almost as hostile as those of the old Puritans and Roundheads. Throughout the pulpits of parish churches the Americans were reviled in the most opprobrious language. The rebellion was compared to the sin of witchcraft; Franklin was likened to Achitophel, and Washington to Jeroboam.§ Porteous preached a fast-day sermon upon the subject before the king, and defended the doctrines of

---

* "Observations on the Nature of Civil Liberty, the Principles of Government, and the Justice and Policy of the War with America." By Richard Price, D.D., F.R.S. 1776. pp. 6, 8.

† "Observations on the Nature of Civil Liberty, the Principles of Government, and the Justice and Policy of the War with America." By Richard Price, D.D., F.R.S. 1776. p. 98.

‡ "Letter to T. Cushing," Franklin's Correspondence, iii. 359.

§ Lord North's Correspondence, ii. 3.

arbitrary power with such zeal that he was rewarded with a bishopric for his service. The clergy carried their Tory principles so far as to call down a rebuke in the House of Lords from the Duke of Grafton, who referred, in the strongest language, to the despotic spirit which they, and especially Archbishop Markham, "preached up."* The election for which Priestley wrote his "Address" resulted in large majorities for Lord North—majorities which were furnished by the country gentlemen and "the clergy." Every measure for carrying on the war, and for adding renewed oppression to the colonies, was supported, throughout, by the Episcopal Bench. "Twenty-four bishops," wrote Franklin, "with all the lords in possession or expectation of places, make a dead majority that renders all debating ridiculous." †

It must always be a subject of regret, although not of surprise, that John Wesley sided with the High Church party on this occasion. In a "Calm Address to the Americans" Wesley firmly upheld the right of the English Parliament to tax the Colonists; and in his advocacy of the doctrines of arbitrary power went as far as Markham himself. But Wesley, both by education and by constitution, was a Tory. He, however, was not allowed to remain unanswered. It was found that his Address was for the most part a plagiarism from Dr. Johnson's "Taxation no Tyranny"; and Toplady, who hated Wesley with all the hate that it was then considered proper for a high Calvinist to bear to a low Arminian, rushed, with eager haste, into the field to expose the literary theft. Never particular in his choice of language, Toplady's bad taste led him to entitle this production "The Old Fox Tarred and Feathered." The

---

* Horace Walpole's "Last Journal," ii. 117.

† "Memoirs of Franklin," i. 493.

Rev. Caleb Evans, Baptist minister, of Bristol, next addressed to Wesley a spirited and pungent reply,* which brought a rejoinder from Wesley in the *Gazetteer*, and to this Evans wrote an answer which convicted Wesley of almost incredible inconsistency and disingenuousness. Wesley, in fact, had suddenly turned round upon this question. The probability is that he changed his course because he had found himself in accordance with the views of the Dissenters, and because he thought it would do good to Methodism. His service was so much appreciated by the Government that they distributed his pamphlet from the Treasury; † and whatever may have been the king's feelings towards the Methodists before, he certainly, after this time, never showed an aversion to them.

Wesley, coming out of this controversy with less credit than he came out of most controversies, Fletcher, of Madeley, undertook his defence. Evans had soiled the fair fame of a man whose reputation it was desirable, above all things, to sustain. Fletcher wrote with all the ardent feelings of a generous friend, as well as with undoubted conviction of the justice of his arguments. Whether Wesley was, or was not, a "fox," no one, who knew Fletcher, could attribute to him anything but the most transparent honesty and honour. But even he could not write without a fling at Dissenters. When, however, the war was over, these men perhaps judged that they had after all, taken the wrong side. It is remarkable to find John Wesley then writing of the "very uncommon chain of proceedings" by which the Colonies had been separated from the mother country; and adding, "As our American

* "Letter to the Rev. Mr. Wesley." By Caleb Evans, M.A.

† "Political Empiricism; a Letter to the Rev. Mr. John Wesley." 1776.

brethren are now totally disentangled both from the State and the English hierarchy, we dare not entangle them again, either with the one or the other. They are now at full liberty simply to follow the Scriptures and the Primitive Church. And we judge it best that they should stand fast in that liberty wherewith God has so strangely made them free."* Yet Wesley would have kept them, as he kept the Wesleyans at home, from "full liberty to follow the Scriptures and the Primitive Church." Happily, with respect both to the political and the religious liberty of the world, the Americans were successful in asserting their rights. Had they failed, arbitrary power would probably have been re-established in England after a Tudor pattern. To the descendants of those Puritans who withstood Elizabeth and who conquered Charles, England itself is under an obligation equal to that which their forefathers laid upon the nation.

Towards the end of this century, there were signs of a gradual revival of religion made manifest by the increased interest taken in social questions. John Howard was visiting the gaols of England and Europe, and publishing the results of his investigations. This great philanthropist was a Congregationalist, but, when in London, was an attendant at Dr. Stennett's Baptist Church, in Little Wild Street.† A man of singular modesty, of inflexible moral courage, and of untiring devotion to the good of men, his name is one of the greatest amongst those who adorn the history of the Free Churches. Although society was, at this period, corrupt in morals, and laws, which disgraced humanity, existed and were defended, the revelations made by Howard

* "Letter to Dr. Coke," &c. Coke and Moore's "Life of Wesley," pp. 457, 459.

† "History of the Church in Little Wild Street."

shocked the feelings of the civilised world. The reform of the prison system dates from his labours.

The institution of Sunday-schools also dates from this period. It was about the year 1781 that Robert Raikes, the proprietor and editor of the *Gloucester Journal*, had his attention drawn to the ignorance and depravity of the children of that city. The streets of the lower parts of Gloucester, he was informed, were filled on Sundays with "multitudes of these wretches, who, released on that day from employment, spent their time in noise and riot, playing at chink, and cursing and swearing." Raikes at once conceived the idea of employing persons to teach these children on the Sunday. The idea was carried into execution, and at the end of three years he could write to a friend, "It is now three years since we began, and I wish you were here to make inquiry into the effect. A woman who lives in a lane, where I had fixed a school, told me, some time ago, that the place was quite a heaven on Sunday, compared with what it used to be. The numbers who have learned to read, and say their catechism, are so great that I am astonished at it. Upon the Sunday afternoon the mistresses take their scholars to church—a place into which neither they nor their ancestors ever entered with a view to the glory of God."* The knowledge of this work was quickly made public, and four years afterwards, Mr. Wm. Fox, a London merchant, opened a correspondence with Raikes, concerning the expediency of establishing a society for the support of Sunday-schools throughout Great Britain. On September 7th, 1785, through the co-operation of three well-known philanthropists, Mr. Jonas Hanway, Mr. Henry Thornton, and Mr. Samuel Hoare, this Society was formed. It at once received the support of members of all religious

* "Watson's History of the Sunday School Union," pp. 4, 6.

denominations.* Its income, in the first year of its existence, was nearly a thousand pounds; and in a few years afterwards it had established, or assisted in establishing, Sunday-schools in various parts of the kingdom. At first the teachers of these institutions were paid, but payment was soon found not to be necessary. Voluntary zeal supplied all that was required, and, for the purpose for which Sunday-schools were instituted, supplied it in better quality than any money payment could have secured.

The children of the lower classes, at this period, presented a terrible spectacle of ignorance and depravity. Although possessed of vast revenues, and of a monopoly of power, the Established Church had almost utterly neglected to perform its duty in respect to the religious education of the people. What Hannah More saw in Gloucestershire and Somersetshire was to be found in any county in England. This eminently cultured and Christian lady, to whose written works much of the reformation in manners which subsequently took place in the higher classes of society was owing, established, in her own neighbourhood, day schools for the education of children. The parishes within fifteen miles of her residence she describes as "almost pagan." Thirteen of them were without even a resident curate.† At Cheddar, when, in 1789, she began her work, she was opposed by all the farmers, whom she found to be "as ignorant as the beasts that perish, intoxicated every day before dinner, and plunged," she adds, "in such vices as make me think London a virtuous place." When she first visited Cheddar she went to every house in the place, and found each a scene "of the greatest ignorance and vice.

* "Watson's History of the Sunday School Union," pp. 8, 9.

† "Roberts's Memoirs of Hannah More," ii. 213. Letter to Mrs. Kennicott.

There was but one Bible in all the parish, and that was used to prop a flower-pot. No clergyman had resided in it for forty years. Children were buried without any funeral service; and out of a population of two thousand, eight persons at the morning service, and twenty in the afternoon, was considered a good congregation." The vicarage of this place was in the gift of the Dean of Wells; the incumbent resided at Oxford, and his curate at Wells, twelve miles distant. There was scarcely an instance in the whole town of a poor person ever being visited or prayed with. At Wiveliscombe, the incumbent was intoxicated about six times a week, and was "very frequently prevented from preaching by two black eyes, honestly earned in fighting."* For placing a school at Wedmore, Hannah More was ultimately prosecuted in the Ecclesiastical Court.† Her success in her work was, however, equal to that of Robert Raikes. Her schools contained, within seven years from their institution, between sixteen and seventeen hundred pupils, and the whole district became reformed. What Christian education can, under the most disadvantageous circumstances, sometimes effect, may be learned from the practical results of Miss More's experiment at Blagdon, where, about the year 1800, it was stated that "two sessions and two assizes were past, and a third was approaching, and neither as prosecutor nor prisoner, plaintiff nor defendant, had any of that parish (once so notorious for crimes and litigations) appeared." But in some parishes she dared not

* "Roberts's Memoirs of Hannah More," ii. 207, 209. Letter to Wilberforce.

† Some of the depositions in this case went to prove, as an offence, that Miss More's schoolmaster "had been heard to pray extempore, in private, and that he was a Calvinist." "The Church," says Miss More, "was in danger!" Letter to Wilberforce. Memoirs, iii. 147, 148.

do what she wished, "by reason of the worldly clergymen, who," she states, "are now quiet and civil, but who would become hostile if we attempted, in their parishes, what we do in some others."* Hannah More was a zealous but liberal member of the Established Church, and a personal friend of many of the bishops and clergy. If she met with such difficulties, what must not Dissenters have encountered?

In May, 1787, another movement, having in view the welfare of humanity, was commenced. It was in this year that the Committee for the Abolition of the Slave Trade was formed. The iniquity of this trade had been denounced by individuals for more than a century. Fox, the Quaker, Baxter, the Presbyterian, and Warburton, the Episcopalian, had joined in condemning it as a violation of the principles of the Christian religion, and an outrage on human feelings. The first religious body, as such, that delivered a protest against it were the Quakers. As early as the year 1727 the subject had attracted the attention of the Friends, who, at their general meeting in London, passed a resolution condemning the importation of negroes by any of their members, and declaring such a practice to be neither commendable nor allowable. In 1758 an elaborate resolution was passed by the same body, in which its members were warned not to engage in the slave-trade traffic, nor in any way to make profit out of it. Three years afterwards it was resolved that any member who was engaged in it, and who should "persevere in a conduct so reprehensible to Christianity," should be disowned by the Society. In 1783 they drew up, and caused to be presented, a petition to Parliament for the abolition of the trade—"a petition," said Lord North, "that did credit to the most benevolent Society in the world." In the same year they issued a

* "Roberts's Memoirs of Hannah More," ii. 469. Letter to Newton.

printed address on the subject which was widely distributed. Next, they advised that it should be brought before all their country meetings; and in the same year, a private committee, consisting of six members of the Society, was organised for the purpose of taking steps to secure the abolition of the inhuman traffic. This committee, by publications and by letters to journals, happily succeeded in attracting attention to the subject. In 1787, those who felt the greatest interest in it, formed themselves into a public committee of twelve, nine of whom were Quakers, the others being Granville Sharp, Thomas Clarkson, and Philip Sansom. In the next year the matter was first brought before Parliament. The subject had received, during the interval, the support of another religious body—the General Baptists, who were the second formally to identify themselves with it. At the annual meeting of that body, in 1788, two of its members were appointed to wait on the Abolition Committee, and to inform them that they approved of its object, and should countenance it.* The Baptists now threw themselves with peculiar ardour into the movement. Sermons in its favour were preached by their most eminent ministers; and the names of Booth, Dore, and Robert Robinson, at this early period of the agitation, shone with a lustre as great as that which belonged to the members of the same body in the subsequent agitation against slavery itself. The Western and Midland Associations of Baptists formally connected themselves with the London Committee.† They did not, however, stand alone, for when the iniquity of the trade was fully understood, all denominations of Christians joined in denouncing it. None gave the movement a greater support than some of the bishops of the Established Church—

* Clarkson's "History of the Abolition of the Slave Trade," vol. 1.

† Ivimey, iv. 63.

Porteus, Bishop of London, standing pre-eminent in this respect amongst his brethren; Paley also lent to it the weight of his clear and calm reason. Churchmen and Dissenters forgot their religious differences, and joined hands all over the kingdom in its support.* To the Quakers, however, belonged the honour of its initiation, and the principal management of the agitation. Nine-tenths of its first coadjutors in England were members of that body,† and of other denominations the Baptists were the first to identify themselves with the movement after it had been formally commenced.

Nearly two generations having passed away since the last appeal to Parliament for the abolition of the Test and Corporation Acts, the Committee of Deputies now determined to bring this subject once more before the Legislature. What reasons they possessed for supposing that their application would be successful are now unknown, but it is on record that they considered such success to be at least probable.‡ Backed by a large and powerful committee, the Deputies waited on Pitt and Fox, and other leading members of the House of Commons, and solicited their support. The measure was placed, by unanimous decision, in the hands of Mr. Beaufoy, who, on March 28th, 1787, brought it before the House. The debate which followed was remarkable for the high character of its eloquence, and for the advanced sentiments on the subject of religious liberty which were expressed by the supporters of the motion. Mr. Beaufoy placed in the strongest light the gross injustice to which Dissenters were subjected, especially illustrating it by the case of John Howard. "He," said the speaker, "upon whom every kingdom in Europe, England excepted, would

---

* Clarkson's "History," i. 492, 572. † Ib., p. 445.

‡ "Sketch of the History," &c., p. 46.

gladly confer at least the common privileges of a citizen and whom the proudest nation might be happy to call her own; he of whom a right honourable member of this House* has said, 'He has visited all Europe, not to survey the sumptuousness of palaces, or the stateliness of temples; not to make accurate measurements of the remains of ancient grandeur, nor to form a scale of the curiosity of modern art; not to collect medals, nor to collate manuscripts; but to dive into the depths of dungeons, to plunge into the infection of hospitals, to survey the mansions of sorrow and pain; to take the gauge and dimensions of misery, depression, and contempt; to remember the forgotten and attend the neglected; to visit the forsaken; and to compare and collate the distresses of men in all countries'—he, even he, is denied, in England, the common rights of a subject; he is incapable of legal admission into any office; and the consequence is that his zeal for his country having led him, a few years since, to brave the penalties of the law, and to serve her in a troublesome and expensive civil employment, without the sacramental qualification which his religious persuasion would not permit him to take, the penalties of the Test Act are still hanging over him, and I fear that even now, on his return to his native country, amid the plaudits of an admiring world, it is in the power of any desperate informer, who is willing to take that road to wealth and damnation which the Legislature has pointed out and recommended to his choice—I fear it is in the power of every such informer to prosecute him to conviction, and to bring upon him those dreadful penalties which contribute to the punishment of an outlaw." Quoting, next, some solemn passages from the communion service, Mr. Beaufoy observed how religion was degraded, hypocrisy encouraged,

* Alluding to Burke.

and clergymen placed in the most painful position by the law—a law whose object, he said, was "to strengthen the Church of England by the debasement of the Church of Christ." Sir Henry Houghton having seconded the motion, Lord North expressed his opinion that it "prayed for the repeal of an Act which was the great bulwark of the constitution, and to which they owed those inestimable blessings of freedom which they now happily enjoyed. They all knew," he added, "the powerful nature of the cry of 'The Church in danger!' and an incendiary watching his opportunity might make as much mischief by that cry as by the cry of 'No Popery!'" Lord North therefore indicated his intention strenuously to oppose the motion. William Pitt dwelt on the alarm which the sanction of the motion would create in the Church. "The Church and the State," he said, "are united upon principles of expediency, and it concerns those to whom the well-being of the State is entrusted to take care that the Church be not rashly demolished. It has been said, if you grant this, they will soon come to you to grant something more. This will not weigh with me. I will not object to concede what I ought to concede, because I may be asked to concede what I ought not to concede; and yet this concession may be coupled with the danger of being pressed by future demands." He alluded to the fact that some of the Dissenters were opposed to all establishments of religion, and cited Robinson of Cambridge as an illustration. Fox* replied to

* In the separately published copy of this debate in my possession, there is an interesting note, written evidently at the time, concerning Fox's speech. The writer says—"On the day of the debate Dr. Rees waited on Mr. Fox with a deputation to engage his support in their cause. He received them courteously, but, though a friend to religious liberty, was evidently unacquainted with the principal bearing of their peculiar case. He listened attentively to their exposition, and put

Pitt, vindicating the character and the public services of Dissenters; and, in answer to what had been observed regarding the sentiments of the bishops and clergy, protested against the opinions of the heads of the Church of England being taken as a rule for the political conduct of the House of Commons. After a seven hours' debate the motion was rejected by 178 to 100 votes.*

But this defeat did not discourage the committee, who immediately issued an address calling upon Dissenters to pursue their object with steady assiduity until their rights were conceded. During the next two years they employed their resources and organized an agitation on the subject throughout the country. The language in which they requested the assistance of their brethren shows how much the theory of religious equality had recently grown. "We feel," they said, "as fellow citizens, unjustly deprived of civil privileges, and are equally sensible that what we claim is not a favour, but a right." In response to their appeals meetings were held in different counties, and resolutions passed in favour of making another demand upon the Parliament. But, as is generally the case, the sense of injustice which had been quickened afresh by the rejection of their claims, led to a review by the Dissenters of the privileges which the Established Church enjoyed over the members of the Free Churches, and, for the first time, questions were discussed which, but for this rejection

---

forth a few searching questions. They withdrew after a short conference, and, as they walked up St. James Street, Mr. Fox passed them booted. From the gallery they saw him enter the house with whip in hand as if just dismounted. When he rose to speak he displayed such mastery of the subject, his arguments and illustrations were so various, his views so profound and statesman-like, that a spectator must have imagined the question at issue between the High Church and the Dissenters to have been the main subject of his study through life."

* Debate on the repeal of the Test and Corporation Acts, 1787.

would probably have slept for many years. This is the almost inevitable consequence of delay in the concession of popular demands. The agitation in favour of particular rights is not only made the occasion for making other claims, but it provokes an inquiry into the justice of the principles on which such claims have been refused. The country Dissenters, in their resolutions, demanded not merely the repeal of the Test and Corporation Acts, but the abolition of all penal laws whatsoever on the subject of religion.* Some of the pamphlets and tracts which were issued took a still wider range. Dr. Priestley, who was in the gallery of the House of Commons during the debate on Mr. Beaufoy's motion, addressed a letter to Pitt on some of the sentiments contained in that statesman's speech.† In this address he avowed himself to belong to the class of Dissenters who were enemies of all ecclesiastical establishments, and, he said, "I glory in it. I have even no doubt," he added, "that when Christianity shall have recovered its pristine purity, and its pristine vigour, it will entirely disengage itself from the unnatural alliance which it is at present fettered with, and that our posterity will even look back with astonishment at the infatuation of their ancestors in imagining that things so wholly different from each other as Christianity and civil power had any material connection." He also frankly acknowledged that if Dissenters gained this they would aim at something more. They would ask for the repeal of the statute which made it blasphemy to impugn the doctrine of the Trinity; for liberty to be married by their own ministers; and to be relieved from subscriptions at the national Universities. They would ask for the

* "Sketch of the History," &c., p. 49.

† A letter to the Right Hon. William Pitt on the subject of Toleration and Church Establishments, &c. 1787.

bishops to be relieved of their seats in the House of Lords; they would ask for the tithe system to be abolished. "Much, very much," he remarked in conclusion, "is to be done in this country, and in due time there will not be wanting men who will have the head, the heart, and the firmness to do it." Another writer on the same subject, of almost equal vigour and breadth, was Mrs. Barbauld, the author of "Evenings at Home." In an address to the opponents of the repeal of the Test Corporation Acts,* that lady also characterised the alliance between the State and the Church as an "ill-assorted union," and protested against Dissenters being merely "tolerated" by the State. "What they call toleration," she said, "we call the exercise of a natural and unalienable right." There is no proof, however, that Dissenters, generally, held such sentiments, but the resistance offered to them and their rights was provoking the more advanced and courageous section to attack the institution to whose existence they owed their state of legal degradation. Cowper also joined the throng of writers, inquiring, in indignant interrogation—

> "Hast thou by statute shoved from its design
> The Saviour's feast, his own bless'd bread and wine,
> And made the symbols of atoning grace
> An office-key, a pick-lock to a place,
> That infidels may prove their title good
> By an oath dipp'd in sacramental blood?
> A blot that will be still a blot, in spite
> Of all that grave apologists may write;
> And though a bishop toil to cleanse the stain,
> He wipes and scours the silver cup in vain."†

Having thoroughly prepared their measures, the Dissenters resolved in 1789 on again appealing to the Legislature. As before, Mr. Beaufoy took charge of their Bill, and, on

* 1790. † The "Expostulation."

May 8th, brought it before the House of Commons. He endeavoured, in his speech, to conciliate the opinion of members by stating that the "unsanctioned asperities" of some persons amongst the Dissenters ought not to be charged to the general body, who, as a whole, were friendly to the Established Church. "Its teachers were," he said, "undoubtedly enemies from principle to the revenues of the Church, and if the Bill should pass, would still be excluded from the offices of the civil government by their refusal to take the oath of allegiance." He then, in an eloquent speech, set forth the arguments for the repeal of the laws, which, he said, degraded the sacrament to "a qualification for gauging beer barrels and soap-boilers' tubs, and for seizing smuggled tea." Sir Henry Houghton seconded the motion, and was followed, on the same side, by Sir James Johnstone and Mr. William Smith. Lord North took the same position as formerly. Fox then rose. Some of the sentiments advocated by the great Whig orator on this occasion were as advanced as those that would have been expressed by any Dissenter. He declared that, in his conception, religion should always be distinct from the civil government, and that it was not otherwise connected with it than as it tended to promote morality amongst the people. He held that no human government had a right to inquire into private opinions. In reply to those who said that the political opinions of Dissenters were inimical to the Constitution, he compared their history with that of the Church, vindicated their religious opinions as favourable to civil liberty, and said that the principles of the Constitution had been asserted by them at times when they had been forgotten, perhaps betrayed, by the Church. The comparative moderation of sentiment in the Church itself he held to be owing to the Dissenters, who had compelled the members of the Establishment to oppose argument, instead of force, to argument. Pitt replied in a brief speech, in which he again referred to the opinions of those who held that there should be no Church Establishment whatever. Mr. Windham rejoined that he did not believe the Dissenters had any disposition to shake the Establishment. The motion was negatived by 122 to 102 votes.*

The favourable character of this division acted as a stimulus to all classes of Dissenters. Their energies were redoubled. Committees were formed in different parts of the kingdom; country voters communicated with their members, and large numbers came up to London as delegates from churches and public meetings, to give encouragement and strength to the Committee of Deputies. Some Churchmen also joined the Central Committee, but in the country at large, the opposition to the efforts of Dissenters assumed as vigorous an attitude as that which had been taken by the Deputies and their friends. Where Dissenters' meetings were summoned, the clergy summoned meetings of Churchmen, at which the proposed relief was denounced, in the old style, as dangerous to the Church, and Dissent itself as equally dangerous to the State. Notwithstanding the excitement thus aroused, which gave little prospect of success to their measure, the Deputies determined, in 1790, to submit their motion once more to the House of Commons. Fox, on this occasion, took it in his charge. As soon as he had given notice of his intended motion, Pitt moved for a call of the House, which took place on the 1st of March. On the following day, the measure was debated. Probably no speech of Fox's surpassed that which he delivered on this occasion. His denunciation of all kinds of persecution, his vindication of religious liberty, and of the public services of Dissenters; his exposure of the

* Parliamentary History, xxviii. 1—41.

sympathy of the Established Church with arbitrary authority, were enforced with a power which belongs only to the highest order of eloquence. He said that he had always understood the leading feature of true religion to be charity, but when he viewed the Church, and saw Churchmen evincing a spirit directly opposite to the religion they professed, he must consider them as men who were ambitious of a monopoly of power, under the mask of an affected apprehension of danger. The Christian religion had existed for centuries without any assistance from the secular arm, but, according to a new-fangled doctrine, the Church was not to depend upon its own merits, nor was religion to be established by the truth of its own evidence, but was to be supported by the assistance of civil authority. He warned the House that if the Test laws were maintained, there would be stronger exertions in defence of civil rights, as well as other applications to the Legislature. The cause of the Dissenters was identified with the universal rights of mankind, and although he might be denounced as another Oliver Cromwell for undertaking its defence, the time was not far distant when the world would do justice to his motives. Fox's principal opponent on this, as on most similar occasions, was Pitt, who protested in vehement language, that toleration did not mean equality, and denounced the conduct of the Deputies in advising electors to support those men only, as Parliamentary candidates, who should prove themselves favourable to civil and religious liberty. He believed that the safety of the Church and the Constitution would be endangered if the equality which was demanded was granted to Dissenters, for their next application might even extend to a claim for exemption from Church-rates. Mr. Powys said that the principles of toleration advocated by Fox would admit even Jews to hold offices of trust; to which remark the Whig orator cried,

"Hear, hear." Burke afterwards spoke, and, holding in his hand two catechisms for Dissenters, one written by Robinson, of Cambridge, and another by Palmer, of Hackney, quoted several passages to show that the doctrines which were being taught by Dissenters, tended to the subversion of all Church Establishments, and possibly to the alienation of Church property. Mr. Wm. Smith, a Dissenter, who followed Pitt, denied, and no doubt correctly, that the doctrines which had been alluded to were doctrines held by Dissenters generally. Mr. Wilberforce said that it was now a question of Church Establishment or no Church Establishment, and therefore he should vote against the motion. Fox, in his reply, vindicated the right of Dissenters to avow their opinions concerning the utility of the Church Establishment, or any other civil institution, and expressed his willingness to take the field for them again on any future occasion. On a division there appeared 105 votes for the motion, and 294 against it.*

The decisive majority against Fox's motion, after a debate of unexampled length, was owing to two causes—first, the avowal by several of the most eminent Dissenting ministers of their antipathy to all Established Churches; and, secondly, the well-known sympathy of Nonconformists with the earlier proceedings connected with the French Revolution. The upholders of the Test Acts affected to believe that the ultimate object of Dissenters, in seeking to obtain employment under the Crown, and admission to offices of civil dignity, was to destroy the Church. The red flag of "The Church in danger!" was, therefore, again raised, and with all the success that had hitherto attended that device. The bishops and the High Church clergy did nothing, during this memorable agitation, but

* Parliamentary History, xxviii. 387, 451.

point, with gestures of frantic excitement, to the old banner, and shout aloud the old cry.

The second cause of defeat, namely, the avowed sympathy of Dissenters with the earlier proceedings of the French Revolution, was equally operative with the first. It was frequently alluded to during the debates, and was not disowned either in or out of Parliament. In expressing their opinions on this event, the Dissenters did no more than all the lovers of freedom throughout the world. It was impossible for them to see the most corrupt State-Church, and the most corrupt Government in Europe, suddenly overthrown without feelings of the most intense gratification. Nor did the character of the Government, which immediately succeeded to the old monarchy of France, at all tend to diminish such sympathy. At its head were men, some of whom were of spotless integrity and fame, and nearly all of whom appeared to be animated by a pure and lofty patriotism. The principles of government which had been laid down seemed to promise a return to the golden age. A priestly order, which had hitherto been sustained by persecution, ignorance, and superstition, and stained with the foulest moral vices, had been dismissed, and perfect religious equality had been proclaimed in France. An oppressive and odious civil tyranny, which had brought the nation to a state of almost abject despair, had given way to a free and pure government, based in sentiment, and at first in action, on the highest principles of justice. Was it possible for any but arbitrary rulers, and their followers—men of a naturally despotic mind, and men belonging to other priestly orders—not to hail such a change with almost rapturous enthusiasm? Fox, in impassioned eloquence, expressed his joy at the event; Mackintosh wrote in its vindication; and the whole Liberal party in England stretched out the hand of friendship and congratulation to the new Government and the people of France.

But, undoubtedly, most conspicuous in this sympathetic movement were several members of the Dissenting bodies. Amongst the foremost were Price and Priestley. There existed in London, at this time, a society for commemorating the Revolution of 1688, commonly called the Revolution Society. On November 4th, 1789, Dr. Price preached, by request of the society, a discourse, to which he afterwards gave the title of "A Discourse on the Love of our Country." This address was an eloquent eulogium, characterised by a vigorous style and a philosophical precision of thought, on the three national blessings of intelligence, virtue, and liberty. On the last subject Dr. Price expressed sentiments which created feelings of exasperation and anger in Court, Tory, and High Church circles. After defining the constitutional relations of king and people, and severely deprecating the adulation with which it had been customary in England in public oratory to address the King, he called upon his hearers to exert

---

* Wordsworth has admirably expressed the feeling predominant in most liberally educated and religious minds at this period—

But now,
To the wide world's astonishment, appeared
A glorious opening, the unlooked-for dawn,
That promised everlasting joy to France!
Her voice of social transport reached even him!
He broke from his contracted bounds, repaired
To the great city, and emporium then
Of golden expectations, and receiving
Freights every day from a new world of hope.
Hither his popular talents he transferred;
And from the pulpit zealously maintained
The cause of Christ and civil liberty
As one, and moving to one glorious end.

—*The Excursion*, Book II.

their utmost influence to increase the civil, political, and religious liberties of the nation; to agitate for complete religious toleration, and for Parliamentary reform. With an unconcealed application to the condition of England, he concluded a peroration of magnificent power by calling upon all governments to consider what had occurred in France.* On the same day the Revolutionary Society held its anniversary meeting, with Earl Stanhope in the chair, at which an address of congratulation to the National Assembly of France was agreed upon. This address was read in the Assembly, and acknowledged by public vote. French Patriotic Societies followed the precedent set by the Assembly, and a correspondence was at once established between the leaders of the Revolutionary party in France and the Liberal party in England. At the next anniversary meeting of the Revolutionary Society Dr. Price gave the toast, "The Parliament of Britain—may it become a National Assembly." Burke now attacked the government of France and the principles advocated by Dr. Price, arousing Mackintosh to confute him; but before Mackintosh, Dr. Priestley was in the field to reply.† The nature of Burke's "Reflections" gave Priestley occasion to treat of almost every branch of political government. He asserted and defended the rights of the people as against despotic governments on the one hand, and Church Establishments on the other; and in his last letter expatiated on the "glorious prospect which, by the example of America and France, was now opening upon the world." So calm and judicious a man as the leading Baptist minister in London, Dr. Stennett, did not hesitate to express his full sympathy with such views.

* "A Discourse," &c., pp. 50, 51.

† "Letters to the Right Hon. Edmund Burke," &c., 1791.

If the Church had been in danger before, it was in greater danger now. It was enough that Dissenters had applauded a revolution which had led to the separation of Church and State, and the application of ecclesiastical revenues to secular purposes. They were accordingly denounced as Republicans and levellers. The spirit of Sacheverell seemed again to walk the earth. In 1792 an Association was formed at the Crown and Anchor, by which Nonconformists were charged with being enemies to the Constitution—an aspersion which the Deputies met with a prompt and vigorous denial.* Bishop Horsley also maintained that Dissenters were necessarily Republicans,† and advised the Government not to yield, in the smallest degree, to any of their demands. Popular ignorance, excited by the seditious harangues of the clergy, reached its climax at Birmingham in 1791, when Dr. Priestley's house, with his library and philosophical apparatus, were burned to the ground, and the houses of other Dissenters burned and damaged; the populace, led by the clergy, shouting, as they set fire to the property, "Down with the Dissenters!" "Down with the abettors of the French Revolution!" "Church and King!" ‡

Priestley was selected for this act of vengeance on account of his acknowledged eminence, and his equally acknowledged opposition to the Established Church. The rector of Stourbridge, and the prebendaries of the diocese, illustrated the temper of the times. The former compared Priestley to the "devil himself;" the latter, when a clergyman remarked that, if Priestley were mounted on a pile of his publications, he would set fire to them and burn him

---

* "Sketch of the History," &c., pp. 54, 55.

† "Review of the Case of the Dissenters."

‡ London Chronicle, lxx. 64.

alive, said that they would be ready to do the same.* He was threatened in letters with burning before a slow fire. It is gratifying to know that, while George III. expressed his pleasure at hearing of the treatment which Priestley had received, these barbarous proceedings were denounced by all but the Church and Court bigots. "Never, sure," wrote Cowper, "was religious zeal more detestably manifested."† From all parts of the kingdom came addresses of sympathy. The Protestant Dissenters of Great Yarmouth—Congregationalists, Baptists, and Presbyterians—addressed him, saying, "Differing in various matters of opinion, we all agree in warm admiration of your high abilities, your zealous researches after Christian truth, and your distinguished exertions in the cause of civil and religious liberty. These qualities, which have made you the peculiar mark of the vengeance of bigotry, render your safety and welfare proportionably dear to us."‡ The Committee of the "Revolution Society" wrote to Priestley, characterizing the act of the rioters as "nothing but the most execrable bigotry."§ The Committee of Dissenters of the county of York addressed him, saying, "However some of us may differ from you in several doctrinal opinions, we are well convinced of the integrity of your character. In this cause we respect you as a confessor, and admire the magnanimity and meekness, equally honourable to the man and the Christian, with which you have borne the losses which you have sustained." Addresses couched in the same style were adopted at Derby, Bath, Bristol, Essex, and Exeter, most of them signed by Dissenters. In France the Academy of

* "Memoirs of Priestley," p. 158. 1806.
† Letters to Rev. W. Bagot, Aug. 2, 1791. Letters iii., 340.
‡ Rutt's "Life and Correspondence of Priestley," ii. 126.
§ Rutt's "Life and Correspondence," p. 143.

Sciences and the Jacobin Society voted addresses to him, and he was elected a member of the National Convention. But with the spirit which had been roused, Priestley felt that he was no longer safe in his own country. Three years later, therefore, he left, as the Puritans before him had done, for America, where the welcome he received was as honourable as his treatment by some of his own countrymen had been to the last degree shameful.*

The spirit which animated the Court was now made sufficiently conspicuous. The principal agent in the riots at Birmingham was Dr. Spencer Madan, rector of St. Philip's, who had charged Dissenters in general, and Priestley in particular, with being enemies to the State as well as to the Church. A few months after, Madan was nominated by the King to the bishopric of Bristol. Nor was the feeling against the Dissenters confined to Priestley or to Birmingham. At Yarmouth and other places the Dissenters were compelled to arm themselves for the defence of their houses.† In many districts Churchmen refused to deal with them, and farmers and artisans were dismissed because they would not attend the Established Church. In such a state of public feeling there could be no immediate prospect

---

* Coleridge, in his "Religious Musings," written in the year that Priestley left England, expresses the indignation which all men now feel at the conduct of the Court, the clergy, and the mob:—

> "Pressing on his steps,
> Lo! *Priestley* there, patriot, saint, and sage,
> Whom, that my fleshly eye hath never seen,
> A childish fancy of impotent regret
> Hath thrilled my heart. Him from his native land,
> Statesmen bloodstained, and priests idolatrous,
> By dark lies maddening the blind multitude,
> Drove with vain hate; calm, pitying, he retired,
> And mus'd expectant on these promised years."

† Rutt's "Memoirs of Priestley," ii. 173.

of a relaxation of the Test Acts or any similar laws. Agitation for all such purposes, therefore, gradually ceased. The organizations which had been established were dissolved, and the work which they had undertaken was left to be completed by a succeeding generation.

CHAPTER IX.

FROM THE SECOND AGITATION FOR THE REPEAL OF THE TEST AND CORPORATION ACTS TO THEIR REPEAL.—1792—1828.

BEFORE the eighteenth century had closed, a work of the greatest spiritual interest and importance was undertaken by a denomination whose claims on the respect and gratitude of Englishmen have always been greater than their numerical power. It was on October 2nd, 1792, that, in the parlour of a widow living at Kettering—Mrs. Beeby Wallis—the Baptist Missionary Society was formed. Two members of this body may claim an almost equal share in the successful foundation of this society—William Carey and Andrew Fuller; but to Carey belongs the honour of its original conception. Years before, from reading Cook's voyages, he had been vividly impressed with the degraded state of the heathen. The idea of sending men from England to preach the Christian Gospel to them took possession of his thoughts. He obtained all the information with respect to their condition that could be gleaned from books of travel; and, while mending shoes, he would sit and contemplate a map of the heathen kingdoms, in which this information was carefully noted down. Gazing at it from time to time, his soul became absorbed in contemplation of the moral darkness of the picture. At the next meeting of ministers at Northampton, Carey proposed, as a subject of discussion, the duty of Christians to attempt the spread of the Gospel among heathen nations. It is stated that when this subject was mentioned, another Baptist minister—the Rev. John C. Rylands, of Northampton—rose to denounce the proposal. 'Young man," he said, "sit down; when God pleases to convert the heathen, He will do it without your aid or mine.' Notwithstanding this rebuke, Carey did not abandon his purpose. Although he and his family were at the time in a state bordering on starvation, he published a pamphlet upon the subject, replete with information, and written with all the ardour of a mind possessed by the loftiest Christian benevolence. Year after year he continued to press its importance upon the ministers of his denomination. He brought it again before them at a meeting at Clipstone, when it was again avoided, and once more, in 1792, at Nottingham, where he preached a sermon which, by the force of its pathos and its indignation, broke down the indifference and almost contempt with which the scheme had hitherto been entertained. The next meeting was held in the same year, at Kettering, when a series of resolutions was passed, forming a "Baptist Society for Propagating the Gospel among the Heathen," appointing a committee of five persons to direct the enterprise, and at once opening a subscription, which amounted to thirteen pounds two shillings and sixpence. Within little more than eight months, Carey had sailed to India, where he translated the New Testament into Bengalee, and laid the foundation of the successes which have since attended missionary enterprise. Aided soon afterwards by William Ward and John Marshman, who had been sent out by the Society, an establishment, complete in its organisation, was formed. To these three fellow-labourers, all of them men of masterful enterprise, and of a lofty heroism, belongs the honour of being the apostles of modern Christian missions.*

Had it not been, however, for Carey's own vigour and determination, this work would probably have been delayed. For many years he stood alone; his brethren in the ministry had neither faith nor sense of duty until they were quickened by his unceasing expostulations; and it was with difficulty that money could be procured to send out Carey and his earliest associates. The association, however, when it was formed, was in the hands of men of untiring zeal. First amongst these was Andrew Fuller, of Kettering, who had himself, in some measure, prepared the way for the acceptance of Carey's scheme. The Baptist denomination at this period—as, to a considerable extent, it has since been—was largely pervaded by an ultra-Calvinistic spirit, which questioned the necessity of offering the Gospel for the acceptance of the unregenerate. The "elect" only were to hear the message of salvation. On this subject Fuller preached a sermon entitled "The Gospel worthy of all acceptation," in which he urged that every man was under a moral obligation to receive it, and that no natural nor physical inability existed in the human constitution to prevent its acceptance. The bearing of this doctrine on missionary enterprise was obvious, and they were eminently calculated to strengthen the hands of those who believed in the duty of preaching the Gospel to "all the world." These views were brought into greater prominence than Fuller's own reputation at that time would have given them, by the controversy which the publication of this sermon provoked. Ultra-Calvinists, Arminians, and

* "The Story of Carey, Marshman, and Ward." By John Clark Marshman. T. E. Fuller's Life and Writings of Andrew Fuller. Ivimey's "History," vol. iv. "History of the Baptist Missionary Society." By F. A. Cox, D.D.

Sandemanians joined in denouncing it. In meeting these antagonists, Fuller established his almost unrivalled power as a theological controversialist. Possessed of an intellect of extraordinary grasp and ability—which by its sheer momentum bore down with an irresistible force upon his opponents—and acute in detecting the smallest sophistries, he was a man whose sympathy and active aid were worth the assistance of troops of ordinary adherents. On the Unitarian question, he was one of Priestley's most successful antagonists, but the vigour and fulness of his varied powers were chiefly lavished on missionary enterprise. He was elected the first secretary of the new society, and he held that office until his death. All through England and Scotland his voice was heard enforcing the claims of the heathen upon the Christian Church; and to his ardent advocacy the general arousing of a missionary spirit may be largely ascribed.*

Two other ministers bore a subordinate share in this work. The first was the Rev. John Sutcliff, of Olney, a man of great activity, prudence, and calmness of judgment, whose advice in the practical conduct of the affairs of the mission was of eminent service. The second was Samuel Pearce, of Birmingham, whose zeal was boundless, No Church ever possessed a man of holier and more sanctified character than Pearce. He was to the Baptists what Fletcher was to the Methodists. His friends compared him to the disciple "whom Jesus loved." Wherever he went, the "beauty of holiness" accompanied him—a beauty recognised even by the half-heathen colliers of the Forest of Dean, to whom, above all others, he delighted to preach.†

---

* Lives of Fuller, by Ryland, A. G. Fuller, and T. E. Fuller.

† Fuller's Memoir of Samuel Pearce.

The example set by the Baptists was quickly followed by other bodies of Christians. In 1795, the London Missionary Society was founded. By its constitution, this society was on its establishment of an unsectarian character. Evangelical Churchmen, Scotch Presbyterians, Calvinistic Methodists, and Congregationalists took part in its formation, and had their representatives on the committee. Proposals for the establishment of such an institution appeared in the "Evangelical Magazine" during 1794 and 1795, and on September 4th of the last-named year, a conference, summoned from all parts of England, was held at the Castle and Falcon, Aldersgate Street, London, at which it was resolved to establish the society. On the following day a service, attended by no fewer than two hundred ministers, was held at Spafields, and a preliminary committee appointed to draw up a constitution for the society. Amongst the most prominent members of this committee were David Bogue, the Congregationalist of Gosport, and Haweis, the Episcopalian. The constitution being adopted, several meetings were held during the week. At the Tabernacle, Finsbury, where William Jay, of Bath, preached, thousands were unable to obtain admission. Rowland Hill preached, at Surrey Chapel, on the following morning ; and, on the fourth day, David Bogue addressed an immense congregation, at the Tottenham Court Road Chapel. The enthusiasm was almost unexampled. "We are called together this evening," said Bogue, in his sermon, "to the funeral of bigotry ;" a sentiment which elicited one movement of approbation from the whole of the vast audience.* But, although this society was avowedly unsectarian, and was honourably conducted on these principles, its working power soon became concentrated in the hands of members

* Evangelical Magazine, iii. 421, 425.

of the Congregational body. This was inevitable from the formation, in 1799, of the Church Missionary Society by the Evangelical section of the Establishment, led by Simeon and Venn. The Wesleyan bodies followed the example set by other Christians, and established a similar society of their own. Thus, all denominations were found working for Christian purposes which could only indirectly serve denominational interests. As was natural, home missionary labour grew with foreign missionary labour; and, for the first time in the ecclesiastical history of England since the Reformation, there was shown an earnest and general desire for the evangelisation of the heathen.*

Foremost in depreciating the increased activity of Dissenters in religious labours at home and abroad was Samuel Horsley, successively Bishop of St. Davids, Rochester, and St. Asaph, and, perhaps, the ablest prelate at this time upon the Bench. He had already measured weapons with Priestley, and obtained a great—although a scarcely deserved—reputation by his controversial power. He possessed a clear and vigorous intellect; a mind well stored with learning, and a weighty, although somewhat too sonorous, style; but he was of a domineering and intolerant disposition. He believed in no Christianity that was not of the Church, and strictly limited by its rules. Hence the field-preaching of the most zealous evangelist was to him nothing better than "bellowing"; † the labours of the Methodists were only "great crime and folly."‡ Six years after Priestley had left England, Horsley, in alluding to the

* The Society for the Propagation of the Gospel in Foreign Parts was founded some time before the Baptist Missionary Society, but until the year 1813, its fields of labour were limited to the British Colonies and possessions. The Moravian Missions date back to 1732, but its founders and agents were of German nationality.

† Horsley's Charges, p. 39. ‡ Ib. p. 39.

Unitarians, could not refrain from the expression of a vulgar triumph over his old adversary. "The patriarch of the sect," he said, "is fled, and the orators and oracles of Birmingham and Essex Street are dumb."* The efforts of various denominations to plant the Gospel in neglected districts excited his most vehement indignation, although the scandalous neglect of their duties by the clergy of his own diocese was the subject of comment and rebuke in all his Charges. Non-residence, according to his own testimony, was a very general practice, and all parochial duty was indifferently performed. Clerical laziness was even gaining ground.† Yet, when Dissenters attempted to supply the deficiences of the clergy, he denounced them in the most unrestrained language. Addressing the clergy of the Diocese of Rochester, he said that "in many parts of the kingdom, new conventicles had been opened in great numbers," and congregations formed of "one knows not what denominations." Persons of real piety occasionally connected themselves with these congregations, but, in doing so, they were lending their aid to the common enemy, and "making themselves, in effect, accomplices in a conspiracy against the Lord and against His Christ."‡ Horsley expressed, in these words, only the general feeling of the bishops and clergy—a feeling so largely shared by the ruling powers that it was in actual contemplation by Pitt's ministry, in 1801, to bring in a Bill for the legislative suppression of all village preaching and all Sunday-schools.§ Horsley was at once replied to by Rowland Hill in a sermon preached at Surrey Chapel.‖ Hill stated, in the preface to this discourse, that he published it because he found that

* Horsley's Charges, p. 144. † Ib. p. 82, 159. ‡ Ib. pp. 145—147.

§ Robert Hall's Letter to the Rev. James Phillips. Works, i., p. 277. Ed. 1850. Wilberforce's Life, vol. iii.

‖ "An Apology for Sunday Schools," &c. 1801.

Horsley's Charge was already bearing fruit, for families of rank were dismissing servants who were Dissenters. Robert Hall wrote on the same question, but, unfortunately, did not publish what he wrote.*

In the year 1804 another movement, destined to exercise the most beneficial influence upon the human race in every part of the globe, was commenced. Towards the close of the eighteenth century a great want of Welsh Bibles was felt by ministers of religion in the Principality. Few families were in possession of a single copy of the Scriptures. So urgent was the need of a supply that the Rev. Thomas Charles came to London to place the matter before some religious people. Having been introduced to the committee of the Religious Tract Society, it was suggested by the Rev. Joseph Hughes, a Baptist minister, who was present that there might be a similar dearth not only in Wales, but in other parts of the country, and that it would be desirable to form a society for the express purpose of circulating the Scriptures. Inquiries were made in various parts of England as well as on the Continent, and it was found that people everywhere were almost destitute of the Bible. "The British and Foreign Bible Society" was the result. This society was founded on unsectarian principles, it being resolved that one-half of its committee should be elected from amongst Churchmen, and one-half from amongst Dissenters. Mr. Hughes, as a Dissenter, was also elected one of the secretaries.†

The establishment of this Society provoked a controversy of almost unprecedented heat and continuance. For nearly fifteen years the religious world was agitated by two ques-

* Works, iii. 331. Ed. 1832.

† "History of the British and Foreign Bible Society," &c. By the Rev. Joseph Browne. Cap. I. "A Vindication of the British and Foreign Bible Sociey." By the Rev. W. Dealtry.

tions—first, whether it was expedient for Churchmen and Dissenters to unite in circulating the Scriptures; and, secondly, whether it was desirable, under any circumstances, that they should be circulated without the Book of Common Prayer. Charges, pamphlets, letters, and speeches, almost without number, appeared on both sides of these questions. Excepting those who were opprobriously stigmatised as the "Methodist" clergy—or, in other words, the leaders of the rising Evangelical party—nearly the whole body of the bishops and ministers of the Established Church arrayed themselves against both the formation and the constitution of the Bible Society. Amongst those who, in the earlier stages of its history, with all the weight of his high influence, and all the zeal of a mind of the largest charity and the most benevolent disposition, supported the new movement, was the Duke of Kent, father of Queen Victoria. Of all the sons of George III., this prince took the most active interest in questions of a religious or social character. He identified himself with almost every institution of a charitable nature which, at that period, existed in England, but there were two or three societies which engaged his peculiar interest. One of these was the Bible Society, for his unqualified adhesion to which the Archbishop of Canterbury openly rebuked him before the King.* Unfortunately

* "In spirit and feeling the Duke was one of the most benevolent of men. His desire to do good was unremitting. But in speaking and writing of him, you will bear in mind that he lived at a period in which a mark was put upon any man, however high or low in station, who supported liberal institutions, and entertained charitable feelings towards others, out of the Established Church. And it was quite sufficient, at the time to which I allùde, for even a private clergyman to have the door of preferment closed upon him, if by a certain clique suspicion was entertained, and a rumour was propagated, touching his orthodoxy, which orthodoxy was made a matter of question, *if he lent the slightest support to a Bible Society*. The Duke once told me

for his own interests, his Royal Highness had early in life imbibed liberal political principles, and had therefore incurred the severe disapprobation of his father. Rebuke, however, was the mildest form in which the opposition to the Society was clothed. Denunciation followed upon denunciation. The Bishop of London opposed it because Dissenters of any sect could be admitted upon its committee, "and when," he said, "admitted into religious society with us, they will—and it is natural for them—endeavour to gain the ascendancy, and to supplant us whenever they find an opportunity."* The Bishop of Winchester denounced it because it "was not framed with a sufficient security to the Church of England."† Dr. Herbert Marsh, Margaret Professor of Divinity, and afterwards Bishop of Peterborough, addressed a memorial to the Senate of the University of Cambridge, protesting against the constitution of a society where an equality of power and interest between Dissenters and Churchmen was admitted, in which there was an "evident danger that the pre-eminence of the established religion would be gradually forgotten and lost."‡ The Society, it was said, would have only a "baneful" operation, calculated to interfere with,

that, on a visit to Windsor, he met with the then Archbishop of Canterbury. The subject on the tapis—the King was present—was the Bible Society. The Archbishop said to the King, but meaning his remark for the Duke, 'He that is not with us, is against us.' To which the Duke rejoined, 'Your Grace, there is another saying of our Lord, "He that is not against us, is on our side."' The prelate frowned, but made no reply."—"Life of the Duke of Kent." By the Rev. Erskine Neale, M.A., Rector, of Kirton, &c., p. 320.

* Letter to the Rev. R. Yorke. "Anti-Jacobin Review," vol. xxxvi. p. 108.

† Letter to the Rev. H. Venn. "Papers relating to the Bible Society."

‡ Memorial, &c., ibid., pp. 7—11.

impede, and entail the inestimable interests of piety, and peace, and true religion."* "Supply these men," cried a country clergyman, "with Bibles (I speak as a true Churchman), and you will supply them with arms against yourself."† It was gravely argued that, without the Liturgy, men were left in doubt whether the principles of the Established Church should be embraced by them or not; that they wanted a guide to lead them into the Church, and that unless they were supplied with the Prayer Book, the Bible might be misapplied to doctrine and discipline most discordant with those of the Church.‡ It was further urged, that the political consequence of such a society would be damaging to the very stability of the State.§ For these and similar reasons Churchmen were exhorted not to support the new institution. If an additional argument were needed, it was conveyed in the statement that the two archbishops, by far the greater part of the bishops, and the majority of the clergy had shown a repugnance to acting with it.‖

The most able writers amongst the opponents of the Society were Dr. Wordsworth,¶ Dr. Marsh, Archdeacon Daubeny, and Dr. Edward Maltby, afterwards Bishop of Durham. Dr. Marsh's pen was the most prolific, and pamphlet after pamphlet issued from it. On the other side, the Rev. William Dealtry, the Rev. Charles Simeon, and the Rev. Dr. Isaac Milner, were its most conspicuous

* "Reasons for Declining to become a Subscriber to the British and Foreign Bible Society." By Christopher Wordsworth, D.D., p. 9.

† "A Country Clergyman's First Letter to Lord Teignmouth," p. 12.

‡ "An Inquiry into the Consequences of Neglecting to give the Prayer Book with the Bible." By Herbert Marsh, D.D., p. 18.

§ "Objections of a Churchman," etc. By the Rev. F. Nolan, p. 41.

‖ "Twenty Facts in addition to Twenty Reasons for not supporting the Bible Society," p. 19. 1819.

¶ The late Canon Wordsworth.

defenders. It was not a controversy in which Dissenters were called to take a prominent part, but the Rev. Robert Hall, in a speech delivered at Leicester, presented perhaps the ablest argument in favour of the circulation of the Bible, and the Bible alone,* which appeared during the whole of the fifteen years' conflict. To rebut the distinct charge, made in very offensive language by a clergyman of the name of Woodcock, that Dissenters had connected themselves with the Society for the purpose of "carrying on their evil designs against Church and State," Mr. John Bullar, of Southampton, wrote a vigorous defence of them.† The influence of the controversy, as a whole, undoubtedly tended to increase the popularity of the new Society. It emerged from it with vast pecuniary resources, and with the unquestioned adhesion to it of the greater part of the members of the Established Church.‡

While these great religious agencies were being strengthened and extended, another work of equal national importance was undertaken. It is difficult, at the present time, to form an adequate conception of the neglected state of education amongst the poor at the close of the eighteenth century. Not one in twenty of the children of England was at school. It was a rare circumstance to meet a poor man who could read. This ignorance was accompanied, as is generally the case, by depraved minds and brutish manners. But in the year 1796 a young Quaker, Joseph Lancaster opened a school in his father's house in Southwark for the

* Speech on April 13th, 1812.

† "A Refutation of the false assertions against the Dissenters," &c. By John Bullar.

‡ The library of the Bible Society contains twenty volumes of pamphlets, besides several detached publications, on this controversy. I have read one half of them, or rather more than seventy publications. No one need do more than this.

education of the children of the poor. Lancaster's motives sprung from an ardent and benevolent disposition. So strong was his zeal, and so successful his labour, that in two years his scholars were more than a thousand in number. The impossibility of personally teaching the whole of these suggested to him the idea of employing his elder and better educated boys as monitors to the younger scholars. Some years afterwards an angry controversy arose as to whether Lancaster was the originator of the monitorial system, the invention of which was claimed for Dr. Bell, formerly of Madras, who certainly used monitors in the military school in that city as early as 1792. There was some difference, however, between Lancaster's and Bell's systems; and whatever may be claimed for the latter, it is certain that Lancaster, knowing nothing of Bell's theory, introduced the practice into England.* Its extraordinary success soon attracted general attention, and it became one of the fashions of the day to visit Lancaster's schools. Royalty even took an interest in them, and George III. did honour to himself by the open and constant encouragement he gave not only to the young Quaker, but to the unsectarian principles upon which his schools were founded. In 1808, after years of devoted, although sometimes ill-advised, labour, Lancaster had the satisfaction of seeing the formation

* "The system was first introduced, into this country at least, by Joseph Lancaster, a man so well known to all our readers that it would be impertinent to detain them with any praise of his universally acknowledged merits. This much is admitted on all hands: whether he invented the plan himself, or only imported it from Madras, or took a hint from that scheme and improved upon it, is an open question; but there is no one who has ever denied that he was the first who established in England (we may say in Europe) a system of education whereby one master can teach a thousand, or even a greater number of children, not only as well, but a great deal better than they can possibly be taught by the old methods, and at an expense of less than five shillings a year for each."—*Edinburgh Review*, Nov., 1810, p. 67.

of "the Royal Lancastrian Institution for Promoting the Education of the Poor," which subsequently received the title of the "British and Foreign School Society." Through his own personal exertions, and the aid of this society, schools of an unsectarian character were soon established in all the principal towns in England.

But this work was not effected without the most formidable opposition. The bishops and clergy of the Established Church, as soon as Lancaster's scheme became popular, at once sounded the note of alarm. It is almost incredible that not merely an unsectarian education, but education of any kind for the poor, was opposed by some of these parties.* The King was gravely remonstrated with for the countenance he had given to Lancaster; but, happily, the remonstrance failed of its intended effect.† Finding that it

* "The charge most constantly brought against the Church, in the course of the discussions respecting education which have arisen within the last twelve years, has been that of disinclination to have the poor taught. If, instead of disinclination, carelessness or indolence in the cause had been alleged, the accusation would have been better founded as far as regarded the general body of the Church, both lay and clerical, and as far as regarded the beginning of the period to which we are referring. That some leading persons in the hierarchy were averse to education cannot be doubted, but, upon the whole, there was rather a want of diligence than of good-will, until the great exertions of the Dissenters stirred up a corresponding spirit in the Church."—*Edinburgh Review*, March, 1821, p. 228.

† "The press and the pulpit in vain sounded the alarm, with which those reverend personages were willing to reform the Church and the State. It was proposed to wean the sovereign from his unfortunate predilection in favour of those who wished to diffuse, on the cheapest terms, the most useful kinds of knowledge amongst the poorer subjects. Persons were not wanting, nor those in the lowest ranks of the Church, who volunteered their services on this occasion. They remembered the excellent use which had been made of the *No Popery* cry; and vainly imagining that the King had been the dupe of that delusion—that his royal mind had in good earnest been alarmed for the safety of the Church—they concluded that it was peculiarly accessible

was impossible to check the success of the new schools, the old cry was once more raised. The Church was again "in danger." In Charges and pamphlets almost without number, Lancaster was denounced, and his schemes were derided in the most unmeasured terms of abuse. It was enough, it was said, to observe that the new plan had for its author a Quaker,* who could only be compared for mischievous-

to alarms of this description; and they took every means to magnify the dangers which must result from his Majesty's continuing to patronise a sectary who taught reading, and put the Bible itself into children's hands, without the safeguards of proper gloss and commentary, and a regular assortment of articles. We are credibly informed that the utmost effect of these artifices was to provoke the steady contempt of the exalted personage in question; and that he never could, by any efforts, be induced to get over the first difficulty, which met him in the fine-spun Jesuitical reasonings of those ghostly counsellors, '*the evils of being able to read*,' '*the dangers of reading the Bible*.' The tempters soon perceived that they had made another mistake; and once more they shifted their ground. . . . If the poor *must* be educated let them be educated by the clergy of the Establishment. If anything so unworthy of his station as patronising the teaching of ragged beggarlings *must* occupy the mind of the Sovereign, let him bestow those favours exclusively on the members of the Church. What though Dr. Bell's plan is more limited in its efficacy, infinitely inferior in economy, crude and imperfect in many of the most essential points, still, it comes off a right stock, and is wholly in regular Episcopal hands."—*Edinburgh Review*.

* "Mr. Lancaster was a sectary, a respected and cherished member of that peaceful body of Christians who alone never either persecuted, nor fought, nor intrigued, nor ruled; and who, having no establishment, nor, indeed, any order of priests, are not much in favour with such as delight to mingle with the pure clerical functions of Christian ministers, the enjoyment of patronage, wealth, and power. If, then, the first alarm was given by the idea of '*the poor being taught*,' a louder note was soon sounded when it was found that '*the poor were to be taught by a Quaker*.' What more deadly attack upon religion than teaching children to read the Bible without prescribing also the gloss and commentary which Episcopacy has sanctioned?"—*Edinburgh Review*, Nov., 1810, pp. 67, 68.

ness to the apostate Julian* ; that it must, therefore, operate to the disadvantage of the Establishment ; that it was "a wild, absurd, and anti-Christian" scheme, and "calculated to answer no one purpose so much as that of amalgamating the great body of the people into one great deistical compound."† "The plan," said another writer, "was the plan of a Quaker," and Quakerism "meant nothing but Deism, and a disgusting amalgam of all those anti-Christian heresies and blasphemies which were permitted to disgrace and disturb the Church in her primitive days."‡ This style of attack, however, assisted rather than hindered Lancaster's scheme.§ His system was carrying all before it. It was spreading with immense rapidity through the kingdom,‖ and seriously affecting the interests of the Church. "It cannot be dissembled," wrote Dr. Bell, "that thousands in various parts of the kingdom are drawn from the Church by the superior attention paid to education out of the Church. The tide is fast setting in one direction, and, if not speedily stemmed, it may run faster and faster."¶ "A few years hence, were Mr. Lancaster's plan to be fully adopted," wrote Mrs. Trimmer to Dr. Bell, "the common people would not know that there was such a thing as the Established Church in the nation."** In

* Charge of Archdeacon Daubeney, 1806, p. 33.

† Daubeney's "Sermon at St. Paul's Cathedral," June 1st, 1809, p. 17.

‡ "Letter to the Archbishops, &c., on Joseph Lancaster's Plan." 1806.

§ "Many attacked him because he was a Quaker, and the ignorance and bigotry with which he was thus assailed gave him all the advantages he could wish."—Robert Southey, in the *Quarterly Review*, Oct., 1811.

‖ Ib., Sept., 1812, pp. 1—4.

¶ Letter to Dr. Barton, Chaplain to the Archbishop of Canterbury, March 30, 1807. "Southey's Life of Bell," ii. 182.

** "Southey's Life of Bell," ii. 135—138.

Bell's reply to this letter, the germ of a Church Society for the education of the people is first seen. "I know of but one way effectually to check these efforts," he said, "and it is by able and well-directed efforts of our own hands. A scheme of education patronised by Church and State, originating with the Government, and superintended by a member of the Establishment, would most effectually promote our views." "I cannot," wrote Mrs. Trimmer to Bell at another period, "see this Goliath of schismatics bearing down all before him, and engrossing the instruction of the common people, without attempting to give him a little check."* Something, it was urged, must now be done.† "If," said Dr. Herbert Marsh, Margaret Professor of Divinity, "we cannot recall the thousands who have deserted the Church, let us double our efforts to retain the faithful band which rally round her standard. Let both the clergy and the laity, who are still attached to the Church, combine for mutual defence."‡

The "check" ultimately devised was the formation of the National School Society in the year 1811.§ Lancaster's

---

* Letter to Bell. "Southey's Life of Bell," 1807.

† "The cry, therefore, now became prevalent among the same persons, that it was the province of the Establishment to educate the poor; that a sectary could only teach sectarianism, or, at any rate, latitudinarian principles. Therefore, in order to supplant the sectary, there must be found a Churchman; and the irregular empirical scheme, already spreading with the rapidity of error, and the steadiness of truth, must be succeeded by some more correct, orderly, clerical system which should at once resemble it, and coincide with the Establishment."—*Edinburgh Review*, Nov., 1810, p. 70.

‡ Sermon on the "National Religion the Foundation of National Education," June 13, 1811.

§ "The friends of the Establishment have been roused. The enemy set up their song of triumph before they had won the field. This insolent minority dared even to menace the Establishment."—Robert Southey, in the *Quarterly Review*, Oct., 1811, p. 302.

principle, which he had ardently and successfully advocated, was, that education ought not to be made subservient to the propagation of the peculiar tenets of any sect. To meet, however, the feelings of some persons, he was willing that religion should be taught. "Either," he said, "let the religion of Quakers be taught if a Quaker school is founded upon this method of teaching writing and reading; or I will confine myself to those general practical principles which are suitable to all sects, if you choose to found a general school for the instruction of the indigent; or I will meddle only with the temporal instruction of my pupils, and you may confide their religious instruction to whom you please."* The British and Foreign School Society was, therefore, founded upon the broadest and most unsectarian principles; the National Society, on the other hand, made it a condition that all children should be instructed in the liturgy and catechism of the Church, and be compelled to attend the public worship of the Establishment on the Sunday. The founders of this Society, which included most of the prelates of the Church, advanced, at the outset, the principle that if any education was to be given to the poor, the Established Church alone had the right to give it. But when Dr. Bell first urged that something should be done, he deprecated the poor being taught either to write or to cypher. The diffusion of general knowledge amongst them he stigmatised as "utopian;" as calculated to confuse the distinctions of ranks and classes of society, and to make those who were doomed to the drudgery of daily labour discontented and unhappy in their lot.† This narrow scheme had, however, when Lancaster's great success made it imperative to outbid him, to be abandoned, and the author of

---

* *Edinburgh Review*, Oct., 1807, p. 65.

† Bell's Madras School, 3rd Ed., p. 90.

the Church system of education finally consented that both writing and cyphering should be taught. All classes, therefore, were now being instructed. Instead of opposition to education, the strife was who should educate the greatest number, until, ultimately, from being the opponent, the Church became the principal agent of popular instruction.

Taking into consideration the general character of the Established clergy at the commencement of the nineteenth century, it is not difficult to understand the opposition which they gave to all movements for the moral and religious improvement of the people. With the exception of the Evangelical section—now numbering, perhaps, nearly a thousand ministers—it is no exaggeration to say that personal religion and a personal sense of duty were almost unknown amongst them. Racing and drinking were their favourite occupations, and comparatively few were resident upon their benefices.* It is only just to state that their opposition to the more zealous members of their own profession was equal to that which was encountered by the Dissenters. The most eminent for piety amongst its bishops was Beilby Porteus, Bishop of London, the friend of Hannah More and Wilberforce, and a leader in most of the religious and charitable enterprises of the time. The see of Canterbury was filled by John Moore, who considered it to be his chief duty to provide for his relatives. North, Bishop of Winchester, Tomline, Bishop of Lincoln, and Bagot, Bishop of St. Asaph, were conspicuous for the same tendency. The scandalous malpractices of these prelates, in respect to the appropriation of Church patronage and the management of their Episcopal revenues, were some of the chief points of comment when the state of the ecclesiastical

* The state of the clergy at this period has been vividly described in chap. iii. of the "Memoir of Bishop Blomfield," and is indicated with equal truthfulness in Dean Stanley's "Life of Bishop Stanley," p. 8.

revenues of England was subsequently brought before the nation. Hurd, Bishop of Worcester, was, in most respects, superior to these. He possessed both scholarship and piety, but in love of personal display he surpassed all his brethren. It was his custom to travel in a coach and six, attended by twelve liveried servants.* Watson, Bishop of Llandaff, was far more qualified to sit on the Episcopal bench, and in replying to Paine's "Age of Reason" he did the work appropriate to a father of the Church. Archdeacon Paley, of Carlisle, illustrated the low tone of moral opinion by basing the Church establishment and moral conduct on principles of expediency alone. The amount and administration of Church property, and the origin, character, and unjust incidence of the tithe system, now began to be discussed in many pamphlets, and an impetus was given to Church reform in this direction.† But the high character of the arduous labours of the Evangelical section of the Established Church were as conspicuous as were the negligence and the laxity of the majority of their brother clergymen. Through such men as John Newton, Richard Cecil, Joseph Milner, and Charles Simeon, and rural clergymen like Legh Richmond, the Established Church wielded a spiritual power which probably equalled in its influence for good that of all other denominations.

Nearly all classes of Dissenters were now rapidly increasing in number. The sole exceptions were the Presbyterians and the Unitarians; and the former had become almost identified with the latter. The most eminent of

---

* Watson's "Life of Warburton."

† The early pamphlets on this subject are well worth perusal. There is a large collection of them in the library of the "Liberation Society." The estimates of the value of Church property which they contain are very exaggerated, but they point to many reforms which have since been accomplished.

their ministers were Dr. Abraham Rees, Theophilus Lindsey, Thomas Belsham, and Joshua Toulmin. Dr. Rees, who was a Welshman by birth, had succeeded to the pastorate of Chandler's Church, in the Old Jewry, but he was more eminent as a scholar than as a preacher. The forty-five volumes of the "Cyclopædia" which is distinguished by his name—the greatest work of its kind which had up to that date been published, and the whole of which was projected and the greater portion written by himself—testify to the immense extent of his learning and industry. Nor was Dr. Rees less zealous in ecclesiastical than he was in literary labour. Whenever the liberties of Dissenters were attacked, he threw all his energy into their defence. He was one of the most active members of the Committee of Dissenting Deputies, and was a liberal benefactor of his own countrymen. Few men rendered more valuable public service, and none surpassed him in dignity of character and appearance. He was pastor of the Jewin Street Church from 1783 to 1825, when he died. Theophilus Lindsey was one of the clergymen who left the Established Church at the time of the Subscription agitation, after which he became pastor of the Essex Street Church. Here he occupied one of the most influential positions in connexion with Unitarianism in England. His popularity as a preacher was very considerable, and he was the means of converting to his own views the Duke of Grafton, who attended his ministry. The characteristics of his mind were natural devoutness and transparent conscientiousness. The latter quality compelled him to leave the Church, and gradually to abandon, as evidence—in his judgment conclusive—was brought before him, the doctrines of the Evangelical faith.* Thomas Belsham was the biographer of Lindsey. After

* Belsham's "Memoirs of Theophilus Lindsey."

an interval of six years he succeeded, at the request of Mr. Coward's trustees, to the office of Principal of Daventry Academy, nearly the whole charge of which devolved upon him. He left this honourable post in consequence of the decisive change of his doctrinal views, and succeeded Priestley as pastor of the Hackney congregation, at the same time accepting the post of theological tutor at Hackney New College, which had recently been established on avowedly "liberal" theological principles. Next he succeeded Lindsey in the pastorate of the Essex Street Church, which Lindsey had raised to a position of great denominational eminence. Belsham, like Lindsey, was a vigorous defender of Unitarian doctrines; but he brought to that defence a greater philosophical power, and a better trained mind than Lindsey possessed. He was also the author of several works bearing upon the nature of civil government and upon English history. In these, and in three sermons on "The Connexion of Christianity with the Civil Power," the author defended, with great laboriousness, the principle of a State Church in all its applications, excepting the penal punishment of Dissenters. But he subsequently admitted that he made very few proselytes to his principles, and that, amongst his old friends, he did not know one who thought with him. Dr. Joshua Toulmin, of Taunton, and subsequently of Birmingham—where he became pastor of Dr. Priestley's Church—was not less eminent than either of these men. He was both an able preacher and an industrious writer. His "History of Dissent to the Year 1717" is one of the standard works in Dissenting historical literature. His edition of Neal's "History of the Puritans" superseded all previous editions, but in a controversy with Andrew Fuller upon Calvinism and Socinianism he exhibited less ability than in his historical studies.

The prominent position of Unitarianism at this period—as has been the case throughout its history—was owing for the most part, not to the extent to which its doctrines had been received—for they were declining in influence—but to the high character and great abilities of a few preachers and writers. On the religious thought of the nation at large, however, unless by the destruction of the old Presbyterian interest, Unitarianism may be said to have exercised little positive influence.

In the number of remarkably useful, if not great men, the Congregationalists stood far more conspicuous. Dr. David Bogue, Samuel Palmer, George Burder, William Bengo Collyer, William Bull, William Jay, Thomas Toller, and John Clayton the senior, stood pre-eminent amongst their brethren. Dr. Bogue, when a young man, had employed his pen in defence of the rights of Dissenters in connexion with the Test and Corporation Acts, but his greatest service to Christianity was his efforts for the advancement of missionary enterprise. To this work he gave the best energies of a good and able man. As one of the founders of the London Missionary Society his zeal in its behalf increased with his years, and he was selected to preach the first anniversary sermon of that institution. One who knew him best has said that "it would require a volume to record his labours in that great cause."* His peculiar fitness for such a post led to his appointment as Principal of an academy at Gosport for the training of young men for the ministry. Many of the most eminent missionaries of the London Society were educated by him. Dr. Bogue died, where probably he would have chosen to die, at a meeting of the Society, in 1825.

* "Dr. James Bennett's Life of Bogue." "History of Dissenters," p. 144.

No name was more familiar to the Congregational Churches of England at the beginning of this century than that of Samuel Palmer, of Hackney, who served, equally in the pulpit and in literature, the interests of spiritual religion and of Christian freedom. In the "Protestant Dissenter's Magazine," in the "Nonconformists' Memorial"—an improvement on Calamy's well-known work—and in the "Protestant Dissenter's Catechism" he still lives to serve the principles which he held to be more precious than life itself.*

George Burder, the author of "Village Sermons," and in earlier life, when at Lancaster and Coventry, a most active evangelist, was now at Fetter Lane Chapel, and one of the secretaries of the London Missionary Society, as well as editor of the "Evangelical Magazine." He died at nearly eighty years of age, in 1832. Dr. Collyer, of Hanover Chapel, Peckham, was one of the fashionable ministers of his time, a little given to personal display, but a useful preacher. This popular religious author and minister was, for twelve years, one of the most intimate friends of the Duke of Kent, over whom he had great personal influence, and who occasionally attended his chapel.† William Bull, who enjoyed the friendship of Cowper and Newton, and was the first Principal of the Newport-Pagnell Institution, was content to devote some of the highest of human abilities to apparently moderate uses. Although a man of untiring energy and of great pulpit power—which, if he had chosen, would have placed him in one of the most eminent positions in the metropolis as pastor of the Weigh-House

* There is a memoir of Palmer, in two parts, in the "Congregational Magazine" for 1819, but the writer, singularly enough, omits all reference to the "Nonconformists' Memorial."

† "Erskine Neale's Memoir of the Duke of Kent," Preface; Collyer's Funeral Sermon for the Duke of Kent, 1820.

Church—he saw that the spiritual interests of the few hundreds of a country town were enough to absorb the whole labour of a Christian minister.* Three generations of William Bull's family have now filled for a hundred years the same pulpit at Newport-Pagnell. The same can be said of another family, one member of which now occupied the position of pastor of the Congregational Church at Kettering. Thomas Northcote Toller was at this time the most eminent minister in the Midland Counties. A man of rare devotional spirit, of intense zeal in Christian work, of unusual eloquence, and of unblemished integrity and consistency of life, he exercised an influence over his own congregation, and in the neighbouring district, which few men of even the highest mental qualifications have obtained. Into the work of the Bible Society he threw all his spiritual force, and by his eloquent and unremitting advocacy of its claims greatly aided the success of that institution. Living in the same town with Andrew Fuller, the two ministers united in all common Christian enterprises, and, when the Baptist leader died, his Congregational brother was chosen to preach his funeral sermon.†

At Bath William Jay, the favourite of the almost equally celebrated Cornelius Winter, though young in years, was already rising to the height of that remarkable reputation as a Christian preacher which crowded the Argyle Chapel, and every place of worship where he preached. Jay's published discourses have exercised a remarkable influence in England and America.‡ John Clayton, senior, of the

* "Memoir of William Bull." By Josiah Bull.

† A. G. Fuller's Memoir of Andrew Fuller. Robert Hall's Memoir of the Rev. T. N. Toller. Mr. Hall's Estimate of Mr. Toller's character in this memoir is one of the most exquisite productions of the kind in the English language.

‡ Jay's Memoir of Cornelius Winter. Cyrus R. Jay's Life of William Jay.

Weigh-House Chapel, had been one of the favourite students of the Countess of Huntingdon, but, from conscientious motives, he left the Established Church. An active pastor, an effective preacher, and a man of strict holiness of life, he contributed, more than most of his contemporaries, to the dignity and reputation of the Congregational ministry. Mr. Clayton, however, was a Tory, and his opinions on political subjects were therefore opposed to the sentiments of most Dissenters. As the father of three equally celebrated ministers, his name has lived more familiarly than is common in the memory of the generation which he preceded.*

High character, but not the highest order of genius, belonged to the Congregational ministers of this period. There were many of singularly equal powers, but none who stood on the loftiest intellectual platform. It is remarkable that some of the most eminent Independent preachers stood aloof from the public controversial advocacy, and even from the expository statement, of the grounds of their Dissent.

The Nestor of the Baptist denomination was Abraham Booth, who, in very early life, had been brought under religious influences through the ministrations of some General Baptist ministers in Northamptonshire. Booth was originally a weaver, but, while pursuing his occupation, was encouraged to preach in the villages around his residence. Separating, afterwards, from the General Baptists, he composed, while working at his stocking loom, a work on the "Reign of Grace," the manuscript of which, coming into the hands of Henry Venn, the Evangelical minister of Huddersfield, that eminent clergyman visited the author, whom he found at his ordinary occupation, strongly urged the printing of the production, and secured him from all

* Memoir of the Clayton Family. By T. W. Aveling.

pecuniary loss. The remarkable ability shown in this work attracted the attention of the denomination, and he was invited to become the pastor of the Prescott Street Baptist Church in London. By severe and unremitting application to study Booth now made himself master of the classical languages and of nearly the whole range of ecclesiastical and theological literature. He was one of the first Dissenting ministers who identified himself with the anti-slave-trade agitation, and was recognised as the leader of the close communion party in his denomination. The question of admitting members of anti-Pædobaptist churches to the privileges of the Lord's Supper was warmly debated in Booth's time, and, after Kiffin, he was the ablest advocate for the exclusion of all persons who had not received adult baptism by immersion. Bunyan's catholic principles on this subject were received by few churches except those which he had himself founded in Bedfordshire. Andrew Fuller agreed with Booth, and the joint intellectual authority of these two great men was sufficient to preserve, for years, the maintenance of that exclusive practice by the large majority of Baptist Churches. Booth's reputation as an extensive and accurate scholar placed him in the front rank of the ministers of the Free Churches. A man of majesty of demeanour and of profound learning, he was also as remarkable for the humility of his disposition and the simplicity of his life.*

Dr. Rippon, of Southwark, stood, in London, next to Booth. He was known for his literary, poetical, and musical qualifications. As the projector and editor of the "Baptist Register," an occasional periodical devoted to the interests of his denomination, he rendered effective service not merely to his own distinctive principles, but to the work

* Ivimey, iv. 364—379.

of the Christian Church. He was a poet of accurate taste, if not of vigorous thought, and he was the first person to compile, on an extensive scale, a book of tunes, with a companion Hymn-book, suitable for religious worship. A hundred years before this time, a Baptist minister who had performed such a work would probably have been unable to obtain a pastorate.

Dr. John Ryland, formerly of Northampton, and the son of the Rev. John Collett Ryland, of the same town, afterwards pastor of the Broadmead Church, Bristol, and theological tutor to the Baptist Academy, from the extent of his erudition, his lofty integrity, and the maturity of his judgment, was held in the highest veneration. Ryland followed Bunyan and Robinson in defending the practice of open communion. His son, the friend and biographer of John Foster, also named John Ryland, and also of Northampton, inherited his father's principles and abilities. Dr. John Fawcett, one of the converts of Grimshaw of Haworth, for a long period the minister of a church at Hebden Bridge, where he was John Foster's pastor when Foster was a child, and then the president of the Bristol Education Society at Bristol, was an author of religious works of considerable usefulness, and a Christian poet, whose hymns are to be found in almost every selection.* At Oxford James Hinton,† a man of an exquisite susceptibility to devotional feeling, and of inflexible moral courage, ably sustained the reputation of Dissent in the principal University town. "What energy," inquired Foster, writing to Joseph Hughes, "does fire Pearce, Hinton, and yourself?"‡ Joseph

* Ivimey, iv. 568—575.

† Father of the late Isaac Taylor Hinton and John Howard Hinton, M.A.

‡ Foster's Life and Correspondence, i. 113.

Kinghorn occupied a similar position at Norwich, where he remained a pastor for forty years. This Baptist minister was almost the last persistent literary opponent of open communion. For eleven years he endeavoured to blunt the force of Robert Hall's arguments on this question, but lived to see all his endeavours frustrated.*

Two names, in addition to these, threw a lustre on the Baptist denomination, and on all the Free Churches of England, which neither death nor time has dimmed. Amongst all the preachers of Christianity, from the time of Chrysostom to his own, Robert Hall is pre-eminent for majesty of thought and dignity of language. Others have equalled, but few have excelled him, in freedom of utterance and facility of diction; still fewer in the lofty height to which his mind would ascend when speaking of the transcendent glory of the Christian scheme of redemption. To his self-chosen work as a preacher of the Gospel amongst one of the least popular of the Christian sects, he brought not merely the natural genius with which he had been endowed, but a mind trained to the familiar consideration of the most abstruse philosophical problems. In the region of thought which the intellects of other men would scarcely find without his guidance, he appeared to be a customary inhabitant. But he had the rare and precious faculty of making all who heard him live while they heard, according to the measure of his mental and spiritual life. If his own mind, by the touch of a sacred fire, was transmuted, the fire was felt by all who came within its range. Nor did Hall sacrifice the duty of his office to the exhibition of his marvellous mental powers. He was not—what South, to some extent, was—a mere showman of his abilities. The message he had to deliver was ever upon his heart, and

* Wilkins's "Life of Kinghorn." Kinghorn's "Baptism, &c."

was the power that, in the secret chambers of the soul, drove forth his eloquence. At the age of forty Robert Hall's principal published works had been his "Apology for the Freedom of the Press," and his sermons on "Modern Infidelity." In the first he vindicated political liberty, and especially the public rights and services of Dissenters; in the second he examined, held up to light, and exposed the causes, features, and tendencies of the unbelief then characteristic of a large class of educated men. His fame while occupying Robert Robinson's pulpit at Cambridge had already extended far beyond the circles of his own people. It is remarkable that in his writings there are none of the one-sided deficiencies that often attach to great orators. Burke could compose almost unequalled speeches, but when he spoke what he had written, he spoke to a gradually diminishing audience. Fox could speak with a fulness and power of eloquence which transfixed his hearers, but when he wrote he became weak, tame, and loose. But Hall was an equally finished writer and speaker. The rhythm of his thought lost none of its perfection because it was not perfectly spontaneous; his sentences lost none of their natural force because they were exquisitely polished; his thought lost none of its freshness and weight because it had been considered and reconsidered. Hall's greatest reputation was yet to be made. He had yet to preach the discourse occasioned by the anticipated invasion of England by Napoleon, when, picturing to his imagination the possible effects of its success, he appealed to the people, with an eloquence that rivalled the loftiest oratory of Greece and Rome, to save the liberties of their country. He had yet to vindicate the connexion between Christianity and the love of Freedom, and ye to break down the barrier that fenced in all Baptist churches—the immersed from communion with the sprinkled. He had yet to make the old city of Bristol famous, as though it were the cathedral town of the Free Churches, and to make Leicester the heart of English Dissent, whence for a time flowed its best and richest blood. The special influence of Robert Hall upon his own denomination has never been fully considered. When it comes to be, it will probably be judged that, in modern times, that body has owed more to him than to any other man. Through him the Baptist churches gained an elevation in the eyes of their countrymen which they had not before enjoyed. It was impossible to sneer at the sect with which such a man had deliberately chosen to identify himself.

In the first year of the century John Foster, then settled as the pastor of the small village church of Downend, near Bristol, met and heard Robert Hall. He wrote, after hearing him, "In some remarkable manner, everything about him, all he does or says, is instinct with power. Jupiter seems to emanate in his attitude, gesture, look, and tone of voice. Even a common sentence, when he utters one, seems to tell how much more he can do. His intellect is peculiarly potential, and his imagination robes without obscuring the colossal form of his mind."* Foster's parents, and, through them, Foster himself, afford another illustration of the practical effect of the Methodist movement. They had been brought to a sense of religion by Grimshaw of Haworth, but subsequently connected themselves with the Baptist Church of which Dr. Fawcett was pastor. Their son, though he had preached here and there, was, as yet, unknown to the public; but his correspondence gives proof that, in all the essential respects of personal disposition and habits of thought, he was what he was throughout the remainder of his life. The predominant tendency of his intellect was to indulge in analysis. As regarded himself this tendency took a some

* "Ryland's Life and Correspondence of John Foster," i. 74.

what morbid turn. His self-introspection, or what may be described as his curiosity about his own character and abilities, is exhibited in almost every page of his earliest, as well of his latest, familiar letters. But he judged others with the same minute discrimination. In thus giving way to the bent of his natural genius, he was, unconsciously, preparing himself for the peculiar service which he afterwards rendered to religious and critical literature, when, in his "Essays," in some of his contributions to the *Eclectic Review*, and in other writings, he dealt, in his exhaustive manner, with several of the most important problems affecting the political, social, and religious welfare of the people. It would have been remarkable if, excepting as a writer, Foster had been popular. He did not believe in eternal punishments; he shrank from ordinary church life; he assailed, with pitiless severity, the connexion between Church and State, and all that such a connexion involves; and he was a "Radical" in politics. With the just balance of his intellect and the frankness of his mind, he viewed abuses in ecclesiastical and political life with a moral abhorrence which he never hesitated to express. It was, however, in his case, the abhorrence of conscience and reason—not of passion. He described, with a kind of surgical minuteness, dispositions, characters, symptoms, and tendencies; but his judgment concerning injustice was the judgment of a righteous moral indignation. Foster's peculiar function was to give sincerity of tone to the inner life—an office that he will render as long as his writings are read.

Wesley died in 1791, beseeching his adherents not to leave the Established Church. On his decease there were two hundred and seventy-eight ministers in connexion with the Wesleyan societies. Scarcely was he dead when a spirit of revolt against the ecclesiastical subserviency of the societies to the laws of the Church arose. Wesley had been careful that no meeting for religious worship should be held at the customary time for public worship in the Establishment: the ministers and people now demanded that they should hold their assemblies at any convenient time, without being restricted to the mere intervals of the hours appointed for the Church services. Wesley had been careful not to allow the celebration of Baptism and the Lord's Supper by the ministers: the people now claimed the right to receive these ordinances at the hands of their own ministers, in their own places of worship. A similar revolt arose against the semi-sacerdotal power which Wesley had lodged in the body called the "Legal Hundred," or Conference, by which all the affairs of the societies were governed. The itinerant preachers and laity now claimed a share of that power, so that there might be some form of popular government in the body. After four years' dispute the former two rights were conceded, and thus the Wesleyans became separated from the Church. Some minor concessions were made, in 1797, relating to the right of the laity to decide as to fitness of persons wishing to become communicants, but their claim to be admitted to the Conference was peremptorily rejected. That is to say, the ministers were willing to increase their own power, but not to give power to others. A secession, led by the Rev. Alexander Kilham, of Epworth, at once took place, and the "Methodist New Connexion" was established. The rights claimed by the laity were fully conceded by the new body, which, though small at first in numbers, gradually grew to a position of considerable ecclesiastical importance.*

In the beginning of the present century the number of members in connexion with the old Methodist Society had increased to four hundred and fifty-two. Amongst them were some men who, for piety and ability, had few equals.

* "Smith's History of Wesleyan Methodism," Vol. ii. "Cook's History of Kilham."

The ecclesiastical successor of Wesley was Dr. Thomas Coke, who had been educated at Oxford for the ministry of the Established Church; but, at South Petherton, becoming zealous in his religious work, and adopting out-door preaching, he was first admonished by his bishop, then dismissed by his rector, and lastly rung out of the town—a victory over him which the mob celebrated by drinking barrels of cider in the streets. In zeal Coke was equal to Wesley himself; he was the soul of the foreign missionary enterprise of Methodism, and he was the founder—ordained a "Bishop" by Wesley—of the Methodist Episcopal Church of the United States. Coke had some of Whitefield's as well as of Wesley's qualities—the impulsiveness and ardour of the one, united to the sagacity of the other.* Joseph Benson was lost to the Church in the same fashion as all the founders of Methodism. He was refused orders on account of Methodistic tendencies, and at once began field preaching. Benson was remarkable for his Biblical scholarship and his active literary enterprise. The humorous but sublime preacher, Samuel Bradburn—"the Demosthenes of Methodism"—followed next in order of power. The joint biographer of Wesley—Henry Moor—who died in 1842, the patriarch of the denomination, and the last surviving preacher who had been ordained by Wesley, was esteemed not less for his literary qualities than for his sound judgment. Adam Clarke, the commentator, the linguist, the unwearied preacher, the genial companion, the man who combined more than any other in the denomination a capacity for power with a most eminent love of liberty,† may fitly close a list of the immediate successors of John and Charles Wesley.

---

* Stevens's History, ii. cap. v.

† "Adam Clarke Portrayed." By William Everett.

But extensive as was the work in which these men were engaged, and great as were their zeal and strength, they were far surpassed, in some of the highest qualities of Christian orators, as well as in the results of their work, by the second generation of the Calvinistic Methodists of Wales. During ten years the people of that country were subject to an extraordinary series of revivals of religion, which, if attended on some occasions with extravagant manifestations that were productive of religious results, had no parallel in the British dominions. Susceptible, more than any other people, to the influence of religious emotions, the fire of the Divine Word penetrated the hearts of multitudes, who, by their after life, witnessed to its purifying as well as its exciting powers. The history of the progress of religion in Wales is a record of the success of lay evangelisation. The few clergymen, not exceeding four or five in number, who during its first period were in the front of this movement, were merely the staff of the army. Those who carried on the warfare throughout all the mountains and villages of Wales were, like Howel Harries, self-ordained preachers. If the clergy had been wholly inclined, as Wesley once was, to keep the work in their own hands, they could not have done so. As has often been the case, they exhibited some jealousy of their lay helpers. Amongst other symptoms of this feeling, they gave them the title of "Exhorters" instead of preachers. But amongst these "Exhorters" were men who, in the rarest gifts of the Christian preacher, surpassed all the ordained clergymen, Daniel Rowlands, perhaps, excepted. The precedent of the English Wesleyans was followed in Wales. The people, recognising the call of God, if not of men, inquired why they should not administer the sacraments. It was after this period that the inquiry met with a reluctant response from the clerical leaders of the movement. The clergy resisted it to the utmost of their power,* but in 1810 the Rev. Thomas Charles promised to consent to the ordination of preachers for the administration of the sacrament, and the performance of all the other offices of the Christian ministry. Others of the clergy, imagining that the people would follow them, drew back from the proposals, and were left in sudden and unexpected obscurity. As the most rapid success of English Methodism dates from the decision of the Conference of 1795, so the most rapid success of Welsh Methodism dates from the Association meeting of 1811. It is owing to the labours of the unordained "Exhorters" that Welsh Methodism obtained a permanent hold upon the people. They, and the few clergymen who abetted them, were, of course, charged with irregularity; but to their irregular labours is owing a state of society in Wales which, in regard to the high character of religion, purity of morals, the activity of religious enterprise, and the creation and use of the means of religious worship, has no parallel in Great Britain. Of the clergymen who were connected with the second generation of Calvinistic Methodism, Thomas Charles, of Bala, stands pre-eminent. Before the year 1784 Charles had been ejected from three churches, when his Christian instincts compelled him to break through canonical rules, and take the Gospel to whomsoever would hear it. After he had gained the hearts of his countrymen, he was offered promotion, but he wrote, "I really would rather have spent the last twenty-three years of my life as I have done, wandering up and down in this cold and barren country, than if I had been made an archbishop." Charles threw himself with intense ardour, not merely into the ordinary

* Life of the Rev. T. Charles, of Bala. Sir T. Phillips's "Wales," p. 151.

work of the Church, but into the work of all benevolent institutions. By him, through the agency of the Bible Society—which might justly have been termed *his* Bible Society—the love of the Scriptures was planted in the hearts of the people, and from him popular education in Wales received a fresh impetus.

John Elias was, in an Episcopal sense, a layman, but was the equal of Charles in all the divine qualifications necessary to the awakening of a whole nation. Of this apostle of Anglesea a recently deceased writer has said, "In all my journeys through Wales I have not heard of any one minister whose preaching has been so universally blessed to the conversion of sinners as John Elias. In almost every country place, village, or town you can find some person who will ascribe his conversion to one of his sermons. This I have witnessed in very many cases. You know that we are accustomed to very powerful preaching in Wales; indeed, I may say with truth, that there is no ministry on earth that can compete with the Welsh in solidity, warmth, and energy. Yet John Elias was remarkable amongst the Welsh."* After Charles, he was the most efficient co-operator amongst his people in the work of the Bible and the London Missionary Societies.

In South Wales religion owed most of its power and progress to the agency of three men—Ebenezer Morris, David Charles, and Ebenezer Richard. The princely presence and the majestic oratory of Morris are still a tradition; but he is more to be remembered for the fearless courage with which he withstood the indignant Church Methodists, who charged the people with the sin of schism for desiring ministers of their own. To his self-possession, calmness of judgment, and inflexible firmness was owing, in a great

* The Rev. Dr. Charles, of Trevecca, in the Rev. J. K. Foster's "Memoir of John Elias," pp. 152, 153.

degree, the success of the laity over the clergy on this occasion. David Charles was chiefly eminent for might and influence in council; but, amongst all the three, the Rev. Ebenezer Richard,* of Tregaron, contributed most to the success of Methodism in South Wales. He had much of Whitefield's pathos, and Wesley's faculty of organisation. He was the principal organiser of the new Methodist body, and, by the recommendation of Thomas Charles, was appointed general secretary to the South Wales Association. To his rare skill and indefatigable exertions was, also, principally owing the extraordinary success of the Sunday-school system in South Wales.

The character of Dissent, as such, at the beginning of the century, was less obtrusive than it had been in most former periods of its history. The odium which had been incurred by the participation of its leaders in the opposition to the American War, and by their sympathy with the earlier struggles of the French Revolutionists, had induced the same feeling that had characterised their predecessors in the latter years of the reign of Queen Anne. The Five Mile, Conventicle, and Blasphemy Acts were still on the statute book, and it was competent for any man, as Mr. Beaufoy had said in one of the debates on the Test and Corporation Laws, to "earn damnation" by putting them in force. The King's ministry was known to be favourable to some restriction of the practically unlimited right of preaching that existed. It was, therefore, deemed politic to keep silence concerning the serious legal disabilities which attached to the profession of Nonconformity. Even Robert Hall deprecated the idea of Dissent becoming, in any way, "political," or of its being based upon any but the "old grounds."† There were

* Father of the late Henry Richard, M.P.

† Letter in Olinthus Gregory's Memoir. Works, i. 92. Ed. 1832.

others—chiefly those who had been under the Countess of Huntingdon's influence—whose sympathies with the Church were almost as strong as their sympathies with Dissent. Rowland Hill, although he had been cast out from communion with the Church, avowed, to the end of his life, his attachment to it, and his approval of its civil establishment. John Clayton, although from conscientious motives he had declined to become one of its ministers, had little sympathy with the deepest grounds of Dissent, and did not hesitate, in political action, to separate himself from his brethren. The Jays, the Collyers, and nearly all the most eminent of the Congregational ministers, were in intimate intercourse with the leaders of the Evangelical party; and, in that intercourse, as was natural, community of faith and sentiment kept out of sight diversity of principles. There was a tacit compact that the Church should not be attacked. Its intolerance met, therefore, with no rebuke; its liturgy was praised; and its Evangelical clergy were affectionately reverenced. The Methodists, with charming simplicity, still denied that they were Dissenters at all. The phase in the history of religion in England which was exhibited at this period, in the cordial, although necessarily unequal, intercourse which existed between a section of the clergy of the Established Church and some of the more conspicuous members of the Free Churches, had two equally operative causes—first, identity of faith and aim, and, secondly, similarity of position. Both parties believed in the same truths, and both were equally convinced of the supreme importance of these truths. The product, to a large extent, of the same revolution in religious thought and life, they occupied, in doctrinal belief, and in characteristically religious action, almost the same position with respect to the predominant High Church and Indifferent parties in the Establishment. They believed in the same modes of action—in Sunday-schools, in Tract Societies, in Bible Societies, and in evangelization. Their union was, for certain purposes, and for a time, of advantage ; but it was a union that could not, in the nature of things, be lasting. Its condition was silence on one side respecting a fundamental principle. At this period, the silence was honest, but it was impossible that it could remain so. When silence became dishonest, and the touchstone of "religious equality" was applied to the union, the two parties drew asunder, and Nonconformists saw that, under the mask of fraternity, there had ever been concealed the hateful features of ecclesiastical supremacy and pride. Dissent, however, owed much of its increase to the labours of the earlier Evangelical party. This was the case in town as well as in country districts, where, when an Evangelical minister was removed, and was replaced by a man of another character, the people, in almost all instances, turned Dissenters.* Such persons, however, could not be supposed to have a very intelligent appreciation of the reasons for Dissent.

Several circumstances soon contributed to strengthen the tone of most of the Free Churches in this respect. Towards the close of the previous century the Rev. William Graham, a Presbyterian minister at Newcastle, published an elaborate "Review of Ecclesiastical Establishments in Europe,"† in which he traced the rise of the system, and its disastrous influence upon the religious, social, and political character of the people, and argued that all alliances between the Church and the State had deeply injured both of the parties to it. He proceeded to advocate their tota separation as a just and necessary thing if religion was to

---

* Andrew Fuller, on "The Decline of the Dissenting Interest." Works, p. 845.

† "A Review," &c. 1792.

be advanced as it might be, and the Head of the Church to be given the honour that was exclusively His due. The work of this author was remarkable as well for the vigour of its tone as for the comprehensiveness of its argument, and had an unquestionable influence in forming the opinions upon this subject of the generation that succeeded him. In the periodical press, and especially in the *Congregational Magazine* and the *Eclectic Review*, able service was done in the same direction. No man contributed more to this than John Foster, who demanded that the last-named, and, at that time, powerful, journal should be based on opposition to all Church Establishments.*

But, while some of the reasons of their separation from the Established Church were freely stated, little disposition was exhibited by the Free Churches practically to assert either their ecclesiastical or their civil rights. The sole exception, for some years, was a tardy but ultimately effectual protest made by Abraham Booth, Andrew Fuller, and Robert Hall, on behalf of the Baptist Missionary Society, against two Acts of the Jamaica Assembly, which virtually suspended the Toleration Act, and prohibited all Dissenters from preaching to the slaves. Backed by the Committee of Deputies, the memorialists succeeded in obtaining, in 1809, the reversal of these laws by the King in Council.†

In 1808 an occasion arose for enforcing the right of burial against a clergyman who had refused to inter a child baptized by a Dissenter in the parish churchyard, and advantage was taken of the opportunity to procure an authoritative decision respecting the law upon this question. The refusal by High Church clergymen to bury the children

---

* Ryland's "Life," &c., i. 375.
† "Sketch of the History," &c., pp. 61—64.

of Dissenters was a matter of ordinary occurrence, but hitherto it had not been necessary to enforce the law against the offending person. In this year, however, the rector of Wardly-cum-Belton, in Rutlandshire, the Rev. John Wright Wickes, openly and persistently refused to give burial to a child. The Committee of Deputies, after giving him the opportunity of complying with what was believed to be the law upon this question, instituted proceedings against him in the Court of Arches. On December 11th, 1809, Sir John Nicholl, Chief Judge of the Court, delivered judgment. He decided that persons who had been baptized by Dissenters, or by any layman, were baptized within the meaning of the law. "Is it just," Sir John Nicholl further inquired, "to exclude from the rites of the Church persons who are obliged to pay tithes, church-rates, Easter offerings, and other dues, and contribute to the support of the Church and its ministers?" Whether just or not, it was not legal, and Mr. Wickes was therefore condemned to suspension for three months from his office, and to pay the whole costs of the suit.*

In 1810 an event occurred which at last aroused the Dissenters from their comparative apathy. On February 27th, Viscount Sidmouth, in the House of Lords, drew attention to the returns of preachers and places of worship who had been licensed between the years 1760 and 1808.† On June 18th he indicated that it was necessary to restrict the liberty which persons enjoyed of becoming preachers of the Christian religion, and announced his intention of bringing in a Bill upon the subject.‡ On April 29th, in

* "The Judgment of Sir John Nicholl," &c., 1810. "Sketch of the History," &c., pp. 68—82.

† Parl. Debates, xv. 633.

‡ Parl. Debates, xvii. 750.

the following year, the noble lord gave notice of his purpose to call attention to the provisions of the Toleration Act of the 19th of Geo. III. cap. 44, with respect to Dissenting ministers. On May 9th his lordship brought in a Bill upon this subject. Prefacing his speech with an avowal of his attachment to religious liberty, he proceeded to say that the mode in which Dissenting ministers assumed their offices was an abuse of this liberty. It was, he said, a matter of importance to society that persons should not be allowed, without some check, to assume the office of instructing others in the Word of God. He stated that many improper persons had assumed the office—persons who were "cobblers, tailors, pig-drovers, and chimney-sweepers;" and he proposed that, in future, no person should be allowed to obtain a certificate as a minister unless he were recommended by six respectable house-keepers of his own denomination. He concluded by calling attention to the claims of the Church, and stating the necessity for new church edifices.*

As soon as notice had been given of this measure, the General Body of Protestant Dissenting Ministers met, passed resolutions to oppose it, and decided to organise a special agitation with reference to the danger by which they were threatened. Into this movement the Methodist body—acting, for the first time, with other Dissenters in a political question—threw the whole of their influence. At a public general meeting, held early in 1811, which was attended by Dissenters from all parts of England, a committee, consisting, amongst others, of the Rev. Robert Aspland, Unitarian; Henry Burder, William Bengo Collyer, John Leifchild, Thomas Raffles, and John Pye Smith, Congregationalists; Rowland Hill, of the Countess of Hunt-

* Parl. Debates, xix. 781, 1128.

ingdon's Connexion; and Matthew Wilks, of the Calvinistic Methodists, was appointed to conduct the agitation.* The brief notice given of the second reading of the proposed measure compelled the committee to use the most vigorous measures to oppose it. No time was lost in waiting upon members of Parliament, and in forty-eight hours three hundred and thirty-six petitions against it were procured from Dissenting congregations within a hundred and twenty miles of London.

On May 21st, Lord Sidmouth moved the second reading of the Bill, when the table of the House of Lords was loaded with petitions from all parts of the country against it. Lord Holland, Earl Grey, and Earl Stanhope required some of those which they presented to be read. There were petitions from all parts of England, with an "immense number" of signatures. The Marquis of Lansdowne presented more than a hundred, several of which he said were signed by beneficed clergymen of the Established Church. Viscount Sidmouth then arose, and defended his measure against the charges which had been brought against it, declaring, at the close of his speech, that his wish had been to render a benefit to Dissenters, by proposing a measure intended to promote the honour, the dignity, and the sanctity of religion. The Archbishop of Canterbury, while he approved of the Bill, considered it unwise to press it against the wishes of those who were the best judges of their own interests. Lord Erskine, venerable alike for age and learning, vehemently declaimed against it, saying that it was aimed at two millions of persons, whom he recollected as having been in the bosom of the Church, but who had been driven from it by persecution. He moved that it be read a second time that day six months. Lord Holland

* *Evangelical Magazine*, 1811, p. 241.

denounced it as opposed to the principles of the Toleration Act. Earl Stanhope pointed to the immense heap of petitions that was strewed upon the floor and piled upon the table of the House, and declared that he would not argue upon a measure that was evidently beyond human help, for it was already "dead and gone." There were three hundred laws respecting religion, he said, in the statute book, which would disgust the members of the House, and make them ashamed of their ancestors, if they were to read them, as he had done. He stigmatized this proposal to add to their number as detrimental to the best interests of religion, and dangerous to the existence of any Government. The Bill was thrown out without a division, and Lord Erskine's amendment declared to be carried.

Three days after the defeat of this Bill another general meeting of Dissenters was held, when it was resolved to form a new society, to be called the "Protestant Society for the Protection of Religious Liberty," Mr. Thomas Pellatt and Mr. John Wilks, member of Parliament for Boston, being appointed its honorary secretaries.* The formation of this society was hailed with unbounded enthusiasm by all classes of Dissenters. On an appeal for subscriptions being made, two hundred congregations gave collections for its support. The object of this society as publicly announced was to "obtain the repeal of every penal law which prevented the complete enjoyment of religious liberty." † The chief leader in this movement was Mr. Wilks, whose high personal character, commanding eloquence, and unswerving devotion to the principles and interests of Dissent, naturally pointed him out as the most fit person to occupy such a position. John Wilks was the son of the

---

* *Evangelical Magazine*, 1811, pp. 278—284.

† Ib., 1812, p. 446.

Rev. Matthew Wilks, of Moorfields, and was one of the most popular and effective speakers of his generation. At the annual meetings of the Protestant Society his presence would draw thousands of hearers, whom he would hold for three hours in eager attention. The objects of the Protestant Society were, however, of a more limited character than its constitution would appear to indicate. It aimed at the repeal of the Test and Corporation Acts, and the reform of the Marriage, the Burial, and the University Laws. Church-rates, as Mr. Wilks remarked on making his official statement at one of the later annual meetings of the Society, were not considered to involve any injustice to Dissenters, nor was it intended to ask for their repeal.* The Society took notice of illegal acts on the part of Churchmen, such as refusals to bury Dissenters, or to marry unbaptised persons, or refusals of certificates to ministers, and of prosecutions for the violation of the Five-Mile and Conventicle Acts, which, after having been dead for a hundred and fifty years, were now again being put into force by clergymen in country districts, and heavy fines imposed by the magistrates upon persons who had violated them. The number of such cases at this time was extraordinary; and, wherever they occurred, legal proceedings were promptly instituted, and the defence of prosecuted persons undertaken by the Committee.

Before the Society had been in existence a year it had succeeded, acting in conjunction with the Dissenting Deputies, in obtaining the repeal of the Quakers' Oaths, the Conventicle, and the Five-Mile Acts. Communications were opened with the Ministers of the Crown, and in July, 1812, a Bill was brought in by Lord Castlereagh in the House of Commons, and Lord Liverpool in the House of

* Speech of John Wilks, Esq. *Congregational Magazine*, 1824.

Lords, for the repeal of these Acts. It met with no opposition, and at once passed into law. By this Act* the three statutes of Charles II. were abrogated, and the Free Churches were placed, in respect to legal protection from disturbance during times of public worship, on an equality with the Established Church; it being provided† that any person who should wilfully, maliciously, or contemptuously annoy any Dissenting congregation, or any preacher while officiating to such congregation, should, upon conviction of the offence, pay a penalty of forty pounds. The terms of this Act were drawn up by the Wesleyan Methodist Society. During the brief conversation on the Bill, Mr. Vansittart, Chancellor of the Exchequer, remarked that he could not understand how religious liberty could now proceed any further.‡

In 1813 the Free Churches were called upon to make another united effort on behalf of the liberty of preaching the Gospel. In that year the Charter of the East India Company expired. The Baptist missionaries in India had hitherto been subject to the arbitrary caprices of the East India Company, who, besides refusing them permission to go in English ships to their territories, suspended and imprisoned them at their discretion, and showed the utmost opposition to their labours. When the renewal of their Charter came under the consideration of the Government strenuous efforts were made to procure the insertion of a clause giving the missionaries the right of passage to India, and protection when there. The Company opposed this proposal with all the power at their command. They asserted that the preaching of Christianity in their territories would destroy the Empire, and that it was impossible

* 52 Geo. III., cap. 155. † Ib., sec. xii.
‡ Parl. Debates, xxiii. 1107.

to convert the people. At their instance the evidence of "old Indians" was taken, week after week, in the House of Commons, in support of these allegations. The Rev. Sidney Smith came to their assistance in the *Edinburgh Review*, sneering at the "consecrated cobblers" who had undertaken to convert a heathen people. But the obstinate attitude of the Company only served to stimulate the enthusiasm of the Dissenters. The rights of the missionaries were defended by all classes of Christians. Petitions from the Protestant Society, the Dissenting Deputies, the London, the Baptist, and Church Missionary Societies and congregations throughout the country, poured in upon the Legislature, until, upon seeing their magnitude, the Prime Minister exclaimed, "It is enough!" and consented to insert the desired clause. Thus the Legislature resolved that it was really desirable that useful knowledge and the means of religious and moral improvement should be introduced amongst the native inhabitants of India, and that "sufficient facilities should be afforded by law to persons desirous of going to and remaining in India for the purpose of accomplishing those benevolent designs." The Company was defeated, and the Christian missionaries were given their Christian rights.*

In the next Session of Parliament, Mr. William Smith brought in a Bill for the repeal of the statutes of William the Third and George the Third, which made it blasphemy for any person to deny the doctrine of the Trinity, and exempted all such persons from the benefit of the Toleration Act. During the whole time of their existence the Unitarians had been under the ban of the law, and had not merely conducted their worship, but published their

* Parl. Debates, vols. xxv., xxvi.; Ivimey iv. 134—157; Marshman's "Carey, Marshman, and Ward," cap. vi.; Evangelical and Baptist Magazines, 1813.

opinions, by sufferance. It was competent for any informer to bring them under the severest penalties, next to death, which can be inflicted upon any human being. Mr. Smith's Bill passed* with almost the same ease as the new Toleration Act. The Unitarians now enjoyed all the rights which belonged to other classes of Dissenters.†

These liberties may, however, be said to have been purchased. Recent Parliamentary returns had shown that while half the incumbents of the Established Church were non-resident, a large majority of the benefices were of an extremely small value; out of the whole number, 3,998 were proved to be worth less than a hundred and fifty pounds per annum. At the same time, it was shown that the Free Churches were increasing in far greater proportion than the places of worship belonging to the Establishment. It appeared that in the parishes containing more than a thousand inhabitants, while there were only 2,547 places of worship connected with the Establishment, there were 3,457 places, besides many private houses for religious worship not enumerated, connected with the Free Churches. In only five dioceses did the Church possess a majority of public edifices in such towns.‡ It was accordingly urged that the State should go to the rescue of the Establishment, by building new churches, and increasing the incomes of the poorer clergy. While the former proposition was postponed, the Government decided to adopt the latter, and in the yearly Appropriation Bills brought forward successive measures for granting £100,000 to increase the revenues of Queen Anne's Bounty. In 1810 this grant was strongly opposed by Lord Holland and Earl Stanhope; the latter peer remarking, in reply to the Earl of Harrowby, who had

* 53 Geo. III., cap. 160. † Parl. Debates, xxv., 1147.
‡ "Annual Register," 1810, p. 268. App.

dwelt at length upon the poverty of the clergy and the increase of Dissent, that Dissenters would continue to increase while they found that the advocates of the Established Church conceived that the best means of securing it was to be continually applying for public money. "Whether," said the noble earl, "you vote six millions or sixty millions, whether you build churches or no churches, whether you calumniate Dissenters or otherwise, the number of communicants of the Established Church will decrease, and that of Dissenters increase, so long as the Church of England is made the engine of State policy, and its prelates are translated and preferred, not for their religious merits, but for their staunch support to the minister of the day."* In 1812, the grants for the augmentation of Church livings had, according to the statement of the Chancellor of the Exchequer, amounted to over £400,000; besides which the land tax on livings had been relinquished to the extent of £200,000.† No opposition was made to these grants by the Dissenters, whose silent acquiescence in them appears to have been taken as a matter of course.

The continued increase of the Free Churches, combined with the apathy, in respect to church extension, of the Establishment, led to the proposal, in 1818, of a special grant for building new places of worship in connection with the Church. The Prince Regent, in his speech on opening Parliament in that year, directed particular attention to the deficiency which had so long existed in the number of places of worship belonging to the Established Church, and earnestly recommended that the subject should be taken into the consideration of the Legislature. In accordance with this recommendation, the Chancellor of the

---

* "Parl. Debates," xvii., 769. † Ibid., xxiii., 1107.

Exchequer brought forward a Bill for the appropriation of a million pounds for this object, to be invested in a Commission called the "Church Building Commission." The minister remarked that the Church had, by an unfortunate train of circumstances, shut her doors upon the people,* as though this were a reason for increasing the number of closed doors. No adverse criticism was passed upon the proposal, except by one member, who observed that, according to his experience, where there were the most churches belonging to the Establishment the people were the least moral. When the Bill reached the Upper House, Lord Liverpool, in introducing it, declared that its object was to "remove Dissent," and enforced its claims by asserting that it was the duty of the Legislature to afford the Church the means of balancing the efforts of Dissenters; upon which Lord Holland said that its language, as regards Dissenters, was "You, gentlemen, who pay for yourselves, who pay for your own chapels and your own clergy, in addition to paying tithes to ours, shall also contribute to the erection of these churches, in which you have no interest whatever." The Bill passed without a division, but, singular to say, it did not effect the "removal of Dissent."

Whether or not encouraged by the acquiescence of the Dissenters in such measures, Mr., afterwards Lord Brougham, introduced, in 1820, a Bill for the Education of the People, which, but for the unexpected opposition that it encountered, would have secured to the clergy the sole control over all the schools for the poor. Mr. Brougham stated the nature of his Bill in an elaborate speech in the House of Commons, on June 28th. After giving some of the educational statistics of the country, as shown in a recent Parliamentary inquiry, he proceeded to propose the

* Parl. Debates, 1125.

levy of a parochial school rate, by means of which school houses should be built and teachers supported. Every schoolmaster was to be nominated by the clergyman and two or three parishioners, and was to be a communicant of the Established Church, and the clergyman was to fix the whole course of teaching. On this point, he feared "the sectaries" would be against him, and he "dreaded their opposition, but it appeared to him that the system of public education should be closely connected with the Church." After vindicating this position at considerable length, he moved for leave to bring in his Bill.* But, whatever else might have been borne by Dissenters, it was impossible to accept such a proposal for increasing the power and privileges of an already too powerful and too greatly privileged Church. An opposition was accordingly organized against it, before which the author of the measure was reluctantly compelled to give way. In withdrawing his Bill, Mr. Brougham passed a high eulogium on the character of Dissenters,† which would have been of greater value if he had not shown such utter contempt of their public spirit.

During the succeeding eight years the claims of Dissenters were, by means of the Protestant Society, kept prominently before the public. It had become a recognized power in the State. The leaders of the Whig party now formally identified themselves with it. In one year the Duke of Sussex took the chair; in another, Lord Holland occupied the same position; Sir James Mackintosh delivered from its platform a defence of religious liberty, such as had scarcely been given to the English people since the time of Locke; and Lord John Russell, boldly identifying himself and his party with the political interests of Dissenters, came

* Parl. Debates, New Series, vol. 2, 50—90. † Ib. 366.

forward, as chairman in another year, to advocate the full civil and religious rights of the three millions who were now openly connected with one or other of the Free Churches.* The period of the Revolution, when Somers, Halifax, Burnet, and their associates, laid the foundations of constitutional government, seemed to have returned. The whole Whig party entered, once more, into a close and hearty alliance with Dissenters, an alliance that, as far as regards the express purpose for which it was formed, was honourably and faithfully preserved.

One subject which, at the meetings of the Protestant Society, was more frequently referred to than any other was the Test and Corporation Acts. The claims of the Roman Catholics to be emancipated from the disabilities to which they were subjected was, at this time, engaging the prominent attention of statesmen. Ireland was threatening rebellion, and, in the person of Mr. O'Connell, had found a leader who possessed both the will and the power to wrest from a reluctant and panic-stricken Government a concession to the demands of his countrymen. It was while the cabinet of Wellington and Peel were deliberating upon the course which they should pursue with respect to the Roman Catholics that the Protestant Dissenters put forth their claim for a total repeal of the Test and Corporation Acts. On the 9th of March, 1827, the Committee of Deputies, who had long been watching for a favourable opportunity, held a special meeting for the purpose of considering the propriety of adopting immediate measures for securing that object. It was then stated that the British and Foreign Unitarian Association, the Board of Congregational Ministers, and other representative bodies

* The *Congregational Magazine* of the period contains very full reports of the meetings of this Society.

were prepared to take action. At a second meeting of the Committee it was resolved to summon a conference consisting of the Committee of the Deputies, and deputations from the Protestant Society, the Unitarian Association, the Ministers of the Three Denominations, and the Board of Congregational Ministers.* On the 26th of the same month the subject was formally brought before the Committee of the Protestant Society, which passed a series of elaborate resolutions setting forth the injustice to which Dissenters were subjected, and it was decided that, in obedience to the instructions which they had repeatedly received from their constituents, consisting of many Liberal members of the Established Church, and of several hundred congregations of Dissenters and Methodists of all denominations in England and Wales, an application should be made to Parliament. On the 28th the proposed conference was held, the chairman of the Committee of Deputies, Mr. William Smith, M.P. for Norwich, who, forty years before, had, in his place in the House of Commons, supported the motions of Mr. Beaufoy and Mr. Fox, presiding. It was unanimously resolved that the proposed Bill should be placed in the hands of Lord John Russell, and that, with a view to secure combined action, a united committee, drawn from the various public bodies, should be formed, and invested with power to take all the measures necessary to obtain the desired object. The committee consisted of forty-three members, including Mr. William Smith, M.P., chairman; J. T. Rutt, Benjamin Hanbury, Dr. Baldwin Brown, Serjeant Bompas, William Brodie Gurney, and Mr. Wilks, from the Deputies; the Rev. R. Aspland, Dr. Rees, Dr. Winter, Dr. Humphreys, Dr. Cox, and Dr. Newman, from the Three Denominations; Mr. Christie, Mr. Bowring,

* *Test Act Reporter*, p. 2.

and Mr. Edgar Taylor, from the Unitarian Association; and the Rev. Dr. Waugh from the United Associate Presbytery of London.* The Protestant Society subsequently joined the united committee, being represented amongst others by Dr. Styles, Mr. Pellatt, and Mr. Wilks.† Petitions to the Legislature were at once drawn up and presented, a statement of the case of the Dissenters was sent throughout the kingdom, and a periodical,—the *Test Act Reporter*,—was established to give information concerning the proceedings taken in connection with the movement. Towards the close of the year it was resolved, in deference to the judgment of several members of Parliament and others, to postpone the Bill, of which Lord John Russell had already taken charge. During the following winter the Committee were in constant communication with Lord John Russell, Lord Holland, the Marquis of Lansdowne, Lord Althorp, Lord Milton, Mr. Henry Brougham, Sir Francis Burdett, Sir James Mackintosh, and other leaders of the Whig party, concerning measures for securing success. The establishment of the *World* newspaper, an unsectarian ecclesiastical journal, edited by Mr. Stephen Bourne, aided, at the time, very considerably in increasing public interest in the question. Early in the year 1828 the Common Council of London, on the motion of Mr. Favell, supported by Mr. Peacock and Mr. Apsley Pellatt, set an example to other municipal corporations, by resolving to petition in avour of the Bill.‡

As soon as Parliament assembled, Lord John Russell, amidst loud cheers, gave notice that on the 26th of February he should move for a repeal of the Test and

* *Test Act Reporter*, pp. 5, 6.

† Ib. pp. 439--445.

‡ *World* newspaper, January, 1828. *Test Act Reporter*.

Corporation Acts. Petitions at once began to pour in from all parts of England, Ireland, and Scotland. City and borough Corporations, members of the Established Church in England, the Roman Catholics of Ireland, and of every Dissenting community, helped to swell the number. Before the measure was brought forward, it began to be seen that the Established Church would offer no opposition to it. Even the Universities were dumb, and scarcely a voice was heard to cry that the Church was in danger. Lord John Russell brought forward his measure on the day appointed. In the course of a bold and animated speech, he reviewed the history of the Acts, but stated that he could not agree with the abstract principle upon which Dissenters based their claims. This principle, he stated, was, that every man should be allowed to form his own religious opinions, and that, when formed, he should be at liberty to worship God according to the dictates of his conscience, without being subjected to any penalty or disqualification whatever; and that every restraint or disqualification imposed upon any man, on account of his religious creed, was in the nature of persecution, and was at once an offence to God, and an injury to man. He thought that when the religion of any body of men was found to contain political principles hostile to the State, a restrictive test was justifiable. The noble lord did not appear to see that, in making this exception, he was justifying all the penal statutes that had ever been passed against any body of religionists. He proceeded to enforce the propriety of the demands now made, and concluded by appealing to the House to render this act of justice to three millions of their fellow subjects. Mr. John Smith, who seconded the motion, in enlarging on the loyalty of Dissenters, called attention to the fact that two hundred thousand persons of various bodies volunteered for the defence of the kingdom when an invasion seemed imminent. In the debate which followed, Sir Robert Inglis led the High-Church party, and openly justified the predominance of an established religion, the existence of which implied preference, and preference implied exclusion. The friendly feelings of Dissenters towards the Establishment were frequently alluded to. It was said that they would never be mad enough to conspire for its overthrow, and that, if the tests were abolished, mutual respect and amity must increase. On the part of the Government, the Bill was opposed by Mr. Huskisson and Mr. Peel. Lord Althorp and Lord Nugent effectively supported it. Towards the close of the debate, Mr. Brougham delivered the most powerful speech that had yet been made in its favour. When he sat down, Lord Palmerston argued that it was due to the Roman Catholics that their claims should receive a prior attention, and he announced that he should vote against the Bill. On a division there appeared 237 votes for the motion, and only 193 against it, showing a majority of 44 in its favour. On February 28th, the Bill, on Lord John Russell's motion, was considered in Committee, when Sir Thomas Acland suggested a compromise by the introduction of a Declaration pledging all members of corporations, and other persons holding civil offices, not to use their power to the injury of the Established Church. Lord John Russell said that it was possible something might be introduced which would be palatable and welcome to the Church, and, at the same time, not wound the feelings of Dissenters, and he was ready to agree to a form of words having that object, if the Government would pledge itself to them. Mr. Peel replied that the majority in favour of the measure had been so decisive that he should not persevere in an opposition which was calculated to engender religious animosities, and that, if a modified measure were proposed, he should not object to it. He suggested that the Bill should be postponed, a suggestion which called forth indignant denunciations from Lord Althorp and Lord Milton; the latter saying that the only object of such a proposal was to enable the Government to regain the vantage ground they had lost, and, by delay, to defeat the Dissenters. In the angry turmoil which followed, Mr. Peel declared, on his honour, that his suggestion had been made with an honest intention, and that, after what had occurred, he should not vote upon the motion. Followed by all the members of the Administration, Mr. Peel then walked out of the House, and the Committee, without going to a division, agreed to report in favour of the Bill. On March 18th, the clauses were discussed, when Mr. Sturges Bourne suggested the insertion of a Declaration in substitution for the Test, providing for the security of the Church; a Declaration which Lord John Russell at once said he could not accept. Mr. Peel supported Mr. Bourne, recommending an arrangement which would give a reasonable proof to the Church of England that in the repeal of these Acts the Legislature still required a security for its predominance. The Church, he held, had a right to demand such a security, and, if it were given, he hoped that the question would be at once, and for ever, settled. He then proposed a form of Declaration to be made by all municipal officers and magistrates, pledging the declarator never to "exert any power nor any influence" which he might possess, "by virtue of his office, to injure or subvert the Protestant Church, by law established, or to disturb it in the possession of those rights and privileges to which it is by law entitled." Mr. Peel's suggestion having received a general support from both sides of the House, Lord John Russell stated that, although there might be something in the imposition of such a security calculated to raise doubts in the minds of Dissenters, he indulged the hope that those doubts would be removed by a conciliatory conference. The Bill then passed through Committee.

The introduction of Sir Thomas Acland's and Mr. Peel's amendments was viewed with considerable alarm by the Dissenters. At conferences with Lord John Russell, and other supporters of the measure, on the 25th March, the noble lord stated that with a moderate Declaration the measure could be carried through both Houses of Parliament, but that, if no Declaration were inserted, it would be thrown out by the House of Lords. Upon this the united committee resolved to leave the question in the hands of those who had the conduct of the measure in Parliament, and at the same time passed a resolution stating that they considered such a plan unnecessary, impolitic, and inconsistent with the course taken towards Irish Dissenters. Subsequently a formal protest against it was adopted, and it was resolved "that if the Dissenters be reduced to the alternative of submitting to the incorporation of a declaratory test into the Bill of Repeal, or of risking the defeat of the measure, it is the judgment of this committee that the Declaration should be so shaped as to be least injurious and offensive, and that it should be fully explained to the Legislature and the country that it is imposed upon them, and not devised by them nor agreeable to their mature sense of right." If the Declaration could not be so modelled as to be considered comparatively innoxious, it was, at the same time, resolved that the Bill should be abandoned.* When the form of Mr. Peel's Amendment was printed the Committee again met and resolved that it would be inexpedient to oppose it, although they objected to any new Test or Declaration whatsoever.† On the 24th of March the Bill came up again before the House of Commons, when Lord

* *Test Act Reporter*, pp. 450, 453. † Ibid., p. 457.

John Russell stated that he should not offer any objection to Mr. Peel's Amendment. The Bill then passed, and went through its final stage on the 27th of the same month.

Lord Holland took charge of the measure in the House of Lords, where it was read a first time on April 1st. On the 17th of the same month, after some hundreds of petitions had been presented, the noble lord, in a speech remarkable for its comprehensive reach and exhaustive character, moved the second reading. It was significant of the great change which had taken place in public opinion, that the peer who rose immediately upon Lord Holland resuming his seat was the Archbishop of York, who, in a brief speech, declared that he felt himself imperatively bound to vote for the repeal of an Act which led to the profanation of one of the most holy ordinances of the Christian religion. The Bishop of Lincoln and the Bishop of Durham, in speeches remarkable for their generous as well as their just tone, followed on the same side. The Bishop of Chester added that it was the interest of the Church itself to put an end to the odium which this Act had occasioned. One speaker only, Lord Eldon, spoke in opposition to the whole Bill. The Duke of Wellington stated that the Government accepted the measure in the interests of religious peace. The Bill then passed a second reading without a division.

The ease with which this rapid progress had been made if it lulled the friends of the Bill into a feeling of security, had an effect which was very speedily dissipated. For four nights the House of Lords was occupied in dealing with hostile amendments. Lord Eldon proposed nearly twenty of these amendments, and spoke, in their support, no fewer than thirty-five times. With impassioned zeal and pertinacious obstinacy he endeavoured to destroy all that was of value in the measure. He denounced it as a virtual separation between the Church and the State, and said that no consideration on this side of the grave should ever induce him to be a party to it. It was "formed upon principles which no man could deny were revolutionary," and he "would rather suffer death than have it told that he supported such a Bill." Lord Eldon's first amendment was, however, lost by a vote of 100 to 32, and a similar fate befell every other amendment that he moved. The Whig peers, backed, when necessary, during the discussions, by the whole authority of the Government, combated, with untiring perseverance, every proposal calculated to affect the integrity of the measure. Foremost amongst them were Lord Holland, the Marquis of Lansdowne, Lord Ellenborough, the Earl of Harrowby, and Earl Grey. One of the last speakers against it, as it was nearing its final stage, was the Duke of Cumberland, who, striking his breast, declared that his conscience compelled him to oppose it. At a little before eleven o'clock on the 28th April, after all the amendments had at last been disposed of, Lord Holland rose and said, "My Lords, it now becomes my duty to move your lordships that this Bill do pass. In so doing I hardly know whether I should make use of the language of congratulation or gratitude. Both are equally becoming the present occasion and circumstances. I express my gratitude to your lordships for the manner in which you have acted. I congratulate the country on the event of the night. I congratulate also your lordships on the manner in which you have discharged your duty to the country; and I congratulate both the House and the country in the achievement of so glorious a result." The motion having been put, the Bill passed without a division. The Lords' amendments having been agreed to in the Commons, the Act received the Royal

Assent on the 9th of May, and immediately became law.*

The United Committee, to whose vigorous conduct the success of this measure was mainly due, as soon as the Bill had left the Legislature, passed votes of thanks to their Parliamentary supporters, including the bishops and the Government. The services of Lord John Russell and Lord Holland were acknowledged with the grateful expressions which were certainly their due. Reference was also made to the liberal and conciliatory spirit evinced by the Bench of Bishops, and by the Church generally, in abstaining from opposition to the measure. In acknowledgment of the services of their secretary and solicitor, Mr. Robert Winter, the committee voted that gentleman the sum of two thousand guineas.† On the 18th June there was a public dinner at the Freemason's Tavern, presided over by the Duke of Sussex, and attended by four hundred gentlemen from all parts of England. The assembly was addressed by Lord Stourton for the Roman Catholics; Lord John Russell, Lord Holland, Mr. William Smith, Lord Althorp, Mr. Brougham, Lord Carnarvon, Lord Nugent, Sir Francis Burdett, and Mr. Spring Rice, amongst the members of the Legislature; and by the Rev. Dr. F. A. Cox —who proposed a vote of thanks to the bishops and clergy—and the Rev. Dr. Aspland and Dr. Baldwin Brown amongst Dissenters. One subject was alluded to by nearly every speaker — the necessity of continuing

* The most complete report of the debates on this measure is contained in the *Test Act Reporter*, where nearly every speech is given verbatim.

† The total expenses incurred were £3,000, of which £2,000 was given by the Committee of Deputies, and £1,000 by the Protestant Society.

public exertion until complete religious liberty was attained.*

The principal characteristic of this last and successful struggle for the repeal of the Test and Corporation Acts was the friendly attitude assumed by the members of the Established Church towards the Dissenters. After a controversy that had extended over 140 years, the representatives of that Church had finally become convinced that the prostitution, for its own apparent protection, of one of the most sacred acts of religious worship for the purpose of obtaining public office and employment, was acting in a manner that was detrimental to the interests of the Church itself. It may appear extraordinary that this should not have been seen and acknowledged before; but every page of history shows that ecclesiastical prejudices exercise a stronger influence in blinding the judgment, and in hardening the heart and conscience, than any other influences, except the operation of moral iniquity, that can be brought to bear upon the minds of men. It is natural that, in a Church endowed with special privileges, elevated by law into a predominant position, and attacked on all sides, as it must be, by those who dissent from it, such prejudices should last longer and exhibit themselves in a more marked degree than in any other Christian community. The love of power, fostered by the superiority of position, has invariably become, in such a case, a vice which only change of position has been effectual to root out. After the judgment has been convinced, and the conscience enlightened, the will is reluctant to give effect to the discoveries which have

---

* *World* newspaper, June 23, 1828. This vigorous journal, originated by Hone, was subsequently merged in the *Patriot*, which advocated the same principles, and continued in existence for a great number of years, as will be seen further on.

been made. The arguments upon this question were exhausted in the debates which took place towards the close of the previous century, but the generation which listened to them had to pass away, and another to rise to full manhood, before practical effect could be given to them. It is a usual characteristic of English politics that the thought of one generation should be embodied in the action of the next. In not waiting longer than this, and in assuming, for the most part, a passive attitude, the Established Church, on this occasion, gained the first victory over her inherent tendencies that it had gained for five generations.

It is very probable, however, that the importance of the step which was now taken was not seen by the majority of those who took it. Lord Eldon scarcely exaggerated when he said that it was a virtual separation of the Church from the State. It was an abandonment by the Legislature of the principle of protection to one sect. All other reforms in the same direction could, henceforward, be merely instances of the practical application of this principle. That conceded, as it now was, the removal of all ecclesiastical disabilities remaining on the statute book of the kingdom could safely be left to the sure progress of intelligence and the religious conscience and affections of the people.

CHAPTER X.

FROM THE REPEAL OF THE TEST AND CORPORATION ACTS TO THE CENSUS OF RELIGIOUS WORSHIP.—1828—1851.

IN the year following the repeal of the Test and Corporation laws the Roman Catholics wrested from the Government, by the Catholic Emancipation Act, a concession similar to that obtained by the Protestant Dissenters. In return for the support which Mr. O'Connell and many of his co-religionists had given to their Protestant fellow-subjects, the leading representative bodies of the Dissenters gave their hearty assistance towards the successful passage of this measure. There were some who, in view of past history, but not remembering the change which had taken place in the relative positions of different faiths, as well as in the character of the people, saw, with undisguised apprehension, the increase of political and civil power given to the members of a Church whose annals had been written in the blood of their ancestors. But in the most influential sections of the Free Churches there existed no such fear; and, if there had, there existed, at the same time, a sense of justice which could not refuse to others what had already been bestowed upon themselves. Protestantism stood, in relation to the Roman Catholics, in the same position that the Established Church had stood in relation to Dissent. If it was right for the latter to make a concession, it was equally right for the former. Catholic emancipation was, therefore, as far as the majority of Dissenters were concerned, hailed with an openly-expressed satisfaction.* The service which they rendered was acknowledged, in the same year, by Mr. O'Connell, on the platform of the "Protestant Society," when he said, "I have come here as the representative, not of the intellect—for of that I am incapable—but of the warm-hearted feelings of the people of Ireland. I stand here, in the name of my country, to express our gratitude, in feeble but in sincere language, for the exertions made in our behalf by our Protestant Dissenting brethren."†

Relieved from the strain of agitation for a special object, it was now thought desirable to establish anew the foundation principles upon which the Free Churches were based. After one or two preliminary conferences it was resolved to establish a society to be termed, "The Society for Promoting Ecclesiastical Knowledge," the work of which should be the publication and dissemination of essays and tracts upon the principles of Dissent. The Society was formed at the King's Head, Poultry, in May, 1829, when Mr. Benjamin Hanbury occupied the chair, and Dr. James Bennett read a preliminary address. None of those who took a public part at this first meeting for the creation of a literature of Dissent are now living. They included Mr. Hanbury, whose own literary service to the Free Churches, in his laboriously compiled "Memorials of Independency," and in his notes to Hooker's "Ecclesiastical Polity," was of no mean order; Dr. James Bennett, the historian of Dissent, the vigorous writer, the full scholar, the man of liberal intellect, and upright mind; Dr. F. A. Cox, the active,

* See Reports of the Dissenting Deputies, and of the Protestant Society, for the years 1829 and 1830, in the *Congregational Magazine*, for these years.

† *Congregational Magazine*, 1829, pp. 336, 337.

busy, zealous worker in all philanthropical and religious movements; John Blackburn, of Pentonville, then editor of the *Congregational Magazine;* Samuel Murch, of Stepney College; and the Rev. Robert Vaughan, afterwards Principal of Lancashire Independent College, and editor of the *British Quarterly Review*, then of Kensington. Others who connected themselves with the Society were the Rev. Dr. Andrew Reed, whose name and labours now adorn one of the brightest pages in the history of philanthropy in England; Dr. Thomas Price, then of Devonshire Square Chapel, afterwards the historian of Nonconformity, and the editor of the *Eclectic Review*, to whose sagacity, wisdom, and judgment the civil liberties of Dissenters will always owe thc profoundest obligation; Dr. Pye Smith, author of "Scriptural Testimony to the Messiah," and one of the greatest theologians of the Free Churches; John Burnet, of Camberwell, the grave and solid preacher, and the happy, genial, and humorous orator on every platform where political, social, civil, or religious rights were to be advocated; Thomas Binney, Arthur Tidman, Apsley Pellatt, John Hoppus, and John Matheson. In their first public address, the Committee of the Society stated, as one of the reasons of their organisation, that the principles of Dissent had been found to be imperfectly felt and understood by the majority of their fellow-worshippers. They accordinaly projected a series of original and re-printed works, explanatory of the nature and history of the Christian Church, and of the claims of religious liberty. Works on Tithes and Church Establishments, and biographies of eminent Dissenters were added. The project, under Dr. Bennett's guidance, was carried into execution with great ability and success, and during the subsequent ecclesiastical agitations, many of the publications of the society, especially those on Tithes and Religious Establishments, were referred to as indicative of the "revolutionary" spirit and aim of the Dissenters.*

Scarcely was this Society organised than events occurred which indicated that the principles it was intended to promote would be the subject of discussion throughout the kingdom. A demand for political reform suddenly arose, and for two years the whole nation was convulsed with the agitation of this great question. The Dissenters, with scarcely a single exception, supported the Liberal party; the Church, with equal unanimity, gave the weight of its influence to the Tories.† When, in 1831, the second reading of the Reform Bill was thrown out of the House of Lords by the votes of twenty-one bishops, the nation began to inquire into the condition and the expediency of the Established Church. The conduct of the Episcopal Bench exasperated the people to a state of fury. "Will no question," asked the *Times* newspaper,‡ "occur to the people of England touching my lords, the bishops? Will nobody ask, What business have they in Parliament at all? What right have these Tories *ex-officio* to make or mar laws for the people of England? Let them confine themselves to

* *Congregational Magazine*, 1829, 1830, &c.

† "The clergy, especially, remembering the fate of the French priesthood and the spoliation of the French Church, were almost unanimous in their hatred of the proposed innovation. Already highly unpopular, partly on account of the determined opposition which as a body they had offered to every proposal for the extension of civil and religious liberty, and partly on account of the vexations and disputes attendant on the collection of tithes, they rendered themselves still more odious by their undisguised detestation of the new measure. . . . Under the influence of terrors thus excited, the clergy set themselves to oppose that which the nation fondly and almost unanimously desired."—"History of the Reform Bill of 1832." *By Rev. W. N. Molesworth, M.A., Incumbent of St. Clement's, Rochdale. Second Edition. Pp.* 156, 157.

‡ Oct. 10, 1831.

superintending the souls of the faithful, and let them begin with their own." Large public meetings were held, at which their expulsion from the Legislature was demanded; congregations in their own dioceses would not hear them preach; they were hooted wherever they went, and burnt in effigy by the mob. Earl Grey had previously warned them, but in vain, that if they should assist in the rejection of the Bill, they must "set their houses in order," and the Archbishop of Canterbury replied, that if popular violence should result from their vote, he, at least, would cheerfully bear his share of the general calamity.* After the division, Lord King took occasion to remind the country that the bishops had invariably supported every arbitrary Government. The Bishop of Exeter complained that never had they been so vilified and insulted, and they were ready to brave the censures of the mob.† A year afterwards, what the bishop had described as the "censures of the mob" had so enlightened the consciences of the members of the Episcopal Bench, or so tamed their courage, that they consented, as a body, that the Bill should pass. But the opposition they gave to the Reform Bill was never forgotten by their generation, and to it the subsequent rise of the demand for Church-reform, and the rapid increase of Dissent, may chiefly be traced.

While the Established Church was thus the object of increasing odium, an agitation arose which threatened, for some years, to uproot her very foundations. In a sermon preached in 1830, by the Rev. Andrew Marshall, a minister of the United Secession Presbyterian Church, at Kirkintilloch, in Scotland, the author assailed, with great vigour, the principle of Church Establishments, declaring them, especially, to be contrary to the Word of God, and an

* Speeches, Oct. 7, 1831. † Ib., Oct. 11.

invasion of the rights of Christ.* The sermon gave occasion to one of the most memorable controversies that have taken place either in England or Scotland since the Reformation. Mr. Marshall was promptly replied to. A rejoinder followed. The controversy widened and deepened as it grew, until most of the eminent ministers of the Established and the Voluntary Churches of Scotland were engaged in it. No men could have been more peculiarly fitted for the defence of the Voluntary argument than were the Presbyterian and Congregational ministers who conducted their side of the controversy. The intimate knowledge of, and great reverence for, the Scriptures, which has always distinguished the Scottish ministry, was a special qualification for such a work. The remarkable culture of the reasoning faculties, which had, for many generations, characterised the Scottish mind, and the high academical training of all sections of the Presbyterian ministry, was a second qualification. Their historical antecedents, and their peculiar relation to the Scottish Establishment, offered another advantage. Such a controversy could not, as in England, be confounded in the popular mind with questions of theology or ecclesiastical polity. Both parties, with one or two exceptions, were Presbyterians, having a common ancestry, accepting the same standard of faith and order, and worshipping in the same manner. The sole difference between them was that one party was considered to have surrendered to the State, for the sake of its support and patronage, the necessary rights of a Christian Church, while the other received and maintained an unfettered ecclesiastical and spiritual liberty. Then those who on Scottish soil fought the battle of Church Establishments were men of exceptional spiritual and intellectual endowments. The

* "Ecclesiastical Establishments Considered," &c.

names of Andrew Marshall, Dr. John Brown, Dr. David Young, Dr. David King, Dr. John Peddie, Dr. Harper, Dr. Ritchie, Mr. Ballantyne, Andrew Coventry Dick, Dr. Ralph Wardlaw, Dr. Heugh, and Greville Ewing adorn the history of British Christianity, as well as Scottish Presbyterianism and Congregationalism. Dr. Chalmers, Dr. Andrew Thomson, and John Inglis, on the other side, gave to the controversy the reality as well as the aspect of a grave and formidable discussion of the greatest question connected with the politics of Christianity, and the rights and duties of a Christian State.

At an early period of this controversy, the Voluntaries of Scotland were aroused to an active expression of sympathy with their leaders. Voluntary Church Associations were formed in Glasgow, Edinburgh, and all the larger towns. Public meetings were held, and lectures delivered throughout the country. A periodical—*The Voluntary Church Magazine*—was established to aid the work. Year after year, the pulpit, the platform, and the press, were used to enforce, on the loftiest religious grounds, the duty of separating the Church from the State. The enthusiasm excited by the controversy almost equalled that evoked in England during the Reform agitation, but it differed from the English movement in being characterised by a deep religious feeling, and an entire absence of the more vulgar incidents of popular agitation. In Scotland—where every Church member has, more or less, thought out most theological and ecclesiastical problems—the people are easily excited upon questions affecting the character and constitution of the Christian Church; and upon this question there were found to exist profound and well-defined convictions. But it was impossible for the Scottish Dissenters alone to bring the argument between their antagonists and themselves to a practical issue without the aid of their

English brethren, who were at first quiet, if not indifferent. Although the Ecclesiastical Knowledge Society was issuing, with great rapidity, works of considerable value, marked by comprehensiveness of design and boldness of thought, upon the very fundamental question that was agitating the people of Scotland, there existed in England no public movement at all similar to their own. This Society limited its labours to the issue of publications; the Protestant Society had performed the chief work it had undertaken; the Dissenting Deputies never contemplated anything beyond the removal of certain practical grievances, and the defence of certain already recognised legal rights. Information, however, of the proceedings of the Scottish Dissenters was widely distributed in the south, and, in 1834, Voluntary Church Associations began to be formed. In a few months there were societies at Birmingham, Liverpool, Ashton, and many of the larger towns. Young Men's Associations were established in conjunction with them. The whole machinery of popular agitation was put in motion, and it appeared that English Dissent was at last organised for the overthrow of the Church Establishment.

In the midst of this agitation the Congregational Union of England and Wales was established. Proposals for such an organisation had been discussed for some time previous in the pages of the *Congregational Magazine*. In 1831, a provisional committee, composed of the most eminent ministers of the body, met in London, and resolved upon summoning in the next year a meeting of Dissenters from the various country associations for the purpose of discussing the plan of the proposed Union. At this meeting, which was held in May, 1832, it was resolved to form such an organisation. One question, however, was postponed. It was a matter of doubt whether, in accordance with the example of their Nonconformist ancestors, it was desirable for Congregationalists to adopt a declaration of the leading articles of their faith and discipline. A proposed Declaration was submitted, and the opinion upon this question of the associated ministers and churches was invited. The difficulties and dangers of such a Declaration were obvious. A Congregational Union could never be more than a fraternal meeting. Whatever creed it might adopt, could only carry with it a moral influence, and could be merely the general belief of the persons adopting it. But did not Presbyterianism grow from such a root, and did not Episcopacy ultimately spring from Presbyterianism? And would not this voluntary creed have as tyrannical an influence as one that could be enforced by pains and penalties? Such were the difficulties which stood in the way of the proposed Declaration, but they stood equally in the way of the proposed Union. At the first annual meeting of the Union, in 1833, however, the Declaration was adopted, but with the distinct understanding that it was not intended as a test or creed for subscription. Indeed, the fourth article affirmed, in the most explicit language, the independence of every distinct Church; and the tenth declared that no Church, or union of Churches, had any right or power to interfere with the faith or discipline of any other Church. In the ninth article the principles of the Union with respect to Established Churches were set forth. "They believe," said this article, "that the power of a Christian Church is purely spiritual, and should in no way be corrupted by union with temporal or civil power." This was the first occasion that any general assembly of the Congregational Churches of England had accepted such a principle. The last Assembly, held in Richard Cromwell's time, had affirmed the opposite. One of the subjects brought before the meeting of 1833 was the grievances of Protestant Dissenters, which Dr. Baldwin Brown urgently pressed upon the attention of the Union. On the motion of that gentleman, a series of elaborate resolutions, affirming the voluntary character of a Scriptural Church, the unjust oppression of the Establishment, and the rights of Dissenters with regard to all ecclesiastical dues, including Church-rates and tithes, University education, Burial and Marriage, was passed. Finally, the Congregational body were called upon to make strenuous efforts to obtain relief from the humiliating impositions which they, and all other Dissenters, had so long endured.*

A circumstance occurred soon after the Congregational Union was organised, which contributed to deepen the spirit expressed in these resolutions, as well as to quicken the yet slowly-rising agitation. In laying the foundation of the new Weigh-House Chapel, the Rev. Thomas Binney, the eminent minister of that place of worship, delivered an address, which he afterwards published with some remarks upon the characteristics of the times, and the duty of Nonconformists in relation thereto. The passage relative to the Establishment provoked so bitter a controversy that it is better to give it in the speaker's own words. Mr. Binney said: "I have no hesitation about saying that I am an enemy to the Establishment; and I do not see that a Churchman need hesitate to say that he is an enemy to Dissent. Neither of us would mean the persons of Churchmen or Dissenters, nor the Episcopal or other portions of the universal *Church;* but the principle of the national religious Establishment, which we should respectively regard as deserving, universally, opposition or support. It is with me, I confess, a matter of deep, serious religious conviction, that the Established Church is a great national evil; that it is an obstacle to the progress of truth and godliness in the land;

* *Congregational Magazine*, 1831-1833. *Patriot* newspaper, 1833.

that it destroys more souls than it saves; and that, therefore, its end is most devoutly to be wished by every lover of God and man. Right or wrong, this is my belief; and I should not feel the slightest offence if a Churchman were to express himself in precisely the same words with respect to Dissent."

One at least of these sentences has been as often cast in Mr. Binney's teeth, as Mr. Bright's words, "Perish Savoy," were quoted in their fragmentary but untrue form against the great tribune of the people. Again and again Mr. Binney replied to the charges made against him, and showed the true import of his statement.*

* Mr. Binney published a pamphlet in 1837 (Ward & Co.), in the shape of a letter to a clergyman of Worcester, entitled, "What? and Who says it? Edited by John Search"—his *nom de plume*—and subsequently, "Strike, but Hear," a correspondence with the editor of the *Christian Observer*, and "John Search's last Words," and a letter to the Bishop of London (Dr. Bloomfield), who had attacked Mr. Binney in the notes to his Charge of 1834. The drift of this defence is briefly this—that in Mr. Binney's opinion his description was true; that supporters of the Establishment had spoken as strongly against Dissent as himself, and that they *also* had done the same in respect to their own Church; quoting copiously from the *Christian Observer*, the *Record*, Dr. Chalmers, and various English clergymen; and that his language had been rather less decided relative to the Establishment than had been used by Dr. Wardlaw and Dr. Pye Smith, of whom the bishop says:—"The testimony of such a man, for or against us, is of more weight than the invectives of ten Binneys." These various extracts are given in full, and, it need hardly be said, prove the case of the Weigh-House minister, as he put it, up to the hilt. It is curious to note that, in his "Strike, but Hear," Mr. Binney expressed a hope that the Church of England, when freed from State trammels, might absorb into herself, or lead in her wake, minor communities, and advance to be the chief minister and missionary of mankind. What had since occurred had, however, compelled him to recall this hope. He says, in writing to Dr. Bloomfield, "The Church, I fear, as distinct from the Establishment, has within her the elements of incalculable evil. Her mere apprehensions of the shaking of the Establishment have led her to betray *that these very elements* are just the things that she loves most—which she identifies with herself—and will die in defending, rather than relinquish."

The agitation of Nonconformists soon assumed a practical character. The first sign of this was the demand for the abolition of Church Rates. One after another of the city and suburban parishes refused to make a rate. Manchester, Leeds, Rochdale, and Birmingham, in contests which excited national attention, stimulated the larger towns to adopt the same course. In 1834 the first of a series of Church Rate Abolition Bills was brought into the House of Commons by Mr. Divett, then member for Exeter. This measure, which contemplated total and immediate abolition, was withdrawn at the instance of Lord John Russell, who wished that the Liberal Government should have the opportunity of settling the question. The nature of the settlement contemplated by his lordship was indicated in a Bill introduced by Lord Althorp the same year, which proposed to transfer the burden of repairing churches to the land tax. This unexpected compromise encountered the vehement opposition of the friends of the Dissenters. Both Mr. Hume and Mr. Wilks divided the House upon it, but lost their amendments, though the measure was suffered to drop.

It was universally felt by Dissenters, at this period, that the Liberal Government had attempted an unworthy artifice by bringing forward such a measure, and that the Whigs, having obtained power through their means, now intended to desert them. The public affairs of Dissenters were in the hands of three bodies—the Committee of Deputies, the Protestant Society, and a United Committee—the last being similar in constitution to that established during the Test and Corporation agitation. This Committee summoned, in May, 1834, a General Convention from all parts of England, which was attended by several hundred delegates. The Convention resolved that only by a full and complete separation of Church and State could equal rights and justice be secured to all classes of the people; that they deeply regretted that the reasonable expectations of the Dissenters, founded on the admissions of his Majesty's Ministers of the equity of their claims, had been frustrated by the Ministers; that Lord Althorp's proposals respecting Church Rates would only change the name, while they prolonged the burden of the impost; and that the Established Church possessed, in the property then at her disposal, and in the wealth of her individual members, resources abundantly adequate to defray the entire expense of upholding the edifices in which her members worshipped. The Convention claimed the entire abolition of Church Rates on the principle of the measure for doing away with Vestry Cess in Ireland—that is to say, the transfer of the charge to the ecclesiastical revenues of the Kingdom. Finally, the formation of Voluntary Church Societies was recommended, and a deputation was appointed to wait upon the Government.*

This Convention was one of the most influential that had ever been held in connection with the public interests of Dissenters. Mr. Edward Baines, Member of Parliament for Leeds, occupied the chair, and amongst the names of speakers were John Angell James, Josiah Conder, Thomas Wilson, Thomas Stratten, William Howitt, Richard Winter Hamilton, Dr. Baldwin Brown, Dr. Payne, John Howard Hinton, John Robert Beard, and Charles Hindley. This assembly fairly indicated the existing state of feeling with respect to ecclesiastical reform. While advocating the separation of Church and State, it virtually indicated the opinion that Church property belonged to Episcopalians alone. This, however, was not the view held by the Ecclesiastical Knowledge Society, some of whose most valuable and widely-distributed publications went to

---

* *Patriot* newspaper, 1834. Circular of the time.

prove the secular origin and national ownership of all the revenues of the Established Church. The Convention had, however, one good effect—it compelled the Government to withdraw their Church Rate Bill, and to introduce measures relating to other practical questions: the Registration of Births, Deaths, and Marriages, and the Solemnisation of Marriages by Dissenters.

Measures for the accomplishment of these objects had been discussed for several years. Before the Test and Corporation Acts were abolished, Mr. William Smith, at the instance of the Unitarian Association, had, on several occasions, got a Bill through the Commons for the relief of Unitarians, to whom the marriage service was especially distasteful. As uniformly, however, as the Bill had passed the Commons, it was rejected by the Lords. In the early part of the Session of 1836, after having been pressed on all sides by the Dissenters, Lord John Russell brought in two Bills for their relief. Up to this period the births of Dissenters were not registered, and the only means that existed of legally proving the dates were by entries in family Bibles, or by voluntary registers, usually kept by ministers, and deposited, in some instances, with the trustees of Dr. Williams's Library. Nor did parochial church registers give any evidence of birth, the sole fact certified in them being the fact of baptism. Lord John Russell's Bill provided for the uniform registration of births, deaths, and marriages, and appointed public officers to carry out its provisions. It passed both the Commons and the Lords without a division.

The measure for the reform of the marriage laws met with no greater opposition. In introducing it Lord John Russell stated that the grievance of Dissenters on this question was justly regarded by them as very serious. They could be married nowhere but in the parish churches of the Establishment, and with no service but one to which they conscientiously objected. Marriage he held to be a civil ceremony only, and he thought that people were entitled, if they chose, to have it performed by civil officers. His Bill provided that, under certain restrictions, the registrar might perform this ceremony within his own office, or in any Dissenting place of worship. Sir Robert Peel said that he had no objection in principle to offer to such a Bill, and it passed without a division. The Registration Bill was read a third time in the House of Lords on August 1st, and the Marriages Bill on August 4th, 1836. One more step towards the removal of the practical grievances of Nonconformists was thus taken, but Church Rates were still left, and it was resolved to organise, at once, a special agitation for obtaining their repeal.

In order to accomplish this purpose the means were adopted which had been found to be effectual in previous agitations. After some preliminary meetings it was resolved, in October, 1836, to form a Church Rate Abolition Society. On the 29th of that month a public meeting was held in London, Mr. Charles Lushington, member for the Tower Hamlets, in the chair, when resolutions were passed expressive of disappointment at the conduct of the Government, condemning the impost, and declaring that nothing but "utter extinction" could be accepted. A Society was then formed, with instructions to summon a general conference of delegates from local societies prior to the opening of Parliament in the next year. The principal founders of this Society were Mr. Joseph Hume, M.P., the Rev. John Burnet, Daniel Whittle Harvey, M.P., the Rev. Thomas Adkins, of Southampton, Mr. William Ewart, M.P., the Rev. John Howard Hinton, Mr. T. S. Duncombe, M.P., Mr. John Easthope, Mr. John Childs, Mr. Benjamin Hawes, M.P., and Mr. Josiah Conder. Previous to holding the Conference, meetings of Congregational and Baptist Associations, of Voluntary Church Societies, and of inhabitants and ratepayers, took place in all parts of England and Wales, at which the rate was condemned, and petitions against it adopted.* These vigorous proceedings at last induced the Government to move. When the Parliament of 1837 met, upwards of two thousand petitions, some of them praying for the separation of the Church from the State, were presented. On the part of the Liberal Ministry, Mr. Spring Rice (afterwards Lord Monteagle), then moved a resolution to the effect that the expenses provided for by Church Rates should, in future, be paid out of the Church lands and pew rents, the rate itself ceasing altogether. After a debate of several days, this resolution was carried by 273 to 250 votes. But when the resolution was afterwards brought up, although the number of its supporters was increased, the number of its opponents was increased in greater proportion, and it was only carried by 287 to 282, the majority having sunk from twenty-three to five. A few days afterwards, Lord John Russell announced that the Government had abandoned its intention of taking the question to the Upper House. From this period the Whigs, as a party, not only dropped the subject, but opposed, for many years, all the attempts of private members for its settlement. When Mr. Harvey subsequently moved a resolution for abolition, both sides of the House of Commons combined to defeat him; when Mr. Duncombe, in 1839, moved for leave to bring in a Bill for the Relief of Dissenters, the Whigs opposed and again defeated it; when Mr. (afterwards Sir John) Trelawny, in 1849, brought forward a similar resolution, Lord John Russell's ministry led the opposition to him, and

* *Voluntary Church Magazine*, 1836-7. *Patriot* newspaper, *ib.*

secured his defeat also, as well as that of Mr. Page Wood's amendment in favour of the exception of Dissenters alone. At this point the Parliamentary agitation was suspended, and remained so until another and a stronger force than had yet been used was brought to bear upon the grievance. Meanwhile, the supporters of Church Rates were increasing its unpopularity. By the imprisonment, for non-payment of the impost, of Mr. John Thorogood of Chelmsford, of Mr. John Childs of Bungay, of Mr. William Baines of Leicester, and of Mr. John Simonds of Aylesbury, they added a feeling of exasperation to a sense of injustice. When, at the same period, the Churchwardens of Braintree denied the right of a majority of rate-payers to refuse a rate for Church purposes, they provoked a contest which, whatever might be its legal issue, could only result in the ultimate extinction of the rate. Eventually the Courts of Law decided, in connection with the Braintree case, that a Church rate could not be laid without the authority of a majority of the vestry.

When this agitation was commenced, both the political and ecclesiastical state of the nation appeared eminently favourable to its being conducted to a radical and satisfactory issue. The Church was in the depth of its unpopularity. A Government Commission appointed to examine into the value and the administration of the ecclesiastical revenues of the kingdom had been appointed. Popular indignation at the abuses which had been disclosed was at its height. The immense wealth of the bishops, amassed by granting leases at the expense of the future welfare of the Church, had brought the highest officers of the Establishment into very great disrepute. Pamphleteers derided both their office and their character. The public journals teemed with exposures of their malpractices and with ironical criticisms of their consistency. Any lampoon was popular the subject of which was a bishop. It was felt to be impossible that, with a reformed Parliament, the Church could be allowed to continue in a condition which was a reproach to the State and a dishonour to religion. When, however, the Commissioners of Ecclesiastical Revenues came forward with a scheme of reform, which included a reduction of the incomes of the bishops and other dignitaries, and the application of the surplus revenues to the extension of religious agencies in popular districts; and when the Government carried a measure in harmony with these recommendations, the passions of the people cooled. What had been antagonism turned to indifference, and there seemed to be a tacit consent that the Establishment should be allowed another trial.

The same course was taken with the Irish Church. The measure of reform with reference to the Church of Ireland was more comprehensive, as well as more severe, in character, than that in England. It included the abolition of the Irish Church Rate and the extinction of several bishoprics, and was intended by its authors to include, also, the partial secularisation of its revenues. The former two proposals were carried; the latter was surrendered by the Whig party, who, having come into office upon this question, as soon as they obtained it, ignored the very principles by which they had regained their Parliamentary ascendancy. But the Church was unquestionably reformed, and public agitation, as in the case of the English Church, died with the death of its greatest administrative abuses.

The course taken by the Government upon another question assisted to confirm this state of feeling. The direct levy of tithes, both in England and in Ireland, was abolished. For forty years public economists and Church reformers had insisted on the expediency of providing a more equitable and less offensive mode of collecting the clerical revenues than that of seizing them in kind at the point of the bayonet, or by the aid of the bailiff's staff. When Church Reform became necessary, this subject also was dealt with, and tithes were converted into rent-charges. Before this took place, the abuses under the old system had converted almost every payer of these onerous ecclesiastical dues into an enemy of tithes in any form; but as soon as their incidence was changed the enmity was perceptibly lessened. By these politic measures the Establishment was saved, and, when its safety was assured, the Dissenters were, as usual, ignored.

But some causes of their failure existed in the condition of the Free Churches themselves. While they were urging their claims for greater liberty, they were engaged in another agitation which, to a great extent, absorbed their energies. They had resolved upon the abolition of slavery, thus following in the footsteps of Clarkson and Wilberforce, whose vigorous and successful agitation had done away with the slave trade. Joseph Sturge, John Burnet, Daniel O'Connell, and all the leaders of the anti-slavery party were, for the most part, the leaders, also, of the party of religious freedom. The eloquence of Knibb and Thompson was heard by the same people who listened to the eloquence of Wilks. In achieving the liberty of the slave the force of agitation was, in a large measure, spent. Men cannot be always straining their moral strength to the utmost pitch, and it is not surprising if, after years of public struggle, they should suffer from a natural relaxation.

There was also, at this time, a want of unanimity in the councils of Dissent. Some, and those amongst the most conspicuous members of the Free Churches, deprecated the manner in which the agitation for an extended liberty was conducted. A celebrated and fashionable Congregational minister wrote to the Bishop of London to express his entire disapproval of what was being said of the Established Church, and he stated that he did not stand alone in his sentiments.* Another eminent man, Mr. Josiah Conder, who, from his literary abilities and his position as editor of the then two principal organs of the Free Churches—the *Eclectic Review* and the *Patriot* newspaper—occupied a post of considerable power and influence, avowed his antipathy to the Ecclesiastical Knowledge Society, and congratulated himself upon having induced some persons to withdraw from it.† The Wesleyans, although a few of their members petitioned for the abolition of Church Rates, held all attacks upon the Church itself as so contrary to the constitution and purpose of their society, that, after a formal trial by the Conference, they passed an official vote of censure upon one of their ministers, the Rev. D. R. Stephen, of Ashton, and suspended him from the ministry, for taking part in the organisation of a Voluntary Church Association in that town.‡ With such want of unity and such elements of weakness few parties can successfully contend.

Yet there undoubtedly existed a strong feeling that the union between the Church and the State was utterly unscriptural, opposed to the best interests of religion, and contrary to the sense of justice. Whether or not animated mainly by a dislike of the Ecclesiastical Knowledge Society, Mr. Josiah Conder, in 1838, proposed a general union for the promotion of religious equality. The plan was com-

* Letter of the Rev. John Clayton to Bishop Blomfield. "Memoirs," vol. i.

† "I eschew the Ecclesiastical Society and all its works, and glory in having induced Vaughan and some others to retire from it." Life of Josiah Conder, p. 275.

‡ Smith's History of Wesleyan Methodists. Vol. iii., book 4.

prehensively conceived and well defined, and met with such favour that, in May, 1839, it was resolved, at a general Conference of Dissenters, to establish the "Religious Freedom Society," the fundamental principles of which should be a declaration of the inalienable right of every man to worship God according to his own religious convictions; that all compulsory support of religious institutions was manifestly unjust, and at variance with the spirit and principles of Christianity; and that State establishments of religion were to be condemned on every consideration of Scriptural teachings, and social and political equity.

The time for forming such an association was well chosen. Dr. Chalmers had recently been in London, and had been delivering a series of lectures in defence of Church Establishments, to which Dr. Ralph Wardlaw, of Glasgow, had replied. The subject was engaging the attention of all the most thoughtful minds in the various religious communities. The claims of the Church with respect to national education were, then, specially and offensively prominent, and a new party was rising at Oxford, afterwards known as the Tractarian party, which seemed likely to bring the Church into disrepute even amongst some of her most zealous members. There was a readiness, on the part of some Dissenters, for action, if action could be well sustained. And if apparent solidity and extensiveness of organisation could alone have made the Religious Freedom Society successful, it might have succeeded. Mr. Charles Lushington was chosen chairman, and upon its council were the well-known names of Edward Baines, F. A. Cox, Josiah Conder, John Howard Hinton, David King, Thomas Price, and Ralph Wardlaw. It was inaugurated at a public dinner, when Churchman and Dissenter, Catholic and Protestant, Christian and Jew, united to attest their determination to use all available means for the separation of the Church from the State. No uncertain sound went forth from this meeting. Mr. Charles Lushington, Mr. Charles Langdale, the Rev. John Burnet, Mr. Remington Mills, Dr. Ralph Wardlaw, Dr. David King, Dr. Cox, Mr. Ewart, M.P., Mr. Charles Buller, M.P., Mr. Baines, M.P., Mr. Hawes, M.P., and Mr. Goldsmid avowed their cordial sympathy with the principles and objects of the Society.* Local organisations also were connected with it. Yet it did not last so long as either the Protestant Society or the Ecclesiastical Knowledge Society. It failed for lack of practical wisdom and strength of leadership.

The same fate befel another and somewhat similar society, entitled the Evangelical Voluntary Church Association, of which the principal members were Sir Culling Eardley Smith, a member of the Established Church, the Rev. Dr. John Young, Dr. F. A. Cox, and Dr. John Campbell. The distinctive characteristics of this society were abstinence from political agitation, and the exclusion from it of all persons but such as professed Evangelical views. It received little public support, and disappeared soon after the dissolution, in 1843, of the Religious Freedom Society.

If Dissenters themselves had been animated by a stronger faith in their own principles; if they had had a greater consciousness of the injury done to religion by its connection with the State; or if they had shown a little more moral courage, it is possible that these organisations would not have declined with such rapidity. Many amongst their supporters were, however, alarmed at the prospect of such agitations separating them from some of

* "Plan, &c.," 1838. "Proceedings, &c.," of the Religious Freedom Society, 1839. *Patriot* newspaper, *ib.*

their political allies in Parliament. The hereditary attachment of Dissenters to the Whigs had been greatly strengthened by the manner in which the leaders of that party had acted in the final Test and Corporation struggle. It was true, and felt to be true, that the service then rendered had been more than repaid, and that the Whigs had afterwards deserted them upon the Church Rate question; but large numbers of Nonconformists still looked up to that party for the removal of their remaining "grievances," and were afraid of doing anything that might cause offence. The political leader of this class was Mr. Edward Baines, senior, then member for Leeds, who succeeded Mr. John Wilks as the representative of the Dissenting interest in the House of Commons. Probably the majority of the Dissenting ministers at that time sympathised with the apparently politic course pursued by this class. They had a sentimental attachment to their principles, but they shrank from the attempt to embody them in practical legislation.

With the avowed purpose of stimulating the faith and the energies of Dissenters to more consistent and extensive action upon the question of Church and State, Mr. Edward Miall, a Congregational minister at Leicester, came to London in the year 1841, and established the *Nonconformist* newspaper. A great portion of the columns of this journal were devoted, week after week, to the exposition of the fundamental principles of Dissent, and the exposure of what was considered to be the unchristian, unjust, and mischievous character of the Established Church. It was, however, seen that there was little prospect of a radically-improved system of legislation upon ecclesiastical matters unless the Legislature itself were re-constituted; and therefore, side by side with the question of ecclesiastical reform, was urged that of political reform, not, however, merely as a means to an end, but as, in itself, a just and necessary step. In the year 1843 an event occurred which aroused the Free Churches to a renewed sense of danger, and to revived action. On the 28th of February in that year Sir James Graham introduced into the House of Commons a Bill for the Education of Children employed in Factories, some clauses of which appeared to be drawn with the distinct purpose of increasing the power and influence of the Church. Sir James Graham proposed to establish district schools throughout the country, to attach to each school a chapel with a clergyman, who should teach the Litany and Catechism of the Church; the children of Dissenters, however, being exempted from attendance upon the clergyman's ministrations, and allowed to receive religious instruction from any licensed minister of their own denominations. The management of all such schools he proposed to invest in seven persons, three of whom were to be the clergyman and two churchwardens of the parish, the remaining four being nominated by the local magistrates. So undisguised an attempt to hand over the education of the people to the clergy, with such a marked distinction between Church and Dissent, excited the most vehement opposition of all classes of Nonconformists to the proposed Bill. Nothing that had occurred since Lord Sidmouth introduced his measure for restricting the liberty of unlicensed preaching had produced such exasperation. This feeling was probably stronger than it would have been from the fact that the measure received the open support of the leaders of the Whig party. When Sir James Graham had made his explanatory statement, Lord John Russell immediately rose, and expressed his opinion that, as between Church and Dissent, it ought not to be opposed by any person who had the object of education at heart. In other words, the Dissenters, in his judgment, ought to sacrifice themselves. A few days after the speech of Sir

James, the *Patriot* sounded the note of alarm, and published a series of masterly articles analysing and exposing the scheme, and was vigorously supported by the *Nonconformist.* An opposition to the measure was at once organised. Meetings were held throughout the kingdom; petitions poured into the Houses of Legislature; and, eventually, Sir James Graham, after a vain endeavour to modify it, reluctantly withdrew his Bill.

The editor of the *Nonconformist* followed up this agitation by a series of articles urging the necessity of establishing a national association for securing the separation of the Church from the State. During the latter part of the year 1843 and the commencement of the following year these proposals were actively discussed in various parts of the country. Local meetings were held to consider them, and in many districts, especially in the midland counties, resolutions in their favour were passed with unexampled enthusiasm. Ultimately it was resolved that a Convention of Delegates should be summoned to meet in London in the month of April, 1844, with the view of openly forming an Anti-State Church Association.

Independently of the excitement which had been produced by Sir James Graham's proposals, several circumstances combined to favour the establishment of such an organisation. The Oxford Tractarian party, headed by Dr. Pusey, Dr. Manning, and Dr. Newman, by their bold attacks on the characteristically Protestant doctrines of the Established Church, had excited a just alarm amongst Churchmen themselves for the doctrinal securities of the Establishment. The secession of some of the more prominent leaders of this party to the Roman Catholic Church had suggested the inquiry whether some of the formularies of the Church did not encourage Romanism amongst its members. But what was most serious in this movement was the undisguised sacerdotalism which was professed by all who joined it. There can be little doubt that the rise of sacerdotal pretensions at this time is to be attributed to the attacks which, in previous years, had been made upon the Established Church. It was the refuge of men whose Church, as it stood, had suffered by the test of reason, and who therefore fell back for support, as Churchmen in all ages have done, upon superstition and authority.

The remarkable secession, upon the ground of undue secular control in spiritual matters, of four hundred clergymen of the Church of Scotland, with Dr. Chalmers at their head, and their formation of a "Free Church," gave additional impetus to the proposed agitation. One of the Established Churches was now rent in twain. The Dissenters of Scotland were constituted, by this secession, a large majority of the inhabitants of that kingdom, and it was not difficult to foresee that the time could not be distant when it would be impossible to maintain the Northern Establishment in its position of ecclesiastical supremacy.

The proposed Anti-State Church Conference was held in London, on April 30th, and May 1st and 2nd, 1844. Nearly eight hundred delegates responded to the summons which had been issued. Such a meeting, of such a character, and for such a purpose, was without precedent in the history of English Dissent. Nevertheless many of the most influential members of the Free Churches held aloof from it. The only general representative body which sent delegates was the Baptist Union. Only three conspicuous ministers of the Congregational Churches of London were present—Dr. Pye Smith, the Rev. John Burnet, and Dr. John Campbell; the last-named declaring himself "almost a reluctant convert, but a real one." The Congregational Union of Scotland sent, however, several representatives, including the Rev. Dr. Wardlaw. The unendowed Presbyterian bodies of Scotland sent the Rev. Andrew Marshall, of Kirkintilloch, Dr. Adam Thomson, the Rev. Dr. Ritchie, Professor M'Michael, of Dunfermline, and the Rev. Dr. Young, of Perth. The Friends were conspicuously represented by Mr. Joseph Sturge and Mr. Stafford Allen, and the Unitarians by Dr. John Bowring and the Rev. Dr. Hutton. The Jamaica Dissenters requested the Rev. William Brock, of Norwich, to represent them. The Toller family sent one of its members, the Rev. Henry Toller, of Harborough. The veteran controversialist, the Rev. William Thorn, of Winchester, was also there. The section of England which sent by far the greater proportion of delegates was the midland counties. There were also present Dr. Thomas Price, the Rev. James Phillipo Mursell, of Leicester, Dr. F. A. Cox, Mr. Edward Swaine, Mr. Josiah Conder, Mr. Apsley Pellatt, Mr. Thomas Russell, of Edinburgh, the Rev. Charles Stovel, of London, and Mr. Edward Miall—names all of which now belong to the past history of Dissent. At the first meeting Dr. Cox presided, and read a history of the circumstances which had led to the Conference, and a justification of the movement. A resolution was then passed to the effect that the period had arrived when a mere defensive policy, on the part of Dissenters, had failed to meet the requirements of their position, and that an effort to diffuse their sentiments with the view of preparing the public mind for the cessation of the union subsisting between the Church and the State was enforced by their interests as Dissenters, and imperatively called for by their obligations as Christian men. A paper, by Dr. Wardlaw, on the Principle of Voluntaryism, was also read. On the next day Mr. Miall read a paper upon the Practical Evils resulting from the union of Church and State; and the Rev. J. W. Massie, of Manchester, a paper on the External Forms in which the Established principle manifested itself. On the third day papers were read by Mr. J. M. Hare, on the precise meaning of the phrase, "The Separation of the Church from the State, and the legal changes which such separation involved"; and by the Rev. J. P. Mursell, on the "Means of Promoting the Object of the Conference, and on the spirit in which they should be employed." The proceedings of the Conference were throughout of a calm and deliberate, yet enthusiastic, character. As the practical result of its labours a society was formed, to be called "The British Anti-State Church Association," the object of which should be the liberation of religion from all governmental and legislative interference. An Executive Committee of fifty, and a Council of five hundred, persons were appointed to conduct the affairs of the Society, Dr. Cox, Mr. Miall, and Mr. J. M. Hare being, as a temporary arrangement, honorary secretaries, and it was resolved to hold a Triennial Conference.*

Immediately succeeding this agitation, the Free Churches were greatly excited by the proposal in Parliament of the "Dissenters' Chapels Bill." The origin of this measure dates back twenty years from the time when it was brought forward. In 1824, at a meeting held at Manchester, a Unitarian minister, the Rev. George Harris, took occasion to assail, in the most vituperative strains, the character and tendency of "orthodox" Christianity. His speech provoked a local controversy, in which it was suggested that the Unitarians had no legal right to many of the buildings which they used for public worship, and that they were prostituting the funds of several charities left by Lady Hewley, of which, in course of time, they had become the exclusive trustees, to the sectarian purposes of their own

* Of the members of this Executive of fifty members, who comprised ministers and members of all the principal denominations, only two now (1891) survive—Mr. J. M. Hare and the Rev. Dr. Kennedy.

denomination. Inquiry being made into the administration of the funds of the charities, some gross abuses were detected. A list of the old Presbyterian chapels in England occupied at the time of the controversy by the Unitarian descendants of the early founders and worshippers was drawn up, and it was contended that the whole of these chapels belonged of right to the orthodox Protestant Dissenters. It so happened that a case was then pending in the courts of law, the decision of which would probably establish the accuracy or inaccuracy of this allegation. There was at Wolverhampton an endowed chapel which, at one time, had been occupied by the early Presbyterians. In 1782 this place had been forcibly taken possession of by the Unitarian portion of the congregation, who held it until 1816, when the minister, the Rev. John Steward, announced his conversion to Trinitarian views. One of the trustees of this place of worship, Mr. Pearson, was a Unitarian; the other, Mr. Benjamin Mander, was a Congregationalist. After some violent proceedings by both parties to obtain possession of the building, and suits and cross-suits for riot and disorderly conduct, in which Mr. Mander was victorious, the case was, in 1817, brought before the Court of Chancery, and, on a suit for an injunction to stop the ejectment of Mr. Steward, Lord Eldon gave his decision in favour of Mr. Mander, directing at the same time an inquiry into the nature of the trusts. Before this inquiry was instituted Mr. Benjamin Mander died, and his son, Mr. Charles Mander, succeeded to the suit. For nineteen years following the case remained in that grave of equity, the English Court of Chancery, when it was heard on appeal by Lord Chancellor Cottenham, who postponed his decision until the judgment of the House of Lords in the case of Lady Hewley's charities should be pronounced.

The litigation relative to Lady Hewley's charity was commenced in 1830, at the instance, amongst others, of Dr. James Bennett, then of Rotherham College, Mr. George Hadfield,* who had taken a leading part in the Manchester controversy, and Mr. Joshua Wilson. In the suit which was then instituted Mr. Hadfield, Mr. Thomas Wilson, Mr. Joseph Read, of Sheffield, Mr. John Clapham, of Leeds, and Mr. Joseph Hodgson, of Halifax, were made the plaintiffs, and the trustees of the charity the defendants. The object of the suit was to establish the right of orthodox Dissenters alone to the charities founded by Lady Hewley. It was maintained that when Lady Hewley executed her trusts in favour of "poor, godly preachers of Christ's Holy Gospel," for "poor widows of poor and godly preachers of the Gospel," for "the preaching of the Gospel in poor places," for "educating young men for the ministry," and for similar purposes, she must have referred to orthodox persons only, because, first, she was a Presbyterian, and the Presbyterians of that time were orthodox, and because, secondly, she could not have intended to include Unitarians, for Unitarianism, at the period when she lived, was a proscribed faith, and the trusts would therefore have been illegal. The trustees, in reply, endeavoured to show that Lady Hewley left her charities without any exclusive regard either to peculiar forms of Protestant Dissenting worship, or to the particular doctrines inculcated by the different denominations, and they pointed to the fact that the Presbyterians of her time were distinguished by their opposition to all formal creeds and confessions of faith. The plaintiffs brought a mass of evidence to prove the orthodoxy of the Presbyterians; the defendants, on the other hand, met this by the quotation of passages in their writings which

* Afterwards M.P. for Sheffield.

might imply their indifference to theological beliefs. Begun in 1830, the case went through the whole of the tortuous proceedings of a Chancery suit, which was fought on both sides with the utmost pertinacity, combined, in some instances, with the most intense acrimony of feeling. From the first the decisions were against the trustees. The final judgment was pronounced in the House of Lords, in 1842, when six out of seven judges, who had been called in to assist, gave their opinion in favour of the plaintiffs. Lord Lyndhurst then pronounced judgment to the effect that orthodox Dissenters only were entitled to be trustees of the charities, and to participate in the funds. New trustees were subsequently nominated by the Court of Chancery. The Wolverhampton case was decided in accordance with the law which had now been laid down, and its endowments—or such of them as were left—were, in effect, restored to what had thus been declared to have been their original use.

If the orthodox party was delighted at the result of these prolonged contests, the feelings of the Unitarians was one of mingled indignation and dismay. The worshippers in more than two hundred chapels saw themselves in danger of being ejected from the places in which they and their ancestors had worshipped, in some instances for three or four generations, which they had themselves repaired, and where their nearest and dearest relatives lay buried. They at once, therefore, took proceedings to procure such an alteration in the law as should leave them in possession of their edifices, and which, at the same time, should prevent the repetition of any similar suits by any sect against other sects. In response to their appeals, a Bill was brought in by Sir Robert Peel's Government in 1844, the principal object of which was to secure the possession of any place of worship, which had been occupied by a certain congregation for twenty-five years, to the undisturbed use of such congregation. The measure was brought in by Lord Lyndhurst on the 7th of March, and, being supported by the Government and all the law lords who had given judgment in the recent case, passed by a majority of 41 to 9. It encountered the strenuous opposition of the majority of the bishops, and, out of Parliament, of the Congregationalists, Baptists, and Wesleyans, who petitioned largely against it. In the House of Commons, where it was supported, not only by Sir Robert Peel, but by Mr. Gladstone, Lord John Russell, and Mr. Macaulay, it was carried by 300 to 119, and finally passed the Legislature on the 15th of July. The Act, as it was ultimately settled, provided that the usage of twenty-five years should be taken as conclusive evidence of the right of any congregation to the possession of their place of worship, and of the schools, burial grounds, and endowments pertaining thereto.*

The wisdom as well as the charity of the Legislature in this remarkable case will now probably be questioned by very few of those who, at the time, most strenuously opposed it. Whatever legal title the orthodox bodies might have had—and unquestionably did have—to this property and however wrongfully, although naturally, the Unitarians may have become possessed of it, other questions than those of original title were necessarily involved in the case. Litigation such as that which must have taken place if the Unitarians were to be dispossessed of nearly the whole of their chapels, however it may apparently have served the purposes of a sect, could not have served the purposes of Christianity, nor have conduced to that public peace which

* "The Manchester Socinian Controversy." By George Hadfield. "Debates on the Dissenters' Chapels Bill." "The History of the Litigation and Legislation respecting Presbyterian Chapels and Charities." By T. S. James.

it is one of the principal functions of the Legislature to preserve. Nor was it desirable that a greed for mere property should take possession of any religious denomination. How much the possession of these places of worship had contributed, and still contributes, to the spread of Unitarian doctrines it is impossible to say, but it is possible to believe that even successful litigation may do more harm to the Christian character and influence of any sect than possession of the coveted property will do them good. The Act, so far as it limited inquiry into the right to property, was in harmony with previous laws, and, so far as it was calculated to prevent litigation, with the best civil and religious interests of society.

One of the first subjects to which the attention of the Anti-State Church Association was drawn was the *Regium Donum*, and measures were at once adopted for bringing it before Parliament. For ten years past the feeling against this grant had been increasing. It had been condemned by the express resolutions of some of the representative bodies of Dissenters, and Dr. Cox, who had been one of its distributors, felt himself compelled to withdraw from that office. The defence of the grant was undertaken by Dr. Pye Smith, himself a member of the Anti-State Church Association, and one of the distributors of the grant, and a warm public controversy between the Committee of the Association and Dr. Smith upon this subject took place. When Mr. Charles Hindley proposed a resolution in the House of Commons, in 1845, for the rejection of the grant he was followed into the lobby by only three members. Year by year, however, the minority increased. In 1848 and 1849 the question was debated at great length in the House of Commons, and on July 17th, 1851, the Chancellor of the Exchequer announced that, as the opposition to the continuance of the grant had so greatly increased among Dissenters, the Government would not again place it upon the votes. Henceforward, therefore, the Free Churches could protest against national endowments of religion without being themselves charged with accepting them.

The introduction, by Sir Robert Peel's Government, in 1845, of a Bill to increase the State endowment to the Roman Catholic College of Maynooth, gave to the adherents of the Anti-State Church Association an opportunity of placing their principles before the Legislature and the public, of which they took a signal advantage. Sir Robert Peel's proposal excited the especial opposition of two parties—one composed of the Evangelical members of the Established Church, the Wesleyans, and the more Conservative portion of Dissenters, who based their opposition upon Protestant grounds only; and the other mainly composed of the more advanced section of Dissenters, who, while holding fast to Protestantism, based their opposition to the Maynooth Endowment upon the principle that all endowments for religious purposes, whether for Protestantism or for Romanism, were unjust, unscriptural, and mischievous.

The openly-expressed determination of the Prime Minister to proceed with his measure, notwithstanding the expressions of indignation and alarm it encountered, led to the formation of a "Central Anti-Maynooth Committee," of which Sir Culling Eardley Smith was appointed chairman, and which was composed of representatives of all the Evangelical denominations. Failing even to delay the progress of the measure through the Legislature, it was ultimately decided to summon a General Council of Protestants from all parts of the kingdom to adopt measures for securing the defeat of the Bill. The prominence that had recently been given to anti-State Church principles led the

Committee to intimate that, as there was known to be a diversity of sentiment concerning the particular grounds upon which the grant was disapproved, they deemed it to be of supreme importance to "bear with one another in regard to minor differences." The Conference, which numbered more than a thousand deputies from upwards of four hundred cities and towns, met on the 30th of April, 1845. It included some well-known Dissenters. At the second sitting it appeared that liberty of speech on the special subject of ecclesiastical endowments would not be allowed; and some of the members, headed by the Rev. J. P. Mursell, of Leicester, accordingly left the Conference. The Dissenters at once took steps to summon a Convention of their own. At a meeting held at Salter's Hall Chapel, presided over by the Rev. Dr. Cox, of Hackney, it was resolved that it was a matter of high importance that the principles on which they objected to the proposed endowment should be clearly and distinctly understood by both Parliament and the country, and that it was expedient to convene a conference of the friends of religious freedom, to adopt measures, not only to oppose the Maynooth Bill, but all other State-endowments of religion. A committee of thirty-five gentlemen, including representatives from all sections of Evangelical Dissenters, was appointed to make arrangements for such a meeting. The proposed Conference was held on the 20th and 21st of May following. It consisted of nearly a thousand members. The Rev. John Burnet occupied the chair. Many who held aloof from the British Anti-State Church Association now felt compelled to appear upon what was virtually the platform of that Society. The Conference passed a series of resolutions in harmony with the object of its meeting, and adopted a petition of its own to the Legislature. Its proceedings attracted universal attention, and gave to public men a distinct indication that bigotry, at least, was not the feeling by which Dissenters were moved in opposing this measure. Sir Robert Peel had avowed that his object was political, not ecclesiastical, and was met, therefore, on his own ground; for it was argued that the political peace of Ireland would not be secured by any endowment of Roman Catholicism, but only by the disendowment of the State Church.*

The principle upon which this Conference based its action was acknowledged to be both just and intelligible. The continued efforts of both sections of opponents, however, were insufficient to prevent the success of the Maynooth Bill. That measure, supported by the leaders of all parties, passed both Houses of the Legislature by overwhelming majorities. Whatever may have been, up to this time, the fundamental theory upon which a State-establishment of religion was based, it could not, henceforth, be said that it was the duty of the State to endow "the truth." An inevitable result of this Conference—but one that was fully anticipated by its promoters—was the wider separation of Evangelical Churchmen and Evangelical Dissenters. It had become, for some years, more and more obvious that it was impossible for the two parties to work harmoniously together. When union could only be achieved by the exercise of supremacy by the one, and of subserviency by the other, and when it became obvious in relation to this measure that the Evangelical Church party had chiefly in view the salvation of the Irish Establishment, and through it of the institution which was pressing with intolerable weight upon the liberties of Evangelical Dissenters, the time had come for the proclamation of honest differences.

* "Proceedings of the Maynooth Conference." *Nonconformist* Newspaper, 1845.

If, however, there was disappointment at this apparent strengthening of the compulsory principle in matters of religion, the members of the Free Churches had cause to rejoice, in the following year, at the freedom that was given to trade, Sir Robert Peel's Act, which virtually abolished the Corn Laws, being the end of an agitation in which Dissenters had taken a peculiar interest. At a Free Trade Conference held in Manchester in January, 1843, three hundred ministers of the Free Churches were present to promote the success of the movement. At that Conference there were not six ministers of the Established Church. As in the Reform movement, and all similar agitations, the Church was again ranged on the side of monopoly.

Before the last year of the half century had arrived the Methodist body was once more divided. To the "Methodist New Connexion" had already succeeded the "Primitive Methodists," who set up an independent organisation because the Conference, proving more Conservative than Wesley himself, and forgetting the origin of the denomination, discouraged the general practice of field preaching. The Bible Christians, established mainly in Cornwall, through the influence of Mr. William O'Bryan were another offshoot of the old body. In all the new Methodist organisations the power of the laity was fully recognised. In 1849 another secession, originating in the arbitrary proceedings of the Conference, took place. For some time previous to this a few persons had expressed, through various publications, their dissatisfaction with the government of the Wesleyan community, which was then principally lodged in the hands of one successfully ambitious man—the Rev. Dr. Jabez Bunting. At the Conference of this year three ministers, the Revs. Messrs. Everett, Dunn, and Griffith, were summoned to answer the question, whether they had not written some of these publications, viz., the "fly sheets." Declining to be parties to a proceeding which savoured more of the Inquisition and the Star Chamber than of any modern English or Christian court, and refusing to reply to such a question, they were forthwith expelled the society. The Methodist laity did not, however, unanimously endorse the sentence which had been passed upon them. In the year after the expulsion the number of members of the society had decreased to the alarming extent of more than fifty-six thousand. The expelled members soon afterwards became known as the Wesleyan Methodist Reformers, and under that name existed when the Census of Religious Worship was taken in 1851. Subsequently they amalgamated with the Wesleyan Association, and the two bodies, with some additions, constituted the United Methodist Free Churches.

CHAPTER XI.

FROM 1848 TO 1860.

THE publication of the Census of Public Worship taken in 1851 placed the Free Churches in so new and unforeseen a relation to public opinion as to require special notice in this history. But not till the beginning of 1854 were the facts and conclusions deduced from these statistics by Mr. Horace Mann given to the world, and it may be expedient not to anticipate the revelations which then astonished all sections of the Christian Church. Some antecedent ecclesiastical events excited much interest among both Churchmen and Dissenters. One of these was the suggestion that in order to counteract the chronic discontent of the Irish people, the Roman Catholic priests of that country should be endowed by the State, a policy—if so it may be called—which since the time of Catholic emancipation had been aired by weak public men, who considered it a stroke of statesmanship to relieve ecclesiastically-discontented people at the cost of the law abiding. Lord John Russell, then Prime Minister, and always fond of makeshifts, at this time favoured the scheme with the tacit assent of the leaders of the Opposition, though at every Liberal and Liberationist meeting towards the close of 1848 it was vehemently denounced. Before the end of that year, the impracticability of such a policy had been demonstrated at the memorable election for West Riding. The Tory candidate on that occasion was Mr. Beckett Denison, a resident and wealthy landowner in the county, and Sir Culling Eardley was induced to stand in the Liberal interest avowedly as a decided opponent of Roman Catholic endowment. The great families of the district coalesced in support of the Tory, whose adherents, unable to agree in advocating the Catholic nostrum, took up the cry of "no chapel," in reference especially to the leanings of the *Leeds Mercury*. That influential paper threw all its influence on the side of Sir Culling, who unfortunately, before the contest was over, succumbed to illness, and who had also declined to pledge himself to the disestablishment of the Irish Protestant Church. In the end, after a hard struggle, Mr. Denison was returned by a majority of nearly 3,000, but his opponent polled close upon 12,000 votes. Though Sir Culling was not elected, the policy of the Government was practically defeated, and nothing more was, for some time, heard of Roman Catholic endowment; which was practically abandoned after Mr. Miall's motion for disestablishing the Irish Church, and could not be resuscitated even by the specious pleas of Mr. Matthew Arnold.

A still more exciting event at this period was the secession from the Established Church of the Hon. and Rev. Baptist Noel, a popular, devoted, and highly connected Evangelical clergyman, which took place at the close of 1848 after a laborious ministry of twenty years. The report of Mr. Noel's intention* having reached the ears of the Bishop of London (Dr. Blomfield), that prelate peremptorily forbade him again to officiate in his diocese; but on Mr. Noel's refusal to consent, he was allowed to take leave of his congregation on the following Sunday (December 3), when an overflowing congregation listened to his farewell

* Mr. Noel was proposing to retire at the following Midsummer, so as to give his people ample time to choose a successor; St. John's Chapel, Bedford Row, being a proprietary chapel.

sermon. In about a month Mr. Noel published a volume of 600 pages,* the first edition of which was bespoken before it was issued. The reader might suppose that the author had been a Dissenter all his life but for the Preface, in which he states that the book is an attack on the Church and State connection, but that he believes as much in the entire sincerity of his "beloved and honoured brethren" who adhere to the Establishment as in his own in quitting it. In the treatise itself the arguments are directed exclusively to the merits of the case, and traverse nearly the whole ground, while the volume indicates not only the depths of Mr. Noel's convictions, but his courage in stating them, and the necessity that was laid upon him as an honourable man of breaking away at all costs from a system which he believed to be unchristian. Mr. Noel—who, it may be said, accepted the doctrine of believers' baptism—continued to minister almost to the day of his death in John Street Chapel. He took little part in any public movements, and refrained from joining the Liberation Society, or appearing on its platform. In 1855 he presided at the annual session of the Baptist Union, his subject being, "Growth of Grace, the Want of the Churches." In the course of his address he said:—"Since Churches have come under State control by the action of the State, they must be released by the same action; and it is the duty of Christians who see the mischief which State patronage of the Churches does to the cause of Christ, to persuade the State to withdraw it." Mr. Noel went on to indicate that, in his view, political action was always dangerous to Christians, peculiarly so to pastors, and that eminent piety in pastors and churches would, in a

* "An Essay on the Union of Church and State." By Baptist Wriothesay Noel, M.A. (Nisbet & Co.)

few years, do more to free the Church of England than thirty years of political warfare—surely a very illogical and unsound conclusion.

Soon after this, the warlike Bishop of Exeter came prominently before the public in one of those congenial occupations which had earned for him the title of the Hildebrand of the Episcopal Bench. In 1849 the Rev. James Shore, an Evangelical clergyman of the diocese, preached several times in an unconsecrated building, for which he was prosecuted by Dr. Philpotts. To avoid further interference by the Bishop, Mr. Shore subscribed before a magistrate of Totnes such oaths and declarations as he thought would qualify him for becoming a Dissenting minister. But this did not satisfy his zealous diocesan prelate. Acting upon the principle that holy orders were indelible, he obtained decisions against Mr. Shore in various ecclesiastical courts. His victim, unfortunately, appealed to the Judicial Committee of the Privy Council, and was unsuccessful. Being mulcted in heavy costs, he refused to pay, and, thereupon, was one day arrested for contempt of court, after preaching in Spa Fields Chapel, London, and was conveyed to prison. An influential meeting of London ministers, including the Revs. T. Binney, Brock, Kennedy, and Burnet, and Drs. Campbell, Leifchild, and Pye-Smith, was held in Exeter Hall, at which a resolution was passed protesting against the treatment of Mr. Shore as "unjust, cruel, and unchristian" and recommending an alteration of the law. A large committee was nominated to take such proceedings as might be necessary. At this meeting, Mr. Binney, in reference to the letter of Dr. Philpotts' secretary that the costs only applied to the appeal to the Judicial Committee, remarked that Mr. Shore would still be liable to the costs in the Arches Court if the others were paid. There was, he said, purple and fine linen in every line of the Bishop's letter. Mr. Shore was liberated after being in prison two months.

Of far more importance from a public point of view was the celebrated case of Gorham *v.* the Bishop of Exeter, arising out of the refusal of the respondent to induct the plaintiff into the living of Bramford Speke, on the ground that Mr. Gorham held unsound doctrine; he believing that spiritual regeneration did not always follow the administration of the sacrament of Baptism. The Court of Queen's Bench granted a rule; and the Court of Arches, by the mouth of Sir H. Jenner Fust, decided that the Bishop was justified in refusing to induct the plaintiff, the articles and offices of the Church Baptism and Confirmation saying everywhere the same thing—viz., that children invariably and always were spiritually regenerated by the act of Baptism, which Mr. Gorham in the absolute sense denied. This decision excited the greatest excitement among the Evangelical party in the Church of England, and there were many and loud threats of secession in the event of this judgment being confirmed. It was reported to be the anxious wish of the Government, said Mr. Binney, "to keep the nation from being embroiled by a split in, and secession from, the Church, and to keep the Church one and indivisible by assuring its apparently discordant elements that they were alike within the meaning of its liberal institutions, and equally embraced by its loving catholicity."* The case was carried to the highest tribunal —the Judicial Committee of the Privy Council—who, in March, 1850, decided that Mr. Gorham's doctrine might lawfully be held by a clergyman of the Church of England, and had been so held by some of its brightest ornaments,

* "The Great Gorham Case." By a Looker-On. P. 126. (Partridge & Co.)

and that he ought not, by reason of that doctrine, to have been refused admission to the vicarage of Bramford Speke. The printed judgment was read by Lord Langdale, and there were present of the members of the Judicial Committee, Lords Lansdowne, Campbell, and Brougham, Dr. Lushington, Mr. Pemberton Leigh, Baron Parke, Vice-Chancellor Bruce, and Sir Edward Ryan. The two archbishops and the Bishop of London were also present, though they were not actually members of the Committee, and did not sign the report presented to the Queen. The Bishop of London and Vice-Chancellor Knight Bruce dissented from the decision of the Court, though the other prelates acquiesced.

The judgment of the Judicial Committee was variously received by the daily press, but, on the whole, it was approved. As the *Times* remarked, in all probability it saved the Church and the country "from a great calamity," although the majority of Churchmen might accept the orthodox doctrine of the Bishop of Exeter; while the *Daily News* taunted Dr. Blomfield, who had held aloof, with having saved his reputation amongst the High Church clergy at a cheap rate, and pronounced the judgment to be a great blow "struck on the right side." The *Morning Post* ("Puseyite"), while regarding the decision of Sir H. J. Fust, in the Arches Court, as "unanswerable," pronounced that of the Judicial Committee to be "singularly weak and inconclusive," and "an evasion of every point in the case." On the other hand, the *Morning Herald*, then the organ of the Low Church party, was delighted at so "clear and satisfactory a decision," which showed that "the Church of England had always allowed a certain degree of liberty on some points, of which this was one." This was substantially the view of the *Record*, the weekly organ of the Evangelical party, and of the *Christian Observer*, its monthly advocate.

It may seem almost superfluous after this lapse of time to make any lengthened reference in this history to what was then called "The Great Gorham Case." But at that period the litigation excited the most profound interest amongst Nonconformists, as well as Churchmen, and the legal proceedings in connection with the case were as eagerly discussed in their newspapers, such as the *Patriot*, the *Christian Times*, the *British Banner*, and the *Nonconformist*, as in the Church papers. The last-named of these journals thus pithily draws the moral from the final decision of the Judicial Committee :—

"In the same Church, therefore, patronised and supported by the same State, and conjoined together in the same apostolical body, and both conforming their religious opinions to the same standard of faith—for baptismal regeneration as taught by Dr. Pusey is not decided to be no doctrine of the Establishment, nor, indeed, is it likely to be—we have two large sects, differing with each other on what each regards as fundamental to Christianity, and sharing the temporalities set apart by the State for the religious instruction of the people. Well, now, whilst this fact stares us in the face, whatever may be urged in favour of a National Establishment, let us not be told any more that the Church of England is an united, holy, and apostolic *church*. If its code of faith, its rubric, and its formularies are so constructed—and that, too, purposely—as to comprehend in one body teachers or members who differ *toto cœlo* on the very essentials of religious belief, to all intents and purposes it must cease to be regarded as a Church in any sense. It offers no common bond of union."*

In the Gorham case—as, indeed, in most ecclesiastical questions—Mr. Binney took the keenest interest. At this time he wrote much, if somewhat discursively, in the *Christian*

* *Nonconformist*, March 13th, 1850.

Times, an unsectarian religious newspaper, under the title of "The Observatory, or Crows' Nest," which he supposed to be beside the cross of St. Paul's, and from this elevation he tried to mark and interpret the movements around him, with special reference to their religious bearings and ecclesiastical tendency. His papers on the Gorham case were afterwards republished in a separate form, though not with his name attached.* They were issued at intervals during twelve months. Mr. Binney was present in the Court of Arches when Sir H. Jenner Fust delivered his judgment, and again in the Court of Appeal when the Judicial Committee gave their final decision. He describes the two scenes with much picturesqueness, analyses and humorously comments upon both the State papers with great subtlety and all the acumen of a lawyer, traces the theories of baptismal regeneration to their roots, contests the soundness of Mr. Gorham's hypothesis, proclaims his conviction that the position taken by the Court of Arches is, regarded from the point of view of the Canons, Prayer Book, and Offices of the Church, unanswerable; and exposes the gross inconsistencies of the *Christian Observer* and *Record*. The weekly Evangelical organ had previously, on many occasions, denounced "the deadly error" of the High Church theories; and, even after the judgment of the Judicial Committee, spoke of "the grand error of the day," "than which none is more dangerous or more destructive"; while, at the same time, the *Record* was "abundantly thankful" for that decision, which affirmed that "either view of the subject [baptismal regeneration] may be held *and promulgated* without infringing the declared code of

* "The Great Gorham Case: a History in Five Books, including Expositions of the Rival Baptismal Theories." By a Looker-On. (London: Partridge & Oakey.) 1850.

the law of the Church."* It is remarkable, as Mr. Binney points out, that, on the day following the publication of the judgment, a new edition of the Primate's volume on "Apostolical Teaching"—in which Dr. Sumner asserted and maintained absolutely the doctrine of baptismal regeneration—was brought out without any alteration.

What the Court of Final Appeal decided in 1850 in respect to this great question remains binding to this day. This is an adequate reason for giving the following scathing quotation, which has quite a flavour of Carlyle, from the preface to Mr. Binney's little volume. It is signed "John Search," the *nom de plume* which the author was in the habit of assuming in ecclesiastical controversy, when, as he says, he was very frequently called upon to explain or defend the religious grounds of Nonconformity :—

"The time has come for the truth to be spoken,—and to be *so* spoken as that it shall not easily be either missed or forgotten. A whole world-full of modern men, with the thoughts to think and the work to do belonging to their age, have been obliged to listen for weeks and months to the jargon of the schools, to metaphysical distinctions and theological niceties that *they* only can regard as important, who draw the pabulum of their internal life from the past —*man's* past, not God's—the times of councils and popes and priests, who suspended eternity on whatever attached importance to themselves! Why, who cares what this council, or that, or the other, thought or determined? What is it to us, who have got something else to think about and do, in this nineteenth century of the Christian redemption (and society nothing like redeemed yet) than to hear what was thought, hundreds of years ago, on matters, it may be, which nobody believes, or about which we can judge better ourselves than any old ecclesiastical conclave could judge for us? I believe, for my part, that not only did the arguments and explanations in the Gorham case

* *Record*, March 11th, 1850.

amaze and disgust vast numbers in general society, by the things it revealed as important to Churchmen with which others could have no sympathy, but that the judges themselves who decided the dispute, did so professionally as lawyers, but with utter incredulousness as to the substantial reality of what was professed, or the value or worth of it, on either side. It is a terrible state for society to be in, when that is inculcated or professed by its teachers, or included in its creeds and forms of belief, which it itself does not believe. Now I am firmly persuaded that that is the case with what constitutes the basis of both the theories of baptismal grace of which we have lately heard so much, and are destined, I fear, to hear more. What I refer to is this:—They alike assume the liability of all infants, *as such*, to GOD'S EVERLASTING WRATH AND DAMNATION; that every babe is born into the world fitted for HELL; fitted for, that is, or *righteously* exposed to intense, inconceivable, immitigable, and conscious eternal anguish! Gloss, disguise, modify, extenuate it as they may, this is the naked and simple truth; both parties hold and avow it,—and they do so consistently, for the Prayer-book expressly teaches the doctrine. I will not judge other men, or speak of individuals as identical with their belief. But I will say for myself that, with my views of the Divine character, the meaning of the Bible, the redemption of Christ, and the probation of mercy, if I were to adopt and to profess this doctrine, I should, in my own estimation, be a traitor to humanity, a denier of the Gospel, an apostate from Jesus, and an infidel to God. Seeing that I should think thus of myself, I dread to think what may have been passing in the mind of the nation with respect to others, who, for months and more, have been publicly proclaiming *this* idea to be the necessary basis of both their systems of religious belief."

It may be added in relation to the Gorham judgment that the enraged Bishop of Exeter, in a letter to the Primate, pronounced it to be "a grievous perversion of justice," protested against his support of Mr. Gorham's "heresies," and renounced communion with Archbishop Sumner. The friends of Dr. Phillpotts, including Pusey,

Manning, Wilberforce, Keble, and Bennett, encouraged him to strive to obtain a reversal of the legal decision. The case was carried from one court to another, and in each case the application to prohibit the Court of Arches from giving effect to the judgment of the Privy Council was rejected. The Bishop having finally protested against the innovation of the Arches Court, had the mortification of being obliged to permit the induction of Mr. Gorham to the living of Bramford Speke, which was done amid the jubilations of a large portion of the laity in the diocese of Exeter. But the militant prelate had yet to fire a parting, but not very effective shot—a solemn warning to the churchwardens of that parish against the heretical teaching of Mr. Gorham. Shortly after the Bishop of London brought into the House of Lords a Bill to establish a new tribunal for ecclesiastical appeals, instead of the Judicial Committee—viz., a Court of Bishops. Chiefly on the ground that it interfered with the royal supremacy, the measure was rejected by the peers by a majority of 33 (84 to 51 votes), and the whole question was left as a puzzle to exercise the minds of clerical High Churchmen in succeeding generations.

Not long after there set in that mysterious mania, arising out of what was generally designated "the Papal aggression," which led to a most extraordinary outburst of "No Popery" feeling, stimulated, no doubt, by the spread of Tractarianism among the clergy,* still more by the

* Shortly before there had been a great aggregate clerical meeting at St. Martin's Hall, under Dr. Pusey's auspices, to protest against Mr. Gorham's "heresies" and to petition the Queen for a revival of synodical action. This was responded to somewhat later by an address to Her Majesty, signed by 230,000 Churchmen, recommending measures for preventing innovations in the forms of public worship. By the Queen's directions Sir G. Grey transmitted the address to the Archbishop of Canterbury.

encouragement it received from influential statesmen, who had, only a year previously, made abortive attempts to establish diplomatic relations with the Roman Pontiff. The Vatican thought the opportunity favourable for doing away with the vicars-apostolic who governed the English branch of the Roman Catholic Church, and establishing dioceses with bishops who took their titles from the chief towns, with an Archbishop of Westminster at their head. This notable scheme was brought over from Rome by Dr. Wiseman, who was created a cardinal by Pius IX., and placed at the head of the Romish hierarchy, and who issued a grandiloquent manifesto on the subject. There were signs of a rising storm, which Lord John Russell, who was mortified by recent opposition to his Episcopal appointments, lashed into a tempest by his celebrated "Durham" letter—indited in that city. In this missive the Premier spoke of the Papal claim of supremacy over the realm of England as being inconsistent with the Queen's supremacy, with the rights of the bishops and clergy, and with the spiritual independence of the nation. His lordship concluded by an appeal well adapted to arouse Protestant indignation. "I will not," he said, "bate a jot of heart or hope so long as the glorious principles and the immortal martyrs of the Reformation shall be held in reverence by the great mass of a nation which looks with contempt on the mummeries of superstition, and with scorn at the laborious endeavours which are now making to confine the intellect and enslave the soul." In a short time, from the end of 1850, and far into the next year, there were Episcopal and clerical remonstrances and objurgations, followed by innumerable public meetings and addresses to the Queen all over the country, in which Dissenters vied with Churchmen in the strength of their protests against "Papal aggression," and even Jews assisted to defend "our common Protestantism." It was stated by the *Publishers' Circular* that no fewer than seventy-eight works on the subject were issued from the press. Some Nonconformists who held aloof or condemned "every kind of alliance between the priestly and the magisterial power," were denounced as Jesuits in disguise.* When Parliament met in February the Queen's Speech referred to the Papal scheme; and, shortly after, Lord John Russell brought in his Ecclesiastical Titles Bill, which forbade the assumption of territorial titles by Roman Catholics, and rendered void all acts done by parties under these titles. Although his Lordship was, for other reasons, obliged to resign, on his again resuming office, the ill-fated measure was persisted in. An immense majority carried the revised Bill through the Commons, and, although it was shorn of its penal provisions, and was almost innocuous, it was opposed by such eminent men as Graham—who delivered a most telling philippic against the Bill—Gladstone, Roundell Palmer, Cobden, and Bright; and the Premier was cheered only by the Tory members, who had been most persistent in opposing his policy of civil and religious freedom.† The Lords passed the Bill with little debate—almost with contempt. There was, ere long, a complete revulsion of public feeling on the subject, and the

---

* So strong was the excitement of the moment that, at an Islington meeting, the vicar presiding, Mr. Miall, who was a resident in the district, was rising to move an amendment, when two clergymen hurled him off the platform. No great harm was done, but these doughty champions of Protestantism had to make a public apology for their violence.

† The English Catholics, as represented by the Duke of Norfolk and Lord Beaumont, disapproved of Cardinal Wiseman's scheme as uncalled for, while they expressed their regret at the introduction of "the ill-advised" measure of Lord John.

statesmen and Nonconformists who manfully stood firm against the popular clamour were justified by the result.* The measure became a dead letter, and has only since been remembered by *Punch's* felicitous cartoon of "The naughty little boy who chalked up 'No Popery!' and then ran away." After the disestablishment of the Irish Church, at a time when a new bishop was chosen, it was found necessary hastily to repeal the Act, Episcopal titles outside the Establishment being then nominally illegal.

The Religious Census of 1851 stands out as one of the landmarks in the ecclesiastical history of England and Wales. No such information on so complete a scale had been previously supplied. In the preface to the official report —long since, we believe, out of print—the confident hope is expressed that "at each decennial period the returns on 'religious worship' will form a valuable part of the Census, and serve as a powerful aid to the highest interests of the community"—a sanguine anticipation, not destined, it appears, to be realised. But that Census has become a "great fact" in the country's annals, and although passing into the realm of tradition, the influence of its revelations is more or less abiding. More especially was the inquiry remarkable for the justice done to religious bodies outside the pale of the Establishment. For the first time, perhaps, in the annals of England, Dissenters were dealt with in a State paper in accordance with their actual professions and deeds. The introduction of public worship as a feature of the Census was due to the

* One of the immediate effects of the measure was the withdrawal of Archdeacon Manning and other clergymen to the Church of Rome, on which Lord Shaftesbury writes in his diary ("Life and Work of the Earl of Shaftesbury," Cassells), "Lord, purge the Church of these men, who, while their hearts are in the Vatican, still eat the bread of the Establishment, and undermine her."

initiative of Major Graham, who held the position of Registrar-General at that period, and who, during his long official career, effected many statistical reforms, for which he deserves to be held in grateful remembrance by his countrymen in general, and by the Free Churches in particular. It was he who persuaded Lord Palmerston, then Home Secretary, to assent to the information being obtained, and to Mr. Horace Mann, who was employed in the Registrar-General's office, was assigned the onerous task of arranging the returns in a tabular form, accompanied by "explanatory remarks." The statistics were obtained under the auspices of a staff of nearly 40,000 enumerators; and although it was optional for the clergymen, ministers, wardens, or deacons to supply the information in the tabular forms sent to them, their co-operation was general and cordial; so that the necessity to make good defective returns was very limited. Thus, "for the first time," to quote the Report, "there was given to the country a full picture of the state of its religion as exhibited by its religious institutions."

The "explanatory remarks" referred to were in fact a luminous, masterly, and impartial survey of the entire mass of information that came into the hands of Mr. Mann; prefaced by an admirable "Introductory Sketch of the Progress of Religious Opinions in England till the Period of the Revolution of 1688," a record the main points of which are embodied in the foregoing pages of this volume. The returns were obtained from 14,077 churches belonging to the Established Church, and 20,399 places of worship belonging to all other religious bodies. There were in 1851 thirty-five different religious communities or sects in England and Wales; twenty-seven native and indigenous, and nine foreign. Substantially, however, they could be reduced to twelve—viz., the Church of England—*primus* *inter pares*—Presbyterians (with three varieties), Independents or Congregationalists, Baptists (five varieties), the Society of Friends, Unitarians, Moravians, Methodists (seven varieties), Calvinistic Methodists, New Church, or Swedenborgians, Brethren, and Roman Catholics. The rest were, and continue to be, insignificant in numbers and influence.* In the aggregate, both as respects the number of churches and attendants they are an insignificant proportion of the whole, and may for statistical purposes be combined under the designation, "all others."

Before proceeding to refer to the returns in a denominational sense, it may be desirable to speak of the general results; premising that the accommodation in such place of worship was given by the responsible officials, and that the attendance—morning, afternoon, and evening—on Census Sunday was taken by the Government enumerators.

Accommodation in England and Wales.

	Buildings.	Sittings.
Church of England	14,077	5,317,915
All other denominations . . .	20,399†	4,894,648

Attendance at Public Worship.

	Morning.	Afternoon.	Evening.
Church of England .	2,541,244	1,890,764	860,543
All other denominations	2,106,238	1,293,371	2,203,906
	4,647,482	3,184,135	3,064,449

* The old sarcasm of Voltaire that the English had a hundred religions and only one sauce is therefore no more than a striking epigram, though such a taunt often passes muster for argument with opponents of the Free Churches.

† It is to borne in mind that only a proportion of these were permanent places of worship; a great many being of a temporary and fragile character.

By assuming that of the afternoon attendants one-half, and of the evening attendants one-third, had not been at the morning service, Mr. Mann obtains a total of

Worshippers in the Church of England . .	3,773,474
Worshippers of other denominations . .	3,487,558

Or in the proportion of fifty-two Churchmen to forty-eight Nonconformists and others.*

The number and variety of tables compiled by Mr. Mann from the material placed before him, each subserving a specific purpose, were sufficient to satisfy any amount of statistical craving, and were extremely suggestive. Most of them were utilised generally or locally after the issue of the Census of Public Worship, and are to a large extent, after the lapse of forty years, out of date. They showed, for instance, that in the manufacturing districts the Nonconformists were everywhere in a majority, and that in Wales nine-tenths of the people attended Dissenting places of worship. The

* This nearness of equality will not appear so surprising if th relative position of Church and Dissent from 1801 to 1851 is compared. The facts are as follows:—

England and Wales.

		Church of England.	Other Denominations.
Sittings	1801 . .	4,069,281	963,169
Increase to	1831 . .	412,610	1,953,135
,,	1851 . .	836,024	1,969,178

The actual increase in Church of England sittings between 1801 and 1851 was at the rate of 30·6 per cent. In the case of all the other religious bodies it was much larger. We quote these figures from "Voluntaryism in England and Wales," 1854 (Simpkin, Marshall, & Co.), but a little investigation will indicate that they can only be approximately correct. It may, perhaps, be accepted that during the first of these decades, as well as in the second, there was a remarkable development of Dissent as indicated by church building, and that between 1831 and 1851 the Established Church doubled its efforts in that direction.

following table, somewhat enlarged in scope, may, however, have some historical value :—

Proportion of Accommodation provided by fifteen Religious Bodies.

	Sittings.	Proportion to whole.	Most numerously attended service.	Proportion per cent. of Attendants to Sittings.
Church of England .	5,317,915	52·1	2,541,244	33
Presbyterian . .	86,692	·8	47,582	30
Independents . .	1,067,760	10·5	524,612	38
Baptists . . .	752,343	7·3	365,946	39
Friends . . .	91,599	·9	14,364	8
Unitarians . .	68,554	·7	28,483	24
Wesleyans . .	1,447,580	14·1	667,850	35
New Connexion .	96,964	1·0	39,624	34
Primitives . .	414,030	4·0	100,125	41
Bible Christians .	66,834	·7	34,612	37
Methodist Assoctn..	98,813	1·0	40,655	32
Reformers . .	67,814	·7	44,953	45
Calvinistic Mthdsts..	211,951	2·1	125,244	41
Lady Huntingdon's.	38,727	·4	21,103	38
Roman Catholics .	186,111	1·8	252,783	—

This last column is taken from one of Mr. Mann's tables, from which it appears that in the proportion of attendants to sittings in 1851, the Established Church stood tenth on the list. The attendance at Roman Catholic chapels actually exceeds the sittings, which is accounted for by the fact that in such places there are several congregations during Sunday forenoon.

The publication of the Religious Worship tables, and especially of Mr. Mann's important Report, in the early part of 1854, gave rise to not a little indignation and controversy on the part of zealous adherents of the Established Church. They could not brook that the "National" Church should be put on the same footing as the "sects," and it was painfully characteristic of their animus that they made far more of the enormous growth of Nonconformity and its successful efforts in—to put it mildly—supplementing the work of the Church of England, than of the revelation of the fact that the mass of the population never attended public worship. They accused Dissenters of having packed their chapels on the Census Sunday, and of having overrated their sitting accommodation. Dr. Wilberforce, Bishop of Oxford, was foremost in the vehemence and offensiveness of his criticism from the Episcopal Bench of the Upper House; although Lord Palmerston was able, in "another place," to give the assurance that he had "no doubt as to the accuracy of the returns with regard to all the facts to which they refer," and that such inaccuracies as there were "could have no sensible effect upon the general results arrived at." *

One of the chief deductions of Mr. Mann from the statistics marshalled by him was the fact that, in spite of the great increase of places of worship on all sides, the available accommodation provided was quite inadequate to the needs of 58 per cent. of the population—the estimated number who ought to attend public worship.† Of still graver import was his conclusion that, on the Census Sunday, 5,288,294 persons, able to attend religious worship once at least, neglected altogether to do so. ‡ In reference

* Reply to Mr. Apsley Pellatt, July 20th, 1854.

† The actual provision in 1851 was for 46 per cent., less than one-half of this being customarily used. The deficiency of accommodation was found to be greatest in the large and densely-peopled towns. It appears from Mr. Mann's Report (p. 62) that in the urban parishes the proportion of sittings to the population was only 46 per cent., while in rural parishes the rate was 66·5 per cent., "with sometimes superabundant provision."

‡ Mr. Mann is careful to observe that all these must not be regarded as habitual neglectors of public religious services, because they are not always composed of the same persons.

to this serious fact, Mr. Mann remarks: "That neglect like this, spite of opportunities of worship, indicates the insufficiency of any more addition to the number of religious *buildings;* that the greatest difficulty is to fill the churches when provided; and that this can only be accomplished by a great addition to the number of efficient, earnest religious *teachers*, clerical and lay, by whose persuasions the reluctant population might be won."

In what respects the author of this suggestive Report thought that this great work might, to a considerable extent, be accomplished, is not obscurely indicated, and it is remarkable that not a few of his suggestions had been more or less carried out, as in the operations of city missions, ragged schools, and other unsectarian agencies, and that, for the most part, they are as applicable now as they were some forty years ago. Amongst the causes of non-attendance of the working classes at Divine worship, and of the ill-success of the Christian Church, he mentions their dislike to social distinctions, the indifference of the churches to the social condition of the poor, their misconception of the motives of ministers, poverty and crowded dwellings, a genuine repugnance to religion itself, and the parochial system. Some of the remedies propounded are the sub-division of parishes, a greater use of lay agency, the increase of undenominational evangelical societies, the extension of Sunday-schools, and an increase of the Episcopate by the revival of suffragan bishops.*

Roughly stated, these census returns suggested that, from an ecclesiastical point of view, the nation might be divided into three not very unequal classes—Churchmen, Dissenters,

* Report, pp. 91—102.

and Absenters.* While the strength of the religious bodies outside the Establishment created general surprise, the fact that more than five million persons in England and Wales held aloof from places of worship excited serious concern, especially among Nonconformists. It was the frequent theme of pulpit discourses and addresses at Union assemblies and religious meetings, and not a few Dissenting churches increased their agencies already in action for reaching the masses of the population, or started new ones. Amongst those who were specially impressed with the census returns was Mr. Samuel Morley, who called a conference of leading ministers and laymen, upon whom he urged the necessity of awakening every church to a proper sense of its duty by holding itself responsible for the evangelisation of the people round about, and of all within reach of its influence. "This view prevailed," wrote the Rev. J. H. Wilson † at the time, "district conferences in London were called, most of which he attended; and, being held under the auspices of the Christian Instruction

* In illustration of the perversity or prejudice that sometimes obtains in these matters, it may be mentioned that, later on, when the present writer was engaged in an amicable controversy as to the relative position of Church and Dissent with Mr. J. G. Hubbard, M.P. (afterwards Lord Addington), the hon. member claimed that a large portion of the absenters belonged to the Established Church, and were not to be reckoned as Dissenters. No doubt some would come under that category, and would write themselves down Churchmen if there were to be a census of religious opinions. They are Churchmen in the sense of Lord Eldon, who boasted that he was an outside buttress of the Establishment.

† Mr. (now Dr.) Wilson was shortly afterwards appointed Secretary of the Home Missionary Society (Congregational), of which Mr. Morley was treasurer, and was for many years associated with that gentleman in his frequent evangelistic visits throughout England and Wales, working in conjunction with the several county associations.

Society, Baptists and Independents were conjoined in the work. This may be said to be the beginning of a new era in the history of home evangelisation, the outcome of which is seen in the aggressive work of every denomination in London." *

What could the Church of England do in this grave emergency? The lack of flexibility in its machinery was specially manifest in connection with the revelations of the Census, and the parochial system did not admit of any minister intruding into the ecclesiastical domain of a clerical brother. Aggressive work, such as Dissenters were more and more engaged in, was all but impossible.† Bishop Blomfield, however, did what he could by starting a fund, the object of which was to raise half-a-million in ten years, to promote the formation of one hundred new ecclesiastical districts, towards which the great landowners of the metropolis handsomely contributed; but it was not largely taken up. Lord Shaftesbury and his Evangelical friends were, however, thinking of less costly and dilatory measures. A Bill was brought into the House of Commons, where it passed without opposition, repealing the Conventicle Act of George III.—well-nigh obsolete—forbidding under heavy penalties the meeting for worship of congregations of more than twenty persons (apart from households) except in registered buildings. In the Lords the measure was taken in charge by the Earl of Shaftesbury, but was opposed by

* "Life of Mr. Samuel Morley, M.P." By Edwin Hodder. Fifth Edition. 1889. (Hodder & Stoughton.)

† Just about this time Dr. McNeile had been prevented preaching on the flagstones in front of the Liverpool Exchange, by a hint from the Rev. Rector Campbell that the said flagstones were in his parish, and an intimation that if he (Dr. McNeile) wished to extend his usefulness, several churches were at his disposal. Liverpool had then no bishop of its own.

the Episcopal Bench, on the ground—as stated by Bishop Wilberforce—that it "would interfere with the parochial divisions of the Church of England, upon which, after all, they must depend for evangelising the people"—he having heard of a proposal to form a Free Church. The Bill was referred to a select committee, on which Lord Shaftesbury refused to serve, and his lordship would have nothing to say to the new measure, fathered by Lord Derby, which proposed to remove the prohibition only by the authority of the incumbent, his representative, or the bishop. It was thought that a serious storm would arise, especially as the "good earl" stoutly protested, demanding entire freedom for Churchmen and Dissenters. But this Bill was withdrawn, though patronised by the Bishop of London, and Lord Shaftesbury revived his own measure, accepting a compromise. The restriction was retained, but it was graciously allowed that congregations might meet in dwelling-houses, the incumbent or his deputy presiding, and "occasionally" in buildings not usually appropriated to religious worship. Curiously enough, Dissenters were ignored by this Bill, and it seems that both Archbishop Whately—though so liberal a man—and the Bishop of London objected to the City Mission and other town missions, because their agents did not act in subordination to incumbents, the State-appointed ecclesiastical functionaries.

Ere long it appeared that Lord Shaftesbury and his Low Church coadjutors could be foiled with unexpected ease. In the summer of 1857 it was decided by them, with the sanction of the Bishop (Dr. Tait, who had lately been appointed), and of the incumbent of the parish, to institute evangelistic services in Exeter Hall, on Sunday evenings, and the clergy who took part in them, including Bishop Villiers, Canons Miller, Cadman, and other Evangelicals, dispensed with the Prayer Book—the Litany only being used—in order to preach the simple Gospel to the thousands who crowded that spacious building on twelve successive Sunday evenings; the working classes who "were not habitual church or chapel goers" being specially invited. There were no reserved seats and no collections, and says Lord Shaftesbury, in his diary,* "Many have been the proofs that we have had of happy fruits; of persons attending who never in their lives before had been in any place of public worship." As the summer advanced, the services were discontinued, and were to be resumed in October. But the Committee had neglected to ask permission afresh from the incumbent of the parish, the Strand district, who—prompted, no doubt, by others—issued an inhibition, and declined to withdraw it. Lord Shaftesbury, doubting the legality of his action, was for going on, but he was overruled. The freer Nonconformists promptly and fraternally stepped forward to continue the services, and his lordship, echoing the sentiments of the committee, lauded "the delicacy and forbearance" of these ministers, who included the Revs. Dr. Stoughton, Dr. Allon, Dr. Brock, and Dr. Landels—especially their desire that there should be nothing to suggest a contrast with the preceding services.†

Lord Shaftesbury never neglected a remedy if he could find one. He promptly gave notice of a Bill to amend the Act of 1855, with the general approval of men of varying views in the Establishment, except the High Church party. The measure proposed that the power of inhibition should not be operative in parishes with a population of over 2,000, and that it should not be valid unless sanctioned by the bishop of the diocese. Having been present at some of the

* "Life of Lord Shaftesbury," p. 542.
† Speech in the House of Lords, December 8, 1857.

services conducted by Nonconformists, Lord Shaftesbury said with pathetic candour:—"I confess I was almost overwhelmed with shame to think that the Church of England alone, which is constituted the Church of the Realm, and to which such a duty is peculiarly assigned, should be the only body among believers or unbelievers which is not allowed to open a hall with the view of giving instruction to the people." His lordship stood his ground till he discovered that the clergy, "with few exceptions, were either openly or secretly against him,"* and that twenty-four bishops were hostile; † and then he withdrew his measure in favour of the Bill for legalising special services in unconsecrated buildings in connection with the Church of England, introduced by Archbishop Sumner. This measure, which emphasised the sanction of the bishop of the diocese, was passed. Subsequently halls and theatres in London and elsewhere were used on Sundays for this purpose, Churchmen and Dissenters mostly, though not always, co-operating.‡ Though these services have somewhat lost their novelty, they are continued to the present day.

As stated in a preceding chapter, the various organisations

---

* Life, p. 344.

† If the bishop-maker were dethroned by the fall of Pam, our white elephants might become manageable.—"Life of Bishop Wilberforce," Vol. II., p. 376.

‡ There were seven such theatres thus utilised in 1860, at which Lord Shaftesbury more or less "assisted"—that is, read the lessons; the Victoria Theatre being his favourite. The same year he had to defend them in the House of Lords in a speech of more than two hours' duration, in the course of which he quoted overwhelming evidence to show the good that was effected by these agencies. Lord Shaftesbury, though not a Nonconformist, was far nearer to Dissenters in his mode of carrying out his religious enterprises than to the High Anglicans.

for asserting and defending the rights of Dissenters, all of which had more or less done a specific work, disappeared one by one, except that of the British Anti-State Church Association, formed in 1844, and destined to last, not less because it was based upon an elementary principle which was founded on Christianity itself, and appealed to the sense of justice, than because it was the offspring of popular representation; its life being, as it were, renewed every three years by an appeal to its constituents throughout the country. Although from the outset the constitution of the association was broad enough to embrace, without restriction, all who desired to see the separation of Church and State, it was—and still is—substantially a Nonconformist movement. It is essential, therefore, that the Society's operations, conflicts, and successes should receive prominent notice in these pages, there being no other permanent institution of a strictly ecclesiastical character which obtains the support of members of *all* sections of Dissenters. Its history as a modern propagandist organisation is absolutely unique. The Anti-Corn Law League surpassed it in the extent of its influence, the intensity of its agitation, and its hold on public opinion; but, happily, the League was short-lived, having been disbanded when its chief end was attained. The primary object of the Liberation Society* has yet to be realised; but, short of that, it has carried, or materially assisted to carry, nearly all the outworks of the citadel of ecclesiastical monopoly. This

* In 1853 the name of the British Anti-State Church Association was changed for "The Society for the Liberation of Religion from State Patronage and Control," and subsequently was simply known as "The Liberation Society." The earlier title was abandoned because of its alleged pugnacious character.

ecclesiastical struggle entailed from thirty to forty years of agitation, during which period the British people were being indoctrinated in the true principles of religious freedom and equality.

The Liberation movement was, as we have said, greatly strengthened by the holding of triennial conferences in London, which renewed its life and brought in fresh recruits. The first of these took place at the Crosby Hall, in May, 1847, when the Committee were able to report active operations in the provinces and the distribution of some 160,000 tracts bearing on the relations of Church and State. This was followed by a change in the executive of the Society; Dr. Cox, Mr. Miall, and Mr. J. M. Hare, who had acted as honorary secretaries since its formation, having retired, and Mr. J. Carvell Williams being appointed sole secretary, a position for which some previous experience, as well as devotion to the cause of religious equality, well fitted him. In that capacity Mr. Williams has been able to render to the Society and its objects unexampled service during the lengthened period of forty-four years, and amidst all the difficulties and vicissitudes of the movement his faculty of initiation, fertility of resource, thorough reliableness, indomitable resolution, and facile pen and voice have throughout been simply invaluable.*

* In 1854 a Parliamentary Committee was formed, of which Dr. Foster, Professor of Jurisprudence in London University, was appointed Chairman. In that capacity he was able to give much assistance to the Society, till his retirement in 1863, when he left England. The Rev. E. S. Pryce was also for some time, till 1859, Electoral Secretary, and these offices were subsequently amalgamated, their duties being discharged by Mr. Williams, who, in 1877, resigned the Secretaryship, after thirty years' service, and was appointed Chairman of the Society's Parliamentary Committee and Deputy-Chairman of the General Committee.

Prior to the meeting of the Second Triennial Conference in 1850, the *British Banner* announced, in a characteristic and prolix manifesto, that its editor, Dr. Campbell, had retired from the committee of the Society, of which he had only been a nominal member, on the ground that a "school of anarchy" was being formed, that its leaders were using the Society for the promotion of their own objects, and that if the principles they advocated should prevail, they would "for a season" expose "true religion to the peril of extinction."* The Conference was probably all the better attended, and its proceedings were more lively in consequence of this groundless attack. But the Society had to deplore the retirement, owing to declining health, of Dr. Thomas Price, who had rendered conspicuous service as treasurer, an office undertaken by Mr. William Edwards, who, for more than twenty years, devoted himself with rare fidelity to the work of the Association.

Space will not allow of any but the most cursory reference to the succeeding conferences held during this decade. In 1853, when the attendance and enthusiasm were greater than ever, the Executive Committee had to congratulate their constituency on the return of forty Protestant Dissenters to the House of Commons; on the adoption of a Bill authorising the secularisation of the Canadian Clergy Reserves; on the cessation of ecclesiastical grants in one of the Australian colonies; and on the final decision of the

* The primary cause of this defection was the publication of a series of lectures delivered by Mr. Miall on "The British Churches in Relation to the British People," in which the failure of "organised Christianity"—established and non-established—to meet the needs of the great masses of the population was elaborately described, the social and political hindrances to the success of the churches candidly set forth, and a variety of remedial suggestions were made, many of which were subsequently adopted by a number of the Free Churches.

House of Lords in the Braintree case, invalidating church rates made by a minority.* Among those who were elected at the general election of 1852 was Mr. Edward Miall, who had been recommended to Rochdale by his friend, Mr. John Bright, and proved to be so acceptable to the Liberal party that he secured a majority of 154 out of the 904 electors who voted. Not being "obliged to give a holiday to his discretion," he for some time silently studied the habitudes of the House of Commons, though always voting for his principles, and was not sorry somewhat to relax the frequent platform work which had greatly taxed his strength. Mr. Miall soon discovered that in the House of Commons, in respect to Nonconformists, "the sneer of contempt had been changed for the silence of respect," though he forbore to lay any claim to be the spokesman of Dissenters as such. "I stand here," he said, in a debate on the improvement of Church property, "as one of the nation, and in the eye of the law a member of the National Church. I may choose to forego the ministrations of that Church, but I do not, therefore, surrender my legal right in it. I claim the better distribution of its revenues, not for Dissenters, but for the nation at large. . . . That

* This signal success—the capture of the Malakoff of church rates—was mainly due to Mr. Samuel Courtauld, of Bocking, a leading Unitarian of the district, whose "wisdom, courage, and public spirit conducted the Braintree Church-rate contest through sixteen years of litigation from 1837 to 1852, and formally established the necessity of vote in vestry to legalise a rate, and the right of a majority to negative its imposition." This is part of the inscription on a handsome silver testimonial, valued at 700 guineas, presented to that gentleman in the autumn of 1855 at a public dinner in Braintree, over which Sir Wm. Clay presided. Mr. Courtauld was chairman of the Anti-Church Rate Committee of that town. When the protracted conflict was over, the parish church, which had been allowed to fall into decay, was renovated at a cost of £4,000, all raised by voluntary contributions!

property is national, and should be employed for national objects."

But Mr. Miall did not ignore Dissenting grievances in the House of Commons. He cordially co-operated with Mr. James Heywood in supporting a clause in the Oxford University Bill, abolishing oaths and declarations on matriculation, which was carried against the Government,* and, strange to say, accepted by the Lords. The session of 1854, notwithstanding the absorbing interest of the war with Russia, was prolific of discussions on ecclesiastical questions, and Mr. Miall was able to rejoice that Sir W. Clay's Bill for the abolition of church-rates was carried on the second reading, by a majority of twenty-eight in a House of 400 members—a fruitless victory as it turned out. The member for Rochdale had also the satisfaction of helping to defeat (200 to 102 votes) the resolutions of Lord John Russell—who seemed almost to revel in defeats on these questions—extending the Minutes of Council relative to education, which would have enabled the Charity Trusts Commission to apply their funds to the education of the middle and poorer classes, and also the quarter sessions to meet the deficiencies in school districts by the imposition of a school rate. Oddly enough, Sir James Graham and Mr. Gladstone were, on this occasion, his lordship's chief opponents. The latter showed his growing tendencies by the remark that if you wish to "raise men to the standard of Christian life, you must depend on the voluntary principle system, whose spring is found deep in the human heart, in the heart of Christian philanthropy, and you

* At this time the Coalition Government of Lord Aberdeen was in office, Lord Palmerston being Home Secretary and Mr. Gladstone Chancellor of the Exchequer.

cannot supply by legislation that which comes from a different source."

Within a few weeks Mr. Miall himself came to the front, by moving a resolution in favour of the disestablishment and disendowment of the Irish Church and the cessation of the *Regium Donum*, which he supported in a speech of two hours' duration. This was on the 27th of May, when the attendance was comparatively thin, owing to the peace celebrations on that day. Among the reasons for now taking action was the carrying a few weeks before of Mr. Spooner's resolution in favour of the repeal of the Maynooth College endowment. Mr. Miall was not satisfied with advancing general reasons in favour of his motion, but unfolded a scheme of disendowment—the first ever presented to the Legislature—which differs little from that brought forward and carried by Mr. Gladstone thirteen years later. But in 1856 the House of Commons was in no mood to grapple with so serious a problem, and after a perfunctory reply from Lord Palmerston, the resolution was rejected by 143 to 93 votes. This was the last considerable act or service in Parliament for some years to come of the member for Rochdale. In less than a year, at the general election precipitated by Lord Palmerston, in consequence of the hostile resolution of the House of Commons on the Chinese War, Mr. Miall, like Mr. Cobden, Mr. Bright, Mr. Milner Gibson, and other Radical members, lost his seat, and the champion of a "spirited foreign policy" triumphed all along the line. Mr. Miall was absent from Parliament till 1869, when he was returned for Bradford.

At the Liberation Conference in 1856, held in the London Tavern, Mr. S. Morley, who had for several years taken the keenest interest in the affairs of the Society, especially in its parliamentary and electoral action, presided. It was a thorough business assembly, and a considerable increase in the income of the Society was reported, as well as a great expansion of outdoor operations; while the accession of well-known M.P.'s, ministers, and laymen was very marked. There were congratulations on the further stoppage of ecclesiastical grants in several of the colonies, and on the starting of the *Liberator* as the monthly organ of the Society. But the most prominent topic was the proposed Government compromise on church rates, which will be noticed further on. The next—that is, the Fifth—Triennial Conference, in June, 1859, was a little delayed in consequence of the general election under Lord Derby and Mr. Disraeli, which gave some advantage to the Government, though it did not very decisively alter the state of parties. The friends of religious equality had not much reason to complain, their supporters in the House being more reliable, Mr. Frank (afterwards Sir Francis) Crossley, for example, having gained a brilliant victory in the West Riding. The hon. member was himself present at Freemasons' Hall, where the Conference was held; and on the platform with him were many fresh faces, such as Mr. Mellor, M.P.—who said that nothing could exceed the ability, intelligence, and skill with which the executive of the Society was doing its work—Mr. Adam Black, M.P., Mr. Whalley, M.P., Mr. Ayrton, M.P., Mr. Crum Ewing, M.P., Mr. Lindsay, M.P., Dr. Archer, Dr. Halley, Mr. Gilpin, M.P., and Mr. Remington Mills, Mr. James Spicer, Mr. Grimwade, and Sir Morton Peto, M.P., who had, some years before, rather drawn off from the Society, owing, as he said, to the lack of considerate treatment of some opponents. But Sir Morton now frankly admitted that the management of the Society had, for three or four years past, been admirable, and he thoroughly identified himself with it. The report, speaking of the past three years, noted that Ministers' Money had been abolished in

Ireland; Jews had been admitted to Parliament;* secular courts substituted for ecclesiastical courts in testamentary and matrimonial business; the Burial Laws materially modified; the Church-rate Abolition Bill passed through the Commons and sent up to the Lords; and an Endowed Schools Bill † had been brought in by Mr. Dillwyn, who said at one of the meetings that he was a Churchman, and did not regard the Society as a Nonconformist Society, but as a common centre to advance the principles of religious freedom. The supporters of the Establishment had by this time become seriously alarmed at the progress of the Society, and Church Defence Societies were springing up throughout the country.

The Church-rate struggle in and out of Parliament was one of the most remarkable and interesting political events of modern times. Its significance and curious vicissitudes have slipped from the public memory, and nothing like a continuous record of its incidents and fluctuations has appeared in print. We have seen how it was commenced in Parliament, in 1839, by Mr. D. Whittle Harvey and Mr.

* This question had been for many years before Parliament, the Commons voting for the admission of Jews, and the Lords opposing; while Mr. Salomons and Baron Rothschild had in vain attempted to take their seats as elected members. In July, 1858, Lord John Russell proposed a conference between the two Houses, and eventually a Bill passed through enabling each House to modify the form of oath. Shortly after Baron Rothschild took his seat for the City of London. Lord Shaftesbury yielded on this matter very reluctantly, for he held that the admission of Jews unchristianised the Legislature. But the Hebrew members did everything but vote, and his lordship says, "I yield to force, not reason."—"Life," p. 553.

† This measure arose out of the decision of the Court of Chancery in the Ilminster Grammar School case, excluding Dissenters from the governing body, though it was not an exclusively Episcopalian trust. Next year (1860) a Bill removing the disqualification of Dissenters was passed, and in 1869 further concessions were made.

Duncombe, whose proposals followed upon the Bill of Mr. Spring Rice to pay the tax out of the Church lands and pew rents—a proposal which, being supported by dwindling majorities, was dropped before it reached the Lords. Had it been carried, some thirty years of vigorous and extended agitation, most injurious to the Established Church, would have been saved.

The country itself supplied the steam that kept the anti-Church Rate machinery in accelerated motion. The Liberation Society, when it resolved to energetically take the question in hand, had only to give momentum to forces already in action, and the decision in the Braintree case checkmated the obstinate upholders of Church Rates. Year by year the number of recusant parishes increased, and hundreds of vestries were the scenes of excitement, and often of bitterness, while ever and anon illegal rates were passed or disputed, ratepayers hauled before the magistrates, and distraints effected. The indignation on one side encountered obstinacy on the other, and in many cases the clergy and their adherents fought with tenacity, not so much for the rate, as for supremacy; while the vestries became training schools of religious freedom. At a calm distance from these excitements it is now easy to see that the mass of Nonconformists, and of many more outside of them, learned from these object-lessons the injustice and intolerance of a State Church, and soon came to regard the Liberation Society as a protector. That organisation, moreover, pursued its course with untiring energy. It gave legal advice freely to the opponents of Church Rates, circulated leaflets with necessary information by hundreds of thousands, often undertook the defence of persecuted Dissenters before the magistrates, and made the question a prominent test question at the hustings and in the polling booth. Whilst Church Rates were being tenaciously defended to save the

Establishment, they were steadily vanishing, and the Established Church was being weakened. Whereas in 1827 that impost yielded £519,000, it had fallen in 1859 to £261,000—nearly one-half—and was no longer levied in any of the large, and in few of the second-rate, towns.*

In Parliament itself this wide-spread out-door agitation told with increasing effect as time went on. It was in 1853, when the impending war with Russia was overshadowing political life, that Sir William Clay, one of the members for the Tower Hamlets, introduced his Church Rate Abolition Bill; but it was rejected on the second reading by a majority of 48 in a House of 392 members. Next year the adverse majority was reduced to 27. In the succeeding four years the movement was so well managed that majorities were secured at this stage of the measure of 28, 48, 74, 63, and 74 respectively. The question had now reached the compromise stage. In 1856, Sir George Grey, the Home Secretary, after the second reading of Sir W. Clay's Bill, drafted some new clauses, suggested by the Primate, to the effect that persons declaring themselves in writing not members of the Church should be exempted from the rate; that rents on sittings should be legalised for church rate purposes; that rent-charges might be given; and that, with a view to carry out these objects, incumbent and churchwardens should be a corporation. The proposal was not then discussed at length, though the Committee of the Liberation Society carefully considered it. While expressing a decided preference for total abolition, they came to the conclusion that Sir G. Grey's plan would have the effect of abolishing the rate in a large number of

---

* During this portion of the abolitionist campaign important service was rendered by Dr. Foster, who, with legal knowledge and great acumen, systematised the Liberation Society's tactics in regard to proceedings in the vestries and before magistrates.

parishes, and enable others to get rid of them, while in those where it was still levied Dissenters would be exempted. They, therefore, approved of the amendments, reserving the right of proposing further measures to secure complete abolition. At the ensuing Triennial Conference of the Society this decision was endorsed by a large majority, though there was a considerable minority—a large section of the majority acquiescing in the amendments of the Government in the belief that they would destroy the nationality of the Church, and give the Society an effective leverage for prosecuting their ulterior aims. The Bill however, did not re-appear that session, Her Majesty Ministers were not eager for a settlement, and Sir G. Grey's clauses were not again heard of in Parliament. The golden opportunity was lost by the Government, total abolition resumed its sway, and new elements, including a general election, had to be dealt with. In 1858—the Conservatives being then in power—the Bill introduced by Sir John Trelawny, who took it in hand in place of Sir W. Clay, was pushed through the Commons, in spite of the opposition of the leaders of *both* parties, and was sent up for the first time to the Lords, where the Duke of Somerset moved the second reading, and was flanked by a host of petitions.* The Bill did not meet with much support during the debate—Earl Granville being its most conspicuous advocate—but the general tone of the discussion was in favour of compromise; even Lord Derby, who had assented to the Jews Bill only the night before, acquiescing in the exemption of Dissenters on their foregoing any claim to the services of the Established Church. Sixty-two peers voted in favour of the Bill and 213 against, the majority includ-

* 1,800 petitions adverse to Church Rates were presented on this occasion.

ing the Earl of Shaftesbury and nearly all the bishops—"Palmerstonian" and otherwise—whilst amongst its supporters were the Dukes of Bedford and Argyll, and Lords Ebury, Wodehouse, Macaulay, and Fitzwilliam.

The tenour of the debate in the Upper House encouraged Mr. Walpole, who succeeded Sir G. Grey as Home Secretary, to try his hand at a settlement, which was, he said, "a message of peace." In 1859, he brought in a Bill "ticketing" Dissenters by exempting them from the rate, and enabling landowners to charge their lands, in perpetuity, with the average amount charged during a given period, but he was beaten by 84 in a House of 464 members. Although he distinctly declared that the question at issue was compromise or abolition,* no serious attempt was subsequently made by the ministers of the Crown to present a "compromise" scheme to Parliament during the decade under review.

After the general election of 1859 the tide began to turn. This change was due not so much to the decrease of Liberal members as to the attitude taken by Mr. Disraeli, the increasing activity of the Committee of Laymen and other Church Defence societies, and the adroit use made by the champions of the Establishment of the evidence given before the Lords' Select Committee on Church Rates, of which the Duke of Marlborough was chairman. That committee, without making a report, hurriedly published the evidence it had received, and so enabled Church

* On this occasion, Lord John Russell criticised the scheme as subversive of the principle of a National Church; for the Church of England, he said, would then become simply the strongest sect of the community. It was only six days after this defeat of Mr. Walpole that Sir John Trelawny's Bill was carried by a majority of 74 votes (244 to 170). The ensuing general election prevented further progress with the measure.

defenders to make known the "ulterior objects" of the opponents of Church Rates, as though they had not been proclaimed from the house-top since 1844, when the British Anti-State Church Association was established. "Nothing," remarked the *Daily News*, in reference to this Committee, "was more obvious than the expedient of calling the principal members of the Liberation Society before a Parliamentary Committee, asking them questions to which they were sure to give plain answers, and then proclaim that, by the confession of the leaders of the movement, the demand for the abolition of Church Rates was no less than a demand for the separation of Church and State. This was the device adopted. Mr. Morley and Dr. Foster were examined and cross-examined before the Lords' Committee by the Bishops; their answers, carefully noted down in the Blue Book, were despatched to every country rectory, and many worthy persons doubtless believed that a grand conspiracy had been unmasked. A temporary success has crowned this manœuvre." This remark refers to the reduction of the majority on the Church Rate Abolition Bill to only twenty-nine.* It was the largest division ever taken on the subject, and there were as many in favour of abolition (265) as had ever supported it. Later on in the year (May) there was, on the third reading, a majority of only nine in a smaller House (461 members), sixty members who had previously supported the Bill being absent. The measure fared better when it went to the Upper House—Lord Lyveden introducing it. The total number of peers in its favour was sixty-seven, including pairs—an increase of five on the vote of 1858; its opponents being 164. There was still talk of

* On the occasion 5,000 petitions, with 600,699 signatures, were presented in support of Sir John Trelawny's Bill.

compromise—the Primate being willing to give up taxing Dissenters; but who could then have thought that the struggle was yet to be prolonged for eight years before compulsory Church Rates were abolished, or that Mr. Gladstone, who still persistently went against abolition, would have given the impost its *coup de grâce?*

The growing necessity of union among Nonconformists, and of a common centre for social intercourse, led to the formation of the Milton Hall and Club, for which premises were secured on Ludgate Hill at a cost of £40,000, of which £10,000 was on mortgage to the vendors. It appears that 600 debentures were required, of which the greater part were taken up in the large towns by Congregationalists, Baptists, Friends, Wesleyans, and Presbyterians; but the Nonconformists of London were—as in respect to many other public objects—much behindhand in supporting the scheme. The Club, comfortably furnished, was opened in the autumn of 1855, and amongst its prominent supporters were Mr. S. Morley, Sir Thomas Chambers, Mr. Miall, Dr. Foster, Mr. H. Bateman (who was its chief promoter, and was specially active in securing debenture holders), Mr. J. M. Hare, and the Revs. T. Binney, Dr. Campbell, and C. Stovel. Its secretary was Mr. John Bennett, who, as a lawyer, for some time took an active part in Church Rate contests. At the outset there was considerable difference as to the adoption of an evangelical test of membership, against which Mr. Miall and others strongly protested, but without success. The Club remained in existence for several years, and meetings of the Liberation Society, the Congregational Union, and other Dissenting organisations were from time to time held there. The share subscription did not suffice for the erection of a Hall, which would have cost £10,000. If this part of the scheme had been carried out, it would probably have prolonged the existence of the Club, which was, after some years, closed owing to inadequate support.

About the middle of this decade an event occurred which, though hardly remembered by any but contemporaries, led to no little controversy in the religious world. The Rev. T. T. Lynch, a thoughtful, godly, and very retiring Independent minister, had gathered a select congregation in Mortimer Street, London—removing afterwards to Grafton Street—by whom his services were highly appreciated. During a period of domestic affliction—and he was a frail man, who never enjoyed robust health—Mr. Lynch composed a number of hymns, which he published at the close of 1855 under the title of "Hymns for Heart and Voice. The Rivulet." They were favourably noticed in the *Eclectic Review*, which greatly provoked the ire of Mr. James Grant, editor of the *Morning Advertiser*, the organ of the licensed victuallers, who denounced the book as containing "not one particle of vital religion or evangelical piety," nearly the whole of which "might have been written by a Deist, and a very large portion [of the hymns] might be sung by a congregation of Freethinkers," &c. He required the editor of the *Eclectic* to repudiate all sympathy with the reviewer, to which that gentleman responded by expressing his disgust at the reckless injustice with which Mr. Lynch had been treated. As Mr. Grant continued his reckless attacks, fifteen London ministers issued a protest, declaring their utter hatred of that writer's mode of dealing with the book, and their love and reverence for the author. The names of the protestors were the Revs. Messrs. Allon, Binney, Baldwin Brown, Fleming, Newman Hall, J. C. Harrison, Jukes, Kent, S. Martin, Newth, Nunn, Smith, Spence, Vaughan, and E. White—the very cream of the Congregational ministry in London—who said, "If this is suffered to pass current as a specimen of Christian reviewing, then Christian reviewing will become an offence to all good men." This protest added fuel to the fire. The "Rivulet Controversy" assumed larger dimensions. Soon the *British Banner* entered the lists, and the two self-elected champions of orthodoxy were irreverently likened to Gog and Magog. After telling all the world how forbearing he had hitherto been, Dr. Campbell—"set for the defence of the truth," as he said, and asserting, with ludicrous exaggeration, that "nothing like it had occurred within the memory of the present generation, or, perhaps, since the days of the Reformation"—published a series of letters on "Nonconformist Theology," addressed, in his customary style, to the "Principals and Professors of the Independent and Baptist Colleges of England," in which he maintained that "The Rivulet" was "incomparably the most unspiritual publication of the kind in the English language"—with a great deal more to the same effect in seven voluminous letters. Other papers took up the cry, such as the *Record** (Low Church) and the *Watchman* (Wesleyan); while the *Patriot* (though owned by the same proprietary as the *Banner*), the *Nonconformist*, the *Freeman*, and the *Wesleyan Times* were adverse to Dr. Campbell. Even the good, but narrow, Earl of Shaftesbury deplored "the horrid epidemic which had seized upon some of the brightest Nonconformist divines"—words which Mr. Grant did not fail to parade in the seventh edition of his pamphlet; and Mr. Spurgeon, though then new to ministerial life in London, partially condemned Mr. Lynch; though, with characteristic candour, he confessed that he could "scarce see

* The *Record* spoke of the theology of "The Rivulet" as "better suited to the Ojibbeway Indians, who worship the Great Spirit, than to those who believe in the living truth of the Gospel covenant."

into the depths where lurked the essence of the matter."*

The "Rivulet Controversy" was still a burning question when the Congregational Union met in the spring of 1856, on which occasion the Rev. J. Baldwin Brown, amid general applause, protested against Dr. Campbell's shameful and cruel treatment of Mr. Lynch. At a subsequent private conference, Mr. Binney strongly urged that the contemplated issue of the *Banner* articles as a pamphlet should be abandoned, on the ground that nothing but evil could be expected to result from the continuance of the controversy, "in which he thought there had been errors on all sides." The response to this conciliatory suggestion was unanimous, and Dr. Campbell promised that the publication should be suppressed. Nevertheless, within a fortnight, the pamphlet appeared, ostensibly without the author's sanction. Mr. Binney published a remonstrance on the subject,† to which Dr. Campbell responded in a series of nine letters on "Negative Theology," in which he maintained, contrary to his previous explicit statements, that heterodox theological views were widely prevalent amongst Congregationalists, both ministers and laymen.

---

* The only shadow of an excuse for the fury of Mr. Lynch's assailants—if excuse there could be—was that they judged the man by his book, which they wrongly interpreted; while his friends judged the book from the man. Amongst the latter was the Rev. Edward White, who, writing after the death of his friend, speaks of the monthly devotional meetings at each other's houses of North London ministers, where the author of "The Rivulet" used to be present. "It was there that we came to understand how 'mighty in the Scripture was this self-taught—or, rather, heaven-taught—student of truth; and there, best of all, that we learned, from the outpouring of his soul in his addresses to God, the depths from which his wisdom sprang."

† The whole subject was dealt with in a published letter from Mr. Binney to the members of the Union. (Ward & Co. 1856.)

The controversy went on with increasing animosity during the autumn of 1856. On the one side, Mr. Grant and Dr. Campbell maintained these charges with increasing vehemence and wearisome iteration; while an influential layman, Mr. Thomas Thompson, of Bath, treasurer of the Home Missionary Society, actually sent a warning to Mr. Binney and his friends that they would not be received if they came to the West of England as a deputation on behalf of missions. On the other side Mr. White and Mr. Newman Hall manfully stood to their guns, and a considerable fund was subscribed to circulate "The Ethics of Quotation," a pamphlet which proved to demonstration that the charges against Mr. Lynch were to a large extent founded on garbled and twisted extracts.* Thus matters went on till the special meeting of the Congregational Union in January, 1857, at which Dr. Stoughton presided. There were two days of heated discussion, during which Mr. Binney proposed that the "men, brethren, and fathers" whom Dr. Campbell had addressed should have a separate meeting to talk over the matter face to face with that minister and editor. Of course, nothing was done in this direction. Though it was agreed that the relations of Dr. Campbell to the magazine should be dealt with by a large committee, there were some strong expressions of feeling.† Several speakers denounced the scandal that had arisen, Mr. Morley expressing his loathing of what had been going on amongst them, and contending that it ought to be put on record that gross calumnies had been uttered which were not

---

* The disgust felt on the subject may be judged by the fact that Mr. Mudie, the Librarian, who very rarely occupied a public position, could not refuse to act as treasurer to this fund.

† It is only fair to say that neither the *Christian Witness*, nor the *Christian's Penny Magazine*, both of which were originated, as well as edited by Dr. Campbell, ever contained a word on the "Rivulet."

believed. Eventually, a mild resolution was adopted to the effect that the charges of unfaithfulness made against the body of Congregational ministers were "unfounded and unjust," and that religious differences should be dealt with in a Christian spirit. At the regular meeting of the Union in May, an unsuccessful attempt was made to erase Dr. Campbell's name from the list of the committee, and a proposal to remove him from the editorship of the magazines did not find a seconder. But these publications were, in accordance with the advice of the Special Committee, transferred from the Union to a body of forty-eight trustees, half of them laymen. It may be as well to add here that for many years Mr. Lynch survived the virulent attacks made upon him, and that before long, Dr. Campbell, owing to strained relations with the proprietors, found it necessary to resign the editorship of the *British Banner*, and start an independent paper of his own—the *British Standard*, of which he remained editor till the close of 1866.

'The outrage on Mr. Lynch," says the writer of his biography,* "rendered similar outrages from henceforth impossible. His suffering was the means of widely enlarging the spiritual liberty of the Nonconformist ministry." The following remarks on the same subject in the *Nonconformist*, elicited when the excitement on the subject had, to a large extent subsided, are not without relevance to the present times, though there has in general been a vast improvement in the toleration of theological differences:—

"We call upon all good men to unite with us in discouraging those noisy, overbearing, vituperative practices which have so fatal a tendency to paralyse sensitive spirits and confuse tender consciences, unfitting them thereby to

* Memoirs of Thomas T. Lynch. Edited by Wm. White. (Isbister & Co. 1874.)

catch with distinctness the 'still small voice' for which they would fain listen. In presence of such majesty and such mystery, it is a desecration to be obliged to hear the proposition of schools, whether old or new, vociferated with rude energy, and enforced upon belief by an unfeeling denunciation of awful penalties. So have we been pestered sometimes while standing beneath the roof of some ancient and magnificent temple, and wishing to give way to the sentiments of veneration which its associations have awakened in our bosom, by the vulgar bawling of a guide or verger whom nothing could persuade to quit our side. . . . Oh, it is a pitiable case thus to have living thoughts thrust away by dead formulas, and be compelled to swallow, whether you will or no, crude and hard theories which your soul refuses to digest. We enter our protest against this intrusion upon individualism and liberty. We do not believe in its necessity. We feel no respect for its results. It has made us and kept us children, apt to be scared by every unaccustomed appearance as if it were a spectre. The time is ripe, we think, for a better order of things. . . . These social visitations of the right of private judgment are brought chiefly to bear against the thoughtful and ingenuous, for there is little fear of heterodoxy in the unthinking, and little likelihood of its being professed by the calculating, we mean as a change from orthodoxy; it is this class that intolerance first assails and ultimately disgusts." *

By far the most striking phenomenon in the religious life of the period under review was the advent of Mr. Spurgeon—or as he was for a while designated, Pastor Charles Haddon Spurgeon—in London. With the career of no modern minister of the Gospel has the public been so familiar. Both his father and grandfather were in the Congregational ministry, and at the age of sixteen the gifted young man commenced preaching in village chapels and hired rooms with singular acceptance, and during this time he became convinced of the scripturalness of believers' baptism. The

* *Nonconformist* of July and August, 1856.

"boy preacher" was, at his father's suggestion, to have entered Stepney College, but having, through some misunderstanding, failed to see Dr. Angus, the principal, at Cambridge, that scheme was given up, and Mr. Spurgeon accepted a pastorate in the village of Waterbeach, Cambridgeshire. But his fame had already reached the metropolis, and an invitation to supply the pulpit of New Park Street Chapel, Southwark—then at a very low ebb—could not be resisted. The youthful minister took the place by storm; the congregation at once doubled; a proposal for a six months' probation was superseded; and Mr. Spurgeon was forthwith invited to, and accepted, the pastorate. In three months the young Baptist preacher, though not twenty years of age, was the talk of London. How Park Street Chapel soon became too small for the crowds that flocked to it; how, when it was closed for enlargement, even Exeter Hall would hardly hold the multitude that went to hear him; how subsequently his own enlarged place of worship would not suffice; and how the huge music hall in Surrey Gardens was taken for his Sunday evening services, resulting in a terrible calamity arising from a false alarm of fire,* is well known. For a time Mr. Spurgeon was utterly prostrated by this catastrophe, but on recovering his wonted health, the services at the music hall were resumed in the morning instead of the evening. This led the *Times* to ask, why St. Paul's and Westminster Abbey were comparatively empty whilst this young Nonconformist preacher could gather around him 10,000 persons to hear the Gospel at the Surrey Gardens? That building was soon after vacated, and was not long after destroyed by fire. There had been some talk of Mr. Spurgeon becoming

* Seven persons were killed and twenty-eight others injured during this panic.

an itinerant evangelist; but his people resolved to erect a spacious edifice in some suitable locality. While the Metropolitan Tabernacle was being built, the young pastor was married to Miss Susannah Thompson, in New Park Street Chapel, by Dr. Alexander Fletcher, in the presence of an overflowing congregation. In the summer of 1859 the foundation stone of the new place of worship at Newington was laid by Sir S. Morton Peto, and it was opened in the spring of 1861; Mr. Spurgeon having used the interval to preach all over the country, and receiving half the proceeds of every collection for his new tabernacle. This imposing building, which seats over 5,000 persons, with standing room for 1,000 more, cost nearly £32,000, and was opened free of debt.* Mr. Spurgeon's subsequent work will hereafter be referred to in connection with his Jubilee services in the summer of 1884.

When the health of the Rev. Thomas Binney broke down in 1858, he paid a visit to Australia—then a long three months' voyage—and was received with distinction and enthusiasm by people of all classes, who crowded to hear him preach or speak. He went out for health and rest, but did not find rest, and had to embark in a controversy, for which he perhaps had almost as much relish as for quiet and repose. Among those with whom Mr. Binney was brought into contact was Dr. Short, Episcopal Bishop of Adelaide, who, it appears, had made up his mind how to act when the great representative of Congregationalism reached the Australian shores; for he said in a letter, afterwards published, that, although perfect religious equality now obtained in the colony (South Australia), neither Mr. Binney's

* This brief statement of facts is gathered from the "Sketch of the Life of C. H. Spurgeon," published in a cheap form by Messrs. Passmore & Alabaster.

"power of intellect, nor vigour of reasoning, nor mighty eloquence, nor purity of life, nor suavity of manners, nor soundness in the faith" would justify him (Dr. Short) in departing from the rule of the Church of England—a tradition of eighteen centuries, which declares that Mr. Binney's "orders are irregular, his mission the offspring of division, and his church system—he would not say schism—but *dichostasy*" (standing apart). But he added, "My feelings kicked against my judgment." When Mr. Binney was staying with Sir Richard Macdonald, Governor of South Australia, he saw the bishop's letter—already in print—and his Excellency, being a liberal Churchman, originated, or at least promoted, a memorial to Dr. Short, which was signed by a large number of the leading Episcopalians and high officials, requesting him to invite their distinguished guest to preach in Adelaide Cathedral, "in the belief that Christian union and Christian love will be thereby promoted and diffused in the hearts of those who, holding like faith in the great saving doctrines of our common religion, have been hitherto kept asunder by differences in matters of form and discipline." Although the great majority of the colonists cordially sympathised with this movement, there was a section of High Churchmen who did not; and they adopted a counter-memorial, expressing their deep regret that "the invitation of an unordained minister, and of a denomination in separation from our Church to teach in her pulpits," should have been urged on the bishop by certain other members, "professing at the same time attachment to her ritual and government."

Bishop Short, as may be supposed, was prepared to stand his ground. He mildly censured the Governor and his officials for going out of their way to sign a memorial—it was done in their private capacity—recommending if not an actual "at least a virtual transgression of the law of our Church." But, while declining to sanction the opening of Episcopal pulpits to Mr. Binney, the bishop expressed a hope that the inability might at some future time be removed, if the following "indispensable" conditions were agreed to:—(1) The acceptance in common by the Evangelical Churches of the orthodox creed. (2) The use in common of a settled Liturgy, though not to the exclusion of free prayer, as provided for in the Directory of the Assembly of Divines at Westminster; and (3) an Episcopate freely elected by the United Evangelical Churches. In discussing these terms in a subsequent letter, Mr. Binney remarks:—"Some would regard the first as unnecessary, seeing that 'Evangelical Churches' must, as such, have already accepted, and be known to hold, the orthodox creed; others would think the second inexpedient to be insisted upon as a first step, and without preparation, with the present fixed habits of different parties; while the third (to say nothing of its requiring in some the abandonment of what they hold *as principles*), would appear to many to demand what it would require the interposition of a miracle to secure." To the bishop's argument as to the admission of "heretical preachers," Mr. Binney replies that "the stringent and solemn subscriptions of your Church are no security against most serious doctrinal difference among the clergy. There are Romanists in everything but the name, and on the other side men who deny, or explain away, all the essential verities of the Gospel." Exchange of pulpits is a matter of mutual knowledge and confidence, not of re-organisation. Disguise it as they might, the "ecclesiastical gap" still remained, and it was best honestly to recognise the fact "that the Episcopalian clergyman *cannot* recognise the 'orders' of the ministers of other Evangelical churches—he cannot regard the men as ministers of Christ in the full and proper meaning of the words—he cannot admit their official standing," though he may respect and love them as Christian men, and as earnest advocates of the truth. They are, in the view of the Anglican clergy, laymen and nothing else, and this view follows from the "tradition of eighteen centuries." That gulf can never be bridged over till there are buried in it a goodly number of the "customs" and "traditions" of past ages. Till then Dr. Short's "Church of the Future" is only a pleasing vision. Subsequently, Mr. Binney fully explained his ideal of the "Church of the Future" in an address to the Tasmanian Congregational Union.* It need hardly be said that the controversy created at the time a profound impression throughout Australia, and, to a less extent, in England.

The record of the ten years ending 1860 would hardly be complete without some reference to the retirement of Dr. Davidson, one of the Professors of Lancashire Independent College, of which Dr. Vaughan was then the Principal. That learned theologian had published, in 1857, a volume of "Horne's Introduction," which Dr. Campbell, the great heresy-hunter of the day, at once urged the College authorities to examine. They eventually passed a resolution expressing entire confidence in Dr. Davidson's religious sentiments, and sincere sympathy with him in the trials to which he was exposed; but asking him to explain certain expressions in his volume to which some persons had taken exception. The Professor published his "Vindication," which asserted that parts of the Bible are fallible; that the Imprecatory Psalms were not inspired; that the Psalms generally contained, but were not themselves, the Word of

* This address was incorporated in the volume which Mr. Binney published after his return home, under the title of "Lights and Shadows of Church Life in Australia." (Jackson & Walford. Second Edition, 1860.)

God; that inspiration belonged to the men, not to the writings; and that believers of that day had only a glimmering hope of a future state, &c. The views put forth in this book were, to a large extent, those more recently advocated by Professor Robertson Smith, for which he was condemned by the Free Church Assembly. One or two pamphlets on either side were published, and Dr. Campbell, according to his wont, hammered away at Dr. Davidson. When the General Committee of the College met to consider the subject, the Rev. John Kelly, of Liverpool, moved a resolution of want of confidence in the author; but an amendment was carried that a deputation should be appointed to confer with Dr. Davidson. Meanwhile, party spirit had risen so high that Dr. Vaughan considered it necessary to retire from the College, and subsequently Dr. Davidson asked what were the charges against him. But, as the request was not complied with, he resigned his chair, to the great satisfaction of the exultant editor of the *British Standard*, who had been incessant in his attacks, and who declared that, in defence of "the faith once delivered to the saints," he was "prepared to forego the first names and the most brilliant talents." Dr. Campbell's next quarry was New College, which had some time before expelled three students who held views similar to those of Dr. Davidson. But the champion of orthodoxy was not satisfied. After the lapse of a few years he published an anonymous letter from a student, preferring certain charges against the same college, which, on investigation, proved to be utterly groundless, and the tables were turned on Dr. Campbell and his paper.

Not a few eminent men, with whose names and services the Free Churches were familiar, were called to their rest during this decade. The list includes Dr. Collyer, of Peckham, of whom mention has already been made in these pages, and who belonged to a past generation of ministers, as did also the learned and accomplished Dr. Wardlaw, of Glasgow; Dr. Pye-Smith, of Homerton, who was renowned both as a theologian and a scientist; the Rev. W. Jay, of Bath, one of the most incisive and popular preachers of the day; the Rev. John Angell James, of Birmingham, author of several popular religious works, such as the widely-circulated "The Anxious Inquirer," and on intimate terms with the foremost Evangelical Churchmen of the day; the Rev. Algernon Wells, one of the founders and first secretary of the Congregational Union; and Dr. Morison, of Brompton. In this list is also to be included Dr. Harris, Professor at Cheshunt College, and afterwards, in 1850, Principal of New College—a man of gentle and generous nature, an eloquent preacher, and author of Dr. Conquest's prize essay on covetousness, entitled "Mammon," one of the best-known treatises of the day, as well as "The Great Commission" and "The Great Teacher;" the Rev. Mark Wilks, of Paris, and the Rev. Dr. Jenkyn, an eminent college professor. Hardly less eminent than any of these men, for the services he rendered to the cause of Christ and the interests of Dissenters, was Mr. Josiah Conder, who, as already indicated in these pages, filled a large space in the literary and journalistic world. As far back as 1814 he became proprietor of the *Eclectic Review*, a monthly religious journal, which he continued to edit till 1837, when it was transferred to Dr. Thomas Price. Amongst the contributors during his *régime* were John Foster, Robert Hall, James Montgomery, Dr. Chalmers, Isaac Taylor, Dr. Vaughan, and other literary celebrities. His well-known work on "Protestant Nonconformity" was issued in 1818. "The Modern Traveller," which he undertook, was completed in thirty volumes. More responsible was his work as editor of the

Patriot, which extended from 1832 to 1855, when he was succeeded by Mr. J. M. Hare. Mr. Conder was also the editor of "The Congregational Hymn Book," published under the auspices of the Congregational Union, in 1836, and both he and his wife composed some standard hymns, which still retain their popularity. At his funeral in Abney Park Cemetery, in 1856, Dr. Morison thus adverted to Mr. Conder's forty years' incessant toil, undertaken mainly for public objects:—"As their correct and enlightened annalist—as the conductor for many years of the only review they could call their own—as the author of not a few productions which had earned for him the reputation of a scholar, a theologian, a Biblical critic, and a man of general knowledge and accomplishments—and as the wise, the prudent, and energetic editor of one of their best newspapers, Josiah Conder will deserve a name and a place among Nonconformists as long as the world lasts.

CHAPTER XII.

1860—1870.

BEFORE the session of 1860 expired, her Majesty's Ministers prepared a surprise for Nonconformists. Lord Palmerston, who ought to have known better, consented, at the instigation of his Episcopal friends, to a scheme requiring, under a penalty, a statement of "religious profession" from the population in connection with the forthcoming Census, in lieu of returns of attendance at public worship, as made ten years before, which were now found to be impracticable in consequence of Church opposition. The Bill for that purpose was brought in during the month of May by the Home Secretary, Sir G. Cornewall Lewis, with the promised support of Mr. Disraeli and his party, which the Prime Minister unwisely accepted. There was instant action on the other side. To oppose the plan of the Government a large and influential committee was formed, composed of some forty M.P.'s and other gentlemen of mark,* who communicated with the friends of religious freedom throughout the country. A large deputation of members, headed by Mr. Bright and Mr. Baxter, waited upon the Home Secretary, who had evidently

* Mr. Frank Crossley, M.P., was chairman of the Committee, Mr. James Heywood treasurer, Mr. Charles S. Miall acted as honorary secretary, and a committee room was taken at Fendell's Hotel, Westminster.

been deceived on the subject, but who promised that the penalty for refusing the information should be dropped. A great meeting to protest against the fourth clause of the Bill was held in the Freemasons' Hall, and similar meetings were held throughout the country, at which memorials to the Government were adopted, and more than a hundred members sent a memorial to Lord Palmerston urging that the proposed inquiry as to "religious profession" would be unreliable, and that it should be withdrawn; but the deputation made no impression on his lordship. In this case the Wesleyans joined the other Nonconformist bodies in protesting against the scheme, their Committee of Privileges objecting to it as likely to be made "the occasion of intimidation and wrong"; that the returns would necessarily be "defective and inaccurate"; and that the result would be "worthless and misleading, either as to the state of the different denominations, or the religious condition of the country at large." Even Lord Shaftesbury declared that the plan was "impracticable," seeing that in many cases no returns would be made and in others they would be "very fallacious."

When the Bill went into committee on July 11th a shoal of petitions was presented against the scheme,* and Mr. Edward Baines, in an admirable speech, moved an amendment striking out the obnoxious "religious profession" clause. Sir George Lewis then made an angry statement, but he wound up by saying that as it was "useless to contend with the master of forty legions," he would withdraw the clause. An animated debate followed, in which Messrs. Bernal Osborne, F. Crossley, Sir S. M. Peto, and Sir C. Douglas censured the Home Secretary for his speech, and leading members of the Opposition contended that the returns of 1851 were irre-

* 932 petitions with 80,979 signatures.

trievably damaged, and that the Dissenters were afraid of any others. Lord Palmerston was still obstinate, and in his reckless way insisted that the opponents of the scheme had not a shadow of reason on their side. Nevertheless the words were struck out of the Bill without a division. Mr. Baines had given notice of an amendment for authorising a census of accommodation and attendance, as in 1851, but as he was likely to be defeated, he reluctantly agreed not to press it. Afterwards it was hastily proposed that the words struck out of the English measure should be inserted in the Irish Bill, which was not objected to. Ever since 1860 there has been a census of religious profession in Ireland; but though similar returns for England have been suggested at every decennial period by staunch members of the Established Church, the proposal has never been accepted; statesmen as well as Nonconformists having come to see that such an inquiry would, in the present state of things, be wrested to political purposes, with a view to claim all who did not write themselves down as Dissenters to be members of the Church of England.

Heretical questions were as rife in the Established Church—"the bulwark of orthodoxy"—during this decade as they had been a few years before among Nonconformists, and the prelatical Campbells were as little successful in dealing with the Colenso and "Essays and Reviews" cases as had been their prototype in putting down Mr. Lynch and his supporters. Dr. Colenso was consecrated Bishop of Natal in 1853, and, in his sermon on the occasion, Dr. Wilberforce used expressions which were long remembered against him. After referring to "the undying certainty of power and love" through the Holy Ghost to which they were trusting the new bishop, he went on to say, "We add you as new links to the ever-lengthening chain of Christ's anointed witnesses." Alas! for the efficacy of Episcopal benedictions. Within nine years not only the Bishop of Oxford, but nearly every other English prelate, had closed the pulpits of his diocese against this "anointed witness. This was in 1862, when Dr. Colenso startled the world by the publication of his book on the age and authorship of the Pentateuch, which was entirely at variance with the received belief. Some of the clergy applied to the Primate for advice, but Dr. Sumner could only deplore the publication of Dr. Colenso's "crude sentiments," and promised to spare no effort "to vindicate the faith of the Church." As soon as possible both Houses of Convocation—which had only lately been allowed to resume their sittings—appointed committees to inquire into the heterodox publication; but, in a charge to his own clergy, the Archbishop of Canterbury condemned the book, while informing them that primary jurisdiction in the case rested in the Bishop of Cape Town, the Metropolitan of South Africa; but he enjoined his clergy to keep the erring bishop out of their pulpits, and from administering the Sacrament. Thereupon Dr. Colenso protested against the conduct of the bishops in condemning him before he had been tried as illegal, and contrary to the first principles of the Reformation, and said that he stood upon his rights as an Englishman. He was tried in the Colonial Court, and deposed by his Metropolitan, Bishop Gray. The sentence was appealed against, and the pleadings were heard during four days by the Judicial Committee of the Privy Council. That tribunal, in March, 1865, decided that the proceedings before the Bishop of Cape Town were null and void, on the ground that the Crown had no power to constitute a bishopric in any colony possessing an independent legislature, and that the sees of Cape Town and Natal did not in law exist, nor had their respective bishops any jurisdiction whatever. After this judgment Dr. Colenso returned to South Africa; but, in the following year, the Master of the

Rolls decided that the trustees of the Colonial Bishoprics' Fund were bound to set aside £10,000 to secure the Bishop of Natal's income, and to pay him his salary of £362, which had been withheld since 1864. Dr. Colenso continued to exercise his Episcopal functions at Natal for some years, in spite of the opposition of Dr. Macrorie, whom Dr. Gray had nominated as his successor; and he lost no opportunity of befriending the Zulus, by whom he was greatly reverenced.

In the midst of the uproar caused by Bishop Colenso's publication, another remarkable volume, produced by clergymen of the Church of England, was launched. "Essays and Reviews," written severally by Dr. Temple (now Bishop of London),* Dr. Rowland Williams, the Rev. H. B. Wilson, and three others, created much excitement throughout the country, especially among Evangelical Churchmen and Dissenters, in consequence of the latitudinarian views advocated in its pages. These, according to the report of the Joint Committee appointed by Convocation, "contained teachings contrary to the doctrines of the Church of England, in common with the whole Catholic Church of Christ." Both Houses con-

* Though Dr. Tait, then Bishop of London, acquiesced in this censure, he did not, as he admitted to Dr. Temple and Mr. Jowett, think ill of their own Essays, whose only fault was that they did not lay sufficient stress on positive truth. Both Dean Stanley and Dr. Temple condemned Bishop Tait's policy in Convocation. The former, in a letter published in the "Life of Archbishop Tait," remarks: "You could not have adopted a measure more calculated to injure the cause of Christianity or of the Church in this country." And Dr. Temple says to Dr. Tait: "I for one joined in writing this tract in the hope of breaking through that mischievous reticence which, go where I would, I perpetually found destroying the truthfulness of religion. I wished to encourage men to speak out. I believed that many doubts and difficulties only lived because they were hunted into the dark, and would die in the light."

demned the book, though some members of the Lower House wanted fuller and more explicit information as to its statements before such action was taken.* Some time before the Primate had received a memorial from 8,000 of the clergy asking him to take measures to drive away false doctrines from the Church; to which His Grace replied that a suit in the Ecclesiastical Courts would prolong objectionable discussion for three years at least, and that it was better to wait and see if adequate replies were not forthcoming. But the Bishop of Salisbury stepped forward, and commenced proceedings against Dr. Williams and the Rev. H. B. Wilson in the Court of Arches.† Dr. Lushington after fully hearing each case, rejected twenty-seven of the charges; but on the four ultimately retained, he sentenced the defendants to suspension for one year, and condemned them in costs. The defendants appealed to the Judicial Committee of the Privy Council, who, on February 8th, 1864, gave judgment, the two Archbishops dissenting. Substantially it was charged against Dr. Williams that the passages cited from his review contravened the doctrine of the Church of England in regard, first, to Inspiration, and, secondly, to Justification by Faith; and against Mr. Wilson that, in his essay, he had challenged the authenticity of certain parts of the Canonical Books, and that he had expressed himself adversely to the eternity of future punishment. The judges held that the passages impugned and condemned by the Court of Arches did not sustain the conclusions based upon them. They had nothing to do, said the Court, with the general tendency of the writings

* Dr. Temple's essay was in such general terms, and was so expressly claimed to stand by itself, that it was not particularly condemned.

† The Essay of the former was a review of "Bunsen's Biblical Researches"; of the latter, "Séances Historiques de Geneve: the National Church."

from which the selections had been culled; they confined their judgment exclusively to the extracts placed before them, and, comparing those particular extracts with the Articles and Formularies of the Church of England, they could not pronounce the one repugnant to the other. The appellants were allowed the costs of their appeal, but not the costs of the Court below.*

In commenting on the decision of the Judicial Committee, the *Nonconformist* remarked:

"The issue of this celebrated case conclusively establishes the position that the orthodoxy of a Christian Church, even where its own articles and formularies are assumed to be the standard of orthodoxy, cannot safely be trusted to the guardianship of law, or its right thinking and believing be guaranteed by legal processes and decisions. The judgment effects a most momentous change in the position of the Church of England and her clergy. It explicitly lays down, for instance, that 'the proposition or assertion that every part of the Scriptures was written under the inspiration of the Holy Spirit is not to be found either in the Articles or any of the Formularies of the Church; a decision which, so long as a clergyman maintains that 'Holy Scripture containeth all things necessary to salvation,' gives him full liberty to tear any portion of it to tatters by unfriendly criticism, and to secure such writers as Bishop Colenso from all legal censure. . . . There is nothing requiring the Court to condemn as penal the expression of a hope by a clergyman that the ultimate pardon of the wicked may be consistent with the will of Almighty God. It is impossible to avoid seeing that these decisions place in an insecure position the entire system of faith usually and distinctively designated 'Evangelical'—saps the foundations of the arch, and removes from it the keystone."†

This important decision does not appear to have involved

* Amongst the crowded audience to hear the judgment delivered were the Duke of Argyll, Mr. Gladstone, and Mr. Binney.

† *Nonconformist*, February 10th, 1864.

any serious practical results in the Established Church, though there was much talk amongst High Church adherents of an early secession, which came to nothing. There was, indeed, a Free Episcopal Church of England formed, but its clerical adherents were few, and the movement languished. But the decision of the Judicial Committee led to a renewal of the friendship between Lord Shaftesbury and his cousin, Dr. Pusey. The latter having written to the *Record* calling upon all Christians to forego minor differences in mutual resistance of the great doctrina errors of the day, his lordship heartily responded. "For God's sake," he said, "let all who love our blessed Lord, and His perfect Word, be of one heart, one mind, one action, on this great issue, and show that, despite our wanderings, our doubts, our contentions, we yet may be one in Him."*

Towards the close of the session of 1864 Lord Houghton inquired in the Upper House, in reference to "Essays and Reviews," whether it was legal for Convocation to pass a synodical judgment on books written either by clergymen or laymen. Lord Chancellor Bethell evidently enjoyed the opportunity of having a fling at the bishops. Convocation could only, he said, be put in motion by the Crown, and could do nothing valid without the sanction of the Crown. Otherwise it would incur the penalties of *præmunire;* and he drew an amusing picture of the members of the Episcopal Bench appearing at the bar as penitents in sackcloth and ashes, and paying heavy fines—bishops, deacons, archdeacons, canons and vicars, all involved in one common crime, all subject to one common penalty. What was called a synodical judgment was simply a series of well-

* "Life and Work of Lord Shaftesbury." By Edwin Hodder. (Cassell & Co.)

lubricated terms—a sentence so oily and so saponaceous* that no one could grasp it. It was simply nothing. The Bishop of Oxford angrily protested against "such ribaldry," and said he would a thousand times rather face any amount of invective and insinuation than, on his own death-bed, have to look back on himself as one who had not striven for the truth "of our Established Church."

There were at this time other indications of widespread theological strife. By some of the more orthodox papers Professors Kingsley and Maurice were denounced for their heresies, but the greatest excitement was caused by the publication of "Ecce Homo: a Survey of the Life and Work of Jesus Christ." The authorship was never acknowledged, though it was known to be written by Professor Seeley. Edition after edition of this work was called for,† and it was vehemently condemned by Lord Shaftesbury and the Evangelical Church press.‡

The year 1862 was memorable for the celebration of the Bicentenary of the Ejection of 2,000 ministers from the

---

* This was a covert allusion to the popular nickname of the Bishop of Oxford—"Soapy Sam." Dr. Wilberforce is said to have been innocently asked by a lady the meaning of the *soubriquet*, to which the good-natured and witty prelate replied: "Because I am always in hot water, and come out with clean hands."

† One now before us, dated 1881, is the sixteenth.

‡ In his diary, under date May 12th, 1860, Lord Shaftesbury says:—"Speaking at a meeting of Church Pastoral Aid Society, I denounced 'Ecce Homo' as a 'most pestilential book.' This expression I well recollect. The report adds: 'ever vomited from the jaws of hell.' No doubt, then, I used the words. They have excited a good deal of wrath. They were, perhaps, too strong for the *world*, but not too strong for the *truth*. It escaped in the heat of declamation—justifiable, and yet injudicious. The book is as much admired and bepraised in England as Rénan's in France; except that the French have not, as far as I know, found a bishop to endorse M. Rénan; while we have found one, so I hear, to become surety for 'Ecce Homo'!"

Established Church in 1662. In no movement of that era did Nonconformists of all sections so heartily co-operate. Early in the year two central committees were formed in London—one by Independents, under the auspices of the Congregational Union, which decided on the preaching of special sermons in August, district conferences, the holding of special thanksgiving and prayer meetings, the wide diffusion of information illustrating British Nonconformity, and upon a Bicentenary Memorial Fund, with a view to the erection of new places of worship and a memorial hall, to found college endowments and scholarships, &c. The United Central Committee was formed at a meeting held at the Baptist Library, not a few Congregationalists being present, and a strong feeling being shown in favour of general co-operation.* The two committees acted apart, but that of the Congregational Union agreed to unite in the tuitional work, and to issue a memorial volume. At the outset Dr. Stoughton suggested that they should not take the principle and practice of the Liberation Society as their basis; but this timid policy did not meet with general favour. The Rev. J. G. Rogers, of Ashton, Mr. Morley, and the Rev. Samuel Martin (Chairman of the Congregational Union for the year, and a recent adherent of the Liberation Society) thought there should be no compromise, the last-named stating that he was quite prepared for the denunciations of the Evangelical clergy; and Mr. Rogers urging that, in Lancashire, at least, there was a rare opportunity of disseminating their principles. A separate organisation was formed in Wales, the practical object

* The Committee included Dr. Vaughan, Mr. Binney, Mr. S. Morley, Mr. W. Edwards, Mr. Stafford Allen, most of the leading Baptist ministers in the metropolis, and the Rev. Samuel (afterwards Dr.) Cox, who proved to be a most efficient secretary.

being the erection of a new college at Brecon. Most of the Unitarian churches entered heartily into the movement, and a great many of the Methodists.

Both of the central committees issued addresses. That of the Congregational body sketched the events that led to the Ejectment, denounced the Act of Uniformity, with its harsh and sectarian provisions, "as a disgrace to our national Church," and declared that Christianity should never have been an affair of the State. The United Central Committee remarked that their commemoration did not require identity of ecclesiastical or theological faith between the Nonconformists of 1662 and 1862, for it was not the opinions, but the heroic spirit, of the ejected that they desired to honour. They promised the most rigid impartiality in the publication of historical facts on the subject, and appealed to Evangelical Nonconformists for their hearty support. The Liberation Society did not directly take part in the movement. There were doctrinal limitations in the way, and it was manifest that, under any circumstances, the movement would further the objects of the Society, and that the adherents of the Establishment would suffer from and resent it.

For quite six months the Nonconformist agitation continued. In nearly every town, large and small, to say nothing of villages, there were either sermons, lectures, public meetings, or discussions on the subject, in which the story of the Two Thousand was told in every conceivable form, and its lessons inculcated. Never before had there been among Dissenters such widespread instruction on any ecclesiastical subject, or such powerful appeals to "the Nonconformist conscience." Everywhere ministers and influential laymen of most denominations gave their willing aid; not the least cordially those who usually held aloof from the Liberation Society. The Congregational Committee had a great meeting in St. James's Hall, at which Dr. Stoughton read a paper, and Dr. Vaughan, Dr. Edmond, and Mr. Alfred Rooker gave addresses. During May and June there was a series of masterly lectures at Willis's Rooms, under the auspices of the United Committee, the lecturers being Dr. McCrie (Presbyterian), Rev. A. McLaren (Baptist), and the Rev. R. W. Dale and Dr. Halley (Congregationalists).

Almost from the first there was a counter-movement, marked by great and increasing excitement of feeling; and, making due allowance for the embarrassment of their position, the asperity and personalities of the Evangelical leaders, clergy, and editors were such as should not have been possible. Conspicuous among them were Canon Miller, Canon Stowell, and the Bardsleys. During the conflict the first-named renounced co-operation with Dissenters in connection with the Birmingham Bible Society, of which he was chairman. The Rev. R. W. Dale replied to him; and the whole of the Midland capital was for weeks in a ferment on the subject.*

The United Committee published a very masterly essay

* The Rev. James Bardsley described Mr. Miall's "Nonconformist's Sketch Book" as an "infamous publication"; while his brother Joseph spoke of him as "an admitted Socinian," and when challenged to make good his statement, said that Mr. Grant, of the *Morning Advertiser*, had challenged Mr. Miall to deny that he was a Unitarian, and that he had not replied! Sir Culling Eardley also entered into the fray. Deprecating "imputations on either side," he besought Mr. Dale to say "something kind and generous in reference to the clergy"; to which that minister responded: "What I meant is that the Evangelical clergy, whether they number seven, or eight, or ten thousand, obtained orders by declaring their approbation of services which, taken in their plain grammatical sense, embody doctrines and express principles which their hearts condemn"; though Mr. Dale did not accuse Dr. Miller and men like him "of a conscious and habitual violation of the authority of conscience."

on "English Puritanism," by Mr. Peter Bayne, as an introduction to the valuable historical documents they had brought out; three prize essays of fifty guineas each, written by Dr. Angus, Dr. Waddington, and Rev. A. Lord; and the "Ejection of the Episcopalians" by the Commonwealth, from the pen of the Rev. J. G. Miall, of Bradford. The Congregational Committee brought out the memorial volume of Dr. Vaughan,* who had taken a very active part in the Bicentenary commemoration. The learned author deals with the whole period of early English Dissent and with the events connected with the passing of the Act of Uniformity † in a robust and manly style, and shrinks from no conclusion, however adverse to his own predilections, to which historical facts lead him—in this instance indubitably, that the State Church system has been disastrous to the Church of Christ.

St. Bartholomew's Day (August 24th) fell on a Sunday, and it proved to be one of the most memorable religious commemorations recorded in English history. Nearly every minister of the several Dissenting bodies delivered discourses on the subject. Three days after, the *Nonconformist* contained references to upwards of three hundred and fifty sermons preached in more than a hundred and fifty towns, their general subject being a Scriptural justification of Dissent, and its present relations to the Established Church.

---

* "A History of English Nonconformity." By Robert Vaughan, D.D. (Jackson & Walford.)

† It is worthy of note that during this year (June, 1862) Lord Ebury, in the House of Lords, moved an amendment of the Act of Uniformity in order to relax the terms of subscription. But although Lord Shaftesbury said that unless something of the kind were done, it would be impossible to maintain the integrity of the Church, the Bishops of London and Oxford opposed the Bill, which was withdrawn.

The demonstration received full justice in the daily press; the *Times* leading the way with an elaborate and discriminating article, followed by the *Daily News* and *Morning Star*, which expressed unqualified approval of the principles on which the movement was based. Copious extracts were given in the press from the sermons or lectures delivered by such eminent ministers as Dr. Vaughan, Dr. Raleigh, Dr. Angus, Dr. James Hamilton, Dr. J. R. Campbell, and Revs. T. Binney, Edward White, T. T. Lynch, A. M. Henderson, E. R. Conder, Mark Wilks, T. Adkins, S. W. Aveling, Paxton Hood, &c.; * and in summing up results, the *Liberator* remarks:—"The doctrine of the Liberation Society has seldom or ever been more pointedly expressed, or aptly illustrated, than it has been by nearly all the preachers and lecturers who have taken the Ejection for the

* Quotations might be indefinitely multiplied, but only the following significant extract can here be given. It is taken from a lecture by an eminent eloquent and beloved Presbyterian minister, Dr. Hamilton, who, for the most part, held aloof from controversy:—"The tendencies of the time are," he said, "democratic. The olden Nonconformity is replaced by modern Dissent. Reluctant Nonconformists, like myself, are neither so numerous nor so vigorous as those ardent anti-Churchmen, whose cause Tractarianism and Essayism both have strengthened, and whose watchword is *Carthago est Delenda.* A church truly national is, now, perhaps impossible; and should the existing establishment at last come down, its ruin will be still a monument. History will say: 'There lies the institution which understood neither how to retain its friends, nor how to shut out its enemies. There lies the house in which the martyrs lived and which Bartholomew's Day left desolate. There lies the Church which expelled the Puritans, and kept them out so long that they would not come in again—the Church which, by making the Puritans Nonconformists, made the people of England Dissenters; and which thus, forfeiting its State connexion and coming down to the general level, at last carried out its own idea of undistinguishing uniformity by leaving no Dissent in England. Should Dissent continue to make progress in the ratio of the last thirty years, the disendowment of the National Church must follow."

subject of discourse. Those who have never identified themselves with this society have, perhaps, even exceeded our warmer friends in this matter."

One of the most noteworthy ecclesiastical events of the succeeding period was the rupture between Mr. Spurgeon and the Low Church clergy and Evangelical Alliance. The great Baptist minister was now a potent factor in the religious life of the nation. His Tabernacle was the centre of many powerful evangelistic and philanthropic agencies, such as the Pastors' College for training preachers and the Stockwell Orphanage; and his sermons were printed weekly, and had an unexampled circulation in all parts of the world. In the summer of 1864 Mr. Spurgeon preached a very strongly-flavoured sermon on Baptismal Regeneration, in which he charged the Evangelical clergy with having subscribed to opinions they did not believe, with being "dishonest," and being given to "shuffle and equivocate," &c. He was taken to task by the Hon. and Rev. Baptist Noel—himself now a Baptist and a Dissenter—for being "rash and uncharitable." He asks Mr. Spurgeon whether his charges are consistent with the word and will of Christ, and whether he is not contravening the resolution of the Evangelical Alliance, of which he is a member. The Rev. Dr. Winslow, of Bath, though abhorring the doctrine of Baptismal Regeneration, also censured Mr. Spurgeon for his intolerance, and expressed his conviction that not one of the good Evangelical clergy really believed that dogma, and he knew many of them who had declared that, if the decision in the Gorham case had been adverse, they would have seceded from the Church. On the other hand, the Rev. W. Landels, of Regent's Park Chapel, justified the position taken up by Mr. Spurgeon, declaring that, in his view, the Prayer Book does teach Baptismal Regeneration, and that, though he did not condemn, he could not understand the Evangelical clergy. If free, would they accept that doctrine, or why were they so anxious for a revision of the Prayer Book?

The controversy excited profound interest, no less than a score of replies to Mr. Spurgeon, apart from newspaper articles having been published. The pastor of the Tabernacle did not respond, except in a caustic letter to the Committee of the Evangelical Alliance, in which he repeats his opinion that "the subscriptions of many Evangelical clergymen are dishonest in the highest degree," though he does not imagine they are conscious of the enormity of their act. He quotes a pungent passage from Noel's "Essay on the Union of Church and State," which is a terrible indictment of the State Church, and ends—"All these enormous evils are tolerated and concealed." Mr. Spurgeon formally withdrew from the Alliance until such time as the brethren whom he had charged with duplicity cleared themselves of the sin, and he added, with emphasis: "I impeach, before the bar of universal Christendom, these men, who, knowing that baptism does not regenerate, yet declare in public that it does."

Without waiting for further replies, Mr. Spurgeon launched another thunderbolt at the Church. In September of the same year he preached a sermon again denouncing the errors of the Established Church, choosing for his text the words, "Thus saith the Lord." Taking up the Book of Common Prayer, he read extracts from the baptismal, confirmation, and burial services, the visitation of the sick, the ordering of priests, and the consecration of bishops, all of which he declared to be opposed to the Word of God, and he called upon the ministers and members of the Established Church to show him a "Thus saith the Lord" for their proceedings. He alluded with much warmth and vehemence to the rubrics—such as for burying every baptized thief, harlot, rogue, drunkard, and liar, who might die in the parish "in sure and certain hope of the blessed resurrection"; to the "absolution" in the visitation of the sick; and to the imparting of the Holy Ghost in the consecration of bishops by the laying on of hands. He then quoted one or two of the canons, but only a few—"they were too bad, too full of malice and all uncharitableness." There was, he said, an opportunity given them of pushing another Reformation, of which if they did avail themselves they would be verily guilty. With great energy he called upon Protestant England no longer to tolerate such blasphemy. Having once sounded the trumpet, it should ring till his lips were dumb. He was told not to meddle with other people's churches. But the National Church claimed him as a parishioner, and would compel him, if it could, to pay Church Rates, and did exact tithes. He asked the laity of the churches especially, whether they intended for ever to foster such abominations.

Mr. Spurgeon's attack on the Evangelical clergy led to an interesting correspondence between Lord Shaftesbury and Mr. Samuel Morley. His lordship in a brief letter asks his friend whether there is any hope of staying "the sad controversy" raised by Mr. Spurgeon. A good part of his life he had been trying to promote co-operation between Nonconformists and Churchmen, "and this unhappy outbreak will tend to undo what has been done, and introduce bitterness and antagonism." He denies that the Popish doctrine is taught "by our Church." Enough has been said in attack and defence, and he hopes the discussion will cease. Mr. Morley replies with much care, candour, and courage.* He thinks that they have by no means

* His full and admirable letter—probably one of the longest private etters he ever wrote—appears in "The Life of Mr. Morley," pp. 236, 237.

arrived at the end of the controversy. How can they keep silence when they see that the Romanising movement finds its main support in the ambiguous language of the Church formularies, which sanction a Romanist doctrine, and by keeping the people in ignorance and superstition, prepare them for Romanist teachers? He fears there is "a deadly weakness" in the Evangelical party as compared with former times, and they seem to be paralysed by the decisions of the courts that different doctrines may be held and taught in the same Church. Mr. Morley goes on to say:

"I am afraid that, having been frequently reminded of the formularies to which they have given assent and consent, they have felt bound to defend them, and have adopted the words until they have slid into a partial belief, at least, of the erroneous doctrines which these formularies 'grammatically and naturally' express. You yourself, my lord, I am sorry to find, do not feel the force of the objection to the words of the Prayer Book, and many others adopt your lordship's views. The effect of all this is, that we have, in the maintenance and defence of Evangelical truth, unbelief, hesitancy, and all sorts of apologetic explanations within the Church, which greatly perplex the common people, at a time when the need is greatest for a simple, vigorous, and distinct utterance; and can you wonder that such a man as Mr. Spurgeon, seeing this thing from a point of view in which he is untrammelled by any Church ties and clerical subscriptions, should be 'zealously affected,' and even angry, at the magnitude of the evils to which he thinks it gives rise? . . .

"Do not let us be satisfied with the formularies as they are now. They are a dreadful snare and stumbling-block to many consciences. I am deeply concerned to find your lordship regarding them as requiring no alterations."

Lord Shaftesbury responds that he does not blame Mr. Spurgeon for the free expression of his opinions, but for his coarse language, the imputation of the worst motives, and his utter disregard of charity in refusing to admit that men of the present day might be as true and conscientious in their interpretation of the formularies as men of a former day, whose orthodoxy not even Mr. Spurgeon would call in question. By variance between Churchmen and Nonconformists, the progress of vital religion proportionately suffers. No one would eventually gain by these terrible extremes but the Jesuits. "The Church of England, betrayed by its leaders, will sink the first in the mire of division—Ritualism, sacramental systems, and sacerdotal assumptions. The Nonconformists will soon follow, caught in the very same snare, but by a different bait—the bait of Rationalism and self-confidence." Liturgical reform would not avert or abate the evil at a time when the majority of educated people are "of the do-nothing, care-nothing spirit." Here, apparently, the correspondence ceased, Mr. Morley, it must be admitted, having decidedly the best of the argument.

There had been from time to time a great deal of discussion in the *Nonconformist* as to the holding aloof from Christian institutions of the skilled artisan classes. This was brought to a head at the close of 1866 by the Rev. Edward White, who proposed a conference between the leaders of that industrial section of the community and prominent ministers of the Gospel and others in London. Several preliminary meetings of about a dozen on each side were held in Bouverie Street and at Anderton's Hotel, the Rev. F. Denison Maurice, Mr. White, Mr. Hughes, Mr. Ludlow, and Mr. Miall being foremost in promoting the object; and the result was an arrangement to hold a conference at the London Coffee House, Ludgate Hill. This unique meeting took place on January 21st of the following year. So representative an assembly on such a subject had never before been mustered—could not, indeed, have been held even ten years before. Mr. Miall was unanimously called upon to preside. On one side of the chair were about sixty working men, who were not supposed to reject Christianity *per se*, though they might entertain objections of various kinds to existing religious organisations; and, on the other, a number of clergymen, ministers, and laymen of various denominations. The Church of England was represented by the Dean of Westminster, Canons Miller and Champneys, the Revs. F. D. Maurice, J. C. Mackenzie, James Amos, J. E. Kempe, the Hon. A. Kinnaird, M.P., Thomas Hughes, M.P., J. M. Ludlow, and J. Macgregor ("Rob Roy"); the Congregationalists by the Revs. T. Binney, J. Stoughton, J. C. Harrison, Dr. Raleigh, Dr. Mullens, Dr. Spence, Newman Hall, A. Mackennal, A. Hannay, J. Kennedy, Mark Wilks, G. M. Murphy, and J. H. Wilson; the Baptists by the Revs. Dr. Brock, F. Trestrail, S. Manning, Dr. Burns, and C. Bailhache. Other denominations were represented by Dr. Edmond (Presbyterian), Mr. Penrose (Primitive Methodist), R. Spears (Unitarian), and H. Solly (of the Working Men's Club and Institute Union). Among influential laymen were Messrs. W. Edwards, H. R. Ellington, Edmond Beales, C. E. Mudie, G. F. White, H. Spicer, Josias Alexander, W. H. Watson, and John Finch. There were also present the Rev. Christopher Nevile—who had lately resigned two livings in the Church, and who was very active in promoting cordial relations between the clergy and Nonconformists—and representatives of the City Mission, Open-Air Mission, Theatre Services, and other religious organisations in the metropolis. Amongst the gentlemen who had signed the preliminary circular, but were unavoidably absent, were Dr. Guthrie, of Edinburgh, Mr. Samuel Morley, Mr. Goldwin Smith, and the Revs. J. Baldwin Brown, S. Martin, and A. McAulay (Wesleyan).

Mr. Miall opened the proceedings with a lengthened explanatory address, for which Canon Miller, who seems to have entirely got over his anti-Bicentenary ebullitions of 1862, expressed the deepest obligation; nothing more apposite to the occasion, or better adapted to throw their deliberations into the right form, could have been said. The succeeding speakers were, to a large extent, artisans, some of whom stated, with great plainness but with evident restraint, the reasons why working men had been alienated from religious institutions. The first of these was Mr. Patterson, cabinet maker, who had signed the circular, and had, with Mr. Guile, been very active in promoting the conference. He expressed a hope that that meeting might form an epoch in which a new form of an old agency might be introduced, and help to elevate mankind and spread Christianity. About a score of prominent working men, including Mr. George Potter—whose remarks were redolent of sound Christian advice—had their say, and the ministers present listened with exemplary patience, though they must have had a bad eight hours; the exchange of views lasting that time, with an interval for refreshment. These speeches* were interspersed with addresses from the Rev. Newman Hall (who pointed with emphasis to the fifty millions a year spent on intoxicating drinks); Mr. Macgregor; Dr. Miller; Mr. Edmond Beales, who, with much earnestness, said that he would endure ten thousand more sacrifices than he had done in order to make them all perfect Christians, and expressed his belief that the working classes—"the common people"—were not in the main opposed to the Gospel of Christ; the Rev. G. M. McCree, well known for his evangelistic work in London; Mr. Penrose, who had

* The speakers included a cabinet-maker, two or three engineers, a plasterer, a bookseller's porter, a carpenter, a scavenger, a house-painter, an ironfounder, a licensed hawker, a warehouseman, a railway signalman, a bookbinder, and a hatter; and some of the addresses were able and racy, as well as pungent.

worked among the very poor; and the Rev. Mr. Whitmore, an East-end clergyman. Before the adjournment, Dean Stanley said a few words, remarking that, like many others of the ministers of religion present, he came to listen to the arguments that had weight with those whom they desired to influence, and not to speak. He did not agree with them all, but would be glad if any of his working-class friends would explain how the services in Westminster Abbey could be made more attractive or useful. Subsequently there was a greater variety of speakers on the left of the chairman. They included Mr. White (who, when Mr. Miall was obliged to leave, succeeded to the chair), and who insisted on the value of brotherly kindness to the toiling masses on the part of church-goers, spoke of the hateful class-feeling as tending to alienate the working community from Christian institutions, and strongly advocated giving workmen the franchise. Mr. Maurice pleaded like Dean Stanley that he came to listen, and thought they should lay inwardly to heart what was being said. Mr. Henry Lee, of Manchester, made a useful contribution to the discussion by describing his own experience as teacher of a large class of married men in a Sunday School. But the weak point in all their Christian organisations was, he said, the working women. Mr. Harris Cowper, a lecturer in defence of Christianity, also drew upon his experience; the Rev. C. Nevile praised the conduct of the peasantry of Lincolnshire and Nottinghamshire, whom he well knew, and who did not believe that the clergy had faith in what they preached; the Rev. H. Solly thought there was much apathy among working men in relation to spiritual things; the Rev. J. H. Wilson, Secretary of the Congregational Home Mission, recommended for imitation the arrangement at Surrey Chapel, where secular means were consecrated to a religious end;

the Rev. G. M. Murphy referred to his experience as an evangelist; and Mr. Charles S. Miall (who acted as joint secretary with Mr. White) strongly urged that similar conferences should be held in all the large towns of the country—advice which was very largely followed, meetings of the same kind being held at Bristol, Leicester, Ipswich, &c., before the year closed. In fact, there was quite a rage throughout the country for preaching sermons and delivering addresses in theatres and public halls to the working classes, and a verbatim report of the proceedings was published in a pamphlet form, and very widely circulated.

Some facts had recently been brought to light which suggested that, in the metropolis at least, there was much larger provision for the spiritual wants of the poorer sections of the population than in 1851, not only in the way of church accommodation, but by a multitude of external agencies that carried the Gospel to their homes. About this time a member of the staff of the *Nonconformist* newspaper obtained information as to all the places of worship in the thirty-six parishes within the Registrar-General's district, with the kind assistance of the Bishops of London and Winchester—Dr. Tait and Dr. Harold Browne—which was published in a statistical form in that journal, and summarised and amplified in the *British Quarterly Review.** These returns showed that the proportion of sittings supplied in London by the Established Church was 56 per cent. of the whole, and by the Free Churches 44 per cent., against 59 and 41 respectively in 1851. The comparative increase of supply by the four principal denominations during the fourteen years was in the following ratio:—Church of England, 25 per cent.; Congregationalists, 30 per cent.; Baptists, 61 per cent.; and Wesleyans, 19 per

* January, 1866.

cent. Other bodies, such as the United Methodists, the Methodist New Connexion, and the Primitive Methodists —who were spoken of as the flying corps of the Christian army, which was waging perpetual warfare against the kingdom of unrighteousness in the benighted regions of the metropolis—showed a much larger proportionate increase. Still the fact remained—or it was estimated—that in the aggregate 33 per cent. of the accommodation was not used at the most numerously attended service. But waiving further statistical deductions, it was roughly estimated that from 1851 to 1865 the Free Churches of London expended some £800,000 in church extension; a very substantial proof of the efficacy of Christian willinghood. Of course the paramount influence of Mr. Spurgeon—who was said to have provided seven per cent. of the entire sittings of the Baptist denomination in London—and the princely liberality of Mr. Samuel Morley, Sir Morton Peto, Sir Francis Lycett, and other wealthy Nonconformists, greatly helped to realise this result.

In discussing the significance of the facts elicited, the *British Quarterly* pointed out the evils that had sprung from the unequal distribution of the religious provision, and especially the destitution of the belt of suburban districts, while the wage-receiving classes, at that time, did not more systematically neglect public worship than in 1851; the Church of Christ having awakened to a sense of its responsibilities and opportunities, especially in respect to home evangelisation. The pulpit was the first, but not the only agency. Ministers had been, to a large extent, forward in enforcing a higher standard of Christian obligation in "proclaiming the truth that the outside operations of our churches are to be prosecuted, not by themselves alone, but by pastors with the active co-operation of the members of their flocks." The writer speaks from personal observation of the active district mission work which was then being carried on in connection with many of the Free Churches of London, which, he says, "have become local missionary organisations, pushing out their roots into the soil around, and, by the operation of a beautiful providential law, imbibing a more vigorous sap by means of their external growth. For a church to be without these appliances, and to live a life of religious luxury and exclusiveness, is held to be a sign of spiritual unhealthiness." The *British Quarterly* passes in review the resources provided by the irregular or supplementary agencies in London—such as the City Mission, with its four hundred evangelists, nearly doubled since 1851; the Ragged School Union, which at that time had more than 2,000 volunteer teachers working in the most degraded districts of London; the Theatre and Hall Services Committee, which then commanded congregations of some 20,000 every Sunday; and the Sunday School Union, which, apart from kindred organisations, provided in the metropolis for more than 150,000 children. "This kind of work," frankly admitted Lord Shaftesbury about this time, "cannot be done by the Established principle; it must be done by the Voluntary principle, and by the Voluntary principle only." And in closing his review of the religious resources of the metropolis in 1865, the *British Quarterly* reviewer more cogently urges the same conclusion: "The wondrous growth of the Free Churches of England from the beginning of the present century down to the present day—all the more astonishing when we consider their comparatively meagre resources, and the gigantic obstacles in their path—is it not a sign that to them more particularly is committed the grand enterprise of converting England; and that the principle which more or less underlies them all is the only principle able to compass the task?"

In 1864 there was great reason to fear that the Bunhill Fields Burial Ground, City Road—the Campo Santo of Dissenters, as Southey expressed it—was about to pass into the hands of the Ecclesiastical Commissioners; the lease of the Finsbury Prebendal Estate, of which it formed a part, which had been held by the Common Council for more than 500 years, being about to expire, and the land, it was said, to be let for building purposes. The report gave rise to much indignation, and a memorial was sent to the City Corporation, signed by a number of members of Parliament and the most eminent Dissenters, including several Unitarians, of the metropolis, asking that body "to take whatever steps may be necessary to secure the ground for ever against any possible perversion to other uses than those to which, for two centuries, it has been sacredly appropriated." The memorialists remark:—

"In this burial-ground are interred men whose memory and writings are among the most precious of our national heirlooms; some of the most fearless asserters of civil and religious liberty at critical periods of our history; notable men of all professions and of all religious communities—divines, artists, reformers; a crowd of worthies and confessors whose learning, piety, and public services not only adorned the age in which they lived, but have proved a permanent blessing to the land, and whose names the world will not willingly let die. The Nonconformist bodies, especially, look upon this as the holy field of their illustrious dead, because here lied buried those whose remains were refused interment in the grave-yards of the churches in which they had long faithfully ministered, and whose memory is reverently cherished in the hearts and homes of their religious descendants."

Mr. (afterwards Sir Charles) Reed took up the matter with great energy, and he was effectually supported by Mr. S. Morley. For a long time it seemed that their efforts would be unavailing, and the Ecclesiastical Commissioners would not relent. Among those who took action in the matter was Lord Shaftesbury, who, forgetting the "homily" that had lately been read to him, wrote to Mr. Morley at the beginning of 1866 asking if he could be of service in vindicating the right of Nonconformists for the preservation of Bunhill Fields, for he felt very warmly on the subject. To this letter his friend replied that it seemed to him "a very suitable opportunity for showing friendly consideration towards Nonconformists, which may allay controversy and be most important in our national history." Mr. Morley, however, quite over-estimated the "friendly consideration" of the Ecclesiastical Commissioners, albeit they were about to come into possession of £60,000 a year in connection with the Finsbury Estate. It seems that the Corporation referred the memorial alluded to above to the City Lands Committee, who reported that, in response to the offer of the Corporation to take the ground in trust for the public as an open space, the Commissioners claimed that the property was worth £100,000, and put forward the monstrous demand that the burial-ground should be handed over *free of the remains of those interred there*; but as that could not be decently done, they claimed compensation, to be decided by arbitration. They also required an account to be rendered to them of any sums received during the tenancy of the Corporation, although one-half of the fees received had been from time to time handed over to the Prebend. This claim was made after the Corporation had been in occupation of the property for 500 years. When this was reported to the Court of Common Council in January, 1867, there was a great outcry by Churchmen, as well as Dissenters, against such an outrage on public decency. One deputy, who was a commissioner with the Bishop of London for the amalgamation of City churches, denounced the "avarice" of "these grasping ecclesiastics," and, amid general cheers, the Court, by 70 to 3, refused to "arbitrate," and unanimously adopted the report of the Committee. Great pressure was brought to bear upon the Ecclesiastical Commissioners, who were eventually obliged to relax their terms—which, perhaps, it may charitably be hoped, had more to do with driving a hard bargain with the rich Corporation than any desire to outrage the feelings of Dissenters. Before Parliament rose, in 1867—at the end of which year the lease of Bunhill Fields expired—a short Bill was passed, securing the ground in perpetuity to Nonconformists under the ægis of the Corporation, which in this case, as in many others, manfully stood by their Dissenting friends. It was natural, though not less meritorious, that Sir Charles Reed should have taken a paternal interest in the suitable repair of this interesting spot.*

The successful Bicentenary agitation of 1862 was naturally a topic of hearty congratulation at the Sixth Triennial Conference of the Liberation Society, whose objects had been so materially advanced by that movement. Not a few influential recruits appeared on its platform at Freemasons' Hall; its funds were reported to have been largely augmented; and it was stated that,

* Among those whose remains have been interred in this hallowed burial-ground are Lieut.-General Fleetwood, Cromwell's son-in-law; Dr. Owen, the Protector's chaplain; Dr. Goodwin, Dr. Watts, Bunyan, "the immortal dreamer"; and Defoe, the fascinating story writer, as well as champion of religious freedom; Daniel Neal, the historian of the Puritans; and Daniel Williams, whose library still perpetuates his honoured memory; Mrs. Susannah Wesley, mother of the Wesleys; Mather, Bradbury, Kiffin, Hanserd Knollys, Gifford, Ivemy, Richard Price Hughes (the founder of the Bible Society), Dr. N. Lardner, Kippis, Theophilus Lindsay, Dr. Grosvenor, and many others whose names and deeds will be familiar to the readers of this "History."

although the increasing activity of the Church Defence Institution had brought into Parliament a larger number of opponents, no less than 157 members had affirmed the principle of throwing open the parish churchyards to the ministrations of Nonconformist ministers. Three years later (1865) the Society entered upon its twenty-first year, and Mr. Miall, who presided at the first day's conference, took occasion to pay a touching tribute to the memory of some of its leading founders and supporters who had passed away,* and to review their progress through its successive stages. Abundant proofs were forthcoming of the thoroughness of the organisation in all parts of the country, which was managed by a number of local agents; and of the intensity of hostility on the part of the clergy, which had risen to such a height in Manchester that the question had been seriously discussed whether Dissenters should be recognised and associated with as Christians. On this occasion it was resolved to raise a special fund of £25,000 for the extension of the Society's operations, and one of its noteworthy features was the last appearance on that platform of the venerable John Howard Hinton—now in his seventy-fourth year, and the son of a minister that had zealously upheld the same flag—who, in a pathetic valedictory address, solemnly charged the younger section of Nonconformists, "Let this cause of religious freedom be next to the cause of the Gospel itself."

From the beginning of this decade the conflict on behalf of religious equality was mainly waged around the Church Rate question. This was partly owing to the great activity of what was called the Committee of Laymen, afterwards

* These included Dr. Price, Dr. Cox, Dr. Young, Dr. Adam Thomson, Dr. Hutton, Rev. J. Burnet, Joseph Sturge, John Childs, and Robert Norris.

merged in the Church Defence Institution, but most of all to the declaration of Mr. Disraeli—who was at that time, as leader of the Opposition, casting about for a policy—that the question of Church Rates involved the existence of a National Church, and that the clergy must see to it that it was not a party question. This manifesto of the Tory leader did not please many of the defenders of the impost; while all the Liberal journals, the *Times* included, regarded the Amersham manifesto as a grand mistake. The *Guardian*, the High Church organ,* regretted that Mr. Disraeli had raised the cry of "Church Rates and no surrender," and thought that the question would look "more hopeful under the guidance of some less audacious and self-confident champion." Mr. Roundell Palmer, afterwards Lord Chancellor, and a staunch Churchman, also objected, and Mr. Beresford Hope took the same line. There might be some reaction, he said, but how long would it last? By exasperating Dissenters they would be hastening "a day of heavy reckoning for something more than Church Rates." In this instance Mr. Hope proved to be a seer. While the Church Defence people were chuckling over their improved prospects, the Anti-Rate party promptly took action. A great Anti-Church Rate Conference was held in Freemasons' Hall, in February, 1861—convened by Mr. Bright and a dozen other M.P.'s, by the Secretary of the Congregational and Baptist Unions, the Congregational Board, the Dis-

* Just about this time the *Guardian*, in an article on the "Organisation of Dissenters," was very complimentary: "The celerity of the Church Rate petitioning movement, and the energetic and skilful as saulton the Census clause, were triumphs of political organisation of which the Voluntary party in general, and the Liberation Society in particular, may be justly proud. There are many practices and habits of Dissent which none of us would like to copy; but from its political organisation we have already learnt much, and may yet learn more. *Fas est et ab hoste doceri.*"

senting Deputies, and the officials of the United Methodist Free Churches, the New Connexion, and the Unitarian Association—at which gentlemen from all parts of the country were present. One of the features of this assembly, which was presided over by Mr. Scholefield, M.P., was the presence of an unusual number of members of the Moderate Liberal party; a second, the presentation of a declaration signed by 10,000 members of the various Methodist bodies, many of them ministers and office-bearers, declaring their emphatic disapproval "of this unjust and obnoxious impost." Dr. Steane, of Camberwell, who rarely took part in political movements, was present; so also was Mr. Binney, as "a moderate Dissenter," and though he had been favourable to a compromise, they must now, he said, have abolition. Another "moderate" man was Lord Henley, who said that the anti-rate ship had struck on the bar of the House of Lords, because it contained a quantity of ballast (separation of Church and State); to which Mr. Miall aptly replied that the heavy ballast was now on their wharf, though it was their property. But the Committee of the Lords had put on board some of that ballast, with a view to sink the ship. As a matter of fact, Church Rates was a practical grievance which, standing in their way, had been taken up, but they never identified it with the larger question. Resolutions were proposed demanding the total extinction of Church Rates, and condemning Mr. Disraeli's policy. A committee to co-operate with other bodies was appointed, with Mr. Charles Curling as treasurer, and the Rev. N. T. Langridge as secretary, and it was resolved to raise a fund of £3,000, one-third of which was subscribed before the conference closed.

When Sir John Trelawny's Bill* came before the House

* In the preceding session it was carried in the Commons by a majority of nine, and thrown out in the Lords by 123 to 31 votes.

of Commons soon after, there was a significant debate, in the course of which Mr. Gladstone said that, as representing Oxford University, he could not be expected to surrender their claim to the machinery of Church Rates, though he was favourable to an acceptable settlement. Mr. Bright, in one of his most impressive speeches, replied that such compromises were too late. They should have been made twenty or thirty years ago. Nonconformists objected *in toto* to the payment of a tax which recognised the supremacy of a Church to which they objected, and he proceeded to show what that Church was in their estimation. Mr. Disraeli declared that it was a mistake to suppose he should oppose a compromise if abolition was out of the way. But it was clear after Mr. Bright's speech that what Dissenters chiefly objected to was not Church Rates, but the State Church. Lord John Russell now "put his foot down." He thought the time for exemption schemes was passed, and that the agitation would eventually extinguish the whole system. Mr. Disraeli must have been disappointed with the result—281 voted for the Bill, and only 266 against, indicating a reaction. But, as Sydney Smith says, "nothing dies so hard and rallies so often as intolerance."

When the third reading came on, in June, the Opposition mustered more strongly than ever. There were 274 votes on each side, a large number of Irish members being absent and seven fewer supporting the Bill. In accordance with custom the Speaker gave his casting vote with the "Noes," and the Bill was rejected, though Lord Palmerston, Lord John Russell, and most of the members of the Government supported it. Next year the circumstances somewhat varied. Mr. Estcourt moved, as an amendment, that a substitute ought to be provided, to which Sir G. C. Lewis, an eminently practical man, replied that there had been some twenty-three failures in that direction, and they must now accept abolition. Mr. Bright was again to the front, and spoke much to thep urpose. First, he suggested what proved to be the ultimate form of settlement, the withdrawal of the compulsory power; and next, he declared that the Liberation Society was an honest society of earnest men, and that every vestry meeting was an excellent school to train ratepayers to look at something beyond this tax. Mr. Disraeli also was not above snubbing the Primate. The principle of an established Church, he said, was in question, and it was a matter to be settled by statesmen and not by archbishops. A majority of one decided against Sir John Trelawny, though the opponents of the rate had never received so many votes (286 against 182 in 1854). Mr. Estcourt's amendment, now a substantive resolution, was carried by a majority of fifteen, many of the Liberals having hastily left the House. About a month later that right hon. gentleman produced his scheme, which had an exemption clause, and substituted owner for occupier for the purpose of a voluntary rate. This, however, did not please Lord Robert Cecil and other Tories, and Mr. Disraeli having again suggested that the Government should take up the question, Mr. Estcourt withdrew his resolutions. In 1863 the Church Rate Abolition Bill did not find audience till the end of April, when it was rejected by a majority of 10 (285 to 275); the Conservatives being, as the *Liberator* said, "savagely in earnest, and the Liberals lax and apathetic." "We must go on fighting in the parishes till the friends of the Establishment wake up to the conviction that there is nothing left worth fighting for." The rate was every year diminishing by the refusals of the vestries, and the cases of litigation before the magistrates, who had a wholesome fear of Liberation lawyers, were constantly augmenting. The question was in abeyance in 1864, so far as Parliament was concerned, but the rejection of Mr. Coleridge, the Liberal candidate for Exeter, at a bye-election, by the abstention of Dissenters, because he would not support total abolition, created a great impression in ministerial circles. In 1865 Mr. Newdegate made a feeble attempt to carry a Church Rate Commutation Bill, but was beaten by three to one, upon which the *Times*, which had all through opposed the fanaticism of militant Churchmen and advocated an equitable settlement, plainly told the hon. member and his friends: "The Church Rate is gone, and nothing can save it. Let people subscribe for the parish church as they do for many thousand district churches and chapels, and the parish church will be all the better for the alteration."

But in this session Church Rates gave place to the Bill for the Abolition of Tests in Oxford University, the second reading of which was moved by Mr. Goschen—replacing Mr. Dodson, now Chairman of Committees—who, in a very able and exhaustive speech, contended that the Universities were national institutions; that the education given in them was general in the widest sense of the term; that by law they were lay corporations, not spiritual nor ecclesiastical; and that the claim of the clergy, founded on an indissoluble connection between the University and the Church, rested upon an utter fallacy.* Lord Robert Cecil † led the opposition to Mr. Goschen's Bill, and it was opposed by Mr. Gladstone and Mr. Hardy (afterwards Lord Cranbrook). The second reading was carried by a majority of 16 votes (206 to 190). On this occasion

* Mr. Goschen soon after had to abandon his leadership on this question, by taking office as Chancellor of the Duchy of Lancaster.

† The present writer happened to be in the Press Gallery during the debate, and an experienced reporter whispered to him that, while Lord Robert was speaking, news had arrived of the death of his elder brother, by which he became Viscount Cranborne. In 1868, by the decease of his father, he succeeded to the Marquisate of Salisbury, and is now (1891) Prime Minister.

there were seventy-two pairs, and no less than ninety-one Liberal members unpaired. But the dissolution of Parliament in July * prevented further progress with the Bill. Mr. Gladstone lost his seat for Oxford University, and was replaced by Mr. Gathorne Hardy; but was subsequently elected for South Lancashire, and was thus freed from clerical obligations. In October the death of Lord Palmerston † led to a reconstruction of the Cabinet, with Earl Russell as Premier; and although the next session was almost entirely absorbed with the question of Parliamentary reform, time was found to pass the second reading of the Oxford Tests Bill (217 to 103), introduced by Mr. J. D. Coleridge,‡ and also of the Church Rate Abolition Bill (285 to 252), which Mr. Hardcastle had taken in hand. In 1868 came the end of this remarkable and protracted conflict, which had been waged, with varying fortunes, for no less than thirty-four years. The last scene of all is best fitly described by Mr. Carvell Williams, who, together with Dr. Foster, took so prominent a part in the prolonged struggle, and has been obliging enough to furnish the following notes on its unique close :—

"The Anti-Church Rate agitation ended in an altogether unexpected fashion. In 1866, the second reading of Mr. Hardcastle's Bill for total abolition was carried by a majority of 33, and for the first time it was supported by Mr. Gladstone. His support was, however, qualified by a desire to effect a compromise, and his idea of compromise was, the retention of the existing Church Rate machinery, *minus* the

* In the ensuing General Election 367 Liberals and 290 Conservatives were returned, the former gaining a balance of twenty-four seats.

† As for many years Lord Palmerston had indirect relations with Nonconformists, it may be desirable to put on record his complimentary remark that, "in the long run, English politics would follow the consciences of Dissenters."

‡ Now Lord Chief Justice Coleridge.

power to enforce payment by unwilling ratepayers. I have said *his* idea; but it really originated with Lord Robert Grosvenor (now Lord Ebury), and was embodied in a pamphlet, entitled 'The Only Possible Compromise.' The proposal placed the abolitionists in a dilemma; for here was a practical concession of one item of the Liberation Society's programme—the discontinuance of 'compulsory exactions for religious purposes,' accompanied, however, by conditions which might practically prove mischievous. But, with what may now appear to some uncalled-for moderation, the Society's Committee in their report for that year thus expressed themselves:—'If the primary object of the opponents of Church Rates can be realised by a method less simple and decisive than their own, but more in accordance with the feelings of yielding antagonists, the triumph will lose none of its lustre because graced by a spirit of generous moderation.' There was no corresponding graciousness on the other side; the *Guardian* denouncing Mr. Gladstone for acting in conjunction with the Liberationist leader, while the Conservative Government (Mr. Disraeli's) tried to prevent the second reading of Mr. Gladstone's measure, and avoided a division only to escape inevitable defeat. Further progress could not be made that session, and next year the Bill re-appeared in an improved form. Some of its provisions were objected to by abolitionists, and as I had to conduct the negotiations with Mr. Gladstone and Mr. Roundell Palmer, I am able to bear testimony to their perfect readiness to loyally abide by the main principle of the measure, while making the needful reservations in regard to rates for the repayment of debts, and to some other special cases. The debate on the second reading was of a lamb-like character, in comparison with that of the previous session. It was felt to be the very last chance of passing a conciliatory measure to close a protracted controversy, and the now yielding supporters of Church Rates accepted it with dignified serenity, if not with cheerfulness.* There

* On this occasion Lord Cranborne, who had been so persistent an opponent of abolition, admitted that no gain would result to the Church from prolonging the contest. He thought it wiser to accept the terms now offered. They might go farther and fare worse.

was no division, and the Bill was improved, and not damaged, by the hazardous process of amendments in Committee. Its treatment by the Lords was curious rather than eventful. Their lordships gave the Bill an unfriendly reception; but, in the face of what had occurred in the Commons, did not venture to reject it. They referred it to a Select Committee, from which it came back unharmed; the Bill in its final form embodying the simple advice of its promoters, 'Abolish the constable, and leave everything else.' The Act came into force on July 31, 1868; and when Mr. Gladstone received the thanks of the Liberation Society's Executive for his share in these final efforts to close the Church Rate war, his acknowledgment contained this passage: 'We may not be quite certain that we have heard the last of Church Rates in Parliament; but the teeth and claws of the controversy are drawn.' And besides paying a much-appreciated compliment to myself, he also wrote: 'I must add that nothing could be more loyal and considerate than the conduct of the abolitionists in and out of Parliament, throughout the proceedings on this Bill, from 1866 to the final close.'

"As a matter of fact, Parliament has not since been troubled with the subject, and, as the debts contracted on the security of rates are being paid off, compulsory Church Rates are gradually dying out. And none of the dire results predicted by the advocates of the compulsory system have followed. Instead of churches being in ruins, and service being discontinued, the edifices never were kept in so good a condition, and the services held in them were never so numerous."*

Thus Lord John Russell proved to be a true prophet when, some time before, in the heat of the agitation, he said, "I know the Dissenters. They carried the Reform

* It must be admitted that in some parishes where voluntary rates are made they are paid involuntarily by ratepayers who are afraid to offend by refusal. There have also been cases in which parochial officials have sent "demand notes" for Church Rates; but, when appealed to, the Local Government Board peremptorily forbids the practice.

Bill; they carried the abolition of slavery; they carried Free Trade; and they'll carry the abolition of Church Rates."

Even before this settlement had been effected, Mr. Gladstone had resolved upon the Disestablishment of the Irish Church. In vain did Mr. Disraeli (just become Premier by the retirement of the Earl of Derby) propose, through Lord Mayo, during a debate on Mr. Maguire's motion, the endowment of a Roman Catholic University in Ireland,* and declare that the policy of taking away ecclesiastical endowments in that country "would add immensely to the elements of discord, violence, and confiscation." As soon as his great antagonist uttered the oracular words, "When the case is proved, and the hour is come, justice delayed is justice denied," everyone knew what the issue would be. Before many days had elapsed Mr. Gladstone produced his resolutions, proposing that the Church of Ireland should cease to exist as an Establishment, on which Lord Stanley moved as an amendment that the question ought to be reserved for the new Parliament. The debate lasted four nights, Mr. Disraeli, amongst other things, complaining that hardly had he taken his seat than he was confronted with a "national controversy," which showed the High Ritualists and Romanists in open confederacy for the separation of Church and State, and they attacked the Crown itself. The division showed a majority of 61 against ministers on the first resolution. The second and the third were carried without a division after a debate, in which Mr. Bright charged Mr. Disraeli with deceiving his Sovereign, which was as bad as the conspirator who would dethrone her. This, said the Premier, was

* It was in reference to this nostrum that Mr. Bright told the famous story of the mountebank who offered to sell the people in a country town pills against the earthquake.

"indulging in stale invective." Mr. Gladstone next introduced a Bill suspending for a limited time the exercise of patronage in the Irish Church, the second reading of which was carried by a majority of 54. Soon after, at a City banquet, Mr. Disraeli discoursed on the alliance of Church and State as conserving the two great blessings of freedom and order, by giving them an order of pious and learned men who "assuaged the asperities of conflicting creeds." In the House of Lords, the Suspensory Bill was after three nights' debate thrown out by a majority of 95 (192 to 97), and in July Parliament was dissolved.

The General Election in November was a memorable event. Mr. J. Stuart Mill was ousted in Westminster, Baron Rothschild in the City, and Mr. Gladstone in South-West Lancashire; but he had previously been returned for Greenwich, and was able to rejoice in the magnificent majority of 121 in the new Parliament, which included no less than ninety-five supporters of religious equality, of whom sixty-three were Protestant Dissenters. The Liberal list comprised nearly all the representatives of Scotch constituencies. Still more remarkable were the Liberal successes in Wales, where, in place of seventeen lukewarm Liberals, some twenty-three staunch adherents of Mr. Gladstone were returned. At the head of them was Mr. Henry Richard, who in various ways had for a long time devoted his energies to a political revival among his countrymen, and had been the efficient interpreter of Welsh feeling and aspirations to the English people. Both Mr. Morley and Mr. Miall were candidates at this election—the former for Bristol, in place of Sir Morton Peto, who retired from Parliament; and the latter for Bradford. Curiously enough each of these gentlemen was unsuccessful at the poll, and the opponents of both were unseated. Mr. Morley—who, for the first time, entered

Parliament—and Mr. Miall were again candidates. They were returned by large majorities, and had the pleasure of supporting their leader in the Irish Church struggle.*

Mr. Disraeli having promptly retired, Mr. Gladstone took the helm, and was able to meet Parliament in 1869 with a thoroughly Liberal administration, Mr. Bright becoming President of the Board of Trade. His Disestablishment scheme for Ireland was of course the great measure of the session, and, in spite of persistent opposition, it was carried almost intact on the lines proposed through its several stages in the House of Commons. Of course the provisions as to disendowment were very elaborate, and the ultimate settlement was much hastened by facilities being given for the formation of a Church Body by the Irish Episcopal Church. In June the Bill, which had passed the Commons by a majority of 114, reached the Upper House, and was read a second time by a majority of 33 (179 to 146 votes); the Primate, though objecting to the measure, advising that course. In moving its rejection, the Earl of Harrowby said that Mr. Gladstone's scheme was substantially that propounded by Mr. Miall in 1856; while Lord

* Soon after entering Parliament Mr. Morley resigned his membership of the Executive Committee of the Liberation Society, of which he had been an earnest and munificent supporter. He did not, he said, feel less interest in its main object from a religious point of view, but he objected to the secularisation of the endowments of the Established Church. The Committee, through Mr. Carvell Williams, replied that that principle was held by them in common with some of their ablest statesmen and writers. They could not agree that proposals for legislative changes in a matter affecting the whole community should be limited to members of churches, nor was there anything in the character of passing events to indicate that it was safe to abandon the Liberation movement. Subsequently Mr. Morley loyally supported in Parliament the various measures advocated by the Liberation Society, and voted for Mr. Miall's Disestablishment motion in 1871.

Derby traced the large majority at the command of the Government to the unceasing efforts of the Liberation Society, which, as the Duke of Argyll subsequently said, had become one of those political forces which statesmen could neither ignore nor despise.

A great deal of light is thrown upon this critical ecclesiastical period by the recent publication of the Life of Archbishop Tait,* one chapter of which is devoted to "The Disestablishment of the Irish Church," and contains the correspondence on the subject that passed between the Queen and the Primate. From this it appears that Her Majesty was from the first very anxious on the subject, and, though not approving of disestablishment, she was ready to recognise popular feeling. Mr. Gladstone, the Queen reported to Dr. Tait, showed a most conciliatory spirit, and the Archbishop was requested to "meet him in the same spirit." The interview took place before the Bill was explained in the Commons, and the Archbishop was agreeably surprised to find Mr. Gladstone so complaisant.† After the second reading Mr. Disraeli wrote to the Primate

---

* "Life of Archbishop Tait." By Dr. Randall Davidson and Canon Benham. 2 vols. (Macmillan & Co.) 1891.

† When the Bill was being discussed in the Commons, His Grace and Mrs. Tait came upon Mr. and Mrs. Gladstone one Sunday morning in a little church in Windmill Street, and he says, "As we all walked home together, I had some most amiable conversation with him. I wish he was not so strangely impetuous, for he is certainly a good and true man." Contrast this with the account of Dr. Tait's interview some time before with Mr. Disraeli, when he offered him the Archbishopric: "He harangued me on the state of the Church; spoke of rationalists, explained that those now called Christians did not follow Paulus. He spoke at large of his desire to rally a Church party, which, omitting the extremes of rationalism and ritualism, should unite all other sections of the Church; alluded to his Church appointments as aiming at this—Champneys, Merivale, Wordsworth, Gregory, Leighton, myself, Jackson."

that the "mechanical majority" in the Commons could not be wholly relied on, and that he favoured "unfaltering resistance" in the Peers' Chamber. Her Majesty fearing a collision between the two Houses, urged a compromise; but Mr. Gladstone declined to accept any hostile amendments. Then the Queen writes to the Archbishop expressing "the greatest alarm" as to the "probable effect" of the absolute rejection of the Bill, and urges that there was no reason "to believe that any fresh appeal to the people would lead to a different result," and that His Grace's great influence should be brought to bear. Somewhat later, Dr. Tait writes to Her Majesty that the Conservatives had decided to reject the Bill; further on, that the opponents, owing to defections, could not reckon upon a larger majority than twenty; and, finally, that the Conservative leaders were willing to reserve their strength for Committee. When the second reading was carried, notice was given of a series of hostile amendments, and again the Queen urged concessions "on both sides."

For four days, at the beginning of July, the Bill was considered in Committee by the Lords. A large number of amendments, which taken together emasculated the Government scheme, were carried. Most of them were rejected by the Commons at a single sitting; the Government having been fortified in their resolution by a remarkable demonstration of public opinion, seven Free Church denominations combining in a great meeting to protest against the action of the Lords. The Peers, stimulated no doubt by the Royal hints, angrily insisted upon most of their amendments, including the excision from the preamble of the words that no portion of the surplus should be applied for "the maintenance of any church or clergy, or other ministry, nor for the teaching of religion," for which the ecclesiastical leaders and their allies fought with strenuous tenacity. The resolution of

Mr. Gladstone in resisting this and other proposals to absorb, if possible, the whole surplus—one being to give parsonages and glebes to the Romish and Presbyterian clergy—is worthy of the utmost admiration. On the 20th of July, when the "no surrender" spirit was at its height, Lord Granville suggested a two days' adjournment, and before the House again met, Lord Cairns appeared as *Deus ex machinâ.* He proposed on behalf of the Tories to give up the additional private endowments, the Ulster glebes, the clerical tax, and the concurrent endowment device,* while the Government consented to modify the provisions as to commutation, and the curates, and to defer legislation as to the surplus. The Irish Church, "sent naked and bleeding into the wilderness," got eight millions sterling by the Bill, and an additional million by the compromise, in lieu of four millions demanded by the Peers. This settlement was accepted in both Houses, and on July 26th the Bill received the Royal assent. From January 1st, 1871, religious equality in Ireland was recognised by law—a political revolution and an important precedent.

It has already been stated that during this decade there was a remarkable political revival in Wales, the foundation of which was laid in 1862, when Mr. Richard accompanied Mr. Miall and Mr. Carvell Williams to attend a Conference at

* The infatuation in respect to this proposal was extraordinary, and by no one was it always more strongly pressed forward than by Lord John Russell. The bishops of our "Protestant" Church—by fourteen to five—supported it, perhaps for the reason blurted out by Lord Hardwicke, that concurrent endowment would help to strengthen the claim of the disestablished Church to a "larger slice" of the property. The *Record* "with grief and shame" remarked that in this case the bishops "invited the bitter gibes of Liberationists like Mr. Miall, who have said that the 'almighty dollar' and not Christian Protestantism is now the watchword of the bishops."

Swansea in order to stir up the people of the Principality to a fuller sense of their duties as citizens. Leading Liberals in the Principality heartily co-operated in the work, and several other conferences were held, and at Carmarthen a South Wales Registration Society was formed, Mr. Morley entering heartily into the movement. The result appeared in the great electoral triumph of 1868. There was a simultaneous educational movement in the Principality, which resulted in the establishment of a Normal College at Brecon, and subsequently in a University College at Aberyswith. An attempt was made on a large scale to originate places of worship in South Wales for the English-speaking population, in connection with which Mr. Morley contributed £5,000 in three years in aid of local efforts, which led to the erection of twenty-three Congregational chapels in six different counties, with accommodation for some 10,000 persons. These were ultimately increased to fifty churches, many of which became powerful centres of Christian work. A similar course was pursued in North Wales—with the generous assistance of Mr. Morley, and the late Mr. Hudson, of Chester—the Rev. Burford Hooke organising the movement.

Sir S. Morton Peto, Bart.—who, as has already been said, retired from the representation of Bristol, having previously been member for Norwich and Finsbury—had done good service in Parliament, by taking in hand the Burials question, and getting a Bill passed to facilitate the appointment of Dissenting trustees. He was foremost in promoting the interests of the Baptist denomination, of which he was a prominent member, and for many years he was treasurer of the Baptist Missionary Society. He erected Bloomsbury Chapel, and was the means of bringing to that pastorate the Rev. Dr. Brock, of Norwich, who formed an influential church, and took a foremost position among metropolitan Nonconformists. Sir Morton also gave substantial assistance to the Metropolitan Tabernacle, helped to found the Diorama Chapel, Regent's Park, of which Dr. Landels was the first pastor, and also the Tabernacle at Notting Hill, where for a time the Rev. J. A. Spurgeon was the minister, besides contributing largely to other places of worship. But in the great financial panic that swept over the City on "Black Friday" (May 11, 1866), the colossal contracting firm of Peto and Betts went down—its liabilities being estimated at four millions sterling. After this catastrophe Sir Morton Peto, for the most part, retired from public life, though he never lost sight of the interests of the religious community with which he had a life-long connection, and with the remnant of his fortune he, to some extent, continued to assist in the work of the denomination. His baronetcy was conferred on him in recognition of his enterprise in constructing a railway from Balaclava to Sebastopol during the Crimean War. Sir Morton lived to be fourscore years of age.

During this decade the Baptist denomination—of which little has been recently said in these pages apart from the work of Mr. Spurgeon and Sir M. Peto—steadily increased in numbers and influence, partly owing to the popularity of Mr. Spurgeon, partly to the growing strength of the Baptist Union of Great Britain and Ireland, and indirectly to the great success of the Baptist Missionary Society. The Union, though formed as far back as 1832, did not for some time secure the general support of the denomination. "Its existence," said Mr. Hinton, "was a continual struggle." But it gradually grew in strength under the auspices of such men as the Hon. and Rev. Baptist Noel, Dr. Steane, Dr. Gotch, Dr. Brock, Dr. Underhill, Dr. Price, Dr. Landels, Dr. Clifford, and the Revs. C. Williams, J. T. Brown, J. P. Chown, C. Vince, and others. For a long time Dr. Steane and the Rev. J. H. Hinton acted as Secretaries of the Union, and when they retired, in 1864, they were requested to sit for their portraits. Mr. Hinton resigning after a quarter of a century of active service, the Rev. J. H. Millard succeeded him in the office. The annual meetings were, for the most part, held at the Mission House in Moorgate Street, which having been sold, a commodious and suitable building was erected in what is now Furnival Street, Holborn, which has become the headquarters of the denomination. At its several meetings the Union received reports from the country associations, which were always of a varied, and not seldom of an interesting, character; and the chairmen discoursed, not only on the specific claims, projects, and shortcomings of the denomination, but on public religious questions; and it invariably sent delegates to the Triennial Conferences of the Liberation Society, and passed resolutions relative to the chief ecclesiastical questions before Parliament. Not till 1865 did the Union deem it expedient to have autumnal sessions, which began at Birmingham and were successively held in Liverpool, Bristol, Bradford, Cardiff, Leicester, and other large towns. Mr. Noel twice occupied the chair, and prior to the last occasion, which preceded his retirement from the pastorate of John Street Chapel, he was presented with a very cordial and eulogistic valedictory address, signed by sixty gentlemen holding official positions in the Baptist denomination, and presented to him by an influential deputation. Mr. Noel had made an earnest appeal for 5,000 evangelists to assist the regular ministry in preaching the Gospel throughout the land, but there does not appear to have been any decided response to it. Not till 1865 does Mr. Spurgeon seem to have regularly attended the meetings of the Union, and then he took little part in the ordinary discussions. But he and the London Association of Baptist Churches hospitably entertained the delegates at the Metropolitan Tabernacle at the annual meetings, and usually the Union sermon in the great towns where the autumn assembly was held was preached by Mr. Spurgeon.

The Baptists at this period made steady progress. They were little affected by the religious controversies of the time, though their leading ministers at the Union meetings dealt with Ritualism on the one hand and Rationalism on the other. In 1863, the Committee adopted a series of resolutions elicited by Bishop Colenso's work on the Pentateuch and the publication of "Essays and Reviews," in which they deeply deplored such efforts, "because their force is greatly augmented through the alliance of the Church of England with the civil power, by virtue of which the teachers of error are supported out of national property, and from the taxation of English citizens, multitudes of whom abhor the error, and are thus compelled to uphold and maintain it." The courts of law, they went on to say, "are not only impotent to bind the clergy to Divine truths as taught in the Scriptures, but even to secure a right construction of the Articles and Formularies they have sworn to believe; while prosecutions wear the appearance of persecution." The Committee, therefore, earnestly deprecated all attempts to guard the people against the teaching of error by penal laws, and this could only be effectually done by "leaving both the advocates of error and the defenders of Divine truth to the free and voluntary support of their several adherents." The same theme was, at the autumnal meeting at Bristol, towards the close of the decade, dealt with by Dr. Gotch, his remedy being "Christ the Centre"; as well as by Dr. Brock, in his subsequent weighty and characteristic inaugural address in London. In reply to the warnings that decrepitude was coming upon their religious institutions from within, and disfavour from without, and that they had become hindrances instead of helps, the President urged the perpetuity of the oracles of God, of the salvation of God, of the Church of God; in view of which the destruction of all present Church organisations, both the denominational and the geographical, the congregational and the hierarchical, would amount to nothing; but they had an immovable belief in "the predestined reality of a glorious Church, without spot or wrinkle or any such thing."

At this and other meetings of the Union the Rev. Charles Williams introduced the question of a fund for augmenting the incomes of the pastors of the smaller and poorer churches. At first the Union declined to make such a fund its own, and recommended the establishment of a separate society. Mr. Spurgeon, Dr. Brock, Mr. S. R. Pattison (the first treasurer), the Rev. John Aldis, Drs. Maclaren and Landels, the Rev. H. C. Leonard, and others, entered zealously into the project, and the society was formed. Ultimately, in 1877, however, the Union undertook the work, and one of its funds is devoted to this object. A fund was also created, suggested by the Rev. C. M. Birrell, of Liverpool, for providing annuities for aged and infirm ministers, and for the widows of ministers. Dr. Landels and Mr. Williams, assisted by other leaders of the denomination, devoted much time to this project, and were successful in their efforts. On December 31, 1890, the Union reported that the investments of its Annuity Fund were worth £125,269. At the close of 1869 the members of Baptist churches were estimated at 213,506, against 85,245 in 1855; thus showing a very substantial advance during the intervening fourteen years.

Of eminent Nonconformists who were gathered to their rest during this period, the most conspicuous was Joseph Sturge, who died in 1861, and whose whole life was consecrated to benificent public objects. His unceasing efforts to put an end to slavery, his equally meritorious labours in the cause of universal peace and every kind of social reform, and the assistance he gave on behalf of religious equality and voluntary education, place him in the foremost rank of the philanthropists of the age. Equally conspicuous, though in a more limited sphere, was Dr. Reed, the founder of many orphan asylums, whose faculty of organisation was remarkable, and who lived to a great age. The Rev. John Clayton, of whom mention has already been made in these pages, also attained a patriarchal age, as did Dr. Tidman, for a long time the astute Secretary of the London Missionary Society, Dr. Bennett, the historian, and the Rev. James Sherman, of Surrey Chapel. Dr. Vaughan, who died in 1868, figured conspicuously among Congregationalists, and in the Christian Church at large. For some eight years he was the acceptable minister of Kensington Chapel, and was for some time Professor of Modern History in London University, and during this period he wrote many valuable works, one of which was "The Life of Wycliffe." For many years he was Principal of Lancashire Independent College, and upon him devolved the honour of starting, and editing for twenty years, the *British Quarterly Review*. He was a great power both in the pulpit and on the platform, and all bore witness to the decidedly evangelical tone of his own personal religion. In his latter years, Dr. Vaughan ministered for a time to the Congregational Church at Torquay, where he died. Some years before he had to mourn over the loss of his young and gifted son who had commenced a brilliant career as a Congregational minister at Birmingham. Dr. Leifchild was a preacher of great power and unimpeachable orthodoxy, with a somewhat sensational style, who gathered crowded congregations at Craven Chapel, Regent Street; in some respects a contrast to the milder, but not less effective,

John Alexander, of Norwich, who exercised a potent influence as a minister and a man throughout Norfolk and other eastern counties. He was for nearly half a century the pastor of a single church, and one of his foremost aims was to unite all Christian men in works of practical benevolence. Hence he prominently supported the Evangelical Alliance. His friendship with men who greatly differed from him in opinion was well known, and it is a curious fact that Dr. Stanley, Bishop of Norwich, regularly sent to him the questions proposed to candidates for Episcopal ordination. Dr. Raffles may be said to have ruled almost supreme among the Dissenters of Lancashire by reason of his abounding labours in connection with the county college and the county union; but it was a genial and refined rule. Throughout his brilliant ministerial career, during which he always held aloof from politics, his sermons at Great George Street Chapel, Liverpool, always attracted crowds of people; his life as a minister and pastor was most laborious; and his church was a centre of religious influence. Amongst other remembered ministers who passed away about this time were Dr. Urwick and Dr. Alliott; Caleb Morris, whose fascinating pulpit eloquence in Fetter Lane Chapel charmed an appreciative congregation; Dr. Stowell, of Cheshunt College; and the Rev. Quinton Stow, of Adelaide, the father of Australian Congregationalism.

With more decided political leanings than most of the above was the veteran John Burnet, "whose kindly and playful humour, robust intellect, unswerving allegiance to truth, unpremeditated eloquence, and broad Catholicity, have made his memory fragrant to the Free Churches of the United Kingdom." Like but yet how different was Dr. Thomas Price, who for a time, till his voice failed him, was pastor of the Baptist Chapel, Devonshire Square, and who wrote an admirable "History of Protestant Nonconformity," and was for many years editor of the *Eclectic Review*. Besides being an accomplished and weighty writer, Dr. Price was a man of mature judgment, and of warm affection. He was one of the originators and guides of the Liberation Society, and for many years its treasurer.

The Rev. Dr. Campbell, who had been "a man of war from his youth," ceased from his labours in 1867, in the seventy-second year of his age. Some of his prominent characteristics have already been indicated. It has been seen that he was a Boanerges, who was under the delusion—not seldom shared by others, even in this day—that he was specially "a witness for the truth." Consequently, he was, as he boasted, "ever on the watch tower as to every appearance of heresy." If he wielded the tomahawk after a merciless fashion that has become almost obsolete—at all events among Congregationalists—his enormous energy and facile pen gave him immense though transient authority. It was impossible to look in his face in his palmiest days—with "an eye like Mars to threaten and command"—and to listen to his sonorous periods, without discovering the sources of his domineering influence, and also the secret of his decline. His "men, brethren, and fathers'" style of address, which was the particular aversion of Mr. Binney, belonged rather to the rostrum than to the editorial chair. While his *Banner* and *Standard* were the fitting receptacles of the outpouring of his busy brain and burning invective, he showed a great capacity for gaining the public ear, under other conditions, by his editorship of the *Christian Witness*, which he also originated, and his ability to stimulate missionary zeal by his "Jethro." Dr. Campbell was capable of great self-sacrifice and enthusiasm in promoting the Gospel of Christ, and he showed a generous sympathy with all sorts and conditions of men in distress. In his day—even in his later years—he had a large following and many cordial friends, while his home-life is said to have been redolent of affection and benignity. The fact that such eminent men as Dr. Raleigh, Dr. Vaughan, and Dr. Halley took part in his funeral obsequies is a sure indication that Dr. Campbell possessed sterling qualities of heart and mind, which were rarely revealed during his public crusades, or in his jeremiads proclaimed from the housetops.

During this decade more notice was taken of Nonconformist movements of all kinds by the London daily press than had heretofore been the case, for they were now of more than denominational interest. The *Times* did not fail to deal with Church Rates and other Dissenting grievances brought before Parliament, generally in a liberal spirit; and in the *Morning Star*, which had been launched as an organ of the "Manchester School," these questions found a cordial supporter as long as it existed. For various reasons the *Star* did not prosper, even when Mr. Justin McCarthy, and afterwards (for a short time) Mr. John Morley, took the helm, and it eventually—in 1868—became merged in the *Daily News*, the price of which was reduced to a penny. For eleven years Mr. Thomas Walker had been the editor of that journal, and during that period Nonconformists found in him a cordial and reliable, but discriminating, supporter, whose intimate knowledge of the questions in which they were interested, sound judgment, and thorough sympathy with religious freedom, were invaluable in giving a right direction to Liberal opinion, and in spurring on the somewhat lethargic Liberal leaders. When, in 1869, Mr. Walker retired from his responsible position in Bouverie-street, Dissenters lost in him a potential friend, though the *Daily News* did not, in that respect, alter its policy, and has continued to support their claims with faithfulness and ability.

CHAPTER XIII.

FROM 1870 TO 1880.

EARLY in this period there were many signs, besides those already noticed, of anxiety on the part of all the churches, but especially those of the Evangelical type, concerning the state of religion in England. The powerful impulse given to commercial, and manufacturing enterprise, with the enormous increase of wealth and luxury, and the aggravated social inequality which followed; the emancipation of the press from the fetters by which it had been hampered, leading to the rapid multiplication of penny newspapers and of all kinds of periodicals throughout the United Kingdom; as well as the great progress of scientific discovery, the incessant political agitation for an extended franchise and for ecclesiastical reforms, and the sure advance of democratic ideas—all tended to promote freedom of thought, and to give scope for boundless speculation on all questions of human interest, including church creeds and religious institutions generally. The foundations of society were being examined anew, and there was no little disquietude as to what might be the outcome of this extraordinary mental development, and restless spirit of inquiry.

The Free Churches had to lay their account with these important and varied phenomena. Ever since the beginning of the century belief in the strict dogmas of Puritanism had been slackening. The fierce controversies of Calvinist and

Arminian had almost subsided. "In trust-deeds, in traditional dogmas, and in confessions of faith at ordinations," says Dr. Allon, "the older forms of Calvinistic thought continued, but vital conviction was dying out of them. Men were beginning to doubt both traditional Calvinism, and traditional Antinomianism, as adequate exponents of the mysteries of the Divine thought and purpose; and, indeed, whether they could be formulated at all. Since then this feeling has grown, and has caused the almost total cessation of the controversy. Men leave these great mysteries in the unscrutableness common to both the theological and the philosophical aspects of them." Moreover, the Free Churches did not, as in former times, occupy an isolated position. They were now brought into contact with the same seductive influences as affected the outer world, and to a greater extent than ever found disciples amongst the great middle class, whose political power and social importance had been gradually increasing, and their ranks recruited by dissatisfied members of the Church of England. Even the Wesleyan Methodists, whose system had been so exclusive, and their discipline so rigorous, felt the change; still more the Congregational body which, besides possessing a freer organisation, could claim a greater number of independent, educated, and cultured adherents. But while bishops and dignitaries of the church—even Dr. Pusey—held out baits to the multitudinous adherents of Wesley to conform, no such policy was pursued in respect to Congregationalists. The Tractarianism and Rationalism that pervaded the Church of England were an effectual stumblingblock to the former; while the latter still held fast, though perhaps less tenaciously, to their traditions of freedom, and never ceased when occasion required to protest against the bondage and unscriptural character of State Episcopacy.

The firm attitude and increasing influence of the Congregationalists in the country at this time was apparently due to two causes—the wise action of their Union, and the high reputation and timely counsels of their leading representatives. The potent influence exercised by such ministers as Mr. Binney, Drs. Raffles, Stoughton, Halley, Harris, J. R. Campbell, Allon, Raleigh, and the Revs. S. Martin, Newman Hall, R. W. Dale, J. G. Rogers, A. Mackennal, J. Baldwin Brown, and Henry Richard, as well as by eminent laymen like Samuel Morley, Joshua Wilson, Henry Lee, the Salts and the Crossleys, was very far from being limited to their own denomination. To a very large extent they reflected the views of all the principal Free Churches. Dr. George Smith was then, in succession to the Rev. Algernon Wells, secretary of the Congregational Union, the duties of which he discharged with much efficiency. Nowhere could be heard more admirable and timely addresses on the great religious problems of the time than were delivered by the several chairmen at the annual and autumnal assemblies, as recorded in successive numbers of the "Congregational Year Book." They were at the time widely circulated in newspapers and in pamphlet form, and can hardly have failed to produce a deep and permanent impression, clearing and broadening the views, removing the doubts, strengthening the faith, and quickening the religious zeal of those who heard or perused them. Passages of great power and beauty might be given from these inspiring addresses, but it would be difficult to know where to begin or to leave off. Nearly all of them advocated the utmost freedom of thought, and all insisted, in various forms, on the paramount duty of loyal allegiance to Christ as the all-sufficient author of man's redemption, and a sure guide in all the religious perplexities of life; while some faithfully described the defects and shortcomings of current Congregationalism as compared with the demands of its great ideal, and the possibilities of a more exalted Christian course on the part of its adherents. Most of the religious problems affecting the efficiency of the Free Churches in general, and Congregationalists in particular, which are now being dealt with—such as the best style of preaching, the employment of lay agency, nonconformity as a spiritual force, the relations of pastors and churches, the importance of doctrines, Christian union, the Church of the Future, and the support of rural pastors—were then discussed with certainly as much insight and vigour as in these latter days. As space will not allow of more detailed reference to these memorable addresses, it may be useful to quote the resolutions adopted at one of the sittings of the Union after a paper read by the Rev. A. Hannay, on "The present Ecclesiastical condition of England":—

"That this Assembly, having regard to the efficiency and honour of the Church of Christ, and to the spiritual interests of the people of England, has observed with much regret the progress of errors within the pale of the Established Church—Romanistic errors, which invest the ministers of religion with the prerogatives of a priesthood, degrade the commonly acknowledged rites of Christians to a superstitious use, and depreciate the preaching of the Gospel, which, according to apostolic precedent, is the leading function of the Christian ministry; and Rationalistic errors, which rob Christianity of the peculiar honours and the impressive claims upon the faith of men, which it owes to its supernatural origin, and the inspiration of its records.

"That, as the Established Church has, to a large extent, practically ceased to have any distinctive creed, or form of worship, this Assembly desires to put on record its deliberate opinion that the authority and power of the Church as a national institution are being largely abused, to the unsettlement of men and faith, and the hindrance of pure and Scriptural religion in the land.

"That this Assembly, believing, in view of the tendencies of modern thought, that no Established Church is now possible in England, which shall not comprehend all the diversities and contradictions of teaching and ritual, which are distracting the existing Established Church, desires to renew its testimony, as embodied in the Declaration of Faith and Order, adopted in 1833—namely, that 'a Christian Church is purely spiritual, and should in no way be corrupted by union with the temporal or civil power,—and to express its deep conviction that only the separation of the Church from the State can, under present circumstances, prevent the national sanction of superstition and unbelief."

As already remarked, the *odium theologicum* since the failure of Dr. Campbell, had become a comparatively feeble weapon among Congregationalists, and it had never been favoured by their more eminent ministers. But it was not altogether unheard of, even during the decade under review, though charges of unsoundness were raised rather by ephemeral and unimportant newspapers, and Evangelical Church journals, than by the accredited Dissenting organs. Many people will remember that a hue and cry was raised against the Rev. J. Baldwin Brown, an eloquent and thoughtful minister in the south of London,* who wrote a number of helpful and masterly theological—or rather spiritual—works, such as "The Fatherhood of God," and chose to give expression to his elevated and really orthodox views in a form differing from current religious phraseology. His mind was largely imbued with the teachings of Maurice, Kingsley, and Robertson, though too original and independent to slavishly follow these eminent Christian teachers. Once and again Mr. Brown had to stand on the defensive. He lived down detraction, and in 1879 he justified the confidence of his brethren, who had elected him to the

* Mr. Brown was for many years pastor of the church meeting at Claylands Chapel, and subsequently his congregation erected a handsome new building in the Brixton Road, where he ministered for the remainder of his life.

chair of the Union, by giving an address "On theology in relation to the intellectual movement of our times."

Foremost among the "men of light and leading" in the Congregational denomination, as already indicated, was the Rev. Thomas Binney.* Before the year 1870, the King's Weigh House Chapel, so endeared to the Christian Church by many sacred memories, was marked for destruction for railway purposes, and the now venerable pastor retired on a pension, provided by the purchasing company, which, however, subsequently abandoned the scheme.† Although Mr. Binney formally retired from the ministry in 1869, he occasionally preached elsewhere—his last sermon being at Westminster Chapel in 1873. An affection of the heart obliged him to seek relief in rest and foreign travel. On February 24th, 1874, Mr. Binney was released from his sufferings. His remains were interred in Abney Park

* Although he had received the honorary distinction of LL.D. from the University of Aberdeen, and afterwards that of D.D. from an American College, Mr. Binney preferred not to use these distinctions during his lifetime.

† The chapel was utilised for many years under the pastorate of Dr. Bevan, Mr. Braden, and subsequently that of Mr. A. Sandison. The old historic chapel having been at length purchased and pulled down, its name has been perpetuated by the new Weigh House Chapel, a handsome and most commodious edifice, of which Mr. Sandison is still the pastor. This fine place of worship, which stands midway between Duke Street and Grosvenor Square, was opened on July 7th and 8th, 1891. On the first day Dr. Pulsford preached in the morning, and Mr. Sandison in the evening, while at an intervening Communion Service, Principal Reynolds, of Cheshunt College, delivered a dedicatory address. On the following night there was a public meeting at which speeches were delivered by the Revs. J. Viney (the chairman), Dr. Mackennal, J. G. Rogers, Edward White, Dr. Bevan (Melbourne), J. C. Harrison, and Dr. Bradford, of the United States. In the same month the principal meetings of the remarkable International Congregational Council were held in the New Weigh House Chapel.

Cemetery, and the funeral was preceded by a devotional service in Stamford Hill Chapel, in which the Revs. Dr. Halley, Dr. Raleigh, E. Mannering, and L. C. Bevan took part, the Rev. J. C. Harrison delivering an address. The service in the cemetery was read by the Rev. Dr. Allon, who gave a short address, and the concluding prayers were read by Dean Stanley. Many thousands of spectators gathered around the grave, and deputations from the principal religious societies joined in the long procession. On the following Sunday funeral sermons were preached in the Weigh House Chapel by the Revs. Dr. Stoughton and W. Braden.

Although seventeen years have elapsed since the death of Mr. Binney, it is not surprising that at the public meeting in connection with the opening of the new Weigh House Chapel loving references should have been made to the great preacher whose name is inseparably associated with the old Weigh House, and that the elder speakers indulged in so many tender reminiscences of its revered minister. It is to be expected that, as time goes on, such cherished recollections will gradually fade; but the spiritual teachings of Thomas Binney will abide. There must be hundreds still surviving who were by his instrumentality brought into newness of life, his chapel having been a training school in Divine things for a multitude of young people. "He soon," says Dr. Allon, "came to be recognised as especially a preacher to young men, hundreds of whom, from City houses, gathered around his pulpit. He soon felt that this was both his aptitude and a necessity of his position, and to this ministry he specially addressed himself." It is on record that when he went to Australia and to the United States he found quite a number of men who had been his hearers at the Weigh House—"men often high in commercial, political, or social life, and who, in numerous instances, testified to the determining and permanent power of his ministry upon their lives." Mr. Binney was the prince of preachers, and "a king among men." All who have heard him, especially in his prime, must retain a vivid remembrance of his tall, manly, and commanding form; of his quiet but emphatic, if not eccentric, action in the pulpit; of the fervency and elevation of his prayers, which often ushered his fellow-worshippers into the Holy of Holies; and of the vividness of his discourses as he dwelt on the way of salvation. Of his preaching, which was unsensational and opposed to the pulpit style then in vogue, Dr. Allon says:—

"It was the day of stilted rhetoric, elaborate climax, and wrought-up passion. The form of the sermon was as artificial as an epic poem would have been. It was constructed on a conventional model, it was elaborated into grand rhetorical sentences and paragraphs, it moved like a procession, and came to an end like a tragedy. Mr. Binney, in his own preaching, changed all that. He began not only to preach the common things and thoughts of practical life, but to preach them in ordinary colloquial language. As a rule, he did not write his sermons, although he carefully by writing prepared them for speaking. Generally without a note, save in his waistcoat pocket, and with characteristic attitude—the fore-finger of his right hand very frequently in the palm of his left—his sermons were as familiar in respect of language as ordinary conversation. At times there was an appearance of hesitancy, or deliberation, as if casting about for the best way of presenting his thought; at other times, the gradual and unconscious swell of thought and feeling would rise into forcible and even grand eloquence. It was in no sense colour put on, but always the glow induced by exercise. The eloquence was not made, it grew out of the kindling fervour of the speaker; and sometimes description, demonstration, and appeal rose to magnificent heights, and took on the forms of imagination and passion. . . . Mr. Binney's realistic preaching very powerfully affected Nonconformists, although it was only one influence among many."*

Dr. Allon further speaks of Mr. Binney as a great preacher rather than a great prophet, and of having a firm, critical, penetrating, and judicial, but unspeculative, mind; and, above all, of his intense humanity. His was emphatically a ministry of Divine things to human necessities. He would not venture into domains that could not be tested, and he was never a Calvinist.

"He was one of the earliest of his generation to maintain the broad, universal purpose of the Divine Father's love, and of the salvation that is offered through Christ. And for the same reasons he rejected the dogma of eternal punishment; which seems passing through the same stages of instinctive shrinking from it, traditional affirmation, subtle disintegration, and religious abandonment. While Mr Binney shrank from propounding any alternative theory of the destiny of the wicked, he distinctively refused to believe in eternal torments. He felt that conclusions from which, not in their sinful and alienated, but in their best and holiest, feelings, good men instinctively recoiled, could not be possible to the holy and loving God. He felt, too, that it was not possible, as with some mysteries which are simply things unknown, to bow in silence before these conclusions. They involve a necessary appeal to moral judgment and feeling; and if in this appeal repugnance, and not sympathetic conviction, is produced, there must be reason to doubt their correctness. . . . He thought that the

* "Sermons preached in the King's Weigh House, London. By T. Binney, LL.D. Edited by Henry Allon, D.D. Macmillan & Co., 1875." Mr. Binney, in his will, prohibited any biography of himself—that is, any collection of the minute details of an uneventful life. But the afore-named volume is prefaced by a "Biographical and Critical Sketch," extending over more than fifty pages, written by Dr. Allon at the request of Mr. Binney's family, which is a charming and masterly, as well as elaborate estimate of the great preacher's life-work, and of the noble qualities of heart and mind that marked his public career.

exegesis of Scriptural representations needed a thorough re-examination, and that a reasonable and reverent interpretation of the strong language of Scripture was possible which would not necessitate the dogma of eternal suffering."*

Since Mr. Binney's time this suggestion has been amply carried out. Mr. Binney's supremacy in his own denomination was unquestioned. He was twice called to the chair of the Congregational Union, and for many years before his death he was the recognised Nestor of that section of the Christian Church.

Mr. Binney shrank from theologic polemics, but he was always careful in his pulpit and published discourses to justify his doctrines to the moral conscience of men. He was, however, often drawn into ecclesiastical controversy somewhat against his will, although there are manifest signs that he relished the gentle excitement of pulverising Church bigots. His pamphlets and tracts on these subjects constitute a small library. Some of them have been already referred to in the course of this narrative. "When his vitality was at its height," says Mr. Miall, "there was a voice at the King's Weigh House which went straight into the heart of the people, and there was a hand which could strike with a will at social and ecclesiastical iniquity. And not a little of the general turn of thought which has rendered possible the many reforms subsequently effected by direct legislation is fairly traceable to the vigorous arguments of 'John Search,' and of the author of 'Dissent and Schism.'"† Though Mr. Binney was an

* "Biographical and Critical Sketch," p. 54.

† Outside the Congregational body Mr. Binney had a great reputation, though he was often misunderstood, partly in consequence of his independent attitude. In the published extracts from Lord Shaftesbury's diary ("Life," &c.), there is this curious entry :—"1853, May 13. Mrs. Stowe dined with us here last night and all her party; very successful. I rejoice, as a peace-maker, to have brought together the

uncompromising enemy of Church and State connection, he never took an active part in the Liberation movement, partly because his nature was averse to rough platform agitation, except in extreme cases. He was no politician, and if he was a "Political Dissenter," it was in writing only and not in speech, and he cared for Disestablishment mainly as a means of putting a check on sacerdotalism. In this respect he only shared the feelings, and observed the neutrality, of many eminent Congregationalists of the day, such as Dr. Stoughton and Dr. Raleigh. "In the case of Mr. Binney," says Dr. Allon, "his warm affections, his ingenuous and almost womanly delight in human love, made him shrink from polemical conflicts into which others eagerly threw themselves, and sometimes kept him silent when he ought to have spoken."

During this decade the proceedings of Parliament in relation to the Free Churches were of great importance. By the disestablishment of the Irish Church, the ardent supporters of the English State Church were greatly discouraged, and not a few of them in high position believed that the same fate in respect to their own religious communion was within measurable distance. Both they and

Archbishop of Canterbury and the Rev. Thomas Binney, a flaming Dissenter. After dinner we had many Dissenters, many clergy, the editor of the *Patriot* newspaper, Josiah Conder, shopkeepers, lawyers, peers, &c., &c., all with their ladies. It was quite 'a happy family,' and every one seemed mightily pleased." In the same year, under date March 28, Dr. Tait, then Bishop of London, had this characteristic record in *his* diary:—"I received in the Guard Room a deputation from 4,000 Dissenting ministers eager to have the sanction of Parliament for marrying their deceased wives' sisters. Old Binney was there, looking and speaking like a king of men, but —— talked egregious nonsense, as did some of the others; I heard all they had to say, and gave no answer." This decision was perhaps a prudent one. It is not easy to imagine so liberal a prelate as Dr. Tait having to defend the attitude of clerical bigots on this question.

the Liberation Society somewhat underrated the tenacity of the Establishment, though the rapid education of public feeling on the subject seemed to warrant such an expectation. There were, however, several outworks to the main citadel yet to be razed to the ground. Soon after the Irish Act had been passed, a measure for the further opening of grammar schools to Dissenters received the royal assent, and not long afterwards the Bill for abolishing all ecclesiastical tests in Oxford and Cambridge Universities became law.

This Bill had now become a Government measure, and was still in the hands of Sir John Coleridge, Solicitor-General in the new administration. In the Commons no one opposed it. In the Lords, on the plea of Lord Salisbury that the safeguards for religion required careful consideration, it was hung up for a year. When in 1871 the same measure was again presented to the Upper House, the Tory peer aforesaid moved sundry amendments which were, by Mr. Gladstone's advice, decisively rejected by the Commons. When the Bill came back again to the peers, Lord Salisbury advised them once more to throw it out. But they declined to insist on his lordship's mischievous declaration—which was the essence of his "amendments"—by a majority of forty (129 to 89), most of the bishops present, to their credit, supporting the Government. The other amendments shared a similar fate, and in June the University Tests Abolition Bill—Durham being included—received the royal assent. All degrees, all emoluments, and all offices in these seats of learning were thus thrown open to Nonconformists after a prolonged and bitter contest.* As recorded in this History, it was nearly a hundred and fifty years since formal application had been made to admit

* It was not, however, till 1882 that the heads of colleges and fellowship in Oxford and Cambridge were freed from clerical restrictions.

Dissenters to these seats of learning, which, till 1871, remained a Church monopoly. Whether in the earlier or later period, the opposition to this equitable concession was stubborn and unreasonable. It might have been still further delayed but for the firmness of Mr. Gladstone and Sir John Coleridge, as well as the invaluable assistance of eminent University reformers, such as Professor Goldwin Smith, Professor Jowett, Professor Bryce, and Mr. Charles Roundell. It need hardly be said that the Act has worked well.* Prior to this vigorous Parliamentary action, Lord John Russell had, in 1850, secured a Royal Commission on the Universities, whose report was the foundation for the various Bills promoted successively by Mr. Heywood (the pioneer in this work in the House of Commons), Mr. Dodson, Mr. Bouverie, Mr. Goschen, and Sir John Coleridge. Out of doors the Liberation Society was always active in backing up this great reform, especially the Chairman of the Parliamentary Committee, Dr. Foster, whose efforts in this direction were untiring, although, owing to removal to New Zealand, he was not destined personally to see the consummation of his labours.

* The beneficial effect of throwing open the universities cannot be gainsaid. In both of them Nonconformists have successfully competed for their distinctions. Nineteen times in thirty years a Dissenter has won the position of Senior Wrangler at Cambridge—that is, between 1860 and 1889—once four years in succession. Conspicuous in the list were the sons of the Rev. J. Aldis—the third was Senior Wrangler and Smith's Prizeman in 1861; the fourth, Sixth Wrangler, with classical honours, in 1863; the fifth, Second Wrangler and Prizeman, with classical honours, in 1866. At Oxford also many Nonconformists have gained high honours, amongst whom were the Rev. R. F. Horton, M.A., now of Hampstead, whose appointment as examiner in Theology was vetoed by Convocation. It may also be noted that the abolition of tests in that University led to the establishment of Mansfield—of which something will be said further on.

How strongly the tide had set in against Church exclusiveness was shown by the redress about this time of other ecclesiastical grievances. Mr. Hadfield's Bill for abolishing the declaration required from municipal officers, that they would not use their official influence to the detriment of the Established Church—a mere vexatious symbol, a kind of Gesler's cap—was allowed to pass, after having been rejected half a dozen times by the Hereditary Chamber, mainly, as was avowed by the late Lord Derby, to put a bridle on Nonconformists. Two other measures of a different kind, though not less necessary in the interests of religious equality, were the Acts abolishing the declaration against transubstantiation, removing religious disabilities in the choice of Lord Chancellor of Ireland, and allowing all corporate officers in that country to attend their own places of worship with the insignia of office.* A little later the ecclesiastical tests in Trinity College and Dublin University were done away with. Meanwhile, the colonies had been following suit. State-aid to religion was dispensed with in New South Wales, Queensland, and Tasmania, and after the lapse of a few years Jamaica and other West Indian dependencies, Victoria, the Cape of Good Hope, and Ceylon took the same course—thus freeing almost all our colonies in every part of the globe from the connection between Church and State. The impulse in favour of voluntaryism in religion which originated in the mother country went round the world, and now the mother country awaits the return tide.

In 1870 occurred the memorable struggle in the House of Commons in reference to national education, which, in view of recent legislation on the subject, reads like a piece of ancient history. In February of that year Mr. W. E.

* Notwithstanding the strenuous but unsuccessful efforts of Mr. Gladstone in the spring of 1891, the offices of Viceroy in Ireland and of Lord Chancellor in England still remain closed to Roman Catholics.

Forster, Vice-President of Council, introduced his Bill on primary education, the cardinal feature of which was the creation of School Boards to supply deficiencies. Some of Mr. Forster's colleagues rather dreaded the ordeal. "My responsibility," says Mr. Gladstone, in the *Nineteenth Century* (1888), "is that of concurrence rather than authorship. It might have been otherwise." But public opinion was ripe on the subject, and Mr. Foster, better than his colleagues, saw his way how to bring about a settlement, for already he had the Established Church on his side. It was not long before the hostility of Dissenters became manifest. On the motion for the second reading, in March, Mr. Dixon, who was more an educationalist than a Churchman, moved as an amendment that no measure could be regarded as a permanent settlement which left the question of religious instruction in schools supported by public funds and rates to be determined by local authorities. The debate, which lasted over three evenings, revealed very serious differences in the Liberal ranks. The favour shown to the Denominationalists was unsparingly condemned by Mr. Winterbotham, an influential Dissenter, in a speech of great power, and he was followed on the same side by Mr. A. Illingworth, Mr. Miall, Mr. Henry Richard, and other Nonconformists. At length Mr. Gladstone found it necessary to interpose, and promised that the clauses to which they objected should be reconsidered. On this assurance Mr. Dixon withdrew his amendment, and the Bill was read a second time. The alterations proposed by the Prime Minister embraced, among other things, the abolition of inspection, so far as religious instruction was concerned; the adoption of a time-table conscience clause; the freedom of local boards in respect to religious teaching; and the exclusion from all elementary schools of catechisms or formularies "distinctive of any particular denomination." The denominational schools were also cut off from the rates, but were allowed as compensation an increased annual parliamentary grant to the extent of fifty per cent. Further, it was provided that the building grants from the Treasury for "voluntary" schools should, after a short interval, be stopped, and that the election of School Boards by the ratepayers should be by ballot.

These alterations, though considerable, did not satisfy the chief supporters of unsectarian education and religious equality. At their suggestion, Mr. Richard, on June 17th, moved the following amendment to the motion for going into committee :—

"That the grants to existing denominational schools should not be increased and that in any national system of elementary education the attendance everywhere should be compulsory, and the religious instruction supplied by voluntary effort, and not out of the public funds."

This proposal had the effect of bringing out serious differences among the opponents of the Government scheme. For many evenings it was debated; but Mr. Richard's position was greatly weakened by the adverse attitude of Mr. Samuel Morley, Mr. Edward Baines, Dr. Playfair, Mr. Vernon Harcourt, and others, who not only contended for the reading of the Bible, but for religious teaching in schools; though opposed to its enforcement. Mr. Richard secured only 60 votes out of 481, the mass of the Conservatives on this occasion, as on all others, supporting the Government on the education question. On the third reading of the Bill, which now embodied in substance Mr. Gladstone's amendments, Mr. Winterbotham and Mr. Richard entered a final protest against its strong denominational bias; the member for Merthyr declaring that it was easy for a Government to carry any measure by using the votes of its adversaries to defeat the wishes of its friends; but such a policy would prove very disastrous to the Liberal party.* This warning was prophetic. As time went on the preponderating advantages conferred on the Established Church by the Education Act became increasingly apparent, while the unexpected and irritating operation of the celebrated 25th clause,† which did, after all, allow the rates to be expended for specific purposes on denominational schools, and the great efforts of the clergy, often successful, to secure ascendency in the School Boards, further alienated Dissenters against an administration that had in this matter so signally played into the hands of the Church. The result was seen in the great overthrow of the Gladstone Ministry at the general election of 1874, which was in no small measure due to the lack of thorough Nonconformist support.

During the session of 1871, Mr. Miall, who, three years previously, had been restored to the House of Commons by

---

* It was on this occasion that there was an altercation between Mr. Gladstone and Mr. Miall, which excited much public comment. The latter having, in the heat of debate, used an angry and not a happy expression, implying distrust of the Government, the former indignantly replied. It was a momentary outburst on both sides, and did not in the least impair the loyalty of Mr. Miall to his political chief, who, indeed, a year later, when the Disestablishment question was under discussion, referred to Mr. Miall in terms of generous eulogy. Seventeen years later Mr. Gladstone, in the course of a private conversation with the present writer, expressed great regret at the *rencontre*, and sorrow at his share in it. It would not now be recalled—though there is no violation of confidence in doing so—except as an illustration of the great statesman's fine feeling and tender conscientiousness in small as well as great things.

† There is abundant evidence that this clause was particularly obnoxious to Dissenters, and in 1874 Mr. Richard proposed to repeal it. Although Mr. Forster would not listen to the suggestion, the minority of 128 included such ex-Ministers as Lord Hartington (then Liberal leader), Mr. Goschen, Mr. Lowe, and Mr. Campbell-Bannerman.

his triumphant return for Bradford, introduced his first motion for the disestablishment of the English Church—or rather, of the British churches—and he was the more anxious to do so as it would afford an opportunity of placing the question before the country, not on sectarian grounds, but as a question of justice and nationality. While he himself had made the most careful preparation for the event, his hands were greatly strengthened by many public meetings, organised by the Liberation Society, whose primary object was now recognised on all hands, though, as a matter of fact, it had never been concealed. Mr. Miall had secured Tuesday, May 9th, for his motion; the circumstances were favourable, and the hon. member was at his best. The debate was preceded by the ostentatious presentation of a petition against the motion, by Mr. Gathorne Hardy, from 21,000 inhabitants of Bradford. Though Mr. Miall spoke for an hour and a half, he was throughout very attentively listened to, and he sat down amid very hearty applause. The impression produced upon his friends around him—and they were many—is thus described by Mr. Richard, who sat by his side and seconded the motion:—

"When the time came for bringing it forward there was a crowded House. Mr. Miall's position was, in many respects, a very difficult one, for a large proportion of his audience was in anything but a propitious mood. He had to contend with every kind of prejudice. He was not only a Nonconformist, but he was a typical and representative Nonconformist. He was the editor of a Nonconformist newspaper, and, worse than all, he had been at one time a Nonconformist minister; all which points were very repugnant to the ordinary secular politician. He was about to assail an institution which was regarded by many with very sincere, if somewhat superstitious, veneration. But I believe the House was greatly taken by surprise by the speech which Mr. Miall delivered. They had to listen to a strain of refined, almost subtle, thought, temperate in spirit, calm and measured in tone and language, and very far removed from what many of them probably anticipated. Mr. Disraeli was the first to pay a very honourable tribute to Mr. Miall. 'The hon. gentleman,' he said, 'who introduced this question, introduced it with an intellectual power and a maturity of thought worthy of the occasion. I listened to his speech with interest. I felt it was an address which maintained the character of the House of Commons.' And Mr. Gladstone further spoke of him as having treated the subject 'in a tone which has drawn the most just eulogies from every quarter of the House.'" *

It is impossible within a brief space to do justice to a lengthened speech, the essence of which escapes in condensation. But as a specimen of the speaker's style of treatment the following quotation may be given—the specific point being that the State Church in England is an anachronism :—

"During the thirty years that I have given special attention to the State Church system, all the main arguments by which it rooted itself in the public mind have been rent asunder by facts—all the theories (from that of grand old Hooker downwards) which gave it a hold upon reason, conscience, affection, have been pitilessly exploded. The Anglican Church *quâ* a State Church, a Church established by law, a Church lifted by the constitution into political ascendency, has now its only *raison d'être* in the past. It continues to stand among us for no other reason than that

* "Life of Edward Miall." By Arthur Miall. Macmillan and Co., 1834, pp. 316-7. In the same volume are recorded the words used by Mr. Miall some months later in reference to this, his first speech in Parliament on the separation of Church and State. "I have been sustained," he said, "by the sympathy and by the prayers of the Nonconformists throughout the country; and it was in the faith that those prayers would be answered that I rejoiced in the experience which I have never before had in my life, that on the morning of the day on which I was to bring forward the motion, the clouds all lifted off my mind. I can take no credit to myself. I can only say that I have attempted to perform a duty from which I shrank, and that I was assisted in the performance of it."

it has stood so long. Logically speaking, the spring and stay of its life is gone. An institution of which this may be truly said lacks the foremost and most indispensable condition of perpetuity. But look at other conditions. The Church is convulsed by internal dissensions. It must needs become more desperately so in proportion as thought becomes more active, and inquiry more searching, and conscience more energetic; and we know as a matter of fact, what we should have anticipated as a matter of conjecture, that where differing and even opposed schools of theology are dominated by the same legal standards of doctrine and discipline, each will denounce the others as unfaithful, and severe conflicts within will exhaust the strength needed to cope with unfriendly elements without. Then look outside the pale of the Establishment. There are first the various Nonconformist bodies. I will not estimate their numbers absolutely or relatively, because any estimate of mine would be disputed; but nobody will deny that they reach a very considerable aggregate; and to all of these bodies the State Church, in the very nature of things, presents itself in the light of a monopoly, sometimes barefaced and repulsive, sometimes veiled and unobtrusive, but always unjust. Then glance for an instant at the great wage-earning class, both in the large towns and in the rural districts—a goodly proportion, too, of whom possess the elective franchise. It is confessed on all hands that to the great majority of them the Church has ceased to have any attractions, though as yet it may not have called out any very active hostility."

Mr. Miall was ably supported by Mr. Richard in an admirably-arranged address, abounding in apt illustrations and details, eloquently and forcibly delivered. Subsequently Mr. Leatham delivered a sparkling speech, full of epigram and well-turned phrases, describing, for instance, the Church as "a paradox in legislation and an excrescence in our political system." The motion was opposed by Mr. Disraeli, Sir Roundell Palmer, Mr. Bruce (the Home Secretary), and Mr. Gladstone. The Prime Minister gave a sure indication that he did not regard

Irish Disestablishment as a precedent to be followed. But he avoided the principle at issue, and fully and frankly acknowledged the political strength of Nonconformists, who had the power to shatter the whole Liberal party. In conclusion, he "ventured to say to his hon. friend what he was sure he would not resent, that if he sought to convert the majority of the House of Commons to his opinions, he must begin by undertaking the preliminary work of converting to these opinions the majority of the people of England" —a declaration that was rapturously applauded by the Conservatives, and a fair challenge that has not been forgotten by those whom it more nearly concerned. The motion was rejected by a majority of 285 (374 to 89 votes). Including the tellers and five pairs, the total minority in favour of the resolutions was 96 members, among whom was Mr. Samuel Morley, who was unable to resist a motion made in so elevated a religious spirit, though he had already stated that he could not support such a settlement as commended itself to Mr. Miall.* As usual, in relation to such questions, the Irish Roman Catholic Liberals walked out of the House without voting.

To a large extent the comments of the daily and weekly press on the debate were sympathetic. The *Times* thought it hardly to be doubted that this century would see the consummation Mr. Miall so devoutly wished. The *Daily News* remarked that very few could disbelieve in the eventual adoption of the policy recommended by the hon. member. Mr. Miall repeated his motion, varying its form, in 1872 and 1873, but the interest was less sustained, and the historical value smaller, though, on the second occasion, the number of his supporters was increased to 109,

* Mr. John Bright voted for the motion. Mr. Baxter and Mr. Winterbotham, members of the Government, were allowed to be neutral.

including tellers and pairs. The motion for a Commission of Inquiry into the resources of the Church, with a view to disendowment, enabled the hon. member distinctly to maintain that the Establishment was a national institution, and that as the mass of its property belonged to the nation, it could be dealt with by Parliament; while the amendment of Mr. Thomas Hughes only raised the question of Church Reform as an alternative, the mover glorying in the fact that the Church of England embraced every body; but when his amendment became a substantive motion, he had very few votes. Mr. Gladstone was a little contemptuous, and spoke of the "unreality" of the motion, and the "debating society" character of the discussion. In 1873 the debate was cut short by a manœuvre, sixty-one members only voting for it—making, with pairs, &c., a total of ninety-nine, while nearly forty votes were lost by the early closing of the discussion.* This was the last

* At the end of this session, Mr. Miall intimated, in a letter to Sir Titus Salt, his intention to retire from the representation of Bradford, owing to growing physical weakness, and his inability to stand the wear and tear of another contested election. He was requested, in flattering terms, to suspend his decision till the General Election of 1874, when he ceased to be a candidate for that constituency, though for some time taking part in public movements. He was, however, for several years in his quiet seclusion, a deeply interested observer of the course of public events. On the anniversary of his seventieth birthday in May, 1879, a party of friends, including Mr. John Bright, M.P., Mr. Richard, M.P., and about a score of his old colleagues, waited upon Mr. Miall at his residence, Honor Oak, to present him with an address of congratulation, and to assure him of their unabated personal regard, to which he responded with a touching address, in which, after indicating that he had lost the power of active service without losing his interest in the work, he said: "My great and enduring solace is this—that the movement for the liberation of religion from State patronage and control is now beyond the reach of personal changes. It is a moral force which has its life and vigour in itself; it is sure of triumph, though many of us, perhaps, will not live to see it."

time the question was raised in Parliament. Mr. Richard was to have taken it up when his colleague retired from Parliament, but the course of events, and especially exciting foreign complications, prevented him from carrying out his intention.

A glance at some phases of opinion in the Established Church of England at this period seems necessary in order to understand the general attitude and surroundings of the principal Free Churches. There were now three well-defined parties in the Church of England — the Ritualists, the Evangelicals, and the Broad Church. The first and last were, for the most part, gaining ground at the expense of the second, although the clergy connected with each became somewhat united—or, at least, exchanged views—at the Church Congresses, which were held every autumn in one or other of our great towns. This happy device for strengthening the self-developing power of the Church was first adopted in Manchester as far back as 1863, and became increasingly important as time went on; and, as may be supposed, consummate skill was necessary to preserve harmony in their proceedings, and to avoid fiery controversies. The attendance at these free assemblies—which, in many respects, corresponded with, if they were not copied from, the freer meetings of Baptists and Congregationalists—yearly increased; and it is worthy of notice that, in most of the large towns, leading members of the Free Churches so far co-operated as to offer hospitality to the clergymen who attended them—a feeling reciprocated as occasion offered—thus softening, by means of personal intercourse, denominational differences. In one or two cases, as at Leicester, sympathetic addresses from local Nonconformists were formally presented, but the result was not promising. Still, the internal strife in the bosom of the Establishment went on. A large section of

Liberal Churchmen, for instance — Sir John Coleridge leading the way — agitated for the comprehension of Dissenters in the Church of England on favourable terms, but the movement died away. Other Broad Churchmen—perhaps the same—denounced the continued use of the Athanasian Creed, and Archbishop Tait showed considerable sympathy with their protests. But in April, 1872, the Lower House of Convocation gave four days to a discussion of the subject, and in spite of the efforts of Dean Stanley and others to make the public recital of the Creed permissive, it was resolved, by an overwhelming majority, to retain it as prescribed by the Rubric; and thus it has remained to the present day. Soon after, the Primate, in the course of a speech at Tonbridge, complacently referred to the comprehensiveness of the Church of England, as combining the perfection of civil and ecclesiastical society, and as giving shelter to such famous and free-spoken ministers as Arnold, Maurice, and Robertson, "who had done a good work in their day and generation, but who, under another system, might (he said) have been expelled, and not have found a home 'in any of the ordinary sects.'" There is no doubt that the Archbishop had a leaning to the Broad Church party, which was yearly growing in numbers, and striving with much earnestness, but with little results, to bring about radical reforms in the Church.

But the Primate was a little premature in his boasting. Within two years his Grace brought into the House of Lords a Public Worship Regulation Bill, which, when it came down to the Commons, Mr. Disraeli, then Prime Minister, described as a measure "to put down Ritualism."* Opinion

* The supposed necessity for the Bill was forcibly stated by the *Times*, which said that it was "now recognised that a clergyman of the Church of England might teach any doctrine which only extreme subtlety could distinguish from Roman Catholicism on the one side,

on the subject in the Cabinet being divided, it was regarded as an "open question," and Lord Salisbury (then Secretary for India), having vigorously opposed the Bill, was described by the Premier as "a great master of gibes and flouts and jeers." Mr. Gladstone also took the same course, and moved six resolutions, the effect of which, he contended, would afford sufficient protection to congregations from sacerdotal excesses, while leaving the clergy ample freedom in the ordering of Church services. Though these resolutions were defeated, one of them, enlarging individual freedom, was afterwards accepted by the Lords, and retained in the Bill. When the measure was before the Commons, Mr. Henry Richard made a very weighty speech on the subject. Referring to the clergy who were denouncing the Reformation, he taunted the majority of the House of Commons with doing all they could to throw the entire education of the young, both secular and religious, into the hands of these men; and in respect to Sir W. Harcourt's laudation of the Act of Uniformity, he pointed out that that enactment was adapted to do violence to conscience, and to sap morality. In conclusion the member for Merthyr said —and it was truly "a word in season"—"All I desire for the Church of England is that she should enjoy the same

---

Calvinism on another side, and Deism on a third side." Ten years earlier there were scenes of great turmoil at Exeter, when Bishop Phillpotts insisted upon the clergy wearing the surplice, and in London also on a smaller scale when Bishop Blomfield took the same course. But this was a thing of the past. Things had now gone so far among the clergy that many of them, including Church dignitaries, did not hesitate to proclaim 'the Catholic Revival' as an antidote to the Reformation"—"the Tudor Settlement," as it was contemptuously described. About this time, also, Cardinal Manning publicly said that the Church of England clergy had relieved the Catholic clergy of the necessity of defending transubstantiation and the invocation of the saints.

privileges that I myself enjoy; that the fetters by which she is bound to the State be cut asunder, so that she may possess that which the humblest Christian community in this land possesses—freedom to order her own affairs, according to her conception of what will most conduce to her edification, and is most in harmony with the will of her Divine Master."*

The Public Worship Bill—which was said to have been instigated by the Court, and by the passing of which Mr. Disraeli to a large extent forfeited the confidence of the High Church party—soon after received the Royal assent. It has, to a large extent, been a dead letter, because its provisions can only be made operative with the assent of the bishops, who are very reluctant to give it. It has not availed to prevent Ritualism from becoming more and more the fashionable mode of embodying the religious sentiment of the upper circles of society and a large section of the middle classes, nor has it prevented our ecclesiastical tribunals from stamping with legal sanction, to a considerable extent, the Romish ceremonials of the ritualistic priesthood.

The advent to power of the Conservatives in 1874, with a majority of fifty at the back of Mr. Disraeli, was hailed by Church defenders as a fatal blow to "Political Dissenters." But Nonconformists were not greatly affected or discouraged by the change, though this Parliament began as an ecclesiastical Parliament. They were not much excited when, during the first session, they saw the House of Commons turned into a Church Convocation to discuss a new Lectionary—the Prayer Book itself being appealed to; "everything," said Mr. Richard, "but the Bible." They could look with composure on the passing of the Scottish

* "Henry Richard, M.P. A Biography" (Cassell & Co.), p. 251.

Patronage Bill, which was intended to draw the Presbyterian dissenting laity into the Established Church, but actually drove the Free Church into the arms of the Disestablishment party. They could discover a tribute to their influence in the withdrawal of Lord Sandon's Endowed Schools Acts Amendment Bill, which substantially abrogated Mr. Forster's excellent Act. In this case there was a tempest, in the midst of which the Premier "with incomparable audacity" withdrew the obnoxious clauses for amendment; and in the end nothing remained but the substitution of the Charity Commissioners for the Endowed School Commissioners.

Later on there was, however, greater reason for Dissenters to be angry. In 1876 the Vice-President of Council brought in a Bill to amend Mr. Forster's Act of 1870—the basis of which was compulsory education, now demanded by public opinion. Of course there were provisions for strengthening and extending denominational schools, of which there were 12,000 outside the boroughs. The very grave objections to the details of the Bill were considered at a special conference convened by the Liberation Society and Dissenting Deputies jointly, and embodied in a series of resolutions, which were laid before the Liberal leaders. On the second reading Mr. Mundella moved an amendment, which secured only 160 votes, and on going into committee, Mr. Richard submitted a further amendment to the effect that the public management of elementary schools ought to be coupled with universal compulsion; and in the course of an elaborate speech, the hon. member showed how extensively the denominational schools were used by the clergy for proselytising purposes. But the amendment was rejected by 317 to 99 votes, and eventually the Bill passed. In the following session, Mr. Cross, with curious infatuation, brought in a reactionary Burials Bill, offering Nonconformist ministers the privilege of conducting silent burials, without a religious service, in the parochial churchyards, but it was indignantly repudiated. Eventually the Home Secretary had the mortification of withdrawing his ill-omened measure. Thenceforward, to the end of the Beaconsfield *régime*, Parliament was absorbed with questions of foreign policy.

The 9th of May, 1878, was the jubilee of the repeal of the Test and Corporation Acts, which was brought about in 1828 mainly by the agency of Lord Holland in the House of Lords, and Lord John Russell in the Commons. The veteran leader of the Whig party had long since retired from public life, and by favour of the Queen was calmly spending the last days of his protracted life at Pembroke Lodge, Richmond. With the approval of his lordship's family, a deputation from the Deputies of the Three Denominations, consisting of Messrs. S. Morley, M.P., H. Richard, M.P., Mr. Edward Baines, Sir Charles Reed, Mr. J. R. Hill, and the Revs. J. Baldwin Brown (Chairman of the Congregational Union), and J. G. Rogers, representing the Independents; Rev. G. Gould (President), Dr. Underhill, and Rev. S. H. Booth (Baptists); Dr. McEwen (Presbyterian); and Messrs. New and Aspland (Unitarian), went down to Richmond to present Earl Russell with an address congratulating him on his conspicuous share in carrying that great measure, and on his life-long advocacy of religious freedom. They were cordially received by the Countess, who regretted that her husband was too feeble in health to be able to welcome them in person. The deputation was introduced by Mr. Richard in an appropriate speech, and after brief and laudatory remarks from Mr. Morley, Mr. Brown, Mr. New, and Mr. Baines, her ladyship read a reply in which Earl Russell, after gratefully expressing his thanks, said that in none of the national struggles in which he had been engaged had he a stronger conviction of the justice and greatness of the issue than in the effort to secure the emancipation of Dissenters from odious disabilities, and of the victories which he had helped to gain, none was dearer to him than the repeal of the Test and Corporation Acts. Subsequently, Lord Rollo Russell and Lord Edmond Fitzmaurice, in grateful terms, addressed the deputation. The more public celebration of the jubilee was postponed in consequence of Earl Russell's critical condition. In a few weeks the end came, and the decease of his lordship gave rise to general demonstrations of regret and respect; his widow, who had received a great number of addresses from public bodies, gratefully declining the offer of a State funeral.

On the 18th of June there was a public banquet at the Cannon Street Hotel to commemorate the repeal of the Test and Corporation Acts. Earl Granville presided. Mr. Richard was placed in the vice-chair, and there was an unprecedented attendance of Liberal members of all shades of opinion, and of Nonconformist ministers and laymen. The Chairman, in giving the first toast—"The Event we Commemorate—the first of those triumphs of religious liberty which have made the half-century memorable"—dwelt with much felicity upon the national services of the recently-deceased statesman, and upon the valuable support given by Nonconformists to the Liberal party. Mr. Samuel Morley, M.P., proposed the second toast—"The Protestant Dissenting Deputies, and the other public bodies who initiated and carried to a successful issue the agitation for the repeal." To this Mr. Richard responded, and in the course of his speech he produced a medal which had been struck in 1828 in connection with the event they were celebrating; and at the request of their secretary (Mr. Shepheard) placed it in the hands of their chairman—one who had already guarded, and would no doubt in the future courageously and eloquently defend, those principles of religious liberty which that medal might be said to symbolise. "The revered memory of Earl Russell, the patriotic and consistent champion of the rights of conscience," was responded to by Lord Arthur Russell; and then Mr. W. E. Forster proposed the memory of the Parliamentary associates of the departed statesman, dwelling to a great extent upon the grand example of the old Puritans—a safe topic for a statesman who had been somewhat at war with their descendants. "The Health of Mr. George Hadfield," whose persistent advocacy of the Qualification for Offices Bill swept away the last relics of the Test and Corporation Acts," was proposed by Lord E. Fitzmaurice, but the feebleness of the veteran Nonconformist prevented him from being present. Among the other speakers were Mr. Osborne Morgan, Lord Cork, and the Hon. E. Lyulph Stanley, whose significant reference to "religious equality" afterwards drew from Mr. Goschen the remark that there were Church as well as Nonconformist advocates of religious liberty, and who hinted that it was undesirable to invite the secession of any portion of their army by summoning them to a cause for which they had not been enrolled. As may be imagined, the proceedings at this feast were somewhat protracted, but by no means to the extent of the banquet of 1828, which lasted till half-past one in the morning!

Although from 1874 to 1880 the supreme Government of the United Kingdom was in the hands of Lord Beaconsfield and his colleagues—who cared little for domestic legislation, except for reactionary purposes, and strove to dazzle the nation with their "spirited foreign policy"—the Liberation Society, which now represented the great mass of Nonconformists in their combined action, the Wesleyans (or rather their ministers) excepted, profitably employed that period in seed-sowing on an extensive scale. At the Triennial

Conference of 1877 the Executive Committee were able to report very favourably of this movement. During the three preceding years between five and six millions of publications of various kinds had been issued. There had been 2,600 meetings and lectures, some of them on a large scale. These were attended by Dr. R. W. Dale and the Rev. J. G. Rogers, who, in an exemplary spirit of self-sacrifice, and of devotion to the cause of religious equality, consented to attend a series of demonstrations in the large centres of population, which were invariably crowded, and aroused much enthusiasm on behalf of Free Church principles wherever they went. In 1874 it had been resolved to raise, during the next five years a special fund of £100,000, and before the close of that conference nearly a quarter of that amount had been subscribed. This was subsequently swollen to £42,000, which was expended during the next three years, and it was reported that by this means a network of agencies had been established throughout the kingdom, and that the society "had never been so well organised; had never worked on a scale of such magnitude; and had never attracted to its great objects so much attention."* The prospect of an ultimate triumph suggested the preparation of a practical plan of disestablishment and disendowment of the Church of England. This scheme was the work of a large and representative committee, who devoted much time and labour to its consideration. It

* Soon after this Conference Mr. J. Carvell Williams, whose services have several times been adverted to, resigned the position of Secretary on the completion of his twenty-fifth year in that position, and was appointed Chairman of the Society's Parliamentary Committee, and deputy-Chairman of the Executive Committee, which offices he still holds. At an earlier period, Mr. H. R. Ellington and Mr. Illingworth, M.P., became joint Treasurers, and eventually the last-named gentleman, together with Mr. Evan Spicer, undertook the same duties.

was published as a separate paper, under the title of "Suggestions," which dealt with the whole subject, some of the topics discussed being "To whom Compensation is to be Given," "Mode of Compensation," "Disposal of Buildings," and "Disposal of Surplus Property."

One of the tangible results of the Bicentenary Commemoration of 1862 appeared in 1875, when the Congregational Hall and Library in Farringdon Street, which had been erected in memory of the ejectment of the Two Thousand, was publicly opened. The ceremony took place on January 19th, Mr. John Remington Mills presiding, and was attended by the leading ministers and laymen of the denomination, including Mr. S. Morley, M.P., Mr. James Spicer, Mr. G. F. White (treasurer), Sir Charles Reed, Mr. Henry Wright, Mr. Edward Baines, Drs. Stoughton, Allon, Mullens, Parker, Hannay, Newth, and the Revs. J. G. Rogers and J. C. Harrison.* The dedication service was followed in the evening by a public meeting, Mr. Henry Lee, of Manchester, in the chair, at which the Rev. J. Baldwin Brown spoke on "The Heroic Age of Nonconformity," the Rev. J. G. Rogers on "The Spiritual Work of Nonconformity," and Mr. Richard, M.P., on "The Contention of Modern Nonconformity for Religious Equality." The subsequent speakers included the Rev. Dr. Moffat and Mr. Henry Wright. At the conversazione on the following

* The Memorial Hall was intended to be a centre for all the religious societies connected with the Congregational body. Its total cost was about £80,000, towards which Mr. Mills contributed £12,000, Mr. Morley £5,000, Mr. John Crossley £5,000, Sir Titus Salt £5,000, several other gentlemen £1,000 each, and the Congregational Union £3,000. When the opening took place there was still a debt of £10,000, the greater part of which was cleared off in the next few days. The Library is hung with portraits of leading Independent Ministers from the days of the Commonwealth to the present time, and the large hall at the top of the building is used for public meetings.

evening, there was an overflowing attendance of ladies and gentlemen. Mr. Morley occupied the chair, and there were present the Rev. Samuel Minton, and other clergymen and laymen of the Church of England. After a Catholic-minded address from Dr. Allon on "The Relation of Congregationalists with other Churches," a resolution welcoming the presence of distinguished representatives of other Evangelical denominations, and urging co-operation in Christian work, was moved by the Rev. Alexander Thomson, Chairman of the Congregational Union for the year, seconded by Sir Charles Reed, and responded to by the Rev. Dr. Angus (Baptist), the Rev. Dr. Fraser (Presbyterian), and the Rev. Morley Punshon (President of the Wesleyan Conference).

Within a little more than a week of the opening of the Memorial Hall, Mr. Richard, M.P., was elected Chairman of the Deputies of the Three Denominations for the next three years, in succession to Sir Charles Reed, who had found it necessary to vacate that position in consequence of having been chosen Chairman of the London School Board. In his opening speech the hon. member presented an interesting historical retrospect of the action of the Deputies, whose successes were the result solely of their sleepless vigilance, and not of confiding trust in political parties, and he strongly deprecated a cringing attitude at the present time, Nonconformists having won the right to stand erect and to hold their own. That Mr. Richard proved to be a most vigilant and laborious chairman was attested by his popularity among the Deputies when the annual address was delivered, and by the fact that he was triennially re-elected to that position to the day of his death. The readers of this History will be familiar with the great service rendered to religious freedom by this ancient body in times long since gone by.* Little more need be said of the Deputies than that their work during the last half-century in promoting good legislation, and in shielding Nonconformists from oppression for conscience sake, especially in the rural districts, has been as meritorious as that of their predecessors in the eighteenth century.

The Autumnal Session of the Congregational Union in 1877 was held at Leicester, and was marked by an unprecedented and memorable event. The Chairman for the year was Mr. Richard, M.P., the first layman who had occupied that position, though, after all, he was an ex-minister. For the first time, also, the autumnal sermon was preached by a member of another denomination, Dr. Alexander McLaren, of Manchester, who spoke some timely words, and made a great impression on his hearers. The subject of the Chairman's address, which was pervaded by an earnest, healthy, and sanguine tone, was "The Application of Religion to Politics," in the course of which he traced many of the evils of society to the fact that the teachings of Christ had nowhere been fully applied to politics, and said that he had no hope for the future of this world that was not connected with Christianity.

The novelty referred to was another conference, held on the evening of the second day, at Wycliffe Congregational Church, of "those who value spiritual religion, and who are in sympathy with the principle that religious communion is not dependent on agreement in theological, critical, or historical opinion"; there being an understanding that no one was committed either positively or negatively to more than the words quoted imply. The Rev. Mark Wilks, of Holloway, presided, and there was a large attendance of ministers

* The Deputies were organised in 1732 (see p. 270), and now number more than 250 members.

and laymen, the majority apparently being members of the Congregational Union who did not sympathise with the object of the meeting; nor did all of them manifest a becoming spirit, some regarding the conference as an unseemly challenge. It is not easy in a small compass to give an adequate idea of a conference so unique and indefinite in its scope. A hymn having been sung, and prayer offered by the Rev. J. Hunter, of York, the chairman explained the object of that assembly. He disclaimed a spirit of hostility to the Congregational Union. People generally, he contended, were either indifferent to theology as compared with religion, or in serious doubt as to the truth of the doctrines to which they might, nevertheless, give a formal answer, or had arrived at the conclusion that theology was absolutely false. Those had been invited to that conference who were in substantial agreement that religious communion is independent of intellectual identity, and that Christianity is a life, and not a system of belief.

Mr. J. Allanson Picton, M.A., of Hackney, then read an able, elaborate, and rather metaphysical paper on "Some Relations of Theology to Religion;" its object being to show that, while theology has always been of practical importance to religion, the same office has, at different stages of human progress, been performed by various theologies, and that experience does not justify us in insisting that any one set of theological opinions is necessary to spiritual life. Religion was older than theology, but without theology religion never could have known itself. People should be satisfied with their theology if it purified and elevated their hearts. The Great Master touched it lightly, and with a marvellous insight into human needs. To call God "our Father" was not to define Him; and with the doubtful exception of the words "God is a Spirit," Jesus never went further. Therefore, in this age, when many systems are in a state of flux and about to assume forms which no one can foresee, it could not be insisted that any one theology was necessary to religion. Mr. Picton's paper was very well received, and, according to the report, many who did not accept the conclusions of the speaker were struck with his earnestness and the beauty of his style.

After another paper had been read, the expression of opinion was invited, and the Rev. S. Hebditch asked a number of pointed questions, and remarked that from what they had now heard it seemed that the personality of God, the truth of the Gospels, and the resurrection of our Lord were to be regarded as open questions, and that persons differing upon them were eligible to what was called religious communion. This seemed to him very undesirable and absolutely impossible. This view was substantially endorsed by Dr. Simon, of Springhill College, who differed from his old friend and fellow-student, Mr. Picton, whose sincerity he profoundly respected. They did not want to be bigoted, or to suppress liberty of thought, but it was only fair they should know what they were doing. So long as a man's face was truthwards; so long as he was evincing a sober, earnest, and devout spirit in pursuit of truth; so long as he did not preach simple denials, but that positive truth which God had given him to know, be it merely morality, or religious spirituality, or the Fatherhood of God, then churches should exercise a large patience. Dr. Allon went to the heart of the subject, when he remarked that men must be agreed in great fundamental principles, or else they could not act together. It was not intolerance that limited the communion of men who thought differently in religious matters; it was the necessities of human nature and of practical life. The two succeeding speakers put the issue in a concrete form. The Rev. Joseph Wood, of Leicester, felt that Dr. Channing, Dr. Martineau, and the Rev. J. J. Tayler had the same spirit of spiritual goodness and Christliness in them as could be found in the members of their own evangelical churches; and the Rev. Page Hopps (Unitarian) said that when he heard the glorious prayer of Mr. McLaren and the sermon that followed it on the preceding night, there was an answer of Amen in his own heart—and he asked, Why then was he shut out? One or two other speakers followed, and Mr. Picton, in the course of a general reply, said, that what they wanted was, not theological agreement, but that the churches generally should recognise openly what each individual Christian, for the most part, recognised privately—that there was a spiritual drawing of heart to heart where there were the widest differences of theological opinion. By the criticised term, "the grand totality of being," he meant that, as the very basis of faith, the creature was nothing whatever but as the ray out of a candle; the central light of the eternal substance being God Himself, whom he would worship as a person, because he could not picture anything higher.

The Leicester Conference, as was, of course, intended by its promoters, created among the several churches much discussion, and, as Dr. Mellor afterwards put it, "great uneasiness"; and, whether rightly or wrongly, the Committee of the Congregational Union helped to give the utmost publicity to its objects. They appointed a special and comprehensive committee to consider the whole question, who, by a large majority, adopted a resolution to be submitted to the annual meeting. This, together with an amendment to be moved by Dr. Parker, having been published beforehand, there was unusual excitement and a crowded attendance when the Assembly met in May, this time in Union Chapel, Islington, as being more commodious than most other edifices. The chairman for the year was the Rev. J. Baldwin Brown, who was well known to have a great repugnance to religious tests of every kind, and the subject of his inaugural address was, "Our Theology in Relation to the Intellectual Movement of our Times." With great force he vindicated the freedom of Congregationalism, which, because it was free, was flexible and full of vitality, and worked with, as well as for, the people. He referred at some length to the assaults of Atheism and Materialism on Christianity, spoke with discrimination of their foremost champions, and condemned those Evangelical Christians who offered a theological creed or ecclesiastical system instead of a Gospel. At the crisis that was upon them they must, he said, bring more humanity into their Gospel. But the Gospel was not a noble and beautiful speculation about God, about life, about duty, but the tale of what the God who made the world had, in His own living person, done and suffered for the world. Here was the firm, strong, broad basis of Christian communion. From the demand somewhat imperatively made upon them for religious communion on a basis independent of doctrinal ideas, as well as from the way recommended to the Union to meet it, he utterly dissented. Mr. Brown thought they were taking a very unwise step in suffering any course of action on vital matters to be forced upon them by a Conference outside their pale. They had best consult their own dignity and the true interests of their churches by refusing to recognise the action of a knot of individuals, whose number and weight they had no means of estimating, who carried on operations outside their fellowship. He denied that there was "a dangerous laxity" among them, and went on to say, with much emphasis: "No demand which can be made on the one hand, and no resolutions which can be passed on the other, will in the least cripple our liberty of action, as churches or as ministers, in giving large and loving extension to our fellowships where vital sympathy demands it, or in refusing it where, under cover of specious phrases, we feel that there is radical difference within." What need was there that they, whose ministers were among the ablest and most successful preachers of the Gospel, must pray the world to believe that they were loyal to the Gospel, and must hearten their faith by repeating their creed? There was no necessity to pass such a resolution as was to be proposed. They were saying the same thing in a hundred nobler and more effectual ways, and the world heard them. Declarations and confessions were valuable documents when men knew little of each other beyond a narrow circle. They meant nothing now.

This dignified, vehement, and formidable protest from the chair was naturally an embarrassment to those who were about to take action. There was, however, substantially nothing else done during the two days' sittings of the Assembly, besides the discussion of the programme of the Leicester Conference. It was opened by the Rev. Dr. Mellor, of Halifax, who moved the following resolutions, which, for the sake of completeness, may be quoted *in extenso* :—

"That, in view of the uneasiness produced in the churches of the Congregational Order by the proceedings of the recent Conference at Leicester on the terms of Religious Communion, the Assembly feels called upon to re-affirm, that the primary object of the Congregational Union is, according to the terms of its own constitution, to uphold and extend Evangelical Religion.

"That the Assembly appeals to the history of the Congregational churches generally, as evidence that Congregationalists have always regarded the acceptance of the Facts and Doctrines of the Evangelical Faith revealed in the Holy Scriptures of the Old and New Testaments as an essential condition of Religious Communion in Congregational churches, and that among these have always been included the Incarnation, the Atoning Sacrifice of the Lord Jesus Christ, His Resurrection, His Ascension, and Mediatorial Reign, and the Work of the Holy Spirit in the renewal of men.

"That the Congregational Union was established on the basis of these Facts and Doctrines is the judgment of the Assembly, made evident by the Declaration of Faith and Order adopted at the Annual Meeting in 1833, and the Assembly believes that the churches represented in the Union hold these Facts and Doctrines in their integrity to this day."

The speaker only incidentally referred to the chairman's arguments. He effectively dealt with some of the claims of the Leicester Conference, vindicated the right of the Union to adopt a declaration on the subject, insisted that it was not a question of individual freedom, but of association and fellowship, and asked how could they have communion with each other when they did not worship the same being, co-operate in the same work, or preach the same Gospel. The dignity of Dr. Mellor's address, which was very earnest, and, towards the close, full of feeling, was, in the estimation of many present, greatly lowered by his categorical questions on the points at issue, to which he invited a "Yes" or "No," the emphatic response being an irregular anticipation of the more decorous vote. The resolution was seconded by the Rev. Charles Wilson, of Plymouth. Dr. Parker's amendment was to this effect :—

"That, whilst this Assembly views hopefully every honourable effort to extend the terms of personal religious communion, it is of opinion that co-operative fellowship on the part of Christian churches, as between churches and any of their organised forms, can be made complete and useful only by the acceptance of a common doctrinal basis, and, therefore, the Assembly solemnly re-affirms its adhesion to those Evangelical doctrines which the Congregational Union has maintained throughout the whole period of its existence."

The mover said that it was because of his deep attachment to the Evangelical faith that he objected to such a thing of shreds and patches as the second resolution, which omitted all reference to some of their leading doctrines. Too much had been made of the Leicester Conference, and to legislate or resolve in a spirit of panic was to take a false position. The members of that Conference, who had conducted the proceedings with temper and moderation, had been well answered, if not vanquished, on the spot, and that was enough. He ridiculed Dr. Mellor's method of settling problems, which caused many men so much heart-agony, by a loud "Yes," or "No." He believed they had the truth so far, but God had more light and truth to break forth from His word, and if anyone had anything new to show them, let there be the most unrestricted liberty. They ought to recognise diversity of thought and difference of temperament, and his amendment did send out a brief message to those who were thinking whether the terms of religious communion might not be enlarged. The amendment having been seconded by the Rev. F. W. Aveling, Mr. Picton came forward, and, there being some show of opposition, the Chairman declared that, as a member of the Union, he had a right to be heard. The meeting acquiesced. Mr. Picton said that it was not the object of the Leicester Conference to cast discredit on the doctrines held by most of the members of the Union. Why did not the extreme left of the body leave the Congregationalists and go over to the Unitarians? To this he replied that there was no other body with which they had so much sympathy, or with whom they felt so much at home. He had himself been brought up under the blessed influence of Evangelical traditions, and gloried in the spiritual life derived from Christ, and it was not without a struggle and suffering that he had come to occupy his present position. The rejection of creeds was a principle of Independency, and they should trust to the spirit of freedom that always animated them. If it were asked, Were there to be no limits? he replied that these were selective spiritual affinities [at which there was a slight murmur], which to him had a meaning. But those only who loved Congregationalists would wish to adhere to their fellowship. It would be better to trust to the power of truth to overcome what was wrong. He and those acting with him were not alone. Many in their churches and families sympathised with them, and if the Union set its seal to those resolutions, they would do more than affirm what nobody doubted, viz., that the Congregational Union was Evangelical in sentiment—for they would also cast a forbidding shadow upon the path of many suffering and struggling souls, who feared to give up their living faith, but who could not reconcile their scientific instruction and their historical knowledge with the external framework in which that faith had been embodied. If pain or uneasiness had been caused by the Leicester Conference, it had been unintentional. Looking back, and seeing what had occurred, he for one could not help feeling regret that the meeting should have been held at that time. The Rev. Eustace Conder briefly expressed his admiration of Mr. Picton's manliness and deep feeling. He could have seconded Dr. Parker's amendment, but either that or the resolutions—which were not a creed—were necessary, seeing that Congregationalism was not merely a form of government, but involved certain historical beliefs.

The adjourned discussion was resumed at the Friday's sitting of the Assembly. Union Chapel was as crowded as before, and the interest in the proceedings was sustained to the last. Dr. Raleigh, in a speech full of incisive points, said that their chairman had enunciated every item of Evangelical faith named in the resolutions. Why should he object to the Union as a body doing the same?—a question answered by loud cheers. Was silence to be maintained lest somebody's liberty should be infringed? They stood where their fathers stood, and that was all that the resolutions recognised. The argument that they were attempting to impose a creed was not worthy of consideration. They simply made an historic testimony. Some had thought that a proposal like Dr. Parker's would serve, but the feeling of the country required such resolutions as had been submitted.

Mr. Ackland—the only layman who took part in the debate—deprecated any action at all, and contrasted the speech of Dr. Mellor, which insinuated that those who did not accept the policy of the Union did not believe in Christianity—an inference protested against—with the following quotation from the Congregational Declaration of "Faith, Church, Order, and Discipline":—"Disallowing the utility of creeds and articles of religion as a bond of union, and protesting against subscription to any human formularies as a term of communion, Congregationalists are yet willing to declare," &c. Mr. Dale thought that the matter must be dealt with, though he preferred no action to the amendment, which gave a quasi-sanction to the Leicester Conference, against which he protested. If the Union did not act, people would be left in the dark. The Rev. W. Dorling made a palpable hit by saying that Mr. Dale and Mr. White did not believe in the immortality of the soul in full measure, and yet he regarded them as worthy members of the Union, and did not want them expelled. Then followed Dr. Kennedy, who, referring to a quotation from

John Robinson made by the preceding speaker, asked what that Puritan divine would have said if he had been asked to recognise those who did not believe in God as a person and in a divine Christ. Mr. Wilks hinted that if the resolutions were carried he might feel bound to withdraw from the Union, painful as it would be. The promoters of the Conference ought not to be regarded as delighting in scepticism, because it was borne by them as a burden. Then the Rev. J. G. Rogers said he thought they had no option but to pass the resolutions, for the Conference had thrown down a distinct challenge, to which the Union was bound to give a distinct answer. They did not enter the Union as inquirers, but as having a full belief. There must be a strong reason for separating from so estimable a man as Mr. Picton, but there was also a strong reason for not suppressing their testimony against his teaching, and for making it known that they believed in Jesus Christ. The Rev. J. Wood, of Leicester, one of the conveners of the Conference, having vindicated that movement, the Rev. Edward White said he admired Mr. Picton's speech, but contrasted it with some of his writings. The atmosphere had now grown somewhat electrical, and there was a call for a vote, which was taken as soon as Dr. Mellor had made a brief reply. About fifty hands were held up for Dr. Parker's amendment, and the resolutions were carried by an overwhelming majority. Instantly the Doxology was sung, and this remarkable meeting was at an end, having been marked (says one of the reports) by singular forbearance and good temper, the majority being by no means intolerant.

Subsequent experience can hardly have changed the views of many who thought, at the time, that the promoters of the Conference adopted a wrong method—as indeed was admitted—and that the principle of "selective spiritual affinity" was as applicable to one side as the other. The recollections of that remarkable episode are fading into the distance, but the general tone of feeling—at all events outside the Established Church—is, in the present day, inimical to anything like proscription to religious beliefs and to rigid creed-definitions, and recognises the superiority of the spiritual aspects of Christianity to those which are technical and material. The importance of this controversy, and the fact that both sides were fairly heard, seems to be an adequate reason for giving it a full and impartial record in this History.

The losses by death, during this decade, of eminent ministers and laymen associated with the Free Churches were very heavy. First and foremost was David Livingstone, the illustrious African missionary and explorer, whose romantic life—which began with his sojourn at Kuruman, with his honoured father-in-law, Robert Moffat—strange adventures, stupendous discoveries, heroic devotion to his Divine Master and to the down-trodden people of the "Dark Continent," in his strivings "to heal the open sore of the world" are universally known. Truly says Professor Drummond, in "Tropical Africa," "Wherever David Livingstone's footsteps are crossed in Africa, the fragrance of his memory seems to remain." What can be more pathetic than that memorable twelve months' journey from the interior of Africa of those faithful blacks to carry the remains of their dead master to the coast. As is well known, his body was brought home and interred with somewhat incongruous though well-meant parade in Westminster Abbey, the "national mausoleum." Livingstone was a missionary first and an explorer afterwards; and in the zenith of his reputation he resolutely declined to subordinate the one to the other.

Of a like mind, and destined to a like fate, was Dr. Mullens, who was for many years a successful missionary apostle in Hindostan, and sent home to the *Nonconformist* the most realistic sketches of the terrible Indian Mutiny that appeared in print. His remarkable faculty for ruling men, his indomitable resolution, his genius for organisation, and his tact in carrying out his plans, marked him out, on his return home, as the best man to fill the position of Foreign Secretary of the London Missionary Society. In this responsible sphere Dr. Mullens fulfilled all the expectations that had been formed of him. When, at his own earnest entreaty, in the summer of 1879, he was deputed to re-organise the Central African Mission, on behalf of the Society with which he had been identified for more than thirty-five years, there was considerable misgiving lest his ardent nature should strain the cautious instructions which had been laid down for his guidance. On arriving at Zanzibar, he came to the conclusion that he must go forward. He tried to thread his way through the pestilential and pathless wilds of Central Africa to Lake Tanganyika, only to be stricken down not far from the region where Livingstone had expended his last breath for the welfare of the down-trodden natives. Like his illustrious predecessor, Dr. Mullens was enrolled as an African martyr.

The names of Sir Titus Salt, of Bradford; John Crossley, of Halifax—younger brother of Sir Francis, who had earlier gone to his rest—and George Hadfield, of Manchester, may be classed together as earnest Christians, munificent supporters of Congregationalism, and sincere "Political Dissenters." The first, by his successful enterprise, created a manufacturing model town (Saltaire) which became the pride of the West Riding; the second won for himself a name far beyond the limits of Yorkshire, by his extraordinary devotion to religious and philanthropic enterprises; and the third, while pursuing a similar course of generous co-operation in Lancashire, was a foremost and fearless

supporter of religious equality in the Legislature, and the author of at least one useful measure—the Qualification for Offices Act—which, after about a dozen defeats, was inscribed on the Statute Book of the Realm.

Other conspicuous laymen during that period terminated their earthly labours—William Howitt, the genial and accomplished Quaker, whose high literary qualities were, to a large extent, consecrated to noble ends; George Thompson, whose eloquent voice was so often heard on behalf of slave emancipation and religious freedom; and Henry Vincent, who spent the best years of his life in indoctrinating his countrymen in all parts of the land with Puritan principles and elevated social and political ideas. Before the dawn of 1880 was also called away Mr. John Remington Mills, a wealthy representative of traditional Nonconformity, who helped many a good cause with his purse, and was in many ways useful in the House of Commons, and to his fellow-Dissenters.

Besides Mr. Binney — who, as already stated, was a tower of strength among Dissenters for two generations—many eminent ministers completed their life-work during this decade. Not a few survivors will remember the holy zeal and magnetic influence of the venerated Samuel Martin, for whom Westminster Chapel was not too large a temple in which to minister in spiritual things to all sections of society; and many can bear witness to the massive force, varied erudition and genial humour of Dr. Halley, whether in the pulpit or the professor's chair. Charged with similar duties, but more gifted in a literary sense, was Professor Henry Rogers, who was, indeed, a pupil of Dr. Halley at Highbury College. For some reasons the pastoral office did not suit Mr. Rogers. During six years he was Professor of English Literature in London University, and he afterwards occupied a similar position at

Spring Hill College, and was subsequently Principal of Lancashire Independent College. In 1871 growing infirmities obliged his retirement, though he survived till 1877. Henry Rogers, though a man of retiring habits, was a familiar name in the Christian world twenty years ago. He was a frequent contributor to the *Edinburgh Review*; but his literary fame rests on such well-known works as "The Superhuman Origin of the Bible" and "The Eclipse of Faith."

Not a few living men will remember the fervid and torrent-like preaching of James Parsons, of York; the brilliant qualities of George William Conder as a preacher and lecturer; the silver-tongue and sound judgment of Joseph Fletcher; the spiritual insight and consecrated life of Thomas Lynch; the high theological tone, literary finish, and critical acumen of G. W. Bubier; the skill and perseverance of William Thorn, of Winchester, in setting forth the true principles of a New Testament Church; the potent influence exercised in a wide sphere by Dr. Henderson; the University services of Dr. Hoppus; and the laborious life of Dr. Unwin as head of the Homerton Training Institution. The list of faithful ministers and pastors whose careers had now closed might be greatly extended, for it includes Dr. Massie, of Manchester; T. Adkins, of Southampton; W. Braden and J. S. Pearsall, of London; W. Parkinson, of Rochdale; and J. Shedlock, who laboured so diligently on behalf of Protestant religion on the Continent.

The Baptist denomination also lost not a few eminent men during this period. The services to the Christian Church of William Brock and Baptist Noel have already been referred to. Dr. Burns was best known as an untiring temperance reformer; Mr. Francis Clowes as a man of mark in literature; Dr. Hoby was zealous in denomina-

tional matters; Dr. Leechman stood high in the ranks of devoted missionaries; W. Robinson was a zealous political Dissenter, as well as a conscientious pastor; and the pulpit services of Charles Vince, of Birmingham; C. M. Birrell, of Liverpool; and Dr. Haycroft, of Leicester, are not forgotten to this day.

CHAPTER XIV.

1881 TO 1891.

IN the autumn of 1867 was held the first Pan-Anglican Synod at Lambeth Palace. It had been suggested by the Primate that the sittings should take place in Westminster Abbey; but Dean Stanley, in reply, with malicious frankness, offered the use of the Abbey for the promotion of some special object "of unquestioned importance," such as "the promotion of brotherly goodwill and mutual edification amongst all members of the Anglican Communion." The Archbishop regarded this letter virtually as an intimation that the Abbey was not open to them. There were seventeen British prelates present on the occasion, twenty-one from the United States and twenty-three from the British colonies. The proceedings lasted over several days, and dealt with common objects affecting the relations of the Episcopal bodies represented.

The second of these ecclesiastical assemblies was not held till 1886, when the Lambeth Conference—as it was now called, at the suggestion, apparently, of the American bishops present—adopted a resolution expressing their readiness "to enter into brotherly conference with the representatives of other Christian communions in the English-speaking races, in order to consider what steps can be taken either towards corporate reunion or towards such relations as may prepare the way for fuller organic unity hereafter." The basis for consideration was acceptance of the Holy Scriptures as the rule and ultimate standard of faith, the Apostles' Creed, the Nicene Creed, the Sacra-

ments of Baptism and the Lord's Supper, and "the Historic Episcopate, locally adapted in the methods of its administration to the varying needs of the nations and peoples called of God into the unity of His Church." These overtures—if so they may be called—were forwarded by the Archbishop of Canterbury to the Congregational and Baptist Unions, the Wesleyan Conference, and the English Presbyterian Church, with a courteous letter, in which he stated that the sentiments of the whole assembly on the subject were most real and heartfelt, and concluded by saying: "We know that, under whatever diversities of opinion, a true and loving hope of oneness in Christ Jesus is a living power in the hearts of all His people." It need hardly be said that in each case the response was in effect substantially the same. The subject was considered at the autumnal meeting of the Congregational Union, held at Hull in October, 1889, at which a reply laid before the assembly was approved of and signed by the chairman, the Rev. Dr. Falding. In this document it is stated that fraternal relations and cordial Christian co-operation are "of profound practical interest to the Congregational churches of the country," which deplore ecclesiastical divisions, such as, it is hoped, will ere long "cease to break the unity of the Spirit." With that view it is suggested that preliminary meetings might be arranged to consider measures of practical co-operation, though such a course was not suggested in the Encyclical Letter, but only some form of ecclesiastical incorporation. Approval more or less decided is expressed of the articles proposed as a basis, except the last on the Historic Episcopate, the objections to which are "an insuperable obstacle in the way of conference." On this point it is said:—

"What the Archbishop proposes is that the Congregational churches abandon their distinctive testimony, and accept,

not union with a sister church, but incorporation into a system against which they have been an historical and continuous protest. There is a sense in which we not only hold the 'Historic Episcopate,' but maintain that it is fully realised in our midst and by our churches. Our pastors are bishops, and we strenuously affirm and teach that their 'episcopate' is at once primitive and historical—*i.e.*, after the form instituted by Christ and enjoined by His Apostles. This office our pastors hold by Divine authority and through Divine appointment, their institution being of Christ, who acts through the voice and by election of the churches, whose one and common Head He is. This view of the episcopate is our historical inheritance, and we construe it as no mere matter of polity or ritual, but as of the nature or essence of the Church, necessary to its complete dependence on Christ, and involving its no less complete independence of the State. This conception of the Church, held as a matter of deep and settled conviction by Congregationalists, and derived, as they believe, from the New Testament, is the very thing it is here proposed that they surrender as a condition preliminary to a conference on 'Home Reunion.' This is a surrender they cannot make, and ought not to be expected to be able to make; and we therefore feel compelled to decline a conference which would allow such a surrender to seem possible."

The resolution adopting the reply was moved and seconded by the Revs. Dr. Conder and J. G. Rogers, who, while approving of its spirit, expressed their gratification that the heads of the Episcopal Church had made the overture in so cordial and gracious a manner. It does not appear that any further action was taken in the matter, though it has been a great deal discussed in the American churches.

But it is necessary to go a little further back in relation to the Establishment. Within the space to which this supplementary record of the Free Churches is necessarily limited, though it is impossible to do full justice to parallel

events in connection with the Church of England; yet it is a matter that cannot be ignored. Far apart as the two great divisions of professing Christians may be, they are, in a sense, interwoven—or, at least, overlap each other, as well as being adherents of the same religious faith. Nominally at least—the Act of Uniformity not being repealed—all British subjects south of the Tweed are members of the Established Church. For many reasons, as we have seen, Dissenters took a vital interest in the decisions of the law courts in the Gorham and "Essays and Reviews" cases, each of which greatly enlarged the liberties of Churchmen The ecclesiastical prosecutions which have since occupied our legal tribunals have aimed at restricting the boundaries of High Churchism, and were mostly initiated by the Church Association, though, curiously enough, the venerable—in a double sense—but exceptionally rigid, Archdeacon Denison has figured both as plaintiff and defendant. In the Bennett case the question at issue was the doctrine of the Real Presence, for advocating which view Dr. Pusey had, some time before, been suspended for two years by Oxford University. When the subject came before the Court of Appeal some of Mr. Bennett's opinions were condemned, and his words pronounced to be "rash, ill-judged, and perilously near to a violation of the law." It seems that, in the first edition of the pamphlet before the Court, he had spoken of "a real, actual, and visible presence"; but, in the second, he omitted the word "visible"—a change which, as his judges said, saved him from condemnation. On the whole, the suit resulted in the practical acquittal of the vicar of St. Barnabas, Knightsbridge, who not only remained a clergyman of the Church of England, but continued to introduce into his services everything that could attract the eye or please the ear.

"To the true Protestant," says the Rev. J. G. Rogers,

"that which is 'perilously near' is as objectionable as that which would have been, even in the view of the Court, an actual transgression. Both set forth the wonder-working power of the priest; both degrade the entire conception of the service; both make the altar greater than the God; both turned the spiritual religion of Christ into a wretched materialism and an enslaving superstition. The Romanisers triumphed, and the Evangelicals sought to find consolation in the fact that the Court, though it tolerated Mr. Bennett, had not pronounced transubstantiation to be a doctrine of the English Church." *

From this time the litigation of the Evangelical party, represented by the Church Association, took the form of attacks on Ritual. One suit after another followed, but without any very definite results; although, after the passing of the Public Worship Regulation Bill, which reflected the current popular feeling in 1874, Lord Penzance's Court was specially appointed to take cognisance of such cases. Again and again his lordship gave judgment adversely to the Ritualists in relation to the sacerdotal

* "The Church Systems of England in the Nineteenth Century." The Sixth Congregational Union Lecture. By J. G. Rogers, B.A. Second Edition. (Memorial Hall, Farringdon Street.) 676 pp. This valuable treatise is worthy of the careful attention of the student of Church history, and of all who would understand the ecclesiastical controversies of the times. Mr. Rogers has evidently bestowed great labour and research upon the subject. It may have been a disadvantage that the treatise originally took the form of a series of public lectures; but, however that may be, the author describes with masterly skill, keen penetration, and in an impartial, philosophic, and genial tone the various ecclesiastical movements of the age, such as "The Evangelical Revival," "The Oxford School," "The Broad Church," "The Tractarian Struggle," "The Church and the Courts," "The Ritualist Controversy"—topics of profound and enduring interest in connection with the history of England. Further, the church systems of the Plymouth Brethren, Methodism, Presbyterianism, and Congregationalism are sketched and analysed in a critical, but kindly, spirit, though in a somewhat diffusive style.

vestments—a judgment which, in the case of Mr. Ridsdale, of Folkestone, was ratified by the Supreme Court. After prolonged litigation also, there was a decision against Mr. Mackonochie, vicar of St. Alban's, Holborn, who adopted most of the imposing ceremonials of the Romish Church; but the personal issue was frustrated by the Fabian tactics of Archbishop Tait, who consented to an exchange of livings between that High Ritualist and an East-end incumbent.

Subsequent attempts to come to an understanding between the High Church party and the Evangelicals, such as the proposed Irenicon of Dean Perowne, were resultless; but the suit against Dr. King, the Bishop of Lincoln, for his alleged violation of the Rubrics, brought about a new development of the perennial controversy. The Queen's Bench Division decided that the Primate, with the aid of his Episcopal assessors, might legitimately hear the case; after which the Archbishop could not, of course, decline. The pleadings took place in the Lambeth Library, before his grace, and were protracted to enormous length. The tribunal was, in fact, a resuscitation of the Archbishop's Court, which had been in abeyance for some two hundred years—a signal triumph of the Church over the State, reserved for the close of the nineteenth century. After some months' delay the Archbishop delivered the judgment of himself and his Episcopal brethren on the charges brought against Bishop King. His grace decided that the "mixed cup" was not illegal, but the addition of water to the wine must not take place before the Communion Table as part of the public service; while the charge of "ablution"—washing the paten and chalice, and afterwards drinking the water and wine—was dismissed. The Eastward Position at the altar during the sacramental service was declared to be legal, but devoid of doctrinal significance. As to the breaking of bread and taking the cup by

the celebrant with his back to the people, the Court decided that Bishop King had mistaken the true interpretation of the Rubric; but the singing of the "Agnus Dei"—which had no sacrificial significance—was not illegal, neither did the use of lighted candles come under the definition of a ceremony, nor is it to be associated with erroneous teaching in respect to the nature of the Sacrament—thus setting aside the decision of the Judicial Committee. Finally, making the sign of the Cross was declared to be an innovation on the ceremonies of the Church of England.

In his concluding remarks, the Primate endeavoured to minimise the concessions made to the High Church party by admonitions to the clergy on the necessity of acting in harmony with their parishioners, and by dwelling on "the incongruity of minute questionings and disputations on great and sacred subjects, adding that no significance can be attached to a form, act, or usage unless that significance is in accordance with the regular and established meaning of language or symbol, whether liturgical or other." Is this in accordance with the opinion of the Ritualists, who contend that their observances have no meaning but as the expression of dogma, and who scornfully repudiate the term Protestant?

As was to be expected, the judgment of the Archbishop's Court has been appealed against. In some points it is at variance with the decisions of the Judicial Committee of the Privy Council, and it is possible that the Secular Court may override the Spiritual Court. But the Evangelical party is by no means agreed as to the expediency of any appeal at all; a consideration that may weigh with a Court of Appeal which does not, it is thought, shut out questions of policy in deciding cases of ecclesiastical law. Meanwhile, as the *Times* says, "any country village may suddenly have a priest imposed upon it who will transform its familiar and simple

form of worship into an approximation to that of Rome, and every parishioner must either submit to it, or give up his church altogether. . . . If the limits of the Church of England are to be so extended as to include all variations between the Mass and the Puritan Communion, the bands of the Establishment will be in danger of snapping."

At the General Election of 1880 the country threw off the yoke of Lord Beaconsfield, and gave a majority of some 118—independent of Irish Home Rulers—to Mr. Gladstone, whom the Queen somewhat reluctantly accepted as Prime Minister. Of 343 Liberals returned more than a hundred were Nonconformists, including sixteen members of the Executive Committee of the Liberation Society. Of the members for Wales only two were Conservatives, and almost all the Scotch representatives were in favour of disestablishing the Presbyterian Church, or prepared to accept the decision of the people regarding it. The Triennial Conference of the Liberation Society, held immediately after the election, was naturally of a very jubilant character, for the influence of the supporters of religious equality had never been so great, owing no doubt in part to the activity of the Society in the preceding three years, during which no fewer than seven millions of publications had been issued. For the last time Mr. Miall, though in feeble health, appeared on its platform.

During the first session of what was emphatically Mr. Gladstone's Parliament, which did not commence its sittings till the end of April, much time was consumed and passion excited relative to Mr. Bradlaugh taking the oath, and eventually the Premier carried a resolution by a majority giving members the option of making an affirmation instead of taking an oath. Not till June was the Burials Bill of the Government, which had been drafted by Mr. Osborne Morgan and Lord Chancellor Selborne,

brought into the House of Peers. The measure was very feebly resisted in that assembly, although Convocation had just before strongly condemned it. But it was necessary something should be done, after Mr. Gladstone's generous admission of the great services of Nonconformists as "the backbone of the Liberal Party." In the Commons Mr. Osborne Morgan had the powerful assistance of Mr. Bright and Mr. Forster, and the Bill was carried on the second reading by 258 to 79 votes. One or two restrictive amendments of the Upper House were expunged in committee, and, on the clause requiring the burial service to be "Christian and orderly," Mr. Illingworth proposed that the words should be "Christian or other orderly service," which, however reasonable, found but few supporters, owing to Mr. Morgan's assurance that it would wreck the Bill. It was passed without a division. The amendments of the Commons, even including that suppressing the reference to Convocation, were accepted by their lordships; and, on the 3rd of September, the Bill received the Royal assent, and came into immediate operation. The measure, though useful, is incomplete; but Mr. Morgan's attempts to supplement it by further legislation had, up to the close of the session of 1891, been resultless.

The struggle, in and out of Parliament, over the proposal to allow the burial of Dissenters in the parochial churchyards with funeral services by their own ministers was only less protracted and bitter than the struggle for the abolition of Church Rates. The reason for this is evident. In both cases the supremacy of the incumbent in his parish was menaced, and the concession in each was resisted by what Sydney Smith called "a forty-parson power." It is not necessary to describe the many vicissitudes of this strange and not very creditable conflict, which lasted over twenty years; but a reference to its later stages seems necessary,

for, in fact, the battle was virtually won for Nonconformists in the Upper House three years before Lord Selborne brought in his Bill. In 1877 the Duke of Richmond had a measure on the lines of that introduced "elsewhere" by Mr. Cross and withdrawn, and Lord Granville proposed, as an amendment to the second reading, that interments in churchyards should be allowed with a Christian service other than that prescribed by the Prayer Book, and was defeated by a majority of only 39. In committee the Earl of Harrowby, a staunch Conservative, who, with Lord Shaftesbury, was anxious for a reasonable settlement, revived in substance Lord Granville's clause, and, as the two Archbishops concurred that it would be dangerous to keep the question open, the amendment secured additional supporters, and the result was a tie—102 on each side. This unexpected vote greatly alarmed the clergy, and in the course of ten days a declaration, signed by 12,500 ministers of the Church of England, was sent to the Government, protesting against the suggested settlement, and the Bill was forthwith abandoned. Next year Mr. Osborne Morgan's proposal, embodying the concessions to Nonconformists, was only lost by fifteen votes in the House of Commons, and the question was allowed to rest till after the general election of 1880, with the result already recorded.

Even in the midst of harassing trials at home, owing to the obstructive tactics of "the Fourth party" and the Irish Home Rulers, and abroad, as the result of foreign wars and complications, the Gladstone Cabinet did not forget its obligations to the Nonconformists of Wales. In 1882 Lord Spencer, President of the Council, appointed a Departmental Commission to inquire into the condition of the intermediate and higher education of the Principality, of which Lord Aberdare (formerly Mr. H. A. Bruce) was the chairman, and Mr. Henry Richard a member. Based

upon their report, a Bill was brought in by Mr. Mundella, which had to be again and again postponed. After protracted delays, a compromise was arranged by Mr. Stuart Rendel with Lord Salisbury's Government, on behalf of the Welsh Liberal Members, for the appointment of joint committees for each county, composed of three nominees of the Education Department and three representatives of the County Council, but without the power of levying rates, except by consent of the Council, the schemes adopted to be submitted to the Charity Commission and Privy Council. The several proposals were embodied in a Bill, which was accepted by Parliament. At the same time, it was arranged that the three University Colleges at Aberystwith, Bangor, and Cardiff should receive an annual yearly grant of £4,000, these institutions being entirely unsectarian, and an immense boon to the Dissenters of Wales.

The exigencies of space prevent more than a cursory reference to further political and ecclesiastical events affecting Nonconformists. The general election of 1885, following the passing of the Reform and Re-distribution Bill, gave Mr. Gladstone a majority of more than 100, but also resulted in the return of 86 Irish Nationalists. The State-Church question played a prominent part in this election. The republication of "Suggestions on Disestablishment" by the Liberation Society, and what was called "The Unauthorised Programme," embodying them, had thoroughly aroused the clergy, and from several hundreds of pulpits the old cry of "The Church in Danger" was raised, though with little effect; while the *Record* made the disquieting discovery that some four hundred candidates were, more or less, pledged to disestablishment. Added to this was the fact that Mr. Carvell Williams, chairman of the Parliamentary Committee of the Liberation Society, was triumphantly returned for one of the divisions of Nottingham.

That experienced gentleman was now able to render with more effect the service to the cause of religious equality he had for many previous years given in the lobby, and he had the rare opportunity of passing a Bill for the extension of marriage hours from twelve to three.* But in the general election of 1886 Mr. Williams unexpectedly lost his seat, and what was worse the cause he so steadfastly upheld was seriously damaged by the secession of Liberal Unionists in and out of Parliament—numbers of whom were supporters of religious equality—from the leadership of Mr. Gladstone. Five years of Conservative rule with a majority brought about by this alliance has, to a great extent, kept all ecclesiastical questions in the background. But during the interval, disestablishment in Wales and Scotland has once and again been supported by large minorities in the House of Commons; both have been included in the programme of the Liberal party; and both have been endorsed by Mr. Gladstone himself as well as by his influential colleagues; and both are certain to come to the front as soon as some effective kind of Home Rule has been carried. Under the adverse circumstances referred to the claims of Wales to disestablishment were, during the session of 1891, rejected by a majority of only 32, and received the support of no less than 203 Liberals; the official whips being tellers on the occasion, and Mr. Gladstone giving the aid of his powerful advocacy in favour of Mr. Pritchard Morgan's resolution. The more serious English problem remains to be discussed by a future Parliament. Even the most pronounced Churchmen freely admit that the separation of Church and State in England is only a question of time, and it is quite possible either that it may

* The passing of this Bill greatly exercised the Lower House of Convocation.

be the result of internal changes, or that the party which has granted free education in order to "dish the Radicals" will, for the same reason, in due time, pronounce in favour of disestablishment.

The Jubilee of the formation of the Congregational Union of England and Wales was celebrated in 1881 in a very effective fashion. Meetings were held on the subject in various parts of the country, and it was a special topic at the assemblies held in London during May and in Manchester in October. The Rev. Dr. Allon was the chairman for the year, and his second call to that distinguished position was evidently due to its Jubilee associations. The proceedings of the Union on each occasion attracted more than ordinary interest. In May the Assembly held its deliberations at Union Chapel, Islington—that noble and commodious edifice, erected on the site of the old place of worship, which had for years enjoyed, and still enjoys, the great advantages of Dr. Allon's ministrations. On this occasion the chairman chose for the topic of his address "The History of Independency"—a familiar subject on which he expatiated at length, claiming for Congregationalism that, "above all church systems, it trains men to spiritual apprehensions of religion, to the sense of personal religious responsibility, to independence of religious life, to individualism of thought and will and conduct, such as form the noblest type of the citizen and the Christian." After vindicating the principle that the union of churches is for the benefit of the individual churches that constitute it, Dr. Allon faithfully pointed out some of the defects of the Congregational body, including the use of chapel trust-deeds, challenging the policy that permits the property of the world to be regulated by the behests of the dead, and declaring that "it is the living church, and not the trust-deed, which conserves the orthodoxy that our

Congregational churches have so singularly maintained." Subsequently, in a masterly and exhaustive address, which produced a great impression, Dr. Hannay, the secretary, explained the aim of the Special Jubilee Fund, the chief features of which were to secure to all aided pastors a minimum stipend of £150 a year, which would require an additional annual income of £35,000 to the Church-Aid Society; a gross sum sufficient to relieve the churches of about a quarter of a million of burdensome debts; and an open column for subscriptions to be appropriated as the donors wished. Mr. S. Morley and others promised cordial co-operation in the scheme, and in the evening there was a public meeting, at which the Revs. J. G. Rogers and R. W. Dale delivered the first of the addresses on the subject, to be followed up in various parts of the country.

The autumnal meeting at Manchester was decidedly of the Jubilee order. Some 1,600 delegates and four eminent American ministers — Drs. Dexter, Storrs, Magoun, and Hopkins—were present, as well as Dr. Pressensé, of Paris, and the Rev. Griffith John, the eminent missionary from China. The Free Trade Hall hardly sufficed for the needs of the Assembly, and did not suffice for the crowds who beset that commodious building at an evening meeting, which was addressed by Mr. Richard, M.P., Dr. Dale, and Mr. Rogers in their most effective style. Dr. Allon was again chairman, and took for the subject of his opening address, "The Church of the Future," which was discussed with all the logical force, acumen, and elevation of thought which are characteristic of that minister, and the sermon was preached by the Rev. J. Baldwin Brown. As "preliminary to a beginning," Dr. Hannay was able to announce several large contributions to the extent of £50,000, including £20,000 promised by Mr. R. S. Hudson, of

Chester.* In connection with these meetings, which were undoubtedly the most spirited and successful ever held up to that time under the auspices of the Union, the venerable Dr. Stoughton gave some interesting reminiscences extending over the fifty years, partly historical, partly controversial, with a due infusion of pleasant gossip.

Besides a number of public meetings throughout the country, a series of special lectures were delivered in London, the following being the subjects and names of the lecturers:—"Bishop Burnet and Contemporary Schemes of Church Comprehension" (Rev. S. Pearson); "The Struggle for Civil Liberty in the Georgian Era" (Rev. J. B. Brown); "The Evangelical Revival in the Georgian Era and its Effects on the Development of the Free Church Principle" (Dr. Mackennal); "Broad Church Doctrine and Independency" (Rev. E. White); "Clericalism and Congregationalism" (Rev. J. G. Rogers); "Ecclesiastical Polity and the Religion of Christ" (Principal Fairbairn); "Early Independents" (Dr. Dale); "Laud and the Puritans" (Dr. Allon); "Westminster Assemblies" (Dr. Stoughton); "Independents in the Days of the Commonwealth" (Dr. Conder); "The Policy of the Restoration and the Reign of Charles II." (Dr. Kennedy).

The Jubilee Fund was kept open for nearly seven years, and was not in fact closed till 1888. It appears that the aggregate amount reached the large sum of £434,470; the disbursements being thus divided:—To the Church-Aid and Home Missionary Society, General, £27,829; Special, £12,492; total, £40,021; Liquidation of Chapel Debts, General, £117,876; Special, £130,999; total, £248,875; the Welsh churches con-

* This munificent gentleman died before all his promises could be fulfilled, and his executors declined to pay £8,000 which was outstanding.

tributing, in round numbers, £100,000; Metropolitan Chapel Extension, promoted by the late Mr. R. S. Hudson, £93,236; various Congregational societies, £5,544; colleges and schools, £20,218; new chapels and Sunday-schools, £24,372. As may be supposed, the labour in connection with this large fund was very great and complicated. The responsibility of working the scheme was assigned to the Rev. D. Burford Hooke, whose tact, vigilance, and energy shone conspicuously in its management.

Some two years previous to the winding up of this great undertaking there was a special event in connection with the May assemblies worthy of notice in this History. It happened that the spring meetings of the Baptist Union were, owing to special circumstances, held in the same week as those of the Congregational Union. Some time before there had been the expression of a hope that the two bodies, in so many respects identical in faith and usage, might for once meet under the same roof. A suggestion to that effect was made by Dr. Booth, the respected secretary of the Baptist Union, and before May it was definitely arranged that the two Unions should hold a joint meeting in the City Temple on the Friday following the regular assemblies, for acts of common worship, for the free mutual expression of fraternal feeling, and for united testimony to certain truths in regard to the Church of Christ which they held in common. The first of these united assemblies took place on the morning of May 14, and there was a very crowded attendance. The Rev. Charles Williams, president for the year of the Baptist Union, occupied the chair, and, after a devotional service conducted by the Revs. J. C. Harrison and Dr. Green, he briefly explained the character of the meeting. Addresses were then delivered as follows: "The Idea of the Christian Church held in Common by the Two Bodies," by Dr. Conder; "The Dependence of the

Spiritual Power of the Churches on their Practical Maintenance of this Idea," by Dr. Dale; "The Power of the Churches true to this Idea in promoting Sound Theological Thought and conserving Essential Truth," by Dr. Culross; "Fidelity to this Idea in its Bearing on the Upraising and Nurture of a Consecrated Christian Ministry," by Dr. Angus. These papers were followed by a special discourse from the venerable John Aldis, and it was decided that the several addresses should be printed. At the evening meeting, the Rev. Edward White, chairman of the Congregational Union for that year, presided, and, after prayer by the Rev. W. Hewgill, delivered an address. The subjects dealt with by the succeeding speakers were "The New Democracy and the New Testament Church," by Dr. Clifford; "Congregationalism as a Church System," by the Rev. J. G. Rogers; "The Foreign Missionary Work of the Churches," by the Rev. Richard Glover; and "The Larger Congregationalism," by the Rev. Dr. Parker. The religious fervour and fraternal feeling of these assemblies were altogether exceptional, more than justifying so interesting and remarkable an experiment.

The Revision of the Bible was one of the chief achievements of the decade now under review, and its initiation was undoubtedly the greatest boon conferred upon the English-speaking race by the Convocation of the Province of Canterbury. What was involved in this stupendous undertaking may be to some extent inferred from the fact that it engaged attention for some fifteen years. It is not necessary in these pages to refer at any length to the various versions of the Scriptures that have been made since Protestantism became the predominant religion in England. The names of Tyndale, Miles Coverdale, Cranmer ("The Great Bible"), and Calvin ("The Geneva Bible"), are associated with such efforts; and, when James I. ascended the throne, two of these versions were in use—the Bishops' Bible, which was admitted to be very defective, and the Geneva Bible, used generally in British households, and much esteemed by scholars. The idea of one version to supersede those in use was first mooted at the Hampton Court Conference in 1604. The King encouraged, though he did not greatly aid, the project, and six companies of scholars, two at Oxford, Cambridge, and Westminster, respectively, undertook the onerous task. They began their work in 1607; it lasted three years, and, in 1611, the result was published as the Authorised Version, though it was not brought out under direct authority. For upwards of two hundred years this version, which was the fruit of the labours of a most able and learned body of men, has held the field by its own intrinsic merits; but, as time elapsed, and exegetical knowledge increased, the necessity for a new revision became irresistible.

In 1870 the proposal for a new revision of the Bible was submitted to Convocation by the late Bishop of Winchester (Dr. Samuel Wilberforce), seconded by the Bishop of Gloucester and Bristol (Dr. Ellicott), and favourably received by both Houses. A joint committee was appointed to take measures for carrying that decision into effect, consisting of seven bishops and eight members of the Lower House. It was at first intended only to deal with the New Testament, but eventually the Old Testament was included. One of the resolutions adopted was that the committee should be empowered to invite the co-operation of any persons eminent for scholarship, to whatever nation or religious body they might belong. Some members of the Lower House objected to the inclusion of any besides scholars connected with the Church of England, but they were overruled. The joint committee appointed two companies—one for the revision of the Old Testament, and one for that of the New, and laid down the general rules for the guidance of the revisers. The original chairman of the first of these companies was Bishop Thirlwall, and he was succeeded by Dr. Harold Browne; Dr. Ellicott remained chairman of the second company to the end. As members died or resigned, their places were supplied at the pleasure of the joint committee.

Sixty-five English scholars took part in the work, of whom forty-one were members of the Church of England, and twenty-four members of other Christian churches. Of the latter, two represented the Episcopal Church of Ireland, one the Episcopal Church of Scotland, four the Baptists, three the Congregationalists, five the Free Church of Scotland five the Established Church of Scotland, one the United Presbyterians, one the Unitarians, and two the Wesleyan Methodists. The English Nonconformist scholars on the Old Testament Company were Dr. W. L. Alexander, of the Congregational Theological Hall, Edinburgh; Professor Davies, of the Baptist College, Regent's Park; and Dr. Gotch, Principal of the Baptist College, Bristol. Dissenters were represented on the New Testament Company by Dr. Angus, of Regent's Park College; Dr. Moulton, of Wesley College, Richmond; Professor Geden, of Didsbury; Dr. Samuel Newth, Principal of New College; and Dr. G. Vance Smith, Principal of the Presbyterian College, Carmarthen. All the most eminent scholars in the Established Church, whose names it would be superfluous to give, were included in the revisers, and there were subsequently added, amongst others, Professor Cheyne and Mr. S. E. Driver, of Oxford, and Professor Robertson Smith and Dr. W. Wright, of Cambridge. Then in 1872 two companies of American revisers were formed under the auspices of Dr. Philip Schaff, of New York, comprising some of the most eminent scholars of the New World, most of whom were other than Episcopalians. Their conclusions were sent over in time for the second revision of the respective texts by the English companies, no alteration of the Authorised Version being accepted on this occasion except by a majority of two to one.

It appears that from first to last ninety-nine scholars were engaged in this laborious and meritorious work, of whom fifty were members of Christian churches other than Episcopalian. This fact suggests some suitable remarks by the Rev. Dr. Newth—a first-hand authority on the subject—which are well worthy of quotation :—

"Upon no previous occasion have so many scholars been engaged. In no previous revision has the co-operation of those engaged upon it been so equally diffused over all parts of the work. In no previous revision have those who took the lead in originating it, and carrying it forward, shown so large a measure of Christian confidence in scholars who were outside of their own communion. In no previous revision have such effective precautions been created by the very composition of the body of revisers against accidental oversight, or any lurking bias that might arise from natural tendencies or from ecclesiastical prepossessions. On these accounts alone, if on no other, this revision may be fairly said to possess peculiar claims upon the confidence of all thoughtful and devout readers of the Bible." *

The entire labours of the New Testament revisers were prolonged till March, 1880. Those who took in hand the

* "Lectures on Bible Revision, with an Appendix containing the Prefaces to the chief historical editions of the English Bible." By Samuel Newth, M.A., D.D., Principal and Lee Professor of Divinity, New College. (London: Hodder & Stoughton.) 1881. Dr. Newth, having been one of the New Testament revisers, was, of course, specially qualified to deal with so interesting a subject. He has told the story of the recent revision of the Bible, and of those which preceded it, with a simplicity, conciseness, and clearness that enhance its interest.

Old Testament worked for some years after that period, and it was not till the spring of 1885 that a copy of the completely revised Bible was presented to Convocation. It was brought out by the University Presses of Oxford and Cambridge, the authorities of those two seats of learning having undertaken the heavy expenses of production on condition that the copyright was secured to them. The revisers gave their work gratuitously, but the Universities jointly contributed £20,000 towards the expenses of the two companies, and also, of course, found the capital for the subsequent printing, binding, and publishing.*

At the autumnal session of the Congregational Union, at Manchester, in 1881, the question of the Revised Version of the New Testament was introduced by Principal Scott, of Lancashire Independent College, who moved a resolution offering hearty thanks to the scholars of England and America who had thereby rendered an important service to the whole Church of Christ. This was seconded by the Rev. W. F. Adeney, of New College. The resolution contained a special reference to the services of the Rev. Dr. Newth in connection with the revision. At the suggestion of that scholar the reference to himself was expunged, and Dr. Fairbairn then moved a separate resolution recognising the great services of Dr. Newth as their representative on the New Testament company, and cordially thanking him for what he had done. This was seconded by Dr. Stoughton, and carried by acclamation.

---

* The sale of the Revised Bible, both complete and in two separate parts, was for some time prodigious, and was largely increased by being brought out in all sizes, so as to suit the convenience of the public. This great work will, of course, be always in demand; for though it has not superseded, it is used to a large extent conjointly with, the Authorised Version, both in the pulpit and in the household.

The founding of Mansfield College, Oxford, primarily suggested by the abolition of University tests, had been a subject of serious consideration long before it took practical form, not only by leading Congregationalists, but by some of the foremost teachers of that venerable seat of learning. Thus many years ago the late Professor T. H. Green had expressed to Dr. Dale his belief that the throwing open of the Universities had been rather an injury than a help to Nonconformists, because so many of their sons drifted away, not only from Nonconformity, but also from Christianity, and lost all faith; and the young men ought to be followed there in order that their religious life and principles might be defended and maintained. Other eminent members of Oxford University expressed to Dr. Fairbairn similar views, and the prevalent opinion was embodied in a report submitted to the trustees and council of Spring Hill College, near Birmingham, who had already considered the subject. It had also been prominently discussed in the *British Quarterly Review*, by Professor Bryce and Dr. Fairbairn. The former suggested the removal to Oxford of one of the existing Congregational Colleges as a Free Church Theological Hall; the latter proposed a practical scheme which, indeed, foreshadowed what has already been accomplished. Dr. Simon, the Principal of Spring Hill College, whose disinterestedness in the matter was conspicuous, publicly advocated some such plan at Liverpool in 1883, and a month or two later Dr. Paton read a paper on the subject at a sectional meeting of the Congregational Union at Sheffield, where it was fully discussed. Opinion on the proposal matured into the conclusion that Spring Hill was the one college which ought to make the essay at the new departure; that institution possessing the requisite endowments, and being in near proximity to Oxford. The matter was specially taken up by Dr. Dale with great energy and perseverance. Eventually, the authorities at Spring Hill agreed that it should be organised as a Theological Hall, removed to Oxford, that it should be non-residential, and that it should be named after the family of the founders. The Charity Commissioners were consulted, and with great willingness elaborated a scheme, which was finally sanctioned in September, 1885. The Congregational Churches were at once challenged to show their interest in the project by erecting the new buildings—as required by the Commissioners—free of any charge on the endowment or the proceeds expected to result from the sale of the Spring Hill Estate. An influential Building Committee was formed, of which Mr. Edward Spicer was chairman, Mr. Albert Spicer, treasurer, and Dr. Dale and Dr. Hannay were the honorary secretaries. The subscription list was headed with large sums from such influential Congregationalists as Mr. Samuel Morley, Mr. James Spicer, Mr. W. H. Wills, Mr. W. Sommerville, Mr. T. Rowley Hill, Mr. W. W. Pilkington, Mr. W. Crosfield, and Messrs. Abraham and Jesse Haworth. Dr. Fairbairn—who had some time before consented to retire from the headship of Airedale College and accept the position of Principal of Mansfield—as well as Dr. Dale were indefatigable in promoting the object, and numerous meetings were held for the same purpose in the metropolis and provincial towns, and in the end it was announced on the opening day that the munificent sum of £50,000 had been subscribed, and that Mansfield College was opened free of debt.

The objects of the College have been frequently described.* The most important of them is to provide a high-class

* They are stated, with adequate fulness, by the Rev. W. B. Selbie, M.A., in the handsome memorial volume, "Mansfield College; its Origin and Opening." James Clarke & Co., 13 and 14, Fleet Street.

theological education for men intending to enter the Congregational ministry, and the present endowments are restricted to this purpose. The work of the College is purely theological, and its classes are open to members of other colleges in Oxford, and to accredited students of any religious body. All regular students, however, must be members of the University, if they have not already an Oxford degree. The College is non-resident, while it has a corporate life and communion. A further aim is to provide a religious home and centre for the Nonconformists of various denominations in the University. "It is essentially," says Mr. Selbie, "a theological hall, and exists primarily for the study of theology, in a spirit at once constructive, critical, and devout. It is entirely a post-graduate college, and has a purely theological course of three years' duration. The majority of the men who attend it are looking forward to the Christian ministry, and no pains are to be spared in training them for the function of preacher and in preparing them to bear 'the care of the churches.' Above all, the College is a religious institution. It seeks to promote the pure and undefiled religion of Christ and His Apostles by its chapel services, its lectures, and the spirit of its social life."

The inauguration of Mansfield College took place on October 14th and two following days. The occasion was unique in the history of the Free Churches of England, and the services were worthy of the occasion. There was a large attendance of ministers and laymen from all parts of the country. The dedicatory prayer was offered by the Rev. J. C. Harrison, of London; the opening sermon was preached by Dr. R. W. Dale; the Rev. Dr. Reynolds, of Cheshunt College, presided at the communion service; and the inaugural discourse was delivered by the Principal, the Rev. Dr. Fairbairn. These were followed, at various stages of the celebration, by addresses from representative men connected with British and American churches, and from several heads of houses and others belonging to the University of Oxford, such as Professor Jowett, of Balliol; Dr. Fowler, President of Corpus Christi; Rev. W. Jackson, of Exeter College; and Dr. Edwin Hatch. Amongst the speakers at the luncheon and the breakfast on the following morning were Mr. Albert Spicer (who presided at the former); the Rev. J. G. Rogers; Mr. John Massie, of Mansfield; Dr. Charles Ray Palmer, of Yale University; Principal Cairns, of the United Presbyterian College, Edinburgh; Professor Bruce, of the Free Church College, Glasgow; Professor Wilkins, of Owens College; and Principal Simon, of the Congregational College, Edinburgh. Fraternal greetings and congratulations came from many churches, and from eminent men in many lands; and a large and influential assemblage of Nonconformists from all parts of the country showed how wide was the interest felt in this great experiment.

Several of the speeches delivered in connection with the celebrations have more than an ephemeral interest. Professor Jowett, for instance, spoke of the event as a great festival of union and reconciliation. Their points of difference were, he said, few; those of agreement many.

"Do we not use the same version of the Scriptures? Are not many of the hymns in which we worship God of Nonconformist origin? Is there anyone who is not willing to join with others in any philanthropic work? Are our ideas of truth and right and goodness materially different? The great names of English literature—at least, a great part of them—although they may be strictly claimed by Nonconformists, do not really belong to any caste or party. The names of Milton, of Bunyan, of Baxter, of Watts and Wesley, are the property of the whole English nation. This, again, is a tie between us. We may be divided into different sects—I would rather say, into different families—but it does not follow that there is anything wrong in the division, or that there should be any feeling of enmity entertained by different bodies towards one another. These divisions arise from many causes—from the accidents of past history; from differences of individual character; from the circumstance that one body is more suited to deal with one class and another with another. Persons have entertained schemes of comprehension which look well on paper, but they are perfectly impracticable, and they mean very little. But what does mean a great deal is that there should be a common spirit amongst us—a spirit which recognises a great common principle of religious truth and morality. And, as we begin to understand one another better, we also see the points of agreement among us growing larger and larger, and the points of disagreement grow less and less."

The remarkable prestige associated with the opening of Mansfield College naturally increased the sense of responsibility on the part of the Principal and his colleagues. It had been more than once publicly stated that the creation of such an institution would have been hazardous, if not impossible, without the right man to direct it. All who came into personal contact with Dr. Fairbairn, and all who knew of his high reputation as a scholar, his intense devotion to the object, his peculiar organising faculty, his indomitable perseverance, and the charm of his manners, felt that he was exactly fitted to mould the destinies of the infant institution at whose birth he had presided. His first year's report, issued in the autumn of 1890, breathed a spirit of gratulation and gratitude, as the following extract will indicate:—

"We opened with thirty-four names on our books. Of these, six were Art Scholars, whose education proceeds outside Mansfield; twenty-eight were students in Mansfield. They were remarkable for the number of men who had attained high—often the highest—distinctions in many

Universities. We had graduates of Oxford, Cambridge, London, Victoria, Edinburgh, Glasgow, Aberdeen, Melbourne, the Cape of Good Hope. Four had taken first-class honours in Oxford; two had received the gold medal as the most distinguished students of their year in their respective Universities; twenty-one had taken honours or prizes of greater or less distinction. They were a body of men of which any college might well have been proud. They were joined, now for one term and now for two, by men from the Universities of Bonn, Berlin, Geneva, Montauban, and Union College, New York. While the large majority were of our own communion, we had members of the Church of England, the Baptist, Methodist, Presbyterian, French Protestant, and Lutheran Churches. It was an epitome of living catholicity." A chapel experiment had also been successful, quite beyond expectation. "It has," says the Principal, "fitly alike in its pulpit and in its congregation represented and completed the catholicity of the College. Its pulpit has been occupied by four Methodists, four Presbyterians, three Baptists, and twelve Congregationalists; and the congregations have been such that we have been forced to increase our sitting accommodation. And our freer evenings have been useful as our more solemn morning services. The men have there met our preachers as thinkers or practical workers."

The establishment of Mansfield College seems to have been approved, not only by the influential University men referred to, but by leading Anglican theologians at Oxford, and, according to well-informed people, it has already had a perceptible influence on the theological training of the Church of England. It may be remembered that the late Earl Beauchamp highly praised the Mansfield course of study, and a writer in the *Guardian* hints that, seeing the equipment of that College, it might easily happen that Nonconformists may in future take all the theological prizes in the Universities.

Perhaps the chief drawback of Mansfield College is that

there is no adequate endowment for the teaching staff, there being as yet no chair for Homiletics or Church History, both of which are much needed. For the present, at all events, its annual cost is defrayed more by subscriptions and donations than by its scanty endowments.

To the indirect influence of the College movement is owing the interesting University settlement in Canning Town, Eastern London, called "Mansfield House," which has been so actively promoted by the Rev. F. W. Newland, and is under the efficient management of Mr. Percy Alden. A ladies' settlement in the same district is also projected.

When Mr. Spurgeon entered upon the thirty-first year of his ministry in London he was fifty years of age, and it was determined to celebrate the Jubilee in a fitting manner. During the long interval since the Metropolitan Tabernacle was built, it had more and more grown to be a centre of far-reaching evangelistic and benevolent agencies—seeming, as Lord Shaftesbury said, "to be the whole world in a nut-shell," "enough to occupy the minds and hearts of some fifty ordinary men." That a man of such manifold gifts and abounding sympathies should be popular in the metropolis was not so remarkable as that he should be as fresh as ever, and enjoy a much higher reputation after the lapse of so many years of exhaustive labour in and out of the pulpit, chequered by some severe illnesses. In 1879, on the occasion of his Silver Wedding, Mr. Spurgeon had been presented with a testimonial of £6,000, which he expended upon the Almshouses and other enterprises associated with the Tabernacle. On the occasion of the Jubilee he was once and again warned that any further pecuniary tribute must be regarded as a personal gift.

That celebration commenced on June 18th, 1884, with a meeting in the Tabernacle, Pastor C. H. Spurgeon, as he was still called, in the chair. He said that there was nothing about himself that would account for the great and long-continued success attending his labours. He owed it all to the Gospel he had preached, and his attempt to saturate his sermons with the doctrines of grace. A list of the societies represented there on that occasion was then read. It comprised the Almshouses, the Pastors' College, the Pastors' College Society of Evangelists, the Stockwell Orphanage, the Colportage Association, Mrs. Spurgeon's Book Fund and Pastors' Aid Fund, the Evangelist Association, the Country Mission, and more than fifty other societies and missions. After a touching address from Mr. D. L. Moody, the American evangelist, a list was read of addresses of congratulation received from all parts of the world, including France, the United States, Canada, and Australia. Mr. Carr, one of the deacons, read an eloquent address from the Tabernacle Church to Mr. Spurgeon, abounding in gratifying reminiscences and expressions of deep sympathy and gratitude. In response, Mr. Spurgeon said he thought it a very great mercy that he was not expected to speak after that. The Rev. John Spurgeon, his father, followed with a hearty address, rejoicing that he had been able to preach for five-and-forty years, following a parent who had been a minister of the Puritan type for fifty years in Suffolk and Essex. The next speaker was the Rev. James A. Spurgeon, of Croydon, and co-pastor of the Metropolitan Tabernacle, who testified to the enormous amount of work in which his brother was involved in serving His Master, and to his singleness of eye in connection with it, and laid great stress upon his geniality of disposition that lightened his own and others' burdens. The Chairman having attributed what had been done largely to the co-operation of a willing, cheerful, persevering, and zealous people, the Rev. Charles Spurgeon, of Greenwich, spoke on behalf of himself and his brother Thomas, who is pastor of a large Tabernacle at Auckland, New Zealand, and was then on his way home. The Rev. Archibald Brown, a successful minister among the outcast poor of East London, dwelt upon the usefulness of their College, which had sent missionaries to all parts of the globe, and had been the means of adding some 70,000 brethren and sisters to the Church of Christ. An address from the students was then presented, followed by an address from the Sunday-school with a cheque for £63. Mr. W. J. Orsman, "the Lord Archbishop of the Costermongers," was the next speaker, and finally there was an address from the Baptist ministers of France, and a speech from Mr. W. Olney.

On the following evening, June 19—*the* birthday—Lord Shaftesbury presided over a crowded meeting in the Tabernacle. Mr. Spurgeon, said his lordship, stood before them as a marvel. He was the same now as when he began his ministry—the same true, simple man, not puffed up, but rather humbled, by success, and animated to go on in the noble career God had marked out for him for the benefit of mankind. "Jesus Christ and Him crucified"—that was the strength of Mr. Spurgeon's preaching. He was one of the most admirable, amicable, affable fellows Lord Shaftesbury ever knew, and he could only pray that their pastor might go on increasing in service, in depth of feeling, in winning souls to the Lord, and in advancing the heavenly Kingdom. Canon Wilberforce most cordially expressed his sympathy and congratulations, and rejoiced in the real spiritual unity amongst those that were in Christ Jesus, with rather a wide divergence of method and external practice. The presentation of a hearty congratulatory address from the London Baptist Association, by the Rev. Dr. Todd and a deputation, drew from Mr. Spurgeon an expression of the deepest possible interest in the work of that organisation, and this was followed by an address from the Baptist ministers of Boston (U.S.) and its vicinity. Sir W. McArthur, M.P., and the Rev. Newman Hall, LL.B., also offered their congratulations. Other excellent things were said suitable to the occasion, especially by Dr. Parker, chairman of the Congregational Union for the year. Then Mr. T. H. Olney, in some suitable remarks, asked Mr. Spurgeon's acceptance of a cheque for £4,500, which Mr. Murrell, who followed, said was only on account,* and was entirely free from any condition—absolutely at his own disposal, for there were very many calls on his private purse. Three hearty cheers greeted the pastor of the Metropolitan Tabernacle when he rose to reply. What he had heard during the last two days would, said Mr. Spurgeon, melt a heart of stone. He had intended to devote the testimonial to things in connection with the church. Objection was made, but he could not be debarred the gratification, but he would take some portion for himself. Though wanting nothing, he was kept perpetually poor, and as to the idea that he had a large sum laid by, he would take a bid for it. Still he did want money, for he was as a pipe. The money went in at one end and ran out with extreme rapidity at the other, which they could discover by looking around. In concluding a touching address, Mr. Spurgeon said: "The Lord bless you! The Lord bless you! The Lord bless you more and more, you and your children!"

Once and again the world has been informed of the marvellous and unprecedented sale of Mr. Spurgeon's publications. More than 2,200 of his sermons have been issued, with a weekly circulation of 25,000 copies, which are sent to all parts of the world, including the remotest districts of India and Australia. But these are only the

* The amount was eventually raised to £5,000.

most prominent of the multifarious productions of his pen. His most ponderous work is "The Treasury of David," a commentary on the Psalms, in which he has received able assistance. It comprises seven massive volumes. "John Ploughman's Talk," abounds in shrewd and witty common sense, which would be a fortune to any writer. Of this shilling book more than 400,000 have been published.

Within three years of the memorable joint session of the Congregational and Baptist Unions, held at the City Temple—in respect to which Mr. Spurgeon was conspicuous by his absence—the pastor of the Metropolitan Tabernacle, to the surprise and grief of many of his best friends, began what was known as the "Down Grade" crusade in the *Sword and Trowel.* Month after month Mr. Spurgeon reiterated his charges as to the introduction into the denomination of a new religion, in which all the leading principles of the Gospel were discarded. Nothing being done by the Baptist Union, as he seemed to expect, Mr. Spurgeon, in 1887, announced that he should distinctly retire from the Union, but did not intend to form a new denomination. Like another Achilles, he retired moodily to his tent. This statement naturally caused much excitement, not to say consternation. A deputation of the most influential Baptists could not persuade the great preacher to alter his decision, and eventually his resignation was accepted. He appears to have desired the acceptance of a creed based on that of the Evangelical Alliance; but, as such a course was inadmissible in relation to churches claiming individual independence, it was at length agreed, after much consultation among the leading Baptists, to adopt a declaration of what was "commonly believed by the churches of the Union"—the points (apart from those relating to baptism) being those generally received as orthodox, but instead of the affirmation of eternal punishment, there was a reference to the verses in Matthew (xxv. 46), with an explanation that some brethren, "while reverently bowing to the authority of Holy Scripture, and rejecting the dogmas of purgatory and universalism, have not held the common interpretation of these words of our Lord." This formula was accepted at the next meeting of the Union by acclamation, the Rev. J. A. Spurgeon seconding its adoption. From this time his elder brother, though not again joining the Union, maintained towards it a friendly feeling and cordial relations with its leading men. In the spring of the present year there was issued a circular, signed by Mr. C. H. Spurgeon and some thirty other Baptists, in which they expressed their "firmest belief in the verbal inspiration of all Holy Scripture," as against "the supposed discoveries of so-called higher criticism," as well as in "the doctrine of grace and the hopeless perdition of all who reject the Saviour." This is the latest version of the theological views of the pastor of the Metropolitan Tabernacle. Of the dangerous and lengthened illness of Mr. Spurgeon, which excited the most profound sympathy throughout the civilised world, it is only necessary to say here that, as these pages are passing through the press, there is good reason to hope that this devoted Christian Evangelist may be spared to continue his noble work.

One of the cherished objects of Dr. Hannay while Secretary of the Congregational Union was to create and deepen a genuine interest in the principles held by the denomination. Notwithstanding the prominent part taken by him in the commemoration of the Ejectment of 1662 and the Union Jubilee, he was quite ready to turn to account the Bicentenary of the English Revolution—an event which immediately preceded the Toleration Act. During 1888 a statement and appeal were issued by the Committee of the Union in the form of a paper prepared by the Rev. Dr.

Brown, of Bedford, the accomplished author of "The Life of Bunyan," which set forth the chief reasons why that Bicentenary should be commemorated. There was also, in the latter part of the year, a series of lectures in the Memorial Hall on the history of Toleration, the policy of the Revolution, and other topics suggested by the progress of the nation towards religious equality; the lecturers being the Revs. Dr. Fairbairn, Dr. Mackennal, J. G. Rogers, C. A. Berry, and Mr. J. Carvell Williams, whose addresses were afterwards published in a volume and in a separate form. In addition, a number of leaflets were issued embodying more concisely the same views, with the special object of instructing Nonconformists in a knowledge of the principles for which their forefathers contended and suffered. The subject also received prominent attention at the autumnal session of the Union at Nottingham, where a public meeting was held in reference to the Bicentenary (Mr. J. J. Colman, M.P., in the chair), and inspiring addresses were delivered by Principal Fairbairn, of Oxford, and the late Dr. Stevenson, of Brixton.

Since the year 1880 the decease of leaders and other men of distinction connected with the Free Churches has been unprecedentedly large, many of whose names must still be held in grateful recollection by the present generation of Nonconformists. As far back as 1881 Mr. Edward Miall, who had for some time retired from public life, was called away from the scene of his abounding labours at the ripe age of seventy-two. The sketch of his public work in and out of Parliament occupies some space in this History; their results are seen in the Statute Book of the Realm, and the changed aspect of opinion on the relations of Church and State. Probably no Dissenting leader of the era had so many ardent disciples. Some of the prominent features in the meritorious career of his friend and coadjutor,

Mr. Samuel Morley, have also been conspicuously referred to. He combined, in a singular degree, the attributes of a Christian and a philanthropist, and lavished his great wealth in the service of his Master with a rare conscientiousness. To the last he was a munificent supporter of religious institutions and social and political reforms. None who were present will forget the touching and imposing scene at his funeral at Abney Park Cemetery in 1886. It is given to few men, still fewer Dissenters, to act as did Mr. Morley in declining a peerage. At a later period Mr. James Spicer, who so often emulated Mr. Morley's liberality, and was the head of a family that has for many years been a tower of strength to Nonconformity, went to his rest. Sir Edward Baines, of Leeds, who lived to be, in Parliamentary phrase, the father of Nonconformity, began public life before either of his friends referred to above, and attained the advanced age of fourscore-and-ten. The reader will get in the foregoing pages a glimpse—but only a glimpse—of his life-long services on behalf of Christian truth, education, religious equality, temperance, and philanthropy. Equally high in public reputation, and distinguished alike for his impressive eloquence, his statesmanlike grasp of principles, and his amiable qualities was Mr. Henry Richard, the "Apostle of Wales," and *par excellence* its political representative, as well as the Nonconformist leader in Parliament after Mr. Miall's retirement. John Bright survived about a year his friend and coadjutor in the advocacy of the principles of peace, but he lived to see those who were his bitter opponents in the Anti-Corn Law agitation and those who afterwards denounced his policy as a Radical reformer, as a determined enemy of his Church Rates, and as a champion of religious equality, do homage to his greatness as a statesman and his noble qualities as a man. Not a few other Dissenting laymen of this period made their mark in the world, such as the Right

Honourable W. E. Baxter, a Radical reformer as well as a staunch Dissenter, who carried out his economical principles, as far as possible, in influential official positions. The public services of Sir Charles Reed were conspicuous, not the least so as Chairman both of the London School Board and the Deputies, and in connection with Bunhill Fields; and who can forget the terrible Alpine accident which cut short the promising career of his eldest son, Mr. C. E. B. Reed, who was one of the secretaries of the Bible Society? The sterling piety, generous support of religious institutions, and devotional hymns of Mr. Charles E. Mudie were less known than the great library which he founded. Not less conspicuous was Mr. James Clarke, whose business capacity, unique sagacity, and editorial aptitude built up the *Christian World* till it became the foremost of Nonconformist newspapers. Mr. William Baines, of Leicester, will be long remembered as a Church Rate martyr of half a century ago; Mr. Edward Butler, of Leeds, as a thoughtful and humorous essay writer, as well as a laborious Christian worker.

The loss of ministers and missionaries of the Congregational order during this decade has been very serious. The venerable Robert Moffat, of Kuruman, survived for many years his illustrious son-in-law, Dr. Livingstone, and after his remarkable career and self-denying labours in South Africa he was able in various ways to render much service to the Church of Christ at home. About the same time Mr. Sherring, missionary at Benares, went to his rest, as well as the Rev. John Curwen, whose ministerial work in East London was eclipsed by his successful mission as a musical reformer. A little later two distinguished ministers closed their careers—Dr. Raleigh, of Canonbury, and afterwards of Kensington, whose refined and glowing pulpit addresses, some of them published separately, placed him in the first rank as a preacher; and Dr. Mellor, of Halifax and Liverpool, who, like Dr. Raleigh, had occupied the chair of the Union, and was famed for his logical acumen, and much in demand among Congregationalists in the North of England. Dr. Lindsay Alexander, of the Theological Institution, Edinburgh, while eschewing ecclesiastical politics, took the lead of his denomination north of the Tweed, and had a wide reputation for his great erudition. In the year 1888 entered upon their rest several other distinguished ministers. Foremost among them was the Rev. J. Baldwin Brown, whose qualities as a preacher and an intrepid leader of religious thought are indicated in a preceding chapter, and who has left several religious works which are adapted to delight and solace his Christian readers; Dr. Aveling, of Kingsland, who attained to the dignity of Chairman of the Union; Thomas Jones, who was a sublimated specimen of the race of inspired Welsh preachers, and who had the faculty of photographing Gospel truth on the hearts of his hearers—a faculty not wanting to Paxton Hood, albeit an Englishman, who wrote several highly popular works. To this list of honoured ministers must be added the names of John Brown, of Wrentham, the model of a laborious and successful country pastor; Dr. Goodwin, of New College, a learned and much-loved Professor at New College; R. H. Smith, who combined a rare artistic taste with evangelistic zeal; William Leask, whose religious devotion was tinged with mysticism; G. M. Murphy, whose pastoral career showed how influential may be the sphere occupied by an uncultured man, whose actions spring from devotion to God and sympathy with men. H. J. Gamble will be remembered as an intelligent preacher at Hackney; John Corbin, whose disinterestedness was equal to his godliness; E. J. Hartland as the amiable Secretary of the Church-Aid Society; Samuel McAll as the venerable and experienced Principal of Hackney College, now removed to St. John's Wood; D. Jones Hamer and S. Hebditch as men of rare talent and devotion, whose health the milder climate of Australia failed to restore; and J. C. Gallaway, as having devoted his life to the work of chapel building and extension.

Other heavy losses were impending. In 1890 Congregationalists had to deplore the decease of William Tyler, the "bishop" and benefactor of East London; of Dr. Stevenson, the gifted, amiable, thoughtful, and acceptable successor of Mr. Brown at Brixton; of Dr. Macfadyen, of Manchester, a devoted pastor, who was the victim of overwork in his Master's cause; and the unexpected death of Dr. Hannay, who was for nearly twenty years the Secretary, master-spirit, and statesman of the Congregational Union, whose strength was undermined by his ill-fated holiday in Australia, and whose funeral obsequies last October were attended by all that was representative of the denomination that loved and venerated him so well. It is remarkable that his death almost coincided in point of time with that of his friend, Dr. Dexter, the Puritan historian in the United States. Some time prior to his death the Secretary of the Union was much troubled by the loss of another intimate friend on the other side of the Atlantic, Dr. Duff, Principal of Montreal College, and a pillar of Congregationalism in the Canadian Dominion.

In the same period the Baptist denomination lost some of its greatest luminaries, including Dr. Steane, of Camberwell, who had a cosmopolitan interest in the extension of the Gospel; Dr. Samuel Manning, whose labours as a minister were followed by effective service as one of the Secretaries of the Religious Tract Society; George Gould, who successfully undertook the pastorate of Bloomsbury when Dr. Brock retired; Dr. Acworth, whose public life was divided between ministerial and college work in Yorkshire;

J. P. Mursell, of Leicester, whose pulpit gifts made him no unworthy successor of Robert Hall, in that town, who was, at one time, a potent tribune of the people, when the operatives there were in a very restless state, and who was one of the most zealous coadjutors of Mr. Miall in the cause of religious equality; Charles Stovel, whose religious fervour was unquenched even by advancing age; Dr. Stock, of Salendine Nook, in whose life was exemplified the successful minister and the staunch "political Dissenter"; Hugh Stowell Brown, whose witty and luminous addresses, unconventional manners, and strong common sense, gave him a strong hold on the working classes of Liverpool; J. H. Millard, whose work in the Midland Counties and as Secretary of the Baptist Union are well remembered; and Dr. Stanford a man of refined mind, whose charming books are a rich inheritance.

CHAPTER XV.

VARIOUS FREE CHURCHES—A RETROSPECT.

FOR the most part, the foregoing four chapters have relation to the course of events in connection with the Free Churches since 1850. With a view to completeness it is proposed, in this supplementary chapter, to describe, without regard to the sequence of time, the characteristics and operations of various denominations heretofore only incidentally referred to, or not mentioned at all, in the current narrative, adding a few concluding remarks suggested by the historical retrospect.

The last prominent mention in this History of the oldest section of the Methodist family concerned sundry secessions which weakened its numerical strength, though their ultimate effect was to assist in broadening the polity of the Wesleyan community. Consequently, since 1851 the progress of that denomination has, in some respects, been comparatively slow. The total number of "members of Society" in Great Britain in 1851 was 302,209; in 1861 it was 319,780; in 1871 it had slightly risen to 347,090; in 1881 to 380,956; and in 1891 the aggregate number was 424,220. During the same period the number of ordained itinerant ministers has risen from 1,210 to 2,000; that is to say, nearly 800 more pastors are at work than forty years ago; but the local, or lay preachers, who constitute so important a factor in the ecclesiastical life of Methodism, are, in 1891, no less than 16,334. In 1851 the lay element was not sufficiently recognised to secure even a return of the local preachers in the official Minutes. The advance in the membership has, therefore, barely kept pace with—indeed, it is some little distance behind—the advance of population in Great Britain. It is a singular fact that, during this period of forty years, upwards of 600,000 persons have entered the Wesleyan Methodist Society, and subsequently ceased to belong to it. What the explanation of this startling fact may be would require much space to investigate. Possibly it may be found that the privilege of meeting weekly in class for religious intercourse does not counterbalance the financial burdens which are imposed upon members of Society through the medium of the class meeting, and which must always be an important feature in a Church recruited largely, if not chiefly, from the working and artisan classes. Or it may be urged that the spread of religious information through the agency of denominational newspapers, coupled with the increased power of the people to profit by such literature, may account for the unpopularity of the class meeting as a Church test. Whatever the reasons may be, it is curious that a powerful and aggressive Church should insist upon retaining, as its test of membership, an institution which for such a purpose is manifestly an anachronism.

While guarding with scrupulous jealousy the unit of their church life—the class meeting—the Wesleyan body have dealt less tenderly with their chief governing assembly—the Conference. Technically the "Conference" is a body of one hundred ministers legally constituted under a deed of declaration signed by Mr. Wesley; but this assembly of legal ancients is a mere phantom. Their real Conference and chief executive and administrative assembly is a much larger body. This powerful assembly, which exercises all the ecclesiastical patronage of Methodism, and directs its policy, was, up to the year 1876, a purely clerical synod.

No layman could enter its doors. In 1877 the Conference was reformed and divided into two sections—a pastoral section, which concerns itself chiefly with the appointments of the ministers to circuits, questions affecting ministerial character, and matters especially bearing upon the doctrinal teaching of the Church. The representative section of the Conference, comprising 240 ministers and 240 laymen, chiefly elected by the Wesleyan local district meetings, deals with financial, administrative, and social questions relating to Methodism at home and abroad. The result of the admission of the laity into the Conference has been greatly to add to the popularity and strength of the Assembly. One of the most recent resolutions passed by the representative Conference authorises the admission of reporters of the Press to its meetings. The growing requirements of a vigorous and energetic Church, rapidly advancing in the number of adherents and communicants, will, apparently ere long, require that there shall be one joint assembly for the discussion and settlement of Church questions; and possibly it may be found necessary, as in the United States, to have recourse to annual district conferences of smaller dimensions—say, one for London and the Southern and Eastern Counties; a second at Bristol for Wales, Cornwall, Devon, and the West of England; and a third for Lancashire, Yorkshire, and the North; with a Triennial Conference to deal with the more important public questions. In connection with the admission of the laity to the Conference in 1878, a fund called the Thanksgiving Fund, amounting to £297,000, was raised and used to clear off the debts of various departments of Methodist Church work.

If evidence were wanted that the Wesleyan Conference has not shown itself to be tenacious of its rights and authority, but, on the other hand, has manifested a ready disposition to adapt itself to the altering conditions of the age, it might be found in the Methodist Conference Act, 1876. By this Act, Parliament conferred upon the Conference the power of granting Home Rule to its colonial churches. In exercise of the powers so conferred, the Conference has constituted its churches in South Africa, in Australasia, and in the West Indies separate conferences, with full powers of appointment to all colonial chapels; and has thus, by one stroke of the pen, freely and without one penny of compensation, vested in those colonial church assemblies properties valued at many hundreds of thousands of pounds.

The gathering, for the first time in the history of Methodism, of an Œcumenical Methodist Conference in London, in 1881, afforded practical evidence of the close unity of Methodism, notwithstanding the willingness to sever the colonial churches. At this Conference—which is to be followed by a similar gathering at Washington in October, 1891—delegates assembled from seven sections of British and Irish Methodism, thirteen Methodist bodies in the United States, and various Methodist churches in Canada, the continent of Europe, and elsewhere. They represented 4,700,810 registered members, 23,000,000 adherents or communicants, 31,477 ministers, and 85,000 local preachers.

The establishment of four theological colleges for the training of Methodist ministers, at Richmond, Handsworth, Didsbury, and Leeds, coupled with the more exacting requirements of the day, have tended to raise the intellectual standard of the ordained preachers; but the formation of what is termed the "Joyful News" Mission, under the management of the founder, the Rev. Thomas Champness, for the employment of a cheaper class of evangelists, has shown that, both at home and abroad, Methodism cannot afford to depend upon ordained ministers alone, among whom there is a general tendency to develop curious forms of ecclesiastical officialism. The average cost of a Wesleyan Methodist married preacher in England is about £380, that of a village evangelist about £60.

It is a somewhat astounding fact that, with the example of their founder before them, the Wesleyan community should for half a century have devoted so little of their attention to the humanitarian duties of a Christian Church. The excuse for them may be that they were, for the first half of the nineteenth century, torn by internal dissensions, centering round what is always a repulsive subject to English people—ecclesiastical ceremonies and pretensions. The advancing intelligence of the rank and file of the people, the influence of a cheap press, the facilities for quick intercourse, and the rapid interchange of ideas, have shown to Methodist people that they have something more to do than merely preaching the Gospel and saving souls. Modern Methodism feels that, besides being an ecclesiastical organisation and a spiritual power, it must also be a social force striving, by the application of a practical Christianity, to lengthen the lives, improve the homes, educate the minds, and raise the moral and physical standard of the people. This conviction led to the formation of The Children's Home, under the effective management of the Rev. Dr. Bowman Stephenson—the President of the Conference for 1891—with its orphanages, its convalescent homes, its farms, and its emigration agencies. The same spirit led to the Wesleyan "Forward" Movement."

The promotion of primary, middle-class, and higher education have been part of the recognised work of modern Wesleyans. So far as its elementary denominational schools—of which there are 833—are concerned, the policy of the body since 1870 has been to maintain their schools efficiently, but to advocate wherever practicable the establishment of Board schools. The resolutions of the Wesleyan Committee called to consider the Free Education proposals of the Government affirmed the necessity of a free school under public management, within reasonable walking distance of every child; and the Right Hon. H. H. Fowler, M.P., the most eminent spokesman in Parliament among the Wesleyan members, declared on behalf of the body that they were willing to accept on their own behalf the same popular control of their own Wesleyan denominational schools which they asked to have over the National schools of the Established Church. The educational authorities of Methodism would, perhaps, be in a stronger position to-day than they are had they recognised, in a greater degree, their duty towards the million of Methodist children who are compelled to attend the village National school with no other protection than an ineffective conscience clause.

A distinct feature of modern educational work in Methodism has been the establishment of nearly a dozen large middle-class schools, under the management of limited liability companies, in provincial towns, and the erection of a most successful school at Cambridge, called the Leys, which has already attained considerable reputation under the headmastership of the Rev. Dr. Moulton, a member of one of the Bible Revision Companies.

In making the press and literature tributary to the work of evangelisation, the Wesleyans still lag far behind their founder, and do not compare with the Salvation Army. The circulation of their two leading newspapers, the *Methodist Recorder*, and the *Methodist Times*, each of which prints less than 30,000 a week, is trifling compared with what it ought to be. The magazines of the Wesleyan Church are little read, considering the vast constituency to which they can appeal. Her great Foreign Missionary Society publishes a small monthly circular, which is bound up with another magazine, and does not pay its way. Few of her well-known writers publish their books at the official dépôt or "Book Room" of the Church. Her literature is still largely sold by the itinerant preachers, who receive monthly parcels for distribution, much in the same way as Mr. Wesley's preachers used to carry tracts in the saddle bags of their horses. A strict clerical control and censorship are kept over the Press and journalism of Wesleyan Methodism. The Book Room is regarded as the special property and preserve of the ministers, and no layman is allowed on its Board of Management. The *Wesleyan Magazine* is edited and chiefly written by ministers. It was a favourite study of some of the earlier writers upon Methodist economy to compare the ecclesiastical systems of John Wesley and Ignatius Loyola. A parallel might be found between them in the tight grasp which Wesley's successors have kept on the press and journalism of the body.

What are called "Missions" have been established in London, Manchester, Birmingham, Liverpool, and Leeds, and are worked on lines which differ considerably from those of the ordinary circuit system. The superintendent and his ministerial assistants, for instance, are exempt from the necessity of changing their spheres of labour every three years, while the financial affairs are administered by a committee. By these means several large deserted chapels in these towns have been refilled.

The London Mission requires more specific mention. It is divided into four branches—West Central, Central, East, and South. The Central branch includes the Leysian Mission, an evangelistic and philanthropic agency supported by old boys of the Leys School, Cambridge. Adjoining the area occupied by the South branch is the Methodist University Settlement in Bermondsey, which is to be carried on in a manner similar to the work of Toynbee Hall and the Congregational Mansfield House. The foundation stone of the Settlement buildings, which are to cost £13,500, was laid by Lord Mayor Savory in July, 1891. The Rev. Peter Thompson's work at the East-End is largely social in its character, and it is significant that, while the meetings at his "Old Mahogany Bar" and "Paddy's Goose" attract numbers, Spitalfields Chapel, one of the oldest Wesleyan places of worship, has had to be closed. But the branch of the London Mission best known of all is the West Central, the superintendent of which is the Rev. Hugh Price Hughes. Mr. Hughes has become famous for his fervid eloquence, his organising power, his devotion to the social and political interests of the people, and his untiring advocacy of the "Forward Movement." Associated with him, among other "missioners," is the Rev. Mark Guy Pearse, who, besides being a popular author, is not inferior to his colleague as an impressive preacher. There are also a medical director and "Sisters of the People." The latter wear a uniform, and devote their whole time to the work. They visit the slums, nurse the sick, hold mothers' meetings, teach classes, and in a variety of ways help forward the spiritual work of the Mission. Of class leaders and lay preachers there are a large number. Two buildings, known as Wardour Hall and Cleveland Hall, are used for the benevolent work and for concerts, lectures, and smaller meetings; while St. James's Hall is occupied three times on Sunday. Prince's Hall is also engaged for Sunday and week-day gatherings. Music is made a prominent attraction at all the public services, and the orchestral and military bands and the choirs for the various halls furnish employment for the leisure hours of a large number of young people. Outdoor services are held in Soho, and occasionally in Hyde Park. Although the branch has not reported any dukes among its converts, as it was popularly expected to do, it has been most successful in attaching to itself young people from the business establishments at the West-End, as well as persons in other grades of life, and it has a membership of over 1,000. So extended and varied an agency is of course very costly, for £2,000 a year has to be paid in rent and taxes alone, before anything can be expended in aggressive work. Consequently there is a heavy debt to be cleared off, at which, however, Mr. Hughes and his colleagues are not dismayed.

These missions are really an adaptation of Wesleyan Methodism to the necessities of modern life in large towns, especially in London, where the denomination, up to the year 1859, had only sixteen chapels. Since then the Wesleyans have erected eighty-seven places of worship, most of them holding 1,000 people, at a cost of upwards of £650,000. There are still less than 30,000 members of the Wesleyan Societies in the metropolis, and probably not more than 250,000 adherents. To some exten this is possibly explained by the attempt made in many of the London suburban Methodist chapels to produce a sort of bastard Anglicanism—a kind of compound of the liturgical forms of the Established Church and a plain Nonconformist service. Artisans from the densely-peopled cities of the provinces, and labourers fresh from the village chapel, will not tolerate anything savouring of the State Church. Hence, perhaps, one of the explanations of the fact that there are said to be more than half-a-million of people in the metropolis at one time or another connected with Methodism, who are not now associated with it.

The closing years of the nineteenth century present, so far as the Wesleyan Methodists are concerned, a ministry more united, more accomplished, and more tolerant than at any former period of their history. The Wesleyans to-day have preachers excelling Dr. Adam Clarke in classical attainment and biblical knowledge; evangelists of greater power than Wesley's early preachers; and scientists, such as Dr. Dallinger, who are heard with equal respect on the platform of the Royal Society and in the pulpits of their Church. Wesleyan Methodism is, moreover, asserting more loudly and forcibly its claims to be an independent ecclesiastical organisation. It scouts the idea of being a poor relation of the Established Church, and it has finally and irrevocably abandoned any notion of absorption in the Church from which Wesley reluctantly broke free. Holding fast by its doctrinal standards, it has shown the utmost flexibility in mere church forms; while music, art, and literature have, in varied degrees, to suit the taste and temperament of different ranks of society and communities, been freely pressed into the service of the Church.

The Wesleyan Methodist laity have, with increasing responsibility and power, shown themselves keenly alive to the spiritual privileges and humanitarian obligations of Christian citizenship. What may the dying years of the century bring forth? Who can tell? Possibly the union of the severed branches of Methodism into one powerful re-united Methodism. If so, a religious force, instinct with energy, will be created in rural England which is, perhaps, destined to become a new centre of independent English village life, and a shelter from the withering blast of dominant Anglicanism.

Of the several offshoots of the original Methodist Connexion something needs to be said in these pages. The New Connexion Methodists have steadily grown in numbers and influence since the time of Kilham, their founder. They have now 186 settled ministers, 1,175 local preachers, and 31,020 members. In their organisation they most nearly approach the Wesleyans. One of their best known leaders was the late Rev. Dr. Stacey, of Sheffield, who occupied a high position as a college tutor. The United Methodist Free Churches arose, in 1850, out of an amalgamation of the Wesleyan Association and the Methodist Reformers. They have grown rapidly since that period, though of late years their numbers have fluctuated, especially during the last twelve months. The denomination has 346 itinerant preachers, 3,032 local preachers, and 67,200 Church members, with a great many on trial. The United Churches have efficient foreign missionary agencies, especially in China, upon which they expend more than £23,000 a year; and their vitality is indicated by the resolution passed at their recent conference to raise a fund of £15,000 to carry on a "forward" movement, a considerable portion of which has been subscribed. For some time past negotiations have been carried on between these two bodies with a view to amalgamation; but, at the recent conference of the New Connexion, it was decided to break them off "for the present," their members being unable to agree among themselves as to the expediency of the proposed basis of union.

The origin of the Primitive Methodists dates from the beginning of the present century, and in 1851 they had nearly 3,000 chapels, 9,000 local preachers, and 109,000 members. Although exposed to a good deal of rivalry from the evangelistic agencies generally attached to places of worship, and affected also by the great progress of the Salvation Army, this body has now 1,050 regular ministers, 16,317 local preachers, and close upon 200,000 members, and works with much zeal in the rural districts as well as in the towns. The itinerant system is in great vogue among the Primitives, and their mission agents are remunerated not from local sources, but from circuit contributions or from the general fund. The value of the Connexional property is estimated to amount to more than three millions and a quarter. Another branch of the Methodist family is the Bible Christians, or "Bryanites," who are mostly limited to the South of England. While, in 1852, they could count on about 14,000 members, they have now 25,769, with about 180 ministers, and 1,491 local preachers. It is not necessary to do more than mention here the Wesleyan Reform Union and the Independent Methodists, which together number about 15,000.

The various Methodist bodies referred to have a total membership of about 350,000; and if to these be added the Wesleyans, the aggregate members of the Methodist community in Great Britain will be 775,000. They thus stand numerically at the head of the Free Churches, and apparently they are fully as liberal in support of their religious and educational institutions, and not less ready to stand up in defence of religious freedom and equality than any other Nonconformist bodies.

As already stated in these pages, the Calvinistic Methodist organisation, which doctrinally stands apart from the other Methodists, arose out of the zealous evangelistic work of Whitefield; its first leaders being clergymen of the Established Church in the Principality. It is almost limited to Wales, where it is the foremost of the Free Churches. The Countess of Huntingdon's Connexion in England was also the result of the labours of that great Evangelist, in combination with that illustrious lady; but it has, to a large extent, merged in the Congregational body. The Welsh Calvinistic Methodists are governed by their "Quarterly Association," which is invested with all the authority of the Presbyterian "Synod," and annually chooses a Moderator. The ecclesiastical bias of the body is seen in the fact that its recent Conference near Swansea was attended by Dr. Monro Gibson as a corresponding member from the Presbyterian Church of England. The denomination is peculiarly obnoxious to the State Church in the Principality, having been in times past mainly recruited from its ranks; and the clergy of the Establishment indulge in frequent and bitter attacks on the Welsh Methodists. This was a prominent topic at the Conference referred to. In reply to the taunt that the Methodists were fast dying out, it was stated that their statistics were garbled by their opponents; that the Church wanted to get them back again; and that she, as it were, dogged the footsteps of Nonconformist bodies, so that she might lay hold of the laggards. During the past year the Calvinistic Methodists contributed to their Connexional fund the large amount of £202,700. It has been decided that their theological seminary at Bala is to be "open to all, whether Calvinistic Methodists or not, whether candidates for the Christian ministry or laymen, and whether men or women." This is a remarkable revolution, only brought about after protracted discussion. The success of the transformed college will, for a time at least, depend upon its new head, Dr. Thomas Edwards, the late Principal of the University College at Aberystwith, the great-grandson of the celebrated Charles, of Bala, and in many respects the greatest Welshman of the day. For twenty years his skill has guided that institution, until now, as he says, it "is perfectly safe." Principal Edwards has a high reputation alike as a preacher, teacher, and commentator, and there can be little doubt that he will raise the college at Bala Lake to a proficiency not surpassed by the college at Aberystwith. In 1889 the Calvinistic Methodists had 1,258 churches, 134,239 communicants, and 283,629 attendants at public worship; the communicants and attendants being more than double those returned in 1851.

For some time little has been said in this History relative

to Presbyterianism in England, although it has previously occupied a conspicuous space in these pages, and many of its leaders, it will be seen, won for themselves imperishable names in the Christian Church, both before and after the Revolution. Soon after that great event in our annals, however, the organisation of these churches fell off, and their attempted inclusion in the Church of England was not effected. Some became associated with the Congregationalists, some lapsed into Unitarianism, and, in the early part of last century, scarcely seventy independent congregations, out of about 800 that existed twenty-five years after the Revolution, remained. "Until about 1836, well into the nineteenth century," said Mr. Justice Kekewich, in his judgment in the Tooting case, "the Presbyterians had no active life as a body; there appears to have been no return of their chapels, and no other evidence of their identity. It is impossible to suppose that, after such prominent success as they had in the earlier years, and the faith being still strong in Scotland, there were no Presbyterians here and there yearning after the return of what they called the 'good old ways'; but they dropped out as a body."

Within the last half-century, however, there has been a gradual revival of Presbyterianism in England, owing, in a measure, to its renewed life in the North, and to the large and steady migration of Scotchmen over the border. A few congregations were, and remain, associated with the Establishment in Scotland; many more were formed under the auspices of the Presbyterian Church in England; and others were affiliated to the United Presbyterian Church north of the Tweed. As time went on the necessity of union between these two bodies became apparent, and, in 1876, the respective Synods held a joint session in the Philharmonic Hall, Liverpool, with a view to complete amalgamation. On the 13th of June the two

Synods met separately for the last time, and then went in procession to the hall, where there was a crowded audience to see the respective moderators sign the necessary documents, give each other the right hand of fellowship, and hear the Rev. Dr. Dykes proclaim the constitution of "The Presbyterian Church of England." The Rev. Dr. Anderson, of Morpeth, was elected Moderator of the Synod. Subsequently addresses of congratulation were presented from the several Scotch churches, and from forty ministers of various denominations in Liverpool. A dinner at St. George's Hall followed, and in the evening there was a further meeting of the Synod, which was addressed by Professor Chalmers, Principal Cairns and others. A thanksgiving fund was initiated applicable to various church purposes, one gentleman promising £5,000 a year for five years.

The basis on which "The Presbyterian Church of England" is founded is the sufficiency of the Scriptures as "the only rule of faith and duty," and the acceptance of the Westminster Confession of Faith, and the Larger and Shorter Catechisms. A Declaratory Act has been adopted by the Synod setting forth the relation of the present teaching of the Church to the Confession of Faith. A new Creed, entitled "The Articles of our Faith," was subsequently prepared by a committee as a result of labours extending over seven years. It is largely based on the Westminster Confession, which document it is destined to supersede for popular uses. Since the union was constituted the church has greatly prospered; for one reason, there are not a few Englishmen who accept it as a happy medium between Episcopacy with its sacerdotalism, and Congregationalism with its supposed lack of cohesion. The Presbyterians have a highly efficient college in Guildford Street, of which Dr. Dykes is now the principal, assisted by Professors Gibb and Skinner, and to it a great many scholarships are attached.

Several fine and costly churches have been erected in London and its suburbs during the last twenty years, attached to which are many evangelistic agencies, both for the poor at home and the heathen abroad. One important feature of the Presbyterian Church is a Sustentation Fund, which, during the present year distributed £200 to each minister whose congregation had qualified for what is known as an equal dividend. This matter, as well as other questions affecting the welfare of the denomination in respect to order and government, come under the control of the Synod which meets annually in the metropolis or some large town. The Church can boast 289 places of worship and 65,688 communicants, the income being nearly £240,000 a year.

The Presbyterian Church of England can claim more than the usual proportion of ministers whose reputation extends beyond its own limits. Among those who have gone to their rest may be mentioned, Dr. James Hamilton, Professor Elmslie, Dr. Saphir, Professor Graham, Dr. Anderson, Dr. McLeod, and Dr. Symington. Those still able to render conspicuous service in the Church of Christ include Dr. Oswald Dykes, Dr. Donald Fraser, Dr. Edmond, Dr. Thain Davidson, Dr. McEwan, Dr. Morison, Dr. Monro Gibson, Dr. Thoburn McGaw, and the Rev. J. McNeill. The names of some of its distinguished laymen, such as Professor Leone Levi (deceased), Sir George Bruce, Mr. H. M. Matheson and Mr. S. Stitt are well-known to the world.

The hopeful anticipations as to the future usefulness of the English Presbyterians would be somewhat belied if there were to be many such unpleasant incidents as those in connection with the well-known Tooting case, which, however, we can only briefly summarise. It seems that in that suburban district there is what is called a De Foe chapel, built by the widow of Dr. Miles, an Independent minister, who had been pastor of the church from 1731 to 1763, for Dr. Wilton, also an Independent minister, who was her husband's successor. From 1688 to 1731 there were three consecutive Presbyterian ministers, but from that time up to 1879 the ministers have all been Independents, the last being a Dr. Anderson, who was an acknowledged Independent;* but for some reason or other he came to the conclusion that he and his congregation should become Presbyterian, and at the close of 1879 it was decided, by ten of the fourteen persons present at a church meeting, to apply to the Presbytery of London for admission to the Presbyterian Church of England. One of the dissentient members laid the matter before the committee of the London Congregational Union, by whom notice was given that steps would be taken to prevent the alienation of the property Although a conference between the two parties took place, the Presbytery decided to recommend the application of Dr. Anderson to the favourable consideration of the Synod. In April, 1880, that assembly declined it, but in April, 1881, the Synod, by a very large majority, acceded to the petition. After much fruitless negotiation, a basis of compromise was arranged between Messrs. Matheson and G. B. Bruce on the one side, and Mr. Albert Spicer and the Rev. A. Mearns on the other, but in 1884 the Tooting congregation refused to accept it. It was therefore reluctantly resolved—the Congregational Union now co-operating with the London Union —to seek a legal remedy. Next year, however, a fresh basis was found, and accepted by the London Presbytery, but the Synod did not acquiesce. Notice of action was given, and a further scheme was drawn up in conference—the main point being the payment to the London Congregational

* Some ten years previously Dr. Anderson was publicly appealing to Congregationalists for subscriptions to build a "De Foe manse."

Union of £1,000 towards the erection of a new Congregational church in South-west London, leaving Dr. Anderson in possession of De Foe Church—which it was agreed to submit to the arbitration of Messrs. G. B. Bruce and Albert Spicer with power to appoint an umpire, and that in the event of their agreement the Synod should be asked to disclaim by resolution any desire to transfer to their church any chapel property held for any considerable time by Congregationalists. Mr. E. N. Buxton was called in as umpire, by whom an award was given and two additional provisions suggested. In respect to a suggested rider declaring that the award was not in any way based on "the historical claims" on either side, the London Union left it to the decision of its own arbitrator. But ere long Dr. Fraser announced that they were "baulked" by the refusal of Dr. Anderson to concur in asking the Charity Commissioners to alter the trusts. This ended all negotiations, in which, it is only just to say, the London Congregational Union exhausted every device for bringing about an amicable arrangement.

The Tooting case was heard before the Chancery Division of the High Court of Justice on February 23rd, 1888, and was fully argued; Mr. Cozens-Hardy, Q.C., Mr. Aspland, Q.C., and Mr. Lemon being counsel for the plaintiffs, and Mr. Gainsford Bruce, Q.C., and Mr. Pownall for the defendant. The pleadings occupied five days, and a great deal of interesting historical matter, not always reliable, was produced.*

Mr. Justice Kekewich, in delivering judgment, said that the trust required that the property should be "used and enjoyed as and for a meeting-house or place for Protestant

* A full report of the entire proceedings was subsequently published by the London Congregational Union.

Dissenters of the Presbyterian or Protestant denomination"—that is, for the benefit of these bodies exclusively. After laying stress on the twenty-five years limit, which secured possession, his lordship decided that the proper forms for applying for admission to the Presbyterian Church had not been observed by Dr. Anderson. He declined to express an opinion as to whether present Presbyterians are the lineal descendants of the old Presbyterians, or had made a new departure; but it was quite clear that the rules of the Presbyterian Church, as contained in the Book of Order, were inconsistent with the polity of Independents as they existed in the middle of the eighteenth century, have existed ever since, and exist now. He thought that the De Foe church should have consulted the trust deed before they adopted Dr. Anderson's suggestion. That minister was in the wrong, and all this litigation might have been avoided. New trustees must be appointed, and the decision to subject the trust property to the control of the Presbyterian Church of England was null and void. "To unite [De Foe Chapel, Tooting] with the Presbyterian Church of England was," said the judge, "to take a step in contravention of the trust." He did not think justice required an injunction unless circumstances forced him to do it, and he saw no reason for depriving Dr. Anderson of his income, but the judge was pleased that the plaintiffs waived costs except so far as the income in hand would pay them.

As is well known, Dr. Anderson and his friends at Tooting eventually elected to remain in connection with the Presbyterian Church of England, and consequently had to abandon the chapel and its endowments, which have since been transferred to the London Congregational Union.

"The importance of the question to the Independent denomination" (says a statement published in the interests of that body) "arose from the fact that a number of chapels with Protestant Dissenting trusts, which had at one time been Congregational, especially in the North of England, and with scarcely an exception subsidised by the denominational funds, had been at various times times carried over to the Presbyterian Synod; that a much larger number of chapels scattered throughout the kingdom are, while connected with Independents, according to their trusts in a somewhat similar position to the Tooting Chapel; and that the Presbyterians had repeatedly published lists of these in their denominational organs, and in a variety of ways had been, for the last half century, asserting their claims to be considered the rightful successors and heirs of the old English Presbyterian Dissenters, and therefore to be the possessors of these buildings. The chapel at Tooting was consequently typical, and the case a test case whose decision would affect a large number of others."

There is good reason to hope that there will not again arise any necessity for litigation between bodies that have so much in common, and that need each other's Christian co-operation.

For the following notes, relative to the more recent history of the Society of Friends, whose rise and heroism form a prominent feature in the earlier pages of this History, we are indebted to Mr. William Tallack, who has so nobly followed the best traditions of his ancestors, and who is widely known for his meritorious work in connection with the Howard Association:—

"During the last forty years the Society of Friends has put forth an energy in the direction of Foreign Missions, as well as Home Evangelisation, previously unknown; whilst, at the same time, its members have generally divested themselves of those peculiarities of dress and phraseology which, for nearly two centuries, had been popularly regarded as essential characteristics of Quakerism. The adherents of the Society are now incomparably more aggressive in their external operations than they were. They support a large number of missionaries in Madagascar, Syria, India, China, Mexico, Japan, and Turkey. In Madagascar, in particular, the Society has taken a prominent share in the religious and educational elevation of its Christian inhabitants, and has maintained the most cordial relations with the missionaries of other religious bodies there. It has also established a medical mission and a hospital at Antananarivo, the capital. In Syria there are two Quaker mission stations—one at Ramallah, near Jerusalem, and the other (a much larger one) at Brumana, on the Lebanon range, near Beyrout. There also the medical department is an important feature, and a markedly favourable impression has been made by the Friends upon the previously hostile and prejudiced minds of the neighbouring Druses and Maronites. In India and China, the Friends' Missions have been patiently and wisely laying the foundations for a considerable and permanent establishment of Gospel and educational efforts. In the former country, the base of these operations is in the district around Hoshungabad, in Central India. In China the Society has chosen the large and thriving mercantile emporium of Chung-king, in the province of Sichuen, as its chief seat of missionary labour.

"At home, the forty years in question have seen a great wave of educational activity pass over the Society. A training college for its teachers was established at Ackworth, near Pontefract, Yorkshire (a few years before 1851), through the munificent bequest of £40,000 by Mr. Jonathan Flounders, of Yarm, and it is named, after him, the "Flounders Institute." Most of the schoolmasters and teachers amongst the Friends, during the period now under review, have received a training within its walls, and many of them have graduated with marked credit in London University. Meanwhile, the large boarding-schools, termed public schools, because partly supported by subscriptions from the members of the Society generally, have been well maintained. The principal of these are situated at Ackworth, Saffron Walden, Sidcot (near Bristol), York, Wigton (Cumberland), Penketh (near Warrington), Ayton (near Middlesborough), Waterford (Ireland), Mountmellick, with Lisburn and Brookfield, near Belfast; and in all these schools the education has taken a wider range, and become more thorough in character, than previously. Private or proprietary boarding-schools have also been established, during the forty years, at Scarborough, Ilkley, Christchurch, Stoke Newington, Darlington, and other places. A high-class school for the sons of the wealthier Friends has recently been opened at Leighton Park, near Reading. And at Manchester, an important college, named after the eminent Quaker philosopher, John Dalton, the discoverer of the "Atomic Theory," has been established and affiliated with Owens College and the Victoria University. It affords special facilities for the study of science and engineering. Nor have the Friends been unmindful of the claims of the working classes and their poorer neighbours. Their efforts in this direction have chiefly consisted in the establishment of Sabbath-schools for the children, and classes for the adults, in London, Birmingham, Bristol, Hull, and other large towns. The scholars, scarcely any of whom are members of the Society itself, who are thus taught, and in various other ways aided, now amount to about 35,000, or just double the aggregate number of Friends in Great Britain. This extensive educational work has involved the outlay of many thousand pounds, cheerfully contributed by the members of the Society, for this Christian and patriotic service.

"Another feature of the forty years has been the greatly increased participation by Friends in political and municipal functions. It was deemed an extraordinary incident when, soon after the passing of the Reform Bill, the late Joseph Pease, of Darlington, was returned to Parliament as member for South Durham. For some time he was the only person of his own denomination thus honoured, but year by year other Friends also entered the House; the foremost in popularity being John Bright, whose remarkable Parliamentary career covered nearly the whole of the period now under notice. His eloquence and his national services are too familiar to all to need comment here. But it is interesting to note that John Bright retained his Quaker simplicity to the last, and, in accordance with his wish, was buried "amongst his own people," outside the plain meeting-house at Rochdale, where an unadorned slab with its brief inscription marks the resting-place of the "Great Tribune." Mr. Bright consistently carried out, in his own life, the democratic principles he approved, and whilst wearing the honours of a leading statesman he did not refuse to discharge some of the most humble denominational services of the Society in which he had been born. Next to Mr. Bright in Parliamentary repute amongst the Friends of this period was William Edward Forster, who although he had ceased to be a fully-recognised member of the denomination, yet always remained a Friend at heart, and never ceased to cherish and retain his social and sympathetic connections with his old acquaintances. Nor was he separated from them in death, for his body was consigned to its last resting-place amongst the Yorkshire hills, with the solemn simplicity which specially characterises Quaker interments. Mr. Forster was also the last prominent member of a family which, for about three-quarters of a century, had taken a leading part in the religious and denominational movements of the Friends. His uncle, Josiah Forster, was sometimes termed "the King of the Quakers," and his father, William Forster, was one of the most honoured amongst its ministers. Amongst other Parliamentary representatives of the Society, during this period, were Mr. John Ellis, of Leicester, and his son, Edward Shipley Ellis, both of whom had so prominent a share in the development and management of the Midland Railway Company; the latter being for some time its chairman. Another well-known Quaker M.P. was the late Mr. J. F. Bottomley Firth, whose promising career was so unexpectedly terminated by his sudden death in Switzerland. Then, too, there were Charles Gilpin and James Wilson, both of whom accepted office under Government; the former becoming Under Secretary of the Poor Law Board, and the latter Chancellor of the Indian Exchequer. One more M.P. of Quaker training was Frederick Lucas, who joined the Roman Catholic Church, and founded the *Tablet* newspaper. He wrote a curious pamphlet designed to show a vital resemblance between Catholicism and Quakerism.

"Amid the great changes which, in the forty years, have both beset and surrounded Quakerism, it is hardly to be expected that even the religious views and sentiments of the Society should have wholly escaped modification. In America, with perhaps the single exception of Pennsylvania, an absolute revolution has taken place in even the deepest, and as they were formerly deemed, the most essential matters of the Society's convictions. In fact, it is fairly open to question whether Quakerism, as hitherto understood in England, at least, has not entirely disappeared from the Western States of America as a whole, seeing that its professed adherents have generally adopted a paid ministry, pre-arranged services, singing, and even instrumental music, and various other features of the ordinary denominational life outside and around them.

"In Great Britain and Ireland, however, there still remains —at any rate in most places—much of the formerly universal system in Quakerism of a meditative worship, based on silent waiting for the solemnising and impressive influences of the Holy Spirit. But even in this country this is gradually undergoing a perceptible change. It can hardly be claimed by any that there is now such a measure, as there used to be, of dependence, amongst those who take vocal part in the Friends' meetings, upon the sincerely-believed influences and impressions of the Divine presence. There is more of talking and less of real preaching, probably, than of yore. In a few places, even in England, one or two of the members, of the weaker sex chiefly, have occasionally essayed solos, or hymn-singing, in their meetings; but such attempts have not as yet met with any general encouragement. But it has hitherto been regarded of vital importance by all the most honoured and most worthy representatives of Quakerism, that its own distinctive principle shall be prized and practised—namely, that worship should primarily regard what is Divine rather than human, and that prayer should be its essence and basis, especially that mode of prayer, usually termed 'silent waiting.' It was by the long waitings, the humbling visitations, and the gratitude-enkindling influences of this peaceful, inward, and individual waiting upon God, that the most devoted Friends of former generations, as also of the last half-century, became the men and the women that they were. It was this mode of worship and prayerful dependence which was so prized and cherished, not only by the Society's most useful ministers—such as the late Benjamin Seebohm, William Forster, Stephen Grellet, Joseph John Gurney, Daniel Wheeler, John Pease, Robert Charleton, Grover Kemp, John Hodgkin, and many other faithful labourers in the Gospel—but also by not a few of those Friends whose service and acceptance has chiefly been in the line of civil and social usefulness, as, for instance, the late Joseph Sturge,

Joseph Cooper, George Stacey Gibson, George Thomas, Samuel Tuke, Joseph Eaton, Joseph Rowntree, Edward Smith, and many members of this Society whose lives were so effectually devoted to the liberation of the slave, to the prevention and repression of crime, to the promotion of temperance, to the extension of international peace and arbitration, and, in general, to the honour of God and the welfare of His creatures. It is believed amongst thoughtful Friends that, if modern Quakerism is to maintain the honoured reputation won for the Society by its members hitherto, it must combine with the progressive requirements of the present a practical attachment to the powerful and godly influences which have been so fruitful of varied and solid service in the past."

During the last forty years the Unitarian churches in England have increased in numbers, though it can hardly be said that they have done more than keep pace with the population. Some few of their village churches have ceased to exist, and others have decreased in numbers and altered in character. The liberal tendencies at work in orthodox churches, though, in some respects, favourable to the growth of Unitarian opinion, have made some Unitarians lukewarm in respect to the support of their own places of worship. Many of them say that they can hear as good Unitarian sermons in the Episcopal churches or among the Congregationalists as from their own preachers. There has always been an influential section opposed to any kind of denominational extension. The late Dr. Charles Beard, of Liverpool, was a typical representative of this section. He did not believe in "Unitarian" churches, nor would he support the Unitarian Association. He was a devoted adherent of the Free Church principle that no dogmatic definitions or sectarian restrictions should be attached to worshipping societies. Dr. Martineau, though an earnest

Unitarian, has also expressed his strong disapproval of labelling churches with the name "Unitarian."

The manufacturing towns of Lancashire and Yorkshire may be said to have the most active congregations, though London has shown more vigour in recent years, and there are still a few strong churches in some of the out-of-the-way country districts. Theologically, the teachings of the English Unitarians of the present day are a long way removed from the views of Lindsey, Priestley, and Belsham. A few here and there, more particularly in the north of Ireland, are tinged with a kind of Arianism, and cling to what is popularly known as supernaturalism; but the great bulk of English Unitarians are believers in the simple humanity of Jesus, and either reject or ignore the miraculous. Under the influence of Dr. Martineau a higher and purer spiritual Theism is gradually supplanting the colder and more materialistic teachings of the early English Unitarians. Scholarship is still highly esteemed in the denomination, and it was in the interests of an educated ministry that Manchester New College was removed from London to Oxford in 1889; but the necessity of finding preachers for the smaller and poorer churches has compelled Unitarians to admit men into the ministry who are less efficiently equipped than the leaders would desire. It is noteworthy, however, that the Home Missionary College, Manchester, has been extending its curriculum year after year, until it has become quite an advanced theological institution for the training of ministers.

In recent years, influenced by the spirit of the times, and the example of other religious bodies, social work has assumed larger proportions among Unitarians. Domestic missions to the poor, organised on unsectarian lines, have for many years been carried on in Birmingham, Bristol, Manchester, Liverpool, and London. All the churches that are really alive are beginning to perceive that they must bestir themselves with social problems. Unitarians have always been strong educationalists, and so libraries, schools, museums, and picture-galleries have received generous and enthusiastic support at their hands. In proportion to their numbers, they are always well represented in Parliament, as well as on the various town councils and local boards of the country. There is a popular idea that the Unitarian churches are very wealthy. This is a mistake. There are a few wealthy laymen, but the great mass of English Unitarians belong to the artisan and lower middle classes. Many of the churches have great difficulty in meeting their liabilities, and if it were not for the aid rendered by the British and Foreign Unitarian Association, and other missionary agencies, they would find it impossible to retain the services of a settled minister.

Dr. Martineau proposed an organisation scheme at Leeds in 1888, by which these difficulties might be overcome. All were to contribute to a common sustentation fund, and the rich were to help the poor. The scheme was discussed a great deal, but practically nothing came of it. The isolated churches were wedded to their congregationalism, and the notion of joining a kind of free presbytery was foreign to their thought and feeling. The British and Foreign Unitarian Association thus retains its place as the leading society for missionary work. It includes all shades of opinion on its committee and council, so that the word "Unitarian" has ceased to have any narrow, sectarian meaning attached to it, by those who employ it, to describe their theological position. Among the ministers there is very little controversial work or negative criticism compared to what there used to be. The ordinary sermon is more affirmative and practical, and the services are brighter and more inspiring. Some few attempts have been made to reach the masses in theatres and halls by popular Sunday services. Most of these experiments have been singularly successful in drawing eager crowds to listen, though the additions to church membership have not been conspicuous.

It is difficult to forecast the future of English Unitarianism. Some of the orthodox churches practically occupy the theological standpoint of the older Unitarianism, while the average Unitarian has marched forward in the direction of a larger and wider faith than his forefathers reached. Where active, able, earnest men are at work, churches succeed among the Unitarians as well as among other denominations; where men simply repeat the phraseology of a bygone age, and take no living interest in the life and thought of their town or village, Unitarian churches decline and decay just as other churches do. People who wish to believe it, think that the "trend" of modern thought is in the Unitarian direction; but few Unitarians are bold enough to imagine that the Church of the Future will bear their peculiar name. At the present time (1891) they possess 265 churches and mission stations in England, 30 in Wales, 10 in Scotland, 39 in Ireland—344 in all. The "Essex Hall Year Book" contains the names of 356 ministers, 284 of whom are occupied in active ministerial work.

The growth and success of the Salvation Army is one of the most striking ecclesiastical events of the present era. This body was not in existence at the time of the Religious Census of 1851. The movement was originated by Mr Booth, who was brought up in the Church of England, and received his religious impressions among the Wesleyans. Afterwards he became a minister of the New Connexion, and preached with much acceptance in various parts of England; and in 1861, he, together with the late Mrs. Booth, gave himself up to evangelistic work, with the result that their united labours were the means of bringing many people into connection with the various churches. In 1865 Mr. Booth began to prosecute his work in the East of London, where the alienation of the masses of the population from religious institutions, and their degraded social condition, made a profound impression on his mind; and he resolved to consecrate his life to save them from the abyss of misery into which they had fallen. Hence the origin of the Salvation Army, which, although gradually modelled in military fashion with a view to the maintenance of discipline, did not adopt that designation till eleven years after that scheme was set on foot. Their modes of operation are thus described by themselves:—

"1. By holding meetings out-of-doors, and marching, singing through the streets in harmony with law and order.

"2. By visiting public-houses, gin palaces, prisons, private houses, and speaking to and praying with all who can be reached.

"3. By holding meetings in theatres, music-halls, saloons, and the other common resorts of those who prefer pleasure to God, and by turning factories and other available buildings into meeting-rooms, so securing hearers who would not enter ordinary places of worship.

"4. By using the most popular song-tunes and the language of every-day life not only to convey God's thoughts to everyone in novel and striking forms, but in such language as they can easily understand.

"5. By making every convert a daily witness for Christ, both in public and private."

It will thus be seen that one of the cardinal features of the new movement—if not *the* cardinal feature—was publicity. The multitude were not so much invited to attend places of worship, mission-rooms, &c., as followed to their own places of resort and confronted with these intrusive evangelists. Year by year General Booth—as he was now called—and his followers acquired growing influence and notoriety as they were brought into contact with those whom they desired to arouse. Their peculiar organisation; their strange and coarse methods, sometimes bordering on profanity; their clamorous meetings; and their want of reverence, grieved and startled sober Christians, who were quite unable to find in the Word of God or the character of Christianity any warrant for such eccentricities. For a long time the procedure of the Salvation Army was regarded even by the least refined of the regular denominations as a travesty of the religion of Jesus Christ. But whatever the peculiar characteristics of Salvation Army teaching, and however alien many of its methods to those ordinarily used by other Christians, it was not long before it became manifest that the growth of this unique organisation was in no way arrested by opposition or hostile criticism; that it not only reached a class scarcely reached by other evangelistic agencies, but has been the means of transforming numbers who were addicted to drunkenness and vice into examplary citizens; that thousands of the most godless people are among the zealous apostles of the new evangel; that its adherents generally are capable of great self-denial; and that the predictions that the Salvation Army would be only a nine days' wonder has thus far been unquestionably falsified. Facts such as these, apart from all questions as to the soundness of the basis on which it rests, coupled with confidence in the piety, devotion, and rare ability of Mr. and Mrs. Booth and their family, have created widespread sympathy with the movement as a means of elevating the masses of the population, which found remarkable expression in the raising of more than £100,000 to enable the "General" to carry out the extensive social reforms promulgated in his celebrated work, "In Darkest England." That the Salvation Army has, to a large extent, succeeded in its professed object is attested by the foundation of a Church Army on similar lines.

The organisation of General Booth has reached an enormous and unprecedented development. Outside the British Isles there are 2,740 separate "Salvation Societies," which are to be found on the American continent and in all parts of the world. In the United Kingdom there are reported to be 1,383 corps and 152 outposts, with 4,649 officers. The organ of the Army, *The War Cry*, has a weekly issue of more than 300,000, and *The Young Soldier* (for children) circulates about 130,000, while the *War Crys* in foreign lands are published in fifteen different languages.

This is not the place to examine the soundness of the theory at the basis of the Salvation Army, to discuss the various intricate problems associated with it, or to forecast the future of this marvellous organisation. That it maintains a rigid discipline over its multitudinous adherents is notorious. That discipline is, no doubt, one of the sources of its present strength. To what extent it will be maintained when the able and sagacious founder of the movement, now considerably advanced in life, ceases from his labours, can hardly be conjectured. Possibly it is destined to pass through various modifications—perhaps to throw off its despotic attributes, till it approximates to the various agencies of the Free Churches that express the religious sentiments of so large a proportion of the British people.

It is not quite easy to decide whether the Brethren—otherwise known as the Plymouth Brethren—have increased in numbers and influence during the past half-century—for their genesis does not date back more than sixty or seventy years. Brethrenism had its origin in the dissatisfaction of members of the Church of England with the prevalent laxity of life and of spirituality in the Establishment. The Rev. J. G. Rogers* considers it to have been a revolt against

* "Church Systems in the Nineteenth Century."

the spirit of routine and conventionalism which had fallen like an untimely blight upon the Evangelicals in the Established Church, and had affected the Dissenting communities as well. Amongst both the Tractarians and Brethren there was, says the same writer, "a feeling that the idea of the Universal Church had been lost, and a craving for its embodiment in some outward form." The Brethren repudiate all organised forms of Christianity, their *raison d'être* being that each individual may become an organ of the Holy Ghost. They object to a paid ministry, cultivate religious fellowship, hold periodical meetings—oftentimes in drawing-rooms—for the study of the Scriptures, Christian conference, and prayer, and have a weekly observance of the Lord's Supper. Next to the Romish Church, Brethrenism has become, in process of time, an instrument for proselytising from other churches, against whose errors it maintains a protest, though it has no organisations for aggressive purposes. "They make it their business," says Mr. Rogers, "to detach Christians from the churches where they have a religious home, instead of seeking to attract sinners to Jesus Christ." Many converts are made, especially among retired officers and the professional classes among aristocrats who have lost their attachment to the State Church, but are unwilling to identify themselves with anything so vulgar as Dissent ; and among pious people who shrink from contact with the world in the belief that by that means they preserve their spirituality. The Plymouth Brethren have numbered among their adherents not a few persons of eminence, some of whom, such as Dr. Tregelles, Mr. Muller, of Bristol, Mr. A. Groves, and Mr. Craik, have been driven out by internal dissensions, which is one of the chief banes of the sect. It is boasted that, "unlike other sects, they originated not with the lower or middle class of society, but they can enrol among their leaders gentlemen of the learned professions, esquires, baronets, and even peers of the realm."

The adherents in this country of Emanuel Swedenborg, the eminent Swedish theologian, had for a long time been satisfied with disseminating his doctrines by means of meetings for reading and conversation. But, in 1788, a small chapel was rented in Eastcheap, and the New Jerusalem Church was organised. There are now associated with the Church eighty-twc congregations, most of them in England, and many of their places of worship are handsome and commodious. There are forty-three ordained ministers and six recognised leaders connected with the body. The service is liturgical, the form compiled by its Conference being in general use. The denomination has various missionary and publishing societies to promulgate its doctrines. The Swedenborg Society, founded in 1810 for translating, publishing, and circulating the writings of their founder, possesses, besides its own house, an annual income of about £400. The Church has also a National Missionary Institution, with six provincial missionary committees; a training college for students preparing to enter its ministry; and an orphanage equal to the maintenance of forty orphans. The General Conference, which meets annually, holds £66,431, the interest from which is expended in the maintenance of its various churches and for missionary uses.

The rise and progress of Nonconformity in England and Wales is a suggestive and fertile theme that has commended itself as well to the philosophical historian, the practical statesman, and the popular lecturer, as to the pulpit orator. The godliness and self-denial, the sufferings and heroism, of the stalwart Puritans, are, in spite of their ascetism, austere manners, and trivial controversies, a subject almost as fascinating to Churchmen as to Dissenters in these days of ease and self-indulgence, and read almost like a romance.* Their noble deeds and vicissitudes are not only an integral part of our national history, but the source of much of our national greatness, and it is natural for Englishmen in general to pride themselves on the exhibition of solid and sterling qualities which have stamped successive generations at home, and have laid the foundations of a vast commonwealth on the other side of the Atlantic.

It is hardly possible to examine the records of the Free Churches impartially without reaching the conclusion that the connection of Church and State has, from the first, been by far the greatest obstacle to the welfare of the British people. The natural opposition of sovereigns and a feudal aristocracy to the concession of equal rights to the people of this country has always been intensified by the ready co-operation of a privileged Church with arbitrary power. Every concession in the direction of civil and religious freedom has consequently been the outcome of severe and aggravated conflicts. The successful attempts, extending over several generations, to frustrate the intentions of the Toleration Act were the work of the Established

* It is curious that the apostle of "sweetness and light" was fain to do homage to their antique virtues. In his published "Discourses in America," the late Mr. Matthew Arnold remarked: "Then you have had, as we in England have had, but more entirely than we, and more exclusively, the Puritan discipline. Certainly I am not blind to the faults of that discipline; certainly I do not wish it to remain in possession of the field for ever, or too long. But as a stage and a discipline, and as means for enabling that poor, inattentive and immoral creature—man—to love and appropriate, and make part of his being, divine ideas, on which he could not otherwise have laid or kept hold, the discipline of Puritanism has been invaluable; and the more I read history, the more I see of mankind, the more I recognise its value." (Macmillan & Co., pp. 70-1.)

Church alone. This is only an illustration of the persistent resistance of ecclesiastical authority to national progress ; and that resistance has, in the main, proceeded far more from the rank and file of the clergy than from their episcopal rulers. It was the clergy who, in the reign of William III., frustrated the Comprehension Scheme, which was accepted by the bishops, and this malevolent influence has retarded necessary reforms even down to the present era, as when, by almost incredible efforts, the clergy warded off, for many years, such rational reforms as the abolition of Church Rates and the extinction of the churchyard monopoly.

This undoubted fact has the more significance in view of the unnatural revival of mediævalism in the Church of England. The ascendency of High Churchism in the reigns of Charles II. and Queen Anne was coeval with the Jacobite fanaticism and the scandalous scenes associated with "The Church-in-Danger" cry. Though there is no fear that, with a free press and democratic institutions, such a cry could now have the same meaning as in days of yore, it is a serious thing that, in the estimation of a great majority of the clergy, the Reformation is a bye-word ; that they pride themselves on being an exclusive caste by right of apostolical succession ; and that successive decisions of the law courts—not the least that of the recent Archbishop's Tribunal—have left the ministers of the Establishment entire freedom, with or without the sanction of their parishioners, to adopt what ritual they please and to preach whatever dogmas they incline to, unless their diocesan should intervene—a right scarcely ever exercised. Almost more than in the olden times, the State Church is an exclusive ecclesiastical corporation, though it can hardly claim the allegiance of more than one-third of the population. There is progress in every direction except in respect to the Church, where there is retrogression. The sacerdotal claims now revived in our midst can only, in these days of universal education, multiply unbelievers in Christianity, and still further alienate the masses. While privilege is on all sides yielding to popular rights, can it be that an ecclesiastical system, whose claims have become increasingly exacting, is destined to retain its supremacy?

Time is on the side of the Free Churches. The tendency to sub-division is less marked than the tendency to co-operation and ultimate federation, and becomes more manifest now that their unity with the Church of England can only be brought about by marching under the Caudine Forks of the "Historic Episcopacy." So decisive is this reaction that the Comprehension Scheme of two centuries ago, which was favoured by the most eminent prelates of that epoch, would be almost more repugnant to the clergy of the Established Church than to Dissenters themselves. Between most of the Free Churches there is a working Evangelical Alliance, which is visible in the frequent interchange of pulpits, and the exchange of fraternal greetings in their several assemblies. The latest sign of this pervading Christian sympathy is the recent Congregational Council, at which Baptists, Presbyterians, and Methodists were present to offer the right hand of fellowship to their Congregational brethren.

Dissenters, though conscientiously believing in the superiority of their own polity, cannot but view, with pain and disquietude, the disintegrating processes that are impairing the influence of the Church of England as a Christian institution. They, as well as Churchmen, are proud of the illustrious men associated with that Church, whose erudition, luminous criticism of the Scriptures, and theological pre-eminence reflect a lustre on Protestant Christianity generally. They can find some comfort in the belief that the men are better than the system. Leaving out of view the laity of the Church, it cannot be doubted that, among its 20,000 clergy, there is a large minority who are more or less in sympathy with Dissenters, who abhor intolerance, and cheerfully co-operate with Christians outside their pale in evangelistic and benevolent movements. Further, it is, we believe, undeniable that among all sections of the clergy there is more Christian zeal, more devotion to their official duties, and more readiness, spite of repellant dogmas, to recognise the "one touch of nature" than was ever before the case. As the theory of Papal Infallibility almost vanishes into a myth amid the necessities of modern society in Roman Catholic countries, so, it may charitably be hoped, the sacerdotal system which for the most part dominates the Anglican Communion breaks down in practical life. Mediævalism is too unsuitable to the age to be long maintained in a commonwealth where the democracy is in power, where free thought and a free press are predominant, and where an increasing number of Free Churches counteract its influence. But how many people do its discredited pretensions drive into utter scepticism?

There has been of late years abundant speculation as to what is called "The Church of the Future," and no little concern has been expressed as to the ultimate outcome of free Biblical criticism, and a fearless examination of the foundations of the Christian faith. These fears will be dissipated in proportion to the completeness and depth of man's spiritual faith in the Gospel of Christ, such as was realised by the devout Puritans and such as *is* realised—though not exclusively—in the Free Churches of the present era. Christians generally, apart from all denominational differences, may find consolation in the thought so finely and devoutly elaborated by Dean Milman in the concluding volume of his "History of Latin Christianity,"* in which he

* "History of Latin Christianity." By Henry Hart Milman, D.D., Dean of St. Paul's. Vol. vi. Second Edition. (John Murray.)

says :—"As it is my own confident belief that the words of Christ, and His words alone (the primal indefeasible truths of Christianity) shall not pass away; so I cannot presume to say that men may not attain to a clearer, at the same time more full and comprehensive and balanced sense of those words, than has as yet been generally received in the Christian world. As all else is transient and mutable, these only eternal and universal, assuredly, whatever light may be thrown on the mental constitution of man, even on the constitution of nature, and the laws which govern the world, will be concentred so as to give a more penetrating vision of those undying truths. Teutonic Christianity (and this seems to be its mission and privilege), however nearly in its more perfect form it may already have approximated, may approximate still more closely to the absolute perfect faith of Christ; it may discover and establish the sublime mission of religion and reason; keep in tone the triple-corded harmony of faith, holiness and charity; assert its own full freedom, know the bounds of that freedom, respect the freedom of others. Christianity may yet have to exercise a far wider, even if more silent and untraceable influence, through its primary, all-penetrating, all-pervading principles, on the civilisation of mankind." This faith-inspiring passage was written more than thirty years ago, and who can doubt that during the interval its aspirations have already, to a certain extent, been realised?

THE END.

INDEX.

E.

LONDON:
PRINTED BY ALEXANDER AND SHEPHEARD,
27, CHANCERY LANE, W.C.

0=12.50